S0-BOE-087

A Celebration of Community

August 26-31, 1993 • Site: The Evergreen State College, Olympia, Washington

Dear Friends,

The Fellowship for Intentional Community is planning an International Gathering on Cooperative Living, to be held the last week of August, 1993, at The Evergreen State College on the Olympic Peninsula in Washington State.

The Fellowship is a network of intentional communities, community networks, individuals, and other interested organizations across North America.

The purpose of the gathering is to celebrate the diversity and vitality of the intentional communities movement, bringing together participants from all over the planet — to share visions, experiences, and systems for cooperative and sustainable lifestyles — and to create an atmosphere of fellowship and alliance-building which will serve to promote the health and growth of the movement.

Our projected audience is diverse: intentional communities, seekers, cooperatives, collectives, alternative villages, support organizations, and any other individuals or groups which have an interest in promoting this type of progressive endeavor.

Evergreen State College is located in the heart of 1,000 acres of forest, with extensive organic gardens and cooperative housing. The excellent facilities have a capacity of 2,500 on-site participants (including limited camping) with additional lodging available in Olympia, only a few minutes from the campus. We will keep the fees as low as possible; early projections indicate a cost range of $12-$50 per day, depending on lodging and meal choices.

We need your help:

- Let us know your thoughts on such a large gathering of community-minded people.

- Your organizational involvement is welcome, especially suggestions and comments about activities, program, and funding sources.

- Help us get the word out to your community members and coworkers — and to your regional and global contacts.

- Plan to attend— as a local organizer, as a workshop focalizer, and as a participant.

Please complete the following survey and return to: Fellowship for Intentional Community, '93 Communities Gathering, 8600 University Boulevard, Evansville IN 47712.

Please reproduce this form and distribute as widely as possible. Thanks!

11/91

Name: _____ Phone: _____

Community/Organizational Affiliation: _____

Street Address: _____

City: _____ State/ Prov: _____

Country: _____ Postal Code: _____ Date: _____

❑ I'm planning to attend the Aug. '93 Conference; please send me information and a registration packet.

❑ I'd like to coordinate outreach and inquiries in my area (specify country, region, network, or city):

_____

❑ I can help distribute flyers in my area. Please send me ____ flyers for:
  ❑ posting on local bulletin boards, and/or ❑ to include in my/our next mailings.
  ❑ Please send me a flyer master — I/we will donate the copying expense.

❑ Please send me Gathering ad copy so we can run a free notice in our next publication(s): ❑ Display Ad ❑ Classified Ad

❑ I want to help organize the Conference (specify which committee):
  ❑ Structure & Coordination ❑ Fund Raising ❑ International Hospitality ❑ Publicity & Media ❑ Site Logistics
  ❑ Registration ❑ Ride Sharing ❑ Housing ❑ Food ❑ Program ❑ Exhibits ❑ Arts/Entertainment
  Workshop Coordinator (specify): _____
  Other: _____

❑ I am planning to bring ____ children (ages: _____) ❑ I want to help organize/ assist with on-site childcare.

❑ I have enclosed a list of individuals and organizations that might want to
  a) co-sponsor the Gathering; b) provide seed grants or other funding; c) arrange for special needs
  (scholarships, transportation, wheelchair access, signing, etc.); d) help organize events; e) make
  a presentation; or f) attend the Gathering. *Please specify a, b, c, d, e, or f for each referral.*
  ❑ I have special dietary needs (please specify):

❑ I would like to donate the following goods and/or services to the Gathering:

❑ Enclosed is a donation of $_____ earmarked to:
  ❑ Support the development of the Gathering. ❑ Be credited toward payment of my conference fees.
  ❑ Supplement scholarships for conference fees and/or travel subsidies (specify?):
  ❑ Other (please specify):

A Celebration of Community

Our vision of this gathering is an event that will be:

- International in scope
- Diverse in philosophy, culture, and presentation format
- An interactive multi-media means to communicate messages on various themes:

  Learning from the Past, Visioning the Future
  Multigenerational Living, Nuturance in Families & Tribes
  Diversity: Our Strength, Our Challenge
  Cooperative Connections Between & Beyond Communities
  Community Technology: Hardware, Software, Liveware
  Celebrating our Creativity

We are designing the themes and structure to:

- Address issues of ecology and appropriately applied technology, community systems, legal definitions and structures
- Show models of group decision making
- Invite challenges to the movement (especially from social change organizations)
- Facilitate skills and labor exchanges
- Help seekers find community options that could work for them
- Experience the healing aspects of community life (we plan to organize "clans" or "pods" to give the opportunity for small group sharing to happen throughout the Gathering).

> **Please reproduce this form and distribute as widely as possible. Thanks!**

Aug 26-31 1993

Networking & Alliance Building:

"Making Connections" will be a major sub-theme of our celebration. The Gathering will be a fertile environment for:

- Community-to-community contact
- Seekers of community meeting groups with openings
- Contact between the communities movement and the larger society

---

 Media: There will be at least one Media Day which will encourage reporters from all types and sizes of media organizations to cover the activities of our movement. We are also planing to coordinate efforts to create a broadcast-quality documentary of the event, and of the variety of lifestyles represented.

 Forums: The schedule will include many opportunities for people to share their visions of community, and there will be booth and exhibit spaces readily available to communities — where contemporary groups may sell their products and provide information about their daily lives.

 Child Care: Some cooperative child care will be organized. Please indicate on the reply form if you will be bringing child(ren) or if you can help with child care.

 Rides, Housing and Food Subsidies: will be available for those who need them, although we cannot guarantee an endless supply. If you can help with a ride, a gift of food, or a donation for a scholarship fund, please let us know. If you have special needs or require more information, write us at the address below.

 Camping and Dormitory Space: will be available on the campus. Please bring a tent to camp if possible. Also, there is very limited RV space. The registration form will have an option to indicate that this is your preference for lodging. Local motels will need to receive your reservation at least 3 months in advance.

 Do Not Bring: any illegal substances to the Gathering site. Also, do not bring pets. Because of environmental sensitivities, there will be no indoor smoking and we ask that you do not wear perfumes.

WHO WE ARE: The Fellowship for Intentional Community helps to provide a sense of connectedness and cooperation among communitarians and their friends by serving as a network to facilitate trust building and information sharing between intentional communities. We also demonstrate applications of cooperative experiences to the larger society through publications, forums, workshops, and other projects. We seek to increase global awareness of the many alternative communities now in existence, and to make referrals for individuals looking for cooperative resources or a home in an intentional community.

Fellowship for Intentional Community
Center for Communal Studies • 8600 University Blvd. • Evansville, IN 47712 • (812) 464-1727

DIRECTORY OF

INTENTIONAL
COMMUNITIES

·

A
GUIDE
TO
COOPERATIVE
LIVING

·

1991 Edition

·

Co-Published by:

**FELLOWSHIP FOR
INTENTIONAL COMMUNITY**
Evansville, Indiana
&
**COMMUNITIES
PUBLICATIONS COOPERATIVE**
Rutledge, Missouri

·

*With financial support
from the following sources:*

CESCI
School of Living
Unitarian Universalist Fellowship of Twin Oaks
Federation of Egalitarian Communities
Community Catalyst Project
Sandhill Farm · Twin Oaks · Shannon Farm · Ganas

Printed on recycled paper.

Maps & Charts

N. America

International

Resources

Late Entries

Copyright © 1991 by:

Fellowship For Intentional Community, and

Communities Publications Cooperative, a division of the
Unschool Educational Services Corporation

All rights reserved. No part of this book may be reproduced for purposes of resale or republication without written permission from the publisher, except by a reviewer who may quote brief passages or reproduce illustrations in a review; nor may any part of this book be stored in a retrieval system, or transmitted in any form or by any means — electronic, mechanical, photocopying, recording, or other — without written permission from the publisher, unless the information so stored and retrieved is made available to the public *entirely free of charge* (meaning that no joining fees, user fees, handling fees, or access fees may be charged).

However, it is our intent and desire that the information contained in this Directory be made as widely available as possible; therefore, we grant permission to organizations that are strictly non-profit to republish excerpts, provided that the combined length of such excerpts does not exceed 5,000 words, and also provided that each excerpt is accompanied by the credit line: "Reprinted with permission from the *Directory of Intentional Communities* ; c/o Sandhill Farm; Route 1, Box 155; Rutledge, MO 63563."

Furthermore, we grant permission to private individuals to reproduce and distribute this information among friends and acquaintances, as long as the nature of the exchange is non-commercial and the information is provided free of charge save for reimbursement of copying and mailing expenses.

The following articles have been reprinted here with permission:

A Checklist for Those Wanting to Join Community
    Copyright © 1985 by Corinne McLaughlin and Gordon Davidson. All rights reserved.

Cohousing
    Copyright © 1988 by Los Angeles Times. All rights reserved.

Emissary International Communities
    Copyright © 1989 by Foundation House Publications, Inc. All rights reserved.

The Idea of Owning Land
    Copyright © 1984 by In Context. All rights reserved.

Land Trusts offer American Land Reform
    Copyright © 1988 by In These Times. All rights reserved.

Ten Main Aspects of the New Utopian Vision
    Copyright © 1983 by the Tarrytown Group. All rights reserved.

The Tyranny of Structurelessness
    Copyright © 1975 by The Second Wave. All rights reserved.

A Word About Cults
    Copyright © 1985 by Corinne McLaughlin and Gordon Davidson. All rights reserved.

Cover Design & Layout: Rick Bickhart

Drawings: Albert Bates/The Farm (99); Elizabeth Jarrett/Goodenough Community (49); Even Eve/Kerista (34, 36); Jake Kawatski/Twin Oaks (52); Joanie Mitchell/Black Oak Ranch (38); School of Living logo (104)

Cover Photos (Left to Right)
    Back: 100 Mile House/Emissary Foundation International
        Oakwood Farm/ Emissary Foundation International
    Front: 100 Mile House/Emissary Foundation International
        Oakwood Farm/Emissary Foundation International
        Geoph Kozeny/Community Catalyst Project
        Geoph Kozeny/Community Catalyst Project

ISBN 0-9602714-0-6 • First Printing, October 1990 • Printed in the U.S.A.
ISBN 0-9602714-1-4 • Revised Second Printing, June 1991

Welcome...

Welcome to *Communities* Magazine's ninth Directory of Intentional Communities. In our 17 years of chronicling the visions and realities of cooperative living, we believe this is some of our best work.

It's been five years since our last Directory — a longer gap than we intended, and much longer than our readers wanted. Yet, we're excited about this Directory, and hope you'll agree it's worth the wait.

What's Inside

As you can see from the map on pages 146-151, communities are sprinkled all over the continent. We are proud to present about 425 community listings, all freshly confirmed by the communities themselves (that is, we did not reprint *any* old descriptions from previous directories without confirming their accuracy).

This Directory is also more than listings — we are pleased to include nearly 40 feature articles which discuss aspects and issues of community living, and information on more than 200 alternative resources and services, a representative sampling from the thousands in North America.

But the community listings have been our primary focus, and that's where we've worked the hardest. This effort shows in two ways. First, in breadth of representation: this is by far the largest directory we've ever compiled. For its depth and degree of verified information, we believe it to be the most comprehensive communities directory ever produced.

Second, in organization of the material: we've tried hard to present the information in the most useful ways possible. We've been listening for years to what people want to know about community, and have attempted to address those concerns and questions in ways that are both informative and easy to use. This includes maps; cross-reference charts; alphabetized descriptions; and even lists of who's disbanded, who's changed their name, and who didn't answer our inquiries. We've created an extensive index for tracking down groups by area of focus. And if we still didn't get it quite right, there's a form on the last page for letting us know how to do it better the next time.

Our Context

The focus of this magazine is intentional communities, and their interplay with the larger society. Only a tiny fraction of the population lives in community, yet we know that our positive contribution to the culture is out of all proportion to our numbers.

Our years of experience with the magazine and the "movement" have taught us that at any point in time there are thousands of people who are becoming aware of community for the first time, and they are hungry for more information. We believe community is a lifestyle choice suitable for many more people than know it exists. This Directory was created largely with this audience in mind.

Part of the appeal of community (and the demand for directories) is that it is one of the more vibrant, dynamic segments of society. Many people feel that mainstream cultural choices are limiting and don't provide the context or opportunity to lead a full and enriching life. Communities are one segment of the society that's *doing something* to create those opportunities... not as a unified movement, but as a spontaneous and sometimes confusing array of choices — there are nearly as many choices as there are communities.

To a large extent, this vibrancy is the result of being responsive to changing needs. While this flexibility is attractive to many, this same feature means volatility, and is maddening to those of us trying to collect and present accurate information. Sometimes it seems that the information changes faster than we can write it down, much less get it printed.

The Broader Movement

The Directory is not only a reaching out from communities to seekers, but a reaching out from community to community. In creating our questionnaires and soliciting listings, we made a concerted effort to gather information about how each group functions... what, in their own opinion, makes them "tick".

By collecting in this Directory a description of each community's unique vision and systems, we offer the opportunity for other groups to draw inspiration and/or technical support for their own work of community building. This includes the encouragement derived from knowing others are doing the same thing, and the excitement that comes from learning how others have successfully handled a similar challenge. We hope that many groups will be inspired to initiate contact with others where there is a sharing of systems, style, or spirit — for we are in this together.

Values in Action

The challenge of trying to develop an accurate, comprehensive directory was also an opportunity. As the "Journal of Cooperation", we got a chance to put our values into practice in the process of creating this Directory.

In the early planning stages, as the expanding scope and increasing quality of the information ballooned the Directory into a thick, "double issue," it became clear that the magazine's regular staff would need help. The Fellowship for Intentional Community (see article in "Networking") came forward with an offer to combine resources on the project, and a partnership developed.

Through the Fellowship we made contacts which spanned the continent, covering as much ground as the communities themselves. Through this wealth of personal connections, and the pervasiveness of the friends-of-friends network, the responses to our call for participation were much stronger than usual... and the result is in your hands.

This Directory is a triumph of cooperation. A celebration of the maturing of the communities movement, and its increasing commitment to intercommunity contact — building on our common commitment to cooperation. We hope you enjoy it.

Table of Contents

1991 Update:
Address changes and corrections have been incorporated into the main text. Additionally, there are more than 40 new community listings and over 20 new resource groups in the specially tabbed section beginning on page 292.

Dramatis Personae:
Mention of the Main Characters Who Helped Cast this Directory

It takes a large cast to put on a big production … and this Directory is the largest issue we've ever produced. There are a number of individuals who deserve credit for their roles in this effort. We won't be able to mention everyone who contributed, but we insist on naming the major angels.

The biggest round of applesauce goes to Geoph Kozeny, the peripatetic communitarian and networker par excellence of the Community Catalyst Project (have Apple/Mac, will travel). His unflagging effort to draw together the myriad loose ends of information now captured between the covers of this Directory was irreplaceable. We couldn't have done it without him. Really. He stored and organized all the listings in his computer, tracking down many of the listings personally. He also did the layout for both the Listings and Resources sections. He took many of the photos used, and had a hand in editing most of the articles. But there is absolutely no truth to the rumor that he hand-stitched each copy.

Dan Questenberry at Shannon Farm helped line up some of our financing, and headed up the team which selected and edited the Article section. This thankless task proved trickier than we first conceived. In good part, we brought this on ourselves by seeking more in-depth articles than those included in previous directories.

For this edition we wanted to engage on important issues, and to describe some of the challenges and struggles in community, as well as the successes. We did not want promotional pieces, where authors favorably compare their particular community with heaven on earth. We wanted reality, not real estate listings.

Fortunately, many communitarians have something to say about their lives, so there was a lot to work with. Unfortunately, not everyone writes as clearly as they think, or think they think. Worse, it wasn't necessarily easy to get people to write about some of the topics we wanted to cover. In the end, though, Dan held the team together and produced a cohesive, high-quality batch of articles.

While we didn't send the whole production to New Haven for polishing, we *did* send all the articles there — so long-time *Communities* magazine layout wizard Chris Collins could work her magic.

In the category of "quickest with an editing pencil in a community without a modem," Jim Estes from Alpha Farm is the runaway winner. Stand up and take a bow, Jim.

Rick Bickhart, formerly of Twin Oaks, did the cover design, while Jenny Upton of Shannon Farm was in charge of the inside visual effects, matching photos and graphics with appropriate prose.

David Thatcher of 100 Mile Lodge made the initial contacts for the international listings, and did much of the follow-up work — tracking down leads, sending off gentle reminders, and tying up loose ends.

For the best contribution by a community in a supporting role, there are eight nominees: Sandhill Farm, Shannon Farm, Twin Oaks, Alpha Farm, The Farm (TN), Currents, Ahimsa, and Hei Wa House. The first three lent money to the project,

and all eight took turns offering Geoph a warm place to eat and lie down between marathon stretches choreographing the various listings sections, editing copy, and doing substantial sections of the final layout. Thanks also to Geoph's mom, Ginny, and her husband, Don, for providing production space and accommodations during several extended visits. The same goes for Allen Butcher and his daughter, Elaine, for hosting several Evansville stop-overs.

At both Shannon and Sandhill there were a number of community members who formed strong supporting casts for different acts in the drama. In addition to Dan and Jenny, the Shannon editorial team included Julie Mazo, Bill Hirsch, Helen Kimble, and Mike Hill. Mike also pitched in from time to time as a computer technician, as did Charlie Hickox, Peter Robinson, Tony Amico, and the Starburst Computer Group.

Much editorial and organizational work was done at Sandhill Farm, where Elke Lerman, Chris Roth, and Rebecca Krantz all played more than cameo roles. The long distance commuting award goes to East Winder Anne Beck, who made several trips to Sandhill (more than 300 miles away) for the sheer enjoyment of putting in long hours poring over lists, licking stamps, and cajoling groups to send us information about themselves.

In creating a list of communities and resources to contact, we started out with our own list and added any other lead we came across that wasn't more than ten years old. We used every old directory we could find. In this realm, special thanks goes to those individuals who supplied long lists of referrals: Corinne McLaughlin & Gordon Davidson (Sirius), Joe Peterson (CSA), Charlie Kraybill (Ganas), Allen Butcher, Dan Greenberg, Ian St. John (Old Hall), Cerek, and Bob Watzke (Farm Home Center).

We'd also like to thank Lisa Wigoda, Marianne Maurin Kilroy, and the Twin Oaks community — for generously lending their darkroom facilities for print-making marathons, and freely offering their technical expertise.

Steve Kehoe, our liaison at Cushing-Malloy in Ann Arbor (our printer), shone brightly in his role. He performed above and beyond the call, whether tracking down leads for recycled paper, tolerating with grace the frequent slippage in our production schedule, and even countersigning our out-of-town check so we could take prompt delivery of the first printing (when the cashier's check was not made out in the right amount). Thanks Steve.

Several groups supplied the financial backing for this production. Their names are mentioned as prominently as possible on the title page.

The initial mailings for this Directory went out in August, 1988. With a few slow periods here and there, we rehearsed for 26 months, constantly building and improving. It wasn't always easy, but it was a wonderful and unifying experience. We're proud of our work, and we hope you enjoy the show.

Laird Sandhill, for the
Directory Management Team

How to Use This Directory

This table outlines six different paths to take in searching through the information contained in this Directory. Your success with any given approach will vary somewhat depending on:

1) What you already know about (or seek in) a community,

2) Whether you're looking for a specific group (one you already know something about), or

3) If you're interested in *any* group which satifies a number of the characteristics that you specify.

	Do You Know the Name ?	Geographic Region?	Defining Characteristics?
Is it in North America ?	Look for a description in the Listings which begin on page 168, and the cross-reference chart (sorted alphabetically) which begins on page 152. If you don't find it there, try the lists of communities which are "Renamed, Regrouped, Dead, Disbanded, Lost, or No Replies" which begins on page 232.	Look at the maps beginning on page 146 to locate those included in this Directory, or the chart on page 160, which sorts communities by state or province (arranged alphabetically within each region).	Examine the cross-reference charts beginning on pages 152 & 160. Hopefully, the specific characteristics you're seeking are among those reviewed in the chart. If a particular characteristic does not appear in the chart, try locating relevant keywords in the Index at the back of the book.
Is it on Another Continent ?	Check the International Listings which begin on page 242 and the international cross-reference chart which begins on page 240.	Begin with the list on page 241 which sorts communities by country, arranged alphabetically.	Study the cross-reference chart which begins on page 240. If a particular characteristic does not appear in the chart, look for relevant keywords in the Index..

Still can't find it?

If you followed the steps outlined above and still can't find the information you want, there are several possibilities. If it's a North American community, it may be listed in the Late Entries beginning on page 292.

Another possibility is that the group has chosen to downplay its living situation in deference to its "work". Check through the Resources section for groups that are doing relevant work but which may not consider themselves "a community".

If you still can't find it, we suggest you write us with your specific request. We've gathered boxes of information (literally) — far more than we could possibly include in the Directory — and it's possible that at our Fellowship headquarters we still have something for you. There were also over a hundred groups that reported that they "still exist as a community, but don't wish to be listed at this time." Details about how to place a request for information and/or referrals are outlined on the next-to-last page.

And finally — you may have information about a group that we don't know about. If so, please let us know! We'd like to invite their participation in our next directory. Please use the form on the last page to share any new leads you have. Thanks! ❖

7

Paper Chase:

The story about how we make decisions and how we were able to get this printing done on 100% recycled paper (which is a good thing, though perhaps not as wonderful as it first appears ...).

This Directory was conceived and created by a team — a cooperative group recruited by the Fellowship just for this project. There was no staff or system in place. What we needed we made up. Among us we had a lot of experience in community, some experience editing and writing, and almost no experience working together.

The key adjective in the above paragraph is "cooperative." In keeping with the cooperative nature of intentional communities in general and of the Fellowship in particular, we were determined to do our work with this value always in view: *how* we created the Directory was every bit as important as *what* we created.

While we had a common goal — the Directory — members of the editorial team had different ideas about how best to get there. There were choices everywhere. (See the sidebar on Decisions for a sampling of what we faced and how we chose.)

It was particularly challenging to create a process for selecting and editing the articles. We agreed that we wanted articles which examined issues in community living, engagingly written and illuminating — but could we establish objective criteria to accomplish that goal?

What is confusing to an editor may be the heart and soul of the author's appeal to others. To what extent is the medium integral to the message? Because our goal is not homogenization, but a witnessing and celebration of choices and vitality, we faced a tough challenge in deciding where confused writing ends and unenlightened editing begins.

As if questions of style weren't challenge enough, we also discovered that our team relies on a variety of technologies (all the way from paper and pencil to laptop computer, and several stops in between), and these choices have a subtle influence on one's sense of what is "well-written."

Some of our team members write letters nearly every day, while others use the phone almost exclusively. Some are linked by electronic mail, and others are as easily reached by carrier pigeon (which is to say, messages go out on a wing and a prayer). Just as with the movement in general, our editorial team was both diverse and dispersed.

Finding a Printer

To illustrate how all this comes to bear on our work, let's explore the process we went through in selecting a printer for the Directory.

We started out looking at costs. After working up an approximate list of specifications, we shopped around for possible printers, using any and all leads for those who were reliable and reasonably priced. In the quotes we received there was a startling array of prices (in some cases it was hard to believe we were talking about the same project). Based on these responses, we quickly narrowed our search to three possibilities. Then it got complicated.

In comparing the details of the various bids, we had to face several decisions. How should we protect the cover: use the longer lasting film lamination, or the less expensive press

varnish? Is 50-lb. paper stock heavy enough to not have photographs show through on the next page, or should we play it safe and go with 60-lb. stock? Were we willing to pay extra to use a local and more familiar printer? Were we willing to use a more expensive printer if it meant we could get the Directory out six weeks sooner? Were we willing to pay a premium to have the printing done on recycled paper?

After considerable back and forth, we decided to select a smaller, more local printer who was more flexible about using recycled paper. At the last moment, though, this printer had a press breakdown and had to withdraw from consideration. As a consequence of switching to a different printer on short notice, we lost the chance to have the first printing done on recycled stock.

Finding Recycled Paper

For the second printing we were better prepared. With help from Albert Bates and Bob Holzapfel (both at The Farm) and our printer in Ann Arbor, we were able to locate a major paper maker (Glatfelter) who regularly produces batches of "environmentally-friendly" paper stock. It is only produced once a month, and must be special-ordered more than two months ahead of the time you will need it. It is the same paper that Earth Care [see Resource listing on page 264] markets as Minimum Impact™. It is not an ideal paper (we'll get to that below), but on the balance it is the most appropriate paper stock we could locate that is suitable for the Directory. (There is paper available that is more environmentally benign, but it costs considerably more; at some point the loss of accessibility — increased paper cost equals higher cover price — is not offset by the environmental gain.)

OK, so how environmentally sound is this paper? It's 100% recycled, which means it's made entirely from old paper (no virgin wood pulp is used). However, the more telling statistic is that only about 5% of this stock is post-consumer paper. Because pre-consumer waste (printer scraps, trimmings, mill ends, bark, wood, chips, etc.) has traditionally been used by paper manufacturers, its inclusion in recycled paper does not represent a change. It is the post-consumer fraction (for a brief technical definition, read the paragraph on "Industrial Hair Splitting" printed at the bottom of page 325) that impacts the environment — through less cutting of trees, and less materials going into landfills. In this light, "recycled" doesn't mean that much, and 5% post-consumer, while better than nothing, is still a long, long way from perfect.

Why not a higher percentage of post-consumer? We're told there is a glut of paper waiting to be recycled. Paper manufacturers have been slow to build enough plant capacity to process the treasure. Hopefully this is a temporary dilemma, and the next time we print the Directory we'll be able to report a higher percentage of post-consumer paper in the mix.

Now for the good news. Although only slightly post-consumer, this paper is unbleached and has not been de-inked. That means no dioxins or other environmentally objectionable treatments. Because of this, the color of the paper varies slightly from batch to batch, from cream to light grey — and is likely to vary even within the pages of a given book. Interestingly, though less processed, this paper still costs more. For the most part, this is due to economies of scale. Recycled paper is still only a small fraction of the market, and is not yet being made at the most efficient mills. By being willing to pay a premium price, we're trying to do our part to hasten the day when paper that is less processed is also less costly.

Our Different Path to Decisions

In the mainstream culture, there would typically be one person charged with making these decisions about a printer, with one factor to consider above all others — the proverbial bottom line. After getting the initial bids, and perhaps requesting a few clarifications, it might have taken only minutes to make the necessary choices.

This same decision took our team weeks of hard work, gathering information and searching for alternative routes that, as a package, offered the best mix of our chosen values. To be sure, we looked at money. But instead of being the overriding factor, it was just one consideration, along with ecological values and the implications of supporting small, local businesses.

The Directory was not held up while these decisions were agonized over, but our group willingly accepted this extra claim on our time, because we cared about reaching the best possible decisions, in the best possible manner.

We believe it takes effort to learn decision-making in a cooperative way, unlearning the hierarchical patterns of the dominant culture. We believe it is worth taking the time to work on this even when the consequences are not necessarily major, so the habit will be that much further ingrained for decisions yet to come. ❖

Decisions, Decisions, Decisions...

The editorial team for this Directory faced a bunch of choices. Below is a collection of some of the more interesting ones, along with which path we took, and our reasons for doing so.

Should we charge communities and resources for listings? We didn't. We wanted participation as full as we could get, and were afraid that many smaller communities — who make up the vast majority — would not pay to be included. Directories of the larger, more established communities already exist; we wanted something more representative of what's actually going on.

What price should we set for the Directory? The first printing was priced at $12 — a figure set at the very beginning of the project (spring of '88), before a single listing or article was solicited. It was a guess about appropriate middle ground between the need to make money to operate the magazine, and the goal of keeping the Directory affordable.

The more we got into the project, the more we saw ways to improve the product. We found out how poorly old directories had been researched, and how complex a challenge it was to make the information as accessible as possible — recognizing that people approach community, and information about community, in a variety of ways. (The cross-reference charts on pages 152-167 are a good example of this. It took hundreds of painstaking hours to prepare them. In the end we had fully detailed charts, the likes of which have never appeared in directories before. They are absolute godsends to some ... and anathemas to others.)

We worked hard to set a different standard, both in accuracy of information and in how well it is organized. Before we knew it, two years had passed and we had created a $20 Directory ... with a list price of $12. Because

of considerable advance publicity and solicitation of pre-publication orders, we felt obliged to stick with the $12 price for the first printing — even though it meant less income for paying off loans, compensating labor, and funding the Fellowship's other projects.

With the second printing, we boosted the price to $16 (no, we didn't consider $15.95 ... somebody needs to stand up to Madison Avenue gimmickry). The extra four dollars helps pay for several things: 1) better binding (these copies are stitched, where the first printing was only glued; 2) recycled paper (though less processed, it costs more); 3) eight extra pages of material, and lots of updated information; 4) funds that the Fellowship will use to create a whole new edition of the Directory (scheduled for a November '92 release), to organize the international Gathering of communities in June '93, and to pay off thousands of dollars of old debt for Communities magazine.

How do we decide who is a "legitimate" community? While this is a "legitimate" question, we decided not to pick up this hot potato. There is no standard definition of community, and we chose to let groups define themselves. Seekers will have to reach their own conclusions.

Should we print articles representing one viewpoint if we don't have at least one other piece from a different perspective? We did, occasionally. We decided our main goal was to stimulate discussion, without promoting any particular position. Where we had a well-written, stimulating article we tried hard to get additional pieces focusing on the same issue from a different angle. If, however, additional pieces didn't surface, we printed what we had. At the same time, we *did* reject one or two engaging articles which appeared at the last moment, because there wasn't adequate time to solicit writing representing other views. Those articles will have to wait for another edition. ❖

What This Directory Is ... And Isn't

The editorial staff of this Directory worked long and hard to include information about as many intentional communities as possible. We believe it to be the most comprehensive directory ever produced. And yet ... we know that there are many, many communities which are not listed, despite our best efforts.

The fact is, many communities are not looking for contact with others, or prefer that referrals come only by word of mouth. Some groups feel that they're not ready for any publicity. In other cases, a community has been created to meet specific needs of its members — who are more or less happy with what they now have. In any event, we've been in touch with about 75 existing groups that prefer to remain unlisted

The communities we've included are those which (within limits) do want contact with others. They may be looking for more members, they may be curious to find other groups doing similar things, or they may simply be willing to talk about what works for them.

We also believe that this is a highly accurate directory. And yet, no matter how careful we have been ... communities are dynamic, changing entities. Some of the information we have gathered will be out of date even before it's printed, and the inaccuracies are sure to grow with the passing of time.

What Is a "Community"?
Right from the start we were faced with the challenge of defining what, exactly, is an intentional community. There is no uniformly accepted definition. Given that we had no mandate to decide this issue, and no means to verify claims — we chose to let communities define themselves. Basically, any group of two or more adults which chose to call itself a community was welcome to participate.

Our early mailings invited listings from any community which had appeared in past directories. In the beginning we did not qualify our invitation because we didn't want to be in the role of passing judgment on others, or deciding which styles of community were more worthy than others. Since the criteria for such comparisons vary from one person to the next, the responsibility for evaluating the information and determining which leads to pursue has been left to you, the reader.

As we dug deeper for information about additional groups to contact, we realized that we wanted to narrow our invitation somewhat. Instead of leaving the door wide open, we asked communities to submit listings only if they aligned themselves with a philosophy of non-violence and freedom for members to leave the group at any time — but we left it to each community to determine, *in its own view*, exactly what those terms mean. Most (but not all) communities listed in this Directory have been asked to screen themselves in this way.

To the best of our knowledge, we have included no community which has standards contrary to either of these two basic guiding principles. At the same time, it is important to note that very little of the information in the Directory has been confirmed by first-hand observation of our staff. We have included only information that has been recently verified (or at least reviewed) by someone representing the community or organization — and we want to make it clear that we've simply taken people's word for the accuracy of their statements and representations.

"Forming" Communities
As agents of change and voices for lifestyle options, intentional communities are a particularly volatile component of society. They change a lot — especially communities that are not yet settled. Given our interest in having up-to-date information, we struggled with the question of whether to include forming communities at all ... since much of their information will be inaccurate by the time this Directory is distributed. The rate of change (and disbandments) for forming groups is typically much higher than that of more established groups.

Despite this concern, we have decided to include forming communities because: 1) it is important to illustrate as fully as possible the breadth of the alternatives available (or being attempted), and 2) many new communities fail for lack of energy provided by prospective members, or insufficient support from established groups with similar goals and approaches. We hope that the Directory will play an important role in fulfilling both of these needs.

Having decided to include them, we still had to define them. Again we were faced with the dilemma of having subjective terminology ... what some consider stable may appear unsettled to others. For this Directory we have labeled as "forming" any community describing itself as such, and any community with fewer than three adult members.

In many cases, forming communities have only recently coalesced and are looking to grow — but that is not always the case. Sometimes a group has been around quite a while, yet is still working to settle one or more key questions about how to develop. Other groups with this classification were once well established, but have now shrunk and may be wavering between continuing and disbanding.

We have designated forming communities by the ingenious method of printing "(Forming)" after their names in the Listings section, and by labeling them with an "[F]" in the index and in the charts.

Reader Beware ...
It can't be overemphasized that the groups depicted in this Directory are *not* Utopias realized. Many of them are quite wonderful places to live and work, places where the residents share a common vision or purpose. Most are ripe with good

How You Can Help ...

Communities **Magazine invites you to help us help intentional communities and communitarians ...**

Reader Involvement

Feedback is what enables us to take your opinions and preferences into consideration as we continue our efforts to refine and improve our publications and services. We encourage you to send letters to the editor on any topic related to community, cooperation, transformation, etc.

Editorial Support

We invite your participation and editorial input on future issues of the magazine. Responsibility for an issue of *Communities* is often assigned to a volunteer who is interested in editing an issue on a particular topic (with assistance from our staff, as needed). Articles are always welcome on any aspect of community or cooperation, including full-length articles on individual communities and organizations. We are especially interested in articles which substantiate the services communities provide to people outside their membership or group. Articles should be typewritten and double-spaced, and include as many photographs and graphics as possible. We also welcome drawings and photos which depict ideas or scenes related to cooperative living — we can pair these with articles that need additional graphics.

Advertising Support

If you have a product or service that would be of interest to our readers, please send for our advertising rate sheet and place your ad with us.

Subscription/Distribution

In order to increase the circulation of *Communities*, we need the help of every community, cooperative organization, and communitarians everywhere. You can help us by distributing flyers and by suggesting that the bookstores, libraries, and health food stores in your area carry *Communities*. If you publish a newsletter or magazine, you could help by running an exchange ad. If you have a community center or storefront where you could sell copies or display flyers, we would be happy to pay you a commission for every sale and subscription you generate. Another way you can help us *and* a friend is to give a gift subscription to *Communities*. Or you can make a tax-deductible donation to help *Communities* continue to grow and prosper as we help communities and communitarians around the world. ❖

intentions and dedication, and are fertile environments for personal growth and work toward the greater good. Most also suffer occasional bouts of such human failings as egocentric behavior, power struggles, miscommunication, and unrealistic expectations.

The Directory is a forum which allows each group to share its vision, and it's natural that most groups want to put their best foot forward. It's up to each reader to assess the information which describes each group — and try to identify what statements are part of the "grand plan", and which ones reflect the day-to-day reality. May your search be interesting, and fruitful.

Articles Galore

In the pages immediately following, we are pleased to present almost 40 feature articles about various aspects of community living, gleaned carefully from the nearly 100 submitted, and grouped by subject area. We've included about a half-dozen reprints from other sources, but most of the articles are original works.

In soliciting articles we indicated our openness to the full spectrum of community choices and viewpoints. We specified only that "community" be the unifying theme, and that articles be more informative and engaging than promotional and laudatory.

We feel that this collection gives a valuable overview of community living, yet we are aware that all views and topics worthy of attention are not represented. Even though everyone was invited, not everyone was inspired. And in the end we could only choose from among what was submitted.

We invite you to turn the page and sample what we've collected. Our intent is to be more stimulating than definitive. So we ask you to see these articles not as a final word, but as a point of departure. Community is a full participation activity, and we want *you* to be part of the process. ❖

Guidelines for Contacting & Visiting Communities

We're confident this Directory will stimulate inquiries and visits to intentional communities — a development that most communities will welcome. Based on our collective experience with seekers and communities, we offer the following guidance on how to make contacts and visits work well for everyone.

Correspondence

When writing, it's usually a good practice to include a self-addressed, stamped envelope (SASE) and a small donation. These are invariably appreciated, and in some cases they're expected (if we know this to be the case, we have included a note in the group's description).

Unfortunately, not all communities answer all inquiries promptly. There are a variety of reasons for this — sometimes groups are swamped with inquiries; sometimes groups are not currently interested in additional members; sometimes other events have completely overshadowed answering the mail (financial crisis, medical emergency, tension within the group); sometimes letters simply get misplaced or lost. We asked communities, "Can you commit to answering correspondence promptly?" For the groups which answered negatively we have included the code "[cc]" at the end of their listings. So please take note.

The letters most likely to be answered promptly are those which are personable, short to medium in length, and pose interesting and/or thought-provoking questions. Most communities are full of busy people, and many will never get around to reading an initial letter longer than about two pages.

Tell something about yourself: your background, your interests, your needs, your endearing quirks, and what you're looking for in a community. Experience in group living and working situations is not typically required, but it can be a major "plus" when a community is screening for prospective members. Try to be up front about your interest in contact … are you looking for a home, just curious about community, or something in between?

Try to be as specific as possible when asking questions, focusing on what is important to you. Note that you're not likely to get a very revealing response to a general question such as "Please tell me about your community." If that's what you write, often a standard flyer (if one exists) is all you'll get in return. Most communities report that simple one-line inquiries like this rarely lead to secondary contact, much less to visits or new members, and so are given less serious attention. The other extreme — also to be avoided — is a long series of in-depth questions which reads like an entrance exam to a private university. The more time and effort it will take to answer your letter, the less likely it is that someone will get around to doing it.

Visiting

Do *not* assume that a community is open to visits just because it's listed in the Directory. Our questionnaire asked: "Are you open to visitors who make arrangements in advance?" You'll find the communities' answers in the cross-reference charts. If a community you're interested in has answered "Yes"or "Maybe", check their description in the Listings section to see if they have any specific restrictions about visiting.

If a visit seems appropriate, the next step is to contact the community to discuss visiting guidelines, mutual expectations, length of stay, and prospective dates. Keep in mind that while a community may *usually* be open to visits, there may be *particular* times that are not good for the community. The more flexibility you show, the more likely you'll be able to schedule a visit that suits everyone.

If the community suggests guidelines for visiting, try to respect them. Some communities have developed highly-structured visitor programs, while others are very loose. In any event, dropping in on a community without prior arrangements is *strongly discouraged*. Most communities consider this disrespectful, and some will flatly refuse to let you stay.

It may happen that you set up a visit, and then find it necessary to change your plans. Whether you need to alter dates or wish to cancel the visit altogether, it's a courtesy to inform the community. Sometimes communities decide to turn away prospective visitors because others are already scheduled for the dates under consideration. If they are holding a space in their schedule for you, others may be needlessly inconvenienced if you don't report your change in plans.

If you are traveling by public transportation and need to be picked up, try to arrange a convenient time and place of arrival. With some planning, the connection can often be worked into an already scheduled trip. If a special trip is required, it is appropriate to reimburse the community for travel costs.

Communities have varying policies about giving visitors access to community resources, and it is wise to be clear at the outset. Ask about charges for room and board, and compensation for use of the telephone, postage, vehicles, etc. There may be restrictions on using some tools or machines, or eating some food supplies. You may need to bring your own towels, shampoo, bedding, etc., so ask in advance.

Remember, the community is home to the members, and you are a guest. Try to learn and respect the community's norms. Starting off well is often the key to getting the most out of your visit.

[For further perspectives on visiting communities, see the articles on "Finding Your Community" beginning on the next page.]

Feedback

If a community is particularly responsive to your requests, we'd appreciate hearing about it … we want to know who's doing a good job. Naturally, we hope to hear a lot of stories about people's needs getting met and their expectations exceeded.

However, we know that won't always the case; sometimes things won't work out as hoped for. If information in this Directory appears to be incorrect, or if you believe you've been ignored or mistreated by one of the communities we've listed … please tell us about that, too. On the next-to-last page we've included information on how to write us about your experience.

Happy Hunting!

Finding Your Community

How can you, an individual looking for a home in community, find one that satisfies your basic needs and shares your core values? The articles in this section approach this question from a variety of viewpoints.

Kat Kinkade of Twin Oaks gives a communitarian's perspective on visitors, offering practical advice on **How to Visit a Community.** She discusses visiting etiquette, and how to get the most out of one's visit. Based on her many years of community experience, she offers valuable insights about how prospective members may be viewed by existing community members.

Sirius Community's Corinne McLaughlin and Gordon Davidson, seasoned veterans of community living, share their perspective in **A Checklist for Those Wanting to Join a Community.** They address the question "Are you a community person?" (in most cases, they believe, "the answer is probably yes") and offer tips on self-assessment and advice on visiting.

William Schlicht, Jr., himself a community seeker, describes the insights he gained by visiting fourteen communities in the Eastern U.S. in the mid-80s. His article, **Finding a Community to Call Home,** suggests many useful questions for prospective members to consider in evaluating how well a community might fulfill their needs.

Communities for the Mainstream tells of Julie Mazo's search to find a home community in which she could reap the benefits of cooperative living while continuing a fairly conventional lifestyle. Julie, as one relatively new to community, examines her motives for joining, and describes the groups she visited during her search.

A Word About Cults, also by Corinne McLaughlin and Gordon Davidson, elaborates on the differences between growth-enhancing intentional communities and "cults" — groups which may restrict individual free will and personal freedom. Their analysis includes a list of traits common to such groups.

Like all major life choices, finding your community can be one of the most challenging, growthful, and enriching experiences you'll ever have... no matter what your background or what you're looking for. These authors' insights will help you on your way.

Gordon Davidson/Sirius

How to Visit a Community

The author, a long-term member of Twin Oaks, provides practical advice to visitors from the community's perspective. She describes etiquette in communal societies with helpful insights for those seekers wishing to enhance their first visits to intentional communities.

by Kat Kinkade

The mechanics of visiting a community aren't very difficult. One writes a letter, waits for a response, follows directions, and that's that. But assuring oneself of a fruitful and satisfying visit is another matter. Most communities spend considerable time and energy talking and worrying about this. Yet there are still shortcomings and miscommunication from time to time. Visitors can help by doing some thinking ahead of time to set themselves up for a good visit. This article is full of advice to the prospective visitor. Read it with your own plans in mind. Maybe it will give you some ideas.

It is useful to consider the question: Why is this particular community open to visitors at all? What do they want or need from them? I think it's safe to say that most communities who advertise in a directory are keeping an eye out for people who might join them. They may be openly seeking members, or they may be only selectively open, watching for someone with a high degree of compatibility.

There are other reasons for having visitors, and they will vary from group to group. Some may simply need help with their work. Others may welcome stimulation from outsiders. Several groups make their living from welcoming visitors at various conferences and seminars. Some organizations are interested in spreading their philosophy or religion. What you can be sure of, however, is that a group opens itself to receive strangers for its own reasons and its own needs. It isn't just exercising neighborly hospitality.

On your side, you have your reasons for wanting to visit. The sensible thing is to make plans to visit groups who not only have something to offer you, but also have something to gain from your stay.

No matter what a visitor's private agenda may be, helping the community with its daily work is quite likely to make the visit worthwhile on both sides. Work is appreciated, and good work is appreciated a lot! This is true on the smallest commune or the biggest kibbutz. Work opens doors to friendship and mutual confidence that no amount of conversation will accomplish. Most people know this intuitively.

Over the years my community has hosted thousands of visitors, a large percentage of whom have pitched in willingly with everything from collating newsletters to bucking hay, and didn't begrudge the time. They have helped us build what we have today, and I, for one, am grateful. It's one of the reasons we will probably continue to be open to thousands more. The visitor who feels touchy about being exploited during the few days or weeks of a visit just doesn't understand the trade-offs from the community's point of view, and is unlikely to get much from the visit.

Sometimes a visitor is perfectly willing to work, and repeatedly volunteers, but the community members don't seem to take the time or make the effort to find an appropriate job. If this happens, and you aren't the sort who can just intuitively find ways to help out, make sure your offer is clear, and then enjoy yourself doing something else. Some groups are just not well enough organized to use the available resources, and there's no point in bugging them about it.

The mistake to be avoided is treating the communities like a sort of Disney World, put there for the interest of the public. For the most part, intentional communities are not showcases, are not kept up to impress outsiders, and are not particularly interested in being casually looked at. Communitarians may put up with a certain amount of tourism for income, or for outreach; but the main thing they are doing in communities is living their private lives, and they don't really enjoy spectators.

Occasionally an outsider who is not content with a guided tour becomes exasperating by insisting on "talking to the common people to get a real feel for the place." The common, as well as uncommon, people in any community are friendly enough, but they see too many strangers. The only way to get a feel for the place is to stay awhile, and the best way to do that is to invest yourself in a visit that is useful to both parties.

Kathleen Kinkade is one of the founders of Twin Oaks in Virginia, and East Wind in Missouri. She wrote the Twin Oaks history, *A Walden Two Experiment*. Kat lives at Twin Oaks, where she is active in various administrative and clerical functions, as well as choral singing, barbership quartets and community musical productions.

Let us assume, then, that you are prepared to establish your welcome in a community by one means or another, and get on to other issues. One of the main other issues is the matter of expectations.

It's a good idea to read the printed material that a community provides. While no substitute for a visit, it at least gives you an idea of how a substantial part of the community views itself. Of course this material will contribute to your expectations, as it should. This can be upsetting when your actual on-site experiences don't seem to have much to do with the lofty sentiments expressed on paper. Just the same, there is a connection between a group's beliefs and its behaviors, and it is a mistake to ignore it, especially if you think of joining.

Years ago I knew a couple who read the philosophical material of a certain community and were appalled by it. They didn't agree with its tenets and didn't like the tone of the presentation, either. However, they happened to meet someone from the group who was highly personable, so they visited and found the entire group to be friendly, charming, and warm. My friends, figuring actions spoke louder than words, decided to ignore the declared goals of the community and to believe instead the day-to-day behavior of the people they were getting to know and enjoy. They joined up.

But as the months of their membership progressed, they found themselves continually at odds with the community's oldest members. Everybody was warm and courteous, but their goals weren't compatible. Before anybody quite realized what was happening, there was serious internal dissen-

sion, which saw my friends battling with the original leaders for directional control of the community. Eventually the couple left, and so did some other members, who were disillusioned by the bad feelings generated by the philosophical battle.

This left the group weak, angry, and exhausted. It was a community tragedy, and not an uncommon one. I say, before joining a community, read and believe its documents. The chances are they mean what they say.

Of course a visitor will have expectations of some sort, but it's useful to keep them to a modest level. I can think of three common expectations that frequently meet with disappointment.

There's the wealthy community vision. A person who doesn't understand why the community isn't bursting with artistic work or doesn't have its own school or isn't generating its own power or creating original architecture is frequently unaware that such visions depend on financial wealth. "But I expected a rural group to have horses", is a typical case in point.

More common, there's the sense of community vision. This person expects to be included and loved fairly soon after arrival, because of an idea that all the people in a true community love one another. It is a serious disillusionment to discover that this kind of love grows only after time and mutual commitment and cannot be grasped quickly.

Many people expect all communities to be wholehearted in their dedication to food self-sufficiency or healthful eating habits. I have seen some visitors to my community seriously

*Laundry day at
Twin Oaks,
Virginia*

Geoph Kozeny/Community Catalyst

shocked by our casual laissez-faire attitude toward diet. We eat meat and frequently serve desserts, as well as indulging in a small amount of junk food. To us this seems moderate and reasonable, considering our abundance of whole grains and tempeh and vegetables. To some visitors it seems like heresy and backsliding.

A viable community adapts to the needs and desires of its own members much more than it conforms to abstract ideals. The probability is high that it will not, if it is successful, be very fanatical in its ideals. There will be some determined core idealism, but otherwise compromise will prevail. Doubtless some communities don't compromise. Some don't last, either. I suspect a connection.

Many visitors set themselves up for disappointment by expecting their visit to be blessed with a love affair (or relationship). Now, who am I to say this won't happen? In fact it has happened to hundreds of people in hundreds of communities, and maybe it will happen to you. But don't count on it. If you join, that's another matter. The chances of a long-term community member finding, at one time or another, a love relationship within or through the community are quite high if not absolutely guaranteed. But the visitor? My advice is to set the hope firmly aside and enjoy other things. Trying too hard will just make it less likely. As to the notion of finding readily available casual sex in the commune, forget it.

The most interesting community visit is that of a prospective member. Let's say you've read the materials, and you're ready for a change in your life. You've come with modest expectations, and the community looks pretty good to you. Even at this point, there are still things to consider in order to enhance the chances of a good connection to your chosen group.

Take this question: Shall I be on my best behavior while I visit, or shall I let them know what I am really like? By all means put your best foot forward! The experienced community makes allowances. We know that in a year or two you're not going to be jumping up and volunteering to wash the dishes, the way you do when you're just visiting. But the eagerness to make a good impression makes a good impression. We like you wanting to please. It says something good about your social skills. We know that the real you is somewhat more of a mixed bag. So is the real we for that matter.

That's not the same thing as hiding vital information. If you have a serious medical problem or a sticky child custody situation or a history of drug abuse, it just isn't fair to join and lay these problems on a community without its knowledge and agreement.

Then there's the related question: Shall I let them know my real opinions, or shall I just go along with their assumptions? I would say that this depends on the nature of the group. Are you joining a group that essentially has a religion it wants all members to adhere to? If so, it seems to me highly questionable ethically to join such a group without embracing its

Work is appreciated, and good work is appreciated a lot! This is true on the smallest commune or the biggest kibbutz. Work opens doors to friendship and mutual confidence that no amount of conversation will accomplish.

convictions. On the other hand, a group that is essentially secular should not concern itself with your private opinions. It is your behavior that matters. In my opinion, when someone in a secular community asks you whether you believe in this or that doctrine (and you're not sure you do), you could answer to the effect\that you respect the community's stand on it and are prepared to conform to its rules and norms on the subject, and let it go at that.

Nothing is more obnoxious than the visitor who defies the important traditions of a community. Imagine, for example, a visitor surreptitiously passing out candy bars to the children in a commune that makes a big deal about pure food, arguing that this is personal freedom. Joining any community automatically entails giving up certain personal freedoms (different ones at different communities); and it is unmannerly in the extreme, to say nothing of ineffective, to insist on taking for yourself freedoms that the community members have voluntarily given up. A certain amount of "When in Rome" is certainly appropriate.

On the other hand, if you are thinking of joining, and your happiness depends on something that you don't think the community has, judging from what you see, don't give up too easily. Make it a point to ask, without being pushy. It might be that the community is more flexible than it looks. In my own community there are many things that can sometimes be done, within our rules, but aren't done very often for various reasons. If a prospective member looks good to us and wonders aloud if this or that could be arranged, maybe it can. Certainly it's worth bringing up the subject and checking it out.

The community you see during your visit is not the whole community. It is almost impossible for visitors to understand this, but it is profoundly true. A little slice of time cannot give a deep understanding of the nature of the community. Your visit is influenced by many factors that are trivial in relation to the entire membership experience. For instance, a particularly influential member may be absent when you visit. Or there may be other visitors at the same time who by their presence skew your impressions. The seasons have a great impact on community activity, as do such things as getting out a big order of the community's main product, or participating in an emergency, or being there during a birth or a death. The particular ideological issue being discussed avidly when you visit is probably only one of many, and your visit will not give you an accurate impression of either its importance or its outcome. If you visit when somebody is angrily leaving the group, you will pick up on a different feeling from the one you'd get if you visit when things are going well and membership is solid.

Your impressions of the community will also be influenced by the group you hang out with. I strongly advise all visitors to be cautious of information from a member who is angry with the community and wants to air grievances. Such impressions can give a sense of getting the lowdown on the community, but the value of this lowdown is questionable. At a minimum, a visitor who is subjected to it should make a point of bringing up the same issues with a member who is happy with the place. If you're looking for a communal home, give yourself a chance! The disillusioned member on the way out is not an objective informant, by a long shot. No place is perfect, but it's probably not as bad as it can be made to sound.

On the subject of community controversy, there's not much point in a visitor getting involved. In my community, public discussions are carried on in writing, on a bulletin board. The comments of visitors on these controversies are not usually welcome. Other communities argue in meetings, and the same thing is true of visitor comments there. I know that it may seem to the visitor that there is something quite

Pitching in at
Twin Oaks

Geoph Kozeny/Community Catalyst

17

relevant that hasn't been said, and somebody needs to say it. But this is virtually never true. No outsider can really understand these issues after a brief stay.

After joining, new members will still blunder and be gently helped by older members to a greater understanding of the issues; but it is too much to expect for this educational process to be extended to the revolving population of visitors. It isn't quite a matter of "Visitors should be seen and not heard," but there is value in listening a lot and reserving your opinions for later. It can be valuable for the visitor to listen to the controversial discussion and then ask questions privately, outside of meeting time. If your opinion is couched in the form of "But why is it so important that…" or "What would happen if such and such an approach were taken?" it will give you a chance to participate without being resented. Be prepared to hear answers to your questions, however, and don't be hurt if your input isn't taken very seriously.

Every once in a while a community gets a visitor who really does have knowledge that is immediately useful, and offering help in such cases is appreciated. Generally this is technical help. The community is having legal difficulties with a custody case, for example, and you happen to be a retired lawyer from a firm that did a lot of custody work. Or the community is building a house, and you are an experienced construction contractor. Or you are a doctor and notice with alarm that certain community norms are likely to lead to a particular disease you know about. Note that the helpful information is not philosophical in nature. It is practical, and it is the direct result of specialized training and experience.

In between solid technical expertise and personal opinion and philosophy lie many areas that may or may not be useful to the community. The one I notice most often is massage. A lot of people are trained masseurs these days. Good. Offering to give massages is a courteous and friendly thing to do. You may or may not get any takers. The same is true for various schools of conflict resolution, facilitation, and therapy, and for artistic accomplishments that you can teach. If you have such a skill, your best tactic is to offer but not push it. If your guitar playing draws a happy crowd, good, you've added something to the group's happiness. On the other hand, if nobody wants to listen, oh well, try something else.

Any community's favorite visitor is the cheerful, helpful one who is genuinely impressed with the community and not very critical of its flaws. Even if you don't join, leaving the group with a positive feeling about itself is a nice thing to do. Of course it's always possible that some group at a particular time doesn't really need congratulations; it needs a kick in the pants. Even so, be very careful before you elect yourself to the job.

A word about doing the community circuit. People often set out to visit many different communities, but few ever finish their trek. They find out what they need to know after

> *A viable community adapts to the needs and desires of its own members much more than it conforms to abstract ideals. The probability is high that it will not, if it is successful, be very fanatical in its ideals. There will be some determined core idealism, but otherwise compromise will prevail. Doubtless some communities don't compromise. Some don't last, either. I suspect a connection.*

being at two or three. This being the case, it makes sense to look at the list of groups that sound interesting, and visit the most likely-looking ones first. Directories get outdated quickly, too, so write more letters than you need. Some of them may not be answered.

When I mentioned to my fellow communitarians that I was writing this article about how to visit a community, they said, "Tell them this is our home," and "Tell them not to drop in without being invited," and "Tell them they sometimes have to take no for an answer." So I'm passing along all those messages, but while I'm at it, I should explain that 19 out of every 20 visitors are a help and a pleasure to us, and that these growls and groans all come because of the exceptional 20th. Furthermore, virtually all groups who publish their name and whereabouts do want and need a certain number and kind of visitors. So don't be discouraged. If you really want to live in community, you'll find one. ❖

(*A Walden Two Experiment*, 271 pages, is available for $5.95 plus $1.50 postage and handling from Twin Oaks, Rt. 4, Box 169, Louisa, VA 23093.)

A Checklist for Those Wanting to Join a Community

by Corinne McLaughlin and Gordon Davidson

Are you wondering if you're a community person? Do you think you would fit in with a community? No matter who you are, the answer is probably yes, as there's undoubtedly a community somewhere for every type of person. However, here are a few qualities that are generally needed in most communities, so you can see how you'd fare in one:

1. A willingness to think and act in terms of the good of the whole, not just in terms of personal needs and opinions — in other words, good old-fashioned unselfishness (or at least a willingness to grow in this direction).

2. Tolerance for differences and open-mindedness toward different points of view.

3. A willingness to work out conflicts and not hold grudges, with a realistic belief in the possibility of resolving differences to mutual satisfaction.

4. A somewhat adventurous and courageous spirit, open to change, flexible and adaptable.

5. A generally social nature — liking to be with people much of the time (hermit types would climb the wall!).

Although perfection in all of these qualities is hardly expected (and rarely achieved), a willingness to change and grow into these qualities is important.

How would you know if community living was right for you, even if you had the above qualities? What should you look for in a community? This depends on what your personal values are. Here are some things you might want to explore and reflect on as you read about and visit various communities:

1) If you are mainly looking for a supportive and loving environment with lots of good friends, then spend as much time as you can on a one-to-one basis with members of each community you visit. Get to know the members personally to see if you share an easy and natural harmony with them. If you don't feel a good heart-to-heart connection at first, it may be more difficult to become close friends later.

If an active social life is your interest, check out how much harmony or conflict there is among the community members. Observe how much time the members spend hanging out with each other, sharing social activities like parties or sports events. And feel out the "vibes" — the general atmosphere — of the community when you first arrive. Your intuition will tell you whether it could be "home" for you.Even though the community members you visit may be good people with whom you share common ideals and values, you may not have a basic "resonance" with each other on a personality level. So if support and nurturing are high on your agenda, keep looking until you find your "family."

2) If spirituality is a central value for you, then explore the common beliefs and practices of the community. Are these in harmony with your own? Are there regular meditations or prayer times, study groups, yoga practices, a library of spiritual books? Are spiritual practices required or left to individual choice? Are they structured or unstructured? If practices are not required or structured, do you have the necessary self-discipline to practice on your own? If you seek some kind of authority structure or guru, are you ready to submit without rebelliousness?

Notice what happens day-to-day in community life. Do members actually work at *living* their spiritual beliefs? Do they inspire you? Is the general atmosphere uplifting and positive? Although many communities proclaim spiritual

Corinne McLaughlin and Gordon Davidson, former members of Findhorn Community, are founding members of Sirius, a spiritual community in Massachusetts. They have visited over 200 communities and helped organize the New England Network of Light, a grouping of over 60 New Age communities and centers which was active in the early '80s.

Corinne and Gordon are authors of the intentional communities reference book *Builders of the Dawn: Community Lifestyles in a Changing World,* and numerous published articles. They teach courses on community lifestyles through Hampshire College and the University of Massachusetts. Corinne, a former editorial assistant at *Rolling Stone* magazine, is director of Sirius Publishing. Gordon is director of CERES, the Coalition for Environmentally Responsible Economics, which is described in "Home or Activist Community" on page 66. Other versions of this article have been published previously. (Copyright, 1985, Sirius Publishing, reprinted by permission.)

Gordon Davidson/Sirius

ideals — love, sharing, brother/sisterhood — you have to actually spend time in each community to see how their ideals work out in practice.

3) If equality, shared governance and decision-making are important to you, then explore how power and leadership actually function in the community. Again, go beyond the theory and the words and look at the practice. Are there authoritarian leaders or dependent, subservient followers? Who really makes the major decisions? By what process? How involved is the whole membership in decision-making? Is there openness to feedback in the leadership? Are members taking their fair share of responsibility, or leaving it to a few leaders? How decentralized is power in the community?

4) If economic equality and sharing of resources is important, then note how income is generated and where it goes. Are incomes pooled and all bills paid out of a common treasury, or do individuals maintain separate incomes? Is everyone required to work an equal amount of time? Is all work equally shared and valued — including things like cleaning and child care? How are land, houses, vehicles, machinery and other

resources owned — communally or individually? Or is there some mix of communal and individual ownership? How do members feel about their economic system?

5) If privacy and individual freedom are high on your list, then check out housing and financial arrangements. Does everyone live in one big house, or are there individual dwellings? Are these privately or communally owned? If houses are shared, are bedrooms and/or other spaces in the house designated as private? Is there internal soundproofing sufficient to provide privacy? Are members quiet enough when time alone is needed?

Are all meals eaten communally or individually? Is there personal choice of lifestyle? Or does everyone live in the same way? Do all members have the same spiritual and political values, or is there room for diversity? How much time and work energy are required for membership? How frequent are required meetings?

6) If a simple lifestyle with appropriate technology, organic gardening, recycling and "living lightly on the earth" is what you desire, explore how homes are built and how they

Independence Day Celebration at Sirius Community, MA

Gordon Davidson/Sirius

Resonating Values to look for in a community:

- Personal support
- Spirituality
- Equality
- Group Economics
- Privacy
- Simplicity
- Fe/Male Roles
- Child Support

trade-offs between a totally nuclear family setting and an active life in the community? Are there children of similar age to your own? Are there community playgrounds or spaces just for children? Is there a general sense of happiness and harmony among families in the community?

No one community is Utopia, and no one community will meet your ideal arrangements in all of the areas discussed above. Each community has its special focus, based on its own values and philosophy. If you find a community you really like, but are disappointed that it doesn't provide something you feel is important, then perhaps it's a message to you to do something *yourself* to change or improve it, if the community members agree.

It's easy to throw stones from the sidelines. It's harder — and yet more rewarding — to create something better. So, make a gift to all those who will come later to the community. Consider joining to help provide focusing energy for that special something you feel would make the community better... another step closer to Utopia.

If you find that no community seems to live up to your ideals, then perhaps it's best to turn within and ask whether you are living these ideals yourself. Maybe you are searching in vain for something outside yourself that only can be found within. Perhaps that is the place to begin. Otherwise, you may visit any number of communities without ever finding your own community home. ❖

(*Builders of the Dawn: Community Lifestyles in a Changing World*, 365 pages, is available for $17.95 plus $1.50 postage and handling from Sirius Publishing, Baker Road, Shutesbury, MA 01072)

are heated. How many appliances and gadgets are in use? How is kitchen waste handled—is it recycled into compost? Is food home-grown and organic, or is it store-bought? How vital and productive is the garden? Are furniture, clothing, equipment, tools mostly new or recycled (used)? How extensive is the use of wind, water and solar energy?

7) If feminist values are important to you, then observe who does what jobs in the community. Do men share cooking, cleaning, child care? Are women working in administrative and leadership positions and sharing heavier work like construction and mechanics? How is sexuality viewed in the community? Are there a majority of celibates or families? Singles or gays? Are women's opinions as highly valued in the community as men's? Are certain behaviors deemed more appropriate for just one sex? Is there freedom of expression?

8) If a supportive and safe environment for children and/or shared child care is what you're looking for, then observe who has responsibility for children — individual parents, the whole community or somewhere in between? Notice also whether child care is structured or informal, and whether there are good teachers and schools in the community or nearby. Are there adequate accommodations available in the community or nearby for families?

How much time commitment is asked of community members, and does this leave time for family? What are the

Finding a Community To Call Home

by W. J. Schlicht, Jr.

Recently I visited 14 communities in the Eastern United States while looking for a community to join for at least the next few years. During my search a number of considerations emerged which are listed below. Some of these issues are phrased as questions you might ask various members of the communities you visit, or questions you might ask yourself.

Any visit to a community for the purpose of seeking a home will have to be long enough for you to get a good idea of how the community operates. I believe this can be done in two days, but some communities feel that a much longer period, sometimes up to two weeks, occasionally as much as several months, may be required to get to know the community well enough to make decisions about major lifestyle changes.

If you plan on moving into a community with a partner or with a family, I believe it is important that your partner and any children involved accompany you on all visits. Bear in mind during all community visits, particularly when asking questions, that decisions about community membership are necessarily *mutual decisions!* The community has to want you as a member in the same way that you have to decide to be a part of the community.

No doubt the most important issue has to do with the question of how well you get along with the community members. Do you feel accepted generally by the group? Is at least some honest effort made to welcome you? Many communities have a specific member designated to be responsible for visitors. But even when this is not the case, some members, if not all, should make an attempt to meet your effort to get acquainted.

Naturally common sense applies here; if you visit a community that is in the middle of a major project such as completion of large-scale construction, then you should lower your expectations of the amount of time community members will be able to spend with you. Any visitor, however, who expects to be waited on by the community members is no doubt due for a disappointment — and rightly so. Plan on helping out with some of the community work, especially in meal preparation or chores, if your help seems welcome.

In most communities your work contribution is expected and provides a wonderful opportunity to see how well you can work cooperatively with at least a few of the members. Do not imagine that you have VIP status, but do anticipate that at least some of the people will want to know something about you and what you are doing.

It seems to me important to trust your basic instincts about the vibes that community members put out to you. Do they seem simpatico? Are they "your kind of people"? This is not to say that you should look for a community of people just like you. Far from it. There is great benefit to be found in living with people who have divergent backgrounds and viewpoints. But there is no point in trying to fit in with people who are so different that there is insufficient common ground to form a basis for mutual communication.

How well do different members of a community get along with each other? Do they tend to share feelings with each other? Or is there a pattern of covering up feelings and dealing only with material concerns and things that need to be done? Are community members generally supportive of each other? Do you get the feeling that members are genuinely concerned that each of the other members is able to grow along self-defined paths? If a member asks for special assistance, are others eager to volunteer, or is it difficult to get cooperation?

Are there splinter groups within the community who have negative feelings about the community as a whole? The question of equality among the membership is very important. Of course some communities have definite hierarchical structures with designated leadership. But if there is inequality of position, with some members working to support other com-

William Schlicht, Jr., lived for six months in 1984 at Woodburn Hill Farm on Maryland's eastern shore. After practicing and teaching clinical psychology for most of his life, Bill now lives in Key West, Florida, where he edits the literary magazine, *Key West Review*, writes, and leads workshops at Unitarian camps and conferences. His spiritual pathway is a personal variant of Zen Buddhism augmented by what he's learned in his work with psychology.

munity members who exploit leadership positions, the community may not provide support for personal growth among the working members. Generally, a community that gets caught up in viewing some of its members as second-class citizens is a community that is bound to develop serious interpersonal problems.

Is the community you are considering made up mostly of families or mostly of singles? Depending upon your own status, this can be an extremely important consideration. If you are single and a majority of the community is made up of family units, you are likely to be lonely. However, if the community is located close to a fairly large population center, then this need not be a major concern. Likewise, if the community offers frequent programs of some kind that attract large numbers of people who visit for extended periods, such activities may provide the needed social contact with other people who are not in families. Speak to one or two single members about their life in the community.

Many people are drawn to a community that is spiritually oriented. If you fit into this category, then ask yourself whether you want a community that has a specific spiritual orientation or one that has a more general spiritual outlook. For example, you might consider a monastery or a lay community that follows a particular religion.

Alternatively, there are communities with a general spiritual orientation that have great respect for the need of individual community members to follow their own particular spiritual practice. In such communities, you may find Chris-

Do you get the feeling that members are genuninely concerned that each of the other members is able to grow along self-defined paths? If a member asks for special assistance, are others eager to volunteer, or is it difficult to get cooperation?

tians, Sufis, Buddhists or other religious living together with people following spiritual disciplines that are entirely unique.

Just how community-oriented do you want your community to be? Some communities are little more than land co-operatives where people build individual homes around a central building and land owned in common. Co-operative members may see each other only rarely, may hold business meetings monthly or less frequently, and may not know each other very deeply. More intimacy is required among those who frequently share meals and work together inside the community. Based on these and many other factors, the degree of interpersonal involvement and intimacy varies enormously among different communities.

Communities can be found in the hearts of the largest cities as well as in the most remote rural areas. If you want access to museums, concerts, libraries and a varied social life, you won't be as likely to find contentment out in the boondocks.

Climatic changes should be explored when considering intentional communities in unfamiliar regions of the country. What may appear as a beautiful climate in the late spring will look different with two feet of snow on the ground.

What size community are you seeking? If you are looking for some variant of an extended family, then you should probably consider communities of no more than 20 people. That would be a large family indeed! But if you want to live in a neighborhood similar to the small villages existing long ago, then a larger community would be more suitable. Be aware, however, that in a community of 50 or more people, there will be members with whom you are only slightly acquainted, even after you've lived there several years. So you will need to be comfortable with a wide variety of intimacy levels in your social contacts if you choose a larger community.

The practical question of how much it will cost to live in a given community is of great importance. You will need to know the cost of personal maintenance in cash and personal labor. What are the job opportunities available in the community or nearby? It is vital that financial arrangements be clearly understood well in advance of any decision to join a community.

What is the overall economic condition of the community that you are considering? If there is a desperate struggle each month to pay the bills, you will need to decide if you can handle routine financial pressure. Take a careful look at all the buildings owned in common by the community. Are they in good repair? Are the water and heating systems adequate and usually operable? Are tools, appliances, farm implements and vehicles in good shape?

What are the expectations of incoming members about financial and labor contributions to the community beyond the cost of basic food and lodging? Some common treasury, or income-sharing, communities require that new members

Bear in mind during all community visits, particularly when asking questions, that decisions about community membership are necessarily mutual decisions! The community has to want you as a member in the same way that you have to decide to be a part of the community.

turn personal assets over to the community, either permanently or for the duration of their membership. Other communities require the purchase of shares which may be very expensive. And some communities rely on member dues payments or assessments.

It is especially important for a prospective member to know what will happen if a member eventually decides to leave the community. If resigning members have to leave everything behind, leaving can become extremely difficult.

You should have in mind quite clearly how much time and effort the community will expect of you as a new member. In some communities a major part of everyone's day will be devoted to community labor. If you are engaged already in daily spiritual practice or other personal regimens, there may be time conflicts.

When you visit communities, share meals with members so that you learn whether the food meets your dietary preferences. While some communities adhere to strict vegetarian diets, many consume dairy products, eggs and occasional fish and poultry at common meals; a significant number feature a basic 'meat and potatoes' diet.

For many people today ecological consciousness is very important. If this is true for you, then you will be interested in whether the community employs organic agricultural methods, solar power for heating and electricity, energy-saving building design, water conservation and purity testing, and wind and water energy.

Are the relationships healthy between the community, neighbors and nearby villages and towns? A few communities have experienced very poor relationships with their neighbors in the regular world outside their own subculture.

It's important for you to understand the basis and current state of such problems, as well as the plans for improving any negative situations.

This is especially important if you are sensitive and perhaps a little self-conscious. It's one thing to be identified with a group that townspeople think is generally weird. Then, you may be looked at oddly when you go into the local general store. However, if hostility is present in serious proportions, you need to know about it in order to make a decision about your potential place in the community.

Is the community you are interested in part of a national or international movement? The main advantage of affiliated communities is that members are usually able to move easily to different parts of the country or even to foreign lands, while remaining within the affiliation. The disadvantages are that such community networks tend to be doctrinaire in their practice and may limit the autonomy of the local community.

Does the community you are interested in have important ties with the wider society? Some communities operate programs for visitors who may remain in residence for several days, weeks or months. Such programs affect the atmosphere of the community so that it is sometimes not as stable as a community with a population consisting primarily of resident members. If you seek the familiarity of an unchanging group, you should think carefully before joining a community based on active, on-site visitor programs. On the other hand, some people would not be comfortable in a community unless it contributes to the larger society, perhaps even the whole world.

You are looking at intentional communities with the idea of finding a group which meets enough of your needs that you will consider living with them. This article has mentioned a number of important considerations to be included in your decision-making process: emotional climate, spiritual outlook, financial arrangements, employment possibilities, physical living conditions, the way the community is governed, the general health and stability of the community, size and location, relationships with the larger society, ecological practices, and community expectations of new members.

All of these issues are relevant to the person who is looking for a community to call home. But, remember that no ideal, no perfect community, exists today, nor is one ever likely to exist. To complicate the matter, the idea of perfection seems to vary from one person to the next. So evaluating the answers to the above questions may not provide the basis for longer-term decisions until you have visited a variety of communities, and made several follow-up visits to those that catch your interest. If you listen carefully, you will know inside yourself when you have found a community where the chances of creating a happy life are good enough for you to take the plunge. ❖

Communities for the Mainstream

by Julie Mazo

The "maturing" of intentional communities has received considerable media attention in recent years. Articles on cooperative lifestyles have appeared in the *Boston Globe, Denver Post, Los Angeles Times,* and *St. Louis Post-Dispatch,* among other major publications. Even the *Wall Street Journal* found it relevant to report on the evolution of the people and places once called hippies and communes, as gray hair grows more plentiful among the Woodstock generation.

This article tells a related story, the story of a search for community for the middle class. Six intentional communities are described, as I experienced them in 1989. Each is very different from the others. What they have in common is the offering of a viable opportunity for a lifestyle of one's choice, from a home with as many or few "middle-class" accouterments as one may desire to a primitive cabin in the woods. In each of these communities, members can contentedly enjoy whatever they wish that mainstream America has to offer while snuggled in the comforting embrace of communitarian values.

My husband and I were not passionate back-to-the-land advocates, nor were we anti-urban in principle. We had been living the comfortable, relatively conventional existence of middle-class professionals, and were not looking to trade that for an ideal of spartan self-sufficiency. We wanted, however, the sense of "belonging" to something larger than our nuclear family, more consciously interdependent than our circle of friends. And we wanted to express and experience the generic community values described so well elsewhere in this publication.

But how to find "our" community? We used five criteria to help us sift through the masses of available information and identify those places that felt like a "good fit." The criteria were:

1. absence of dogma or leader or required belief system
2. private dwellings designed to the member's taste and means
3. self-responsibility for livelihood
4. proximity to a college town for professional opportunities and for cultural stimulation
5. relatively mild winters

People were intrigued and puzzled by our search. Few of our friends had even heard of "intentional community." Their only frames of reference were the commune scene of the '60s or Jonestown — and they had trouble fitting us into either frame. The more we talked about the large, varied world of the communities movement, the more interested they became, and the more they wanted to know.

That's why this article is being written: to inform people like our friends about the existence of an option for the middle class, an alternative to city dwellings where one is cautious about walking at night, or suburban enclaves where common interests are rarely examined beyond the sports page or the travails of the daily commute; a living environment where doors don't need to be locked, where significant relationships with neighbors are the norm rather than the exception, where generations mix and everyone has a role, where people experiment with commitment to something more than their individual interests; in short, intentional community.

MONAN'S RILL

And so we set out on our odyssey, in February 1989. Monan's Rill, one half-hour from Santa Rosa, California, was the first

Julie Mazo first became interested in joining an alternative lifestyle community in the early '50s, but she never made the jump until 1989, after visiting six communities in a cross-country tour. During the years in between, Julie became a mother, writer, editor, publisher, and business owner. This article was written in response to personal requests from friends she left behind in her recent move from San Diego. A features editor for this Directory, Julie is a writer and editor who also provides consulting services in marketing, conflict resolution, mediation, and training.

*Mainstream embraces
communitarian values*

100 Mile Lodge/Emissaries

stop. The narrow dirt road twisting up the ridge prepared us for a rural experience, but not for the dramatic contrast between the exceedingly rugged landscape and the comfortable, modern, even luxurious homes tucked at different levels into the high land dividing the Sonoma and Napa Valleys.

Founded in 1974, Monan's Rill has 17 adult members, single and coupled, ranging in age from 30s to 70s, and five children. The wooden sign at the entrance gently suggests a 10 1/2-mile speed limit and adds, "We thank thee" — one indication of the Quaker influence on this non-sectarian group.

Some of Monan's Rill's members work in Santa Rosa full or part time (as nurse, teacher, therapist, etc.). Retired members divide their days between various "good works" in town and necessary chores on the land.

To become a member an interested person may apply for year-long visitor status after frequent enough contacts to be reasonably sure of one's desire. More intensive contact during the visitorship enables both the prospective member and the community to make a good long-term decision. It is not a decision to be taken casually, since membership re-

quires a substantial financial commitment based on a formula that includes a non-refundable portion, a lump sum (adjusted by age), and purchase of equity in the total value of the 440-acre property. Title to the land and houses is held by a general partnership of all members.

There are bi-monthly potlucks and community meetings, and work days when members volunteer for tasks decided upon by the Land Plans Committee. We were there for a work day that included chopping firewood for all the households, gardening, road maintenance, and scouring the inside of the water tower. There is an expectation of participation by everyone in community work, but exceptions for good cause seem to be made casually enough. Leadership of the meetings rotates annually, and decisions are made by consensus following the Quaker model.

The Process Committee, whose mandate includes keeping a finger on the social/emotional pulse of the community, brings to the surface issues that may lie beneath the calm, caring surface of personal interactions. After the first death of a member, the Process Committee created an occasion for people to share feelings about their loss, and to explore the implications of growing old in the community.

Monan's Rill is a group of gentle people who care about one another, who live in relative independence and have the security of knowing they belong to a caring, supportive extended family. Friendships grow strong, and acceptance of a range of lifestyles is the norm.

SANTA ROSA CREEK COMMONS

Our next visit represented the other end of the rural-urban spectrum. Santa Rosa Creek Commons is smack in the middle of downtown Santa Rosa, within walking distance of every urban convenience. A limited-equity co-operative founded in the early 1980s, it looks much like a small, two-story garden apartment development set between an original house facing the city street and what is affectionately called "the back 40," a large grassy slope down to the creek with a garden, a circle of tree stumps cut at comfortable sitting height, with plenty of room for children to play and for adults to enjoy the natural surroundings.

The front house has been divided between a private apartment belonging to one member and community space: a kitchen for community meals, a large room for community meetings and other events, and visitor accommodations. This community space was our first stop, since we had scheduled our arrival in time for the Saturday afternoon monthly meeting. These first few hours provided generous evidence of responsible, careful work on the part of committees, consensus decisions, good humor, sharing and caring for individuals and for the community as a whole.

We were particularly delighted by the "Other Friends" project, whereby an adult who wishes to be an "other friend" to any community child posts a notice on the bulletin board in the clean, well-ordered laundry room to announce that "Jane will teach baking to up to three children at a time. Most convenient schedule would be Wednesdays between 4 and 6 p.m.," or "John will take one child for walks around Santa Rosa on Saturdays and tell stories of the town's history," or "Mary will give computer lessons..." What a wonderful structure for the grownups to share themselves and their interests, and for the children to expand their adult relationships.

SRCC consists of 27 apartments in a series of low-rise buildings. Seventeen of the units have been bought by members at full cost; the others are subsidized, and available for rental. The membership includes minorities of all sorts: blind, black, hearing-impaired, Hispanic. The community building has a wheelchair lift, and ramps ensure accessibility elsewhere. The cooperative seeks renters who understand and are interested in cooperation, rather than those who are simply looking for subsidized rent, and the membership

In each of these communities, members can contentedly enjoy whatever they wish that mainstream America has to offer while snuggled in the comforting embrace of communitarian values.

process exposes potential residents to the full experience of SRCC.

The community takes its grievance procedure very seriously. Any member having a problem with a neighbor is encouraged first to speak with the neighbor directly. A three-person mediation team, consisting of a facilitator, a referee, and an active listener, can be called together to meet with the disputants. The belief that all members can develop mediation skills is borne out by the expectation that, after participating in the process as a disputant, a member can then become part of the mediation team, and learn to help others by sitting in with more experienced member-mediators.

SRCC is a successful model of urban community living, with commitment to intelligent, participatory management, sharing in community work, and cooperation in many other areas of members' lives. It turns upside down the stereotypical view that city apartment complexes are necessarily places where a smile and a nod to some of the other residents is the ultimate in neighborliness.

CO-HOUSING

Before we left California, we visited people involved in the burgeoning co-housing movement in San Luis Obispo, Berkeley, San Rafael, Oakland, Palo Alto, and Sacramento. This very exciting concept of intentional neighborhoods with clustered housing and common facilities, designed to enhance social contact, planned and managed by residents, is very worth watching — and supporting. Representing a broad spectrum of ages and income levels, considering both rural and urban sites, the co-housing groups were all highly motivated and dedicated to the challenge of creating their own community. The temptation to stay and work with these wonderful groups of people was strong, but we resisted — and headed east.

Can you continue a conventional lifestyle in community?

100 Mile Lodge/Emissaries

CELO LAND TRUST

We drove as quickly as we could across the country, passing by some very interesting communities along the way for no reason other than their typically harsh winters. By the time we reached Celo Land Trust, near Asheville, North Carolina, we were eager for our next community experience.

Due to a mix-up with our correspondence, no one was expecting us. We found our way to the home of 87-year old Ernest Morgan, son of Arthur Morgan, Celo's founder and long-time inspiration for the communities movement worldwide. Ernest had just come in from cutting firewood and was deeply involved in his next project for the afternoon, filling orders of a self-produced videotape for the far-flung network of the Rural Southern Voice for Peace (RSVP). After a few moments of sorting out who we were and what we wanted, we found ourselves on the receiving end of a full measure of his personal charm. He conveyed the history and spirit of Celo, starting with his parents' purchase of Berkshire Mountain land in 1916 to site their dream of community, and the shift to North Carolina in the 1930s.

Celo members were described as "a bunch of fierce individualists," exurbanites generally, most of whom have chosen to locate their leaseholdings on the 1200-acre land trust in an isolated spot "at the far end of a dirt road," rather than in clusters. The thirty-some households are economical-ly independent except for the few adults on the payroll of community enterprises such as the Health Center which serves the surrounding area, the Arthur Morgan School, a private residential school for adolescents, or the summer camp for children. Many members are craftspeople, possessive of the privacy and time it takes to produce the fine works they market cooperatively. Others commute to work in Asheville, an hour away, or to nearby small towns.

We also learned about many other cooperative activities, such as the RSVP, an active food co-op, a Friends Meeting, work days devoted to community upkeep or to helping neighbors, and community meetings. I interjected with "I'm getting a schizoid picture of Celo: on the one hand, fierce individualists; on the other, a lot of jointly developed, highly participatory activities... " Ernest chuckled in response. "That's Celo!"

Cabin Fever University, another cooperative Celo project, is a sharing of skills and interests open to all area residents, with no distinction between Celo members and others. No money changes hands except when costs are incurred for art supplies, food or the like. Seven photocopied pages listed a rich, stimulating collection of activities: ongoing groups and one-time events during the winter "cabin fever" season. The current offerings included a pizza party at the Health Center, yoga lessons, Games Night for Adults, a colloquy for writers, art lessons, a meeting to organize book-sharing, a support group for mothers of young children, a glass-blowing demonstration at one home/studio, and dozens of others.

The "sane fringe" (Ernest Morgan's phrase) refers to the 100 or more people who live nearby but not on the Celo Land Trust property. Tucked into the river valley, scattered along the flatland, hidden deep in the woods, and perched on the hills that lap against the Appalachian Mountains is an extraordinary, vigorous collection of human talent and energy. Some of the "sane fringe" came because they were attracted to the Celo community, some to the Arthur Morgan School, some to the thriving crafts network (the nearby Penland School of Crafts has a national reputation). Some were attracted by the general acceptance in the area of alternative styles of life; and all are drawn to the beauty of the mountains.

The line between the land trust community members and the surrounding folk is blurred. The food co-op, for example, is on land trust property, sharing space with the craft co-op. Over 90 households belong to the food co-op; Celo members account for approximately a third of that number.

Celo operates according to 50-plus years of strongly cooperative tradition based on slow change, gradually achieved consensus. Respect for the land is a paramount value, as are helping one's neighbors and living a balanced life of work, play, and creativity.

SHALOM COMMUNITY

Shalom Community is situated just at the edge of Greensboro, North Carolina. Each of the eight adult members has an urban career (college professor, social worker, administrator, etc.), and retreats after working hours to the 46-acre rural paradise they own as a housing cooperative. Members are in their 30s, 40s and 50s, and there are two preschoolers and a teenager.

Member housing runs the gamut from the tiny original farmhouse to the newly completed, large, luxurious, ultra-modern dwelling overlooking the community's lake. Another building is an attractive, comfortable duplex which includes self-contained private space for two households as well as a community library/lounge and meeting/dining space used by all. Shalom has a pattern of members moving from one house to another, or moving in with another family for a while, as life circumstances change. Questions about who is to live where seem to have been easily resolvable.

Shalom has stayed small since its founding in 1974, and hasn't had the need for elaborate structure. A new member purchases shares in the co-op, and bears the cost of housing her/himself in a house that the co-op owns. Community issues are considered as they arise, and decisions are made by consensus. Without much attention to formal structure and without members feeling bound by precedent, the land gets tended, new buildings are designed and built cooperatively, specific projects get the time they require as needs surface.

A living environment where doors don't need to be locked, where significant relationships with neighbors are the norm rather than the exception, where generations mix and everyone has a role, where people experiment with commitment to something more than their individual interests... in short, intentional community.

Members have a commitment to attend weekly non-business meetings. This is a time to discuss feelings about current issues in their lives directly bearing either on community relationships or on outside experiences. The point of these honest, often moving exchanges (we were privileged to be invited to one) is to uncover childhood patterns that continue to influence present behavior, and therefore to have the opportunity to let go of old patterns that are no longer constructive. There is neither leader nor agenda for these meetings, simply a group of people experimenting with this means of increasing the harmony of their lives.

We were told of periods in Shalom's history when members had only minimum interaction with one another, and other periods when the group operated as a big family. Our time there included both spontaneous and scheduled socializing (the latter extending to non-member friends), cheerful cooperation on community tasks and assistance to individuals, and very real concern for one another.

NEW LAND

We headed north into Virginia. Our destination: the New Land. Sprawling across 800 acres of magnificent, hilly terrain about 30 miles south of Charlottesville, the New Land is structured as a subdivision rather than an intentional community. The land was bought in 1979 by Bob Monroe, author of *Journeys Out of the Body*, as setting for an educational and research institute dealing with investigation and expansion of human consciousness. A substantial part of the property was subsequently divided into lots of three to 10 or more acres which are for sale to any buyer. This makes of the New Land an open community, intentional in appeal, but without a membership process. However, virtually all of the 25 or so households have been drawn there by the work of The Monroe Institute. Most of the striking, modern, custom-designed homes are sited in splendid isolation, which reflects the independence of New Landers. There is no common responsibility except for the roads, and therefore few issues that affect all the residents.

While the New Land does not fit most definitions of intentional community, there is a very tangible "community of interest" that bonds many of its residents. Some gather regularly in study groups on various topics; others come together to sing, publish a quarterly newsletter, engage in political, social, and personal growth activities, and just to enjoy the proximity of kindred spirits.

A few New Landers work at the Institute; one family operates a llama farm on the property; some are retired; others commute to nearby towns or pursue their business interests around the country and around the globe. New Landers are vital people across a wide age range, intellectually curious and active, who know they can look to their neighbors for stimulation and nourishment and support. To become a New Lander, one needs just the price of a lot and the resources to build a house on it.

SHANNON FARM

Shannon Farm, founded in 1974, is 10 minutes away from the New Land, tucked cozily into the foothills of the Blue Ridge Mountains. About two-thirds of Shannon's 490 acres are wooded; the rest holds gardens, pastures, hayfields, orchards, ball fields, a lake, and one of the seven residential clusters (the other six are in wooded areas). The houses give visual testimony to the wide spectrum of values, lifestyle choices, and financial resources that comprise this highly eclectic community. There are simple cabins, a geodesic dome, more conventional homes, elegant, custom-detailed structures, and a solar-powered group house with ample capacity for eight adults to enjoy their private space and shared living areas equipped with a full range of TV's, computers, sound systems, VCR's, and a well-equipped caterer's kitchen.

The 60 members range in age from 19 up to the 70s, and include nuclear families, single parent households, and individuals who choose to live alone, in couples or with one of the intentional groups. Parents are responsible for their own children (infants to teens), but there is much cooperation in child-rearing. A few of the 21 children have been home schooled, but most of the school-aged children go to nearby public or alternative schools, and parents, grandma, or daycare providers look after the younger ones.

The membership process includes a minimum six-month provisional period; full membership requires approval of two-thirds of the community. There is no "buy-in," but members pay 7 percent of their income as monthly dues. All are responsible for their own livelihood, and for the cost of their own housing, which is owned communally and leased longterm by the householder.

The bulletin board in community space announces weekend work days when needed, anything from filling potholes to cleaning the sweat lodge, or a roofing party for a member's house. On weekdays members scatter to pursue their individual livelihoods in nearby towns, some of them to jobs in the two collectives (woodworking and computers), or work on the land.

Shannon Farm makes decisions by consensus at monthly meetings, after intensive committee work shapes a proposal for consideration by the total group. The community is proud of its decision-making system, which has grown through the years into an effective and potent vehicle to harness energy in pursuit of the common good. Widespread acceptance of difference, high tolerance for individual idiosyncracies, and profound respect for personal freedom are hallmarks of Shannon Farm, as either cause or effect of its processes.

These brief sketches are incomplete. I have not described the challenges and frustrations or the disappointments and the compromises that also come with living in community — as they come, in different guises, with living anywhere.

Living in community is not for everyone; but knowing about the options is important for making an informed decision. So here are six options — and there are many more — where elements from more conventional and familiar environments exist side by side in a comfortable marriage with the rich subculture of the intentional communities movement.

Personal Note —

At this writing, my husband and I are provisional members of Shannon Farm, work at professional jobs nearby, and are both deeply involved in the life of the community. Is our life in community an unending idyll? Of course not. Have we found what we were looking for? Yes: a beautiful, human-scale, peaceful environment; professional and personal stimulation; frequent opportunities to stretch the boundaries of our understanding of human nature; the experience of being part of a larger whole; a place to give of our talents and ourselves and to receive the same from others. ❖

A Word About Cults

by Corinne McLaughlin and Gordon Davidson

This discussion of cults is adapted from part of the fourth chapter of Corinne and Gordon's book Builders of the Dawn: Community Lifestyles in a Changing World (copyright, 1985, Sirius Publishing, Shutesbury MA, reprinted by permission).

At the same time that the hippie communes were attracting major attention in the '60s and early '70s, the so-called "cults" – manipulative, authoritarian mass movements – began growing in popularity and attracting many young people who were burned out on drugs, or generally confused and lost. Today, the cults are still recruiting large numbers of people, and are still sensationalized in the media.

Many people are desperate to change themselves and to change the world. Some are so lonely and alienated from family, religion or friendships, that any group which looks loving and supportive is very magnetic, even if the price is one's personal freedom. The very legitimate search for truth, personal and spiritual values and transcendence is easily exploited by power-driven "cult" leaders.

There is a problem, though, in defining exactly what a cult is. The point at which a group actually crosses the line between what is acceptable and what is not, depends a great deal on a person's values. As Ken Keyes, author of *The Handbook to Higher Consciousness*, expressed it: A "cult" is a term you would use to apply to that which you don't like... so I don't really have much use for that term. I could tell you [about] the groups that I feel are sincerely trying to do something good for the world and that I like... I don't consider them "cults".

It may be hard to define exactly what a cult is since it is such a subjective, emotionally laden label. However, we would warn people about groups that manifest many of the following traits:

- encourages the violation of personal ethics or encourages deception to prove loyalty to the group
- encourages relinquishment of personal responsibility for actions
- restricts access to outside people or information
- inhibits critical thinking so that "group think" predominates, and many subjects are taboo for discussion
- restricts the ability to leave the group
- restricts privacy
- uses intense indoctrination
- demands absolute obedience
- applies intense pressure towards group conformity
- demands stereotyped behavior, physically or psychologically encourages over-dependency
- manipulates feelings in a conscious way
- appeals to fear of not being saved or enlightened
- appeals to greed
- appeals to power
- appeals to the glamour of being the elect
- appeals to vanity and flattery
- uses guilt to control behavior
- uses humiliation to control
- uses intimidation or threats
- plays on low self-esteem or feelings of inadequacy
- encourages sexual relationships with group leaders
- uses high-pressure sales pitches and plays on loyalty of friends to attract members
- evidences extreme paranoia and the stockpiling of firearms for "protection"

In our view, the element that distinguishes a cult from a healthy, participative community is the interference with a person's free will rather than the nurturing of its use. Free will is the most basic and inviolate spiritual principle on Earth. A benevolent community or spiritual teacher will respect a person's free will and encourage members to freely make their own choices, to take responsibility for any mistakes made and to learn from them. ❖

Bibliography

Deikman, Arthur, "The Evaluation of Spiritual and Utopian Groups," *Journal of Humanistic Psychology*, Summer 1983.

Vaughn, Frances, "A Question of Balance: Health and Pathology in New Religious Movements," *Journal of Humanistic Psychology*, Summer 1983.

(Builders of the Dawn: Community Lifestyles in a Changing World is available for $17.95 plus $1.50 postage from Sirius Publishing, Baker Road, Shutesbury MA 01072.)

[Editor's note: Inclusiveness was a guiding value in creating this Directory, and information on a wide array of choices is offered. As editors we have relied primarily on information provided by local community sources, and have taken the position that it is not our place to judge. Still, there are "cult" communities — so the above guidelines may be helpful in distinguishing them from the vast majority of benevolent and self-affirming intentional communities.]

Geoph Kozeny/Community Catalyst

The Evolving Culture

What is the role of intentional community in the evolution of culture?

Griscom Morgan of The Vale Community discusses the relationship between **Individuality and Community,** *maintaining that the societies that survive and endure are those in which membership is based on diversity rather than disciplined conformity to an ideology. Stressing the need for balance, Griscom warns that "the community... must not take the place of a person's direct relationship to the universe."*

Allen Butcher, a former member of both East Wind and Twin Oaks, presents a historical overview of the intentional community as a tool for experimenting with social change options. Noting today's increase in "popular awareness of the need for change", he believes this trend will provide signals for **Community in the 1990s.**

This Directory explores many ways that individual, group, and broader society can interact... and how every person or element in the communities movement is a potential catalyst for the evolution of self, community, and culture.

Individuality and Community

by Griscom Morgan

The author received a letter from a person who had made several valiant attempts at intentional community. That person concluded "human nature is not yet ready for community." Alternatively, we should question whether the conventional concept of intentional community is right for human nature.

Individuality and Community

Certain presuppositions characterize and harm the life and relationships of our dominant Western society, and these presuppositions extend to the revolutionary movements and intentional communities that are outgrowths and reactions to our society. D. H. Lawrence advanced this thesis at length in works such as Studies In Classic American Literature.

Mary Freeman summarized Lawrence's concerns as follows: Lawrence... concluded that abundant life was not to be found in the main currents of our culture... He also found inadequate current versions of social reform and revolution. It seemed to him that they failed to free themselves from the limitations of past ideals, and, as a result, took forms too lean, too barren. Neither established culture, nor our ready-made panaceas for its ills, appeared conducive to more abundant life.

Eugene Goodheart quotes Lawrence:

There must be... love, a wholeness of humanity. But there must also be pure, separate individuality, separate and proud.

In *The Community of the Future*, Arthur Morgan warned that "Mediocrity is at home in the crowd. The discriminating mind and spirit make their best growths when they have opportunity for periods of quiet and solitude."

Elsewhere he wrote:

For the purpose of keeping clear our ultimate aims and of keeping strong our sense of validity in them, it is necessary that we have regular periods of retirement, either alone or with others who have the same purpose. In the quiet and peace of these periods we can renew and refresh loyalty to the ultimate and controlling purpose for which we should live.

Neither the family, the community, the church nor the nation must take the place of each person's direct relationship to the wider reality of mankind, nature and the universe, however that might be conceived. Albert Einstein expressed such a view with regard to his life:

I ... have never belonged to my country, my home, my friends, or even to my immediate family, with my whole heart; in the face of all these ties I have never lost an obstinate sense of detachment, of the need for solitude— a feeling which increases with the years ... (such a person) is largely independent of the opinions, habits and judgements of his fellows and avoids temptation to take his stand on such insecure foundations.

The Origin of Healthy Individuality

The individuality of the child finds its origin in the family. From the small world of the family the infant emerges into the enlarging world of experience and association—the small neighborhood, the community, and then the progressively larger society.

If one of the early steps in this social emergence is broken, a gap is left in the child's personality development. A secure biological family, well-integrated into a secure small neighborhood or community, is essential to the healthy development of both the individual and society as a whole. In fact,

Griscom Morgan is a long-term communitarian theorist, writer and organizer. Gris was a founding member of both Celo Land Trust, North Carolina, and The Vale, Ohio. He followed his father as a leader of Community Service, Inc. (CSI), which provides consulting services, maintains a catalog of mail order books, and holds annual conferences on small community development. CSI founded the Fellowship of Intentional Communities which, in turn, spawned the CESCI business loan fund and this Directory. This article is abstracted from *Guidebook for Intentional Communities*, which Gris helped edit and write, along with a number of other books, including *Hope for the Future*, all available from CSI. His personal interests focus around his activist family — his wife, Jane, and children, Faith and John. Gris' spiritual teacher is the Great Spirit of the Universe known by the original Native Americans, who was called Father by Jesus. (Copyright, 1988, Community Service, Inc., Yellow Springs, Ohio, reprinted by permission.)

the disintegration of small communities eliminates the inter-family support systems which have maintained nuclear families through the ages. When this community-based support is lost through moves or other causes, the modern family becomes ever more isolated and difficult to sustain.

In *Successful American Families* Zimmerman and Cervantes reported on the characteristics of families in American cities that had survived without symptoms of social breakdown. They found that such families had associated themselves with a number of other such families in close bonds like those of small communities, providing mutual aid, common cultural values and a milieu for supportive child development.

The Common Denominator

How are we to achieve the new society, the new community, the new family and the new individuality at the base of the new society? By what kind of interpersonal relationships can we attain harmony of *individuality and community?* The common denominator of people is their universal aspect, their more fundamental being. Lawrence's insight is that, at the level of the deepest self, people can relate to each other without mutual destruction or loss of individuality. But trying to impose unity upon diverse people at the more superficial level, whether by love, coercion or group process, is to do violence, to make human anthills or beehives, as in Orwell's book *1984*.

People may be oriented and attuned to each other only as a family, community or nation. But they can be attuned also to the universe, inclusive of all humanity and nature. Then they can be truly attuned to each other and effectively integrated in community, and beyond into the ever-widening ecology of the universe.

Not only the individual person, but also the family, the community and the nation need similar mutual attunements to be free from imposition, warping or domination by the other levels of society. Each needs integrity and its own orientation to the universe. On the basis of this kind of integrity, each becomes a better family member, neighbor, communiteer and citizen.

Though inspiring to think about, these are general and abstract statements. Ex-

amples will illustrate some of the ways personal egotism can be transcended without communal domination of the individual.

The Common Denominator in Action

Thomas Banyacya tells of an intertribal meeting of Native Americans in Denver. The meeting began with the usual business agenda, but soon degenerated into the factionalism and semi-futility that characterizes so many political procedures. Banyacya then suggested that the meeting start over again, beginning with an Indian orientation to the universe and the powers of life, addressing those powers and giving verbal recognition to them. After this new beginning, the proceedings developed with power and good spirit.

In a very different context, there was a bitter labor-management conflict in Philadelphia years ago. The city was suffering from an extended deadlock in negotiations. A Quaker respected by both sides, Will Biddle, was called in as a mediator. He asked that the two factions join in a half-hour of silence before beginning business. After the shared silence, the conflict was resolved quickly and in good will.

In still another situation this same procedure worked again. A young coal miner agreed to take the pastorship of a church so divided by strife that trained ministers had given up on it. The miner announced at a Sunday service that the following midweek meeting would be held in complete silence. He had no experience with silent meditation, but he knew that the quality of communication within the congregation was such that verbal exchange would certainly continue to be ineffectual. The church members needed to go to a deeper level to achieve unity.

Midweek meeting was fully attended and members were deeply moved during a long period of shared silence. Reconciliation began and the church progressively regained power and vitality.

"Interlocking at certain points."

In each of these situations, people transcended their personal egos and their group inclination toward conflict. They became attuned to a larger reality and to each other. Such attunement is necessary for sound relationships — between individuals, between individuals and community, between groups of people and the rest of the environment.

Awareness of the balance between the need for individuality and the need for community can provide basic insights necessary to the survival of intentional communities. Rather than exclusive conformity to an ideology, such an awareness of balance can provide the basis for communities to encourage a wide diversity of individuals among their memberships.

Community as a Work of Art

We have to learn to balance varied features of community life that have hitherto been considered irreconcilable, either-or alternatives. Herman Melville wrote a poem on art that applies particularly to the art of community development:

> In placid hours well pleased we dream
> of many a brave unbodied scheme
> But form to lend, pulsed life create,
> what unlike things must meet and mate;
> A flame to melt — a wind to freeze;
> sad patience — joyous energies;
> Humility — yet pride and scorn;
> instinct and study; love and hate;
> Audacity — reverence. These must mate,
> and fuse with Jacob's mystic heart,
> to wrestle with the angel — art.

From our intellectual background we tend to have preconceptions of what it takes to make a viable society. Society looks to us so arbitrary and ill-organized that we assume that we ought to be able to create a better one without too much difficulty. Each community that is thus developed tends to be creatively significant in the one area of particular interest and awareness of its original members. But each is handicapped by lack of awareness of developments in other cooperative living groups.

For instance, some intentional communities seek to avoid considerations related to the exercise of power, responsibility and authority. In our revolt against the old, outdated structures of power, we tend to overlook important organizational principles.

Yet, in every group there must be a committed core of leadership within which there is a depth of mutual trust and capacity for teamwork. This core group must be secure in its purpose and impregnable in its dependability and selflessness.

How are we to achieve the new society, the new community, the new family and the new individuality at the base of the new society? By what kind of interpersonal relationships can we attain harmony of individuality and community?

In many successful societies, power is consciously apportioned according to the capacity of individuals and groups to wisely yield it. Such a system evolves by necessity and a long train of natural selection. At best a power structure is free from self-will, arbitrariness, exclusiveness and is shared by all members. Those communities that neglect to develop a responsible and dependable power structure are faced with the alternatives of frequent membership turnover or exhausting internecine struggle.

Another preconception is that the practice of living and eating together necessarily creates brotherhood, intimacy and sharing. But even common ownership of property does not of itself liberate communitarians from the characteristics of selfishness. In fact, a community as a whole can be just as selfish as an individual. Intentional communities can develop a culture of selfishness, or a culture of brotherhood and sharing with each other and with humanity in general.

Openness to Wider Associations

Communities need to maintain an openness to wider associations. The reality of intentional community culture is that the local unit is too small a world for members to live in without other associations in the larger society. The local group is only a small fragment of the total world; when isolated the community may develop personal tensions and internal preoccupations to the point that wider perspectives tend to fade. The result can be a self-centered community that is as pathological as a self-centered individual.

In some cases communities have found that they needed more freedom from interpersonal contact during the workday. So, they deliberately took jobs outside the community to balance the intensity of contact during the remainder of their lives together.

Modern companies and other institutions usually involve outside directors and consultants to bring perspective to the activities of local organizations. Adventist communities, Lama Foundation, Fairhope Single Tax Corporation and Koinonia Partners all have non-community members on their directorates. Communities of the Federation of Egalitarian Communities and the Emissary Foundation International rely on each other for mutual development assistance and member exchange.

Martin Buber referred to the importance of the kibbutz movement in Israel as a "community of communities" that gives a wider context to life in local intentional communities throughout that country. North American communities could benefit from such a communities movement on this continent, or at least a much wider array of community networks than are presently in operation.

Open-Ended Intentional Communities Balance Individualism

A philosophy of balance lies behind the intentional community endeavors that arose from the work of Arthur Morgan and Community Service, Inc. A sociologist studying Celo Land Trust in North Carolina perceived that Celo's longevity since 1939 is based on a wide horizon of diversity rather than disciplined conformity to an ideology. The researcher found this to be anachronistic in that the opposite condition is widely accepted as necessary for the survival of intentional communities.

Beyond the diversity of both Celo and The Vale OH, founded 1959, there was the conception of a deeper base of unity such as D. H. Lawrence envisioned. These communities and a number of others have a similar awareness of the balance between individual and community values. As a result, they have enjoyed stability over the decades and continue to thrive today.

May Valley WA, Alpha Farm OR, Tanguy Homesteads PA and Bryn Gweled PA, as well as Celo and The Vale, are all outgoing in their involvement with the wider society. None of these communities conform to communal stereotypes. Rather, they strive to be open-ended, living organisms. Their group lives are designed around the changing needs of diverse individual members who are continually evolving in the ever-changing order of the universe. Such communities confirm the community development philosophies of D.H. Lawrence and Arthur Morgan, who call us to free ourselves of limitations and look beyond our past ideals of established culture, social reform or revolution.

There must be… love, a wholeness of humanity.
But there must also be pure, separate individuality, separate and proud. ❖

References

D.H. Lawrence, *Studies In Classic American Literature*, Doubleday, pg 17.
Mary Freeman, *D.H. Lawrence, A Basic Study of His Ideas*, Grosset and Dunlap, 1955, pg 2.
Eugene Goodheart, *The Utopian Vision of D.H. Lawrence*, University of Chicago Press, 1963, pg 9.
Albert Einstein, *The World as I See It*, Philosophical Library, 1949, pg. 52
Arthur Morgan, *The Community of the Future*, Community Service, Inc., 1957, pg 79.
Arthur Morgan, *The Small Community*, Community Service, Inc., 1984.
Carl Zimmerman and Lucius Cervantes, *Successful American Families*, Pageant Press, 1960, pg. 65.

(*Guidebook for Intentional Communities*, 41 pages, is available for $5.00 plus $1.00 postage and handling from Community Service, Inc., Box 243, Yellow Springs, OH 45387, 513-767-2161 or 1461.)

Balancing group and individuality.

Community in the 1990s

We are in the midst of a major era of change, as significant as any in our history. The contemporary melange of conspicuous poverty and affluence, of ecological awakening and technological advance, of spiritual renewal and political integration, is effecting every level of society. As in every past era intentional community will play a role. The challenge for us today is to develop communications and a broad-based movement strategy among those involved in community organizing.

Social change. Evolution. New Age. Paradigm Shift. Cultural Transformation. Planetary Awakening. — Each of these phrases speaks of change within individuals, or change in relationships between people, and of change between people and their environment. These words express both our perception of what is happening in the world today and our hope for the future.

Change in society comes gradually, often with two steps forward and one step back. Change can also be described as a progression through waves or cycles, or even as moving in ascending spirals, repeating old themes but in changing contexts.

The futurist and communitarian William Irwin Thompson offers a model of cultural change as a progression through four phases. The first is mystical and cultural awareness. This is followed by the expression of cultural change through art. Then the changes are reflected in technology and economics. Finally, politics and government begin to respond to the forces for change, but usually not until change has spread throughout society. We can illustrate Thompson's model by looking at the progression through history of the ideal of participatory communication and decision-making processes in religion and government.

The theme of the individual intentionally choosing a lifestyle of social responsibility begins (in Western history) with the primitive Christian church inspiring "all those who believe to hold everything in common." This theme of social responsibility was later expressed as the individual electing to follow one's "Inner Light" rather than an external authority. In the 16th century this experience, called "self-election," inspired individuals to become lay leaders, gather congregations, and challenge the spiritual status quo. There still exist today intentional communities with histories dating back to those times: the Hutterites, Mennonites, Amish, and Quakers, each founding different traditions during the period.

These 16th century socio-spiritual movements were part of the cultural transformation we know as the Protestant Reformation.

At the same time, the growth of the market economy began to transform feudal systems and encourage technological developments, including those used in warfare. Technology further spurred on the transformation, and the newly invented printing press made the Bible and reformers' tracts widely available. Religious wars broke the secular power of the Roman Catholic Church.

Revolutions transformed governments. Eventually the concept of individual election, practiced first by the 16th century mystics, moved from religion into politics and law, and became the basis of the democratic tradition written into the constitutions of the United States and many other nations of today.

The concepts of the "inner light" and individual election are inspiring further cultural change today. The issue of worker participation in workplace decision-making is changing the old hierarchical and adversary structures of authority into more cooperative, consensus-based, decentralized-authority models. In some cases worker involvement includes employee ownership and participatory management — a clear trend toward economic democracy. With participatory communication and decision-making processes influencing the business world, and beginning to be practiced in education, we might wonder what this suggests for the future of our government.

Change often begins with individuals purposefully choosing a life of social and environmental responsibility. Com-

Allen Butcher, former member of East Wind and Twin Oaks, is a librarian and historian of contemporary communities. He has been a regular contributor to *Communities* magazine for a number of years. Allen is a member of the Communal Studies Association, and a founding member of the Fellowship for Intentional Community. He has traveled widely among communities and is now studying political science at the University of Southern Indiana, site of the Center for Communal Studies.

*Building a social tradition
tolerant of the differences
among people.*

municating one's convictions to
others leads to the formation of
groups, communities, and networks
— and these often eventually influence the larger society. The
waves of community movements
throughout history have mirrored,
and even influenced, the development of participatory decision-
making processes in the larger
society.

Transformation Today

The transformation we are experiencing today is likely to affect our culture on a scale similar to that of the Renaissance
and the Reformation. Spiritual, technological, economic, and
social forces today are quickening the pace of change.

Peter Russell suggests in his book *The Global Brain* that
the direction of change is toward a mutually advantageous
relationship between human culture and the Earth's natural
systems. The Gaia Hypothesis presents the Earth as a single,
self-regulating organism. Russell presents human awareness
as a gradual spiritual evolution toward planetary consciousness. We are awakening to the realization that we must accept responsibility for our actions as they effect society and
nature.

Russell refers to the complexity of the human brain, necessary for consciousness to evolve, as a parallel to how human
society must also be complex in order to support the evolutionary leap to planetary Gaia awakening. This complexity
involves both the infrastructure of electronic and laser communication technology, and the sophistication of interpersonal decision-making process and spiritual awareness.

The Gaia Hypothesis may be a cultural myth for our New
Age, a paradise that we may continually work toward achieving. The effect of Gaia awakening upon human culture may
have best been projected by William Irwin Thompson in his
concept of a steady-state climax culture. Elements of this future society would be: an integration of Eastern and Western
philosophy, technology, psychology, and culture; innovation
being a permanent feature of science, technology, and
economics; and a multiple political culture composed of nations, world-class cities, citizens' groups, and non-

governmental organizations. All of the characteristics of this
new society would involve the enhanced and expanded role
of participatory communication and decision-making processes among the world's peoples.

We are working toward more individual participation in the
decision making structures that control our society. Flexible social systems encourage a diversity of social patterns and
programs, making options available to fit a wide variety of individual needs. The many different community and co-operative projects of today are a beginning. Expansion and increased
networking among such projects will ensure that the growth of
these ideals will accelerate change in our culture.

Individual participation in social institutions requires
flexible rather than rigid control systems, and tolerance for
differing opinions and lifestyles. The resulting diversity in
human society could then reflect the ecological diversity
that we hope to maintain in our biosphere. As the world
rushes toward greater economic development and integration, there is a parallel between the loss of natural biological diversity and the loss of human cultural diversity. It is
not clear at what point this trend may be reversed, but the
way to effect this reverse is clear. We must accept and encourage spiritual, cultural, technological, philosophical, racial, and other differences among people, sometimes within
our own communities, always among different communities,
regions, and nations.

The futurist Robert Theobald clearly states this point: "Our
need is to discover ways in which we can live together in a
world of diversity, using this diversity to increase our ability
to change and adapt. The need is for flexible systems which
respond to this diversity rather than stifle it. ... We must learn
to move beyond a culture based on violence to one with new
attitudes and values which use conflicts to promote
creativity."

A Coming Wave?

If we hope to see a future of diversity and tolerance among cultures, we need to provide for those values within the intentional communities movement. Too often we are guilty of thinking, in the narrow parochial view of our home community, that ours is the only truly valuable social design. This communitarian chauvinism keeps us apart and limits our potential for creating a larger movement that is greater than the sum of our individual communities. Even as we reach out to each other, we can take pride in our differences and validate the uniqueness of all intentional communities, just as we appreciate the cultural and ecological diversity of our planet.

It is precisely our diversity of communitarian designs that provides our movement's ability to adapt creatively to changing conditions and opportunities. The potential for communitarian development increases as the level of stress in the wider society rises. With the increase in homelessness, single parent families, violence, ecological degradation, and the potential for economic catastrophe, communitarian models of a human scale society will become more and more relevant. Applying various forms of these models to an ever wider span of urban, suburban, and rural lifestyles is the challenge of the next wave of intentional communities.

Communitarian activity has been most noticeable during times of significant social change in the past. Communitarianism has progressed along with the dominant social design, in both pace and sophistication.

In the early 12th century, Catholic monasticism occupied approximately a quarter of the developed lands of Europe and preserved much of ancient culture. In the 17th century, with the opening of the New World, the first wave of North American communitarianism came with the first colonists, the religious sects such as the Puritans and Quakers. The second wave landed in the 1840s as a result of continued religious and political persecution in Europe. The excesses of the European Industrial Revolution encouraged the beginning of economic and social communitarian traditions such as the Owenites and the Oneida Perfectionists.

The third wave came in the 1890s, largely in response to the economic recessions and industrial labor strife of that era. These involved the single-tax, socialist, and anarchist communitarian designs. Forty years later, the fourth wave came during the Great Depression of the 1930s, with New Deal government-sponsored Green Belt towns, as well as the Catholic Worker, Socialist, and Emissary communities (many of which also still exist).

The fifth wave of North American communitarianism crested just 30 years later, in the 1960s and '70s, with the New Age, Christian, back-to-the-land, Egalitarian, and other

Change can be described as a progression through waves or cycles, or even as moving in ascending spirals, repeating old themes but in changing contexts.

movements. Notice that the length of time between waves has grown shorter. Many communities have built upon earlier communitarian experiences, sometimes even occupying the same physical sites.

With each period between waves being shorter than the last, and the most recent wave of the '60s and '70s now being roughly 20 years past, we might expect the 1990s to be another time of communitarian growth. Certainly most of the issues of the '60s are still unresolved, and many new concerns have arisen.

If we are to encourage a new wave of communitarianism in the coming decade, we might do well to focus upon building a tradition of individual participation in, and responsibility for, the institutions that control our lives. In order to achieve a balance between the values of competition and cooperation, we may be most effective by building a social tradition which is tolerant of the differences among people, provides a diversity of lifestyle options, and educates individuals for social and environmental responsibility. Communitarianism anticipates, reflects, and quickens the pace of social change, and the surest way to bring about change is to live it! ❖

Bibliography

Michael Ventura, "Over the Edge of History with William Irwin Thompson," *Utne Reader*, June/July '86, from *Los Angeles Weekly*, 12-13-85.

Peter Russell, *The Global Brain*, Tarcher Press, 1983.

James Lovelock, *GAIA: A New Look At Life On Earth*, Oxford U. Press, 1979.

Robert Theobald, "Recognizing the Change," *Guidebook For The 90s*, Knowledge Systems, Inc., 7777 West Morris St, Indianapolis 46231

The Tribal Vision

Gordon Davidson/Sirius

What vision brings people to community, and what sustains them there?

Eve Furchgott of Kerista Village believes that — in addition to voluntary membership, cooperative economics, and social contracts — every successful community needs a "soul". In **The Soul of Community** *she explores how this "inspirational sense of mission and future vision" is achieved, in part, by "truly dynamic self-development and interpersonal relationships development process."*

Rich Miller, a long-term member of the now defunct Kindred Community, reflects on the challenge of maintaining personal motivation and direction while engaged in the process and goals of cooperative living. In answering the question **Why Do We Do It?** *he gives new meaning to the word 'faith'.*

David and Carol Thatcher of l00 Mile Lodge describe spiritual values common to most communitarians — even those who don't consider themselves to be at all spiritual. Their thoughts on **Why Live Communally?** *point to the wider connections and common values emerging in the far-ranging communities movement.*

Yogaville's Swami Satchidananda speaks about equality, individuality, the basis of inter-religious strife, and the common purpose that can hold us together. **Let's Come...Unity,** *based on one of his Satsang addresses, closes with a dream common to those seeking to rediscover "the tribal vision": "Then we can live harmoniously. That would certainly make a heaven on Earth!"*

Ten Aspects of the New Utopian Vision, *compiled by the Tarrytown Group, is a concise listing of values commonly held by contemporary intentional communities. Though some groups do not share all ten of the values, the list is valuable for highlighting the trends of the overall communities movement.*

Intentional communities emphasize a vision which simultaneously nurtures the individual and works for the common good... so that we can all help create that "heaven on Earth."

The Soul of Community

In the beginning there were tribes. You were born in the midst of your people and lived out your life there, safe in your social niche. The structure of traditional tribal life was clear-cut and static. You belonged by reason of blood relatedness, and you were expected to carry out all the obligations of your social position in the tribe, something that most often was determined at or even before your birth.

Then came the agricultural revolution, followed eventually by the industrial revolution, with radical societal changes and disintegration of old patterns. This has left us, in the Western world, with nuclear families and a continually increasing number of people who live alone. The material and intellectual benefits of our modern civilization are offset by a whole new set of psychological problems, many of which can be traced back to people trying to figure out their place in the world — something a tribal person knows implicitly.

Traditional tribalism — an involuntary form of community — makes no room for the kind of experimental individualism most of us take for granted. On the other hand, freedom to do one's own thing, and access to the technology to carry it out, are of little solace to someone suffering from loneliness, boredom, and feelings of social alienation.

Intentional communities — voluntary tribes — combine the most desirable elements of both traditional and contemporary or even experimental lifestyles. Intentional communities have been around for a long time, dating back to groups like the Essenes in Biblical days, or the community of Pythagoras in ancient Greece. The most successful modern, secular intentional communities, in terms of population, are the Israeli kibbutzim and moshavim. All these communities share at least three things in common: 1) the members are there by choice, 2) they practice some form of cooperation at the economic level, and 3) they agree to live by a code, or social contract, as a condition of membership.

Many communities fit these fundamental parameters, yet lack a quality I describe as "soul," a certain spirit that goes beyond the purely prosaic, economic elements of life.

Most people attracted to group living have some degree of idealistic vision, some expectation of a better way of life. My vision was of a close circle of friends who shared everything, including the inner recesses of their psyches, who were imbued with a "one for all and all for one" expectation in which material sharing was only a small element. The relationship of people to one another and to humanity as a whole was paramount. I wanted to attach my energy to something that could work toward solving humanity's massive problems at the same time that it took care of my own.

Arriving in San Francisco, I first heard about a "gestalt kibbutz." It was an encounter weekend that never ended, an outgrowth of the sensitivity/human potential movement. Having begun to peel away neurotic habits and negative attitudes, people stayed together and took the process further rather than return to the environment which created the unsatisfying habits and attitudes. This was what I was seeking.

Superficially, the gestalt kibbutz model may seem self-indulgent, but it is also eminently practical. Poor interpersonal relations tear communities apart more than any other single factor. Kerista, the community I joined, came up very early with "inability to hold a steady course" as a definition of neurosis. However well you get along with someone initially, eventually you meet her/his "other side," which might be macho, sneaky, schleppy, stupid or stubborn. In many communities, this is what leads to individuals leaving or the group's disintegration. Our solution is a process capable of creating genuine dialogue so that individuals can root out basic issues, see them objectively, and work on them.

Without commitment, such a process will not do the job. Desire has to be very strong; and what fuels that desire is a future vision larger than the immediate situation. When the going gets tough, we have to know that the effort is going to be worthwhile. This inspires us to keep on and nurtures a healthy sense of vanity, a conviction that we are involved in something of significance within the sweep of human history. Without boosts like these, morale could decline and members could be drawn back to isolated lifestyles.

Any intentional community is, to some degree, a utopian experiment, an attempt to create a new model of association that uses cooperation to create a "more perfect union" among

Eve Furchgott, a member of Kerista in San Francisco since 1971, is editor of the Kerista publications *Rockhead* and *The Node*, and is art director of Abacus, Inc., their computer service bureau. She is a graphic artist animator and a community outreach activist who has visited many different communities. She enjoys backpacking and singing in Sex Kult, Kerista's rock band.

Future vision...

people. Any model that holds together, functions harmoniously, and succeeds economically is a potential prototype for future communitarians.

Sometimes members of my community are perceived as arrogant or too critical by other communitarians. We do practice direct confrontation of apparent contradictions when we think we see them — that's part of our operating culture. We believe that debate is healthy and can stimulate deeper thought than bland niceties or tips about composting techniques. We defend our model of communal life enthusiastically, and seek others who do the same.

In my experience, the intentional community movement seems to be characterized by soft-spoken, anti-judgmental interactions, wherein negative opinions or critical analysis of strengths, weaknesses, and underlying motivations are considered gauche. This, I believe, is counter-productive to the development of a strong movement. There is plenty of room for all sorts of people, living in all sorts of co-operative arrangements, and the more dialogue there is about differences the better. I don't believe all intentional communities have to use the communication process my group uses. Nor do we have to agree about other aspects of community life in order to be supportive colleagues and friends.

Intentional communities in the post-industrial world must forge their own ways to success. I maintain that, whatever the variations, the successful models need (1) cooperative economics, (2) a social contract, (3) voluntary membership, (4) a truly dynamic self-development and inter-personal development process, and (5) an inspirational sense of mission and future vision that gives members their raison d'etre. These, taken together, are the soul of intentional community. ❖

Self development for health and direction.

Why Do We Do It ?

by Rich Miller

When people ask us what we do in community, war resistance, service, living simply and so on, it's usually not too hard to answer the questions about details — what, where, when, how. The hard questions are the ones that start with "why": *Why* do we do the things we do? Such questions are so hard we often have trouble asking them of ourselves as a community, and even as individuals. "Why" questions are fundamentally different from the others, and have to be answered in a fundamentally different way.

When we face a Why question, the first thing we have to recognize is the deeper question that lies behind the Why. The

essential question is not "Why live simply?" or "Why do service?"; it is "Why do *anything*?" The question is a universal one. Whether we live on the fringes of society or in the dead center of the mainstream, we all do something. And the same question confronts every one of us: Why do we do the things we do? Make the choices we make? Live the way we live? What is the point to our lives? To life in general? **Is** there a point to any of this?

If one were to ask Martin Luther King Jr. why he did the things he did, and then ask Jerry Falwell why he does the things he does, both might give the same answer: "faith." But

*Sharing a meal at
Camphill Village*

Stephan C. Rasch/Camphill Village

Rich Miller was a member of Kindred Community and writer for their community newsletter. As a peace activist he has participated in demonstrations against U.S. nuclear bomb testing and is now imprisoned as a result of his physical opposition inside the testing zone.

Plowing the garden after a wet spring at Oakwood Farm

Oakwood Farm/Emissaries

they would clearly not be talking about the same thing; what faith means to one is radically different from what faith means to the other.

Faith gives us all assurances that there is a point to life. Faith is also the source of our answers to what that point is. Yet we have to be careful here: "faith" as a word is so abstract and ambiguous that it cannot stand by itself as an answer. We have to find a clear way of showing what we mean. This is where the Why questions differ from the detail questions.

How, then, can we know what a person means when they say faith is why they do what they do? The only way we can really know is simply by looking at how those persons live their lives, at the specific things they do, and the choices they make. For no matter how much we try to add to that basic answer, the words have no life of their own. Unless they are placed in the context of a person's life, the words mean nothing.

This leaves us with a paradox: The answer to "Why do we do what we do?" can only be found in **what** we do.

We do what we do because of faith, yes, and because our faith tells us that there is more to life than meets the eye. But the only way we can give meaning to our answer is to show what this "more" is — to actually do what we are trying to explain: community, service, living simply, and all the rest. Our lives are the clearest exposition of what we mean by faith.

Our lives speak the truth as we see it far more directly than our words ever can. In this sense our lives are the most authentic answers that we can give to the question "Why do we do what we do?" ❖

A construction project at Oakwood Farm, Indiana

Oakwood Farm/Emissaries

Why Live Communally?

by David Thatcher

Why live communally? The answers are as varied as the community residents themselves: to reconnect with deeper personal currents; to get away from our frenetic, overpopulated, yet ironically lonely world; to connect with the rhythms of nature; to follow a particular spiritual path. Yet as varied as the reasons may be, most community residents I know acknowledge their reverence for the sacredness of life. Some living in community don't consider themselves spiritual in the least; others speak of spirit as the very essence of community, of life itself. Beyond such beliefs, I find that this fundamental reverence for life provides the common ground vital to allowing the deeper nature and purpose of community to be seen.

Several years ago I acknowledged that it wasn't valid for me to achieve "enlightenment", or ultimate fulfillment, atop a mountain, isolated from others. I noted that my consciousness, my living experience was and is inextricably intertwined with the rest of humanity. I found myself drawn to participate in a collective process perhaps akin to marriage, in which I acknowledged my responsibility to honor and respect, to love and support my fellows through their ups and downs, and through my own vacillations of clarity and energy. As a certain steadiness has been maintained in my living experience over a number of years — and I know I speak for many others — a depth of fulfillment has been discovered which overflows and connects with others the world around who share a concern for the well-being of the global community.

At my home, the 100 Mile Lodge, we speak of our community as a unit, an essential part of the world community. Webster's Dictionary defines unit as "a single thing or person or group that is a constituent of a whole." This whole initially may be seen as the community of which one is a part; yet living in a collective setting does not separate you from the rest of the world. In fact, as responsibility for the "marriage" agreement just mentioned is assumed, you find yourself more deliberately connected to the world, because your current of respect, of love, for the fellows around you who represent many others worldwide, must consistently be maintained. The purpose of intentional community living is not to pleasantly interact when you wish, and retreat when situations become uncomfortable. Rather, communal living requires continual clarification; it requires expansive, balanced vision and maturity.

The proliferation of communities in the late 1960s and early 1970s has been useful in helping many to release isolated, self-serving habits and open to a more transcendent and consistently loving experience. Such a broad and unifying interrelatedness is undeniable.

The desecration of the Brazilian rain forest, for example, directly affects the ability of the earth's atmosphere to dissipate carbon monoxide generated on Los Angeles freeways; all the world's PCB incineration takes place at a plant near Birmingham, England; the brutal suppression of Chinese students in Tiananmen Square immediately shifted the world stock markets. Such examples are legion. Yet on a brighter note, the heartfelt experience of community, shared by some people in communities worldwide, contributes to the greater experience of world community. This spirit of world community, despite the suppression in China, actually runs deeply in the hearts of people everywhere. So deeply that even barriers between the Soviet Union and the western world, most notably the USA, appear to be dissolving.

Rupert Sheldrake, a well-known British plant physiologist, speaks of the morphogenetic field, the fact that the world doesn't function so much by preordained fate as by precedent. As precedents are set, the way is made easier for further developments of similar nature to occur. Scientists seeking to create new crystalline formations in laboratories are required to painstakingly prepare the components and environment, and may, after numerous failures,

David Thatcher, and his wife Carol, are long-term residents of 100 Mile Lodge, Canadian headquarters for Emissary Foundation International. Carol lived at Findhorn in the middle '70s. David is author of the book *Earthrise: A Personal Responsibility.* Together they have over 35 years of association with the communities, consciousness, and social change movements.

David and Carol's lectures, workshops and seminars have taken them throughout North America, Europe and Australasia. The Emissary Foundation International operates over 200 centers and communities worldwide. The Kripalu Center, also mentioned in this article, has some 75 closely associated support groups, primarily in the U.S.

Young Emissaries from 100 Mile Lodge, British Columbia.

100 Mile Lodge/Emissaries

facilitate the appearance of a new variation of crystalline structure. But once created, such new forms appear as if by magic in laboratories the world around, totally unconnected in any visible way with the initial experiment. I expect this parallels the pioneering being done by many who have chosen to live their lives with reverence for the sacredness of life. Such pioneering surely helps the spirit of community appear more easily throughout the world.

Recently Michael Exeter, who coordinates the International Emissary Community, met with Dr. Amrit Desai, founder of the Kripalu Center for Yoga and Health, headquartered in Lenox, Massachusetts. In an address to these two expansive

We live in a time in which global inter-relatedness is undeniable.

communities, noting the obvious resonance between them and those they represented, they acknowledged the ultimate importance of the consciousness of the individual. On the surface the lives and practices of the residents of these communities are quite different. Yet the deeply shared interest in expressing noble qualities of character through the simple circumstances of daily living revealed a depth of individual communion with the innate design of life which was thus able to be shared collectively. It was acknowledged that "groups" can't come together. Only as communion is known within can it be shared with others. Thomas Merton, a 20th century Trappist monk, recorded in his diary:

> I have the immense joy of being a man, a member of a race in which God Himself became incarnate. As if the sorrows and stupidities of the human condition could overwhelm me, now I realize what we all are! And if only everybody could realize this! But it cannot be explained. There is no way of telling people that they are walking around shining like the sun.

We live in a time that invites, indeed requires, as many as are willing to abide in a living experience which cannot be explained, shining like the sun. As reverence for the sacredness of life is maintained in living, the experience of community long sought on earth is sure to become more present. As sure as the sun rises and shines each day. ❖

(*Earthrise: A Personal Responsibility*, 165 pages, is available by writing to David Thatcher, P.O. Box 667, Lynden WA 98264.)

Let's Come... Unity

by Swami Satchidananda

On March 12, 1988, at Yogaville, InterCommunities of Virginia held its Fourth Annual Conference, which was attended by communitarians from Common Ground, The Gathering, Gesundheit Institute, Innisfree Village, MSH Association, New Land, Shannon Farm, Springtree, Twin Oaks and Yogaville. The day-long conference was followed by Satsang where Swami Satchidananda, founder of Yogaville, spoke on the topics of community, equality, individuality, and interreligious strife:

It was so nice to have the InterCommunities gathering. In a way Yogaville is expanding.

Mohini gave a nice story about the watch and how important it is to recognize and respect even the littlest swinging wheel. That clearly showed that everything is important. Nobody is insignificant. Everything has its own place. And so it is with intentional communities.

But sometimes that philosophy is misinterpreted. Just because everybody is equally important doesn't mean that everybody should be doing the same thing.

We have our own individuality... at the same time, equality.

Equality in function for a common goal. The functions may vary because we're all individuals. But nobody can substitute for you. You have a special purpose, a special mission to fulfill. And you are the only one who can fulfill your mission.

Josh Gitomer

Mount Madonna Center in Watsonville, CA.

Swami Satchidananda is a spiritual leader and yoga teacher, participant in ecumenical religious services around the world and founder of Integral Yoga Institutes (IYI). In the late '60s he moved from India to the United States, where he has founded a number of training centers and intentional communities. Swami Satchidananda leads peace delegations and spiritual pilgramages to major shrines throughout the world. He now resides at Satchidananda Ashram/Yogaville, an intentional community of diversity in the mountains of central Virginia where the international headquarters of IYI is located, as well as the site of the Light of Truth Universal Shrine (LOTUS). The LOTUS is a beautiful South Indian-style shrine which contains the holy scriptures of all the world's major religions and includes public displays of sacred objects dedicated to the ending of strife and violence among all believers. (Copyright, March 12, 1988, Integral Yoga Internat'l, Buckingham, VA 23921, reproduced by permission.)

Common Purpose Vs. Ego

Equality comes in realizing that we are all doing different jobs for a common purpose. That is the aim behind any community. The very name community means let's come together to recognize the unity. Come... unity. We are coming to experience the unity.

I'm very, very glad that at least the communities have a community feeling among themselves. How often that is forgotten or ignored. Take for example the religions. Each religion is a community by itself. But when some of the so-called religious communities function, they seem to inject their own egoism into it and say, "What we're doing is right. What you're doing is wrong. Our way is the best way. Unless you come and get onto our bandwagon, you can never go to the place where we are supposed to be going."

Often we come across this even in the name of Yoga. Some would say only Kundalini Yoga is the way. Others, no, no, only Tantra Yoga. Or Mantra Yoga. There's nothing wrong with Yoga; but we limit it by our own egoism.

In this way so many quarrels, fights and even massacres happen in the name of religion; each one says, "Mine is the only way." If we can only rise above our egoism, we can learn to respect and accept everybody's approach.

The Bhagavad Gita says that you have no business in disturbing somebody's faith. If someone is following a way, help them if you want, to go in their way. Show them how to reach the goal, but in their own way.

If anybody comes and says that this is the only way, "My way is the best," that means they are far away from their own path. They have not reached it, but are only talking about it. Experience is really different from talking about it.

So let us realize the importance of learning to respect each other. Variety is the spice of life. We want variety in people and in communities. But it can be enjoyed only when we recognize the purpose, the common purpose behind life. Then respecting each other becomes easy. We don't criticize the other person. We don't claim superiority. All those things just drop out.

So let us realize the importance of learning to respect each other. Variety is the spice of life. We want variety in people and in communities. But it can be enjoyed only when we recognize the purpose, the common purpose behind life. Then respecting each other becomes easy. We don't criticize the other person. We don't claim superiority. All those things just drop out.

Then we can live harmoniously. That would certainly make a heaven on Earth! ❖

(Books by Swami Satchidananda, including *Kailash Journal: Pilgrimage into the Himalayas,* 148 pages, $6.95 plus $1.50 postage and handling, are available from Satchidananda Ashram — Yogaville, Rt. 1, Box 172, Buckingham, VA 23921, 804-969-1500.)

Gordon Davidson/Sirius

University Program at Sirius Community, MA.

Ten Main Aspects of the New Utopian Vision

by the Tarrytown Group

1. **A dual commitment to transformation**, both personal and planetary: dedication to individual growth and to serving the needs of humanity and society.

2. **Cooperation**: a community based on sharing, pooling of finances and human resources, rather than competition and being "Out for Number One."

3. **A deep respect for the environment**: restoring ecological balance and "living lightly" on the earth; developing organic agriculture, and solar and wind energy.

4. **A spirit of experimentalism** in both work and relationships: committing to "working through" the shadow side of the personality, to confront conflict between individuals and within the self, to bring out the dark side for transformation into affirmative alliances.

5. **A new economics**: finding businesses and ways to manage them that put human values on the bottom line and still return a healthy profit.

6. **Common sense**: determination to find practical solutions for conquering society's problems of pollution, inflation, violence and alienation.

7. **A holistic approach to health**: exploring alternative healing — such as herbs, acupuncture, nutrition and massage — and preventive methods aimed at helping people take responsibility for their own health.

8. **Building a positive vision**: creating examples of a better society, and striving to live tomorrow's world today — then making their insights available, through outreach programs, to local communities and the world at large.

9. **Self-government by consensus**: working with group process and evoking the intuition of community members in the decision-making process.

10. **A world network**: cooperating with similar communities throughout the world; sharing skills and services, taking political action, and forming the vital nucleus of a new civilization. ❖

Editor's Note: This vision statement is reprinted, with permission, from the March, 1983, issue of the Tarrytown Letter. It concisely captures the major trends of today's communities movement, and outlines some of the cultural alternatives frequently mentioned in our research. This vision is VERY general — there is considerable variety in the degree to which any single community embraces any particular value mentioned.

It is our sense that most communities share many of the values listed above, or at least agree substantially with the underlying principles (though not necessarily with the specific forms). This list is offered as an observation, not as an endorsement.

The Tarrytown Group may be reached at Box 222, Tarrytown NY 10591.

Personal Growth

How far-reaching is the effect of community life on an individual's personal growth?

Geoph Kozeny of the Community Catalyst Project depicts the cooperative lifestyle pressures that can induce us to "spread ourselves too thin, and eventually burn out." In **Long On Idealism, Short On Time** he suggests alternative perspectives that can help us become happier, more effective and creative, and more oriented toward personal growth.

Patch Adams is a "happy hippie doctor" from the Gesundheit Institute, a community based on free and bartered health services. In his **Prescription for Community** he describes the personal growth and security he experiences in his own life, and suggests that shared living is a generically sane and healthful lifestyle.

Women in Community, edited by Julie Mazo, combines insights from two conversations — one among women at Springtree, and another among women at Shannon Farm. The participants elaborate on their experiences and growth as individuals in community, and offer thoughts on support, work, security, family, companionship, privacy, and other aspects of community life.

Dan Greenberg is a University of Minnesota student doing graduate work on **Children in Community.** Based on extensive correspondence and visits with North American communities, he concludes that for children and adults alike, "the most important product of intentional communities (may be) process itself... how groups can work and grow together in joyful and humane ways and, at the same time, get things done."

In each of these four articles, personal growth and the process of community are seen as being inextricably and joyfully intertwined.

100 Mile Lodge/Emissaries

Long on Idealism, Short on Time

by Geoph Kozeny

The Doorstep Grocer, a pre-order food co-op launched in the spring of 1985, was a worker-owned food distribution business in which customers placed orders on Mondays and collective members delivered on Thursdays.

It was a tough decision for the collective, but after months of deliberation, we finally decided to fold up shop.

It wasn't that we weren't enjoying the work — we were always laughing and joking with each other as we worked, and it provided a great excuse to socialize with a bunch of friends (our main source of customers) for a couple of minutes every Thursday at delivery time.

When a person feels perpetually overextended, the accompanying feelings of frustration can be thoroughly overwhelming. We need ways to get our lives organized, and to identify new roles to emulate.

It wasn't that the work seemed meaningless — we really believed in the folk ideal "Food for people, not for profit," and our customers often mentioned how much they enjoyed and appreciated our service. Several of them nearly begged us to reconsider our decision.

It also wasn't a question of financial viability — though we were often underpaid or unpaid for our efforts, we accepted that as standard procedure for any small business in the start-up mode. All of our studies and projections indicated that by doubling our weekly volume — by making up to 35 or 40 deliveries per week — we would be able to consistently pay ourselves $6 to $8 per hour. Due to efficiencies of scale, shopping for 40 households takes only slightly more time than shopping for 20.

So what was the problem? — In retrospect, I'm convinced it was the predictable effect of a condition that's widespread throughout the movement for social change: an excess of idealism, a condition that isn't obvious when judging from outward appearances. In effect, it's biting off more than you can chew.

Among the members of the collective we had enough experience and skills to do the actual work, but in reality we weren't getting the work done. Although we'd process the orders and (almost always) get the deliveries done on time, our personal schedules were so seriously overloaded, primarily with commitments we'd made long before Doorstep entered the picture, that our daily lives were in constant stress. So it was usually a strain to divvy up the week's Doorstep chores and wedge them into our individual plans.

This state of chronic overload persisted for a year and a half, and we felt we were smack up against an economic

Geoph Kozeny was a founding member of San Francisco's Stardance (now Purple Rose) in 1978, and has lived cooperatively since 1973. He is a volleyballer and professional communities movement networker. A skilled architect, builder, electrician, photographer, folk singer and guitarist, computer whiz, and philosopher, Geoph's experience as a graphic artist, writer and publisher began with his high school newspaper. Very "long on idealism" himself, he edited and typeset the communities and resources listings for this directory, reviewed feature articles, and provided photos for article illustration from his extensive personal collection. Since January of 1988, Geoph has been on the road with the Community Catalyst Project (see Resources section). He has visited and worked with over two hundred intentional communities across North America. As one of his services to communities and the general public, Geoph makes frequemt presentations of an ever-changing slide show about diverse intentional communities. His shows stimulate consistently fascinating discussions on the philosohy of cooperative lifestyles.

Catch 22: needing more capital to fund outreach, expansion and wages — and needing more customers and volume in order to finance the transition.

Not an overwhelming challenge by any means, at least by itself. There are dozens of ways to come up with seed money (start-up capital), and several deferred-payment plans to fund the front-end labor (including "sweat equity" approaches). But our basic weakness was left unsolved — none of us made the business a priority; none of us pursued it with a passion or a plan.

To be sure, we had an overall long-range plan, but we had neither the focus nor the energy to convert it into a day-by-day, one step at a time program.

We all liked the idea of providing a convenient and affordable health food delivery service, especially the part about being a friendly worker owned enterprise. It also seemed a

viable source of income for meeting our living expenses. Most of the bases were covered.

Unfortunately, our grocery business didn't rank high enough on anyone's priority list, individual or collective. Grocery work fell in line behind our daily chores, behind our relationships, behind other community work, and behind other income-producing activities. We squeezed it into the cracks of our already overcommitted lives.

In this fashion we kept the Doorstep Grocer running along on a shoestring for 18 months, mindful of our noble purpose and enjoying the actual work. Yet we never managed to follow through on detailing long-range plans, much less implementing them. Though we were appreciated and supported by our loyal customers, things didn't just "organically" fall into place — the business didn't take off on its own without any need of management by us.

And so it goes with far too many of our visions — we know what we want to accomplish (or so we think), but we so often fail to get the job done. Not enough time, not enough resources, so many "priorities" that the concept of priorities becomes almost meaningless. It's grease the squeaky wheel, run yourself ragged — reach the point of burnout when you get sick, or go nuts, or simply withdraw, or head off on a much-needed vacation where you relax enough to catch up with yourself. Then it's take a deep breath and climb back onto the treadmill of daily life. It's back to bill paying and making the world a better place. The next cycle has begun.

Interestingly enough, traditional cultural conditioning (including sex roles) has often helped us to avoid or overcome traps, or at least minimize their effects — while some of our creative "alternative lifestyles" tend to compound the problems. [Please note that I'm not an advocate of perpetuating traditional sex roles.]

In the '70s the Women's Movement identified the problem by describing how women were trying to become "Supermoms" — excelling in full-time demanding work, raising several children with love and understanding, and maintaining a clean, well organized house — all at the same time. I think all of us exploring alternative lifestyles tend to fall into a similar trap. We are afraid to be "less" than our image of a man or a woman, regardless of how we choose to define those roles. We don't give up our old roles so much as try to take on new ones as well.

We complicate things further by feeling we need to perform many of these roles simultaneously, especially if we are at a transition point in life. Changing careers, going to school,

*Enjoying
cooperative living*

raising a family as a single parent, re-evaluating primary relationship(s), and trying to earn enough money to pay the bills — any one of these can be a strain, and it's quite common for many of my friends to be working on three or four at once.

One thing the old roles did was limit the number of things any one person had to be good at, or had to devote a lot of time to. Sex roles made it simpler for a lot of people to make sure the basics were covered (dishes washed, money earned, kids diapered, roof fixed, field plowed, car started) without needing to discuss and plan who was going to do what. The role models in our parents' culture offered a technique for avoiding the chaos of trying to do too much at once. If you tried to follow the All-American path of life (get a basic education, go to college, fall in love and get married, begin a career, raise a family, retire), you had at least one thing working strongly in your favor: Your path was laid out in a logical and orderly fashion, and things were lined up more or less sequentially. This type of approach enabled you to concentrate on one major project at a time — hopefully doing it well, then leaving that structure in place (almost on automatic pilot) as you moved on to the next step.

I see the need to limit my focus, to concentrate on getting one project completed (or solidly established) before moving on — and I see how others, individually and collectively, are in similar situations. Many people leave a community or drop out of a collective because of a sense of constant pressure. It's really sad to watch people working on things they find meaningful, trying so hard for so long, but eventually giving up because of this. When a person feels perpetually overextended, the accompanying feelings of frustration can be thoroughly overwhelming. We need ways to get our lives organized, and to identify new roles to emulate.

In looking at how different individuals and groups have addressed this challenge, I've identified several helpful techniques. Here are five common practices for becoming more effective in your daily reality:

1) *Simplify things.* Pay attention to feelings of stress. Learn to feel comfortable in saying "no" to a request that's more than you can (or want to) handle — even if you wish you could help out. Accept temporary imperfections, knowing that things will eventually get taken care of if you (and others) keep a positive attitude and continue working for the needed changes.

2) *Prioritize.* Look for the areas in which you can be most effective, or those that can be stabilized in the future by a spurt of effort now. Schedule a few hours a month to work on community or regional projects, and make sure you spend some time every week on tasks that are moving you toward long range goals.

3) *Be Supportive.* If you encourage others in their efforts, good things can actually happen without you being there to

Call in "well" at work — tell your co-workers that you're feeling too good to come in today — and that instead you're going to do something you've been wanting to do for months, but lacked the time.

do them. It may even become possible for you to let go of a project you're attached to — if you see that it's in good hands. And financial support is definitely in order — for those groups doing the good work you want to see done, but which you lack the time or energy to do yourself.

4) *Stay informed.* Granted this is an age of information overload — so skim a lot, and be selective about the in depth stuff. If you know that your areas of concern are being covered by other people and other groups, you can have more time to focus on your own priority pursuits.

Corollary: Be sure that others know about the projects you are committed to.

5) *Be creative.* Rotate tasks with your housemates or co-workers, or actually swap roles if you find there are some you seldom fill. Have brainstorming sessions. Pretend that you've just moved to town, and imagine where you would really want to live and work, and what projects you'd like to support — then compare your answers to how you're actually living. Call in "well" at work — tell your co-workers that you're feeling too good to come in today — and that instead you're going to do something you've been wanting to do for months, but lacked the time. Corner a stranger and ask them what they'd do if they were you. The possibilities are endless... use your imagination!

Family, community, education, ecology, peace, civil rights, careers, hobbies — they all need attention, but it's so much ground to cover. We need a co-operative system that's decentralized enough to focus on the individual issues within each category, yet integrated enough that the individual efforts complement each other. Then we as a society can accomplish what we as individuals keep trying to do by ourselves. ❖

Prescription for Community

by Patch Adams M.D.

A portrait of the author

For tens of millions of years we primates have lived in tribes. I'm sure we came together because of mutual interdependence in child rearing, food gathering, and security. The fun experienced as a collective came as a powerful side effect. I believe this is so much a part of our primate past that the drive to huddle together has become part of our genetic coding. I think all this is why an intimate health professional like myself finds loneliness to be one of the most devastating illnesses in our culture. Only friendship can cure loneliness.

When we changed from hunter/gatherers to farmers we left the larger traveling band for smaller groups, claiming individual plots of land, and huddling at a distance from the rest by householding in villages. As villages grew into cities, huddling happened in neighborhoods. As we moved further apart our community diminished to the extended family, then to the nuclear family and finally to the solitary dweller. This progression has been heralded in the arts, psychology and sociology as "the alienation of the society."

In my years of being an intimate physician with thousands of folks, I have found very few people who have the intoxicating enrapturement that comes with a circle of deeply committed friends. In fact, I have found the vast majority of

Patch Adams   After he graduated from medical school in 1971 Hunter "Patch" Adams helped found Gesundheit Institute, based on the idea that healing should be a loving human interchange, not a business transaction. Gesundheit provided free and bartered medical care to over 15,000 people from 1971 to 1983, when the group reluctantly stopped seeing patients to concentrate on building their dream — a 40-bed free hospital. Patch has visited over 550 intentional communities and maintains a correspondence rate of 400 letters per month. His other interests include cooking, cleaning, medicine, recreation, fundraising, clowning and working with volunters on construction of Gesundheit's hospital. This article appeared in the health column published in *New Frontier*. (Copyright, September 1987, *New Frontier, The Magazine of Transformation*, Philadelphia PA, reprinted by permission.)

people feeling lucky even to have a few close acquaintances. Even in marriages I don't often hear the serenade of chumship. Very few adults are capable of erasing this cloud of loneliness by turning to God, nature, pets, art, or their work, though the opportunity is there.

Ultimately everything is better with a circle of friends within which to huddle. Without this circle of safety it is extremely difficult to erase the security fears that coat each of our lives, in our economics, health, and relationships. Seeking to resolve these fears as individuals can result in increasing competitiveness and isolation, major stumbling blocks to establishing community. Yet it is in community that we find the basic emotional security we seek.

Community can be experienced in many forms, and I suggest exploring many of them. Live embraced by concentric circles. I am not speaking of collecting membership cards or notches in your resume — but of commitment to individuals by action. I would like to speak out for one form that I love dearly. I have lived in a communal group for 16 years, and it has been the most significant factor in the progression of all my dreams, both personal and public.

I have been with my wife 16 years, and we have known only the communal lifestyle. I am sure that living in community is the major reason we still have a rich, vibrant love for each other.

We are always surrounded by men and women friends. When one of us wants some space from the other we can simply go elsewhere in the house and play with someone else. When a project ties one of us up, the other need not feel neglected and without companionship.

Every day every meal can be a dinner party with conversation sizzling. With shared labor each person in our group cooks one night a week, and with such infrequency can really put their heart into the meal. One's cleaning week comes every six weeks.

And child-rearing... oh, this may be the best! Our child has had such magical input from each member. Sure, time is shared, but much more; talents and personalities are shared as well.

Professionally, communal life has given me the opportunity to chase after rainbows. Gesundheit Institute, our free hospital, has existed because we are a commune. It simply would not have existed at all without group living. Gesundheit was not the quest of one man but the living byproduct of committed friends. I cannot conceive of practicing medicine in today's usual context, but I can practice it otherwise only by the grace of community. Nothing can encourage your dreams more outrageously than chums in mutual support.

By sharing costs and possessions we have been able to do big things for pennies. As we have moved along in building the hospital of our dreams, we have exceeded our ability to pay for it ourselves — but we are slowly building up a community of people from all over the United States who are sending what they can to build the hospital. For five years all the expenses on the land have been paid for by donations.

My personal growth has also been enhanced by community. I graduated from medical school head-smart, but while living in community I have helped construct buildings, farmed, had a goat herd, produced movies, learned rope walking, unicycling, and so much more. The joy I find in this new knowledge is dwarfed, however, by the happiness I feel in simply being alive in the bosom of so many friends.

This is a security that transcends economics.

So how can you take steps toward community? First — be ready to belong with all your heart and soul. Community will not sustain itself casually. Look at your current relationships — discuss their potential beyond your wildest dreams. The clearer your dreams, the happier your journey. Seeing the dream as a journey and not a final product can allow you to feel. You can have it now — your dream is not a thing only of the future.

Two whoppers are patience and flexibility — carry these friends every day in every group process and the hurdles can be flown over. It is important to develop the dream co-operatively with others, because without similar goals no amount of patience or flexibility will suffice; but with similar goals, — ooooh, get ready! Community is like marriage; whatever works great there will work in an intentional community. Consider making that level of commitment to your community. It's scary — but it sure makes the friendships easier.

Find a way to love the meetings. Friendships are again a key here; with deep respect and trust for your fellows, every discussion becomes a brush stroke for the complete picture. If your group makes rules even if you didn't vote for them — give them your active support without grumbling. Grumblers and whiners are community maggots.

Folks, this marriage of friends in community is the most complex and difficult thing you'll ever do — so study the field. There is much practical information available on relationships, loving, and community — digest the material.

Community can be experienced in many forms, and I suggest exploring many of them. Live embraced by concentric circles.

55

"Everything is better with a circle of friends within which to huddle."

Linda Edquist/Gesundheit

Also, use your personal experience and seek to understand the relationships all around you: What works? What doesn't? How do dishes get done? How does the hammer get back to its proper place?

Get involved — hook, line, and sinker. The greater the commitment, the easier the task. Be a self starter — respect how you fuel your life and do it. Have the joy of the labor be its own reward. Crave to do the work of two or three people, not in competition, but in excitement for serving your extended family. Find ways to love the jobs no one else likes. Be a family troubleshooter.

Be sure to know how to play with each member — the broader your contacts are within the group, the more you will feel its security. In this case every one will be a playmate — and every issue will become your issue. Many communities get into trouble because they don't value the group's play as much as the group's work. ❖

(*New Frontier, The Magazine of Transformation* is available for $18 per year — 11 issues — in USA and Canada, $38 per year elsewhere, from New Frontier Education Society, 46 N. Front St., Philadelphia PA 19106, 215-627-5683)

These are two very useful periodicals. It would be helpful to get all the back issues and study them.

1. *Communities, Journal of Cooperation*
   126 Sun Street, Stelle, IL 60919.

2. *In Context, Quarterly of Sustainable Culture*
   Box 11470, Bainbridge Island, WA 98110.

References

1. *Community and Growth*: Jean Vanier, Griffin Press, Ltd.
2. *Volume One*: Stephen Gaskin, The Book Publishing Co.
3. *Mutual Aid*: Peter Kropotkin, Porter Sargeant Books.
4. *Cooperative Communities*: Swami Kriyananda, Ananda Publications.
5. *Builders of the Dawn*: McLaughlin & Davidson, Stillpoint Press.
6. *Utopian Thought*: Manuel and Manuel, Harvard University Press.

Women in Community

by Julie Mazo

Here are the words of women — reflecting on their lives, and on what living in community has meant for them. One conversation took place at Shannon Farm, an economically diverse community with separate households and individual livelihood. The other was transcribed at Springtree, where members live together, share all income, and raise children collectively.

Though these models of community are different, the themes and the quality of the women's experience have more similarities than otherwise. I have woven the conversations together to represent the flavor, rather than to convey the unique personalities and the different life styles they have chosen.

SUPPORT

"Without support to help me through my changes, I'm not sure I'd have had the courage to make some of the choices I've made. The community as a whole, and individual members, have always been there to back me up. Outside, I think it's harder to hook into a group that you can count on consistently being there for you. People in mainstream culture tend to be more mobile; relationships peak and fall; there are always distractions. Of course, there's turnover in community, too, but the community endures, and so does the support.

"And there are more people to look to for support. Before we came, if my husband was down on something I wanted to do, that was it. Now his opinion is not my only point of reference.

WORK

"I'm pretty sure I'd be doing a more traditional job. It's a rare mainstream business that would have taken me on completely unskilled, just because I'm a good person, someone worth working with and training. Expectations of longevity, staying power, had something to do with their enthusiasm about accepting me, too. They encouraged me to experiment until I found something I loved doing and — eventually — learned to do well.

"My work for the community brings me into lots of contact with people from the surrounding area and, with them, I'm constantly having to prove myself, especially with the men. The non-sexist environment within the community makes that stand out even more.

"I'm the only woman in a community enterprise, but it's something I rarely have cause to think about. It's not that I'm one-of-the-boys; I'm one of the workers, and so are each of my partners.

"I work in a community collective, too, where chauvinism never raises its ugly head. There is an elitism, but it has to do with competence and commitment, not with gender.

"I like variety in my work, doing lots of different things, and no one of them for too long. The community values that and makes it possible, while the world values stability. Outside I'd probably be put down as a drifter.

"When I first came to live in community, I knew I wanted to make a contribution — my own contribution — rather than just being here as partner to the man I came with. So I learned plumbing, because the community needed that skill. Then from taking care of my garden I kind of slid into being farm manager, because there was a vacuum the community needed filled. I treasure all the time there is to think while I'm on the tractor. Working on the land is like a meditation for me.

Julie Mazo of Shannon Farm combines excerpts from women in Springtree newsletters of the '70s with the thoughts of Shannon women discussing cooperative life in 1989. Julie recorded conversations among a cabinetmaker, the farm manager, and a computer service representative — all Shannon women of long standing with strong feelings about their lives at Shannon.

Julie is a professional group facilitator, mediator and trainer, as well as a writer and editor. She is currently projects director at Monroe Institute, a research and training corporation engaged in the development of human potential through brain hemispheric synchronization and other scientific aids to the inner search.

*Maintaining the tractor
at Shannon Farm.*

Geoph Kozeny/Community Catalyst

SECURITY

"Living here has probably kept me from being as successful, in the world's terms, as I might have been elsewhere. And that's ok, because I feel secure in so many other ways that living high on the hog can't compete. My only regret is that I can't provide my kids with all that I'd like.

"Financial security isn't an issue for me. I have a sense of owning 500 acres and a house, even though I really don't. But it's mine as long as I live here, and I plan to be here for life.

"I think very little about the future. I used be so concerned about what would happen to me if I lost the security of my marriage. Now I'm pretty optimistic. So what if I were on my own? I think I could make it.

"I used to be lonely, spending a lot of time by myself. Coming here was really a treat for me because it meant that I didn't have to be lonesome anymore. I could have anybody I wanted to talk to, and if my husband left, I'd still have somebody to talk to. It sure gives me a sense of security.

FAMILY

"It seems that for many of the married couples who came here, the women came less willingly, but in the end were more attached to staying. The men decided to come, and the women agreed with varying degrees of enthusiasm, but once we were here, we adjusted better and were happier.

"That's true for me. It was my husband who wanted to come here, not I. And ironically, being in community made it easy for me to end that marriage.

"In my first marriage my role was that of supportive wife. I think I'm still a supportive partner, but now it's because I want to. There are no 'shoulds' attached. In community there have been lots of good models for discarding 'shoulds'.

"If we lived elsewhere I would have wanted more than one child, but there's such a sense of "family" here, and enough other children so that mine has never felt solitary.

"Children are raised differently here. There's more sharing in child-rearing. Wherever I lived I would have sought day care, but it was so easy and natural here. Cooperating and helping are the norm: anything else would have been strange.

"Living in community helped me make the decision not to have my own kids. I can always borrow a child for an hour, or a day, and I enjoy knowing so many children so well. Today's teenagers I knew as babies, and they've always known me. It feels as if I've had a small share in the raising of a big family.

COMPANIONSHIP

"Don't you find that there's less need to plan for social time in community? It just seems to happen. You're having an interesting conversation at the lake — start feeling hungry — "Come on home for dinner." And you have a wonderful evening without having had to arrange for it to happen.

"I've noticed that I don't have to be intentional about developing relationships. Before I came here, if I met someone I liked and wanted to get to know better I had to wait —maybe a long time — until I would meet up with that person again, or else make appointments to get together. Here, we're sure to bump into one another casually. An invitation to take a walk, or sitting near one another at a potluck, or helping weed the garden, or supporting the same position at monthly meeting, or ... Relationships grow naturally with a lot of informal, unplanned contact as the building blocks.

"In some ways the community is like having a ready-made family. No one needs to feel uptight about being alone on Thanksgiving or Christmas or any other time you want company.

PRIVACY

"Outside, the effort is to seek companionship. Here, I have to put forth effort to be alone. It's good to have our houses, our private living space. I need to know there's a place for me to withdraw. My life is so filled with people, there's such social intensity, that I deliberately pull back from time to time.

"Sometimes I feel as if people are too much with me, also. But the flip side of that is when I've gone through a crisis or a large life change. I'll never forget how strongly people reached out. The nurturing attention that's here for us when we're feeling vulnerable and unhappy is a trade-off I'm willing to make any day.

"I used to be a very private person, kept my business to myself. My being ok with a lack of personal privacy amazes my mom. I remember her saying to me, "You mean you want all those people to really know you?" The way everybody talks about everybody did take some getting used to, but now it really doesn't matter. It's comforting to know that people care.

"Members stay in tune with one another's lives. The rumor mill tends to grind away pretty constantly. But if there's little sense of privacy, there's also little sense of isolation.

"The only way anyone can feel isolated is by choice. Those few people who have been alienated from time to time have done it themselves, by isolating themselves from the process of the group.

GIVING AND TAKING

"We've learned that the community needs people who give to it and to one another, not those who are excessively needy, who take all the time.

"It also can be ok not to give a lot, as long as you don't take. As long as the balance is maintained.

"The balance extends over time, too. Sometimes I'm feeling especially needy, and other times I can be one of the givers. People accept my taking, because they know it will be balanced out.

"Only if the imbalance is too great, or goes on for too long a time, does it cause a problem. Otherwise we can live with it. After all, we're here for a long time.

INFLUENCE

"There's another plus for me about the closeness. Having others involved in my life, commenting on it, reacting to it, has helped keep me balanced and centered. I'm less likely to go too far off in a screwy direction before I hear about it. Then I can consider if it's really what I want to do.

"We definitely influence one another by all the talk. Feedback from people I like and trust often influences my choices and my behavior. And input from others makes me search more deeply in myself, makes me more accepting.

"That's very different from kowtowing to someone in authority, isn't it? I can go along with someone else's view if it feels right for me. If it doesn't — I don't. Before I came to community it was always, "Yes, sir, Yes, ma'am." Those days are over.

"The way we make decisions — by consensus — is related to this, I think. In order to be successful in arriving at decisions that the whole community can live with, we have to stretch our sensitivity to others, take the time to understand

The communal kitchen at 100 Mile Lodge, British Columbia

how I choose to live, to people who think in stereotypes. When I'm out in the world I try to blend in, but it's awkward; it's no longer a good fit.

"I've changed from someone always needing to understand, know, and learn from others, to being someone who can teach, who has something to share that others want. I never envisioned myself like that, but I'm having to get used to the idea that people see me that way.

them, learn what will satisfy them. A lot of the decision-making process takes place outside of meetings. With any thorny issue there are dozens of conversations where we inch closer towards the development of the final agreement.

"That's one of our strongest commonalities: our process — and our respect for the process. The more secure we've grown as a community, the more easily we can handle the differences among us. That doesn't mean there aren't wrangles, and hurt feelings, and private feuds. But we do have a process for living and working together, and we know it can be effective. That's a powerful incentive to keep us hanging in as we work it out.

CHANGE

"I'm comfortable now speaking my mind, speaking in groups, speaking to strangers. I remember sitting in Community Meeting when we first came, wanting to say something. My heart would beat so fast and so loud I was sure everyone could hear it. Now, if I have something on my mind I just blurt it out. What a difference!

"I'm less inhibited than I was on the outside, too. It's great to be around groups of people and feel totally natural, comfortable. I can be myself here. People know me and accept me as I am, and there's no need for play-acting in order to fit in or to meet somebody else's expectations.

"I like who I've come to be, and I wouldn't want to be different. But it does leave me feeling like an eccentric when I'm outside. It's hard for me to explain my home, where and

"Living in community has helped me feel stronger and more confident about expressing anger. I can say to myself, 'OK, I know I'm going to get into a hassle, but I'm going to go through with it anyway; it's not going to kill me, and something good may come of it.'

"I think the men in the community are generally more able to express feelings than men outside. It has to do with the atmosphere for all of us.

"I've discovered that men can be neat as friends. It used to be father, husband, or boyfriend — and pretty bad relationships, too.

"I get impatient with women who say, 'But I can't do that.' We can do whatever we want to learn how to do. We just have to do it!

GROWING OLD

"Sometimes I feel uneasy about the fact that so many of us will be getting old at the same time. We need more younger people.

"It's my biggest fear, too, that we'll all grow old together; that community children will choose not to live here as adults. We'll bury one another up on Orchard Ridge until only a handful of us are left -not enough to keep the farm up. We'll be a dying, rather than a living community.

"I have faith in continuity. Others took care of this land before we came. And there will be others after us. It may or may not be an intentional community, but the land will be here and it will be tended by people who love it as we do. ❖

Children in Community

by Daniel Greenberg

Well over 3,000 children live in the North American communities listed in this directory. What are the social, economic, and educational experiences of children living in community? During the fall and winter of 1989-90, I visited 25 and surveyed 219 intentional communities in the U.S. to explore these questions. This article describes some initial themes that emerged from this project. The points made do not apply equally to all communities. My aim is to present a broad range of issues that individuals with children may want to consider before joining a community, or that a community may want to consider before adding children to its ranks.

EXTENDED FAMILY RELATIONSHIPS

In our present North American society, the family arrangement of one or two parents living alone with their children is the norm. Unfortunately, in these settings, children tend to have very little contact with adults who are not either their parents or their teachers. In most intentional communities, however, there is an extended family-like atmosphere, where children and adults alike have ample opportunities to create close, nurturing relationships with people of all ages. Thus a wide variety of role models is available to the children of intentional communities.

In such an environment, the experience of parenting children is far from lonely. An immense amount of emotional support is usually given to mothers and fathers, especially in the first few months of a child's life. Often, in larger communities, pregnancies seem almost contagious, enabling parents with same-aged children to share wisdom and emotional support throughout their children's development.

Even when parents separate or divorce, they are both frequently able to continue living within their community and to maintain close relationships with their

100 Mile Lodge/Emissaries

Young cowhands at play

Dan Greenberg recently spent six months visiting and corresponding with intentional communities across the U.S. This article provides a preliminary summary of information collected for his doctoral dissertation, which is tentatively titled "Children and Education in U.S. Intentional Communities."

Dan has lived cooperatively for four years while studying at the University of Minnesota in Minneapolis. He has a sparkling and engaging way with children, as well as adults, and dreams of helping develop an alternative school in an intentional community.

children. In such circumstances, children don't have to be right in the middle of the fighting and chaos sometimes associated with separations. In fact, they often get to see their parents slowly become friends again as members of the community.

Unfortunately, because the law favors traditional lifestyles, it has been difficult in the past for some communities to achieve legal recognition and support for alternative parenting and childcare arrangements. Legal struggles seem to be fading, however, as more people in the wider society realize that stable intentional communities can provide long-term social and economic benefits for families.

COMMUNAL CHILD REARING

Given the extended family structure of many intentional communities, it is not surprising that most rear their preschool children communally to some degree. Through sharing childcare and related tasks such as cooking, laundry, shopping, and cleaning, parents (most notably mothers) are freed to pursue activities other than parenting. This freedom also allows parents and other adults to interact with children more often when they want to rather than when they have to, which tends to greatly enhance the overall quality of adult-child relationships.

In some communities, the opportunity for parents to share responsibilities for childcare with other members is coupled with an expectation to share rights in making important decisions about their children. This may be difficult for parents who are unwilling to relinquish sole authority over their children.

Another potentially negative outcome of community childcare is that inconsistency among caregivers with respect to discipline and expectations may be confusing for children. This can also be a problem in nuclear families, of course; but in community there are more adults interacting with a child, and therefore a greater variety of child rearing practices may be experienced. Such inconsistency is especially likely to be a problem in the early stages of building a community when child rearing may get less attention than more pressing survival needs such as building residences and establishing a viable economic and social order.

MATERIAL RESOURCES

Unfortunately, even after communities have established their basic physical and socio-economic structures, concerns over the material resources needed to raise children remain. While it may be generally less costly to rear children in community, group childcare and education still takes a tremendous amount of labor and resources — resources that are in short supply and high demand. This situation is especially frustrat-

ing in communities with a high turnover rate among families with children. Adults who are not very interested in having children in their community, or communities that are struggling to survive, may well ask, "Why put all this effort into children when they end up leaving anyway?"

On the positive side, there are some definite economic benefits to parents and children living in community. Most income-sharing communities strive toward the ideal of "From each according to ability, to each according to need." In such communities, wives are not financially dependent upon their husbands, nor are children financially dependent upon their parents. With no purse strings to pull, husbands relate to their wives, and parents relate to their children more from a position of material equality than from a position of power based on what they can provide. In addition, cooperative living is an economic benefit to single parents who do not have to struggle alone to provide basic necessities for their children and themselves.

TURNOVER

America is a mobile country, and this feature of the larger society is characteristic of intentional communities as well. An average family in the U.S. moves approximately once every five years (American Housing Survey, 1987), and it is likely that families in U.S. intentional communities move at around the same rate.

The dynamics of turnover are probably different in rural and urban communities. For example, in rural communities without a school, families may be tempted to leave when their children reach school age if they are dissatisfied with the values or quality of the local public school system. Members of urban communities have more choices about where and how their children will be educated. Yet, despite this flexibility, most urban communities seem to have more transient populations.

Even in relatively stable communities, adults and children still come and go. Research on turnover in communities suggests that when children do not have a strong primary attachment to a parent or other adult, a high turnover rate is associated with children exhibiting an apathetic attitude and an above-average degree of hostility (Johnston and Deisher, 1973). However, in the general case where there is a nurturing and secure attachment with a primary caregiver, the coming and going of people appears to be a positive experience for children. Still, it is difficult when close friends leave, and turnover in intentional communities is generally a source of frustration and sadness for all concerned, just as it is in the wider society.

ISOLATION

Though not to the extent that many people believe, children in community often lack exposure to the broader society.

This may be more the case in rural than in urban communities, and may be especially applicable to children in small communities where there are few peers with whom to grow up. Children whose formal education takes place within the community rather than in an outside school are further isolated from the mainstream.

A positive aspect of communities being somewhat separate from the broader society is that they can provide extremely safe environments for their children. In rural communal environments especially, children can roam about freely with little fear of kidnapping or abuse. In this sense, communities act as safety zones within the broader society, where people watch out for each other and there is less need of police forces or jails.

In communities with few children, isolation from the broader society further limits the size of a child's peer group. As can be seen in Figure 1, most of the 219 intentional communities surveyed (almost 70%) have 10 or fewer children, while just 21 percent have more than 20 children, and only 7 percent have more than 50 children.

Having few children in an intentional community seems to be a mixed blessing. On the one hand, children often seem frustrated about there being so few communitarian peers from whom to choose their friends. Some children even seem to long for the sense of anonymity possible in a large school, or at least a large community. Lack of experience with peers seems to contribute to occasional difficulties with communal children being accepted when they do interact with children in the broader society. On the other hand, having no choice but to associate with a small group of children that is quite diverse in age and personality appears to be a rewarding and stimulating experience for these children.

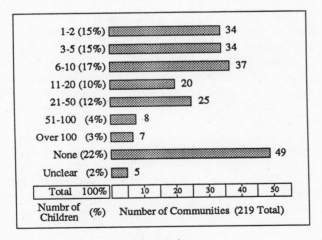

Figure 1:
Number of Children in Intentional Communities

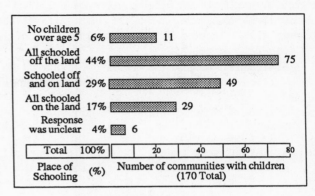

Figure 2:
Schooling of Children in Intentional Communities

FORMAL EDUCATION

Of the 170 communities surveyed that have children, only 17 percent have formal educational programs for all of their children (see Figure 2). However, 46 percent have some sort of educational programs for some of their children, including elementary or home schooling. Largely due to the immense amount of resources needed (facilities and materials, trained and dedicated people), and legal difficulties in some states, educational programs within communities can be very difficult to create. This is especially true among small communities that do not have enough children to justify such a large expenditure of resources.

As might be expected, those communities with over 50 children were three times as likely to have a community school as were those with fewer than 21 children. In small communities home schooling is often a more feasible option. Regardless of size, most communities are supportive of parents who decide to home school.

While communal schools are difficult to create, there are many advantages for communities that do establish them. Through these programs, children can be encouraged to carry on the values and traditions of the community. They can be further protected from undesirable aspects of mainstream society such as prejudice and mass-media values. Student-teacher relationships in community schools are generally based on friendships and understanding developed over many years, and there is usually a high degree of parent and community involvement in such programs. Community schools have more freedom and flexibility to experiment with a variety of educational methods in order to adapt to the changing needs of the children. Some communities accept children from outside the community, which can enrich the school and the community both socially and economically.

However, over eighty percent of the intentional communities surveyed that have school-aged children send some or all of their children to public or private schools outside their communities. For these children it is often a struggle to adapt to the very different peer cultures and value systems of these schools. Consequently, some communitarian children may have problems feeling accepted in off-land schools. In addition, children from communities may occasionally feel victimized by peer prejudice resulting from the negative publicity some intentional communities have received. In such cases, parent involvement with the school system can be especially important in helping children feel comfortable and, at the same time, building positive public relations with the surrounding community.

INFORMAL EDUCATION

Whatever the schooling arrangement is in a community, much of the children's education happens informally. Simply by living in an intentional community, children gain hands-on experience with politics, economics, and group process. Through apprenticeships with adults in their community, children can often acquire a wide variety of practical skills such as gardening, food processing, cooking, construction, and auto mechanics.

Many community children have unusual opportunities to travel widely and to become involved in community projects. These activities range from helping hurricane victims in South Carolina to harvesting oranges in Florida to visiting and developing relationships with other communities all across the continent. Children in community learn skills needed for self-sufficiency, gain a sense of group spirit and self-esteem, and are generally well prepared for life in the community and the broader society.

If there is anything that research on the informal education of children in community has consistently borne out, it is that these children are exposed to a *lot* of social interaction (Lakin, Lakin, & Costanzo, 1979). In addition to all the interaction with community members, the children of communities that are fairly well-known have opportunities to share experiences with visitors from around the globe.

Early independence and autonomous behavior are highly valued in most communities and, as a result, communal children generally learn to talk and reason quite early. There are stories in almost every community about 2- and 3-year-olds surprising adults with their social finesse.

Most children in our society have very little exposure to the world adults live in. In community, however, the joys and struggles of adult work and life are not hidden from children's view. They may witness a birth one day and perhaps help with a funeral another day. Children see adults building houses, building relationships, building political structures

In rural communities children can roam free with little fear

Jim Allen/Vine & Fig Tree

— things that are all too often mysterious during childhood. Children in community have frequent opportunities to come to terms with the realities of life and learn to share, endure, and generally live with others.

CONCLUSION

Having children in community raises many important issues, all more complicated in reality than on paper. In general, communities seem to provide environments for their children that are safe, supportive, and social. While formal educational programs are difficult to create, especially in small communities, simply living in community provides many educational experiences for children.

How well do intentional communities prepare children for the future? A community is a microcosmic society, and can therefore provide children with a broad understanding of group process and adaptation to change. It has been said that the most important product of intentional communities is process itself; learning how groups can work and grow together in joyful and humane ways is as important as getting things done. Given the pace at which our society and world are changing, empowering children with the skills needed to effectively work and grow with others may be one of the most significant contributions that communities can make to their children and to our world's future. ❖

Bibliography

American Housing Survey, 1980 U.S. Census (1987).

Johnston, C.M. and Deisher, R.W. (1973) Contemporary communal child rearing: A first analysis. *Pediatrics*, 52(3), pp. 319-326.

Lakin, M., Lakin, M.G., and Costanzo, P.R. (1979). Group process in early childhood: A dimension of human development. *International Journal of Behavioral Development*, 2, pp.171-183.

Social Action

What is the interplay of intentional communities with the society at large? How does one affect the other?

Jim Estes of Alpha Farm describes how communitarians often struggle among themselves in choosing between a **Home or Activist Community** focus. He then asks, "Does it have to be one or the other?" and provides several examples of communities in action — groups which see themselves as both homes and centers of activism. "If home is where the heart is," he finds, "it can also be where the action is."

Ken Norwood of the Shared Living Resource Center discusses **Innovative Housing Options**, offering legal and practical means for transforming traditional urban and suburban residential areas into more intimate neighborhoods. The author has many years of experience in organizing shared housing and cooperative community clusters — ways in which many of the ideas of intentional community can be transposed into a wider social setting.

Connie Koennen, writing for the Los Angeles Times, examines the **CoHousing** concept which originated in Scandinavia two decades ago, and which has been popularized in this country through the work of Kathryn McCamant and Charles Durrett. In CoHousing, residents start from scratch — working as a team to design houses and common facilities which meet their specific needs. This model offers some of the social and practical benefits of intentional community, while providing an option for economic autonomy.

Communitarians, communal ideals, and cooperative models can all be powerful forces for creating social change — just as involvement in social action can strongly influence the daily life of a community.

Geoph Kozeny/Community Catalyst

Home or Activist Community

by Jim Estes

Communitarians spend a lot of time reinventing the wheel. They also spend a lot of time debating whether the wheel is necessary. Typical of this sort of debate is the discussion, which goes on in probably every community, of whether to put more value on "home," or on service to better the world. The Springtree community's debate, as reflected in a past edition of its newsletter, exemplifies the range of opinions.

Herb: "Springtree, as I see it, is two separate realities. To some people it is Home. ... Here we have a place of satisfaction and security.

"Me, I am of the restless sort... what do I worry about? Culture. Socio/political change. I am not at Home in this world. Around me I see destructiveness, artificiality, confusion, disintegration. So I want to create a world with a cultural and political relatedness that I fit into. What I want is an alternative way of life with an intentional culture...

"It seems that intentional communities are of, meaning in, this world to the extent they address themselves to creating a culture out of the chaos found in our world. It's like I can shut out the world from my house by locking the doors at night, or my home can be more. It can be a light shining in a world of insane technological inhumanity. It can be an intentional community."

Evelyn responds: "What is the purpose of life anyway? To us 'restful' souls it is — to live it. Goals and long-range events are less important than the process...

"Creating a home is important to me. If other people in the world want to follow our example, I am willing to help."

Or, as some existentialist put it: "To be is to do."

But many communitarians — and many non-communitarians — would ask: Is just "being" enough?

Life at Springtree includes hosting interns for training in organic gardening and cooperative living, activism in the Virginia Association of Biological Farmers, and coordination of worldwide research on use of the honey locust tree as a self-harvesting feed for livestock. Community members have also served as regional coordinators for plaintiffs in a successful federal court suit against the Virginia State Police and the National Guard for invasion of privacy. In concluding the three-year court case a federal judge limited helicopter surveillance to above 500 feet, declaring that

Albert Bates, attorney for The Farm, announces suit to halt licensing of the Tennessee Valley Authority's Sequoyah Nuclear Power Plant, Unit 2.

Farm News Service

Jim Estes edits a monthly newspaper in Lane County, Oregon, is a co-founder of Alpha Farm, and is a review editor for this Directory. He is a retired newspaperman.

descent below that level without a search warrant was an invasion of personal privacy (Letcher *et al.* v. Garrett, 84-0174-L, Western District of Virginia, filed 10-25-84).

Koinonia Partners, near Plains, in rural southwest Georgia, began during World War II as a deliberately inter-racial and ecumenical Christian community, living a witness against racial prejudice. Existing in that fashion, in that time and in that place, was a form of doing — and that commitment to equality has remained strong over the intervening 48 years. Beginning in the mid-fifties, under pressure from a local economic boycott and Ku Klux Klan violence, Koinonia began to reach out for support to the wider world through the preparation and sale of pecan and peanut products.

Koinonia incorporated in 1969, becoming Koinonia Partners: "the ministry of some who are beginning to see one way to live a life of service in today's world." In addition to farming hundreds of acres, the Partners operate a nursery and preschool center, tutoring programs, and paralegal services. Many members and Koinonia volunteers are deeply concerned about U.S. policy in Central America and the nuclear arms race, and some engage in civil disobedience to express these concerns.

However, the community is best known for its housing ministry to the rural and urban poor of Sumter County. Since 1969 over 175 three- and four-bedroom homes have been built and sold at cost with no-interest loans — about $700 down and $100 per month for 20 years. A spin-off from this "housing for the poor" program has spread internationally as Habitat for Humanity. Habitat built more than 4,000 homes in the twelve years from 1976 to 1988. 324 local Habitat affiliates (including 68 overseas) raised $30 million in 1989, and built another 2,000 homes in that year alone.

To the northeast but still in Georgia, Jubilee Partners — another spin-off from Koinonia — helps Central American political refugees, and assists Nicaraguan civilians who need artificial limbs and physical rehabilitation after being wounded in the U.S.-financed Contra war (see sidebar).

Aprovecho, near Cottage Grove, Oregon, has gone at the question another way — by sending workers to Third World countries with low-tech innovations to help improve their lives. A mud stove is a good example: every country has mud. Showing people how to build fuel-efficient, wood-fired cook stoves can abate the depletion of local fuel wood supplies, and greatly reduce Third World deforestation and urban air pollution.

In Des Moines, Iowa, lived an urban group active from 1984 to 1989: the Kindred Community, "a group of people who live together and work together. For our work we get

Susan Gravely/Twin Oaks

ECONOMIC REFORM

— Sirius Community —

Sirius community in central Massachusetts has long had members active in organizing Community Land Trusts, Socially Responsible Investments, and intentional community networks. The valuable intentional communities reference book *Builders of the Dawn* was written by Sirius members Corinne McLaughlin and Gordon Davidson. Members of this New Age spiritual community have been active in development of worker-owned Mondragon cooperatives, land trusts and the Social Investment Forum. The forum's Coalition for Environmentally Responsible Economics (CERES) announced the Valdez Principles in September 1989.

The Valdez Principles outline a corporate code of environmental conduct which stresses protection of air, water, and natural resources; proper waste disposal; energy efficiency; damage compensation; and independent environmental audits. Endorsed by 15 major environmental groups and backed by over $150 billion in the Socially Responsible Investment movement, CERES is asking 3,000 major U.S. companies to sign the Principles and help develop specific monitoring procedures. A protocol is being developed for environmental audits, the key compliance provision in the Principles. Such audits will become part of a company's annual report, along with its financial audits. For more information write or call: Ceres Project, Social Investment Forum, 711 Atlantic Avenue, Boston MA 02111, (617) 451-3252.

(*Sirius Journal* is available from Sirius, Baker Rd., Shutesbury MA 01072, 413-259-1505. An optional $5 contribution toward mailing costs is appreciated.)

room and board but no monetary payment. Getting paid for what we do would be inconsistent with the values we are trying to demonstrate for others."

Those values included "caring for humanity through serving those who've hit rough times... we are bound together by faith itself. We have the faith that if we work for the good of the world, we will get what we need to continue that work.

"We address our faith and work in four ways: service, resistance, revolutionary vision and education. Through our service we provide the basic necessities of life to those who need them. ...

"The second aspect... is resistance to a system that puts people on the street and forces many around the world to live under massive oppression and horrendous poverty."

From *Kindred Voices*, Summer 1986: "... of all the chores that I do with the Kindred community, gleaning vegetables and fruits from grocery store dumpsters is my favorite. Imagine filling up a station wagon with gleaned food, getting more and putting it up on top. ... Imagine people starting to come by to pick up this food at 6 a.m. ...

"There are more reasons than the satisfaction of giving to explain my commitment to dumpster diving. Things such as... the adrenaline rush of risking arrest for 'stealing garbage.' We've talked one store out of arresting us three times and they will arrest us the next time they see us. Dumpster diving is just like Christmas morning every time you lift up the lid. You never know what goodies you'll find. It keeps the wonder and joy of unexpected gifts in unforeseen places with me throughout the year."

The *Rainbow Gathering* of the Tribes is a nomadic community which is less intentional than many. Yet Rainbow people share a common identity, care deeply for the consensus process and ecology, and are firmly committed to the belief that the First Article of the Bill of Rights guarantees "the right of the people to freely assemble" on U.S. National Forest land in numerous regional public gatherings each year. During the week of July 4th, 1990, the 19th Annual Rainbow Gathering of the Tribes was held in the National Forests of Minnesota. For more information contact the Rainbow tribal newspaper, *All Ways Free* (see Bibliography).

The Farm in Tennessee has been active in Third World service since 1974. The community has initiated a wide-ranging spectrum of projects, including work with earthquake victims in Guatemala, orphans in Bangladesh, a health clinic in Lesotho, South Africa, and a Native American radio station in South Dakota. The farm has launched volunteer projects in 12 countries on four continents, helping to build several thousand state-of-the-art buildings including giant, earthquake-proof, municipal buildings and large, passive solar homes with thick insulation and photovoltaic arrays on the roofs.

ASSISTANCE TO POLITICAL REFUGEES & WAR VICTIMS
— Jubilee Partners —

For years the Christian service community Jubilee Partners was a dream of the older Koinonia Partners community. Finally, in the spring of 1979 a small group from Koinonia pitched their tents on 258 acres of meadows, fields, and forest in northeast Georgia. From the first the group found inspiration in Jesus' sermon about the "Year of the Jubilee… good news for the poor… release for prisoners… recovery of sight… freeing broken victims."

In the fall of 1980 the first political refugees were hosted at the Jubilee Welcome Center. For the first two years most of the refugees came from Cuba, then Cambodia, Vietnam, and Laos. In 1982 Salvadorian political refugees, some Guatemalans, and later Hondurans, began requesting assistance. According to U.S. law people who come to this country are not to be forced to return to their own countries if they have a "well-founded fear of persecution because of race, religion… social group, or political opinion." In fact many thousands of such Central American refugees are deported from the United States each year.

While the U.S. Government accepts refugees from Cuba and Nicaragua, political refugees from these other Central American countries cannot stay permanently in this country. With the change in Nicaraguan leadership following the February 1990 elections there, U.S. government policy toward Nicaraguan immigrants may change also. It seems that our national government does not recognize the need of political asylum for Central American refugees — unless they are fleeing countries with governments that are in opposition to our government.

However, Canada does accept such political refugees. So Jubilee works with the Canadian government, and individuals and churches all over the United States, to help Central Americans move legally to new homes in Canada. By 1990, with a resident staff and numerous short-term volunteers, this community has hosted more than 1,300 political refugees on their way to Canada from El Salvador, Honduras and Guatemala.

Jubilee partners and volunteers interview Central American refugees in the church-sponsored emergency shelters and the federal detention centers and children's camp on the Mexican border in southern Texas. The community collects tax-deductible contributions for the Paul and Silas Revolving Bail Fund to help free a few of the political refugees held in the overcrowded detention centers ($1,500 to $3,000 per refugee). Jubilee interviewers have to make hundreds of agonizing decisions in trying to discern who is in greatest danger from the government armies or guerrillas in their home countries. Sometimes the "Año de Jubileo" program can accept only one in 50 of the refugees, even while increasing numbers are being deported to the home countries from which they had fled.

A single busload at a time (30–35 passenger capacity), Jubilee provides transportation from the Rio Grande Valley to Georgia for some of those who qualify for Canadian citizenship as political refugees. In Georgia the community hosts the immigrants for about two months in temporary housing built by the community, guides them through the lengthy paperwork process required for immigration to Canada, and helps them learn English and prepare for life in that country. Only when the refugees reach Canada does the U.S. Government return the bail money to the Paul and Silas Fund.

The community reports that the refugees "have a profound impact on our understanding of suffering, courage, and faith. In a very real sense they help us to 'recover our sight.'" People at Jubilee "have been struck by the power of God's healing Spirit as we have watched wounded refugees and war victims from many poor countries of the world meet a different kind of wounded refugee from the rich countries — and each ministers to the needs of the other."

In 1987 Jubilee launched the *Walk In Peace* campaign, which has helped provide artificial legs and rehabilitation therapy to more than 1,000 Nicaraguans. Jubilee works with the Nicaraguan Evangelical Committee for Aid and Development (CEPAD), an ecumenical Christian service group which listed over 2,000 civilian war amputees by the end of 1989. Most of the wounded, including many children and teenagers, were victims of explosive land mines and attacks on civilians by the Contra rebels.

(*Jubilee Partners Report*, Box 68, Comer GA 30629, is available upon request for those interested in what is happening at Jubilee. Donations are appreciated.)

"It seems that intentional communitiies are of, meaning in, this world to the extent they address themselves to creating a culture out of the chaos found in our world."

Herb
Springtree Community

As Albert Bates, one of The Farm's resident attorneys, told a conference of the National Historic Communal Societies Association: "It was, and remains, our commonly held view that how you choose to live should be seamless with what you believe in. It should come as no surprise that no one on The Farm developed an advanced design for a nuclear reactor or a Star Wars shield, although we did develop advanced radiation detection equipment, employed amateur satellite communications, advanced the scientific basis for midwifery, experimented with temperature and mucus methods of birth control, and helped build the first doppler fetal pulse monitor."

At The Farm, social activism can be seen in both the cottage industries that support the community and in the work of The Farm's charity organization, Plenty. At solar Electronics, young Farm School graduates assemble photovoltaic arrays and manufacture super-sensitive geiger counters suitable for civilian use in monitoring nuclear power production facilities. At the Book Publishing Company, printers churn out books about environmental issues, vegetarian cooking, natural health care, Native Americans, children's stories, and pesticide-free gardening. Recent publications include *Climate in Crisis: The Greenhouse Effect and What We Can Do*.

Plenty projects at The Farm include Kids to the Country, a summer camp for underprivileged children; the One World Trading Company, a mail-order business supporting 80 village weaving co-ops in Guatemala; and the Natural Rights Center, an environmental law project. The Natural Rights Center, which has won landmark civil rights and voting rights cases, currently has lawsuits pending against the Army Corps of Engineers, the FBI, several chemical companies, and 250 deployed and operational weapons systems for which environmental impact statements have never been prepared.

From ham radio and television used to communicate with traveling members of The Farm, the community developed a radio system for Greenpeace's ships. These vessels kept tuned to the Farm Net and at one time used that as the principal news link to the international media covering the Greenpeace campaign. Reporters from British or Cambodian newspapers might be aboard the Rainbow Warrior, but their newspapers got the story by way of a ham radio in a horse barn in Tennessee.

Although at first The Farm refrained from voting in local elections, the community eventually came to comprise a majority of voters in its district and elected two of three of the local district commissioners from among Farm members. "We could have elected all three," says Bates, "but we wanted our neighbors to feel represented too." Farm technicians have also set up computer systems to manage successful political campaigns for the U.S. House of Representatives and the Senate, for governor of Tennessee, as well as a primary run for president of the United States.

Stephen Gaskin described The Farm's approach to social activism in his book, *Rendered Infamous*: "I do not feel like letting my country be taken over by a minority of people who... mess over the rest of the world in our name. I resent that being done in my name as an American. I have to become involved because that is the only way I can stop it from happening... which is not as impossible as it seems at first glance, because we have a tremendous amount of justice in our viewpoint."

For communities, it appears that if home is where the heart is, it can also be where the action is.

So Springtree's "two separate realities" are present in every community; and the debate goes on. ❖

Bibliography

All Ways Free, 1989, Box 3481, Madison WI 53704.

Back on the Farm: Living the Gospel at Koinonia, *The Other Side*, Aug. 1985, 300 W. Apsley St., Philadelphia PA 19144.

Bates, Albert, *Climate in Crisis: The Greenhouse Effect and What We Can Do*, 1990, The Book Publishing Company, Box 99, Summertown TN 38483.

Bates, Albert, Technological Innovation in a Rural Intentional Community (The Farm), 1988, *Bull. Sci. Tech. Soc.*, Vol. 8.

Kindred Voices, 1988, Des Moines, Iowa.

Koinonia Newsletter, 1990, Rt 2, Americus, Georgia 31709, 912-924-0391.

Natural Rights Center Annual Report, 1989, Box 90, Summertown TN 38483.

Plenty Bulletin, 1989, Plenty-USA, Box 90, Summertown TN 38483.

Springtree Newsletter, 1976–1990, Rt 2 Box 89, Scottsville VA 24590.

Winbush, Don, Habitat for Humanity: A Bootstrap Approach to Low-Cost Housing, *Time*, Jan. 16, 1989.

Innovative Housing Options for Urban Areas

by Ken E. Norwood, AICP

There's no use pretending the urban housing/jobs/traffic crunch will just go away. It has come about through "normal" ways of functioning in our society, and it's getting worse. We need to transform the choking and outmoded sprawl of the outgoing century's housing patterns into socially and environmentally livable alternatives that will work for us into the future. We have no choice but to seek housing solutions that are innovative and affordable, and have an ecologically positive impact on urban patterns.

The following options for community design could be integrated into the traditional urban pattern, and could well have the result of revitalizing areas of the city.

Transforming traditional urban and suburban residential areas into more intimate cohousing-style neighborhoods

100 Mile Lodge/Emissaries

Ken Norwood has 33 years experience as a city planner and architect, and is active in the American Institute of Certified Planners, a network of city planners. He has lived cooperatively for two decades in a wide range of intentional communities and cooperative houses. In 1987 Ken founded the Shared Living Resource Center as an outgrowth of prior architectural and planning services dealing in alternative technology design, innovative housing and cooperative community. He provides "hands-on" construction management for owner-builders and community groups, serving as both architectural designer and master carpenter with specialized experience in foundation/earthqake retrofitting, passive solar and earth-sheltered design. He was co-consultant in the Ananda Village, California master plan report and architect for the Ananda Community retreat facility and has created renovation and master plan designs for a number of other communities and cooperative houses.

Shared housing and cooperative community clusters can work; sharing can pool time, energy, and money for development; offer emotional support; bring young and old together; and benefit the natural environment — as well as satisfy people's yearning for a sense of family and community.

"VOLUNTARY FAMILY" SHARED HOUSING: through co-ownership and rentals of existing houses and apartment buildings. This is an easy and relatively low-cost way of obtaining the most housing for the money, while simultaneously creating social and ecological benefits. Shared housing has proliferated throughout the country, and is represented by more than 500 nonprofit and public shared housing organizations.

URBAN VILLAGE CLUSTER: joining existing adjacent single-family houses and lots through voluntary partnership (agreeing on shared use of adjacent backyards, for example), co-ownership, or use of a for-profit or nonprofit cooperative housing sponsor. This provides affordability, an enhanced living environment with more amenities, and a resident-managed community atmosphere. Small units, and additional bedrooms for larger group houses can be added, with central community facilities in the joined and redesigned backyards.

FAMILY VILLAGE CLUSTER: a complex of private living suites or master bedrooms clustered around a common kitchen-dining-living space and other shared amenities (for example, home office, small meeting room, TV room, library, children's playroom, etc.) This option can provide a group of people with a 'dream house' that none of them could have afforded as individuals, and which can be cooperatively designed, financed and built or remodeled.

COMMUNITY VILLAGE CLUSTER: newly constructed private units of various sizes, grouped around extensive common facilities in a central house. Such clusters exist in some American intentional communities and in Scandinavian cohousing communities. The latter are advanced, state-of-the-art developments with as many as 50 or more units clustered around village-like streets, self-sufficient gardens, a central kitchen/dining/social hall, work studios, and whatever other shared amenities the residents plan. It can be organized, designed, financed and built by a group acting as their own developer, or sponsored by for-profit or nonprofit developers.

These options have been called visionary, but the work of serving people's needs and visions is very pragmatic. Shared housing and cooperative community clusters can work; sharing can pool time, energy, and money for development; offer emotional support; bring young and old together; and benefit the natural environment — as well as satisfy people's yearning for a sense of family and community. ❖

(Shared Living Resource Center services include slide shows, workshops, lectures and consultations for individuals and groups interested in shared living/co-ownership, Village Clusters, cooperative buildings, and intentional communities. SLRC's address is 2375 Shattuck Avenue, Berkeley CA 94704, 415-548-6608.)

Cohousing

by Connie Koenenn

Kathryn McCamant and Charles Durrett , San Francis-co architects, are authors of "Cohousing, A Contemporary Approach to Housing Ourselves". Their interest in alternative housing arose as they realized how many people's needs were not being met by the available traditional choices. Young couples were spending all their spare time shuttling children to and from day-care centers. Widowed and divorced mothers were living alone in the sprawling six-bedroom homes where they had raised their families. Single career people were going broke making mortgage payments, or sharing a house with other singles often without adequate agreements regarding domestic operations, equity-sharing and decision-making.

McCamant and Durrett learned of a solution — a concept they call "cohousing," which was introduced about 20 years ago in Scandinavia. Until their book started receiving national attention, this cooperative housing alternative was virtually unheard of in the United States.

Cohousing is custom-built neighborhoods, planned from beginning to end by the people who will live in them. In northern Europe, where the numbers of cohousing communities has quadrupled in the past five years, the communities vary in detail and design but essentially provide a mix of privacy and community, combining individual

Charles Durrett/CoHousing Co.

Site plan of Davis CoHousing Community, Muir Commons, by The CoHousing Company in Berkeley, California

Connie Koenenn, journalist for the *Los Angeles Times*, interviewed Kathryn McCamant and Charles Durrett, community designers and authors of the book *Cohousing: A Contemporary Approach to Housing Ourselves*. Inspired by the planned communities described in this book, some 50 U.S. groups have formed to cooperatively design and build cohousing communities. Kathryn and Charles have created The CoHousing Company to work with these groups and others engaged in community building projects (see Resources section). The first two U.S. cohousing groups will begin construction in the San Francisco Bay area in 1990 — a new 26-unit community in Davis named Muir Commons, and a 12-unit conversion of an industrial building in Emeryville. In conjunction with Innovative Housing, Kathryn and Charles publish a cohousing newsletter and offer workshops and consulting services across the United States. This article has been adapted from that news interview (Copyright, December 1988, *Los Angeles Times*, reprinted by permission.)

> *Cohousing is custom-built neighborhoods, planned from beginning to end by the people who will live in them.*

houses with facilities for shared meals, child care and other support systems and amenities as desired by the residents.

At Trudeslund, north of Copenhagen, for example, 33 families live in houses clustered along two pedestrian streets (cars are parked on the periphery). A wooded area makes a natural playground for the community's 50 children. The adults, mostly professionals, range in age from 30 to 69. There are four households with no children, nine one-parent households, and several occupied by singles. A large common house includes a dining hall where most residents eat three or four times a week. Meals are planned and prepared by the adults on a rotating basis (which means each resident cooks one day a month). A cooperative store, laundry facilities, photography darkroom and television room are also located in the common house.

McCamant and Durette offer their experience as consultants to fledgling U.S. groups that might be interested in forming their own neighborhoods. "We coined the word 'cohousing'," McCamant said, "to express the sense of the Danish word, *bofoellesskaber*... 'living communities.'" There was an enormous quantity of experience there, which is why we wrote our book — to put it into useful form."

Their 200-page reference work describes life in eight cohousing communities — richly illustrated with photographs of what appear to be utopian communities of pastel row houses lining pedestrian streets, and solar-paneled houses clustered around village greens. The book offers case studies of the development process and essays on such psychological aspects of community living as body language and candid communication.

Although cohousing developments vary in size (as small as six families and as large as 80 families), location (from inner cities to farm lands), type of ownership, design and priorities, four characteristics are common to all. Durrett outlined them:

- Participatory process: "Residents are involved from the outset in the planning and design process for the housing development, and are responsible as a group for all final decisions."
- Intentional neighborhood design: "Providing small gardens and comfortable sitting places overlooking shared outdoor areas makes it easier for people to meet their neighbors." Cohousing designs encourage sociability with building site layouts similar to African villages.
- Extensive common facilities: "This is what makes cohousing particularly special. Common dinners have proved overwhelmingly successful, with more than half the residents participating on any given evening." Cohousing can also include a large functional workshop, common laundry and teenage room.
- Complete resident management without the intercession of a professional manager: "That sounds burdensome, but they have learned to complete a three-hour agenda in an hour and a half."

During the development process of a new cohousing community, everybody learns a lot about working cooperatively. For example, the Trudeslund organization was launched in 1978. Construction was completed only after 2-1/2 years of hectic and frustrating meetings by a flood of work groups wrestling with the challenges of cooperative development. In the end, residents say, the difficulties of participatory democracy eventually helped to strengthen community spirit.

The first cohousing community in Denmark was developed in 1972, and there are now close to 125. Durrett and McCamant see the potential for similar growth in the U.S. From their workshops, a number of groups already have formed to start the process of forming cohousing neighborhoods up and down the West Coast.

Clearly, they acknowledge, cohousing is not for everybody. Still they are finding that the response of U.S. audiences echoes the mood they recognized in Denmark: "People want to live in a place with a strong sense of community, a place where you know your neighbors." ❖

(Cohousing: A Contemporary Approach to Housing Ourselves, 1988, Ten Speed/Habitat Press, a 202-page book, is available for $19.95 plus $1.50 postage and handling from the Directory Bookshelf, see inside back cover.

Co-Housing: Innovative Housing's Newsletter on Cooperative Communities, is available in two-year subscriptions at $20 for individuals, or $30 for organizations. Contact Innovative Housing, 325 Douherty Drive, Larkspur CA 94939, 415-924-6400.

National CoHousing Referral Network contact lists for your region are available for $10 from The CoHousing Company, 48 Shattuck Square, Suite 15, Berkeley CA 94704, 415-549-9980. If you want to be on CoHousing Network's contact list for those interested in living in a cohousing community, send a 3x5 card to the company with your name, address, phone number, and preferred geographic area. There is no charge for listing.)

Decision-Making

What are the structures and techniques that
contemporary communities use in making decisions —
and are they effective?

Joreen, writing for KNOW, Inc., states that informal
power structures will arise even where explicit structure
is avoided. Many groups, in their efforts to stay away
from the abuses of centralized decision-making,
unwittingly create a **Tyranny of Structurelessness**
which is just as dysfunctional as what it replaces. The
author recommends seven principles for organizing
decentralized, democratic structures — to insure that
the group as a whole will be in control of their
structures and decisions.

Over the past decade, consensus decision-making has
been gaining popularity among a wide range of
communities and grass-roots organizations. In
Consensus Ingredients, Caroline Estes of Alpha Farm
traces the history of consensus process, describing the
basic elements necessary for its success, and offering
insights about how it can be implemented. She
shares her belief that consensus is much more than
a decision-making process: it can bond group members
together, promote understanding, and advance basic
group purposes in ways that some have called
mystical.

Ultimately each group must decide what
decision-making techniques and structures best serve
its purposes — and knowledge of a variety of
approaches provides a group with more options. As
Estes notes, "the lesson... is to have lots of tools in
your toolbox, and use each where it fits."

Lora J. Donahue.

75

The Tyranny of Structurelessness

by Joreen

Absence of structure in many intentional communities is a natural reaction against the over-structured society in which most of us found ourselves, and against the inevitable control this gave others over our lives. The idea of structurelessness, however, has moved from a healthy counter to those tendencies to becoming a goddess in its own right.

Contrary to what we would like to believe, there is no such thing as a structureless group. Any group of people that comes together for any length of time for any purpose will inevitably structure itself in some fashion. The structure may be flexible; it may vary over time; it may evenly or unevenly distribute tasks, power, and resources over the members of the group. But it will be formed regardless of the abilities, personalities, or intentions of the people involved. The very fact that we are individuals, with different talents, predispositions, and backgrounds makes this inevitable. Only if we refused to relate or interact on any basis whatsoever could we approximate structurelessness; that is not the nature of human groups.

For everyone to have the opportunity to be involved in a group and to participate in its activities, the structure must be explicit, not implicit.

The idea of structurelessness does not prevent the formation of informal structures, only formal ones. A "laissez faire" ideal for group structure becomes a smokescreen for the strong or the lucky to establish unquestioned hegemony over others. Thus structurelessness becomes a way of masking power. As long as the structure of the group is informal, the rules of how decisions are made are known only to a few, and awareness of power is limited to those who know the rules.

For everyone to have the opportunity to be involved in a group and to participate in its activities, the structure must be explicit, not implicit. Decision-making must be open and available to everyone, and this can happen only if it is formalized.

This is not to say that formal structure in a group will destroy the informal structure. But it does hinder the informal structure from having predominant control and makes available some means of formal negotiation if the informal leaders are not at least responsive to the needs of the group at large.

Once a group has given up clinging to the ideology of structurelessness, it is free to develop those forms of organization best suited to its healthy functioning. This does not mean blindly imitating traditional forms of organization or blindly rejecting them either. Some traditions will prove useful, some will give us insights into what we should and should not do to meet the objectives of the members. But mostly we will have to experiment with different kinds of structures, both traditional and contemporary.

While engaging in this evolutionary process, there are some principles we can keep in mind that are essential to effective democratic structuring:

1. Delegation of specific authority to specific individuals for specific tasks by democratic procedures. If people are selected to do a task after expressing an interest or willing-

Joreen, Jo Freeman, wrote this article (originally six pages, from which we've excerpted this summary) when she was working toward her doctorate in history at the University of Chicago. During that time she signed her feminist writing with the pen name Joreen. Since then she has completed her advanced degree in history and written a book, *The Politics of Women's Liberation*. Originally printed in *The Second Wave*, Vol. 2, No. 1, a women's movement periodical published in the early '70s, this article was reprinted soon after by Know, Inc., a feminist publishing group active in Pittsburgh PA until the early '80s.

Once a group has given up clinging to the ideology of structurelessness, it is free to develop those forms of organization best suited to its healthy functioning.

ness, they have made a commitment that cannot easily be ignored.

2. Responsiveness of all those to whom authority has been delegated, to those who delegated it. Individuals may exercise power, but it is the group that has ultimate say over how the power is exercised. This is how the group has control over people in positions of authority.

3. Distribution of authority among as many people as is reasonably possible. This prevents monopoly of power and requires those in positions of authority to consult with many others in the process of exercising their authority. Such decentralization also gives many people the opportunity to have responsibility for specific tasks and thereby to learn different skills.

4. Rotation of tasks among individuals. Responsibilities that are held too long by one person, formally or informally, come to be seen as that person's property, and are not easily relinquished or controlled by the group. Conversely, if tasks are rotated too frequently the individual does not have time to learn the job well and acquire the sense of satisfaction of doing a good job.

5. Allocation of tasks along rational criteria such as ability, interest, and responsibility.

6. Diffusion of information to everyone as frequently as possible. Information is power. Access to information enhances one's power.

7. Access to needed resources. Skills and information are resources as much as physical equipment or space or dollars. Members' skills can be available equitably only when they are willing to teach what they know to others.

When these principles are applied, they ensure that the structures developed will be controlled by each community as a whole. Those in positions of authority will be flexible, open, and temporary. They will not be in positions to institutionalize their power easily, because ultimate decisions will be made by all group members. As communities go through various stages of development, they gain experience in determining which of their members can provide the effective leadership needed to meet different challenges. ❖

An informal kids meeting at Twin Oaks: the "Midis" discuss a misunderstanding.

Geoph Kozeny/Community Catalyst

Consensus Ingredients

by Caroline Estes

Decision-making by consensus is a very old process arousing much new interest. Primitive tribes and cultures have used it for thousands of years. Early Jesuits used it in the 17th century, calling it Communal Discernment. The Society of Friends (Quakers) has used it for over 300 years, calling it Seeking Unity or Gathering the Sense of the Meeting. In the past decade or two it has come into use in settings as diverse as businesses, intentional communities, and social action groups.

In simple terms, consensus refers to agreement on some decision by all members of a group, rather than a majority or a select group of representatives. The consensus process is what the group goes through to reach this agreement. The assumptions, methods and results are different from Robert's Rules of Order or traditional parliamentary procedure.

During the past 32 years, since I was first exposed to the use of consensus in Quaker meetings, I have been in some widely different situations in which consensus has been successfully used. In 1965, at the time of the Free Speech Movement in Berkeley, I watched this process being used in both the small council that was the governing body and the large mass meetings of up to 5,000 persons. The council was made up of such diverse representatives as Goldwater conservatives, Marxists, Maoists, Democrats, Republicans, Socialists, hippies, and simple activists. Mario Savio, leader of the movement, said that during all of this tense and dramatic time, the group made only two strategic mistakes in carrying out their sit-ins, marches, and confrontations, and these two occurred when they voted because they couldn't reach consensus. Both votes led them in the wrong direction. In the large mass meetings, there was consistent agreement among those assembled, after they had taken the time to talk and discuss. There is no doubt it was a tense and exciting time — and the unity in the group was very strong.

Since then I have worked with many groups that use this kind of decision-making, whether in community gatherings, neighborhood meetings or family (Alpha Farm) meetings. I have found it works as more than just a decision-making technique, for the unity and understanding it fosters serve in many ways to advance the basic purposes of these groups.

THE BASIS

Consensus is based on the belief that each person has some part of the truth and no one has all of it (no matter how much we like to believe that we ourselves know it all). It is also based on a respect for all persons involved in the decision being considered.

In our present society the governing idea is that we can trust no one, and therefore we must protect ourselves if we are to have any security in our decisions. The most we will be willing to do is compromise, and this leads to a very interesting way of viewing the outcome of working together. It means we are willing to settle for less than the very best — and that we will often have a sense of dissatisfaction with our decisions unless we can somehow outmaneuver others involved in the process. This leads to a skewing of honesty and forthrightness in our relationships.

In the consensus process, we start from a different basis. The assumption is that we are all trustworthy (or at least can become so). The process allows each person complete power over the group. For example, the central idea for the Quakers is the complete elimination of majorities and minorities. If there are any differences of view at a Quaker meeting, as there are likely to be in such a body, the consideration of the question at issue proceeds with long periods of solemn hush and meditation, until slowly the lines of thought draw together toward a point of unity. Then the clerk frames

---

Caroline Estes is a founding member of Alpha Farm. She is a facilitator of mass meetings, a trainer and a conference coordinator. Caroline has served as a conference facilitator for the North American Bioregional Congresses, the continental Fellowship for Intentional Community and various Northwestern alternative groups, especially in the Eugene area and the Cascades Bioregion. As a professional facilitator, Caroline's skills are based in 38 years of experience as a college treasurer, legal secretary, special education teacher and personnel administrator. She leads three Consensus and Facilitation Workshops a year at Alpha, and is writing a book on consensus decision-making techniques. This article is adapted from a published piece. (Copyright, Fall 1983, *In Context: A Quarterly of Humane Sustainable Culture*, Bainbridge Island WA, reprinted by permission).

a minute of conclusion, expressing the "sense of the meeting."

Built into the consensual process is the belief that all persons have some part of the truth in them, or what in spiritual terms might be called "some part of God." We will reach a better decision by putting all of the pieces of the truth together before proceeding. There are indeed times when it appears that two pieces of the truth are in contradiction with each other, but with clear thinking and attention, the whole may be perceived including both pieces, or many pieces. The traditional either/or type of argument does not advance this process. Instead the consensus process is a search for the very best solution — whatever the problem. That does not mean that there is never room for error — but on the whole, in my experience, it is rare.

The consensus process makes direct application of the idea that all persons are equal — an idea that we are not entirely comfortable with, since it seems on the surface that some people are "more equal than others." But if we do indeed trust one another and do believe that we all have parts of the truth, then we can remember that one person may know more of the truth at one time, while another person may know more at another time. Even when we have all the facts before us, it may be the spirit that is lacking; and this may come forth from yet another who sees the whole better than anyone else. Everybody's contributions are important.

Decisions which all have helped shape, and with which all can feel united, make the necessary action go forward with more efficiency, power and smoothness. This applies to persons, communities and nations. Given the enormous issues and problems before us, we need to make decisions in ways that will best enable us to move forward together. When people join their energy streams, miracles can happen.

THE PROCESS

How does the consensus process actually work? It can be a powerful tool, yet like any tool, this process needs to be used rightly. To make the most of its possibilities we need to understand the parts and the process.

Consensus needs four ingredients — a group of people willing to work together, a problem or issue that requires a decision by the group, trust that there is a solution, and perseverance to find the truth.

It is important to come to the meetings with a clear and unmade-up mind. This is not to say that prior thinking should not have been done, but simply that the thinking must remain open throughout the discussion — or else there is no way to reach the full truth. Ideas and solutions must be listened to with respect and trust, and must be sought from all assembled. This means everyone, not just some of the group. Consensus

is the practice of oneness for those who are committed to that idea, or it is the search for the best possible solution for those who are more logic-based.

The problems to be considered come in all sizes, from "who does the dishes" to "how to reach accord on limiting the arms race." The consensus process begins with a statement of the problem — as clearly as possible, in language as simple as possible. It is important that the problem not be stated in such a way that an answer is built in, but that there be an openness to looking at all sides of the issue — whatever it may be. It is also necessary to state the problem in the positive: "We will wash the dishes with detergent and hot water," not "We will not wash the dishes in cold water." Or "We need to wash the dishes so they are clean and sanitary," not "The dishes are very dirty, and we are not washing them correctly." Stating the issues in the positive begins the process of looking for positive solutions and not a general discussion of everything that is undesirable or awful.

The meeting needs a facilitator/clerk/convener, a role whose importance cannot be too strongly emphasized. It is this person whose responsibility it is to see that all are heard, that all ideas are incorporated if they seem to be part of the truth, and that the final decision is agreed upon by all assembled.

Traits that help the facilitator are patience, intuition, articulateness, ability to think on one's feet and a sense of humor. It is important that the facilitator never show signs of impatience. The facilitator is the servant of the group, not its leader. As long as the group needs the clerk, he/she should be there. It is also important for a facilitator to look within to see if there is something that is missing — a person who is wanting to speak but has been too shy, an idea that was badly articulated but has the possibility of helping build the solution, anything that seems of importance on the non-verbal level. This essence of intuition can often be of great service to the group by releasing some active but unseen deterrent to the continued development of a solution.

The facilitator must be able to constantly state and restate the position of the meeting and at the same time know that progress is being made. This helps the group to move ahead with some dispatch.

And last but by no means least — a sense of humor. There is nothing like a small turn of a phrase at a tense moment to lighten up the discussion and allow a little relaxation. Once you have found a good clerk or facilitator, support that person and encourage them to develop their skills as much as possible. Often there are participants who want to talk more than necessary and others who don't speak enough. The facilitator needs to be able to keep the discussion from being dominated by a few and to encourage those who have not spoken to share their thoughts. There are a number of techniques for achieving this. One method is to suggest that no one speak more than once, until everyone has spoken; another is

Sue Hopkins/Alpha Farm

Members of Alpha Farm in Oregon. (Caroline is in the back row, second from the right.)

for men and women to speak alternately if those of one gender seem to be dominating the discussion.

However, it is not good to use any arbitrary technique for too long. These methods can bring balance into group, but artificial guidelines should be abandoned as soon as possible. For instance, the technique of alternating men and women speakers might be used in only one session. My experience is that a single two- or three-hour session using such techniques will establish a new pattern, and there will be little need for guidelines to be continued any longer.

No matter how well the discussion is carried forward, how good the facilitator and how much integrity there is in the group, there sometimes comes a point when all are in agreement but one or two. At that point there are three courses open. One is to see whether the individuals are willing to "step aside." This means that they do not agree with the decision but do not feel that it is wrong. They are willing to have the decision go forward, but do not want to take part in carrying it out.

If more than two or three persons start to step aside from a decision, then the facilitator should question whether the best decision has been reached yet. This would depend on the size of the group, naturally. At Alpha it is OK for one person to step aside, but as soon as others step aside also, the facilitator begins to watch and to re-examine the decision. At such a time the facilitator might ask for a few minutes of silence to see if there was another decision or an amendment that should have been considered but had been overlooked, something that would ease the situation.

Another possibility is to lay aside the issue for another time. Although this alternative always seems to raise serious questions, we need to have some perspective on what we are doing. It is likely that the world will continue to revolve around the sun for another day, week, or year, whether we come to a decision at this moment or at another. The need to make a decision promptly is often not as important as the need to ultimately come to unity around a decision that has been well-seasoned.

Personal experience has shown me that even the most crucial decisions, seemingly time-bound, can be laid aside for a while — and that the time, whether a few hours or days, is wisely allowed if a later meeting can create a better decision than was possible in the first attempt.

The third possibility is that one or two people may stop the group or meeting from moving forward. At that time there are several key considerations. Most important, the group should see those who are withholding consensus as doing so out of their highest understanding and beliefs. Next, the individual(s) who are holding the group from making a decision should also examine themselves closely to assure that they are not withholding consensus out of self-interest, bias, vengeance, or any other such feeling. A refusal to consense should be based on a very strong belief that the decision is wrong — and that the dissenter(s) would be doing the group a great disservice by allowing the decision to go forward.

This is always one of those times when feelings can run high, and it is important for the group not to use pressure on those who differ. It is hard enough to feel that you are stopping the group from going forward, without having additional pressure exerted to go against your examined reasons and deeply felt understandings.

In my personal experience of living with the consensus process full-time for 17 years, I have seen meetings held from going forward on only a handful of occasions, and usually the dissenter(s) was justified — the group would have made a mistake by moving forward.

Sometimes, though rarely, one person is consistently at odds with everyone else in the group. Depending on the type of group and its membership, it would be well to see if this person is in the right organization or group. If there is a consistent difference, the person cannot feel comfortable continuing, so the group needs to meet and work with that person concerning alignment of basic values and goals.

Consensus is a very conservative process — once a decision has been made, another consensus is required to change it. So each decision must be well seasoned and generally be relied on for some time. While decisions should not be made in haste, they can be tried on a temporary basis by including expiration dates. At Alpha Farm we have made temporary decisions on a number of occasions, usually trying the decision for a year and then either making a final decision or dropping it entirely. This necessitates keeping minutes, which is another aspect of consensus that needs consistent attention.

Minutes on each decision should be stated by the clerk, facilitator or minute-taker at the time of the decision, so that all present know they have agreed to the same thing. It is not sufficient for minutes to be taken and then read at the next meeting, unless there is to be another meeting very soon. Copies of the minutes should be distributed promptly, because those who make the decisions are also the ones to carry them out. If the minutes are not distributed until the next meeting, some of the original decision-makers may not be present. The minutes may or may not be correct, but the time for correction is past. This is a particularly important but little respected part of the process.

Several years ago, I was privileged to facilitate the first North American Bioregional Congress, held in Missouri. Over 200 persons arrived from all over the continent, and some from abroad. We worked together for five days, making all decisions by consensus. Some of those present had used the process before or were currently using it in the groups they worked with at home, but many had not used it. There was a high degree of skepticism when we began as to whether such a widely diverse group of people could work in the degree of harmony and unity that consensus demands. On the final day of the Congress, there were very many resolutions, position papers, and policies put forward from committees that had been working all week long. All decisions made that day were made by consensus — and the level of love and trust among the participants was tangible. Much to the surprise of nearly everyone, we came away with a sense of unity and forward motion that was near miraculous.

A Second Point of View

by Ianto Evans

Thirteen years of experience at Aprovecho Institute has taught us some valuable lessons about consensus and our practice of consensus-minus-one.

Initially, coming from conservative backgrounds and fearing an inability to achieve unanimous agreement, we decided to ratify decisions if all but one person agreed. We saw this as a way to get business done without some obdurate individual holding up the whole show. Our bylaws say something like "with one member dissenting." What it means is if two people oppose something, they can block it, but an individual can't.

In fact, we seldom get a dissenter, but we're protected against unaccountable insanity or temporary bouts of grumpiness. Neither has ever been an issue, but we've found that if one person strongly opposes something, we usually try to discuss it to a point where they at least feel OK about the group going ahead. Then the dissenter can say, "Well, I still dissent but I don't feel unsupported in my views."

Effectively, this gives everyone a vote, as of course they have with total consensus, but there's a difference. In total consensus, one individual can gradually take control of an organization by cumulatively swaying what doesn't get done in a direction s/he wants to see it go. By refusing to agree to black, the group is left only with white to dark grey. Later the options can be narrowed further by refusing to support darker shades of grey. Over a period, and sometimes going unnoticed, a single subversive can push the whole group to accepting only white.

Reflections on Consensus-Minus-One

by Caroline Estes

At one level, the differences between these two approaches are slight — in practice probably hardly noticeable. Yet there is a difference in spirit that harks back to the difference between unitary and adversary democracy. Total consensus assumes and requires a high level of trust and maturity. If these qualities can be developed in the group, then using total consensus is well rewarded by a bonding that goes deeper than the reserve implied in consensus-minus-one. But even with the most unpromising groups a good facilitator can do wonders .

On the other hand, there are many groups — especially with loosely defined memberships — where it would be naive to assume that every member will act in "unitary good faith," especially since our society trains us to act as adversaries. Consensus-minus-one can permit these groups to gain many of the benefits of consensus and avoid risking the subversion that Ianto fears. The lesson, it seems to me, is to have lots of tools in your toolbox, and use each where it fits. ❖

Bibliography

Auvine, Brian *et al., A Handbook for Consensus Decision Making: Building United Judgement*, 1981, Center for Conflict Resolution, 731 State St., Madison WI 53703, 608-0479.

Auvine, Brian *et al., A Manual for Group Facilitators*, 1978, Center for Conflict Resolution.

(*In Context: A Quarterly of Humane Sustainable Cultures,* is available for $18 per year, $25 surface or $36 air mail outside USA, from Context Institute, Box 11470, Bainbridge Island WA 98110, Visa/Mastercard accepted.)

Community Economics

100 Mile Lodge/Emissaries

What economic structures are most widely used in contemporary communities, and which ones have proved to be most suitable?

George Ineson's **Reflections on Community Changes** recounts how his home community in Great Britain, Taena, has undergone major changes over the past five decades. The group's original practice of communal income sharing has evolved, through varying cycles, into a diversified economy based on financially autonomous families and single individuals. George finds that going through changes together has deepened personal bonds among members, and helped them better understand the foundations of their community identity.

Peter Robinson describes living in Shannon Farm, **A Mixed Economy Community.** He examines Shannon's values and organizational processes: common land, minimal ideology, consensus decision-making, a dues system for partial income sharing, home equity, a property valuation method, financing, and — most important — people to make it all work.

In **The Wonders of Communal Economics**, Allen Butcher explores the personal and social benefits of living in a community that practices total income sharing. Drawing on his experiences as a member of East Wind and Twin Oaks, he portrays well-established participatory processes for decision-making, economic planning, and labor coordination.

Joel David Welty explains **The Rochdale Cooperative Principles** — a set of fundamental guidelines for cooperatives drawn up in the mid-1800s by English weavers. These principles have endured the test of time, having been used successfully over the past 150 years by thousands of cooperatives around the world.

Albert Bates of The Farm in Tennessee joins Allen Butcher in delineating the range of **Options for Incorporation of Intentional Communities**. They explain how varying approaches to community property, governmental requirements for tax exemptions, and other issues all have implications in selecting the tax classifications best-suited to your community's needs.

Intentional communities are at the forefront of the movement to forge new economic structures that are accessible and human-scaled to meet human needs.

Reflections on Intentional Community Changes

by George Ineson

The critical situation facing the society we live in cannot be understood by fitting it into any of the word categories from the past, such as political, economic or religious. We are having to move into a new level of awareness in order to understand the creative opportunities open to us. The move to form communes and return to a basic pattern of living is one of the more obvious ways of responding to this new awareness.

Before World War II intentional community seemed to be a prophetic gesture outside the mainstream of society. But now the intentional communities movement is one of society's crucial growing points. Yet every community seems to develop its own inbuilt blind spots. Some kind of dialogue between groups will be of considerable value to help each other widen our perspectives. Now is a good time in the history of the movement to reflect on the different experiences that communities have been through, and see if any general patterns are emerging.

The following reflections on the experiences of my community are published in the hope that other communitarians will benefit from our story and be motivated to share their experience, also. In this way, we can come to broader understandings about the new levels of awareness that we are all beginning to experience.

The community I live in is called Taena. It was started by a group of pacifists in 1940. Our outlook was mainly left-wing political and humanist. We had no religious beliefs and understood our intentional community as an experiment in a new form of society and a response to the position of a pacifist in wartime. But we also responded to the common emotional crises that mark the beginnings of any group. We moved away from a purely political position and began a decade long search for a deeper meaning to human existence.

Our search started with Krishnamurti and Jung and led to yoga, meditation and the East generally, Christian mysticism and contact with a Benedictine monastery. During this initial period of about 10 years, we lived together on a communal basis, pooled our possessions, worked on a dairy farm and pottery, and managed our common life from a weekly meeting. There were no elected officers, no sanctions to enforce decisions, and no membership restrictions — anyone who wanted to join was accepted.

Then, over the next two years, we were received into the Roman Catholic Church and a gift of money enabled us to move to a farm in Gloucestershire adjoining Prinknash Abbey. This was the beginning of a second 10-year period very different from the first — we agreed on the objective of building a Benedictine community for lay people and worked out a Constitution with the approval of the Abbot of Prinknash. Members were elected once a year to be responsible for different activities and we instituted a three-year trial period for new members. We recited the Benedictine Office in the chapel at various times of the day, and on Sundays and Feast Days a monk from Prinknash came down to celebrate Mass, which we sang in Gregorian Plainsong.

There were six families with over 30 children and a number of single people. Our work consisted of a dairy farm of 135 acres and various crafts. Community life during this second period was interesting and fulfilling. The daily and seasonal rhythms of the Church's Liturgy were especially useful, revealing a deeper level of meaning underlying the work, prayer and play of our ordinary life.

However, by about 1960 a number of problems arose that were so intractable that we almost despaired of a solution. One was financial — the families had grown to such an extent that the farm could no longer meet our expenses, as minimal as they were. Another problem was a growing sense of frustration because of the need to discuss in meetings anything that involved the expenditure of time and money. We had built a way of living that worked well providing each individual remained a complementary part of the total organism, but our way then allowed little space for the individual to develop as a separate person.

Eventually we were driven to the drastic solution of making each family and single person a separate unit economically (after 21 years of common ownership) and we

---

George Ineson is a founding member of Taena, an intentional community near Gloucester, up the Avon River from the Bay of Bristol on the southwestern coast of Great Britain. In 1955 he wrote a book, *Community Journey*, now out of print. George has at times practiced architecture, and recently, woodcarving and joinery.

83

threw out the Constitution. As four people took work outside the community, we became outwardly more like a very small village — the weekly community meeting, Mass, and the close relationship remained, but now on a voluntary basis. We had in one way returned to where we had started — the attempt to "let things happen."

Since then many things have evolved, but in much more diverse patterns. In addition to the farm workers, some of our members are now silversmiths, wood and stone carvers, potters and architects. A recent experiment involves weekends with people from outside for yoga, meditation and tai chi ch'uan meditation dances from China. Interests have widened and we are more aware of the destructive effects of that occupational disease of communities — a narrow, compulsive fanaticism.

The attempt to look back on all this and gain some kind of perspective is a difficult procedure. Such reflections involve making generalizations which are always in some sense false. So what follows are not conclusions, but rather tentative ideas to be questioned and discussed.

Among the many hidden assumptions we bring with us to intentional community is the belief that if society at large seems unsatisfactory, unjust or morally wrong, then it is up to us to work out and put into practice something better. For most of us it takes a long and laborious journey to reach the understanding that such creation does not spring from thinking and will, or ego, alone.

All life, including group life, evolves from a deeply mysterious energy. If we are led to live in a community, the action asked of us is not to establish dogmatic positions, religious or political, but to open ourselves to see what IS. We must become aware of the ways in which life is blocked, in ourselves and in others, before we can release the creative energies within us. Often, the arising of new patterns of inner and outer relating wait for the meeting of opposites. The tendency for a community therefore to simplify, to label what is right and exclude what is wrong, to pressure members to agree by requiring unanimous decisions, causes its own atrophy by stifling individual creativity and narrowing the perspective of the group as a whole.

The question of common or private ownership is a basic and continuing controversy no matter which economic system, or mix of economic systems, a community decides to use. We felt in the beginning that, unless each of us gave everything we owned to the group, we would be unable to meet others as naked human beings divested of power and privilege. Yet it is just this kind of continuing encounter that is the foundation of community living. Meeting challenges keeps the movement for change in motion.

Common ownership became dogma for the people of Taena; and it was said that without it we could not call our-

selves a community. This feeling was followed by a sense of guilt. Few realized that as the group had been vested with economic power over time, it had become an end in itself, with a tendency to self-preservation that awakened a primitive tribal archetype. Now, the experience of tribalism can be necessary and healing for alienated and rootless people living in our technological world. But I do not believe that contemporary tribalism is the ultimate purpose of community.

The purpose of community is to help each other find the fulfillment that is unique to each person. Such a search may require some degree of economic decentralization over time, and certainly requires recognition that each person must have sufficient inner and outer space. Unless we can be alone, we cannot be together in the right way; individual dependence on the group should be only transitional if we are to experience continuing personal growth.

For many years we consulted with a Jungian therapist to understand more about the underlying patterns of our inner evolution, so we could facilitate the movement of energy rather than block it. For instance, a very common reason for the breakup of communities is the emergence of a collective scapegoat. We learned that group members can become obsessively convinced that everything would be all right if only a certain person could be persuaded to leave. However, sometimes a compulsive dislike arises because the other person has become a symbol of a hidden part of themselves, or the group, with which some have not yet come to terms. If this happens, working out the struggle with the scapegoat can be a very positive way for all involved to become more whole as persons. In such a case, if the scapegoat is persuaded to leave, some members may continue to carry their internal tensions until another scapegoat emerges… or is created.

So we can understand that intentional community can happen anywhere, that it is a space in which life can evolve and create more freely, and that in no sense is it an end in itself to be set up as an idol.

We gather around the growing point in a ritual circle and let it grow outward. The breathing in of concentration and the breathing out of dispersion. Our relating to one another springs from each person's commitment to their own life thread, discovered in their own inner space, and from each person's awareness of their love for the mystery of the other person.

Relating to others on this level of awareness opens us all to a profound and powerful energy which heals and transforms. This opening takes place in different ways for each person, but we bear images for each other that are keys to the opening. We are utterly dependent on each other for opening to happen; yet none of us can know the mode of its happening. ❖

A Mixed Economy Model
for Intentional Community

by Peter Robinson with help from Bernie and Clay

I live in Shannon Farm, an intentional community of 75 adults and children on the eastern slope of the Virginia Blue Ridge mountains. I have watched Shannon grow for 15 years, and continue to marvel at how well it works. Our community grows richer, more beautiful, and generally more harmonious, while turnover is negligible. In the summer of 1987 we burned our mortgage, and last summer we first swam and paddled in the lake we had dreamed of since our founding in 1974.

Much of our success can be credited to many extraordinary members: energetic, creative, patient and fair-minded people. But I firmly believe that the way we structure our community is also essential. This paper details the key elements of our model: land, consensus, dues, agreements, home equity and valuation, credit, and people.

LAND — "This land belongs to you and me..."

All communities need land: the bedrock upon which to build our hopes and dreams. Relationships change; loved ones die; children leave home; but the land is always there. The survival of any community and, ultimately, of the entire earth, depends on our willingness to reinhabit and cherish our land.

Larger pieces of land allow for larger communities which are more likely to thrive for generation after generation. Shannon has nearly 500 acres and we wouldn't mind having more. A new group faced with more expensive land could start with less.

At Shannon we have seen numerous benefits because our land is not subdivided, i.e. individual titles granted to residents. All of our land is held by a non-profit corporation. When I walk this land I feel connected to all of it: nearly a square mile of woods, vistas, springs, creeks, orchards and gardens with the Rockfish River meandering through the middle. As I walk I encounter the homes of some nice folks who own this land with me, but this doesn't diminish my feeling of protected space, of room to roam and expand. If our land were carved into deeded lots, my identity with the community as a whole would be greatly diminished. Without some other shared covenants or trusteeship, our unique community might eventually blend into the surrounding Rockfish Valley.

Also, because we hold our land in common we have more flexibility to shape the entire community, such as reserving prime farmland and garden spots for agriculture. By building our homes in designated clusters, wells and springs can be shared by many residents while large wooded areas are left uncleared. Aesthetic and value-based decisions (solar panels vs. outside power, overhead electric lines vs. underground, raising animals for meat, using chemical fertilizers, shooting woodchucks and deer, allowing mobile homes, etc.) can be decided by the entire community. The necessity and difficulty of making these and other decisions provide the forge and anvil on which the spirit of the community is refined.

CONSENSUS — Getting Your
(and Your Neighbor's) Needs Met

Major decisions at Shannon are made by consensus at an open meeting, "the monthly meeting," usually attended by one-third to one-half of the members. Proposals and discussion items are placed on the agenda by standing committees or "ad-hoc" committees of five or more members.

Two members chair the meeting, bringing up items from the printed agenda. The "content chair" calls on members in turn, keeps the meeting on topic, and listens carefully for the points of agreement. The "process chair" notes the vibes of the participants, ensures that all members wishing to speak

Peter Robinson has lived cooperatively since 1973, first in Birmingham, Alabama and since 1978 at Shannon Farm in Virginia. He works with Starburst Computer Group and has provided frequent technical support for the editing of this directory. He is treasurer of the business loan fund administered by Community Educational Service Council, Inc. (CESCI), and is active in the Charlottesville-based Blue Mountain Greens. **Bernie** and **Clay** are other long-term Shannon members. This article has been recently published. (Copyright, January 1990, *Green Revolution*, School of Living, Rt. 1, Box 185A, Cochranville PA 19330, reprinted by permission.)

> ❖
>
> The creation of even one finely designed community, and the development there of a vital community spirit, probably would lead to that general type of social organization being imitated and reproduced many times. ... To work at creating a good community is not a retreat from national or world affairs, but may be the most vital way of contributing to them.
>
> *The Small Community:*
> *Foundation of Democratic Life*
> *by Arthur E. Morgan*
> *Community Service, Inc.*
> *Yellow Springs, Ohio*

are recognized, and makes decisions on procedural questions. When the chairs believe that consensus can be reached, the content chair restates the sense of the meeting and calls for confirmation: "All in favor... All opposed... All abstaining... Does anyone block?" If even one (full) member blocks, the proposal does not pass. If no one blocks and there are no more than a few opposed or abstaining, consensus is confirmed.

When a proposal has been blocked (which happens every few meetings) the chairs may continue discussion, searching for a way to meet the concerns of the blocking member(s). Non-binding straw votes may be used to show where the weight of opinion is and point the way toward consensus. This is often a time when the quieter voices in the room may be heard and help to integrate the opposing views.

The survival of any community and, ultimately, of the entire earth, depends on our willingness to reinhabit and cherish our land.

If further discussion appears futile, the proposal is sent back to committee for more work. Most blocking members recognize a personal responsibility to see that a new and better proposal is formulated before the next meeting.

If a proposal fails to reach consensus at two successive meetings, our bylaws allow us to set aside consensus and vote. This option provides security for those who fear that a necessary decision might be indefinitely stymied. But votes are rare — it's been at least 10 years since we've had one.

One reason consensus works so well for us is our low turnover. Members are less likely to block out of spite, for they must live with the consequences of poor process. The potential for voting may also discourage abuse of the blocking privilege. Also, the general level of trust has risen gradually as we continue to deal with each other over the years. Consensus builds trust, and trust helps to build consensus.

DUES — The 7 Percent Solution.

How to raise funds for land payments, roads, utilities, common structures, and other essentials such as anniversary parties? Right from the beginning Shannon adopted a dues and labor system. Originally we set a sliding scale of a day and a half of take-home pay plus one and a half days of community work per month. This worked fine for a few years, but it was a little fuzzy in some areas: What if I work part-time? What about interest income? In 1980 we changed it to 7 percent of monthly after-tax income. I think of our dues as income-sharing — 7 percent worth.

After 12 years of membership, dues drop back to 5 percent. I like this provision, because members who contribute to Shannon that long have already paid their share of the land cost and have earned a break. (Note that there is no up-front membership fee or capital requirement at Shannon.) Seniority benefits are seen by some as non-egalitarian, but I believe they encourage longterm membership, which is vital.

In the early years dues could not possibly cover all the needs for money: We had a $50,000 mortgage payment to make each summer for the first two years. Therefore many of us lent money to the community, sometimes at no interest. Now all of those original loans have been repaid, and when we deposit money in the "Shannon Bank" we receive 10 percent interest.

A dues system has an important side benefit: Membership is not dependent on residence in the community. This was vital in the early years at Shannon, since there was no way we could all live on the land at first. Now it provides important flexibility; a member has the option of living away from the land while still maintaining full membership.

One thing that we all agree on is that no one is going to tell us how to think or lead our lives.

IDEOLOGY — Less is More.

Perhaps the unique aspect of Shannon is that we have very little ideology. Members generally share those familiar "New-Age" beliefs in co-operative living, organic gardening, alternative energy, home or private schooling, support groups, etc. But for every cherished notion, one can find a Shannon member who thinks it is bunk. Spiritually we are also quite diverse: agnostics and atheists, former Protestants and Catholics, Jews, a Unitarian, a Jehovah's Witness, a Quaker and others who hold deep but unconventional spiritual beliefs. Lifestyles vary as widely. Housing choices run from small cabins with no electricity, to medium-sized houses with photovoltaics, to more modern homes plugged into the new underground electric lines. Some members are single; some have open relationships; some are married and are raising children. In fact, one thing that we all agree on is that no one is going to tell us how to think or lead our lives.

This commitment to individual freedom and autonomy can be seen in our lease agreement (described later) and in many other aspects of our community: We use consensus with rotating chairpersons; our corporate officers have little power; our standing committees are open to all members; we allow for private incomes and possessions.

The diversity of our membership is a source of strength. Our inter-twining philosophies and lifestyles create a complex ecology of minds, creative and resilient in times of stress. There are also costs to this diversity: Group projects and common meals are harder to arrange, and those moments when we glimpse the spirit of the entire community are rare.

Another important part of our minimalist philosophy is a deep-seated dedication to fairness. In meeting after meeting I have heard and felt the determination of our members to treat each other fairly. I find it reassuring that, as a group, we tend to apply the Golden Rule rather than judging situations and persons according to strict ideological standards.

Given all this, you might ask: What holds us together? Our stewardship of our land, our use of consensus, and our pooled dues income are key. ("Paying your dues" is another of our strongest agreements.) Some of our members work together in democratically run collectives. We are good neighbors, and know that we can call on each other for eggs and milk, lifting a refrigerator, starting a car, or roofing a house. As social animals, we yearn for the bonds that grow during long-term, even lifelong, face-to-face encounters. At Shannon we find a small, stable village of open-minded individuals who manifest their interest in social, economic, and political alternatives.

A peaceful community surrounded by the beauty of the Rockfish Valley, the Blue Ridge Mountains, and a spring-fed lake is sufficient reason to stay for many of us. For others this is just the starting point: Here we can strive to create the ideal life, an even better and healthier habitat for human beings.

An intentional community in the Blue Ridge Mountains.

Geoph Kozeny/Community Catalyst

EQUITY — Combining Private Homes and Common Land

Shannon holds the legal title to all structures on the land including individual homes, but the value of those homes belongs to the builders or succeeding lease holders. If I spend $30,000 on materials and labor to build a house at Shannon, I sign a self-perpetuating lease which recognizes that value and allows me to transfer my lease to another Shannon member for no more than that amount adjusted for inflation. Our aim is to prevent speculative profits on the lease sale which tend to arise because of the success of the community as a whole. We recompute the official value annually to reflect any change in construction costs plus any improvements.

We worked on "The Lease" for about 10 years, and in June of 1989, after more than 2000 person-hours of often heated discussion, we reached final agreement. It is one of our key agreements and an excellent example of decision-making at Shannon. We succeeded in addressing the diverse concerns of individual members while protecting Shannon as a whole.

One of the innovative features of our lease agreement is "the guarantee," but first some background. Originally many members wanted Shannon to eventually assume ownership of all homes, renting them to members for modest amounts. Toward that end we agreed that each time a house changed hands, one-third of the value would go to Shannon, looking to the day when Shannon could buy all of the houses. Later this anticapitalist provision came to be seen as Draconian and led to some horrendous meetings and personal confrontations.

In the midst of this controversy, two long-term members declared that they would not build their proposed home unless Shannon guaranteed them 75 percent of the value of their house should they ever decide to leave and be unable to find a buyer. Some of us thought this was a rather brazen proposal. Still others agreed that the community should guarantee a portion of the equity of departing members. No

one welcomed the idea of members leaving penniless or being held captive to a community they no longer called home.

The desire to keep the two members catalyzed our desire to draft a more widely supported lease. We came up with a synthesis of the guarantee and the percentage to Shannon concept. A brand-new member can choose up to a 30 percent guarantee which goes up to a maximum of 75 percent after 15 years of membership. There is a price, however: When members successfully transfer a home that is covered by a guarantee, they pay a transfer fee to Shannon (up to 15 percent of the transfer value) that is proportional to the guarantee percentage which was chosen. I think of it as a brokerage commission.

Thus the collectivists can opt for the maximum available guarantee, contributing to and benefiting from our common wealth, while the free-enterprise types can avoid the bureaucracy and take their chances.

VALUATION — Beauty is in the Eye of the Lease Committee

Members of the lease committee, in consultation with the leaseholders, place a value on all structures at Shannon based on the square footage, degree of finish, and changes in the building cost index. Since we can't sell our homes for more than this official valuation, you might imagine that we would be forever fighting over what is the proper value. "But these are soapstone floors and look at that full-grain maple in the kitchen cabinets." And you might imagine correctly except for one simple fact: We divide the county property taxes (which are levied initially on Shannon Farm Association, Inc.) according to our internal valuation of our homes rather than the county tax assessor's. So if I convince the lease committee that my house is actually worth $35,000 instead of $30,000, then I buy into a larger chunk of the property tax bill, year after year after year.

CREDIT — I'd Rather Be Rich.

Members at Shannon cannot get traditional mortgages on their homes because they do not hold title to a lot. The disadvantages to this are obvious. The advantages are more subtle. We are much more confident that no outside bank or creditor will ever successfully lay claim to a house at Shannon; less availability of money from the bank inclines us to build modest homes that can be paid for in the near future; and it puts more responsibility on the community as a whole to provide some degree of financing.

About 10 years ago Shannon established a credit line with our local bank for $112,000, using the entire farm as collateral. Then we created credit "chips" of $2000 per member and a credit committee to review applications. After com-

> ❖
>
> The roots of civilization are elemental traits — good will, neighborliness, fair play, courage, tolerance, open-minded inquiry, patience. ... They are learned in the intimate, friendly world of the family and the small community...
>
> *The Small Community*

We know that we can call on each other for eggs and milk, lifting a refrigerator, starting a car, or roofing a house.

munity approval and after raising their own matching funds, members could go to the bank and borrow up to that amount with Shannon co-signing the note. Members could pool their chips and also use other members' unallocated chips. No one has ever defaulted on one of these loans, and the bank considers all of us to be good credit risks (when backed by Shannon), even those members living on $4,000 a year.

We have recently agreed to raise the maximum loan per house significantly (up to $20,000) and to allow for longer payback periods (up to 15 years). These loans are secured by a new $300,000 credit line.

PEOPLE — A Necessary Ingredient

A lot of really dedicated people are needed to form a community — at least 20 adults, in my book. The Shannon dream began when a few individuals advanced the concept of an "Alternative Community," but by the time the Shannon land was purchased, 18 months later, more than 40 members were already involved. With fewer than 20, the group is more vulnerable to domination by one or two forceful personalities. When people leave, it's not as wrenching to a larger group.

Shannon enjoys a reasonably wide age spread: though most of us are in our 30's and 40's, we have members of all ages from 19 to over 70. However, it is vital that we keep adding younger members over the next 30 years so that we don't become a retirement community. Hopefully, we will have space (physical and psychological) for our children in case they decide to build their own homes here.

Shannon has always encouraged self-selection rather than exclusionary methods of member selection. In the early years any person could become a provisional member simply by starting to pay dues. Now the support of one-third of the full members is required. After six months to a year, a provisional member can become a full member with the support of two-thirds. It surprises some that this is one of the few areas in which we do not use consensus, but we wish to avoid a "blackball" method that might exclude the non-conformists who, once integrated into the community, reveal special qualities and skills.

Our membership process is generally very relaxed: Only once in our history has a provisional failed to gain full membership after petitioning (though a particularly flamboyant member had to try twice). Approximately half of the provisional members decide that Shannon is not right for them and never request full membership. However, as making a home at Shannon becomes less risky, and as we become aware of our membership limits, we may be faced with rejecting willing members or establishing a waiting list.

A NEW COMMUNITY — A Chip off the Old Block.

While Shannon can absorb only a few new members each year, there is no reason there couldn't be more communities like Shannon. Should you decide to help organize a new community, you may wish to keep our basic structure in mind:

— Enough land held in common.

— Consensus decision making.

— A percentage dues system.

— A minimum of ideology.

— Equity for leaseholders.

— A method of valuing structures.

— Financing for home builders.

— A bunch of patient fanatics.

If you want to know more nitty-gritty details about Shannon Farm Association, Inc. we will be glad to mail a copy of our bylaws and Lease Agreement. Please send $3 and a self-addressed envelope to: Corinne Le Bovit, Archivist, Shannon Farm, Rt. 2, Box 343, Afton, VA 22920. Tell us if you want us to share your name with others who might be interested in forming a new community. ❖

The Wonders of Communal Economics

by Allen Butcher

Twin Oaks, founded in 1967, has about 70 adult members and 12 children; East Wind, established in 1974, is home to 36 adults and seven children. Both communities maintain communal economies using labor credit systems. Members of these communal societies have free and open access to all of their communities' commodities and services, in exchange for their labor and the observance of other community agreements. The labor credit system, along with participatory government and managerial autonomy, provide a high degree of personal freedom, while also encouraging a sense of personal responsibility.

Community economic agreements, behavior norms, and interpersonal relationships are all based upon trust. The values of honesty and trust are assumed in all community affairs, including politics and decision-making, domestic design, child care, interpersonal relations, and outreach to the external culture.

East Wind and Twin Oaks have purposely designed and continue to support a low-stress ambience, partly through their "radical flex-time" labor systems in which people can change their work schedules on short notice. While everyone is trusted to meet their work responsibilities, it is assumed that each person will take advantage of sunshine, each other's company, and other personal and social opportunities.

Encouraging open and honest communication develops self-assurance, self-empowerment and group process skills. The cooperative lifestyle also develops skills in participatory government, facilitation, and conflict resolution techniques, as well as co-counseling or other interpersonal communication and personal growth methods.

COMMUNAL VALUES

The fundamental ideal of communal economics is that human rights have a greater priority than property rights. Communal economics in an egalitarian community assures a focus upon human rights — the right to participation in decision-making, and the right of access to a fair share of community wealth. In contrast, the private property system places its highest priority upon property rights — the individual's right to accumulate and maintain private wealth, independent of the needs of others.

Communal economic systems emphasize the individual's responsibility to the community; the private economic system focuses upon the individual's responsibility to one's self. In both systems balance must be found. The private property system relies upon good will, charity, taxation, court orders and a police force to cajole or coerce individuals into supporting the community. In contrast, egalitarian communal systems rely primarily upon participatory decision-making processes to assure that the community is responsive to individual needs.

EGALITARIAN GOVERNMENT

Egalitarian government and economics are recognized as the central ideology at Twin Oaks and East Wind. Around this ideal the two communities have created the Federation of Egalitarian Communities, a network that includes eight intentional communities across North America. The Federation provides a mutual support base, including personal visits and labor exchanges, a revolving loan program, a common major medical disaster fund, and joint efforts in member recruit-

Allen Butcher For 13 years Allen Butcher was a member of two communal (total income-sharing) groups, East Wind and Twin Oaks. He has visited and corresponded with a wide variety of communal, cooperative and mixed economy communities, and studied their economies on a comparative basis. Allen is a member of the National Historic Communal Societies Association, and one of the incorporators of the Fellowship for Intentional Community. His wide-ranging interests also include communitarian history, social structure, tax law, single parenting, networking, and writing about these subjects. In 1989 Allen moved to Evansville, where he lives with his five year old daughter and studies political science at the University of Southern Indiana.

ment, outreach and networking programs, and publications (see Federation article in the Networking section).

In the planner/manager system used at Twin Oaks there are three planners, each with an 18-month staggered term. Planners coordinate executive functions including economic planning and make decisions in private meetings after community input is received through open meetings, posted opinion papers, and personal conversations. Authority for day-to-day decisions in specific work areas is delegated to the managers, and they are given the power to spend money and labor budgeted by the community. Managers are appointed by managerial councils, which are groups of managers in related areas. Examples are: Agriculture Council, Industrial Council, Outreach Council, Support Council. Twin Oaks utilizes a form of consensus government in which the community concentrates upon direct member participation in policy development, coordinated by the planners and managers. No voting takes place, but an override petition serves as an appeal process which members may use if they feel certain views are inadequately represented. For instance, planners appoint their own successors, but these and all other planner decisions are subject to appeal.

East Wind changed to a democratic process in the late 1970s. Majority rule voting takes place at weekly community meetings, and managers and planners are elected annually. Both the planner/manager process of Twin Oaks and the democratic system of East Wind are designed to encourage members to develop a sense of self-empowerment and personal initiative.

COMMUNAL ECONOMICS

Major aspects of the communal systems used at Twin Oaks and East Wind communities include the following:

1) Standard of Living

Each community decides through participatory process what programs and services it will support with its labor and money resources. In doing so, trade-offs that affect standards of living must be considered. For instance, shall labor be applied to work that makes money to purchase goods and services from the outside, or shall that labor be applied to self-reliant internal production? In considering the trade-off, the efficiency and appeal of the labor involved in earning money for external purchase is compared with the labor involved in internal production — as well as the relative quality of the goods and services obtained by both methods. The community might value growing all of its own food. However, a trade-off must be made if home growing requires three times as much labor as would be needed to purchase food of comparable quality.

Communal sharing is more environmentally sound than private ownership of property. When people share tools, vehicles, buildings, and land, fewer of these recources are needed. With the world's population increasing, sharing can ease the burden on the earth's natural resources while providing everyone access to the common wealth.

The level at which income, land, buildings and other assets are shared has a major effect upon standard of living. Given a constant income and productivity level, the more sharing, the higher the material standard of living. However, individual needs for privacy eventually cancel out the benefits as the level of sharing is increased. The point of diminishing returns is first a function of the group's morale and collective awareness — the greater the cohesiveness, the more sharing is possible. Second, the conflict between privacy needs and sharing is reduced as the wealth of the community increases.

2) The Labor Credit System

The labor credit system includes a "labor quota" set by the community which defines each member's fair share of time at work. At the beginning of each week at Twin Oaks, individuals fill out their work schedules with creditable labor, that is, hours from managerial budgets. Working more than the weekly labor quota earns extra vacation time, to be taken at the member's discretion. Members who consistently work "under quota" risk losing their membership.

Each hour of work is considered to be worth one labor credit. Labor credits are generally non-transferable; only the person who does the work can claim the credit. There is, however, a provision for members to barter vacation credits in exchange for personal services from other members. These are called "personal service credits." A prohibition against using labor credits as a basic exchange medium preserves the communal ideal that goods and services are available to members on the basis of need and availability, and not on one's ability to pay. If something is not available in sufficient supply, the appropriate response is to work collectively to make it more available to everyone, rather than to have people work individually to satisfy just their own desires.

As an economic management system, the participatory labor credit system makes a clear statement that the people whose lives are affected by the system have direct power and responsibility for managing it. There are no outside interests to challenge the rights of community members. There is, however, the need for individuals to tailor their desires according to what is available within the community, or according to what they can find support for creating. Individuals are encouraged to communicate their hopes and ideas, and through this process contribute to the building of shared understanding and common goals.

3) The Communal Treasury

The focus of communal economics is the development of community wealth, or equity. All income is contributed to the community treasury and controlled by the participatory planning process. This includes income earned in the community's businesses or from outside work, and unearned income such as interest or dividends. No individual member has rights to any part of this equity when leaving, other than what the community agrees to give departing members. Members leave with what they brought with them when they originally joined. Personal financial assets of members are usually lent to the community. Income derived from such loans goes into the common treasury, but base assets remain the property of the individual, with use restrictions during membership.

4) Annual Economic Planning

At Twin Oaks the economic planning process is the basic starting point of the labor credit system. The resulting Annual Plan sets the money and labor budgets for each managerial area. The process also builds community awareness and commitment to the Plan as a result of the shared experience of group discussion and work toward consensus. As of 1989, East Wind no longer budgets labor but now relies upon a work manager to coordinate labor. However, the labor quota is set by the community.

Weaving hammocks at Twin Oaks

Susan Gravely/Twin Oaks

At Twin Oaks the process of arriving at a plan includes presentations by the planners, and by the labor, financial, business, and domestic managers. They and other members discuss what happened in the previous year, and what they would like to see accomplished in the coming year. Any member may propose special projects, such as constructing a new building, raising the personal allowance, or buying a musical instrument. If the community agrees to put these items high enough on the priority list to receive funding, the project is on its way.

At Twin Oaks the planners prepare a first draft annual plan, a copy of which is provided to each member. Members are given a form of "trade-off" game providing specific planning parameters, such as projected income and labor supply, requests for budget changes and proposed new projects along with associated money and labor cost projections. Member "game" responses are tabulated by the planners, who use this information in developing a Proposed Annual Economic Plan. The Proposed Plan is considered in additional meetings until some form of consensus is reached. The plan may be altered in midyear using the same group process.

In the planning process many trade-offs must be made, such as growth versus standard of living, and lowered labor quota (more leisure time) versus increased income-producing work or improved domestic services. The communities' desired income levels are dominating factors, since industry requires 40 to 50 percent of the labor supply. (At Twin Oaks and East Wind the per-capita income from industrial work is between $8 and $12 per hour.) The remaining labor is divided among all of the other work areas: usually about 10 percent for maintenance and construction, 12 percent to 15 percent for child care, 10 percent for food service, 10 percent for agriculture and grounds work, and the remainder for smaller work areas.

The budgets set in the Economic Plan are implemented by the managers. Individual members may follow their job preferences in finding areas to fill their work quotas, but the areas they choose must have sufficient budgeted hours. The weekly work quota is from 45 to 49 hours. All domestic work, such as cooking, cleaning, maintenance, and child care, is included. So the labor requirement at Twin Oaks and East Wind is often considerably less than that required of the average householder outside of community.

5) Communal Process

The labor credit system provides a program of organization and coordination without resort to centralized leadership or overly bureaucratic hierarchies. Participatory governmental processes are designed to maintain a sense of community involvement and high morale. Sharing these processes as their work is shared keeps members in control of their community.

The fundamental ideal of communal economics is that human rights have a greater priority than property rights.

Shared leadership gives an egalitarian community a capacity for endurance and progress.

There are a number of other benefits to the labor credit system. The labor quota brings a common awareness of one's fair share while allowing for differences in efficiency, productivity, and type of contribution. At the same time the community is able to establish common priorities according to a cooperative process. The labor system provides for diversification and specialization while also providing a high degree of flexibility. Labor may be transferred swiftly between programs by notifying members of opportunities such as agricultural harvests, sales of community products, training, travel and recreation, meetings, or political actions. The maintenance of hourly labor records facilitates the computation of dollar per hour figures for comparing income work in the different industries, for comparing the relative value of growing food versus buying it, and for projecting labor cost estimates for new projects. The communal economic system provides support during sickness, after accidents, and in other times of crisis. Security in advanced age is provided by a pension program, which is not in the form of accumulated money but simply a reduction of one's labor quota. Affirmative action programs and access to training opportunities are emphasized, so that individuals can expand their interests and skills, and the community can maintain labor flexibility.

Pregnancy time and child care are provided, allowing women and men more flexibility in maintaining both a family and a career. The encouragement of shared parenting and primary and secondary social groupings, supported by spatial and architectural designs, serves to create nurturing structures beyond those of the nuclear family. Thus, aspects of the traditional extended family, clan or tribe are applied to the needs of people in the contemporary world.

Communal sharing is more environmentally sound than private ownership of property. When people share tools, vehicles, buildings, and land, fewer of these resources are needed. With the world's population increasing, sharing can ease the burden on the earth's natural resources while providing everyone access to the common wealth.

In the experiences of Twin Oaks and East Wind, sharing has actually provided a middle-class lifestyle on poverty-level

*The nut butter operation
at East Wind.*

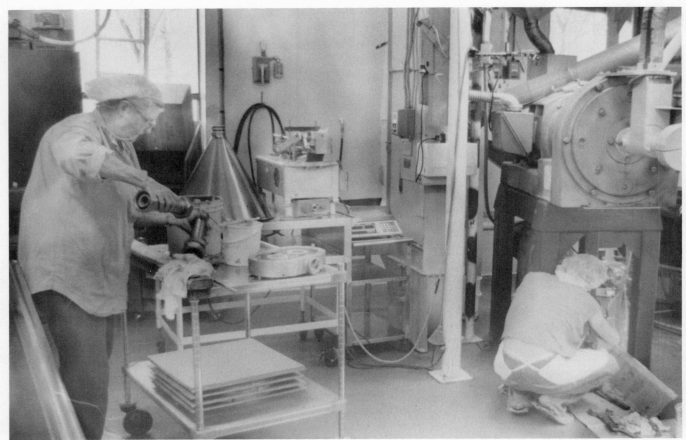

income, while supporting joyful communities. Together members enjoy beautiful rural estates, buildings designed by the people using them, wholesome fresh organic food, and the privilege of taking vacations and returning to a home well cared for in one's absence. New members arriving have access to an impressive accumulation of community resources.

A village-like community encourages a closeness to the earth and to one another, as land use designs stress walking rather than vehicle use. Building interiors and work spaces also are designed to promote interaction among people. Walkways, lounge areas, shady and sunny spots, and work spaces are all designed to be inviting and comfortable. Wild areas of the land are set aside for peace and quiet, while some of the buildings are concentrated in central complexes to create a feeling of vibrancy and social vitality. In the village design, you can walk to work, to celebrations, or to private secluded spots, and return home as unhurriedly as you like. Of course, if you prefer the fast pace, there is an endless array of businesses, meetings, and parties.

Certainly a rural community benefits the children. They learn much about life growing up in the country, especially around the farming activities. Taking regular trips to experience the city without having to live there has real advantages. In a village-like community, child care and education are provided as in an extended family. Children learn cooperation and sharing. They observe and participate in adult work and recreation, and peer groups provide opportunities for children to learn together.

Beyond the sharing of commodities and services with one other, the true luxury of the communal system is the experience of mutual support and caring — a luxury that is often difficult for even the richest people in the private property system to provide for themselves. Friendship is priceless. Perhaps this is the aspect of intentional community most valued by the members — the closeness of other people to share time with on this Earth. In building community people share their life experiences, and through this come to know and appreciate both their own uniqueness as individuals and their common culture as intentional communitarians. ❖

The Rochdale Principles of 1844 in Today's Cooperatives

by Joel David Welty

A co-op village is a certain kind of intentional community, one with a sophisticated organizational structure governed democratically, using a cooperative format rather than a communal, income-sharing economic system. Many people think that the communal model is the only model available for an intentional community. But there are a number of models to choose from, including cooperatives.

Because of the way the laws are set up, a co-op community should organize three cooperatives. A credit union should be created to handle financial matters; and a separate housing co-op is required in order to preserve the right to deduct home mortgage interest and real estate taxes from personal income taxes. The two can't be combined because the tax deductions are lost unless more than 20 percent of the housing co-op's income is in occupancy charges. The third would be a consumer/worker co-op to handle everything else: food, hardware, utilities, clothing, vehicle rental. Of course the co-op members can still be a unified community, even though their economic system is necessarily divided into three co-op corporations.

The cooperative principles provide a clearly defined economic base for community development. Because they were first formulated in 1844 by a group of weavers in Rochdale, a suburb of Manchester, England, we still call them the Rochdale Principles. The weavers organized a multi-purpose cooperative to serve their interests as consumers, workers, homeowners and students. The Rochdale cooperative had seen a good many other co-op projects go belly up, so they included in their bylaws certain principles that enabled them to succeed. That co-op is still prospering today, a century and a half later, and its principles have been successfully copied by thousands of other cooperatives around the world.

There are seven Rochdale Principles. The first is open, voluntary membership, with no religious, political or other test for joining. Anyone who is sincerely interested in benefiting from belonging to a co-op is welcome to join. It doesn't matter what race or class they are, what sex, what political or religious views they hold. Co-ops grow by appealing to and welcoming a wide range of people, building unity in diversity, not in conformity. Indeed, disagreement is expected, and used to develop more balanced decisions.

The second principle is democratic, participative governance. It goes far beyond the allocation of one vote for each member at the annual membership meeting. Participation includes an extensive network of committees to enable members to contribute intimately to the decision-making process. Cooperatives are organized to empower all the members and encourage all to share in leadership.

The third and fourth principles are aspects of the same concept: that no one should exploit any other person. The principles are limited return on capital and non-profit operation. The motive of co-ops is service, not generating a profit for an individual investor.

The fifth Rochdale Principle is education about what a co-op is and how it works, so people can receive the most benefit from belonging to it. And can effectively control it democratically. In a good co-op, every member should be engaged in leadership behavior. To enable that, continuing education in the arts and skills of democracy is necessary. In learning to understand and work with others, people can grow personally, and become stronger, resilient, more decisive personalities. People who would otherwise never get to hold responsible positions find they can do so in a co-op.

Other institutions use education as a means to make people conform and do what the institution wants. Education in a co-op works the other way, to empower people, so they can make the cooperative conform to the wishes of the members.

Joel David Welty, first elected to the board of directors of a cooperative in 1949, has been a co-op manager, organizer, educator and writer. He is author of *Welty's Book of Procedures for Meetings, Boards, Committees and Officers*. Joel has been following the development of intentional communities since the early '50s, and has recently published *Sylviron*, an adventure novel about a cooperative village set in the 21st century. He also conducts seminars and consultations across North America about democratic skills and cooperative development.

Helen Forsey/Dandelion

Working and ...

Whereas the cooperative world contains persons of all religious sects and of all political parties, it is unanimously resolved that cooperators as such are not identified with any religious, irreligious or political tenets whatever, neither those of Mr. Owen nor any other individual.

The resolution passed, and thus people of many different views were enabled to work together for mutual benefit; they may have still argued politics and religion, but the arguments were unofficial, not the official positions of the co-ops. It was an important step toward maturity and strength for the Rochdale cooperative. Independence from partisan issues was an essential step toward unity, for the 1830s and 1840s were years of intense religious and political disputes in England. Each sect wanted the co-op to endorse its own view, and co-op energies would have been spent on promoting personal views, not building the co-op.

What is a contemporary community like if it is organized on the cooperative model? It (1) includes everyone who wishes to join, (2) encourages democratic participation, (3) limits the interest it pays on capital, (4) operates for service instead of profit so no one is exploited by anyone else, (5) educates members in cooperation, (6) cooperates with other cooperatives of all types, and (7) does not permit the community to be used by any other group for purposes outside the co-op. Such a community appeals both to idealism and at the same time to self-interest. A community appealing only to idealism will find most people staying for a while, then leaving to pursue their own personal interests. There's nothing inconsistent in combining idealism and self-interest. If a community doesn't satisfy the individual's needs, what's the point?

There is a wide diversity of successful co-ops. Food co-ops have a million or so members. 1.7 million North Americans live in housing cooperatives, many of them twenty or twenty-five years old and doing well. About 18 million North Americans are members of farm supply co-ops. 24

The sixth Rochdale Principle is cooperation among cooperatives, creating a network of co-ops of all types, working together to maximize the benefits to the members in a worldwide cooperative commonwealth. There are many specialized co-op institutions to help do the job: federations such as the National Association of Housing Cooperatives, and the North American Students of Cooperation, which serves student co-ops; foundations like the Institute for the Development of Cooperation to provide training and consultation and to organize new cooperatives; and the Fellowship for Intentional Community, to provide networking services and a forum for sharing among diverse intentional communities.

The seventh Rochdale Principle is independence from partisan issues, to make sure the co-op's efforts and resources are used to serve the members, and are not diverted by some special interest group to serve other purposes. This last principle was promoted by Robert Owen, known in North America as the founder of New Harmony, a short-lived (1825-1827) but famous intentional community on the Wabash River. (New Harmony near Evansville, Indiana, continues as a thriving town, and a well-maintained historic site. In fact, Historic New Harmony, Inc., provided the impetus for creation of the Center for Communal Studies, which serves as the administrative headquarters for the Fellowship for Intentional Community, co-publisher of this directory.)

Robert Owen was active among the pre-Rochdale co-ops and contributed to the thinking behind the Rochdale Principles. At the London Cooperative Congress of 1832, he offered a resolution:

million North Americans are members of electric co-ops. More than 55 million North Americans belong to credit unions. While banks and savings and loans are having troubles, credit unions are doing well. Worker co-ops are smaller in number, but seem to be growing. Childcare co-ops are popular, too. A remarkable breadth of experience has been developed in the co-op movement since the first cooperative at Rochdale in 1844.

Of course development of villages based primarily on cooperative principles implies major lifestyle changes, but North America has done it before. After World War II, we built the suburbs, about as massive a societal change as can be imagined. But we drifted into that change, without thinking it through, without conducting experiments to see how suburbs worked in practice.

Look at what happened with the building of suburbs. A house on a private lot was every young couple's dream. So we built millions of them. And we got side effects no one had bothered to think about: long commutes, auto exhaust pollution, skyrocketing expenses that require two paycheck earners in every household, loss of a sense of community, for many a haunting sense of isolation, huge public expenses for water and sewer lines, and on and on.

Intentional communities face up to these problems consciously, experiment with ways of coping, and plan development that accounts for the lessons learned from earlier intentional communities. We're good learners. The cooperative movement must evolve consciously, not merely drift into the next century. That is why the Institute for the Development of Cooperation provides continuing education in cooperative methods and seeks to develop the cooperative village model. Rather than relying on government bureaucrats, we can design for social change ourselves, with development policy decided by experienced co-op and community people. ❖

*... living cooperatively in
an egalitarian community*

"No one is born knowing how to function in a democracy, any more than they are born knowing how to drive a car. Co-ops need to train their members continually in the arts and skills of democracy, just as we always need to keep training new drivers how to drive a car."

(*Welty's Book of Procedures for Meetings, Boards, Committees and Officers,* 270 pages, describes a decision-making system that defies traditional rules of order and uses a step-by-step system of negotiating consensus, instead of debate. It can be purchased for $9.95. Joel's novel, *Sylviron,* 603 pages, about a co-op village in the 21st century, can be purchased for $6.95. Please add $1.50 each for postage and handling. Address: 6652 Muirhead Dr., Freeland, Michigan 48623-8847, 517-695-5503.)

Helen Forsey/Dandelion

Options for Incorporation
of Intentional Communities

by Albert Bates and Allen Butcher

Intentional communities generally arise from a specific idea or philosophy. The focus may be the building of a co-operative lifestyle, or co-operation may only be a means toward achieving a wider goal. In either case, once an intentional community arises, attention begins to focus upon what kind of formal organization best suits the group. Certain very persistent imperatives inevitably ensue. In the United States, the main imperative is called the Internal Revenue Service. You'll recognize him. He wears a grey suit, a conservative tie, a white shirt, and black shoes. There are also state and county versions of this person. If you haven't given any thought to formal organization, do not think for a minute that your organization or lack of same will escape official notice.

A lot of people have an inherent aversion to anything ending with "Inc." That is completely understandable. The problem is, the guy in the grey suit loves corporations. He can barely fathom anything else. To get along with the guy in the grey suit, most intentional communities should seriously consider incorporating.

As far as possible, the object of incorporation is not to shape the community to fit the law, but to fashion legal forms that fit the community. Still, we have to admit, sometimes it's easier just to shape the community.

FORMS OF SOCIAL ORGANIZATION

The distinction between intentional communities and other forms of social organization is difficult to define from an in-clusive legal perspective. It's like trying to define a religion in the legal sense — it can't be done in a truly descriptive way. Still, until you understand the different legal forms of organization, it may seem impossible to come up with a definition of what your community is or is not. But if you don't do it, then the guy in the grey suit will.

FOUR FORMS OF
INTENTIONAL COMMUNITY

How is your money channeled? Is your intentional community a collective, a cooperative, or a commune, or does it have a mixed economy? While not legal definitions, these classifications are a good starting point from which to develop an organizational form. The collective community is a form of intentional community in which private property is shared. Cooperative communities hold major property corporately, but co-op members have individual shares of these joint assets. In both co-ops and collectives, members may choose to dissolve the community, divide the assets, and leave nothing behind but memories.

Communal communities hold all of their assets in common. Upon joining, commune members renounce any right to regain their contributions to the community if they leave. This renunciation, or "vow of poverty," originated in monastic orders. It is a feature of some communal societies, although it may not be called a vow, and the members may not live in poverty. Even so, if there is a legally binding contract

Albert Bates joined The Farm in Tennessee in 1972 after graduating from law school. He is a member of the Bar in Tennessee, D.C., and the U.S. Supreme Court; general counsel to Plenty-USA (The Farm's Third World relief and development organization); director of Plenty's Natural Rights Center (a public interest law project); and editor/publisher of *Natural Rights*. Albert has served The Farm as treasurer, archivist, cartoonist, typesetter, computer programmer, and emergency medical technician. He is a member of the North American Bioregional Congress, the Cumberland Greens, the Tennessee Sierra Club, and the Utopian Studies Association; on the boards of directors of the Communal Studies Association, the Tennessee Environmental Council, and the Solar Car Corporation of America; and

author of *Climate in Crisis: The Greenhouse Effect and What We Can Do*. Albert is a Zen Taoist also currently involved in repainting his house and toppling U.S. imperialism.

Allen Butcher became interested in tax law as a member of East Wind. Later, as a member of Twin Oaks, he closely followed his community's long legal struggle with the IRS over its interpretation of the vow of poverty. He has also been involved with the School of Living's Community Land Trust, and is a student of comparative economic systems. Allen has put his extensive knowledge to use in creating Fourth World Services, which provides assistance to local self-reliance efforts. He is currently developing a series of pamphlets about issues in intentional community.

entered into upon joining, and that contract gives up any interest of the member in communal property, then the man in the grey suit considers it a "vow of poverty."

Mixed-economy communities are essentially a blend of collective, cooperative, and communal economic arrangements integrated within one society. The most common form of mixed community is that in which the land and some buildings and equipment are held in common, while houses, cars, and bank accounts are held privately.

As noted above, these are not legal definitions and may relate only indirectly, or not at all, to the organizational categories legislated by the various states.

FOUR LEGAL CATEGORIES OF ORGANIZATION

Theoretically any form of intentional community may be organized under any of the four types of organizational entities normally recognized by state governments — partnership, for-profit corporation, cooperative and not-for-profit-corporation. In fact, mixed-economy communities frequently use more than one of these primary forms in an interactive fashion.

If you are already struggling to keep up with this discussion, take heart! Most states have corporate classifications that keep paperwork to a minimum. State tax exemptions are usually based on federal tax classifications. So local IRS offices make the initial decision to grant or deny tax-exempt status. But first, if you seek tax exemption, the community must register with the state as a not-for-profit corporation. We'll talk more about tax exemptions in a minute, after considering the for-profit alternatives.

Partnership

A general partnership is the simplest form of legal association, and can be thought of as a small group of individual proprietors joining to operate a common business. Each partner takes a share of the profits and pays the taxes on that amount, whether it is actually distributed or retained by the business.

The biggest advantage of the partnership form is its simplicity. In most states no formal filing is required. A partnership can be set up by an oral agreement or a handshake.

The Four Legal Categories

Partnership
For-profit Corporation
Cooperative
Non-profit Corporation

The Four Forms

Collective
Cooperative
Communal
Diverse

The Five Exemptions

Section 501(c)(3)
Section 501(d)
Section 501(c)(2)
Section 501(c)(4)
Section 528

If a community is formed without any formal agreement, the IRS and the courts will usually rule that the community is operating as a partnership.

A second advantage is that partnerships are not taxed, the individual partners are. This avoids the potential pitfall of double taxation into which many organizations fall.

The biggest disadvantage of the partnership comes when something in the community changes; a partner or partners leave, new ones enter, or the agreement dissolves. The property rights and compensation of the partners are established by the partnership agreement. Where the agreement is vague or does not anticipate every contingency, misunderstandings or disagreements can cause problems.

A second problem with partnerships is that general partners are not insulated from legal liability for the debts of the business. For this reason, the business entrepreneurs (robber barons) of the 16th century created the limited liability company, or "corporation."

For-Profit Corporation

A corporation is an artificial person. It is set up to be a legal entity apart from its owners. A corporation can make contracts, accumulate assets, do business, and sue and be sued in its own name. Its owners, or shareholders, vote on the management of the corporation but are not liable for the obligations of the corporation. Limited liability is the principal advantage of incorporation.

The principal disadvantage is double taxation. Corporations are normally taxed on their profits before they distribute them to their shareholders as dividends. The shareholders pay taxes a second time when they treat the dividends as income.

Every now and then the man in the grey suit has taken pity on the poor taxpayer and created a special loophole to enable the little guy to escape unfair situations — like double taxation — while still obtaining the benefits of limited liability. In the world of for-profit corporations, there is such a loophole, the S-corporation, which was created to help small businesses. To qualify for Subchapter S, a corporation must have no more than 35 shareholders, none of whom is another corporation or trust (husband and wife are treated as one shareholder), must operate a business that does not receive more than 20 percent of its income from passive sources such as rents and investments, and must obtain the consent of its shareholders to apply for the classification. Subchapter S corporations pass all profits through to their shareholders, who then take up that income, whether distributed or not, on their tax forms. The corporation itself, like a partnership, is tax-exempt.

Cooperative

For those communities with good state laws governing cooperative corporations, the cooperative form of organization can be easy and comfortable. To qualify as a co-op, the articles of incorporation must usually provide for open membership, democratic control (one member, one vote), political neutrality, and limited return on shares.

There is a federal classification of for-profit cooperative called Subchapter T, but it is only marginally profitable. Its primary purpose must be to serve some public benefit. If a member receives a share of the profits, it must be in the form of a patronage dividend distributed in proportion to the business or labor that each member has contributed — it's more like a salary bonus or purchasing rebate than profit-sharing.

Not-for-profit

Unlike partnerships, for-profits, and co-ops, which are supposed to make money, not-for-profits are not expected to. They are primarily organized to serve some public benefit. Hence they can obtain IRS and state approval for special tax treatment.

FIVE FEDERAL TAX EXEMPTIONS

Most intentional communities, like many traditional municipalities, have elected to organize as not-for-profit corporations and to apply for tax-exempt status. Since their activities are not directed primarily to make a profit, but to create a wholesome environment for themselves and to advance greater social causes, the average intentional community finds that there are significant advantages in becoming tax-exempt.

To qualify for tax-exempt status, the community must register with the state as a not-for-profit corporation. It is best to decide which category of tax exemption you are seeking before you file your articles of incorporation, because the articles may have to conform to certain language.

501(c)(3)

Not-for-profit corporations organized under Internal Revenue Code (I.R.C.) section 501(c)(3) may receive tax-deductible donations from corporations or individuals, and grants from government agencies or private foundations. They are eligible for lower bulk mailing rates, some government loans and favoritisms, and exemption from most forms of property tax. Religious orders that qualify under either 501(c)(3) or 501(d) are also exempt from Social Security, unemployment, and withholding taxes.

In order to qualify for recognition as a 501(c)(3), an intentional community must be both organized and operated exclusively for one or more exempt purposes. The outcome of the organizational test is determined by the man in the grey suit after he reads the articles of incorporation and bylaws. The outcome of the operational test is based on his investigation of the activities of the organization in its first years of operation.

Many communal organizations have difficulty passing the operational test because of the requirement that no part of the net earnings may inure to the benefit of any individual (other than as compensation for labor or as a bona fide beneficiary of the charitable purpose). If the primary activity of the organization is to operate businesses for the mutual benefit of the members, it fails that test. Moreover, even if it passes the operational test by virtue of other, more charitable, public benefits — running an educational center, providing an ambulance service, or making toys for handicapped children, for instance — it can still be taxed on the profits it makes apart from its strictly charitable activities.

This catch — the unrelated business trade income ("UBTI") — prevents tax-exempt entities from unfairly competing with taxable entities. The destination of the income, as well as the source, aids in the determination of UBTI. If a community uses its profits from bake sales to build a community fire station, it may be related income. If the bake sales expand the general operations of the organization, or pay the electric bill, it may be considered "unrelated" and taxed.

There are other restrictions on Section 501(c)(3) corporations. If they are educational in purpose, they may not discriminate on the basis of race and must state that in their organizing documents. A 501(c)(3) is not allowed to participate as an organization in a political campaign or to make substantial contributions in an attempt to influence legislation, other than on issues related to the 501(c)(3) category. They cannot publish political "propaganda," either. Organizations that qualify under Section 501(c)(3) may not distribute their residual assets to their members when they dissolve. After payment of debts, all remaining assets must pass intact to a designated tax-exempt beneficiary.

The 501(d)

If a community has a spiritual focus and a common treasury, it may apply for recognition under I.R.C. Section 501(d). The 501(d) is like a partnership or Subchapter S corporation, in that its net profits, after expenses, are divided among all members pro rata, to be taken up on their individual tax forms. Unlike the 501(c)(3), the 501(d) corporation cannot confer tax deductions for donations.

501(d) corporations have no distinction between related income and UBTI. All income, from any source, is related. However, if a substantial percentage of community income is in wages or salaries from "outside" work, 501(d) classification may be denied. 501(d)s can engage in any kind of business they choose, passive or active, religious or secular. The profits are treated like those of a partnership or S-corporation. But 501(d)s don't have the restrictions of those forms, such as the requirement to reform the partnership with each change of members, or the S-corporation limit of 35 shareholders.

501(d) corporations have no restrictions on their political activity, either. They can lobby, support candidates, and publish "propaganda." They may or may not elect to have a formal vow of poverty. Upon dissolution, assets of the corporation may be divided among the members as far as federal law is concerned. However, state law generally requires that assets remaining after payment of liabilities should be given to another not-for-profit corporation.

The 501(d)'s substantial advantages may be outweighed in communities that would prefer to hold property privately, or to keep spirituality out of the community organization. If the common ground between members is just that — the common ground — one of two other types of exemption may be more suitable.

The 501(c)(2)

Title holding companies are useful devices for owning, controlling, and managing group property. A 501(c)(2) corporation is designed to collect income from property — whether it is a land trust, business, or passive investment — and turn over the entire amount to a tax-exempt parent corporation. To qualify under 501(c)(2), the exempt recipient, usually a 501(c)(3), must exercise some control over the feeder company, such as holding a majority of the voting stock or appointing directors. The two corporations file a consolidated return. Unlike 501(c)(3)s, which may not receive more than 20 percent of their income from passive sources, a 501(c)(2) may not actively engage in "doing business,"except for certain excluded (I.R.C. 512(b)(2)) categories such as renting real estate or negotiating investments. Vehicle leasing, for instance, would be disallowed.

Many community land trusts find that having both 501(c)(3)s and 501(c)(2)s provides a needed form to both run businesses and manage land and housing. The 501(c)(2) limits the community's exposure to conflicts with the IRS over questions of income and inurement.

Section 501(c)(4) and 528 Organizations

The Internal Revenue Code confers tax-exempt status on civic leagues, homeowner associations, and similar organizations under Section 501(c)(4), if they operate exclusively to serve the social welfare or some other exempt purpose. If common areas or facilities are owned or maintained by the group, they must be kept open for the use and enjoyment of the general public. Like 501(c)(3)s, the benefits provided by 501(c)(4)s cannot principally redound or inure to the benefit of members of the group as private individuals. 501(c)(4)s, like 501(c)(2)s and 501(c)(3)s, cannot engage in substantial political activity.

Homeowner associations that qualify under 501(c)(4) or have a narrower scope of public benefit might also decide to skip the paperwork of applying for tax exemption and simply incorporate under I.R.C. Section 528 and file an 1120-H return each year. Under I.R.C. Section 528, homeowner associations are exempt from taxation in acquiring, constructing, managing, and maintaining association property used for mutual benefit. "Association property" may even include property owned privately by members, provided that the private property exempted affects the overall appearance of the community, the owner agrees to keep up the appearance, and there is an annual pro rata assessment of all members to maintain the property. An example of association property would be tennis courts and swimming pools. They would be exempt property under Section 528, unless they were used by non-members. Another example would be meeting places or retreats. Those used exclusively by the association would be exempt. Those leased to non-members would no longer qualify as "association property."

INTENTIONALITY

In designing a new community, or transforming an existing one, it is imperative that mutually respectful relationships evolve among the participants. Often the process of designing the organizational documents is the first opportunity a community has to develop a convivial style of interpersonal relationships. Community members should be aware that creating formal bylaws is of a lower level of importance than the group's associated process of self-definition. This is the crux of intentionality in intentional community. While debate over structure is occasionally the last act of a group, it is often the debate that is most fondly remembered — or deeply regretted — in the years and generations to come. ❖

(*Climate in Crisis: The Greenhouse Effect and What We Can Do*, 195 pages, is available for $11.95 plus $1.50 for postage and handling from The Book Publishing Company, Box 99, Summertown TN 38483.)

Security of Place

Mel Leisure/Common Ground, VA

Each one of us
   has land security.
Within our intentional communities
   we protect each tribe member
   in our touching
   the ground in our place.
Each has security of place
   and identity
   and community.
   We know the truth
   of each other…
   deeper across time.

Each one of our
   intentional community structures
   mirrors our individual self-awareness,
   our unique security needs,
   our self-identities.
Cooperative communities require
   Minimum Unity
   among individual cooperators.
Communes require
   Increasing Unity
   among interdependent communalists.

   Whether commune or co-op,
Land Trusts require
   Inclusive Unity
   among resident communiterrans
   and other Bioregion residents
   who are in touch
   with Gaia.

Each one of us
   defines land security
   in terms of
   individual land tenure
   within the community.
Yet, the community Land title
   in the Court of Records
   places each of us
   at a distance from
   that land title.
Our individual distance
   from the community land title
   is increased directly
   by the degree of
   Unity
   invested in our
   separate tribal structures.

Cooperators enjoy
   Minimum Unity,
   with individual land tenure.
Communalists enjoy
   Increasing Unity,
   with individual land tenure
   shared among the tribe.
Land Trust residents enjoy
   Inclusive Unity,
   with individual
   or shared land tenure,
   with oversight by
   other Bioregion residents
   who are in touch
   with Gaia.

Each one of us
   has an awareness of territory
   that comes not just from documents
   about a surveyed land tract
   listed in a legal name
   at a court of records.
For self-awareness
   thru court records
   is distant, bureaucratic.
   Land titles are symbols
   of distant institutions
   designed to insure
   the security
   and self-identity
   of a transient society
   of individuals…
   adrift…

many without connection
   to extended family,
   tribe,
   community.

Yet, any one of us,
   sometimes,
   may feel our community
   stifling our growth…
   And impel self away.
   Toward what?
   Changing or unknown self?
   Inner self?
Toward different ways?
   More — or less —
   Unity
   in tribal structure?
Toward seeing self
   in new mirrors?
   In different structures?
Each one of us
   seeks Security of Place
   within intentional community,
   in this time.
Ever knowing that
   future changes
   may call us elsewhere,
We intentionally choose
   a community of people
   that mirrors the best
   we choose to see
   in ourselves.

In this time   *Dan Questenberry*

Geoph Kozeny/Community Catalyst

Land Trusts

What are land trusts, and how do they serve the purposes of community?

Jubal Stucki and Artie Yeatman, of the School of Living, discuss the economic objectives of **Community Land Trusts** *and describe the background of the land trust movement. They differentiate between community and private trusts (the latter including some of those created by intentional communities). Jubal and Artie also outline the organization of the School of Living Community Land Trust in the mid-Atlantic region.*

In **The Idea of Owning Land***, Robert Gilman, editor of In Context, looks at historical attitudes toward "ownership" of land, and proposes fresh perspectives which draw from both traditional "tribal" concepts and contemporary thinking about land trusts. He explains land ownership as a "bundle of rights" (which can be unbundled), and shows how trusts can help safeguard the legitimate interests of all parties: the immediate user, the local community, the planetary community, future generations, and all of life. In a sidebar also from In Context, Timothy Clark elaborates on the "stewardship land trust" developed by Turtle Island Earth Stewards in the Pacific Northwest.*

In a reprint from In These Times, **Land Trusts Offer American Land Reform***, journalist Jim Naureckas finds that Community Land Trusts hold promise for combating the high costs of urban housing. Jim reports on the Institute for Community Economics, a Massachusetts-based organization that helps local groups organize CLTs as vehicles for empowering local communities and residents. Other land trust organizing groups are mentioned.*

Dan Questenberry of Shannon Farm traces the history of **Residential Land Trust Organizing** *— from Henry George's Single Tax movement in the 1890s, through the 30s depression, to modern day Community Land Trusts. Dan also provides information about organizations which offer financial and technical support for land reform and land trust development.*

"Who controls the land and resources" is a wide-ranging topic. Community Land Trusts promote local autonomy and social responsibility — to steward the earth in a way that promises an environment for future generations. Land trusting, our authors agree, is an idea whose time has come.

Community Land Trusts

by Jubal Stucki and Artie Yeatman

The Community Land Trust concept was formed out of an underlying principle, one which has been accepted by many people throughout most of history, that land and its resources are given by Mother Nature to all of us. Thus, the land may be said to be owned by all as a common heritage. The concept of private ownership of land is a very recent historical event which has had a serious effect on our sense of personal responsibility for good stewardship of our common heritage.

The Community Land Trust concept is not that each person should have an equal amount of equally good land, but rather that each person should be entitled to a fair share of the income from land and its natural resources, and that each landholder should be restricted only by ecological concern for this our common heritage. The major disparity between the rich and the poor has its roots in the private appropriation of land rent — an economic system which has given a few people major economic advantages, while impoverishing many others who have a right to an equal share of benefits from our common heritage, the land.

Karl Marx saw the solution as state ownership of land. But applications of his theory of communism thus far have empowered only the bureaucrats who run the state, while draining incentive from the rest of the people. With neither private monopoly nor state land ownership systems providing the desired social benefits, the age-old tribal territory or village commons has once again emerged — as a mixed public-private corporation, the Community Land Trust.

SINGLE TAX THEORY

Henry George clearly understood that it was not actually private ownership or private use of natural resources that created the disparity between rich and poor, but rather that the disparity was created by the landholder's private appropriation of unearned increments of common wealth. Late in the last century George advocated that local governments collect this unearned wealth as a common heritage tax, rather than taxing business and personal incomes and improvements on the land.

This idea, known as the Single Tax Theory, maintains that natural resource or common heritage rents, or taxes, would be large enough to support all public functions, eliminating the necessity for any other taxes. Thus, the unearned wealth gained from private use of our common heritage would be distributed to benefit the wider community. Henry George's ideas were so well received that he became a prominent candidate for mayor of New York City in two successive elections, and his major book, "Progress and Poverty," became a best-seller around the world. Single Tax Theory has been the basis for forming a number of intentional communities, originally called Single Tax enclaves. Two such communities, Fairhope AL and Arden DE, are now approaching 100 years of age.

In Denmark, Australia, New Zealand, South Africa and the western provinces of Canada, land value taxation has been adopted by many municipalities. The Georgist move-

*School of Living
established 1934*

Jubal Stucki and **Artie Yeatman** are both long-term board members of the School of Living (SoL). They originally created this article as a position paper published by the SoL. Jubal was an editor of the 1978 *COMMUNITIES Directory* while a resident of SoL's former Deep Run Farm CLT in Pennsylvania. Now he lives in Falls Church, Virginia. Artie is a homesteader, professional gardener, director of the Henry George Foundation, and a former teacher in the Henry George School of Social Science. He resides at Birthright Leasehold, a CLT near Cochranville in southeastern Pennsylvania.

The Community Land Trust concept is not that each person should have an equal amount of equally good land, but rather that each person should be entitled to a fair share of the income from land and its natural resources; and that each of us should be ecologically responsible for this common heritage.

ment continues to be widespread in the United States also. Current initiatives in this country involve shifting taxes away from having equal rates for both land and improvements, moving toward higher rates for land values and lower rates for improvements. Pennsylvania, Henry George's home state, has adopted land value taxation to a greater extent than any other state. As of April 1990, 12 Pennsylvania cities tax land at a much higher rate than improvements, including Pittsburgh, Scranton and Harrisburg. These cities have experienced significant increases in building and renovation following the reduction of taxes on improvements.

One hundred million acres of California farmland are taxed exclusive of improvements. The 12.5 per cent royalty Alaska collects from the use of public oil lands has allowed individual rebates sufficient to cancel personal income taxes in that state.

PRIVATE LAND COOPERATIVE ORIGINS

Despite these successful experiences, many state legislatures have been extremely reluctant to allow municipalities to charge separate property tax rates: reducing taxes on human-made improvements, and increasing taxes on land and resources in proportion to their actual value to society. Ralph Borsodi, founder of the School of Living, SoL, sought to accomplish the same goal through private initiative.

Based on the experiences of Single Tax enclaves such as Fairhope and Arden, Borsodi created a forerunner to the land trust concept — cooperative administration by a board of directors who hold title to the land as a group, and lease plots to themselves as individual leaseholders. Today this type of residential cooperative, or intentional community, is known by some as a private land trust, although that is an oxymoron — a contradiction in terms. The name "trust" signifies administration by one party or group for the benefit of others. When a land-holding organization's board of directors is controlled by the land residents, there is no such trust to guarantee that the land will be used for the mutual and ecological benefit of others beyond the residents.

The first SoL residential cooperative was established in 1936 at Bayard Lane near Suffern, outside of New York City. In the next 10 years others were established, including three still active which are listed in this directory — Tanguy Homesteads and Bryn Gweled Homesteads, both near Philadelphia, and Celo Land Trust near Asheville NC.

COMMUNITY LAND TRUST ORIGINS

By the late Sixties, Bob Swann, a student of Borsodi and community organizer Arthur Morgan, perceived that, over generations, private land trust boards sometimes lost their sense of connection with the wider movement for land reform. In fact, there have been private land trusts that dissolved in order to sell trust lands and divide unearned wealth among the leaseholding board members.

One such community was Cooperative Homesteads, Inc., of Madison Heights, five miles north of Detroit. At the inception of this residential cooperative in 1948, the value of co-op land was $250 per acre. By 1978 that value had increased to $7,000 per acre. Despite a bylaws statement that cooperative lands would not be sold, this non-profit corporation sold out and dissolved in 1978. While Cooperative Homesteads operated successfully for 30 years, the higher purposes of the cooperative were undermined by the lure of unearned wealth. The leaseholders active at the time of the 1978 sale divided the proceeds among themselves without any challenge from the state.

To provide security against such sellouts and express the wider stewardship responsibilities of leaseholders, Bob Swann and others began organizing a new kind of land trust. This new kind of trust was designed to strengthen and broaden the board of trustees by including a majority of non-residents from the wider community, such as specialists in land reform, group process, business, accounting, agriculture, economics and other areas of trust development. Thus, with the wider community in control of the board, the Community Land Trust was born.

*A view through the
onion harvest*

Geoph Kozeny/Community Catalyst

COMMUNITY LAND TRUST TODAY

A primary reason for the term "community" in community land trust, CLT, is to recognize that a significant portion of land value increases are caused by population growth and improvements. For instance, the noticeable increase in the market value of land close to a new highway or railroad is based on the presence of the entire community, and such increased value should be used to benefit the community as a whole.

Another reason for the term "community" in CLT is to differentiate CLTs from "private land trusts", which are owned or controlled by the resident leaseholders. Such land management systems may lose their vitality and wider effectiveness over time. The Community Land Trust board seeks to avoid this possibility by including a majority of trustees from the wider community, while also providing significant representation for leaseholders.

A third reason for the use of the word "Community" is to define a geographical area. In one sense, a World Land Trust might seem to be most fair. But many of those involved in CLTs believe in decentralized structures and favor

smaller trusts limited to a bioregion, a single state, or even a county, where local community control is possible. As the Community Land Trust movement develops and matures, voluntary networks of CLTs can be created to equalize distribution of unearned increments across ever-widening communities.

LAND, RESOURCES AND ECONOMIC RENT

The word "land," as used in Community Land Trust, refers to our common heritage — land and all of the natural resources under or on the land, before human modifications. Land does not refer to improvements and human-made structures. The CLT collects economic rent on this common heritage. Economic rent is the portion of production earnings which is earned by land — just as wages are earned by labor, and interest is earned by capital. When economic rent is not collected by a CLT, nor by government, it is pocketed by the landholders who have not produced that value with their own labor or direct capital. Such private appropriation of unearned economic rent by landholders is an encouragement to speculation — holding land out of optimum use. This causes prices to rise for the reduced quantity of remaining land, contributing to an inflationary spiral.

TRUST HOLDS LEGAL TITLE TO PROPERTY

However the CLT community is defined, the goal of the board of trustees is to represent the interests of the leaseholders using trust land, while being responsible for transferring unearned wealth to the wider community, and exercising stewardship for the land itself. The concept of "trust" as used in Community Land Trust is more complex than the standard legal definition. A trust is a legal title to property for administration by a person or organization for the benefit of another. But CLT trustees have a threefold administrative obligation: first, to protect use rights of leaseholders as defined by a lease agreement; second, to distribute the economic rent collected to the wider community in an equitable manner; and third, to protect our common heritage, the land and natural resources, from ecological abuse and human devastation.

These trust duties are spelled out in the bylaws of the Community Land Trust and in the lease agreement between the Trust and the leaseholders. These legally enforceable documents cannot be changed without the agreement of both parties.

An ongoing objective of the board of trustees is to provide for periodic adjustment of the lease fees. As land values change, the pressures on the board of trustees increase, possibly from all three constituent groups — leaseholders, community members, and the ecology of the land itself. From time to time, even the most effective and virtuous of boards can find itself in deep conflicts, even expensive legal confrontations. Proper fulfillment of trustee responsibilities requires time, energy, commitment, and familiarity with Single Tax Theory, as well as current economic and social issues.

THE SCHOOL OF LIVING AND
OTHER COMMUNITY LAND TRUSTS

The School of Living's membership, or wider community, now includes current and former homesteaders, communitarians, land and economic reform advocates, permaculturists and consensus specialists. SoL has members all over North America, but those active in administration are concentrated in the Philadelphia-Washington corridor and southwest into the Blue Ridge Mountains of rural Virginia, the Mid-Atlantic region where trust lands and SoL headquarters are located. Current School of Living trustees include present or former members of Sonnewald Homestead PA, Shannon Farm VA, Twin Oaks VA, the Yoga Society of Rochester NY, and other trustees who hold SoL leases on Birthright Leasehold PA, Common Ground VA and Heathcote Center

MD. SoL helps organize and finance decentralized, local and sub-state regional CLTs that hold title to rural and urban land, administering long-term leases for residential and commercial use.

The E.F. Schumacher Society, directed by Bob Swann, offers similar services in central Massachusetts; Community Service, Inc., provides CLT management in Ohio (see Resources section).

FREEING THE LAND

More land must be freed from private exploitation of economic rent and moved back into community management. The CLT movement provides a conceptual economic base and legal documentation for recreating the village commons, or tribal territory — updated to the New Age, and corporately administered as a Community Land Trust.

But how does this come to be in today's world? It is certainly not to be expected that a person or group of people will donate a particular piece of land and then pay lease fees to the Community Land Trust for use rights. The School of Living will exempt the donor(s) from lease fees during their lifetime(s). The donors will have the satisfaction of knowing that a particular piece of land has been removed from the speculative market, dedicated to the use of the land trust movement, and used ecologically.

The donor might also be able to take advantage of a tax deduction. Alternatively, those with paid up land on which they plan to live may wish to put the land in trust without making a donation. A credit for the current market value of the land can be issued. If a landholder with credit quits their lease, they would be entitled to return of the credit amount, adjusted for inflation, but not for any speculative increases.

When the Trust leases land not previously owned by the leaseholder, then a fair lease fee equal to the current economic rent is due from all users.

DEFINITION PROBLEMS

The present condition in which private ownership of land and resources has replaced community ownership has been caused in part by a confusion of terms. For example, the legal definition of "real estate" includes both land, associated natural resources, and human-made improvements such as houses and commercial facilities. Likewise, the term "property" includes both land, everyone's common heritage, and buildings which are justly owned privately.

At one time, and even now in some places, human beings were considered as property to be bought or sold. The battle over ownership of humans has been or is being won in favor of individual freedom, the women's movement making the most recent contribution to this cause. A major economic

More of the land must be freed from private exploitation and moved back into community management. The CLT movement provides a conceptual economic base for re-creating the village commons, or tribal territory — updated to the New Age, and corporately administered as a Community Land Trust.

revolution on the road to individual freedom must be over the distribution of unearned increments of wealth derived from the community's failure to collect economic rent from land and natural resources. But in this coming economic revolution, care must be taken to free people's individual incentive by reducing taxes on individual and corporate profits from private labor services and business ventures. Taxes on wages are tantamount to slavery, and therefore, in principle, odious and unfair.

Unfortunately, the confusion over ownership of nature-given resources is widespread, even in some Community Land Trusts. Since CLTs are intended for human use, and not just for preservationist purposes, considerations are usually made in the leases for homes and other improvements. But some CLT lease contracts refer to these improvements without distinguishing between ownership of the improvements and leaseholder use rights to the land itself. This practice does not acknowledge that improvements are properly the subject of commerce, should belong to the builders or subsequent owners, and should be totally under their control, except for ecological and other abuse restrictions.

The CLT, as a land steward, has no legitimate interests in living arrangements, housing, or improvements — except for the impact on the land itself and the possible impact on col-lection of economic rent from the land users. Since improvements are not to be considered when determining the economic rent and setting lease fees, agreements in the lease concerning improvements should be separated from agreements about use of land and natural resources. Mixing these agreements contributes to a general confusion, making it more difficult for people to differentiate individually owned improvements on CLT leaseholds from individual land use rights on those leaseholds.

ACCESS TO LAND, HOUSING, AND LOW-COST HOUSING

Some Community Land Trusts have used the CLT as a vehicle for providing low-cost housing, demonstrating that the trust concept can also be used to discourage speculation on housing. Of course low-cost, subsidized housing should be provided by organizations with that goal. But such organizations would be more accurately described as housing or development trusts.

There is inherent conflict in CLTs subsidizing user fees for leaseholders. Access to land, and even low-cost access, may in some cases be a by-product of the Community Land Trust. However, leaseholder subsidies deprive wider community members of their fair share of the economic rent, or unearned increment, which is in direct conflict with CLT objectives.

CONCLUSION

The Community Land Trust is a long-range solution to many problems, such as poverty amidst plenty, urban blight, unfair and unequal distribution of unearned land rentals, and the disincentive created by taxing human effort. Yet effective CLT administration requires a complex and dynamic three-way balance between leaseholder use rights, distribution of fluctuating unearned wealth to the wider community, and involvement of representatives of the entire community in farsighted, ecologically sensitive land stewardship.

CLT Resources from the School of Living

The School of Living will conduct workshops and seminars and meet with people interested in Community Land Trust organizing throughout the Mid-Atlantic. Contact: *School of Living*, Rt 1 Box 185 A, Cochranville PA 19330, 215-593-6988 or 2346 ❖

The Idea of Owning Land

by Robert Gilman

The idea of owning land is an old notion forged by the sword that is quietly undergoing a profound transformation. However natural "owning" land may seem in our culture, it is a fairly recent invention in the long sweep of human existence. Where did this notion come from? What does it really mean to "own" land? Why do we, in our culture, allow a person to draw lines in the dirt and then have almost complete control over what goes on inside those boundaries? What are the advantages, disadvantages, and alternatives? How is contemporary culture redefining the "ownership" connection between people and the land?

These questions are unfamiliar, perhaps even uncomfortable, to much of our society, for our sense of "land ownership" is so deeply embedded in our fundamental cultural assumptions that some of us never stop to consider its implications or alternatives. Most people are aware of only two choices, two patterns, for land ownership — private ownership, associated with free-enterprise Western countries; and state ownership, as in communist countries.

Both these patterns are full of problems and paradoxes. Private ownership enhances personal freedom for those who are owners. But it frequently leads to vast concentrations of wealth. For instance, in the United States, 75 percent of the privately owned land is held by 5 percent of the private landholders. Such concentration effectively denies freedom and power to those without great wealth. In communist countries state ownership dampens great differences in wealth and some of the abuses of individualistic ownership, but these advantages are often lost to other abuses, such as unresponsive bureaucratic control and corruption.

PREHISTORIC ROOTS

Human feelings about ownership have very deep roots. Tribal groups are connected to particular territories — places that are "theirs." Yet their attitude toward the land is very different from ours. Tribal people frequently speak of the land as their parent or as a sacred being, on whom they are dependent and to whom they owe loyalty and service. Among the aboriginals of Australia, individuals inherit a special relationship to sacred places, but rather than "ownership," this relationship is more like being "owned by" the land. This sense of responsibility extends to ancestors and future generations as well. The Ashanti of Ghana say, "Land belongs to a vast family of whom many are dead, a few are living, and a countless host are still unborn."

For many of these tribal peoples, their sense of "land ownership" involves only the right to use the land and to exclude members of other tribes. But usually they do not exclude members of their own tribe. If there are any private land rights, these are usually subject to review by the tribe as a group, and would cease if the land were no longer being used. The sale of land is either not a possibility or not permitted. As for inheritance, every person has use rights simply by membership in the tribe; so a young person does not have to wait until some other individual dies, or a special fee is paid, before gaining full access to the land.

EARLY AGRICULTURAL CIVILIZATIONS

Farming made the human relationship to the land more concentrated. Tilling the land, and making permanent settlements, meant a greater direct investment in a particular place. Yet this did not lead immediately to our present ideas of ownership. As best as is known, early farming communities continued to experience an intimate spiritual connection to the land, and they often held land in common under the control of a village council. This community land ownership pattern remains to this day in many peasant communities throughout the world.

It was not so much farming directly, but the development of multi-tribal agricultural civilizations that led to major changes in attitude toward the land. Some of the early civilizations were centralized around supposedly godlike rulers, who personalized the tribal idea that "the land belongs to the gods." While this was still a form of common land

Robert Gilman is Editor of *In Context*, a quarterly magazine for exploring what is involved in a humane, sustainable culture — and how to get there. The following article has been adapted from a previously published version (Copyright, Winter 1984, *In Context*, Bainbridge Island WA 98110, reprinted by permission).

The human–human power struggle is hardly the only, or even the most important, issue in our relationship to the land. Whatever happened to the tribal concerns about caring for the land and preserving it for future generations? What about issues like justice, human empowerment and economic efficiency? How about the rights of the land itself?

ownership, privileges of use and control were distributed to emerging ruling elites on the basis of custom and politics.

In such centralized civilizations, land took on a new meaning for the ruling elites as time went on. It became an abstraction, a source of power and wealth, a tool for purposes other than agriculture. The human-human struggle for power gradually came to be the dominant factor shaping the human relationship to the land. This shift, from seeing the land as sacred mother to seeing it as a means to gaining power, required deep changes throughout these cultures. Even the homes of the gods and sacred beings were moved. From hallowed and mysterious places on the land, the gods were moved into the sky where they could be as conveniently mobile as the ever-changing boundaries of the civilizations.

The idea of private land ownership developed as a second step — partly in reaction to the power of the ruler, or sovereign, and partly in response to the opportunities of a multi-tribal economy. The privileges of the ruling elites, or nobility, were often easily withdrawn at the whim of the sovereign, and the importance of politics and raw power as the basis of ownership was rarely forgotten. To guard their power, the nobility frequently pushed for greater legal and customary recognition of their land rights.

Private ownership also developed in response to the break-down of village cohesiveness in the less centralized societies and in the occasional democracies and republics of this period.

By the early days of Greece and Rome, common tribal or village land, state or sovereign land, and private land all had strong traditions behind them. Plato and Aristotle both discussed various mixtures of private and state ownership in ideal societies, Aristotle upholding the value of private ownership as a means of protecting diversity.

TAKING A FRESH LOOK

But the human-human power struggle is hardly the only, or even the most important, issue in our relationship to the land. Whatever happened to the tribal concerns about caring for the land and preserving it for future generations? What about such issues as justice, human empowerment and economic efficiency? How about the rights of the land itself? If we are to move forward toward a more planetary, ecological age, these questions and issues need to be integrated into our relationship with the land. To do this we will have to step outside the narrow circle of ideas and arguments of the past.

"Land ownership" has been discussed as if it were an obvious, clear-cut concept: Either you own and control something or you don't. For most people this has been a useful approximation. But the details of land ownership in the contemporary world are not so simple. As surprising as it may seem, our legal system has developed an understanding of "owning" that is significantly different from our common beliefs. This legal understanding holds potential for a much more appropriate human relationship with the land in the future.

LAND OWNERSHIP IS A BUNDLE OF RIGHTS

"Land ownership" is in fact a whole group of legal rights that can be held by one or more persons with respect to some specific piece of land. In Western countries, this bundle of land ownership rights usually includes the rights to: 1) use or not use; 2) exclude others from using; 3) irreversibly change; 4) sell, give away or bequeath; 5) rent or lease; 6) retain all rights not specifically granted to others; 7) retain these rights without time limit or review. These land rights are usually not absolute, for with them go certain responsibilities, such as paying taxes, being liable for suits brought against the land, and abiding by the laws. If these laws include zoning ordinances, building codes and environmental protection regulations, the rights to use and irreversibly change the land are limited. Nevertheless, within a wide range land owners hold near-sovereign rights over their land.

YET — NO ONE OWNS THE LAND

Each piece in this bundle of land ownership rights can be modified independently of the others, either by law or by

Oakwood Farm/Emissaries

"owners," all of whom will have a claim on some aspect of "your" land.

The land ownership debate is shifting away from rigid state-vs.-individual battles, to the much more flexible question of who should have which land rights. This shift in land ownership practices could be as important to society as the major improvement in governance that came with the shift away from monolithic powers, when sovereigns were forced to share power with semi-independent legislative, executive and judicial institutions.

LEGITIMATE INTERESTS: INDIVIDUAL, COMMUNITY, PLANETARY

A humane, sustainable culture must recognize the legitimate interests of the immediate users of the land, both households and businesses, as well as the local community, and the planetary community, including future generations and all of life. Some of the interests of these groups are:

Immediate users — owners, leaseholders and non-humans — need the freedom to be personally or corporately expressive, creative, and perhaps even eccentric. They need to be able to invest energy and caring into the land with reasonable security that their use of the land will not be arbitrarily taken away and that the full equity value of improvements made on the land will be available to them either through continued use or through resale should they choose to move.

The local community needs optimal use of the land within it. It needs protection from land being arbitrarily held out of use by absentee landlords. The local community needs to benefit from land equity increases caused by overall development of the community, and the community needs security that its character will not be forced to change through inappropriate land use decisions made by those outside the community or those leaving the community.

The planetary community, including future generations and all of life, needs sustainable use practices — the as-

the granting of an easement, or legal restriction, in favor of some other party. In some cases, a bewildering variety of legal conditions develops, challenging the very concept of ownership.

At this point, an important distinction can be made. In spite of the way we normally talk, no one ever "owns land" in the absolute sense. In our legal system you can own rights to land, but you can't own the land itself. You can't even own all of the bundle of land rights, since the state always retains the right of eminent domain.

For example, assume you are forced to grant an easement to the power company allowing it to run power lines across your land. Then it owns rights granted in that easement, but you own most of the other rights — unless the mineral rights, timber rights or other considerations were sold by previous owners. In that case the land rights are divided among several surance that ecosystems and topsoil that have been developed over hundreds of thousands of years will not be casually destroyed; that the opportunities for life will be enhanced; that all non-renewable resources will be used efficiently and for long-term beneficial purposes. The planetary community also needs meaningful recognition that the Earth is our common heritage.

Is it possible to blend these various interests in a mutually supportive way, rather than seeing them locked in a power struggle? The answer, fortunately, is yes. Perhaps the best developed legal form that does this is called a land trust.

THREE TYPES OF LAND TRUSTS

A land trust is a non-governmental organization, frequently a non-profit corporation, that divides land ownership rights between immediate users and their wider communities. Land trusts administer land in a number of places around the world including India, Israel, Tanzania, and the United States. Of the many types of land trusts, three will be described: conservation land trusts, community land trusts, and stewardship land trusts.

In a *conservation land trust*, the purpose is generally to preserve some aspect of the natural environment. A conser-

STEWARDSHIP TRUSTS

by Timothy Clark

One of the models for a stewardship land trust divides ownership of land between two legal entities, two distinct groups of people. One group, the stewards, may inhabit the land and hold title as long as they care for the land according to the covenants and the land stewardship plan. If they fail to do so, ownership of the land reverts to the second group, the land trust board of trustees, who monitor the interaction between the stewards and the land to ensure that the provisions of the trust are fulfilled.

The trustees can be any ecologically skilled and sensitive group that is capable and willing to work with the stewards to create a land stewardship plan, monitor its implementation, and find new stewards in the event that the current ones fail to fulfill the trust agreements. This method more completely ensures the intent and

duration of the trust than if only one group were responsible for the land.

The relationship between the stewards and the trustees is an important and delicate one — yet also fruitful. There is much room for differences in judgment between the two groups. The stewards, through living on the land, may have a greater sensitivity and awareness of it. On the other hand, stewards will have more personal desires attached to land use, and may be tempted to overlook aspects important to the well-being of the land. Recognizing the potential for differences, land trust documents provide for processes to resolve conflicts cooperatively. However, it is our experience that, rather than differences, the partnership between the stewards and the trustees results in a deeper understanding of how best to steward the land.

Timothy Clark was formerly active in Turtle Island Earth Stewards (TIES), an organization which worked with five communities to understand and practice land stewardship. [For more information about TIES see the Resources section.]

vation trust may do this by the full ownership of some piece of land that it holds as wilderness, or it may simply hold "development rights" to an undeveloped piece of land. When the original owner sells or grants development rights to the conservation trust, an easement is placed on the land title that prevents the owners or any future owners from developing the land without the agreement of the conservation trust. The conservation trust then holds these rights with the intention of maintaining the land in an undeveloped state. *The Trust For Public Land* [116 New Montgomery St., 4th Floor, San Francisco CA 91405, (415)495-4014] helps community groups establish conservation and agricultural land trusts.

A *community land trust* (CLT) has as its purpose removing land from the speculative market and making it available to those who will use it for the long-term benefit of the wider community. A CLT generally owns full title to its lands and grants long-term, renewable leases to those who will actually use the land. Appropriate uses are determined by the CLT in a process comparable to public planning or zoning. Lease fees vary from one CLT to another, but they are generally more than taxes and insurance, yet less than typical mortgage payments. The leaseholders have many of the use and security rights normally associated with ownership. They own the buildings on the land and can take full benefit from improvements they make on the land. They cannot, however, sell the land, nor can they usually rent or lease it to others without the consent of the trust. The *Institute for Community Economics* [see Resources section] is one of the major support groups for the creation of community land trusts in both urban and rural settings.

The *stewardship land trust* combines features of both the conservation trust and the CLT, and is being used now primarily by intentional communities and non-profit groups such as schools. The leaseholders using the land, the stewards, may pay less than in a normal CLT, but there are more definite expectations about their care and use of the land. *Turtle Island Earth Stewards* (TIES) is a resource group for stewardship land trusts [see sidebar and Resources section].

In each type of land trust, the immediate users (non-human as well as human) have clear rights which satisfy their legitimate use needs. The needs of the local community and the planetary community are met through representation, along with the leaseholders, on a board of trustees which administers general land use standards. Of course, land trusts are limited by the integrity and the attitudes of the people involved. Even so, by dividing ownership into "stewardship" for leaseholders and "trusteeship" for wider community representatives, land trusts are pioneering an approach that integrates the legitimate interests of the individual with those of society and the rest of the natural world. ❖

We need to recognize that the immediate user of the land (be that a household or a business), the local community, the planetary community, future generations, and all of life, all have legitimate interests.

(*In Context: A Quarterly of Humane Sustainable Culture*, is available for $18 per year, $25 surface or $36 air mail outside USA, from Context Institute, Box 11470, Bainbridge Island WA 98110, Visa/Mastercard accepted.)

Bibliography

Chaudhuri, Joyotpaul, "Possession, Ownership and Access: A Jeffersonian View", *Political Inquiry*, 1-1, Fall 1973.

Denman, D.R., *The Place of Property*, London: Geographical Publications Ltd., 1978.

Institute for Community Economics, *Community Land Trust Handbook*, Emmaus PA: Rodale Press, 1982.

International Independence Institute, *The Community Land Trust* (Cambridge MA: Center for Community Economic Development, 1972).

Macpherson, C.B., *Property: Mainstream and Critical Positions* (Toronto: Univ. of Toronto Press, 1978).

Schlatter, Richard, *Private Property: The History of an Idea* (New Brunswick NJ: Rutgers Univ. Press, 1951).

Scott, William B., *In Pursuit of Happiness: American Conceptions of Property* (Bloomington: Indiana University Press, 1977).

Tully, James, *A Discourse On Property: John Locke And His Adversaries* (Cambridge: Cambridge University Press, 1980).

Land Trusts Offer American Land Reform

by Jim Naureckas

All across the U.S., housing advocates are trying to bring about a quiet revolution in the way land and home ownership are looked at. In response to the housing crunch, neighborhoods in Atlanta, Minneapolis, New York and dozens of other cities have formed urban Community Land Trusts as a way for residents to cushion the inflationary pressures of speculation in their gentrifying neighborhoods.

A community land trust (CLT) is more complex than the standard legal trust: it's a non-profit corporation that owns land. The CLT land is leased for residential use on a long-term basis, but the CLT retains title to the land itself as a hedge against speculation and ecological abuse. By leasing land, people with lower incomes can then better afford to own a home, since the price of the land often accounts for more than a quarter of the price of housing.

Some urban CLTs may take further action to ease pressures on housing costs. The CLT can lease the land to the homeowner with an anti-speculative condition, so that when a home built on trust land is resold, the sale price will not be more than the original cost, adjusted for economic inflation, plus the labor and materials value of any improvements made on the home. Thus, the CLT can blunt the paradox of urban renewal, in which improvements to a low-income neighborhood drive up dwelling costs and eventually drive poorer residents out of the community.

According to the Institute for Community Economics (ICE), an organization in Massachusetts that serves as a godparent to many urban CLTs (see Resources section), the CLT concept is based on the idea that the community has an economic interest in private land and housing. "All property is a public-private partnership," says Chuck Matthei, executive director of ICE. The value of a house depends not only on the private costs of building it, but also on the public's investment in neighborhood streets, schools, and public services. In ICE's view, if the value of a house and lot increases because the public has put money into improving a neighborhood, that increased value should not necessarily act to inflate the resale cost when an individual house changes hands.

The idea of community is reflected in the way a CLT is governed: typically, one-third of a Community Land Trust's board members will reside on land leased from the trust, while the other two-thirds come from local organizations and the community at large. This setup is intended to make the CLT more stable than ordinary residential cooperatives, where rising property values place residents under pressure to dissolve the co-op and sell the land for individual gain.

Some people criticize Community Land Trusts for infringing on the free-enterprise right to speculate. Others have questioned the CLTs' focus on ownership, noting that those who need housing most desperately could not afford to buy even a subsidized house.

But CLTs sell any dwellings purchased with the land to the individuals or groups leasing the land. Land trust advocates believe that continuing the option of private home ownership is important for maintaining the stability of the community. They also note that for most people home ownership is the only feasible form of long-term investment. By selling homes on leased land, CLTs are able to substantially reduce the cost of home ownership. Anti-speculation clauses can act to maintain the reduced costs for future owners. Some urban CLTs, in order to increase the number of people who can participate, lease land for multi-unit apartment buildings in addition to single-family houses. Residents of those apartments usually own the building cooperatively. By curbing land and housing speculation, home ownership costs can be maintained at reduced levels for this and future generations.

GROWING NUMBER OF CLTs

The Community Land Trust concept dates back to the '60s. As of November 1989, Julie Orvis of ICE reports they are in

Jim Naureckas was a reporter for *In These Times* when he wrote the original version of this article.
(Copyright, August 1988, *In These Times,* Chicago, Illinois, reprinted by permission.)

contact with 52 operating urban Community Land Trusts across the country, which provide land for about 1,100 dwelling units. There are 38 more urban CLTs in formation that have not yet purchased land. Development of housing on urban CLTs is expected to accelerate as state and local governments begin to appreciate the urban CLT as a stabilizing influence in the growing housing crisis.

Rising housing costs and interest rates have made home ownership impossible even for many in the middle class. Less publicized is the developing crisis in low-income housing, where rent restrictions on millions of units subsidized by the federal government in the 60s are coming to the end of their 15- or 20-year terms.

Yet at the same time that the need for housing assistance is growing, the federal budget deficit pushes interest rates up and makes home financing almost impossible. "The amount of public money is so much less (today) that people are acutely aware of the need to reuse and recycle what resources there are," says the ICE's Andrew Baker. In the Community Land Trust, says Matthei, "the investment you make to provide affordable housing is preserved when the housing is transferred from owner to owner."

Land trusts are gaining support from various levels of government. U. S. Representative Joseph Kennedy (D-MA), for instance, has introduced legislation mandating the federal government to spend $500 million on programs like land trusts that provide long-term affordability in private housing. The State of Vermont has appropriated $20 million to support land purchases by CLTs and conservation land trusts — legislation pushed by a surprising alliance between housing and environmental advocates. Many municipal governments have also played active roles in forming or supporting both types of land trusts. Governor Dukakis' Office of Community and Development was an important help to developing land trusts in Massachusetts, which has more CLTs than any other state.

RADICAL IMPLICATIONS

The wide base of support for what Matthei describes as "a kind of American land reform" is surprising given the somewhat radical implications. Proponents talk about "decommodification," of changing the way people look at land and housing — not as a commodity for speculation and exploitation, but as a resource to be shared. Land trusts counterbalance the American taboo about inviolability of private property by stressing the historic social rights of the community, successor to the agrarian village and nomadic tribe.

CLTs also serve to provide their communities with clout. "Community Land Trusts are more than benevolent real estate businesses," Matthei says. "They're social and political

The urban land trust is designed to avoid the paradox of urban renewal in which improvements to a low-income neighborhood drive real estate values up and eventually drive poorer residents out of the community.

organizations." Often formed in communities that have histories of community action on issues like rent control, the CLT provides a vehicle through which residents can assert a role in planning neighborhood development.

So far land trusts have made few property developers nervous. "Social ownership is not fundamentally threatening," says Baker, "so long as it is applied only to the poor and those locked out of the housing market."

But with its early signs of success in the housing arena, the CLT is now being looked to as a solution for other problems. Some communities are organizing farm land trusts to protect agricultural land from development. Technical support and financial contacts for this effort are provided by *American Farmland Trust*, 1920 N Street, NW, Suite 400, Washington D.C., 202-659-5170. Other communities form land trusts to save valuable conservation areas or industrial sites when companies pull out of town. As of 1990 there are over 800 land trusts in the United States according to the *Land Trust Alliance*, 900 17th Street, NW, Suite 410, Washington D.C., 202-785-1410.

As the land trust movement grows, it will continue to face legal challenges from dissatisfied leaseholders and real estate interests. The task for the future is to demonstrate in the marketplace and in the courts, possibly with the passage of new legislation, that CLTs provide the legal basis for a kind of semi-public ownership of land, balancing private rights and community interests, in a stable, economical land tenure system. ❖

(*In These Times*, the weekly economics newspaper, may be contacted at 2040 N. Milwaukee, Chicago IL 60647, 312-772-0100.)

Residential Land Trust Organizing

The School of Living, Community Service, Inc. and the Land Trust Movement

by Dan Questenberry

For decades the School of Living (SoL), founded in 1936 by Ralph Borsodi, and Community Service, Inc (CSI), founded in 1940 by Arthur Morgan, have been engaged in economic and land reform initiatives and public education concerning decentralist culture — currency and tax reform, organic agriculture, and small community development including homesteading and intentional community. In more recent years, these issues have also been the focus of the Institute for Community Economics and the Schumacher Society, both founded by Bob Swann, a younger associate of Morgan and Borsodi.

CSI publishes the *CSI Newsletter* and a mail-order book catalog, and hosts annual fall conferences in Yellow Springs, Ohio. SoL publishes *Green Revolution* and a mail-order book list, hosts annual conferences each spring, and periodically co-sponsors the international Fourth World Assemblies. But these alternative institutions have interests far beyond their public education work. For the past half-century SoL and CSI have founded and provided administrative support for decentralist intentional communities. These intentional communities are designed to demonstrate the practical economics of land reform based on the Single Tax theories of Henry George and his predecessors, the classical Scottish economist Adam Smith, and Thomas Paine, the pamphleteer of the American Revolution.

School of Living Land Trust Alliance: Birthright, Common Ground & Heathcote

In 1976, the School of Living expanded its bylaws to create legal and administrative provisions for an alliance of local land trusts in the Mid-Atlantic region of the U. S. The SoL now acts as a landholding company for community land trusts (CLTs) occupied by Birthright Homesteads PA and two intentional communities, Heathcote MD and Common Ground VA. Another CLT held by the School near York PA was vacated in the early '80s when the Deep Run Farm intentional community dissolved. After failing to attract new resident trustees for that CLT, Deep Run was sold and the assets used to create SoL's Land Trust Fund. In this way the Deep Run community, upon its dissolution, became the first independent CLT to recycle its land value back into the wider land trust movement.

SoL administers the $160,000 Land Trust Fund to provide initial or bridging financing for land purchases by community land trusts used by homesteaders, intentional communities and businesses. SoL currently provides financial support to its own regional CLT alliance, as well as the Ozark Regional Land Trust and the Community Land Trust of the Southern Berkshires, which is associated with the Schumacher Society.

The SoL Land Trust Alliance provides homesteaders, communitarians and businesses, both rural and urban, with the opportunity to maintain their land for the benefit of longer-

---

Dan Questenberry, a resident of Shannon Farm since 1976, is treasurer of the School of Living, a Mid-Atlantic regional Community Land Trust with holdings that include land under the stewardship of two intentional communities — Common Ground in the Virginia Blue Ridge and Heathcote Center in suburban Maryland. During his childhood vacations Dan took for granted the sense of personal security and rootednesss provided by a paternal family farm in Alabama's Black Belt region, and a maternal family ranch in the central Texas hill country. After both family homes were sold, it took several years for Dan to become conscious of the losses and realize the significance of family land to his sense of personal identity. While re-establishing a personal land base in Woodstock Nation during the Cultural Changes of the '70s, Dan was influenced by Native American land use values and the historic land reform concepts of Henry George (who first noted the anti-social nature of land speculation). Dan is coordinating features editor for this directory, and an active member of the Fellowship for Intentional Community, InterCommunities of Virginia, Communal Studies Association, and Community Educational Service Council. His other interests include family life in community, new member integration, movement organizing, local/global intentional community development, and politics.

Mel Leisure/Common Ground, VA

The sweat lodge at Common Ground

term land reform and keep it, or its value, from fueling speculation in the land market. In fact, CLTs in central Massachusetts are experiencing such growth that ultimately they expect to reduce the speculative margin on the wider land market in their region. In this manner vision becomes reality in land tenure reform.

Over the years land trust operations and assistance to other land trust developers have been a major SoL emphasis involving a wide diversity of intentional communitarians and urban and rural homesteaders interested in land reform activism. Sitting on the SoL board of trustees are current and former communitarians from Common Ground VA, Deep Run Farm PA, Heathcote MD, Shannon Farm VA, Twin Oaks VA, and the Yoga Center of Rochester NY, as well as homesteaders and other activists with a range of professional backgrounds. The School willingly provides assistance in creating independent trusts apart from SoL's regional CLT. However, emphasis is placed on development of CLTs for ecologically conscious residential and business use, rather than for uninhabited conservation preserves.

The Community Service, Inc., Land Trust now holds title to one piece of land, that used by The Vale, an intentional community in Yellow Springs, Ohio. However, the CSI board is interested in serving as a holding company for other land trusts in the Ohio region.

Land Trust Originators:
Adam Smith, Thomas Paine & Henry George

As land reform institutions, SoL and CSI are based on the ancient land tenure beliefs that have always been common in Native American and other original cultures. As expounded by SoL founder Ralph Borsodi, land and other natural resources, just as human beings, "cannot be morally owned...because none of these...come into existence as a result of human labor." In *The Wealth of Nations*, the classical Scottish economist Adam Smith advocated limiting government taxes to a single source, land value. As a decentralist, he noted that economic growth would be stimulated by freeing improvements, labor income and capital from taxation. Adam

Smith also observed that such a limited, single source tax base would restrict the warmaking power of central governments.

Smith's concepts, and those of the U. S. revolutionary Thomas Paine, were popularized in the anti-speculative Single Tax theories of Henry George, whose best known book, *Progress and Poverty*, was published in many languages and widely read throughout the world around the turn of this century. Beginning in the 1890s, a number of intentional communities were founded in this country based on Single Tax theory. Of that number, several still exist today, including Arden DE and Fairhope AL, which are both now approaching 100 years of age. These historic communities serve as points of origin for the modern land trust movement.

The Henry George School of Social Science in New York City continues to develop and teach Georgist economics, while the associated Henry George Institute promotes the development of Single Tax initiatives. The Institute also monitors the progress of many related tax reform programs, including those in Pittsburgh, Scranton and five other Pennsylvania cities, Southfield MI, San Diego CA, most municipalities in Australia and New Zealand, and the entire nation of Denmark. The Council of Georgist Organizations, also headquartered in New York, coordinates these organizations and related institutions in Chicago, San Francisco, Los Angeles and other places around the Earth.

Georgist Principles vs. Federal
Bureaucracy at Liberty Homesteads

The ideas of Henry George and Thomas Paine were central to the land reform theories of SoL founder Ralph Borsodi. He

Land reform and the related issues of decentralism, small community development, organic agriculture, currency and tax reform have been serious economic issues for many years. With the looming crisis of accelerated centralization in land ownership and economic control, the work of land trusts and decentralists becomes ever more vital.

and his wife, Myrtle Mae Simpson, moved out of New York City in 1920 to began homesteading in nearby Suffern, New York. Borsodi published three books about their experiences and his related land reform visions, culminating with *This Ugly Civilization* in 1928. As those years passed the Borsodis hosted an ever-widening group of neighborhood decentralists at their homesteads, first Sevenacres and then Dogwood Homestead. This group of friends later founded Bayard Lane, the first of a new generation of intentional communities based on the Georgist land reform principles of the 1890s Single Tax colonies.

But before Bayard Lane was started, Ralph Borsodi was asked to come to Dayton, Ohio, in 1932 and help that city's Council of Social Agencies organize the first public CLT, Liberty Homesteads. Borsodi's books promoting land reform, homesteading and decentralism had prompted the Council's Unit Committee to retain him as a consultant to help organize a suburban homestead "colony" for city dwellers hard pressed by the Depression. Liberty Homesteads was chartered as a land trust with leases for individual homesteaders according to non-speculative, Georgist principles.

A 160-acre farm was purchased three miles from Dayton and laid out in 50 three-acre plots. The old farm buildings were rehabilitated as a community center, and within a few months 35 families were building homes and planting crops on their own leaseholds. Initial funding was generated by a local bond issue.

However, contrary to Borsodi's pleas for continuing a decentralist approach, the Council sought additional financing for expansion from the federal government instead of broadening the original base of users' fees, bond issues and other local financing. The Roosevelt Administration had allocated $25 million for the promotion of homesteading. So federal funds were provided by the Subsistence Homestead Division of the Department of Interior under Secretary Harold Ickes. By the end of 1933, $309,000 in federal funds had been lent to the Council for the purpose of developing the first of a ring of 50 homestead colonies around Dayton.

Then, in the spring of 1934, despite specific prior agreements with the Council, Secretary Ickes "federalized" Liberty Homesteads along with all of the other homesteading projects that the Department of Interior was financing. The resulting confusion, delays, increased administrative costs, and loss of control at the local level brought the program to a standstill within a few months. Borsodi said, "After a brave beginning, the palsied hand of bureaucracy had been laid upon it." And "Within a few years abandonment of the subsistence homestead projects began. With but few exceptions, they were incontinental failures (lacking in self restraint) and very appropriately they were finally turned over to the United States Department of Agriculture for liquidation."

**Early SoL Communities:
Bayard Lane, Bryn Gweled & Tanguy**

In 1936 the Borsodis and their friends around Suffern established the School of Living to teach what they had been learning about organic agriculture, homesteading, intentional community design, and other decentralist issues. The purpose of SoL was, and still is, adult education for decentralist lifestyles, ethical economic and land tenure patterns, and co-operative individualism.

An initial project of SoL was the establishment of the Bayard Lane intentional community on 40 acres of land near Suffern. A Dutch colonial structure housed the community center and SoL on four acres surrounded by two-acre family homesteads. Resident members participated in cooperative policy-making, leased homesteads from the community, and paid a modest "economic rent" as conceived in Single Tax theory.

In 1945, after nine years, Bayard Lane was sold as a result of financial problems and land tenure disputes. But well before that, in 1939-40, SoL provided conceptual assistance to some American Friends Service Committee staffers in founding Bryn Gweled Homesteads near Philadelphia. In 1945 Tanguy Homesteads was established, also near

Philadelphia. Both of these intentional communities continue as vital, co-operative land trust ventures to this day. Bryn Gweled and Tanguy continue to share common cause with SoL, placing emphasis on low-cost housing, racial integration, and religious and political diversity.

Leaseholders at Bryn Gweled ("City on a Hill" in Welsh) pay annual lease assessments based on the original 1940 land appraisal of their individual homesteads. During the past 50 years, nearby property costs have skyrocketed from $64 per acre to $6,400. Regardless of the value of the improvements on Bryn Gweled leaseholds, which may range from none to a small $10,000 cottage to an expansive $200,000 home, individual lease assessments are based solely on the land use value. Bryn Gweled has demonstrated the modern workability of Georgist principles in the development of an intentional community with 75 dwellings on 230 acres. Single Tax values have enabled this pioneering group to maintain a wide range of diversity in personal and family incomes and lifestyles. In fact, membership diversity is a primary factor distinguishing Bryn Gweled and Tanguy Homesteads from the other suburban neighborhoods that have grown up around these now historic intentional communities.

CSI Communities:
Celo Land Trust & The Vale

During this same period, in 1937, Arthur Morgan, the first chairman of the Tennessee Valley Authority, helped found Celo Land Trust, an intentional community on 1,200 acres beneath Mount Mitchell, northeast of Asheville, North Carolina. (His son Ernest, a Congressional candidate on the Progressive Party ticket with Henry Wallace, lives at Celo now.) In 1940 Morgan founded Community Service, Inc., as a center where ideas and practices concerning the enhancement of small community life are developed and publicized. CSI work is based on the awareness that maintaining and creating the small community, in its many forms, is basic to the quality of our social evolution and cultural survival.

CSI is located near Dayton, in Yellow Springs, Ohio, where Arthur Morgan served as president of Antioch College and promoted the work-study program in advanced education. In 1961 his son Griscom and Griscom's wife, Jane, founded The Vale intentional community in Yellow Springs with community land placed in a trust administered by CSI. Community members at Celo and The Vale lease their homesteads on a lifetime basis with secure land tenure. Since community leaseholders are tenured land stewards, rather than owners, they do not hold personal land titles. This discourages individual speculation in lease transfers.

Griscom and Jane's children, Faith and John, and Ernest's daughter Jennifer continue the communitarian tradition of the

A good community will not be invented, discovered or "just grow." It must be forged from the purpose and quality of the lives of the people living in it.

— *Arthur Morgan*

Morgan family. Faith is secretary of CESCI and past treasurer of FIC (see below); John is an active member of the Raven Rocks community, founded in the early '70s on 1,000 acres near Beallsville, Ohio; and Jennifer is a resident of Celo.

Fellowship for Intentional Community & CESCI Business Loan Fund

In 1948 CSI established the Fellowship of Intentional Communities (FIC) as a forum for increasing interaction among all types of intentional communities and those seeking places among such groups. During the next four decades, annual Fellowship conferences were hosted by a variety of intentional communities throughout the northeast. In the early '60s the FIC conceived the Guidebook for Intentional Communities, including a listing of contemporary intentional communities. CSI continues to publish the Guidebook, while *Communities* magazine publishes the Directory of Intentional Communities.

During the 1954 conference at the Quaker community of Pendle Hill near Philadelphia, the Fellowship created the Homer Morris Fund to provide short-term financial assistance to intentional community businesses. Today the Homer Morris Fund, renamed the Community Educational Service Council, Inc. (CESCI), is a tax-exempt 501(c)(3) which recently completed its 100th community business loan. CESCI's board of directors includes communitarians from Common Ground, Shannon Farm, and Twin Oaks, all located in the central Virginia mountains. CESCI and FIC, usually meeting jointly, have expanded their historic northeastern base in recent years. CESCI now makes small loans (up to $3,000 to start) to community businesses from coast to coast. The FIC incorporated in 1986 with a slight name change to Fellowship for Intentional Community. Currently, in addition to a number of individual seekers, there are FIC members living in 24 communities across the continent, in both Canada and the United States. Recent board meetings have been hosted by intentional communities in the Midwest, on the Pacific Coast, and in the Mid-Atlantic region, as well as the traditional base area in the Northeast.

Mel Leisure/Common Ground, VA

*Common Ground, a land trust
in Virginia.*

Institute for Community Economics & Schumacher Society

After experiences as civil rights activists in Mississippi in the '60s, Marjorie and Bob Swann were seeking a means of enabling tenant farmers in this country and elsewhere to gain secure land tenure that could not be hornswoggled from them by unscrupulous real estate and financial interests. Swann had experience in the development of cooperative housing from work in his home town, Yellow Springs, where he knew Arthur Morgan. During World War II while in prison as a conscientious objector, Swann participated in a decentralist study course using as texts Morgan's *Small Community* and Borsodi's *Flight from the City*.

So in 1967 the Swanns sought the support of SoL when they joined with some New England academics to form the International Independence Institute. Now named the Institute for Community Economics (ICE) and headquartered in Greenfield, Massachusetts, ICE has experienced phenomenal success in teaching and promoting the methods of community land trusts, as well as assisting in the formation and development of these anti-speculative trusts in central Massachusetts and elsewhere.

ICE synthesized the CLT concept from the experiences of SoL, CSI, the Gandhian Gramdan of India, and the Jewish National Fund (JNF) of Israel, the latter being one of the oldest, largest and most successful land trust holding companies in the world. With land purchases beginning in 1890, the JNF provided agricultural lands for the well-known intentional communities called moshavim (co-ops) and kibbutzim (communes) in Israel and occupied Palestine. These Israeli co-ops and communes now include a quarter million residential members — 7 percent of the population of the entire country.

Bob Swann developed the concept of involving activists and technical experts from the wider community on land trust boards. In order to emphasize this wider participation in land trust policy-making, ICE-sponsored trusts are described as Community Land Trusts (CLTs). (In the ICE view, an intentional community land trust is actually a private trust if only resident communitarians and homesteaders are allowed to serve on the board of trustees.)

As ICE has evolved, the board of directors has not retained the basic Georgist concept of "economic rent." That is, the land rent charged to ICE trust leaseholders is less than the use value of their land. Theoretically, failure to collect the full use value encourages speculation — when a group of people congregates on a piece of land, the site value of the land goes up (in proportion to the increased industry, jobs and services created by the increased population).

Central to the land trust ideal is the belief that when a group increases the site value of their common land, the group should benefit as a whole, rather than individual members. Historically, this increase in site value, or economic rent, has been collected and used to finance common facilities — streets, parks, public buildings — and pay taxes on land, real estate and retail sales, hence the appellation Single Tax. Collection of full economic rent provides common funds for development as well as taxes. The Fairhope Single Tax Association provides paved streets, parks, public utilities and a full range of other municipal facilities.

In earlier years, it also built and maintained a ferry, a dock and a short-line railroad.

In order to get back to economic rent principles, Swann recently left ICE to help form the Schumacher Society, which is headquartered in the Berkshire Mountain town of Great Barrington, Massachusetts. Using CLT concepts, the Society is constructing low-cost houses in a new suburban land trust development, administering a loan fund for urban and suburban land trust purchases, and engaging in public education about land trusts, decentralization and currency reform.

The CLT is designed to avoid the organizational and financial obstacles experienced by some of the early private land trusts, such as Liberty Homesteads, Bayard Lane and many of the local Gramdan units. The difference in CLTs from earlier land trusts is that CLT residents do not comprise a majority on their boards of trustees. The innovative, quasi-public CLT boards of trustees are chartered to hold land in stewardship for all of humanity and the Earth as a whole, as well as the leaseholders residing on trust lands. ICE advocates that CLT boards be composed of one-third residents, one-third local and regional citizens who are not land residents, and one-third professional activists (such as land use planners, ecologists, economists, financiers, and legal and group process experts).

When local CLTs are allied in regional units, their residents can serve as trustees for each other's trust lands, acting to integrate the land reform movement across entire regions. Further, if local CLTs pool part of their growing economic rent in regional CLT alliances, a wider grass-roots financial base can be developed, providing for more secure growth at the local level as well as the purchase of land for new local trusts in the region.

There are now over 30 Community Land Trusts in North America, in addition to others on all of the inhabited continents of the Earth. Thus, this ancient/new land tenure concept has evolved into an attractive and adaptable land reform movement, both across time and across cultures.

Many North Americans do not realize that land ownership in the U.S. is concentrated among a small percentage of the population just as in most older countries. According to 1987 USDA census figures (quoted by Alanna Hartzok in *Green Revolution*, Winter 88) "In the USA today 3 percent of the population owns 95 percent of the private land, land values rise faster than wages, and the resulting maldistribution of wealth is securing the very conditions that our forefathers and mothers had hoped to escape" in their flight from the older countries.

Land reform and the associated issues of decentralism, small community development, organic agriculture, currency and tax reform have been serious economic issues for many years. Since the mid-'30s SoL, CSI and, more recently, ICE and the Schumacher Society have served as bases for substantive theoretical development linked closely with public education and creative reform projects on these issues. With the looming crisis of accelerated centralization in land ownership and economic control, the work of land trusts, and decentralists in general, becomes ever more vital to the quality of our social evolution, even our very cultural survival.

In 1975 at the age of 97 years, Arthur Morgan passed out of this dimension. He was followed two years later by Ralph Borsodi at age 91. For decades they stimulated Community Service, Inc., the School of Living and related organizations to engage in comprehensive, intellectually penetrating analysis and action for basic socioeconomic reform. Now the

The school should not be preparation for life, it should be life.

— *The School of Living*

current generation of theorists and activists in these organizations are implementing futuristic syntheses of the historic land and economic reform visions of George, Borsodi, Morgan and the Gramdan in the evolving New Age. ❖

Addresses of SoL, CSI and Related Organizations

Community Educational Service Council, Rt 2 Bx 343, Afton VA 22920, Peter Robinson, Treasurer, 804-361-2155/1417

Community Service, Inc. Box 243, Yellow Springs OH 45387, Jane Morgan, Director, 513-767-2161

Fellowship for Intentional Community, Center for Communal Studies, 8600 University Boulevard, Evanston IN 47712, Mary Hayden, 812-464-1719

Council of Georgist Organizations, 121 E. 30th St, New York 10017, Mark Sullivan, 212-889-8020

Inst. for Community Economics, 151 Montague Rd, Greenfield MA 01301, Chuck Matthei, Director, 413-774-7956

School of Living, Rt 1 Box 185 A, Cochranville PA 19330, Ginny Green, Director, 215-593-2346

Schumacher Society, Rt 3 Box 76, Great Barrington MA 01230, Bob Swann, Director, 413-528-1737

Bibliography

Alyea, P.E.& B.R. *Fairhope*, 1894–1954 University of Alabama Press, 1956.

Baedeker *Israel: The Ultimate Personal Tour Guide*, New York, Prentice Hall Press.

Borsodi, Ralph *The Challenge of Asia*, Melbourne FL, Melbourne Univ. Press, 1956.

Flight from the City, New York, Harper & Row Publishers, 1933.

George, Henry *Progress & Poverty*, New York, Schalkenbach Foundation, 1980.

Loomis, Mildred *Alternative Americas*, New York, Universe Books, 1982.

Morgan, Arthur *The Small Community*, Yellow Springs, Community Service, 1970, 1984.

The Community of the Future, Yellow Springs, Community Service, 1957.

Morgan, Griscom *Guidebook For Intentional Communities*, Yellow Springs, Community Service, 1988.

Shepard, Mark *Gandhi Today*, Arcata CA, Simple Productions, 1987.

Networking

How do communities build alliances and networks with each other, and what attracts separate groups into a movement?

*In **The Fellowship for Intentional Community: Building Together**, Laird Sandhill of Sandhill Farm reports on an inclusive North American network that offers alliance building, support services, and community referrals for a diversity of intentional communities and cooperative lifestyles. He examines the roots of the Fellowship and its relationship to the broad-based communities movement.*

*Laird next describes the values, objectives, and program of the **Federation of Egalitarian Communities**. This 14-year-old North American organization is based on principles of equality, participatory decision-making, total income sharing, ecological sanity, and commitment to process. The Federation offers special services for groups forming and others in the movement.*

*The **Emissary International Communities** share the philosophy and vision by which Emissaries live their lives, and through which they promote "integrity." There are several Emissary communities, and many affiliated organizations, which combine efforts through a global network for personal and social transformation.*

*In **Regional Organizing: Intercommunities of Virginia**, Isis Ringrose and Benjamin Brown of The Gathering recount the experiences of this network of 10 communities in central Virginia. The ICV has organized regular intercommunity gatherings, and has helped develop a network of friends — for sharing common interests and for exploring the unique differences in the "regional ecology of community."*

*Pam Dawling of Lifespan writes about **Rural Communes in Great Britain**. She describes some of the groups in the Communes Network which recently published* Diggers and Dreamers, *a directory of British communities.*

*Allen Butcher and Laird Sandhill's **Global Networking** reviews the past dozen years, looking at the experiences of the ICN (International Communes Network), which spans much of Europe, and the ICSA (International Communal Studies Association), which originated at a Kibbutz federation in Israel. They explore the divergent interests and orientations of the two groups, compare the experiences of North American networks, and suggest possibilities for the future of global networking.*

*In **Computer Searches for Communities Information**, Bill Pitt, a University of Maryland library professional who teaches librarians how to use computer data bases, shares his knowledge about using this sometimes intimidating technology. In an age of proliferating "computer networking", this is a tool which can help us sort through the overload of information.*

Organizing and communication is happening on many levels, in a variety of forms, and in diverse locales. While sometimes aided by high technology, the growing number of networks and interconnections within the movement attest to the power of what nurtures and sustains them — the person-to-person contact that all of us, as human beings, need.

Geoph Kozeny/Community Catalyst

Building Together:
The Fellowship for Intentional Community

by Laird Sandhill

This Directory represents the fruit borne of a seedling transplanted in the summer of 1986. At that time a small collection of community networkers met at Stelle, Illinois, to re-energize and expand the Fellowship of Intentional Communities (FIC), a relatively quiet network of Northeastern U.S. communities which had been meeting since 1948. At Stelle, we incorporated the FIC under the new name "Fellowship for Intentional Community," replanting it into the fertile soil of the continental communities movement.

Our intent was to build a viable continental organization based on our common values of cooperation, peaceful social transformation, individual initiative, and ecological alternatives. The time seemed ripe for building together.

What Does the Fellowship Do?

There was never any doubt that the Fellowship had work to do. Most intentional communities are working to develop living options which might meet the needs of many who are disillusioned with traditional society. At the same time, many communities are looking for new members. Unfortunately, most North Americans don't know that *any* intentional communities exist today, much less *hundreds* of them. There is a need for better outreach, for telling our story. Hence this Directory, and the Fellowship's Speakers Bureau [see sidebar below].

Communities come in all shapes and sizes, yet share many similar challenges, such as defining membership; succeeding financially and distributing resources fairly; making decisions in a way which feels good to all affected; rearing healthy and happy children; dividing work equitably; choosing an appropriate standard of living. Many also wrestle with questions about right livelihood, spiritual expression, carrying capacity of the land, and the role of service in our lives.

Despite such similar issues, many communities do not know much about what others are doing to answer these chal-

Laird Sandhill is Secretary for both the FIC and the Federation of Egalitarian Communities. During his networking travels around the continent, Laird has done much to develop new FIC contacts and strengthen existing relationships. He has been a member of Sandhill Farm since 1974. In addition to his involvement at home with raising and marketing organic foods, Laird's interests include parenting, facilitation training, outdoor recreation, and public speaking about community.

Need a Speaker on Intentional Community?

The Fellowship has created a referral network of communitarians with many years of experience in cooperative living and public speaking. Their presentations are suitable for lectures, panel discussions, round-table seminars, or the street corner of your choice. (They'll even bring their own soap box!) We can line up someone who cares about the whole community movement, or about the move to holistic health care;

We have people who can describe the intricacies of dealing with Aunt Bertha and traditional family values, or dealing with Uncle Sam and traditional economics;

We can talk about land bases and tenure, or discuss cooperative approaches and techniques of group process;

We can examine the challenge of active leadership in a community of equals, how life in community relates to political activism, or some of the exciting things being done to create new, more appropriate celebrations and rituals.

If this sounds like what you want to hear about, contact Fellowship headquarters and ask for a copy of the Speakers List.

123

Geoph Kozeny/Community Catalyst

FIC members enjoying a meal together at a conference in New Harmony, Indiana

Where to Start?

The first step was to develop an active Board with representation from across the continent, expanding from the Fellowship's traditional base in the Northeast [see History sidebar]. We worked to identify and involve the community people who had already focused movement energy and established connections — the veterans who had been working to make it happen regionally, or in their own communities. Creating a list of names was easy, but it was difficult getting these veterans together (see Member Roster sidebar).

After all, why would this organization be worth people's time? Our answer is that the communities movement is more mature now. Many communities have emerged from the pioneering stage and the days of hand-to-mouth economics. While starting communities are necessarily more absorbed with "how to survive," the more established communities have turned their attention to "how to thrive."

As a movement we are now more comfortable with our choices, and can better afford to spend time looking around at what our contemporaries are doing. We can invest in longer-term projects and broad-based organizations which promote our values.

How Does the Fellowship Operate?

We knew from the start that the Fellowship's strength and dynamism would depend directly on the Board of Directors' ability to build itself into an effective working unit. Based on our years of individual experience with community process, that meant establishing a pattern which supported full expression of views and led to decisions reflecting everyone's input.

In our first few Board meetings, we laid the foundation for how the Fellowship would conduct itself. We wrote bylaws, agreed to make decisions by consensus, and established a membership policy [see Participation sidebar].

There is also a personal advantage to Fellowship involvement. People with movement vision and energy often lack sufficient understanding and support for that aspect of their lives. In working with the Fellowship, our understanding of each other deepens, trust builds, and our meetings become much richer experiences than occasions for just doing business — our gatherings become opportunities to nurture each other and feed our dreams. In fact, the strength of the Fellowship is based on this multi-stranded web of personal connections.

lenges. There is a need to collect and organize this information, making it accessible so all may benefit from the hard work and successes of others. Hence this Directory, and the Fellowship's support of the Communal Studies Archives [see sidebar].

Communities are acutely aware of themselves as different from the mainstream culture, and many choose to highlight these differences. While virtually all communities share a common root value of cooperation, often that deep commitment is limited to only the immediate group.

The Fellowship believes that cooperation should extend beyond boundaries of membership, and even beyond the bounds of common values. For in the end we are all humans, all living on the same planet. We believe that developing a sense of "we" is not dependent on a contrasting sense of "them."

We are learning that differences can be a cause for celebration, and occasion for enrichment and growth. It is the Fellowship's work to help draw the circles of cooperation ever larger, and assist with the personal stretching this requires. Hence our open membership and open meetings.

Cleaning out the Attic? Don't Forget the Communal Studies Archives!

If you're cleaning out your community files, the Center for Communal Studies may want what you're planning to toss out. One reason the FIC selected the Center as its continental administrative office was that the University of Southern Indiana has made a commitment to archive a broad range of information documenting the history and visions of intentional communities. These archives are an obvious bridge linking contemporary communities, historic communities, and scholars interested in both.

Communitarians can benefit from these archives in two ways: first, there is the opportunity to learn from those who have gone before us, to see what others have done when faced with similar challenges; and second, there is the opportunity to increase exposure to your community's notable accomplishments and unique flavor. By contributing materials about your community, you may make it a little easier for those who follow to benefit from your experience.

The Fellowship urges all communities to send suitable archive materials to the Center, including any written documents (such as bylaws, membership agreements, property codes, behavior norms, etc.), newsletters, photos, videos, and selected correspondence. The Archives may be willing to pay for shipping of some materials, though this should be confirmed ahead of time. Submitted material will become the property of the University. Documents will be stored in acid-free containers and secured in a humidity- and temperature-controlled environment, to ensure that these treasures will be around for many years to come.

If there is a concern about confidentiality of the material's content, access can be limited to suit the donor's needs.

The Archives are here to be used, and the staff welcomes inquiries and visits from communitarians, researchers and the general public.

If you have materials to send or questions about the archives, please contact:

Gina Walker, Certified Archivist,
Center for Communal Studies, Box C,
8600 University Blvd., Evansville, IN 47712
(812) 464-1896

How You Can Participate
in the Fellowship

FIC meetings and activities are open. People who agree with Fellowship purposes, and who respect and encourage the freedom and creative initiative of each Fellowship member, are invited to attend meetings and participate in FIC activities.

You may join and support the Fellowship as an associate member. Associates (and others who send $15) receive notice of board meetings, periodic mailings, and annual calendars of public events sponsored by intentional communities throughout North America. Annual dues are:

Individual	$15
Community	$15 (under 10 members)
	$25 (10-50 members)
	$40 (over 50 members)
Organization	$25

The Fellowship is committed to being as inclusive as possible, and as such, associate membership is open to anyone. Information on full membership, a more intentional process, is available to all associate members. Often members of intentional communities or movement groups join first as individuals. Then, as they become more familiar with the Fellowship and its mission, they are encouraged to involve their home communities and support organizations.

Those interested in the Fellowship may contact us at:

Fellowship for Intentional Community
Box D, 8600 University Boulevard
Evansville, IN 47712
(812) 464-1719

❖

History of the Fellowship:
Old Wine in a New Bottle

Networks of intentional communities have been around for decades, and several have had connections with the Fellowship over the years. It's not possible to mention all of these contacts, but what follows is a summary outline of the main path.

1940 — Community Service, Inc. (CSI) is established by Arthur Morgan in Yellow Springs, Ohio, to counsel people about improving the quality of small-town life, and to aid the development of intentional communities.

1948 — Fellowship of Intentional Communities (FIC) is created at a CSI conference to provide annual forums for personal contact among intentional communities with meetings rotated among Northeastern communities.

1954 — FIC receives an endowment to create a revolving loan fund, now called the Community Educational Service Council, Inc. (CESCI), which provides financial assistance for intentional community businesses at lower than commercial rates.

1962 — FIC conceives and CSI publishes the Intentional Community Guidebook, a landmark directory of contemporary communities and related cooperative organizations.

1973 — Twin Oaks Community in Virginia begins publishing Communities magazine, which features a biennial directory of intentional communities.

1975 — National Historic Communal Studies Association (NHCSA) is organized to aid in the study of past and present intentional communities.

1976 — Center for Communal Studies (CCS) is established at the University of Southern Indiana in Evansville to provide administrative support for NHCSA and oversee the creation and development of an archives for the documents and memorabilia of intentional communities.

1979 — Communities magazines publishes "A Guide to Cooperative Alternatives," the most comprehensive directory of intentional communities and related organizations yet compiled.

1984 — Stelle Foundation becomes the publisher of Communities, with financial assistance from CESCI.

1986 — CESCI finances a project to re-energize and expand the Fellowship, leading to an August meeting at Stelle where the FIC is incorporated under the new name "Fellowship for Intentional Community." The name change signals an expanded purpose — the Fellowship actively reaches beyond its roots in the Northeast, and specifically invites participation from those who are not presently living in community but who are nonetheless interested in and supportive of community values. The incorporators include representatives of Communities magazine, CESCI, CCS and NHCSA, Federation of Egalitarian Communities (FEC), InterCommunities of Virginia (ICV), and School of Living.

1987 — The first FIC board meeting is convened at Stelle in May. The board agrees to meet twice a year, in spring and fall, with sites rotated around the continent. The fall meeting is held at East Wind, an FEC community in Missouri.

1988 — The spring FIC board meeting is held at Green Pastures, an Emissary community in New Hampshire. At this meeting the Directory is selected as the first major FIC project, to be co-published with Communities magazine. The fall meeting is held at Alpha Farm, an Oregon community affiliated with the Earth Communities Network.

1989 — The spring FIC board meeting is held at Shannon Farm, an ICV community in Virginia. The board agrees to establish a North American administrative office at CCS, and begins work on the Speakers Bureau. The fall meeting is held at New Harmony, Indiana, site of two historic communities from the 19th century, and near the CCS offices in Evansville.

1990 — NHCSA becomes the Communal Studies Association, reflecting balanced interest in both historic and contemporary communities. The spring FIC board meeting is held at Lost Valley, an Oregon community located on the site of Shiloh, former coordinating center for the Western Intentional Christian Communities.

❖ **FIC Member Communities**

Abode of the Message,
  New Lebanon, NY
Alpha Farm, Deadwood, OR
Camphill Village, Kimberton, PA
Casa Maria Catholic Workers,
  Milwaukee, WI
Celo Land Trust, Burnesville, NC
Center for the Examined Life,
  San Diego, CA
Communia, Iowa City, IA
Comptche Farms, Comptche, CA
Common Ground, Lexington, VA
Cooper St. Household, Vail, AZ
Currents, Glouster, OH
Dunmire Hollow, Waynesboro, TN
East Wind, Tecumseh, MO
Farm Home Center, Milwaukee, WI

The Farm, Summertown, TN
Fellowship Community,
  Spring Valley, NY
Futures, Berea, KY
Galilee, Portland, OR
Ganas, Staten Island, NY
The Gathering, Schuyler, VA
Gesundheit Institute, Arlington, VA
Griffin Gorge Commons, Wells, NY
Harbin Hot Springs, Middletown, CA
Hearthaven, Kansas City, MO
High Wind, Plymouth, WI
House of Lavendar, Milwaukee, WI
Innisfree Village, Crozet, VA
Koinonia Partners, Americus, GA
Lambom Valley, Paonia, CA
Light Morning, Copper Hill, VA

Madre Grande, Dulzura, CA
New Land, Faber, VA
Oakwood Farm, Selma, IN
100 Mile Lodge, 100 Mile House, B.C.
Ponderosa Village, Goldendale, WA
Sandhill Farm, Rutledge, MO
Satchidananda Ashram-Yogaville,
  Buckingham, Va
Skywoods Cosynegal,
  Muskegon Heights, MI
Springtree, Scottsville, VA
Shannon Farm, Afton, VA
Sirius Community, Shutesbury, MA
Terre Nouvelle, Laragne, France
Third Place House, Mt. Vernon, IA
Twin Oaks, Louisa, VA
Union Acres, Whittier, NC
Veiled Cliff, Scottown, OH

❖ **Associated Networks and Support Organizations**

Center for Communal Studies, Evansville, IN
Communal Studies Association, Evansville, IN
Community Catalyst Project, San Francisco, CA
Community Educational Service Council, Inc., Afton, VA
Community Service, Inc., Yellow Springs, OH

Cooperative Resources & Services Project, Los Angeles, CA
Federation of Egalitarian Communities, Tecumseh, MO
International/Communal Studies Association, Evansville, IN
School of Living, Cochranville, PA
Turtle Island Earth Stewards, Issaquah, WA

What Would Be the First Product?

For all our careful preliminary work, we knew that most people would come to know us by our program, and it would be important to choose an initial project which showcased our values, and spoke to as wide an audience as possible. In April, 1988, we selected this Directory as that first project. It had the right ingredients:

OUTREACH — There hadn't been a comprehensive directory produced in several years. Lending a hand with this project would speak directly to our outreach mission, and assist Communities magazine in the bargain.

INCLUSIVENESS — Within the broad diversity of intentional communities, the Directory provides exposure to all, without promoting one over another.

COOPERATION — No single person or community could do as thorough a job as an ecumenical team, and the Fellowship was in a good position to create such a team. It gave us a chance to explore the breadth of our many contacts.

These contacts were fruitful in many ways. For example, the funds to finance this Directory were raised entirely within the communities movement. Also, we relied on movement people to manage, edit, write, and provide most of the other technical skills necessary. It was a special opportunity for interweaving theory and practice, ideals and means. And we have emerged from this effort richer and more self-aware.

What Now?

We are excited about our beginnings and the forging of new ties achieved in the process of creating this Directory. We are, however, not stopping here. We have laid the groundwork for a community Speakers Bureau, are doing preliminary planning for a North American communities conference to be held in June, 1993, and are creating a facilitation training and referral service.

In the summer of 1989 we established an administrative headquarters at the Center for Communal Studies in Evansville, Indiana, to provide continuity between meetings, handle routine inquiries and channel special requests to appropriate FIC members.

Our board holds open, three-day meetings twice a year. We rotate the location of these around the continent, and each time we meet we see a few new faces — steadily expanding our collective base of personal contacts. While we are encouraged by this growth, there remains more work ahead for us as bridge builders. There are segments of the movement not yet represented in the Fellowship. We are still exploring how large we can draw the circle.

Our vision is celebrating our diversity while building on our common strengths. It is learning to be both accepting and decisive, non-judgmental and dynamic — all at the same time. Our vision is building together, and seeing that the fruit of the Fellowship nourishes the entire movement. ❖

The Federation of Egalitarian Communities

by Laird Sandhill

About 15 years ago, five North American communities shared a dream of cooperation. As a result, representatives of these communities got together and founded the Federation of Egalitarian Communities (FEC). Since then the Federation has been evolving and maturing, realizing some of the original dreams, and fostering new ones.

Today the member communities are: *Dandelion, East Wind, Sandhill Farm, Twin Oaks,* and three groups affiliated as communities-in-dialogue—*Ganas (formerly the Foundation for Feedback Learning), Krutsio,* and *Community Evolving.* All together, about 200 people are living in these seven communities.

To Be a Federation Member, a Community Must:

1) hold its land, labor, and other resources in common;
2) assume responsibility for the needs of its members, distributing all goods equally, or according to need;
3) practice non-violence;
4) use a form of decision-making in which members have an equal opportunity to participate, through either consensus, direct vote, or right of appeal or overrule;
5) work to establish equality of all people and not permit discrimination on the basis of race, class, creed, ethnic origin, age, sex, or sexual orientation;
6) act to conserve natural resources for present and future generations while striving to continually improve ecological awareness and practice;
7) create processes for group communication and participation, and provide an environment which supports people's development.

What Does It Mean to Be a Federation Member Community?

In addition to aligning with the seven basic principles, member communities create operating revenues for the Federation by taxing themselves $200 per year plus 1 percent of net revenues. We create a pool of labor by agreeing to commit 10 hours annually for each working member, plus the time it takes for delegates to attend the twice-yearly assemblies. In exchange for these resources, the communities receive a number of benefits.

Recruitment — Most of the time, member communities have been seeking growth. Over the years, we have found it efficient for the Federation to handle a big chunk of the recruitment and outreach for everyone. Every year the FEC places at least $2,000 worth of ads in alternative periodicals, generating hundreds of responses.

To answer these inquiries, an introductory brochure has been put together describing all the member communities in detail. So whenever a letter or phone call comes in to one community, information about all seven goes out. The Federation has also created two slide shows — an introductory version and another focusing on gender roles — and other materials used for lectures and presentations.

When prospective members visit a Federation community, they typically learn something about other member communities at the same time. It is common for visitors of one community to be referred to another as a further place to consider.

The Federation assists in the uniform collection and evaluation of records documenting each community's recruitment efforts. This provides a larger picture for evaluating the overall program, and enables each community to benefit more easily from the experience of the others.

Security Fund — In 1986 the Federation began collecting funds from member communities to create a joint security fund for protection against the economic strain of large medical bills. Taking advantage of combined numbers the risk is spread and the vulnerability of individual communities is reduced. We manage this fund ourselves, self-insuring rather than purchasing insurance from a commercial carrier. In consequence the money remains ours to use for short-term cash needs and other desirable investments, until major medical expenses arise. If necessary, a community can withdraw from the program at any time and get 90 percent of its investment back.

Experience — All of our communities have been around for more than 10 years. The oldest and largest, Twin Oaks, has existed for more than 23 years. Together we have accumulated a wealth of knowledge about community living. Some of this experience has been drawn together in a collection of written materials called the Systems and Structures Packet (see sidebar).

We can help new (and maybe even some not-so-new) communities ease through the struggles of creating appropriate structures, offering models for what to do when good will and the best intentions are not enough. Our communities haven't yet created the perfect social model, but we do have some-

❖
Systems & Structures

Are you forming a community? Or struggling with an existing one?

Maybe the Federation can lend a hand. Our communities have accumulated more than 200 years of experience at figuring out how to make community work. Along the way, we've tried a lot of things, and learned a lot about the kinds of systems and structures that match our values of cooperation and equality.

We have gathered many of the written documents from our affiliated communities and put them together in one collection — the Systems and Structures Packet. There are bylaws, membership agreements, property codes, behavior norms, labor and governance systems, visitor policies, and ideas about what to do when you have too many dogs.

This collection of materials runs to hundreds of pages. We offer any or all of it for little more than the cost of photocopying and postage. For a free catalog describing each document and how to order, write: *Federation Desk,* Box 6B-D, Tecumseh MO 65760

We don't have all the answers, and we may not have an answer for your particular need. But then again — we might. At the least, our work can offer a solid starting place for crafting a system just right for you.

And when you've got it perfected — maybe we can get a copy of what you've done to help when we're in trouble.

---

thing that works. You're welcome to use our experience to get a leg up in your search for something to fit your needs.

Intercommunity Contact — Only a very small percentage of the North American population lives in community. In most communities, especially the smaller ones, it is common to experience a certain amount of cultural isolation — the feeling that we're alone in our alternatives. The Federation provides opportunities for regular contact with like-minded folks, interrupting feelings of isolation, and reinforcing our purposeful choices to not swim in the mainstream. These opportunities take a variety of forms.

Delegates from the member communities get together twice a year to talk about Federation programs and issues. These "assemblies" are open and represent the major forum for getting and giving community news and views. As important as this is, the value of these meetings goes well beyond what's exchanged among delegates in session. The role of host is rotated among the communities; so it's generally enjoyable and stimulating for non-delegates to use the occasion of an assembly to start up or renew acquaintances with members from other communities.

Travel Expenses — FEC pays the cost of delegate travel to assemblies, and offers subsidies for members traveling from one community to another to participate in gatherings or to lend a hand with another community's work. This is especially handy when one community's peak workload occurs during another's off season, and the labor flows back and forth when it's most appreciated. We also set aside some money to foster participation in outside events of general interest to our members.

Staff — Since 1985, the Federation has funded a part-time staff position for one day a week to supplement the labor pool available from member dues. The staff person, called the Secretary, is responsible for streamlining administrative tasks and facilitating communication and understanding among member communities. The Secretary also represents the Federation in work with other organizations. For example, the Secretary serves on the Board of the Fellowship for Intentional Community.

Through pooling resources and building on common values, the Federation has created a presence in each community. It has been invaluable to have many individuals -- staff, delegates, and others — who see and develop opportunities from this wider perspective.

Friends of Community — The Federation created this association for people who are not living in community but who are nonetheless interested in the movement and want to contribute to our continuance and growth. Friends is both an outreach and fund-raising effort, widening our circle of involvement and helping to get out the word about our collective existence and viability.

Can the Federation Help You? — The Federation seeks contact with like-valued communities interested in exploring membership or other forms of regular interchange. However, you needn't be a prospective member community to get our attention. We are happy to share information with any community or interested individual. For information about any aspect of Federation affairs, write or call: *Laird Sandhill,* Federation Secretary, Route 1, Box 155-D, Rutledge, MO 63563, (816) 883-5543 ❖

The Emissary International Communities

by the Emissary Foundation International

A soft rain bathes a spring landscape. Deer play in a lush field, reveling in the cool air. The sun, breaking through the mist, awakens the fertile earth. An eagle rises slowly on living currents of air and beholds a world born anew.

This scene, part of the timeless cycles of life, has been repeated untold times — the mist, the sun, the tableaux of plant and creature — but each time is fresh and vibrant as the first rain. It speaks of the harmony and rhythms of nature, free and pure and as inexorable as the movement of planet and sun.

Now pick up a newspaper. It is filled with the machinations of mankind on this patient earth, the endless round of violence and failure, and the desperate attempts to stop our race to oblivion. Looking at the folly of the human world you cannot help but wonder how the harmony so palpably evident in nature has escaped us.

In the early 1930's a young man, Lloyd Arthur Meeker, began to ask himself a similar question about his meaning and purpose on earth. He had sought understanding through literature, psychology, religion and other avenues available then, as now, and found little peace in the answers found in time- and tradition-worn approaches. He finally looked to himself and began to realize something profound in his own experience: He was completely responsible for the state of his world and the quality of his experience in that world. He knew he could not continue like the mass of humanity, victim or victor in the world of circumstance, but always a pawn in that troubled arena.

He began to see and experience a way of living in which he could simply let go of the vicissitudes of daily existence to find himself at the center of his world, a shining light, steady and unperturbed. As he began to live this vision he wrote and spoke to many, and over years a small number of others began to experience the truth of his words in their everyday living. With their support and under his leadership emerged The Emissaries.

The international headquarters of this program was established on Sunrise Ranch, near Loveland, Colorado, in 1945. A few years later, under the leadership of Martin Exeter, Meeker's close friend, the Canadian headquarters was created at 100 Mile House in British Columbia, where resides Michael Exeter, who has now assumed directorship of the Emissaries. These two places were the first of a number of Emissary centers on four continents.

Although each community is as unique as the country and culture in which it thrives, they all share common purpose and direction. Upon visiting any of the locations you will find what can be described as the atmosphere of home. In each place live individuals who know that this atmosphere cannot be taken for granted, kept to oneself or even limited to the confines of a few buildings and the land around them. It is an atmosphere created by the personal integrity of individuals who are keenly aware of the opportunity, in every moment, to offer light into their environment.

The laws of life are timeless. Even on this seemingly troubled planet, every tree touched by the wind, every drop of rain and ray of sun work in concert to reveal these absolute laws. Emissaries are concerned with the restoration of life's harmony into their own world and thence into the world of human affairs. This concern would be applauded by any sane person, but it takes deliberate individual work to make it a reality. The communities listed below are home to individuals who are living this reality. But for every person who calls one of these centers home, there are many others letting the same spirit of life and love shine through them in cities and villages around the world.

> GLEN IVY, in the Santa Ana Mountains
> an hour from Los Angeles.
> HILLIER PARK, on the Gawler River,
> Adelaide, Australia.
> MICKLETON, in the Cotswolds in the
> heart of England.
> STILL MEADOW, located in the Cascade
> Mountains near Portland.
> OAKWOOD FARM, bordering the
> White River in Indiana.
> KING VIEW, in Canada's most populous
> region near Toronto.
> 100 MILE HOUSE, in British Columbia's
> central interior.
> EDENVALE, in southwest British
> Columbia's Fraser Valley.
> LA VIGNE, in southeastern France near
> Lyon and Grenoble.
> HOHENORT, in the South African
> heartland near Constantia.
> GREEN PASTURES ESTATE, in southern
> New Hampshire.

A wide variety of programs, seminars, classes and conferences are held at Emissary communities and many other centers throughout the year. Many people from all walks of life attend one-day art of living seminars, weekend study groups, and one to three-week classes to develop skills in spiritual leadership. Seven of the communities run Stewardship Farms, a network of farms dedicated to the stewardship and regeneration of the land. Each community also is the venue for seminars on media and art, business, education, agriculture, and health.

Emissary Foundation International supports and participates in activities that magnify the finest qualities of character in every field of human endeavor. Its premise is that all things are manifestations of one universal spirit. The harmony and balance of that spirit become the personal experience of those who find alignment with it. The genuine expression of these characteristics leads to increasing clarity of thought and perception essential to effectiveness in living. The foundation invites all who share the desire to clearly represent this spirit to participate in extending its influence into the world. The quarterly magazine *Integrity* reflects this message.

The Association for Responsible Communication (ARC) represents a growing community of friendships between people in television, radio, film, photography, performing arts, journalism and related fields. ARC members and friends are aware of the influence our lives and our communication have on the world. ARC publishes a quarterly journal *In Touch* and sponsors forums and events in which the nature of this responsibility comes into sharper focus, exploring its practical implications in all forms of media. Remembering why we communicate is essential. Letting creativity sculpt our expression is powerful. Expressing ourselves with clarity and precision is responsible. And associating with others who do likewise deepens the impact. ARC is an invitation to this experience.

Renaissance Business Associates recognizes that the ultimate human resource is quality of character. Without it, true success in any endeavor cannot be known; productivity, effectiveness and innovation all spring from this source. People want to know fulfillment in all areas of their living, including their place of work — and the main ingredient in fulfillment is not what one gets, but what one gives. The workplace should be a primary arena for personal and professional growth. Through public seminars and other programs, local activities, consulting, and its bimonthly journal, *Business Dynamics,* RBA fosters this kind of individual and corporate attitude.

Renaissance Educational Associates has members in England, Ireland, Italy, Korea, Australia, Ghana, South Africa and most states and provinces in the U.S. and Canada. All have a common interest to reveal strength and beauty of character and to fully partake of the adventure of creative living. In doing so, they lead others into the richness and fulfillment of life. Meetings, events, conferences and retreats sponsored by REA give people the chance to explore the practical application of REA's vision. *The Renaissance Educator,* a quarterly publication, carries the REA message to 15 countries. In staff rooms, universities, suburban school districts, prestigious private academies and ghetto schools, REA is rekindling the passion for life that lies at the core of true education.

The Stewardship Community with its conferences, a growing network of Stewardship Farms, and *The Stewards' Journal,* supports a sustainable agriculture, a wholesome food source, appropriate technology, and management systems that work with and enhance the ecological fabric of the planet. It seems almost daily we are told of a new element of environmental concern to add to the already lengthy list of global problems: ozone depletion, deforestation, drought, resource pollution. At one level, the damage that's been done cannot be undone. But the Stewardship Community is providing a network for the application of principles and the practice of responsible care of the earth. In doing this, it is bringing people together from around the world who are interested in renewing their relationship with the earth and its abundant resources.

The Whole Health Institute is concerned to assist in the emergence of a new spirit and vision in the healing arts. What causes the experience of true health? Certainly a wide variety of approaches and techniques are useful, but it is through a transcendent view of the health care field that a central understanding is known regardless of the form of healing used. It is this vision and its practical application — shared at seminars and conferences, and expressed in literature, tapes and the journal *Healing Currents* — that WHI extends to anyone interested in the healing arts throughout the world. ❖

(The above organizations may be contacted by writing to David Thatcher, P.O. Box 667, Lynden WA 98264.)

Regional Organizing:
InterCommunities of Virginia

by Isis Ringrose and Benjamin Brown

The experiences of communitarian activists in central Virginia indicate that intentional communities, across a wide range of diversity, can share with nearby groups, realizing vital social and business advantages. Since 1985 communities around the university town of Charlottesville, Virginia have held joint InterCommunities conferences. These gatherings have served to create lasting interpersonal connections among groups from a variety of intentional community cultures and traditions.

InterCommunities is an informal association of mature intentional communities. Eight of the ten groups have been together for twenty years on the average, and the other two have been established for ten years each. Our home communities are diverse in size, design and intention, including over 500 adults, 100 children, and 3,077 acres of generally very high quality farmland. ICV members share some common values (as described in the book, *Builders of the Dawn*):
— an emphasis on cooperation, sharing and equality;
— a commitment to personal and social change both within and beyond our home communities;
— service to society carried out in a community setting;
— a desire to "live lightly on the earth;"
— an awareness of the oneness of humanity and all life;
— a conscious response to the global crisis through development of social and cultural designs for a more peaceful, ecological and egalitarian world.

InterCommunities of Virginia is not a formal membership organization. All communitarians, seekers and others interested are encouraged to attend ICV conferences and other activities. Minimal communication expenses are financed by donations contributed at our conferences. All activities are voluntary and independent of the policies and particular values of the home communities of participating communitarians.

Geoph Kozeny/Community Catalyst

A network of Virginia communities meets semi-annually to have fun and learn more about each other

Isis Ringrose and Benjamin Brown are long term members of The Gathering, a spiritual group which hosts monthly socials for ICV members. As an active participant in the ICV Open Council, Isis has helped plan ICV conferences and provide continuity to the network. She was one of the founding members of The Gathering in New York City in 1969, and presently serves her group as house manager. Benjamin has been with The Gathering for eight years, and serves as the group's computer programmer and technician. He is medical director of a government supported rural health clinic and an anti-nuclear activist.

ICV Open Council Provides Coordination

Conferences are coordinated by the ICV Open Council, which consists of volunteers who are self-selected members of Virginia intentional communities. The ICV Open Council nurtures an increasing awareness of the common experiences and interests shared among Virginia communitarians, and encourages exploration of the unique differences in the regional ecology of community. This council decides location and time, and coordinates proposed workshop topics, for each conference, in conjunction with the intentional community hosting the conference. Council volunteers also exchange community newsletters and dates for community events to encourage more socializing among ICV communitarians. Formerly referred to as the planning committee, the Open Council renamed itself in the spring of '89 in recognition that ICV had grown to the point of needing a decision-making body. This group, which makes decisions by consensus, has become a forum for various issues that emerge when such diverse individuals organize for unified action.

Open Council meetings are held at different communities to encourage widespread participation. The semi-annual ICV conferences are also hosted by different communities in order that all may experience a bit of the lifestyle and organization of each group. This rotation of sites has been quite fruitful: We find that it's a learning opportunity for everyone to see and experience each community's solutions to the wider issues of cooperative living.

The Benefits of ICV

The original motive for our joint conferences was to broaden our membership recruitment efforts by exposing interested seekers to a number of intentional communities all at one time and place. However, by the end of our second conference it was evident that the primary attraction was the chance to learn more about each other's communities. Of course, this knowledge has enabled us to be more effective in referring community seekers among our communities. But more important for many of us is the opportunity to create relationships with dedicated communitarians outside of our home tribes. Together in ICV we have relieved some of the sense of isolation from wider society that is often present in cooperative living groups.

ICV conferences and shared social, political and business events are especially welcome to young people, single members and communitarian business people. The open-ended exchanges of contacts and information about our businesses, and social, political and financial initiatives, have led to many long-term friendships and joint endeavors. Such exchanges can be developed even more fully now that we are meeting for dinner socials on the first Friday night of each month.

> *[Most] important for many of us is the opportunity to create relationships with dedicated communitarians outside of our home tribes. Together in ICV we have relieved some of the sense of isolation from wider society that is often present in cooperative living groups.*

The basic differences in lifestyle between our communities amply demonstrate the wide range of options that communitarian living can provide. We have both spiritually oriented communities and secular communities. We have large and small communities. We have communities with a variety of guiding interests and economic systems. The common thread linking ICV participants seems to be an interest in expanding the availability of cooperative lifestyles and learning how other communities have responded to the many common problems that face all communitarians. We are gathering around our differences, enjoying and learning from our diversity.

Communities Conference Agendas

ICV's semi-annual conferences have been one-day affairs. Generally, the day starts off with all the participants joining in the Sharing Circle, where we exchange the latest news and get to know each other and each other's home communities. General business from the Open Council is also discussed briefly at this time. At some conferences the Sharing Circle has been preceded by an early morning meditation and healing service.

Late mornings and afternoons are usually divided into various small group workshop periods; topics range from astral travel to regional community land trusts, conflict resolution, spirituality and non-competitive games. Mental, spiritual and physical workshops, and tours of the host community, are scheduled in each period to provide for the wide variety of participant interests. Lunch and dinner provide times for us to discover each other's methods of handling the important issue of diet. Basic foods are usually provided by the host community and potluck dishes brought by others. In the evening we sometimes move into a smaller group that explores the more specific nature of the host community. Those wishing to spend the night generally have that opportunity, both before and after the conference.

InterCommunities History

Central Virginia has long been home for a variety of intentional communities, most with origins in the searchings of the Sixties. ICV had a predecessor in the Inter-Communities Network (ICN) which was incorporated in 1973. ICN had several participants that are now active in ICV, including members of Shannon Farm, Springtree and Twin Oaks. ICN also connected with community members in the Northeast and in Canada. Communication was difficult to maintain over such long distances; even so, ICN lasted for four years.

Central Virginia continues to serve as a magnet for intentional communities. There are several reasons for this attraction: mild climate and proximity to the Northeastern population centers, the Blue Ridge Mountains with their magnetic lay lines and other natural wonders, the cultural riches in the university town of Charlottesville, and relatively inexpensive rural land. By 1985, well over a dozen such groups were located in and around the Charlottesville area (increased to 19 by 1990).

In 1985, eight years after ICN ended, Sevenoaks Pathwork Center near Madison convened a conference of communitarians, in which 11 communities participated. Again in 1986, Sevenoaks hosted another conference, and the name InterCommunities of Virginia emerged. Members of Shannon Farm hosted a spring 1987 meeting, which was attended by 40 communitarians from eight communities.

Deciding to meet more frequently, we gathered at Springtree in late summer 1987. The spring '88 meeting grew to 55 at Yogaville, and in fall '88 we met at Twin Oaks. The Gathering hosted the largest conference to date: more than 100 people attended that publicly advertised meeting in the spring of 1989. Twin Oaks again was host for the fall '89 meeting with about 50 participants. Innisfree Village hosted the latest conference at its new community center in June 1990.

As ICV continues to grow and develop, we are learning from each other, communing in our similarities and debating over our differences. In

Susan Gravely/Twin Oaks

Gathering around
our differences

this fashion, both the comparisons and the contrasts of our separate lifestyles provide insights for enhancement of our unique social visions.

Home Communities of ICV Participants

InterCommunities of Virginia participants come from the home communities listed below. All of these communities are open to new communities movement contacts. Our communities are also open to considering new members. Those who are interested in our activities are encouraged to communicate with us, but it is very important to make arrangements in advance before visiting (see Listings section for contact information).

YOGAVILLE, the international center for Integral Yoga Institutes, is guided by Sri Swami Satchidananda. Our community of 50 monastics and 150 karma yogis has built the Light of Truth Universal Shrine (LOTUS), with an altar for each of the world's religions.

TWIN OAKS is an eclectic group of 72 adults and 10 children who stress equality, cooperation and tolerance. We live and work together on a 300-acre farm, producing about 40 percent of our own food and operating several industries.

SPRINGTREE is a small family-style community on 118 acres. We manage a market garden and an orchard, and offer internships in organic gardening and communal living.

SHANNON FARM is 60 adults and 21 children sharing 490 acres. We are committed to consensus decision-making, sharing of leadership roles, personal independence, group fun, and monthly dues payments. We live as singles, families or groups in 30 custom-built houses and cabins.

REINA del CIELO community numbers 16 adults, including five ministers, and eight children. In 1988 we moved to our 52-acre site east of Lexington. We provide a spiritual atmosphere for the study of ancient wisdom, and plan to build a healing center.

NEW LAND is a loose-knit association of 25 homeowners who have built around the Monroe Institute, a research and educational organization dedicated to the study and development of human consciousness.

The common thread linking ICV participants seems to be an interest in expanding the availability of cooperative lifestyles and learning how other communities have responded to the many common problems that face all communitarians. We are gathering around our differences, enjoying and learning from our diversity.

INNISFREE VILLAGE is a life-sharing community of 65 people. Some have mental disabilities, and others serve as volunteers and staff. We maintain orchards and large vegetable gardens, and operate a bakery, weavery and woodshop.

GESUNDHEIT INSTITUTE is a small group, half living in Arlington and the rest on a 310-acre farm. At the farm we are building our dream — a 40-bed free hospital.

THE GATHERING was founded in New York in response to a spiritual vision. In 1975 we began renovation of an old soapstone hospital in Schuyler. Our 12 members are focused on spiritual development based in a wide range of teachings from Christian, Jewish, Eastern, New Age and other sources.

COMMON GROUND, located south of Lexington, has 11 adults and five children living on 77 acres held in the School of Living's regional Community Land Trust (CLT). We make decisions by consensus, operate a learning center for home schooled children, and provide technical support for land trust development. ❖

Rural Communes in Great Britain

by Pam Dawling

The number of rural, egalitarian, income-sharing communes in Great Britain has remained fairly stable in recent years, with a few new ones forming, and a few unfortunate ones folding. Those established in the early Seventies that are thriving — like *Crabapple, Gleneirw, Lifespan, Monkton Wyld,* and *Shaw* — typically have memberships ranging from six to 12 adults.

People-in-Common community has moved to an old mill building which it has been renovating for many years. It has successfully made the transition from an urban site to a rural one. *Some People*, another urban group, has acquired land just outside of town and started a market garden.

One of the best-known rural groups, *Laurieston Hall*, has dissolved its income-sharing commune in favor of a looser-knit cooperative. Individuals or couples live separately now,

> *The main expansion in communal living in recent years has been in urban cooperatives — both the shared household of mainly single people under 35, and the larger co-ops where families or small groups are housed separately.*

are responsible for their own incomes, and share the work of the cooperative a couple of days a week.

There are some very big rural houses which are divided into family units — including *Old Hall, Whitbourne Hall, Canon Frome,* and *Postlip.* Members cooperate on land use and building maintenance.

Several large religious and spiritual communities are flourishing, including *Findhorn, Manjushri Institute* (Tibetan Buddhists), and the *Darvell Bruderhof* (Hutterites). There are also networks of smaller groups, such as the 15 or so households of *Friends of the Western Buddhist Order.*

Some of the rural communities which live in tipis or caravans (trailers) are being harassed by local government about use of agricultural land for dwellings. One Tipi group is taking its fight to the High Court.

There is a rural women's community, still in the process of formation. Also, a gay men's project, the Edward Carpenter Trust, is gathering funding and members.

The Communes Network (CN) newsletter (see Resources listing) is published quarterly. In the fall of 1989, a small group within the network published *Diggers and Dreamers, A Guide to Communal Living.* This guide has a revised and expanded directory of British communities. The main expansion in communal living in recent years has been in urban cooperatives — both the shared household of mainly single people under 35, and the larger co-ops where families or small groups are housed separately.

There are periodic gatherings of communitarians and CN readers, and the newsletter continues to answer a steady flow of inquiries about communal living. We are interested in contact with communitarians in other countries; so your correspondence is welcome. ❖

(*Diggers and Dreamers, A Guide to Communal Living* is available in North America for $ 9.50 plus $1.50 postage and handling from Community Bookshelf, Rt 1 Box 155, Rutledge MO 63563.)

Pam Dawling has lived in intentional communities since 1973, and for the past eight years has been a member of Lifespan. She is an editor with *Communes Network* newsletter, publishers of *Diggers and Dreamers*, a 1989 Directory of communal living in Great Britain. Her main work areas are printing, gardening, plumbing and building renovation. Apart from communal living, Pam Dawling's political commitments are to feminism, cooperative work and the anti-nuclear movement.

Global Networking:

Trends in European and Israeli Community Networks and
How That Compares with What's Been Happening in North America

by Allen Butcher and Laird Sandhill

O ver the past dozen years, community networking in Europe has been strikingly similar to the North American experience. On both continents there have been regional networks of contemporary communities which gathered annually for a handful of years in the early 1980's, celebrating and sharing, delighting in their common themes and struggles, yet stopping short of developing much structure and common programs. As energy waned, the gatherings stopped, though they left a legacy of lasting relationships within the community movement.

At the same time there has been support among scholars for regular conferences focusing on intentional communities — both historic and contemporary. With institutional backing from universities, this form of networking has proved more enduring.

On both sides of the Atlantic there has been some intermixing between these groups, but not much... so far. Before exploring where matters stand now, let's look at the paths these two trends have described.

INTERNATIONAL COMMUNES NETWORK

Among intentional communities in Great Britain, the Communes Network coalesced as an umbrella organization in the 1970s. Toward the end of the decade Laurieston Hall, in Scotland, was an especially active Network community, and aspired to extend the networking energy beyond the United Kingdom. In 1978, it started publishing a newsletter, and called for an international festival of communities to be held at Laurieston in 1979. The event was well attended, attracting participation by communities from a number of European countries, and the International Communes Network (ICN) was born.

There was strong interest among communities to get together, feel their collective strength, and find out what each was doing. It was an attempt to build trust and unity through informal sharing; these were festivals, not conferences. To be sure, in addition to the parties, there were workshops to explore common issues and challenges, but they depended wholly on volunteers to organize and lead them. There was important exchange of information, but the tone was definitely more celebration than cerebration.

The role of hosting the festivals was rotated among European communities: in 1981 it was held at Mejlgard Castle, Denmark; in 1982 at Hasselt, Belgium; in 1983, back at Laurieston Hall; in 1984 at de Refter, Holland; in 1985 at Le Puy, France.

As the festivals continued, the participants struggled with questions of how, or whether, to develop ICN into a dynamic, self-supporting network. As Bernt Djurs of Jaettestuen, Denmark, put it in an ICN newsletter from February, 1983:

> On the one hand I feel an urge to move on to higher levels of cooperation and wider scopes of activities. But basically we are faced with the problem of formulating a statement of aims and values sufficiently broad to encompass most communes, and yet exact enough to elicit active response and support from those same communes.

The festivals operated on a shoestring budget, and they were a considerable logistical burden for the host community. After six festivals in seven years, the initial enthusiasm had run its course. There was no agreement on how to create a sustainable network, or even on whether a formal structure was desirable at all. Plans for a 1986 festival, in Germany, fell through, and none has been held since.

This flow and ebb of regional networks had close parallels in the United States, where both the New England Network of Light and the Earth Communities Network of the Pacific Northwest flourished in the early 1980s. Just like the

Allen Butcher has attended NHCSA conferences and the ICSA conference in Scotland. He is a former member of East Wind and Twin Oaks communities who has written extensively about the history of networking and intentional community.

Laird Sandhill serves as a networker for the Federation of Egalitarian Communities and the Fellowship for Intentional Community. Both authors are charter members of the FIC.

Laurieston Hall, host of the first International Communes Festival in 1979.

Allen Butcher

ICN in Europe, these regional networks of communities enjoyed a few years of high-energy gatherings and fostered some continuing intercommunity contacts, but did not find a way to translate that initial enthusiasm into a sustaining program.

ISRAELI NETWORKING

At about the same time that the Communes Network was initiating intercommunity contact in Europe, Kibbutz Artzi, one of the federations of the kibbutz movement in Israel, created the International Communes Desk (ICD) and began reaching out to communities outside Israel. Under creator Mordechai Bentov's leadership, the ICD began an internationally circulated newsletter in 1976, and established a scholarship program whereby communitarians from other countries could come to Israel and study aspects of life in kibbutz.

In 1981, the ICD and Yad Tabenkin, an academic institution at Efal, Israel, co-sponsored an international conference on communal living. This attracted participants from communities in Europe and North America, and even some from Japan. The conference was held the same year that the ICN met in Denmark, and there was concern among the Europeans that the ICD initiative would draw energy away from their festival. In addition, some Europeans were concerned about political differences, and questioned the role of the kibbutz in relationship to Arabs. It turned out though that kibbutzniks attended the ICN event in the spring and ICN participants traveled to Israel for the fall conference there. Subsequent-

ly, correspondence from both groups was a regular feature in each other's publications.

The Israeli conference was a very different kind of event from an ICN festival. The program was developed months ahead of time, and featured the presentation of papers with structured discussions and/or question-and-answer sessions. This was the academic style, designed to gather together stimulating thoughts about community life... as opposed to gathering together the stimulating life itself. One "had to be there" to experience an ICN festival, but the personal contacts that were the main attraction of the festivals were only a sideshow at the Israeli conference. If you missed the conference, you could still find out what happened in the sessions by waiting several months and getting a full set of the proceedings.

These differences presented a challenge in how best to move forward with networking. Where the Europeans favored bonding through social interaction, the Israelis emphasized intellectual engagement. There was also a question about how structured a network should be. Uzi El-natan from Kibbutz Gesher offered this perspective in the May 1984 edition of the ICD newsletter:

> ...we held a thorough discussion...on the future of the international network of communes. Two trends stood out. Some claimed that after five years, links should be tightened — and an international center established, at least for the purpose of information and the collation of experiences for the general good. Others argued that the present situation was good enough: "We don't have to create more official frameworks — so as not to be caught up with problems of decision-making, finances, whom to help, and the like." In the background I sensed apprehension that

since the kibbutz movement was older, longer established, and more tightly organized, it might gradually dominate the organization.

CONTRASTING BACKGROUNDS

To a large extent the different networking approaches of ICN and ICD reflect the very different backgrounds of the organizations. On the one hand, ICN was new, and feeling its way. Its main resource was a driving spirit among participants to commune with other communitarians, and to build morale for all. It had no funding source, or affiliation with other, more established organizations. Its events were casual, loosely structured affairs, created largely by the participants, who did virtually all of their own support work.

On the other hand, the ICD was an offshoot of a strong, well-organized kibbutz federation. By the mid-1970s, the kibbutz movement was decades old, and kibbutzniks represented about 3 percent of the nation's Jewish population. They were an established and fully recognized element of Israeli society. Although ICD was new, it had ready access to organizational infrastructure, and with the academic ties through Yad Tabenkin, it was a relatively simple matter to organize a conference every few years.

Having been around, the kibbutzim had a history to look at, study, and project on the basis of. The ICN communities were more concerned with their survival and other immediate issues than with comparing historic trends. Where the European communities were trying to figure out how, if at all, they fit into the society at large, the kibbutzim were more concerned with whether they were being assimilated too much by the mainstream culture.

Israeli kibbutzim are all based on total income-sharing, which lends itself to centralized economies and planning. There was no such common economic structure among the ICN communities. It was a much more diverse group, and this was reflected in ICN's tentativeness in considering an organizational structure or program.

ACADEMIC NETWORKING

After thoroughly digesting their 1981 experience with international conferencing, the ICD moved ahead by setting up a second one in Israel, in 1985. As before, the participants were mainly kibbutzniks, with a sprinkling of folks from other countries. This time representation by scholars was even stronger, and the conference spawned the International Communal Studies Association (ICSA), which inherited from ICD the main thrust of Israeli energy for international networking.

ICSA met next in 1988, at New Lanark, the historic Owenite community site in Scotland. This conference was co-sponsored by the National Historic Communal Societies

Conferences on Communities

For the first time, the International Communal Studies Association (ICSA) will hold a conference in North America. This event is being co-sponsored by the Fellowship for Intentional Community, and is scheduled for July 25-28, 1991, at Elizabethtown College, in Pennsylvania. Everyone interested in learning about intentional communities on the global level is encouraged to attend this important event.

For details about the program and logistics, contact: *ICSA Conference, Donald Kraybill*, Elizabethtown College, Elizabethtown, PA 17022, (717) 367-1151

The Communal Studies Association (CSA) holds annual conferences in the United States. The next CSA conference will be October 10 – 12, 1991, at Aurora, in western Oregon. For details contact program chair, Patrick Harris, Old Aurora Colony Museum, P.O. Box 202, Aurora, OR 97002 (503) 678-5754. Members of the Fellowship of Intentional Communities will be involved in several presentations about living communities, including Community Land Trusts, consensus decision-making, news sharing sessions for contemporary communities, and a slide-show tour of diverse North American intentional communities.

For information about future NHCSA conferences, contact: *Mary Hayden or Don Pitzer, Center for Communal Studies,* University of Southern Indiana, 8600 University Boulevard, Evansville IN 47712, (812) 464-1719.

Association (now become the Communal Studies Association, or CSA) from the United States, which is also essentially an academic association. CSA has been sponsoring annual conferences at U.S. historic communal sites since 1975, and employs a conference style very similar to that of the ICSA.

At both ICSA and CSA events there has been a small, yet persistent presence of representatives from living communities. In the absence of the regional festivals of the early 1980s — on both sides of the ocean — these academic conferences have at least provided an avenue for contemporary communities to gather and learn about each other, even if the format has been more presentation than jubilation.

WHAT'S HAPPENING TODAY?

When ICN and ICD were both fully active in the early 1980s there was considerable and lively exchange between them. By 1985, however, this had tapered off. ICN held its last festival that year, and ICD saw its conference beget the ICSA, strengthening ties with academia. In the United States, the New England Network of Light and the Earth Communities Network had already peaked by 1985, and were slipping into dormancy.

Yet even as the energy was waning among these groups, it was beginning to rise elsewhere. Early in 1985 the Inter-Communities of Virginia met to revive an old association of communities in the central Virginia area. It is a lively regional network today, meeting twice a year [see Isis Ringrose and Ben Brown's article]. On a broader scale, again in North America, the Fellowship for Intentional Community (FIC) convened an incorporation meeting in summer, 1986, and held its first continent-wide membership meeting the following spring. Today FIC is strong enough to both organize the editorial team which created this Directory and put together the financial package to fund it [see Laird Sandhill's article on FIC].

Over in Great Britain, the Communes Network recently published, for the first time in several years, a new directory of communities in that nation [see Pam Dawling's article].

In Israel the ICD, under Nancy Farchi, is being re-funded and is renewing contacts with communities in other countries.

At the same time, the academic networks are aware of the dynamic participation of living communitarians at their events, and there is burgeoning interest at ICSA and CSA for strengthening connections with living communities. CSA recognized this trend by dropping "historic" from its name in 1990.

Through the active support of Don Pitzer, the Director of the Center for Communal Studies, in Evansville, Indiana, the FIC has selected the Center for its continental headquarters, where it shares administrative facilities with NHCSA, which is also headquartered there.

For the ICSA's part, it has extended an invitation to FIC to co-sponsor its next conference, scheduled for July, 1991, in Pennsylvania [see sidebar]. Both ICSA and NHCSA are offering contemporary communities more space on their conference programs.

HOW WILL FUTURE NETWORKING DEVELOP?

While the divergent paths of 1985 are coming together again, some questions remain. To what extent will today's communitarians avail themselves of the offer from the academic networks to work together? Hopefully, as we get to know each other better and gain experience through joint projects, trust will run deeper and doors will open wider.

There are mutual advantages for combining efforts. The academic world offers: a valuable entree to the wider society, which could significantly boost the efforts of communities to achieve their outreach goals; resources, such as information collection and accessing systems; facilities and experience in setting up conferences; and accounting support and financial contacts. Going the other way, regular contact with living communitarians offers scholars an unparalleled opportunity for documenting tomorrow's history today.

Will the current upsurge in support for contemporary networks lead to global networking? The lessons of the past are that successful networks are built a block at a time: strong, stable communities lead to vital regional or special-focus networks, and they, in turn, can be the building blocks of national and international movements.

The communities movement is building all the time, though not at a constant rate. As in the above descriptions, networks tend to go through cycles of greater and lesser energy and harmony. Naturally, the movement tends to build more quickly when the networks are strong, yet activity does not stop altogether when regional gatherings and newsletters cease for a time. Many of the personal contacts, the fundamental elements of networking, continue through the periods of dormancy, and these relationships are the enduring threads with which the movement tapestry is woven.

Communities are a diverse lot, and no single approach to networking is likely to attract them all. Just as there is a plurality of community choices for individuals, it is probably best that there be a plurality of network choices for communities. Time will tell how the networks currently developing will meet the needs of today's communities, and how close we are to realizing the promise of global networking. ❖

Database Searches for Intentional Communities Information

by William Pitt

For many years there have been worthwhile online databases to search for materials on communities. However, their cost ($30 to $300 per hour) has not encouraged the typical communitarian to use them. The emergence of databases on CD-ROM (Compact Disk – Read Only Memory) within the past two years has changed all this by storing information accessible by micro-computers. Many college and university libraries, and larger public libraries, now offer users access to CD-ROM databases and the number of these library databases is increasing rapidly.

ERIC, an educational database and one of the grandfathers in the field, is available on CD-ROM in many versions, including "Silver Platter" and "Dialog-On-Disc." The search

Different search strategies may be required for each database. Use imagination in selecting the databases to search, and in formulating strategies.
Happy hunting.

strategy given below is for Dialog-On-Disc dated 1980 to June 1989. Using controlled vocabulary terms in a free text way will access a great many references on communities:

    SS COMMUNE
    OR COMMUNES
    OR (INTENTIONAL(W)COMMUNIT?)
    OR KIBBUTZ?
    OR (COLLECTIVE(W)SETTLEMENT?)
    OR COMMUNITARIAN?

Entering such a search string (as a continuous line) will produce many relevant journal articles and research reports — plus some things you will not want. The (W) is a proximity operator, so that INTENTIONAL and COMMUNITY must be side by side and in that order. The ? is a truncator, i.e., COMMUNIT? will retrieve items with strings like "Community, "Communities", "Communitarian." Likewise, KIBBUTZ? retrieves "kibbutz", "kibbutzim," "kibbutznick." (The truncator and proximity operators may vary in other software systems.)

This process will produce a "set" (in my example, S11 containing 137 items). Set numbers are automatically generated and will appear on your screen as S1, S2,... You can narrow down your area of search and get more specialized information. For example, if you are interested in children in communities, enter another search string, such as

    SS CHILD?
    OR INFANT?
    OR YOUTH?
    OR YOUNG?
    OR JUVENILE?

This produced a second set for me, S17 with 64,607 items in it. Then, by entering the search string C 11 AND 17, I created a set combining the first two search strings. (C stands

William Pitt visited and worked at the Community for Creative Non-Violence and The Community in D.C., and Gesundheit Institute and Twin Oaks in Virginia. Professionally he worked with the College of Library and Information Services at the University of Maryland.

Bill kept up his interest and support of intentional communities, even in the face of a painful and lingering struggle with cancer. He wrote this article, at our request, in the midst of that distress. Bill passed away on May 8, 1991. His knowledge and support will be sorely missed.

Networking

Geoph Kozeny/Community Catalyst

for combine in this system.) The result will be S18, which has 56 items. The command PRINT 18/5/1-56 will print all 56 items on the printer. (The /5/ means "give me the complete record.")

I judged 52 of the 56 items produced by this search to be of interest to someone looking for information about children in intentional communities. Other searches may not result in such precision. The set numbers and the number of items retrieved will undoubtedly vary, so the combine and print statements must be revised accordingly.

To facilitate your database research:

1. Ask the librarian for help in running your first search.

2. Before you begin, read carefully all directions provided and review the manual, if there is one. After searching one or two databases, you will develop your own productive strategies.

3. If you get only a small number of "hits," examine the items retrieved for other possible search strings. Use them. This is called "pearl growing."

4. Ask the librarian to recommend a book on database searching.

5. Inquire about library orientation sessions on database searching.

There are other pertinent databases for communitarian research available on CD-ROM. These include: AV-online (for audio-visual materials); Infotrac (popular magazines); Dissertation Abstracts (scholarly stuff); Sociofile (for sociology); Psyclit (for psychology); and Newsbank Electronic Index (for newsworthy items). Different search strategies may be required for each database. Use imagination in selecting the databases to search, and in formulating strategies. Happy hunting. ❖

About the Listings...

This section contains 1) a North American map; 2) two cross-reference charts (one arranged alphabetically, the other by state or province) which compare over 30 characteristics of North American communities; and 3) a list of well over 300 intentional communities, including addresses and phone numbers (except for those requesting that contact information remain unpublished). Which of these sections you'll use first will depend on your specific needs and interests — see "How to Use This Directory" on page 7.

The listings are arranged alphabetically for easy overall access — a person whose interests are geographically specific should probably start with the chart that is sorted by state or province (see page 160). Acronyms have been considered as one word even though they might normally be spelled with periods between the letters. Numerals have been treated as if they were spelled out (e.g., 3HO groups are sorted as if spelled "Three HO").

There's a lot of information in the charts that doesn't appear in the listings, and vice versa, so use both for the best overview of each community. You'll usually get a far better sense of a group by reading their descriptive listing — that's where we've given them license to tell their own story ... to share their visions, their histories, their daily life. Many of these descriptions go beyond the facts and figures, and give you a feeling for the community.

Some frequently used abbreviations:

SASE means enclose a self-addressed stamped envelope.

[cc] means that the group cannot commit to responding promptly to written inquiries.

The date in small print at the end of a listing is the date the entry was submitted or, in some cases, the date that the group confirmed that the information is still accurate.

The numbers on the map correspond to an alphabetical numbering of the North American communities included in this Directory, and indicate each community's approximate location. **The index for these numbers** can be found on the cross-reference charts.

The information in the charts is based on community **responses to questionnaires** that we sent out, in at least three slightly different versions, over the 18 months of our research. **An "N/Q" in the "Other Values" column** indicates a group that did not submit a questionnaire; in these cases, we have tried to fill in some of the blanks based on other information (such as the group's descriptive listing, or our own personal knowledge).

The key for the chart codes is on pages 144-145. Since the meaning of some code letters varies from one column to the next, our key explains all the possibilities within each column. It is important to refer to this key when interpreting the chart ... a "C" in the "Decision-Making" column (indicating that the group uses consensus) means something very different from a "C"

(community ownership) in the "Ownership Column" or a "C" (Christian) in the "Spiritual Focus" column or a "C" (celibacy) in the "Sexual Restrictions" column.

A few general disclaimers: As in most questionnaire-based research, different communities may have interpreted the same questions in different ways. It was sometimes impossible for us to tell if groups (including our own research team) had applied the same standards and definitions to each question that appears on this chart. Furthermore, it is impossible to do justice to the vast variety of communities and community experiences by attempting to quantify them in a yes/no or multiple-choice format.

We can't guarantee that the information in the charts and listings is accurate — each community decided what to say about itself, and changes may have happened over the last 6-18 months. We edited only for length and clarity. We caution each reader to verify all information before deciding to get involved with any of the groups listed.

A word of advice for community seekers: do not eliminate a community from your search solely on the basis of a few chart responses which you consider "less than ideal".

First, communities change. Information that was accurate when the questionnaire was answered may now be outdated. The community may be open to change — even desirous of change. Plans for the future are usually not reflected in the chart.

Second — especially in categories like "Pacifist", "Feminist", and "Voluntary Simplicity" — the values of the group may very much depend on the individuals within it at any given time. An individual committed to any particular value may find (or help to create) a climate supportive of that value, even in a group which was reluctant to answer with an unqualified "yes."

Third, various groups may have used different definitions or criteria in answering a question such as "Are you pacifists?" Members of a group that keeps a firearm for self-defense may have answered "yes" because they are against nuclear weapons, while members of a second group, also against nuclear weapons, may have answered "no" because they keep a firearm for self-defense.

Fourth, it's hard to predict what factors will be most important to an individual who is searching for satisfaction in community, especially for a person new to the idea. To choose or exclude communities on the basis of a single factor — diet, for example — may be to exclude a very real possibility for growth, change, new understanding, and happiness. (Are you absolutely *sure* you can't live with meat-eaters ... or vegetarians?)

Ultimately, the interpersonal dynamics and overall "feel" of a community are much more important than any of the narrow categories described in this chart. We encourage you to explore community with an open mind, an open heart, and a willingness to grow and experience — rather than with rigid ideas about what is right for you. ❖

Key to the Chart Codes

About the codes used in this chart ...

They may be intimidating at first glance — but they're really quite simple once you get the hang of them. For a general overview of how to use the chart, and to understand how the chart relates to the rest of the Directory, read "How to Use This Directory" on page 7, and the introduction on page 143.

We originally contemplated a chart that showed a "•" in any column where the community gave a "Yes" response — before we realized that we could pack many times the information into the same space by using code letters. Two major points from the introduction bear repeating here:

1) Different communities may have interpreted the same question in different ways.
2) You'll get a far better sense of a group by reading their descriptive listing.

Generic Codes

A few codes generally mean the same thing throughout, regardless of the column in which they appear. There are a few exceptions, and these are explained in the section that follows on "Special Codes". The generic codes are:

Y   Yes
N   No
M   Maybe
S   Some, Somewhat, or Sometimes
P   Probably, or Preferred
Cb   A combination of the possible options
V   Varies (also "Var")
Q   Questionable
U   Unsure, or Undecided

These last two merit a little further explanation.

A "U" (for Unsure or Undecided) indicates that the group itself has still not decided its position on that issue (for example, a group that is still forming may not know whether it will have a communal kitchen).

A "Q" (Questionable) means that we couldn't figure out the answer based on the information provided; a "Q" in the decision-making column *does not* indicate that we find the group's decision-making process to be questionable or dubious, but simply that it was unclear to us how to categorize the response given on the questionnaire.

A blank space on the chart indicates one of the following: the group chose not to answer the question; the group responded in such a way that we didn't know how to quantify the answer for the chart; we were unable to find the answer to that question through our own research; or the questionnaire we sent to that group was an earlier version which overlooked that particular question altogether (as in the case of the "Acres" category).

Parentheses around an answer indicate that the community prefers, but does not absolutely require, that all members share the belief or practice in question.

Special Codes

What follows is a summary of each of the points we covered in our questionnaire, and an explanation of the special codes used in the chart. A string of code letters at the head of each list (following a "•") indicates the generic values (as described in the previous column) which apply to this question.

Ref: Reference number also used in the State/Province listings, and corresponding to that community's location on the map.

Community: The community names, arranged alphabetically, and followed by an abbreviation for the state or province in which the group is located.

[F]   We classified the group as "Forming"
*   This group has other locations as well
**   A group with several locations

Acres: Early versions of the questionnaire lacked this question, so this column is frequently blank.

ac   acres
Hs   House(s)
Rm   Rooms

Rural/Urban:

R   Rural
U   Urban
B   Both
R*   Rural, but with urban flavor or amenities
U*   Urban, but in a natural setting (includes some suburban sites)

Year: The year the community was established.

Population: The current population in three columns — "Adults", "Children", and "Max" (the community's vision, if any, of a maximum population).

\+   Numbers after a "+" indicate part-time or "extended" community members
F   Families or Households
Incl   In the "Children" column means "included" — the number in the "Adults" column refers to adults and children combined

New Members: Is the community open to new adult members, and to new children?

•   Y,N,M,P,V,Q
S   Soon

School: The type of schooling children receive.

Cm   Community
Hm   Home School
Pr   Private
Pu   Public
Cb   Combination of the above choices

Gender: A BLANK means open to both women and men.

W   Women only
M   Men only

Visitors: Is the community open to visitors who make arrangements in advance?

•   Y,N,M,S,P,Q

Join Fee: What is the fee, if any, for joining? Joining fees may or may not be required only after a trial membership period, may or may not be payable over time, and may or may not be refunded upon leaving — this information is not reflected in this chart. Figures are in dollar amounts.

•	Y,M,S,Var
N	None
AA	All Assets
Negot	Negotiable
Dep	Deposit required

Decisions: How are decisions made?

C	By consensus
M	By majority rule
Cb	By a combination of consensus and majority rule
N	None of the above

Does the community use a system of decision-making whereby one or more members' views are given more weight than others' by virtue of length of membership, special relationship to the group, or other basis of privilege agreeable to the community?

> • Y,N,M,S,Q,U

Note: In some cases these responses refer to members who have already completed their trial periods; trial members may have less weight.

Food/Diet: *GROW?* Does the community grow a substantial amount of its own food? *EAT?* Does the community eat together at least once a week, or prepare food in a communal kitchen? *ORG?* Does the community emphasize organic or minimally processed food? *FLEX?* Is the community willing to make an effort to provide for all dietary preferences and restrictions?

•	Y,N,M,S,P,Q
Cb	Several households within the group — some do, some don't

VEG? Is the community vegetarian (vegetarianism required)?

•	Y,N,M,S
N*	No, but the diet and/or membership is predominantly vegetarian, although vegetarianism is not required
Y*	Members must leave the property to eat meat

Ownership/Housing: [L] Does the community own the land? [B] The houses? [Rm] What is the housing style — or how are rooms allocated?

•	Cb,Q,U
C	Community owned
L	Land Trust
I	Owned by one person or a few individuals
N	Not owned by the community (may be owned by families, individuals, or rented)
F	Family units
R	Individual rooms
D	Dormitory style

Money/Labor: *Share?* Does the community practice total income sharing? (This may refer only to earned income in some cases.) *Labor? Money?* Are members expected to regularly contribute labor or money to the group? Numbers refer to hours or dollars per month or, where noted, a percentage of the member's income or working hours. *Opp?* Are there reasonably attractive income-earning opportunities available on the land?

•	Y,N,M,S,P,Cb,Q,U,Var
Ngo	Negotiable
Vol	Voluntary

Sexual Restrictions: Are there any restrictions on sexual relationships among consenting adult members? The special code letters refer to the practices acceptable in each community.

C	Celibate
H	Heterosexual
G	Gay
L	Lesbian
B	Bisexual
Ma	Marriage only
Mo	Monogamy only
M	Married & Monogamous only
N	No specific restrictions, although several groups stressed that they allow no exploitation, violence, or abuse — others that they particularly value "responsibility"
P	Polyfidelitous
**	Several groups working with mentally disabled adults specified "no staff/client relationships"
( )	Preferred, not required

Spirituality: Does the community have a spiritual focus? Do you recognize a spiritual leader or leaders among your membership?

•	Y,N,M,S,Q
C	Christian
E	Eastern
EDL	Emissaries of Divine Light
HB	Hutterian Brethren
J	Jewish
NAm	Native American
P	Pagan
Qk	Quaker
R/C	Roman Catholic
Ecm	Ecumenical (includes "all religions" and groups who checked most of the possibilities)
Ecl	Eclectic (includes "Yes — individual choice")
O	Other

Pacifism, Feminism, Voluntary Simplicity: Is the community pacifist? Feminist? Do you value voluntary simplicity?

> • Y,N,M,S,P,Q,U

Other: "Is there a value essential to your group which is not reflected in the questions above? Please specify." Some groups left this one blank, others provided lengthy lists. We decided to change the "slant" of this column — and have tried to list a few keywords that describe a primary or significant feature of each group. In many cases this was the group's answer to our original question; sometimes we scanned the group's descriptive paragraph and questionnaire answers, then selected the phrase we felt to be most descriptive.

An "N/Q" at the beginning of the "Other Values" column indicates that the group did not submit a questionnaire. In these cases, we have tried to fill in some of the group's information based on other sources (such as the group's descriptive listing, or our own personal knowledge). *So, on to the charts. ...*

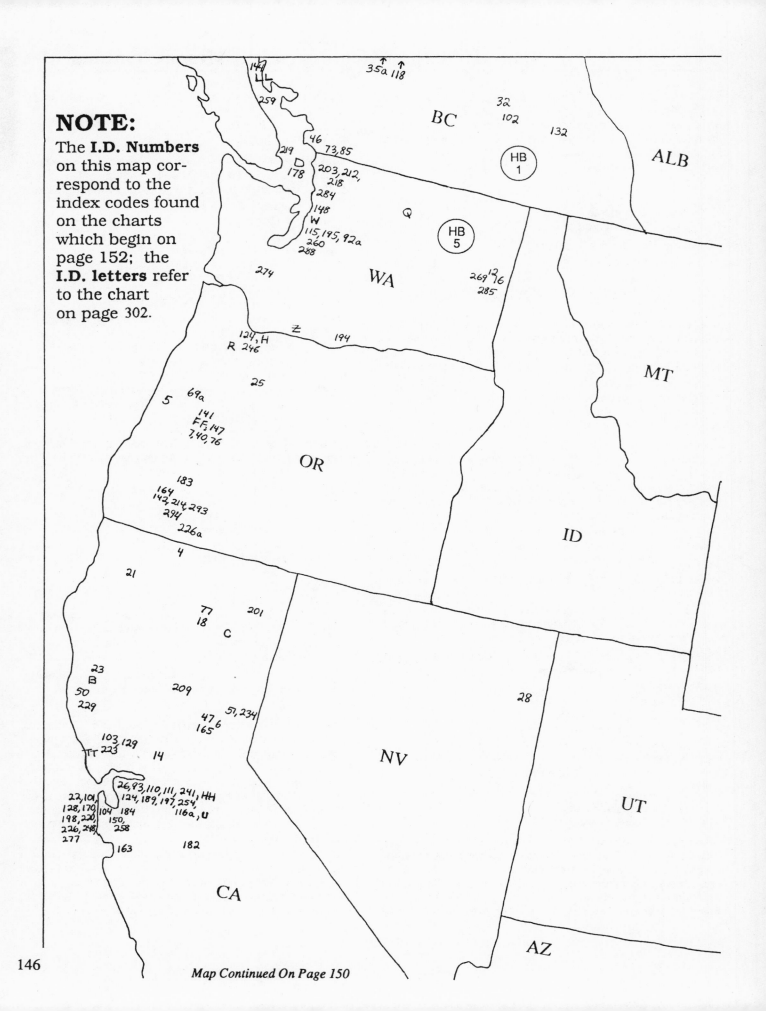

NOTE: The **I.D. Numbers** on this map correspond to the index codes found on the charts which begin on page 152; the **I.D. letters** refer to the chart on page 302.

Map Continued On Page 150

ALB

HB
139

SAS

66

HB
52

MAN

HB
93

55

NOTE:
There are 391
Hutterite colonies
in the great plains
area of the U.S. and
Canada; the circled
"HB" numbers
indicate the count
in each state or
province.

HB
4

HB
6

ND

MT

HB
40

Map Continued on Next Page

HB
51

SD

WY

NB

UT

273

62,116

139

19

CO

S

F

KS

191

155

Map Continued at Bottom of Page 150

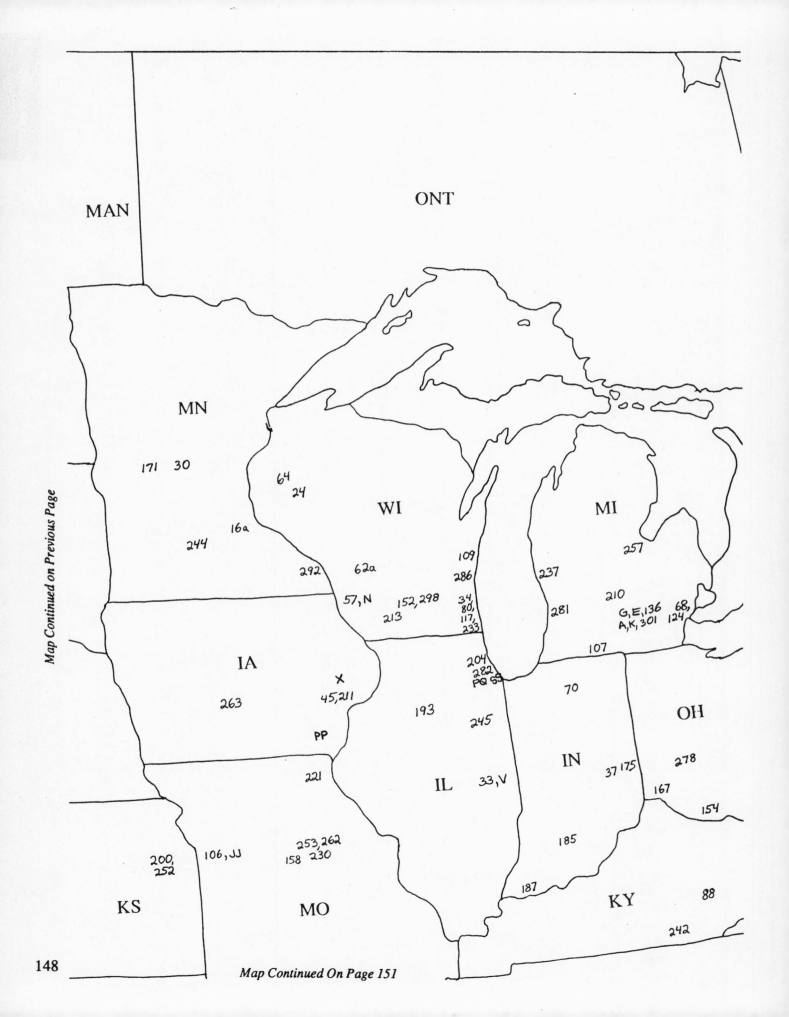

Map Continued on Previous Page

MAN

ONT

MN

171   30

64
24

16a

244

WI

292

62a

57, N

213

152, 298

109

286

34
80,
117,
233

MI

257

237

210

281

G, E, 136
A, K, 301

68,
124

107

IA

X

263

45, 211

PP

204
282
PQ 55

70

193

245

IN

OH

37 175

278

167

221

IL

33, V

154

185

253, 262

158 230

187

187

106, JJ

200,
252

KS

MO

KY

88

242

Map Continued On Page 151

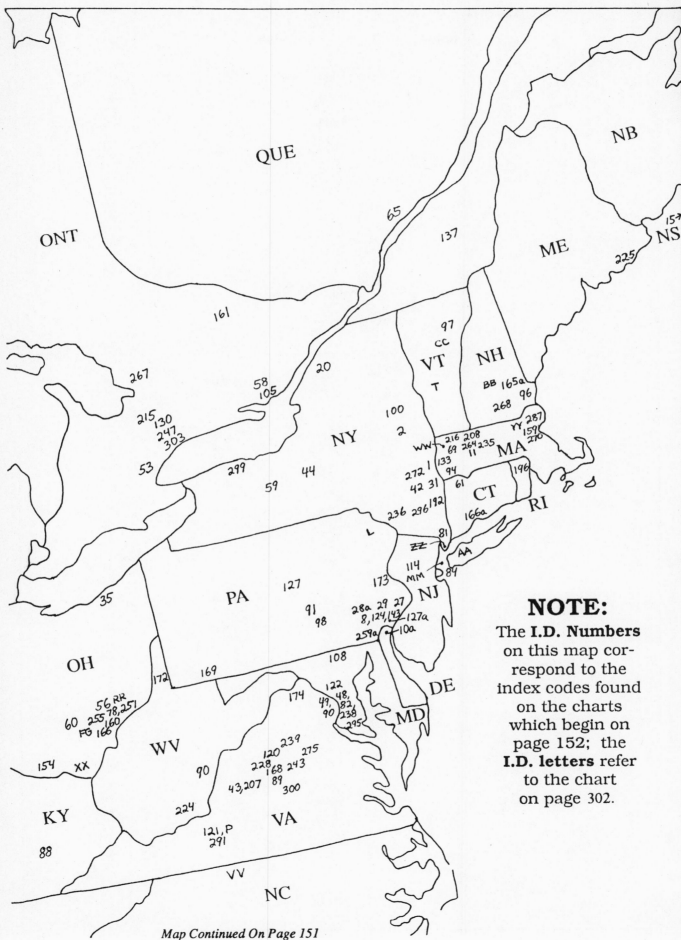

NOTE:

The **I.D. Numbers** on this map correspond to the index codes found on the charts which begin on page 152; the **I.D. letters** refer to the chart on page 302.

Map Continued On Page 151

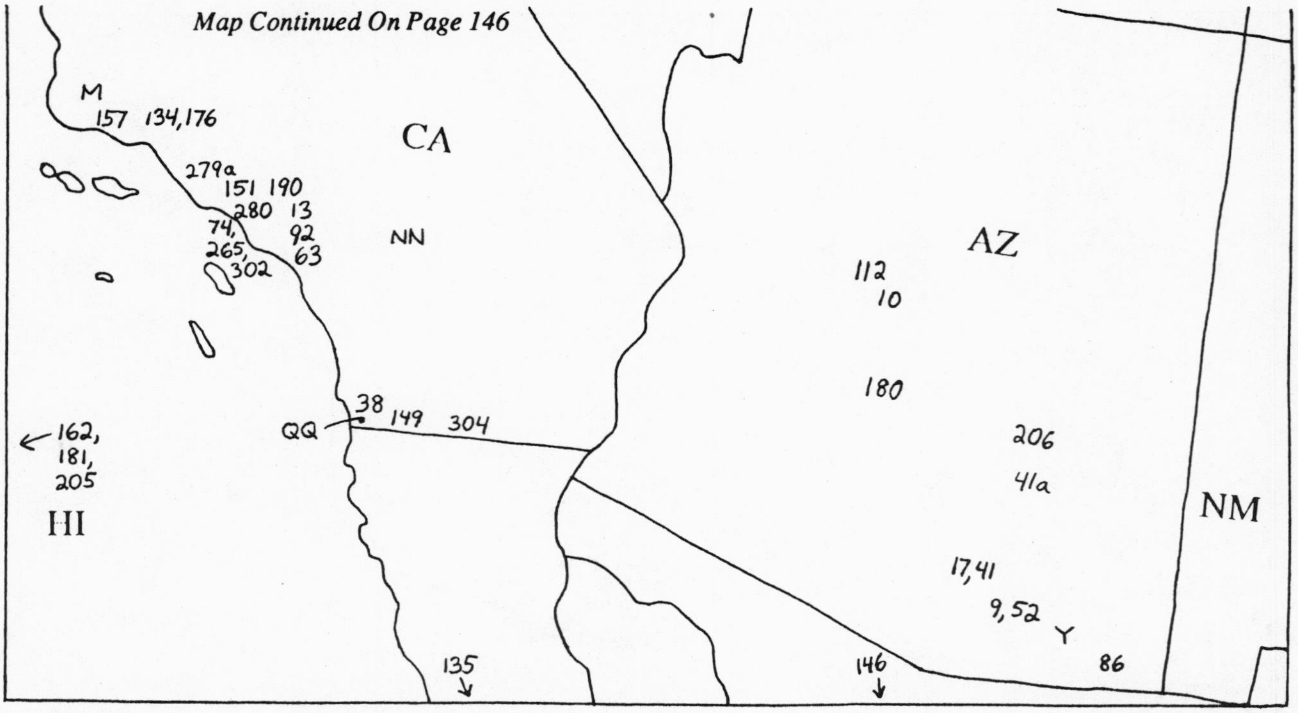

Map Continued On Page 146

CA

M
157 134,176

279a
151 190
280 13
74, 92
265, 63
302

NN

AZ

112
10

180

206

41a

Map Continued Below Left

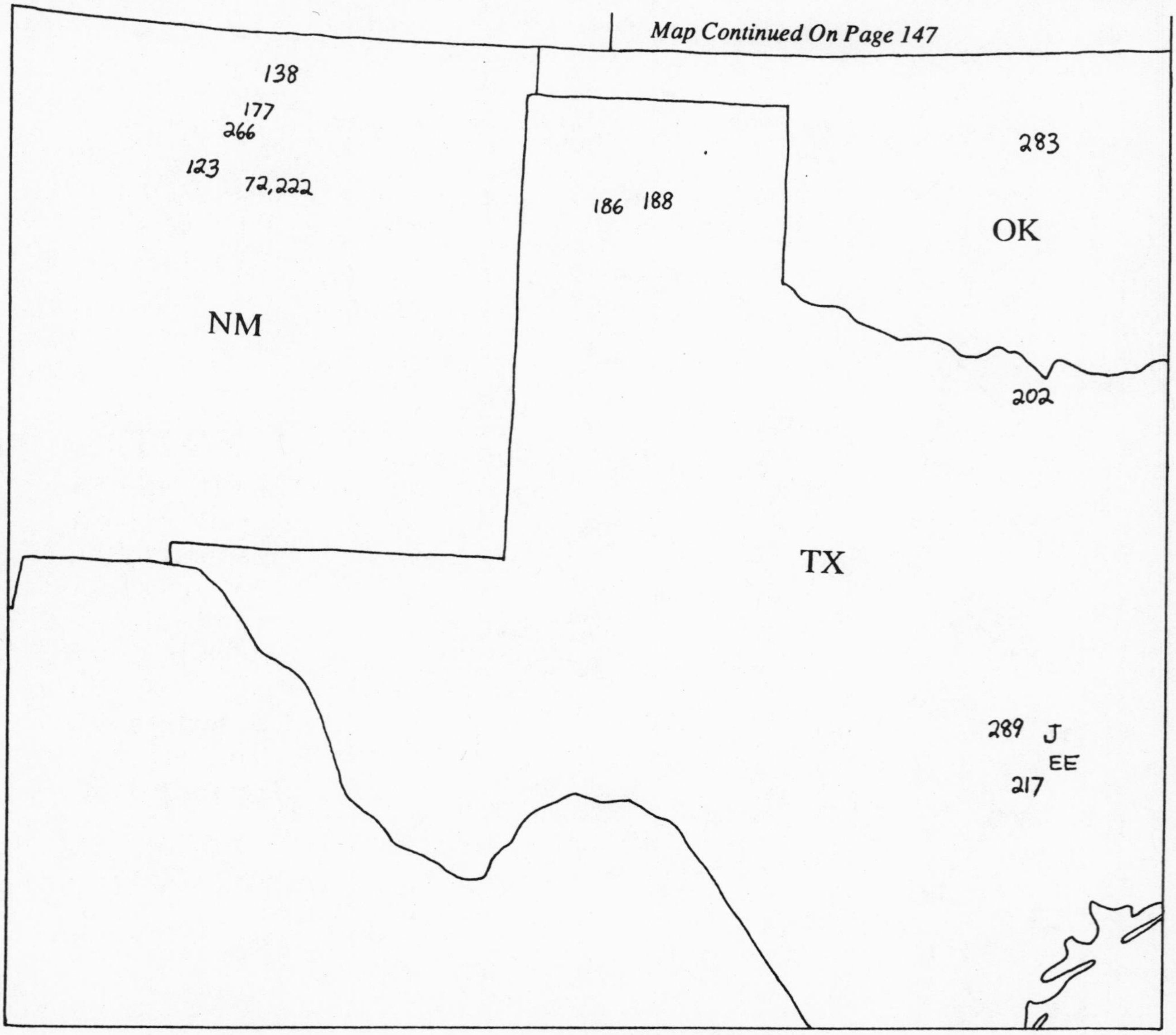

38 149 304
QQ

← 162,
181,
205

HI

NM

17,41

9,52 Y

86

135 ↓

146 ↓

Map Continued On Page 147

138

177
266

123 72,222

NM

186 188

283

OK

Map Continued Above Right

202

TX

289 J
EE
217

Map Continued At Right (Rotated 90°)

150

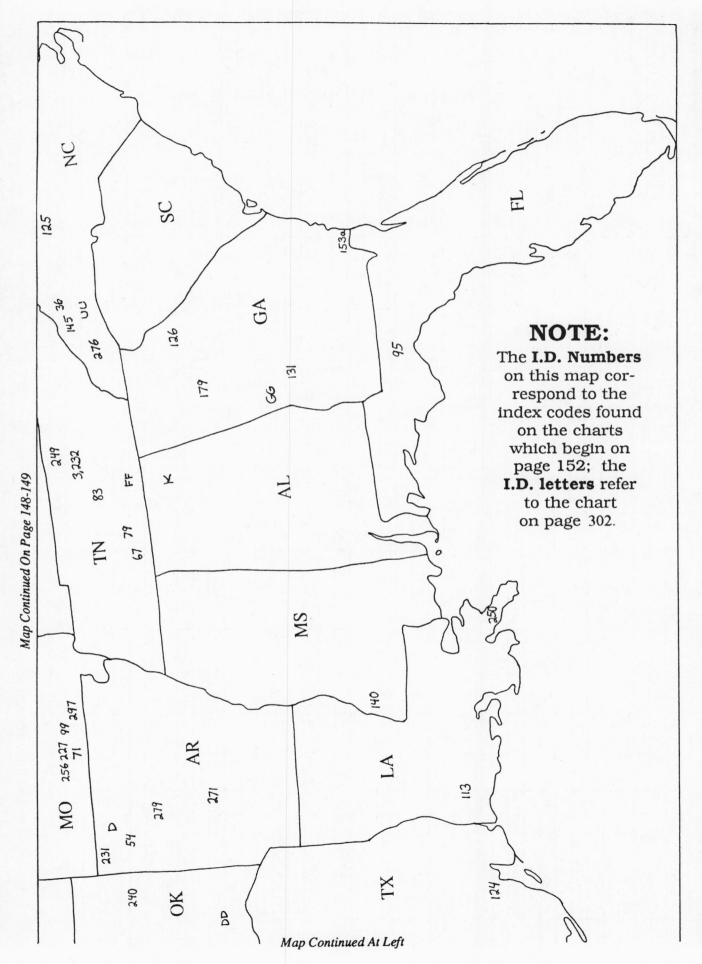

Map Continued On Page 148-149

NC

125

36
145 UU
276

SC

153a

FL

GA

126

179

K

G6 131

95

AL

249
3,232

TN

83
FF

79
67

MS

252

256 227 99 297
71

MO

231 D
54

AR

279 271

140

LA

113

OK

240

DD

TX

124

NOTE:

The **I.D. Numbers** on this map correspond to the index codes found on the charts which begin on page 152; the **I.D. letters** refer to the chart on page 302.

Map Continued At Left

Community Name / Forming?	Map #	State/Prov	Land/Bldgs Ld Ac	Rur/Urb	Year Est?	Pop. Adults	Child	Max?	More? A	More? C	Join Fee	Sch?	Gen? Visitors?	Decis? C/M	Wt?	Food Gr	Ea	Or	Vg	Fl	Own Ld	B	Rm	Econ S?	L/mo	$/mo	Op?	Sexual Restr?	Spirit Basis	L?	P	F	VS	Other Values / Remarks
Abode of the Message	1	NY	430 ac	R	75	43	18	50a25c	Y	Y	500	Cb	Y	M	N	N	Y	Y	N	Y	C	C	Cb	N	16	<405	N	CHLP	Ecl	Y	s	s	Y	Sufism
Adirondack Herb	2	NY	40 ac	R	82	6	0	20	Y	Y	N		Y	N	N	Y	Y	Y	Y	Y	N	N	F	N	64	N	Y		N	N	N	N	N	Conservation
Agape Community (F)	3	TN	300 ac	R	72	2	4	N	Y	Y	N	Hm	Y	Cb	Y	S	S	S	S	S	Cb	Cb	Cb	Y				CMa	C	Y	s	s	Y	Shared Spiritual Life
Alcyone	4	CA	360 ac	R	81	4+16	0	150	Y	Y	Y		Y	C	Y	Y	Y	Y	N*	Y	Cb	Cb	Cb	N	50-8	N	N	CMa	C	Y	Y	Y	Y	Meditation & Unity
Alpha Farm	5	OR	280 ac	R	72	18	4	4	Y	Y	AA	Pu	Y	C	N	N	Y	N*	Y	C	C	C	Y				N	Ecl	N	Y	Y	Y	Group Process
Ananda Village	6	CA	900 ac	B	68	400	125	Same	Y	Y	1,500+	Cb	Y	C	Q	N	Y	N*	Y	C	C	C	N	Vol	Vol	Y	CH	CE	Y	N	N	Y	Non-Denominational
Appletree Co-op	7	OR	23 ac	R	74	13	10	10-25	Y	Y	N		Y	N	s	S	S	Y	N*	N	C	C	C	N	Vol	Y	s		N	Y	Y	Y	Y	Ecology; Communications
Aquarian Research (F)	8	PA	1 Hs	U	69	3	2	N	Y	Y			Y	C	s	S	S	Y	Y	N	R	Cb	Cb	(P)					CO	N	N	N	Y	Concern about World Situation
Aquarius Ranch (F)	9	AZ	30 ac	R	85	3	2	10-20	Y	Y	N		Y	Cb	N	N	Y	S	Y	N	C	N	R	Y	10	100	Y		Ecl	Y	N	N	Y	Preserve Nature
Arcosanti	10	AZ	860 ac	B	70	60	3	5,000	Y	Y	400	Cb	Y	N	Y	Y	S	N	Y	N	C	C	R	N	Y	100	N	N	N	N	N	Y	N	Arcology
Arden Village	10a	IL	<200 ac	U*	00	400	100	Same	N	N		Cb	N	M	N	N	N	Y	N	Y	L	I	F	N	Y	10%	s	N	N	N	s	s	s	Artistic Enclave
Ark/Amherst	11	MA		B	84	10	2	12	Y	Y	N	Pt	Y	C	N	Y	Y	Y	Y	Y	N	N	Cb	N	N		N	N	Ecl	N	s	s	Y	Children
Asponola	12	WA*		R	60	45	Incl		M	M		Cm	P	N	Y	Y	Y	Y	Y	N	C		F	N				Y	HB	Y	Y	Y	N	NQ Agriculture
Atmaniketan	13	CA		B	72	25	6		Y	Y			Y	Cb	N	Y	Y	Y	Q	Y	C	C	D	Y				C	E	Y	E	N	Y	Dedication; Sincerity
Auroville Int'l USA	14	CA*	Network	R*	68	400	200	~50,000	Y	Y		Cb	Y	Y	N	Y	S	N*	Y	L	L	Cb	S	120	(P)	s	E	E	N			Y	[Network] All Life Is Yoga
Baxters Harbour Co-op	15	NS		R	74	15	10		N	N	1,000	Pu	Y	Cb	N	N	N	N	N	Y	C	C	R	N	20		P	Q	Ecm	N	N	U	Y	Individual Lifestyles
Bear Tribe	16	WA	40 ac	R	70				Y				Y			Y	Y	Y	N	N	C	C	C	P					NAm	Y			Y	NQ Permaculture
Bethany Fellowship	16a	MN																						Y						Y				NQ No Info Available
Bhaktiras (F)	17	AZ	Looking	R*	90	4	1	32	Y	Y		Cb	Y	C	Y	N	Y	N	Y	N	L	L	Cb	N	Y		P	CHM	Yoga	N	Y	Y	Y	Bhakti (God Love)
Big Wheels	18	CA	40 ac	R	71	3+10	1+3		Y	Y	N		Y	M	N	Y	Y	Y	Y	N	C	C	F	N	40+	150	Y	Y	N	Y	N	Y	Y	Extended Family
Bijou Community	19	CO		U		3+15	2		M	M		Cm		C		Y	Y	Y	Y	N			L						Ecm	N			Y	NQ Peace & Justice Work
Birdsfoot	20	NY	73 ac	R	72	11	0		Y	Y		Cb	Y	C	N	Y	Y	Y	N*	Y	C	C	Cb	N	18+	160	Y	N	N	Y	Y	Y	Y	Individual Spirituality
Black Bear Ranch	21	CA	70 ac	R	68	5	6	20	Y	Y	Varies	Cb	Y	C	s	Y	Y	Y	N*	Y	L	L	Cb	N			Y	N	N	N	Y	Y	Y	Sustainable Living
Black Cat	22	CA	15 Rm	U	86	9	2	9a,3c	N	N	0		N	N	N	N	S	N	N	Y	C	C	R	N			N	N	P	N	N	N	s	Direct Action Politics
Black Oak Ranch	23	CA*	490 ac	B	65	26+	Y	N	M	M	N	Cb	Y	C*	Y	Y	P	N	Y	N	Cb	Cb	R	Y	250+	Y	N	M	Y	P	N	S	Humor; Friendship
Bounty (F)	24	WI	12 ac	U	89	3	3		Y	Y			Y	C	N	Y	N	Y	N	N	Cb	I	F	P	N		Y	N	P	N	s	s	s	Good Neighbors
Breitenbush Hot Spgs	25	OR	86 ac	R	77	36	10	40a,10c	Y	Y	7,000	Pu	Y	M	Y	Y	N	Y	S	Y	C	C	C	Y	40/w	N	Y	N	Ecl	N	s	s	Y	Energy Self-Sufficiency
Brigid	26	CA	8 Rm	U	85	6	1	Same	N	N	500	Pu	s	C	N	N	Y	Y	S	Y	C	C	R	N	Y		Y	Ecl	N	N	Y	s	Personal Growth
Bryn Gweled	27	PA	240 ac	U	40	136	65	Same	Y	Y	4,500	Cb	Y	Cb	N	N	N	N	N	N	C	N	F	N			Y	N	Ecl	N	N	N	S	Diversity
Builders	28	NV		B	69	40	25		Y	Y		Cb	Y	C		N	S	N	N	Y	C	C	Cb	N	Y		Y	(CHM)	Ecl	Y			Y	Feedback & Free Choice
Camphill Spec'l School	28a	PA	57 ac	R	63	60	80+		Y	Y		Cm	Y	C		Y	N	Y	N	Y	L	L	Cb	N		Vol			O	N			Y	NQ Anthroposophy
Camphill	29	PA	410 ac	R	72	100	30	160	Y	Y		Pt	V	C		N	Y	N	Y	Y	L	L	F	Y	Vol		N**		N				Anthroposophy
Camphill Vill/Minn	30	MN	360 ac	R	80	31	13	~90	Y	Y		Hm	Y			N	Y	N*	Y	Y	L	C	Cb	Y			N**	Y	N			Y	Anthroposophy
Camphill Vill/U.S.A.	31	NY	600 ac	R	61	180	40	220	Y	M		Pt	Y			N	Y	N	N	N	C	C	F	Y			N	C	N			Y	Social Therapy
Caravan Theatre Farm	32	BC	80 ac	R	78	5	5		Y	Y			Y	Cb	Y	Y	Y	N	Q	C	C	Cb	S			N	N	N	P	P	Y	NQ Stewardship
Casa Grande	33	IL		U	70	6	1		Y	Y		Hm	Y			S	S	Y	S	Y	L	C	R	S			N	N	N	Q	Y	Y	Egalitarian; Environment
Casa Maria	34	WI		U	68	15	3		Y	Y	N		Y	C	N	S	S	Y	Y	L	Cb	R	Y	15	200	Y	R/C	N	Y	Y	Y	Non-Violence
Catholic Worker/ Cleve	35	OH	Houses	U	84	20	0		Y	N	N	Cb	Y	C	s	N	Y	Y	Y	Cb	Cb	R	N	Y		Y	N	C/Ecl	N	Y	Y	Y	Live with Poor
CEEDS	35a	BC	400 ac	R	72	15	0	N	S	S	N		Y	C	N	Y	Y	Y	Y	N	N	R	Y			N	Y	N	s	S	Y	Ecology; Agriculture
Celo	36	NC	1200 ac	R	39	43	25		S	S	Y	Cb	Y	C	N	N	Y	N	N	L	I	F	N	Vol	Y	S	(Mo)	N	N	s	s	Y	Community Service
Center/Examined Life	38	CA		U	66	7	0		Y	N	N		Y	Cb	Y	Y	N	N	N	N	C	C	R	N			Y	CHMo	Y	Y	Y	N	Y	Human Potential
Center/Peace & Life	37	IN		R	72?			N	N	N	N	Pu		C	Y	N	N	N	N	N	C	I	F	N			Y	Ma	C	Y	Y	Y	Broader Community

Key to the Headings: **Map#:** Corresponds to numbers on the maps. **More?** [A]Adults, [C]Children **Sch?** Kind of Schooling? **Gen?** Gender: Women or Men only? **Food/Diet?** [Gr]Grow Own? [Wt?]Weighted Decisions? [Or]Organic/Whole Grains? [Vg]Vegetarian? [Fl]Flexible? **Decis?** [C/M]Consensus or Majority? [Wt?]Weighted Decisions? **Economic Sharing:** [S?]Income Sharing? [L/mo]Labor/Month? [$/mo]Cost/Month [Op?]Income-Earning Opportunities? **Ownership:** [Ld]Land? [B]Buildings? [Rm]Rooming/Accommodations Style? **Values:** [P]Pacifist? [F]Feminist? [VS]Voluntary Simplicity? **Spirituality:** [B]Basis? [L?]Leader?

Map #	Community Name	Forming?	State/Prov	Land/Bldgs	Rur/Urb	Year Est?	Adults	Child	Max?	More A	More C	Sch? Visitors?	Gen? Visitors?	Join Fee	Decis C/M	Wt?	Gr	Ea	Or	Vg	Fl	Own Ld	Own B	Own Rm	Econ S?	L/mo	$/mo	Op?	Sexual Restr?	Spirit Basis	L?	P	F	VS	Other Values / Remarks
40	Cerro Gordo		OR	1200 ac	R	73	7F		2,500	Y	Y	Pu	Y	500	M	Q	N	N				L	N	F	N	N	N	Y	N	N	N	N	N	N	Symbiotic Community
41	Child's Garden	(F)	AZ	Looking	R?	88	2+6	1+3	15-50	Y	Y	Hm	Y	V	Cb	N	M	M	Y	M	M	U	U	U	U	U	U	U	U	Ecl	N	N	N	Y	Alt.Childrearing; Pers.Growth
41a	Christmas Star		AZ	41 ac	R	80	12	9	9	Y	Y	Hm	Y	N	C	Y	Y	Y	Y	Y	Y	I	C	F	N	Y	N	Y	N	O	Y	S		Y	Cultural Evolution
42	Common Ground	(F)	NY	70 ac	R	89	3	0		Y	Y	Hm	Y	N	C	N	N	Y	N	Y	Y	N	N	D	N	50	N	Y		N	N	N	N	N	Trust
43	Common Ground		VA	77 ac	R	80	10	5	18 Fam	Y	Y	Hm	Y	Y	C		S			N*		L	I	F	Y		Y			Ecl			Y		Ecology; Non-Exploitation
44	Common Place		NY	300 ac	B	76	7+4	3	40	Y	M	Cb	Y	N	C	N	S	S	Y	P	Y	L	N	F	N	3	60	M		N	Y	Y	Y	Y	11 Core Ideals
45	Communia		IA	6 Hs	B	76	12	6	N	Y	Y		Y	N	C	N	N	N	N	N	N	C	C	F	N	N	25			CE	N	Y	Y	Y	Spiritual Growth
49	Community, The		VA	6 Hs	U	66	5	4		Y	Y	Hm	Y	N	C	N	N	Y	N	Y	Y	C	Cb		Cb	Y	Y	Y	Ecm	N	N	Y	Y	Y	Communication
46	Community Alt'natives	(F)	BC*	9 units	B	77	34	11	~Same	Y	Y	Pu	Y	Y	C		S	S	S	S	Y	C	C	R	N		Y		N	Ecl	N	Y	Q		NQ Cooperative Social Action
48	Community: CCNV		DC		U	70	45	1		Y	Y	Pu	Q	N	C	Q	N	Y	N	N	N	N	N	Cb	Y	Y	Y	Y		N	N	N	Y	Q	Resist Injustice
47	Community Evolving		CA	50 ac	B	88	4	2	32-40	Y	Y	Hm	Y	N	C	N	N	P	Y	Y	N	U	U	R	N		Y			N	N	Y	Y	Y	Intimacy; Deep Ecology
50	Comptche Farms	(F)	CA	100 ac	R	87	6	2	6 Fam	Y	Y	Hm	Y	Y	C	N	P	Y	Y	N	Y	C	C	F	N	40	750	P	HMo	N	N	N	N	N	Diversity; Stewardship
51	Consciousness Village		CA		R	74	8	3	15	Y	Y	Pu	Y	Y	C	Y	S	Y	N*	Y		I	I	Cb	N	75	140	Y		N	Y	S	S	S	Rebirthing
52	Cooper Street		AZ		B	80	6	0	~12	Y	M		Y	N	N	C	N	Y	Q	N	Y	N	N		N	N	Y	Y		N	N	S	Y	Y	Tolerance
53	Crieff Hills		Ont		R	75	2-20	0	N	Y	Y	Pu	Y	N	N	N	N	N	P	N	Y	L	L	F	N	Y	Y	Y	HMa	C	Y	Y	S	Y	Christian Hospitality
54	Crosses Creek		AR		R	85	6	5		Y	Y	Cm	Y	Y	Cb	Y	N	N	Y	N	N	N	Cb	Cb	Y	80	N	Y	Ma	C	Y			Y	Spiritual Healing
55	Crystal Spring		Man	*	R				150?	M	M	Cm	Y	N	N	Y	Y	Y	Y	N	Y	C	C	Cb	Y		88+	N	M	HB	Y	Y	N	Y	NQ Hutterian
56	Currents		OH	163 Ac	R	81	11	6	30	P	P	Pt	Y	13,800	C	N	N	S	Y	N		C	C	Cb	N	12	88+	N		N	N	Y	Y	Y	Cooperation
57	Dancing Waters		WI		R	82	8-10	3	N	Y	Y	Cb	Y	N	C	N	N	Y	N	Y	N	C	C	F	Y	N	140	N		N	N	Y	Y	Y	Communication; Land
58	Dandelion		Ont	50 ac	R	75	4	1	12-15	Y	Y		Y	LoanAA	C	C	Y	Y	N	Y	Y	C	C	R	Y			Y		N	N	Y	Y	Y	EcoFeminism; Self-Sufficiency
59	Dayspring		NY		R	75	8	9	30+	Y	Y	Cm	Y	N	C	N	Y	Y	N	Y	Y	L	L	Cb	Y					Y	Q	Y	N	S	Org.Agricultr; Psych
60	Deep Woods		OH	310 ac	R	78	7	0	30-50	Y	Y	Cb	Y	9,000	C	Y	S	S	Y	N*	Y	C	N	F	N	10+		Y	CMo	Ecl	N	Y	Q	Q	Sharing; Neighbors
61	Deer Spring		CT*		R		10	4		M	M	Cm	Y	N	N	Y	Y					N	N						M	HB	Y	Y	N	Y	NQ Hutterian
62	Denver Space Center		CO		U	79	5	0	N	Y	Q		S	N	Cb	Y	N	Y	Y	N	Y	N	N	R	N	8	150	N		Q	N	S	P	S	Good Company &
62a	DOE Farm		WI	80 ac	R	77			35	Y	Y		W Y	N	C	Y	N	Y	N	Y	Y	C			N	Y	.3%			N		Y	Y	Y	NQ Womyn's Land
63	Dolphin Society	(F)	[HI]	CA now	Q	84?	1+6	0+1	10a+7c	Y	Y		Y				Y	Y	Y	Y		N				Y								Y	NQ Undersea City
64	Dorea Peace Commty		WI	89 ac	R	80	8	8		Y	Y	Pu	Y	N	C	N	N	Y	N	N	N	Cb	N	F	N	Y	175	N	Ma	C	N	N	Y	Y	Justice Issues
65	Dragonfly Farm		Ont	250 ac	R	78	10	1	N	Y	Y		Y	3,000	C	N	Y	Y	Y	Y	Y	C	C		N	N	30	Y		N	N	P	P	P	kAos
66	Duck Mtn Circle	(F)	Man	160 ac	R	87	3	3	10 Fam	Y	Y	Hm	Y	3,000	C	N	Y	Y	Y	N	Y	L	N	F	N	N	60	M		N	N	N	Y	Y	"People Garden"
67	Dunmire Hollow		TN	160 ac	R	74	10	4		Y	Y	Cb	Y	N	C	N	S	Y	N	S	N	C	C	F	N	Y	25	S		N	N	N	N	N	Stewards; Comunity
68	Earth Community		MI	40 ac				8		M	M		M	N			N	Y	Y	N	Y	Cb	Cb	R						Ecl					NQ No Info Available
69	Earthdance		MA	180 ac	R	86	10	3	20-28	Y	Y	Cb	Y	N	C	N	S	Y	Y	N*	Y	C	C	Cb	N	32+	425	U		Y	N				Dance, Joy, Hard Wrk
69a	Earth's Rising Co-op		OR	60 ac	R	70s	<10		>10				M	M	C	N	Y	N	N	Y	N	C	C	F	N	Y				N	N			Y	NQ Simple Living
70	Earthworks	(F)	IN	1 ac	R	88	1+6	0+1		Y	Y		Y	U			Y	Y	Y	N*	Y	N	N	R	N	N	N	M		C	N	Y	Y	Y	Ecology; Art; Prayer
71	East Wind		MO	160 ac	R	74	40	8	300-750	Y	Y	Cb	Y	N	M	Y	S	Y	Y	Y	N	C	C	D	Y					N	N	Y	Y	Y	Egalitarian; Environ;
72	Ecological Village	(F)	NM	Not yet	B	88	20-70	?	700	Y	Y	Cb	Y	25	C	N	Y	S	Y	Y	Y	L	I	Cb	Y					Ecl	N	P		N	Planetary Regeneration
73	Edenvale	(F)	BC*	117 ac	R	73	34	8	Same	Y	Y	Cb	Y	N	C	Y	Y	N	S	N	N	C	C	Cb	N	Y				EDL	Y	N	N	N	Honor Life's
74	Ellis Island		CA	11 BR	U	69	11	0-4		Y	Y		M	N	C	N	Y	N	S	N	S	C	C	R	N	Y				N	Y	N	Y	N	No Dogmas
	Emissar. Divine Light		**	Network						Y	Y		Y	N	Cb	Y	V	V	V	S		Cb	Cb	Cb	Cb	Y	Var	S		EDL	Y	S		S	[International] Global Integrity
76	End of the Road		OR	40 ac	R	81	4	3	12-15	Y	N	Cb	Y	N	C	Y	Y	Y	Y	N*	N	L	L	Cb	N	Y	150	Y		Y	N	N	N	N	De-Consumerizing; 3rd World
77	Essene Mother Earth		CA	140 ac	R	82	4	3	N	Y	Y	Pu	Y	5,000	N	N	N	N	N*	Y	C	C	C	F	N	10	Y		CMo	Ecm	N	N	S		Essene Lifestyle
78	Far Valley Farm		OH	234 ac	R	80	12+2	8	N	P	P	Cb	Y	5,000	C	N	N	Y	N	Y	Y	C	I	Cb	N	10	25			N	N	Y	Y	Y	Organic Structure

North American Communities: Cross-Reference Chart

Sorted Alphabetically

Map #	Community Name / Forming?	State/ Prov	Land/ Bldgs	Rur/ Urb	Year Est?	Adults	Child	Max?	More? A	C	Sch?	Gen?/ Vis?	Decis? C/M	Wt?	Gr	Ea	Or	Vg	Fl	Ld	B	Rm	Econ S?	L/mo $/mo	Op?	Join Fee	Sexual Restr?	Spirit Basis	L?	P	F	VS	Other Values / Remarks
79	Farm, The	TN	1,750 ac	R	71	125	175	800	Y	Y	Cm	Y	Cb		Y	S	Y	N*	Y	C	C	F	S	N 110+	M	3,000	N	Ecm		Y	Y	Y	Universal Oneness
80	Farm Home Center (F)	WI		R	87	3	0		Y	Y		Y	M	U	N	N	Y	N	N	N	N	F	N	U U		U	U	Ecl	N	N	U	U	Alternative Agriculture Center
81	Fellowship Community	NY		U*	67	105	20	N	Y	Y	Pt	Y	N	Y	Y	Y	N	N	N	C	C	Cb	N	Y Y	Y	N	CHM	C	Y	N	N	N	Anthroposophy
82	Finders	DC	Various	B	70	15	2		M	M	Cb	Y		Y	N	Y	N	N	Y	C	C	R	Y	Y Y	Y	Y	N	Ecl	S	S	S	S	Life is a Game
83	Flatrock	TN	27 ac	B	79	8	6		Y	Y	Pu	Y	Cb	N	Y	Y	Y	N*	Y	L	N	F	N	Y 35+	N	3,400	N	N	N	Q	Y	Y	Je Ne Sais Quoi; Funk
85	Fraser Common Farm	BC	10 ac	R	77	4	2+2	35	M	M	Cb	Y	C		Y	Y	Y	Y	Y	C	C	R	Y	Y	Y	Y	Y			Y	Y	Y	NQ Permaculture
86	Friends SW Centr	AZ		R	74	17	0	35	Y	Y	Pu	Y	C	N	N	N	N	Y	N	L	Cb	F	N	2-3	S	N	N	Qk	N	Y	S	Y	Truth; Openness
87	Full Circle Farm	CA	5 ac	R	84	14	4	N	M	N	Cm	N	Cb	Y	N	N	Y	N	Y	I	I	R	N	5-10	N	N	N	N	N	Y	P	S	Non-Violence
88	Futures Inc.	KY	73 ac	R	88	7	1	250	Y	Y	Cb	Y	Cb	N	N	N	S	Y	N*S	L	C	Cb	N	170	S	Varies	U	Ecm	M	S	N	Y	Soul Fraternity
88a	Galilee (F)	OR		R	90	2	0	N	Y	Y	U	Y	Cb		Y	Y	Y	Y	N	U	U	U	P	Y	U	N	N	Ecm	N	N	N	Y	Environmental Consciousness
84	Ganas	NY	7 bldgs	U	78	9+35	0	55	Y	Y		Y	C	Y	N	Y	N	N	Y	C	C	R	S	150+	S	450	N	N	N	S	S	S	Communication & Feedback
89	Gathering, The	VA	10 ac	B	69	14	0		Y			Y			Y	Y	Y	Y	N	C	C	D	N			N	N	Y	Y	Y	Y	N	Spirituality; Communal Life
90	Gesundheit	WV	310 ac	B	71	9	5	150	M	M	Cb	Y	Cb		S	Y	Y	Y	Y	L	L	R	N	Y	Y	N	N	N	N	N	P	P	Serve People & the Planet
91	Gita Nagari	PA	600 ac	R	74	51	23		Y	Y	Cb	Y	N		Y	Y	Y	Y	Y	L	L	R	N	Y	Y	N	N	Y	N	N	N	N	High Thinking
92	Glen Ivy	CA*		B	77	66	10	125	Y	Y		Y	Cb	Y	Y	Y	Y	Y	N	L	L	Cb	N	180	Y	N	CMa	E	Y	N	P	Y	Selfless Service
92a	Goodenough	WA	Non-res	U	81	100	12	300	Y	Y	Cb	Y	C	Y	S	Y	Y	Y	Y	C	N	F	N			25/Yr	N	EDL	Y	S	S	S	Covenant
93	Goodlife	CA	1 hs	U	68	6	2		M	M	Cb	Y	C	N	N	Y	Y	Y	Y	I	I	R	S	300+	Y	100	N	Ecm	Y	N	N	Y	Urban Extended Family
94	Gould Farm	MA	600 ac	B	13	120	18		Y	M	Pu	Y	N	Y	N	Y	N	N	N	Cb	I	F	N	Y	N	N	(M)**	CJ	N	N	S	S	Care for Mentally Ill
95	Grassroots Co-op	FL	40 ac	R	82	44	31	10-12	M	M	Cb	Y	Cb	Y	N	Y	N	N	N	L	N	F	N	10	N	N	N	N	S	S	S	S	Environment; Peace
96	Green Pastures	NH*	160 ac	R	63	68	11	80	Q	Q	Pu	Y	N		Y	Y	Y	N	Y	Cb	N	F	N	Y	N	N	N	EDL	Y	Y	N	N	Stewardship
97	Greenhope Farm	VT	17 ac		83	4	0					W			Y	Y	Y	Y	N	C	C	Cb	N			N	N	Ecl					NQ No Info Available
98	Greening Life	PA	135 ac	R	73	8+2	1+2	30-35	Y	Y	Cb	Y	C	N	Y	Y	Y	Y	Y	C	N	F	N	8-10 95+	Y	5,000	N	Ecm	N	S	N	Y	Growth in Spirit
99	Greenwood Forest	MO	1,000 acRR	R	79	45	8	N	Y	Y	Cb	Y	M		N	S	N	Y	N	I	F	N	Vol	8	N	12,500	N(Mo)	N	N	P	S	Y	Land Stewardship
100	Griffin Gorge	NY	40 ac	R	77	8	3	10-12	N	N	Pu	Y	N		N	Y	N	N	N*	L	N	F	N			N	N	N	N	N	N	Y	Self Esteem; Earth
101	Group W	CA	5 Rm	U	85	5	0	Same	P	N		S	C		N	Y	N	N	N	C	I	F	N	65		N	N	(P)	Y	Y	Y	Y	Political Activism
102	Hailos	Ont	320 ac	R	81?	12+5	0+4		Y	Y	Cb	Y	Cb		N	N	N	Y	Y	L	L	Cb	N	Y		10,000	CM	Ecl	N	N	N	N	Cottage Industries
103	Harbin Hot Springs	CA	1,100 ac	R	71	120	10		Y	Y		Y	N		N	Y	S	Y	P	N	C	Cb	S	50+	Y	1,001	N	Ecl		N	S	Y	Land; Human Potential
104	Harvest Forum (F)	CA		R	87	4	0	12-16	N	N		Y	C		N	N	Y	N*	N	N	N	R	N	12	Y	N	N	Ecm	N	P	Y	P	Alternative Lifestyle
105	Headlands	Ont	1 Hs	R	71	4	2	N	N	Y	Pu		M		S	Y	Y	N*N		N	N	Cb	N	300		N	N	N	N	N	N	N	Ideological Void
106	Hearthaven	MO	1 Hs	U	88	5	0		Y	Y		Y	C		N	Y	N	N	N	C	C	Cb	N	Y	N	N	N	Ecm	N	Y	Y	Y	Peace; Joy; Hospitality
107	Heartlight	MI	35 ac	R	83	12+5	0+4	N	Y	Y		Y	C		Y	Y	Y	Y	Y	N	N	D	N	200+	Y	N	CM	Ecm	Y	Y	Y	Y	Love, Joy, Peace, God
108	Heathcote	MD	35 ac	R	65	4	0	8	Y	Y		Y	C		N	N	Y	Y	S	L	L	Cb	N	30-4 300+	N	250	N	N	N	Y	N	N	Ecology Action
109	High Wind	WI	46 ac	R	81	15	6	60	S	S	Pu	Y	Y	S	N	Y	S	N*	Y	Cb	Cb	F	N	80+ 50+	S	N	N	S	N	S	S	S	Living/Learning Center
110	Hillegass House	CA	11 Rm	U	79	11	0	11	Y	P		Y	C*	Y	N	Y	Y	N*	N	L	Cb	Cb	N	10 450	S	N	N	N	N	N	N	N	Respect; Tolerance;
111	Hog Farm	CA*	490 ac	B	65	26+	Y	N	M	M	C*	Y	Cb	Y	N	Y	Y	Y	Y	C	Cb	R	N	250+	Y	N	N	M	Y	Y	Y	Y	Humor; Friendship
112	Hohm Community	AZ	Non-res	R	75	40-50	Incl		Y		Cb	Y	Cb	Y	Y	Y	Y	Y	N*	Cb	Cb	R	N	Y		Y	Mo	Ecm	Y	Y	N	N	NQ Right Living
113	Holy City	LA	Looking	B	70	33	41		Y	Y	Cb	Y	C	Y	N	N	Y	N	N	Cb	Cb	F	N	10% 10%	N	N	CMa	R/C	Y	N	N	N	Gospel Poverty
114	Homeland (F)	NJ		R	89	9	2	<100	Y	Y	Cb	Y	C		N	P	Y	Y	N	L	C	Cb	N	8	Y	N	N	Ecl	N	Y	Y	Y	Soc. Responsible Development
115	Homestead Co-op (F)	WA	1 Hs	U	89	35+	?	10,000	Y	Y	Cb	Y	C		N	Y	Y	S	N	L	L	Cb	N	V		V	N	N	N	N	S	S	Freedm & Mutul Aid
116	Hooker House	CO	1 Hs	U	77	4	0	8	N	N		Y	C	N	N	Y	N	N	N	C	C	F	N	15	N	N	N	N	N	N	S	S	Middle Class Cooperative
117a	House, The	CA	8 Rm	U	72	6	2		Y	M		Y	S	Y	N	Y	N	N	N	C	C	R	N	10-1 300	Y	N	N	N	N	Y	N	N	Enjoy Shared Living
117	House of Lavendar	WI	1 hs	U	74	7	2	9	S	Q	Pu	Y	M	N	N	N	Y	N	N	C	C	Cb	N	175	N	50 Dep	N	N	S	N	N	Y	Progressive Social Change

Key to the Headings: *Map#?* Corresponds to numbers on the maps. *More?* [A]Adults, [C]Children *Sch?* Kind of Schooling? *Gen?* Gender: Women or Men only? *Food/Diet?* [Gr]Grow Own? [Or]Organic/Whole Grains? [Vg]Vegetarian? [Fl]Flexible? *Decis?* [C/M]Consensus or Majority? [Wt?]Weighted Decisions? *Economic Sharing?* [S?]Income Sharing? [L/mo]Labor/Month? [$/mo]Cost/Month [Op?]Income-Earning Opportunities? *Spirituality?* [B]Basis? [L?]Leader? *Values:* [P]Pacifist? [F]Feminist? [VS]Voluntary Simplicity? *Ownership:* [Ld]Land? [B]Buildings? [Rm]Rooming/Accommodations Style?

North American Communities: Cross-Reference Chart

Sorted Alphabetically

Community Name / Map # / Forming?	State/Prov	Land/Rur/Urb Bldgs	Yr Est?	Pop Adults	Chld	Max?	More? A	C	Sch?/Vis?	Gen?	Join Fee	Decis?	Gr	Ea	Or	Vg	Fl	Ld	B	Rm	Econ S?	L/mo	$/mo Op?	Sexual Restr?	Spirit Basis	L?	P	F	VS	Other Values / Remarks
118 Hundred Mile Lodge	BC*	10 ac R*	48	120	Incl		M	M	Cb	Y		Cb	Y	Y	Y	N	Y	Cb	Cb	Cb	S				EDL	Y	Y	Y	S	NQ Attunement
Hutterian Groups	**	Network R	Var	170	150	400 ea	Y	Y	Cm	Y	AA	C	N	Y	N	N	N	C	C	F	Y			M	HB	Y	N	Y	N	Non-Violence; Brotherhood
120 Innisfree	VA	400 ac B	71	70	1	90	Y	Y	Pu	Y	N	N	N	Y	N	N	N	C	C	F	N		Y	N**	N	N	N	S	S	Disabled
121 Inst Sustain Living	VA	5 ac R	89	10	1	~200	Y	Y	Cm	Y	U	Cb	Y	Cb	Y	N	Y	C	U	Cb	Y			N	Ecl	N	P	Y	Y	Sustainability
122 Intergenerat'n Women (F)	MD	(F) B	89				Y	W	W																					Y	NQ Living/Retirement
123 Jemez Bodhi Mandala	NM																													NQ No Info Available
124 Jesuit Volunteer Corps	**	Network U		Var	0		Y	N		Y	N	C	Y								N		N	N	R/C			Y	Y	NQ Serve the Poor
125 Jubilee House	NC	U	79	13	4		S	S	Pu	Y	AA	C	N	Y	N	N	N	C	C	Q	Y		N	N	C	N	N	Y	Y	Homeless Shelters
126 Jubilee Partners	GA	258 ac R	79	9	6	N	Y	Y	Pu	Y	0	Cb	Y	Y	Y	Y	N	C	C	Cb	Y		Y	CHM	C	N	N	S	Y	Resettling Refugees
127 Julian Woods	PA	140 ac R	75	16	6	N	Y	Y	Y	Y	3,700+	Cb	N	S	N	Y	S	L	I	F	N	Y	21 N	N	Ecl	N	S	S	S	Permaculture; Stewardship
127a Kehillat Mishpakhot	PA	Non-res U	82	6	fam	Families	Y	Y	Cm	N	N	(C)	N	S				F			F	N			J					NQ Tribe of Families
128 Kerista	CA	4 Hs 10U	71	28	4		Y	Y	Hm	N	N	M	N	Y	N	N	N	C	Cb	R	Y		N(P)	Y	N	N	Y	Y	Growth; Communication
129 Kidstown (F)	CA	(F) B	90	1	0	N	Y	M	Cb	N	N	Cb	P	Y	N	N*Y		Cb	Cb	Cb	N	Vol	Var M	N	Ecl	N	N	N	Y	Love One Another
130 King View	Ont*	87 ac R		50	Incl		M	M	Cb	Y		Cb	Y	Y	Y	Y	Y	Cb	Cb	Cb	S		Y	N	EDL	Y	Y	Y	S	NQ Hospitality
131 Koinonia Partners	GA	600 ac R	42	22	10	55	Y	Y	Pu	Y	N	Cb	Y	Y	Y	Y	Y	C	C	Cb	N		Y	CMa	C	N	N	S	Y	Service to Others
132 Kootenay Co-op Land	BC	200 ac R	69	18	9	12 Fam	Y	Y	Cb	Y	25+	C	S	N	Y	N		C	N	F	N	5	N Q		N	S	N	S	Y	Balance Ecology/Economy
133 Kripalu	MA	300 ac R	71	280	7		Y	N	Y	Y		N	N	Y	N	Y	N	C	C	Cb	N	168+	N	CMa	E	Y	N	Y	Y	Service
134 Krotona	CA	118 ac R	24	40															F							Y					NQ Theosophy
135 Krutsio	Mex	80 ac R	76				Y	Y	Hm	Y		Y	Y	Y				C	C	R	Y						Y	Y	Y	NQ Egalitarian; Esperanto
136 Kuntree Bumpkin	MI	80 ac R																													NQ No Info Available
137 La Cité Ecologique	Que	800 ac R	84	102	53	N	Y	Y	Hm	Y	100,000	Cb	Y	Y	Y	Y	Y	L	L	F	N	A lot	200+ Y		N		Y	N	Y	Children's Education
138 Lama Foundation	NM	80 ac R	68	14-70	?	N	V	V	Cb	S	U	Y	S	Y	Y	N*M		L	L	Cb	N		U		Ecc			Y		Awakening Consciousness
139 Lamborn Valley (F)	CO	(F) 120 ac R	89	11	14	40	P	P	Cb	P	U	C	Y	Y	Y	Y	Y	Cb	C	F	N		U	H	CE	S	S	Y	Y	Interpersonal Relations
140 Laurel Hill (F)	MS	(F) 1400 ac R	79	4	1		M	N	Pt	Y	Q	C	N	N	N	N	Y	N	N	Cb	N		Y	HGMo	N		N	N	Y	Honest, Industrious, Clean
142 Lichen	OR	140 ac R	71	3	0	12-15	Y	Y	Pu	Y	3,000	C	N	Y	N	N	N	L	L	F	N	30	Y	(CH)	N		N	Y	Y	Ecology & Environment
143 Life Center Asso.	PA	4 Hs U	71	31	1		Y					C	Q	N	Y	N*		L	L	Cb	N	30	~250 S	N	N		N	Y	Y	Economic Democracy
144 Linnaea	BC	315 ac R	79	8	8	<20	N	N	Cb	N	N	C	N	Y	N	N	Y	L	L	F	N		<50 S	N	N		N	Y	Y	Environment
145 Long Branch	NC	126 ac R	74	6	3								S	N				L	L	Cb	N				N		N	N	Y	NQ Environmental Education
146 Los Horcones	Mex	R	73	20	10		Y		Cm		Varies	C	N	Y	N	Y	N	C	C	Cb	N			Q	N		N	Y	Y	Behavior Change
147 Lost Valley Center	OR	90 ac R	89	13	3	30-40	Y	Y	Cb	Y	100	Cb	P	Y	Y	N	N	L	L	Cb	N	20/w	Y	N	Ecl	N	Y	N	S	Mutual Cooperation
148 Love Israel Family	WA	290 ac R	68	39	46	144,000	Y	Y	Cb	Y	AA	N	Y	N	Y	N	Y	C	C	F	N		Y	N≠	C	Y	Y	Y	Y	Love is the Answer
149 Madre Grande	CA	120 ac R	75	10	3		Y	Y	Pu	Y		C	N	N	Y	N	N	C	C	F	Y		Y	N	Ecl	N	N	S	S	New Age Monastic
150 Magic	CA	1 Hs U	76	8	0	N	Y	Y	Cb	Y	350	S	S	Y	Y	M	N	L	L	D	S	Y - -	450	N	Ecl	N	N	S	Y	Science & Loving
151 Mariposa Group	CA	1 Hs B	84	3	1	40	Y	Y	Pu	Y		Cb	N	Y	N	N	N	C	C	C	N	8	Y	Q	Y	N	N	N	N	Honesty
152 Martha's Housing	WI	1 Hs U	70s	30	+	Same	Y	Y	Cb	Y	35	Cb	N	N	Y	Y	N	C	C	R	N	20-2	200	N	N		N	Y	N	Cooperation; Consensus
153 Meramec	MO	213 ac B	88	40	10		M	M	Cb	Y	Y	Cb	N	Y	N	Y	P	Cb	Cb	F	N	Vol	15	N	C	N	N	N	N	Ecological Practice
153a Metanoia (F)	GA	(F) 1 Hs U	80s	2+2	0		Y						N	Y				C	C						C		Y	Y	Y	NQ Demilitarization
154 Middle Earth (F)	OH	(F) R	76	2	0	5-7	Y	Y	Pu	Y	Negot	N	Y	Y	N	Y	Y	L	L	F	N		Y	HBLP	CP	N	N	N	Y	Community Commitment
155 Midwest Community (F)	KS	(F) 1 Hs U	83	2	0	6	Y	N	Cb	Y		C	Y	Y	Y	Y	Y	N	N	D	N		Y		O		N	Y	Y	Accountability Now
156 Monan's Rill	CA	440 ac R	73	17	6	40	Y	Y	Pu	Y	2,500	C	N	Y	Y	Y	N	C	C	F	N	16	Ngo M	CHLG	Qk	N	N	N	Y	Brother/Sisterhood
157 Monarc-Christiania (F)	CA	(F) R	70	1+	0	Billions	Y	Q	Hm	Y		N	N	M	M	N	Y	Q	N	F	Vo	Vol	Y	CP	CO		N	Y	Y	Free Will
158 Moniteau Farm	MO	465 ac R	79	24	37		Y	Y	Cb	Y	Y	C	S	N	Y	N*		L	N	F	N	8	Q		Cb	Y	N	N	Y	Macrobiotics

Chart Codes explained on Pages 144-145

North American Communities: Cross-Reference Chart

Sorted Alphabetically

Community Name (Forming?)	Map#	State/Prov	Land/Bldgs	Rur/Urb	Yr Est?	Adults	Child	Max?	More? A	More? C	Sch?/Gen?/Visitors?	Decis? C/M	Wt?	Join Fee	Gr	Ea	Or	Vg	Fl	Ld	B	Rm	Econ S?	L/mo	$/mo	Op?	Sexual Restr?	Spirit Basis	L?	P	F	VS	Other Values / Remarks
Montebello	159	MA		U	82	6	0		N	N	Y	M	Cb	N	N	Y	N	N	N	N	N	N	N	Y	243	N	CHM	C	N	N	N	N	Evangelic Christians
Moonridge	160	OH									W																			N	N	N	NQ No Info Available
Morninglory	161	Ont	100 ac	R	69	7	7	7 Fam	Y	Y	Y Cb	Cb	N	5,000	Y	N	Y	N	Y	C	Cb	F	N	N		N	N	Ecm	N	S	S	Y	Respecting Earth
Mother Earth Opihihale	162	HI	9 ac	R	78	7	1	10-12	Y	Y	Y	Cb	Y	Negot	S	Y	Y	Y	Y	C	N	F	S	10-2	125+	N	N	Ecm	ac	Y	Y	Y	Unconditional Love
Mount Madonna	163	CA	355 ac	R	78	~65	~40		Y	P	Y Cm	Cb	N		N	Y	N	N	Y	C	C	F	Y	170	125	Y	Q	E	Y	Y	Y	Y	Positive Thought & Action
Mountain Grove	164	OR	400+ ac	R	70	4+8	2		Y	Y	Y Cb	Cb	N	N	N	Y	Y	Y	Y	C	C	F	S					E	Y	Y	S	S	Non-Doctrinaire
Murphy Street	165	CA	2 Hs	U	85	5	0		M			C	N		S	Y	Y	Y	Y	I	I	F	N					Ecm	N	N	Q	Y	Emotional Healing
Namasté Rainbow (F)	165a	NH	49 ac	R	84?	3	1	N	Y	Y	Y	C		100	Y	Y	Y	Y	Y	I	I			Y			Q	Ecl	Y	Y	Y	Y	NQ Greens Camp
New Covenant	166	OH		R	77	3	1	N	Y	Y	Y Hm	C	C	AA	Y	Y	Y	N	Y	C	C	F	Y				CM	C	Y	Y	Y	Y	Anabaptist
New Haven Zen	166a	CT																															NQ No Info Available
New Jerusalem	167	OH	Non-res	U	71	170	150	N	Y	Y	Y Cb	N	N	N	N	N	S	N	Y	N	N	F	N	N	Y	N	CHM	R/C	Y	Y		Y	Work for Social Change
New Land	168	VA		R	79	37	8	200	M	M	Y Cb	M	Y	N	S	N	S	N	Y	N	N	F	N	Vol	Y	N	M		N	S	S	S	Consciousness
New Meadow Run	169	PA*		R					M	M	Cm	N	Y			Y											M	HB	Y	Y	N	Y	NQ Hutterian
New Moon	170	CA	12 Rm	U	83	10	2		N	N		C	N	N	N	Y	N	N	N	N	N	R	N	N	250+	N	M	N	N	Y	Y	Q	Living Happily w/o Structure
New Prairie	171	MN	10 ac	R	81	4	3	25-30	Y	Y	Y Pu	C	C	AA	Y	Y	Y	N	M	C	C	F	Y				CHMa	C	Y	Y	Y	Y	Sharing & Service
New Vrindaban	172	WV	5,000 ac	R	68	300	120		Y	Y	Y Cb	Y	C		Y	Y	Y	N	M	C	C	Cb	Y	240	Y	N	CHM	Y	Y	Y	N	Y	Surrender to God
Northeon Forest	173	PA&	AZ&	R	73				Y	Y	Y Pu	C	Y		N	N				N	N	Cb	N					O	Y	N	Y	N	Gurdjieff Philosophy
Oak Grove (F)	174	VA		R	89	1	0	12-15	Y	N	S	C	C	U	P	P	P			L	U	Cb					U	Y	N	Y	N	N	Simple Living Center
Oakwood Farm	175	IN*	326 ac	B	73	25	5		M	M	Pu	C	N	N	Y	Y	Y	N	Y	C	C	Cb	Y	N	Y	N		EDL	Y	Y	N	Y	Prctical Spirituality
Ojai Foundation	176	CA	40 ac	R	79	20	2		M	M	M Pr	Cb	N	M	S	Y	Y	N*	Y	N	N	F	N	140	N	Q		Ecl	Y	Y	Y	Y	Education
Ojito	177	NM	20 ac	R	88	1+4	0	8	Y	Y	Y Pt	Cb	N	Negot	Y	Y	Y	N*	M	I	I	Cb	N	40+	S	M	CH	Ecl	S	N	Y	N	Earth; Individual; Spirituality
Old McCauley Farm	178	WA		R	75	15	8+4	N	Q	Q	Y Pt	Y	N	Y	N	N	S	N	S	C	N	F	Y	25	N			N		S	S	S	Owners Agreement
Open Door	179	GA		U	81	32	2	Same	Y	Y	Y Cb	Cb	N	N	Y	S	N	S	N	C	C	Cb	S	A Lot	N		HGMo	N	N	S	Y	Y	Solidarity with Poor
Order Ecumenical	180	AZ*	14 units	U	54	14	7		Y	Y	Y Pu	C	N	N	N	Y	N	N*	Y	C	C	F	N	20	820	N	N	Ecm	N	N	N	Y	Worldwide Diversity + Partic.
Organic Kauai Prod (F)	181	HI		R	89				Y	Y	Y Hm	Hm			Y	Y	Y	N*	Y	L	L	Cb	Y				N	Earth	N	N	Y	N	Simple Living
Our Land (Int'l.)	182	CA		B	80	59	157	N	Y	Y		C	Y		N	N	N	N	N	L	C	Cb	Y				N		Y	Y	Y	Y	Universality:
Owl Farm	183	OR	147 ac	R	76	5	2	N	Y	Y	Y Cb W	C	N	N	N	Y	N	N	Y	L	L	F	N	40-	-100	N	N	P	N	N	Y	N	Earth as Mother
Ozone	184	CA	4 Rm	U	85	4	0	Same	N	N		N	N		N	Y	N*	N	Y	C	C	R	Var	Var	N		N		N	N	N	Y	Eat Together; Family
Padanaram	185	IN	2,000 ac	R	66	100	100		Y	S	Y Pt	Y	S	N	Y	Y	N*	N	Y	C	C	F	Y				CH	Ecm	Y	N	N	N	Internat'l Communal Utopia
Panhandle Permacultr	186	TX		R	88	7	4	N	Y	Y	Y	Y	N		Y	Y	Y	Y	Y	(L)	N	F	Y	7	20	Y				Y	N	Y	Permaculture
Patchwork Central	187	IN	Non-res	U	77	20	6		Y	Y	Y Cb	C	N	N	N	S	S	N	Y	C	N	F	N				N		N	N	S	Y	Urban Mission Work
Peace Farm	188	TX	20 acres	R	86	3	0	6-8	Y	Y	Y	C	N	N	N	Y	P	Y	N*	C	C	R	Y	200		N	Mo	E	Y	P	Y	N	Nonviolence; Peace
Peace Gardens	189	CA	6 units	U	85	8	2	N	Y		Y Cb	C		S	N	N	N	N	Y	L	L	F	N	Y					S	Y	Y	Y	Land Trust
Phoenix	190	CA	4 Rm	U	83	3	0	6	Y	N	Y	Y	N		Y	N	Y	N	Y	C	C	R					N	Ecm	N	N	N	N	Psychospiritual Growth
Planetary Project (F)	191	KS	100 ac	R	89				Y		Y	C								C	C							Y	P		P	P	NQ Integrate Spirituality
Pleasant View	192	NY*		R					M	M	Cm	Cm	N			Y											M	HB	Y	Y	Y	N	NQ Hutterian
Plow Creek Fellowship	193	IL	189 ac	R	71	33	36	N	Y	Y	Y Cb	C	C	N	Y	Y	Y	N	Y	C	C	F	Y				CHMa	C	N	Y	Q	Y	Mennonite
Ponderosa	194	WA	1,000 ac	R	79	36	15		Y	Y	Y Pu	M	Q	N	Y	Q	Y	N	Y	N	N	F	N	N	N			N	Y	Y	Q	Y	Self-Reliance
Prag House	195	WA		U	72	10	5	10a,5c	N	N	M	M	C		N	N	N	N	N	L	L	Cb	Y	8	5%	M				S	S	S	Liberal Politics
Providence Zen Center	196	RI	50 ac	R*	72	10	2	15	Y	N	Y Pu	C	N	350	N	Y	Y	N	Y	C	C	D	N	20	370	N	Mo	E	Y	Y	N	N	Zen Meditation
Prudence Crandall	197	CA	4 Rm	U	72	4	0	Same	N	N	W Y	C	Y	N	N	Y	Y	Y	N	C	C	R	N	Y				N	N	Y	Y	N	Global Conscience
Purple Rose	198	CA	10 Rm	U	78	9	9	9	P	N	P	C	N	50	Y	Y	N*	N	N	C	C	R	N					N	N	N	S	Y	Openness; DIrectness

Directory of Intentional Communities
Page 156

Key to the Headings: Map#: Corresponds to numbers on the maps. More? [A]Adults, [C]Children Sch? Kind of Schooling? Gen? Gender: Women or Men only? Food/Diet? [Gr]Grow Own? [Ea]Eat Together? [Vg]Vegetarian? [Fl]Flexible? [Or]Organic/Whole Grain? Accommodations Style? [S?]Income Sharing? Economic Sharing: [L/mo]Labor/Month? [$/mo]Cost/Month [Op?]Income-Earning Opportunities? Spirituality: [B]Basis? [L?]Leader? Values: [P]Pacifist? [F]Feminist? [VS]Voluntary Simplicity?
Decis? [C/M]Consensus or Majority? [Wt?]Weighted Decisions? Ownership: [Ld]Land? [B]Buildings? [Rm]Rooming/Accommodations?

North American Communities: Cross-Reference Chart

Map #	Community Name	Forming?	State/ Prov	Land/ Bldgs Urb	Rur/ Urb	Year Est?	Pop. Adults	Chld	Max?	More? A	C	Join Fee	Gen? Vis?	Sch?	Decis? C/M	Wt?	Food Gr	Ea	Or	VgFl	Own Ld	B	Rm	Econ S?	$/mo	Op?	Sexual Restr?	Spirit Basis	L?	P	F	VS	Other Values / Remarks
200	Rainbow House		KS	9 Rms	U	81	10	1/2	Same	Y	M		Y		Cb	N	N	S	S	Y	I	I	R	N	2 / 200-		N	N	N	S	S	S	Gender/Ethnic Balance
201	Rainbow Junction	(F)	CA	40 ac	R	89	1-3	0	50+	Y	Y	U	Y	U	Cb	N	U	U	Y	N	C	C	F	N	4 / 20+	M	N	Ecl	N	N	Y	N	No Drugs or Alcohol
202	Rainbow Valley		TX	220 ac	R	80	15	4	50	Y	Y	5,000+	Y	Pu	Cb	N	M	N	Y	N	L	I	F	N			N	Earth	S	N	N	Y	Energy Self-Sufficiency
203	Raj-Yoga Math		WA		R	74	6	0	10-12	Y	N	N	Y		N		Y	Y	Y	N	N	N	D	Var	/	Y	C	E	Y	N	N	N	Directness
203a	Raven Rocks		OH	1047 ac	R	70	11	0	N	Y	Y	N	Y	Cb	C	N	Y	Y	Y	Y	Cb		Ob	S	/	Y	N	QEcl	S	Y	Y	Y	Education; Ecology; Sharing
204	Reba Place		IL	40 Units	U	57	60	35	N	Y	Y	N	Y	Cb	C	S	S	S	Y	N	C	C	Ob	Y			CM	CEcm	S	N	Y	Y	Christian Living
205	ReCreation Center		HI		R	86	6	5	20	Y	Y	300	Y	Cb	N		N	O	s	s	Y	N	N	Cb	40-6 / 300	Y	M	N	N	Y	N	Y	Water Therapy/Birth
206	Reevis Mountain		AZ		R					Y	Y		Y					S												Y			Y	NQ Self-Reliance
207	Reina del Cielo		VA	52 ac	R	72	16	8	N	Y	Y	N	Y	Pu	Cb	Y	N	N	N	N	C	N	F	N	Var / 175	N	Mo	CE	Y	Y	N	Y	Ancient Mysteries
208	Renaissance		MA	80 ac	R	68	12	12	Same	S	S	AA	S	S	M	Y	N	Y	N	Y	C	C	F	Y	/ 375+	Y	CHP	Y	Y	Y	Y	Y	Love
208a	Revolutionary Tomato		CA	1 Hs	U	83	5	2	Same	Y	N	N	N	Cb	N	S	Y	Y	N*	N	Cb			N			N	N	N	Y	Y	Y	Communal Living
209	Riparia		CA	12 ac	B	87	8	7	7	S	S	Sliding	Y	Cb	C	N	N	Y	Y	Y	C	C	Cb	N			N	N	N	Y	Y	Y	Peace Activism
210	Rivendell Co-op		MI	1 Hs	U	74	7	1	7	M	M	200	M		C	N	Y	Y	Y	Y	C	C	R	N	12 / 205	Y	N	N	N	Y	Y	Y	Work on Problems Openly
211	River City		IA	5 Hs	U	77	30	0	75-100	Y	Y	20	Y		M	N	Y	Y	Y	Y	Ob	Ob	R	N	16 / ~250	M	N	N	S	N	Y	Y	Low Cost Housing
212	River Farm		WA		R	71	9	5	12a, 6c	P	P	Varies	Y	Cb	C	Q	Y	S	N	Y	L	L	Cb	N			N	N	Y	N	Y	Y	Pracitcal Homesteading
213	Rock Ridge		WI		R	71	3+3	3		Y	Y		Y		C	N	Y	Y	Y	N	C	C	F	N	8 / 235	N	N	Q	N	P	P	Y	Stewardship; Peace
214	Rootworks		OR		R	70s	~60	~4	N	Y	Y	N	W	Cb	(C)		Y	S	Y	N	N	N	Ob	N			CLP	(P)	N	P	Y	Y	Women's Network
215	Rowanwood		Ont	92 ac	R	80	12	6	30	Y	Y	Y	Y	Cb	C	N	Y	S	Y	N	C	I	F	N	Var / 85	Y	N	Ecl	N	S	S	S	Extended Family Caring
216	Rowe Camp		MA		R	74	7	0	8	M	M	N	M	Pu	N	N	N*	M			C	C	F	N	160+	N	N	UU+P	Y	Y	Y	Y	Hard Work
217	Saint Benedict's Farm		TX		R	56	5			Y	N	N	Y		C	Y	N	N	N	N	C	C	D	Y			C	R/C	Y	N	N	N	Catholic
218	Saint Clares Hermitage		WA		R	80	4	0	12	Y	Y	N	Y		Cb	Q	Y	Y	Y	Y	N	N	Cb	N	80	N	CMa	CEO	Y	N	N	Y	Renunciation; Solitude
219	Salt Spring Centre		BC		R	81	7	2	12-20	Y	M		Y	Cm	Cb	N	Y	Y	Y	N	L	L	Ob	N	100 / 150	M	CHM	E	Y	Y	Y	Y	Daily Spiritual Discipline
220	San Fran Zen Center		CA		U	69	25-40	0	N	Y	Y		Y		C	N	Y	N*	Y	Y	C	C	Ob	N	80	N	Y	Zen	Y	N	N	Y	Daily Zen Medtation
221	Sandhill		MO	135 ac	R	74	7	2	15-20	Y	Y	N	Y	Hm	C	N	N	Y	N	N	C	C	D	Y			N	P	Y	N	Y	Y	Respect for Earth
222	Santa Fe Com. School		NM		B	68	11	13	80	Y	Y	Y	Y	Cb	Cb	Y	S	Y	Y	Y	C	C	F	N	30 – 300	Y	N	N	N	Y	Y	Y	Summerhill Philosophy
223	Santa Rosa Creek		CA	27 units 2 U			27	?	Same	Y	Y	Y	Y			Y					C	I	F	N		Y	N		Y	N	N	Y	NQ Limited Equity Co-op
224	Sassafras Ridge		WV	240 ac	R	72	10	7	15-20	N	N	N	N	Cb	C	S	Y	N			Ob	N	F	N		Y/M	N	PJ	N	Y	Y	Y	Shared Responsibility
225	SEADS of Truth	(F)	ME	Duplex	R	80	5?			Y	Y	N	Y		C		Y	N			L	Cb	F				N	N		Y		Y	Co-op Self-Sufficiency
226	Seeds of Peace		CA		(B)					Y	Y		Y		C		Y							S	50%	Y				Y		Y	NQ Political Action
226a	Seven C's	(F)	OR	160 ac +3R	R	89	6	0	15+kids	Y	Y	U	Y	U	M	Y	Y	Y	Y	Y	I	I	Cb	N	100		N	N	N	S	N	S	Lasting Relationships
227	Seven Springs Farm		MO	120 ac	R	72	10	0	N	Y	N	N	Y	Cb	N	C	N	N	N	N	Ob	N	F	N	2 / 10	N	N	N	N	Y	N	Y	Stewardship; Community Life
228	Shannon Farm		VA	490 ac	R	74	60	21		Y	Y	N	Y	Cb	C	N	N	N	S	N	C	C	Ob	N	12 / 7%	S	N	N	S	N	N	Y	Tolerance; Freedom
229	Shenoa		CA		R					Y	Y		Y		C				Y						S	Y	Y	Ecl	N	S	Y	P	NQ Teach Community
230	Shepherdsfield		MO	95 ac	R	69	<100	Incl	100a	Y	Y	AA	Y	Hm	Cb	Y	Y	Y	Y	N	C	C	F	Y	Y	Y	CHM	C	Y	Y	N	N	Community of Goods
231	Shiloh Community		AR		B	42	25	6		Y	Y	N	Y	Cb	Cb	Y	Y	Y	Y	Y	C	C	F	Q	Y	N	Ma	C	Y	Q	N	Y	Spirituality; Bakery
232	Short Mountain		TN	200 ac	R	80	8	0	N	Y	N	N	Y		C		Y	Y	Y	Y	L	L	Cb	N	75	N	N	PO	N	Y	Y	Y	Radical Faerdom
233	Sichlassenfallen		WI		U		5	0	6-7	Y	Y	N	Y		C	N	N	N	N	N	N	N	Cb	N.	8-10 / 200		N	Ecl	N	S	Y	Y	Democracy; Environment
234	Sierra Hot Springs		CA	600 ac	R	88	10	0	120	Y	M	U	Y		N	Y	Y	Y	Y	N	C	C	Ob	N	Y – Y		N	Ecm	N	Y	Y	Y	Spirituality; Healing
235	Sirius		MA	86 ac	R	78	21	12		Y	Y	200	Y	Cb	N		Y	Y	Y	Y	C	C	Ob	N	32 / 50	Y	N	Ecm	N	Y	Y	Y	Findhom Influence
236	Sivananda Ashram		NY		R	75	10	0	N	Y	Y	N	Y		C		Y	Y	Y	Y	C	C	Cb	N	Var		CMa	E	Y	N	N	Y	Vedanta Yoga
237	Sky Woods Cosynagle		MI		B	72	7	0		Y	Y	N	Y		C	N	Y	Y	Y	Y	C	C	D	Y	Y		N	Y	N	P	Y	Y	Greater Quality
238	Sojourners Community		DC	Non-res	U	75	30	10		Y	?		Y		Y		Y						Cb				N	C	N	Y	N	Y	NQ Neighborhood Service

Chart Codes explained on Pages 144-145

North American Communities: Cross-Reference Chart — Sorted Alphabetically

Map #	Community Name (Forming?)	State/Prov	Land/Bldgs	Rur/Urb	Year Est?	Adults	Child	Max?	More? A	More? C	Sch? Visitors?	Gen?	Join Fee	Decis? C/M	Wt?	Gr	Ea	Or	Vg	Fl	Ld	B	Rm	Econ S?	L/mo	$/mo	Op?	Sexual Restr?	Spirit Basis	L?	P	F	VS	Other Values / Remarks
239	Sojourners' Orchard	VA	211 ac	R	83	6	1	N	N	N		Y	N	C	M	Y	Y	Y	Y	N	I	I	F	N	Y	1200	Q	N(Mo)		N		S	S	N	Tolerance; Environment
240	Sparrow Hawk Village	OK	332 ac	R	81	72	8	300	Y	Y	Pu	Y	N	M		S	Y	Y	Y	Y	N	N	F	N	8	5	N	N	Ecm	Y			Y	Spirituality; Service
241	Spaulding Unit	CA	5 Rm	U	78	6	0	6	Y	Y		Q		Cb	Y	S	Y	Y	Y*	Y	C	C	R	N	8	300	N	N	N				Y	Collectivity
242	Spiral Wimmin's	KY	120 ac	R	81	5	0	10-20	Y	Y	W Y	Y	Y	Cb		N	Y	Y	N*	Y	L	I	F	N	Y	50+	N	N	N		N	Y	Y	Permaculture
243	Springtree	VA	120 ac	R	71	5	2	10	Y	Y	Cb	Y	N	Cb	N	Y	Y	Y	Y	N	C	C	D	Y				N	N		Y	N	Y	Living Lightly; Joy
244	Starland	MN*		R					M	M	Cm	Y		N	Y													M	HB		Y	N	N	NQ Hutterian
245	Stelle	IL	240 ac	R*	73	102	38	250,000	Y	Y	Cb	Y	N	N		N	N	N	N	N	Cb	N	Cb	N	Vol		Y	N	CEO		S	S	N	Self Sufficiency
246	Still Meadow	OR	50 ac	R	76	21	Incl	N	M	M	Cb	Y	N	Cb		N	Y	N	Y	N	Cb	S	R	S		Y		N	EDL				S	NQ RadiantTranquility
247	Stone Soup (F)	Ont	Non-res	U	88	6-10	0	N	P	P		M	N			Y	N	Y	N	Y	Cb	S	R	N		Y	M	N	O				Y	Human Wholeness
248	Suburban Palace	CA	1 Hs	U	82	7	0	Same	N	N			N	C		Y	Y	Y	Y	Y	N	N	N	N				N	N			Y	S	Post-Hippy Anarkids
249	Sundance	TN	7 ac	R	78	2	2	N	P	P	Hm		N	C		N	N	N	Y	N	Cb	C	F	N	N			N	N		Y	Y	Y	Harmony with Earth
250	Suneidesis	LA	117 ac	R	77	11	6	30	Y	Y	Cb	Y	N	C		N	Y	Y	Y	N	N	N	Q	Y				N	Ecm		Y	Y	Y	Self-Motivation/Correction
251	Sunflower Farm	OH		R	75	13	10	30	Y	Y	Pr	Y	5,500	Cb		N	Y	Y	Y	N	Cb	N	F	N		Y		N	N		Y	Y	Y	Self-Reliance
252	Sunflower House	KS	30 Rm	U	69	25	0	30	Y	N	Cb	Y	160	C		N	N	S	Y	N	L	L	R	N	25	150+	N	N	N		N	S	S P	Carry Your Weight
253	Sunnyside (F)	MO	(R)		89	7	2	N	N	N		N	U	U		P	Y	Y	N	Y	N	N	Cb	N		Y	M	N	N				S	Equality; Self-Sufficiency
254	Sunset House	CA	7 Rms	U	77	7	1	Same	M	M	Cb	Y	N	C		S	Y		S		I	I	R	N	5			N	N		S		S	Urban Co-op
255	Susan B. Anthony	OH	152 ac	R	79	4	0	40	Y	N	W	Y	N	C		N	N	N	N	N	C	C		N	150		N	N	N		P		S	Economic & Social Change
256	Sweetwater CLT	MO	480 ac	R	81	6	2	14 Hs	Y	Y	Cb	Y	N	C		N	N	N	Y	N	L	I	F	N	130		N	N	N		N		Y	Environmental Protection
257	Sylviron (F)	MI	Looking	R	89				Y	Y		Y		C		Y	S	Y	Y	Y	C	C	Cb	N		Y		N		Y			S	Co-op Trainings
258	Syntropy Institute	CA	1 Hs	U	86	6	0	40+	Y	Y		Y	N	N	Y	Y	Y	Y	Y	Y	Cb	Cb	R	N	600+		Y	N	N		Y		N	Philanthropic Service
259	Syzygy Cooperative	BC	80 ac	R	73	16	6?	Same	N	N		Y	N	C		S	N	Y			C	I	F	S			Y	N	N		S	S	Y	NQ Cooperation; Trust
259a	Tanguy Homesteads	PA	100 ac	U*	45	?		Same	M	M	Cb	Y	30	C		N	Y	N	N	Y	Cb	I	F	N	Var		N	N	(C)		Y	Y	Y	Racial Equality; Change
260	Teramanto	WA	3 Hs	R	75	7	3	40	Y	Y	Cb	Y	5-	C		Y	Y	Y	Y	Y	C	C	Cb	N Y - or -	75		Q	N	(C)		P	Y	Y	Activism
262	Third Avenue Co-op	MO	3 Hs	U	79	8	4	N	M	M	Pu	Y	100	Cb		N	S	Y	N*	Y	C	C	R	N	85		M	N	N		P	Y	N	Anti-Athoritarian
263	Thoreau Center	IA	3 Hs	U	79	12+	1+	~Same	Y	Y	Cb	Y		C		S	S	Y	N*	S	I	I	R	N	5-4000			N	Ecm		N	S	Y	Art, Environment, Spirit
264	3HO Massachusetts	MA*		R					Y	Y				N	Y	Y	Y	Y	Y		N	N	N	N		Y		Ma	E		P	Y	P	NQ Individual Excellence
265	3HO California	CA*	1+	U					Y	Y				N	Y	Y	Y	Y	Y		N	N	N	N		Y		Ma	E		Y	Y	Y	NQ Righteous Life
266	3HO New Mexico	NM	100	B	69	100			Y	Y	Cb	Y	N	Cb	Y	N	Y	N	Y	Y	N	N	N	N	Var		N	Ma	E				Y	Sikh Religion; Yoga
267	Toad Hollow	Ont	100 ac	R	86	4	3	~20	Y	Y	Pu	Y	Y	C		Y	Y	Y	Y	P	C	I	F	N	Var	50+	Y	LGMo	Y		Y	Y	Y	Support; Deep Relationships
268	Tobias Community	NH		R	88							Y				Y	Y	Y	Y	Y									Y					NQ Anthroposophy
269	Tolstoy Farm	WA	440 ac	R	63	27	22	100	Y	Y	Cb	Y	N	C		N	Y	Y	Y	N	L	N	F	N			N	N	N				S	Organic Farming
270	Top O' The Ten	MA		U		6			Y	Y						N			Y															NQ Urban Co-op
271	Trails End	AR		R	83	5	0	12-15	Y	Q	Cb	Y	N	Cb	N	Y	Y	Y	Y	Y	C		Cb	N			Y	CH	N		N	N	N	Well-Being; Equality
272	Triform	NY	80 ac	R	77	27	6		Y	Y	Pu		N	C		Y	Y	Y	Y	Y	C	C	F	N			Y	N	N		N	N	N	Camphill Community
273	Truth Consciousness	CO*		B	74				Y	Y				N	Y		Y	Y	Y				Cb	N			Y	CH	E	Y			N	NQ Spiritual Growth
274	Twin Brooks	WA	250 ac	R	89	4	1	U	Y	Y	Pr	Y	N	Cb	Y	N	N	N	N	S	N	N	N	N	<100		S	Ecm	Ecm		P	P	S	Casualness
275	Twin Oaks	VA	400 ac	R	67	75	15	200	Y	S	Cb	Y	N	Cb		Y	Y	S	Y	Y	C	C	R	Y				N	N		P	P	Q	Non-Violence; Anti-Racist
276	Union Acres (F)	NC	110 ac	R	89	10	5	50	Y	Y	Pu	Y	Y	C		M	Y	Y	Y	Y	Cb	I	F	N	20		Y	N	Ecl				Y	Spiritual Ecology
277	Urban Stonehenge	CA	8 rm	U	82	5	0	5-10	M	M	Cb	Y	N	C		M	Y	Y	Y	N	N	N	R	N			Y	N	N-(P)		S	Y	Y	AntiAuthority;Humor;Politics
278	Vale	OH	40 ac	U	59	9	10		Q	S	Cb	Y	50	C		Y	Y	Y	Y	Y	L	N	F	N		23		N	Y		S	S	S	Family Oriented
279	Valley of Light	AR		R	78	4	2	14	Y	Y	Hm	Y	2,000	N		Y	Y	Y	Y	Y	N	Cb	F	N		Y		Y	Y		Y			Self-Realization
279a	Vedantic Center	CA																																NQ No Info Available

Key to the Headings: *Map#.* Corresponds to numbers on the maps. *More?* [A]Adults, [C]Children *Sch?* Kind of Schooling? *Gen?* Gender: Women or Men only? *Sch?* [C]Children *Decis?* [C/M]Consensus or Majority? [Wt?]Weighted Decisions? *Food/Diet?* [Gr]Grow Own? [Ea]Eat Together? [Or]Organic/Whole Grains? [Vg]Vegetarian? [Fl]Flexible? *Ownership:* [Ld]Land? [B]Buildings? [Rm]Rooming/Accommodations Style? *Economic Sharing:* [S?]Income Sharing? [L/mo]Labor/Month? [$/mo]Cost/Month [Op?]Income-Earning Opportunities? *Spirituality:* [B]Basis? [L?]Leader? *Values:* [P]Pacifist? [F]Feminist? [VS]Voluntary Simplicity?

North American Communities: Cross-Reference Chart

Sorted Alphabetically

Map #	Community Name	Forming?	State/Prov	Land/Bldgs	Rur/Urb	Year Est?	Pop. Adults	Chld	Max?	More? A	More? C	Sch?/Visitors?	Gen?	Join Fee	Decis? C/M	Wt?	Food Gr	Ea	Or	Vg	Fl	Ownshp Ld	B	Rm	Econ S?	L/mo	$/mo	Op?	Sexual Restr?	Spirit Basis	L?	Val P	F	VS	Other Values / Remarks
280	Villa Sarah		CA		U	73	13	2		S	S		Y	N	C		N	Y	N	N	Y	C	C	R	N	20	170+	N	N	N	N	N	N	N	Group Process
280a	Vine & Fig Tree		AL	240ac	R	86	4	0	N	Y	Y	Cb	Y	Negot	C	N	N	Y	Y	Y	Y				S	Y	Var	S	N	Y	N	P	M	Y	Peace & Justice
281	Vivekananda Mon		MI*	108 ac	R	68	12	0		Y	N		Y	Varies	Cb	Y	N	Y	Y	Y	Y	C	C	Cb	Y		S	N	C	E	Y	S	S	S	Work; Acceptance
282	Vivekananda Soc		IL*		B	30	15	1		Y	M	Pr	Y	25	N	Y	S	Y	N	N*	N	N	C	C	N		Y	N	C	E	Y	S	S	S	Vedanta; Mission
283	Walden Hill		OK		R	81	2	1		Y	Y	Hm	Y	N	Cb	S	P	Y	Y	Y	Y	L	C	Cb	Y		Y	N	N	Y	Y	Y	N	Y	Rainbow Family
284	Walker Creek		WA		R		8	5		Y												L													NQ Evergreen CLT
285	Waukon Inst	(F)	WA		R	87	7	0	20-30	Y	Y		Y		C		Y	Y	Y			C	C	Cb			Y			P				Y	Healing & Nutrition
286	Wellspring		WI	100 ac	R	88	3	0	10-20	Y	Y		Y		C	Y	Y	Y	Y	Y	Y	L	Cb	R	N	5-10	350	Y	N	Ecl	N	Y	Y	Y	Deeply Value Earth
287	Wellspring House		MA		B	81	5			Y	Y		Y	N	C	Q	Y	Y	Y	Y	Y	L	L	Cb			500	Y	C	C	N	Y	Y	Y	Homeless Shelter
288	Wesleyan Christn		WA	68 ac	B	77	28	20	Same	Y	Y	Cb	Y	27	C	N	Y	Y	N*		Y	C	C	F	N	56	293 +		CM	C	Y	N	N	N	Honesty & Integrity
289	Whitehall Co-op		TX	13 Rm	U	49	13	0	13	S	Q		Y	V	C	N	N	Y	S	Y	Y	C	C	R	N	16	360	N	N			N	N	Y	Support; Family Bonding
291	Winged Hrt. Homstd.	(F)	VA	283 ac	R		18	10	20	Y	M		Y	3,000	Cb	Y	Y	S	Y	N	S	N	Cb	Cb	N	Y	30+		N	ECO	Y	Y	N	Y	Sufism
292	Wiscoy Valley		MN	356 ac	R	76	18	10		Q	Q	Cb	Y		C	N	N	Y	N	Y	N	C	N	F	N	4	25	Y	N	N	N	S	S	S	Sustainable Agriculture
293	Wolf Creek Sanctuary		OR		R	85				Y		M	Y									L	L												NQ Radical Faerie
294	Womanshare		OR	23 ac	R	74	4	0	8	Y	Y		W	N	C	M	Y	Y	Y	Y	Y	C	C	Cb	N	40	110+	N	CLP	N	N	N	Y	S	Workshops/Concerts/Gatherin
295	Woodburn Hill		MD	128 ac	R	75	7	3	N	Y	Y	Cb?	Y	Varies	C	N	S	N			S	C	C	Cb	N	12		Y		N	N	S	S	Y	Play; Love; Learn
296	Woodcrest Bruderhof		NY*	100 ac	R	54	300		Incl	M	M	Cm	Y		N	Y	Y					Cb	Cb				Y		M	HB	Y	Y	N	Y	NQ Hutterian
297	Woolcroft	(F)	MO	73 ac	R	88	1	0	10?	Y	Y		Y	Y		Y	Y	Cb	Y			Cb	Cb				Y							P	NQ Permaculture; Livestock
298	Yahara Linden		WI	8 Rm	U	74	4	2	8	Y	M	Pu	Y	N	C	N	N	Y	N	N	Y	L	L	R	N	10	190	N	N	N	N	N	N	N	Cooperaive Diversity
299	Yoga Soc. Rochester		NY		U	73	5	1	7	Y	Y	Pr	Y	N	C	N	N	Y	Y	Y	Y	Q	Q	R	N	8	65	Q	N	Ecl	N			S	Mutual Support
300	Yogaville		VA	750 ac	R*	66	200	50	N	Y	Y	Cm	Y	Y	Y	N	N	Y	Y	Y	Y	C	Cb	Cb	Cb	Y	Y	Y	CM	Ecm	Y	Y	N	Y	Interreligious Peace
301	Zen Buddhist Temple		MI		U		40	3		Y	M		Y					Y											Y	E	Y			Y	NQ Zen Monastery
302	Zen Center (Los Angls)		CA		B	68	40	3	N	Y	Y	Pr	Y	N	N	N	N	Y	N	Y	N* Y	Y	Y	Cb	N	4	40	N	CHLG	Zen	Y	Y	S	Y	The Buddha Way
303	Zen Lotus Society		Ont		U					Y	M		Y					Y											Y	E	Y				NQ Zen Monastery
304	Zendik Farm		TX	300 ac	R	69	40	8		Y	Y	Hm	Y	AA	N	Y	Y	Y	Y	Y	N	C	C	Cb	Cb	Y	Y	Y	N		Y		N	N	EcoLibrium

Chart Codes explained on Pages 144-145

North American Communities: Cross-Reference Chart

Sorted by State/Province

Community Name	Forming?	Map#	State/Prov	Land/Bldgs	Rur/Urb	Year Est?	Adults	Child	Max?	More? A	More? C	Gen?	Sch? Visitors?	Join Fee	Decis? C/M	Wt?	Gr	Ea	Or	Vg	Fl	Ld	B	Rm	Econ S?	L/mo	$/mo	Op?	Sexual Restr?	Spirit Basis	L?	P	F	VS	Other Values / Remarks
Emissar. Divine Light			**	Network	B	48			N	M	M	Y	Cb		Cb		V	Y	V	V	Y	Cb	Cb	Cb	Cb			Var			EDL		S		S	[International] Global Integrity
Hutterian Groups			**	Network	R	Var	170	150	400 ea	Y	Y	Y	Cm	AA	C		N	Y	N	N	Y	C	C		Y				M	HB	Y	Y	N	Y	Non-Violence; Brotherhood
Jesuit Volunteer Corps		124	**	Network	U		Var	0		Y	N	Y						Y							N			N		R/C		Y		Y	NQ Serve the Poor
Vine & Fig Tree		280a	AL	240ac	R	86	4	0	N	Y	Y	Y	Cb	Negot	C	N	Y	Y	Y	Y	Y	N	C		S			Var	N	Y		P	M	Y	Peace & Justice
Crosses Creek		54	AR		R	85	6	5		Y	Y	Y	Cm	Y	Cb	Y	S	Y	Y	Y	Y	N	Cb		Y	80		Y	Ma	C		Y		Y	Spiritual Healing
Shiloh Community		231	AR		B	42	25	6		Y	Y	Y	Cb	N	Cb	Y	N	Y	Y	Y	N	C	C		Q			Y	Ma	C	Y	Y		Y	Spirituality; Bakery
Trails End		271	AR		R	83	5	0	12-15	Y	Q	Y		N	Cb	Y	N	Y	Y	Y	N	C	C	Cb	Y			Y	Ma			N	N	N	Well-Being; Equality
Valley of Light		279	AR		R	78	4	2	14	Y	Y	Y	Hm	2,000	N	Y	Y	Y	Y	Y	Y	N	Cb	F	Y			Y	CH			N	N	N	Self-Realization
Aquarius Ranch	(F)	9	AZ	30 ac	R	85	3	0	10-20	Y	Y	Y	Cb		N	Y	N	Y	S	Y	N	C	N	R	N	10	100	Y	N	Ecl	N	Y	N	Y	Preserve Nature
Arcosanti		10	AZ	860 ac	B	70	60	3	5,000	Y	Y	Y	Cb	400	N	Y	Y	S	Y	N	Y	C	C	R	N	10	10%	N	N			Y		N	Arcology
Bhaktiras	(F)	17	AZ	Looking R*		90	4	1	32	Y	Y	Y	Cb	C		Y	N	Y	N	Y	N	L	Cb		Y			P	CHM	Yoga	N	Y	Y	Y-	Bhakti (God Love)
Child's Garden	(F)	41	AZ	Looking R?		88	2+6	1+3	15-50	Y	Y	Y	Hm	V	Cb	N	M	M	Y	M	M	U	U	U	U			U	U	Ecl	N	Y	Y	Y	Alt.Childrearing; Pers.Growth
Christmas Star		41a	AZ	41 ac	R	80	12	9		Y	Y	Y	Hm	N	C	Y	M	M	Y	Y	Y	I	C	F	N			U	U	O	Y	N	S	Y	Cultural Evolution
Cooper Street		52	AZ		B	80	6	0	~12	Y	M	Y		N	C	N	N	Q	N	Y	Y	N	N	Cb	N			Y	N		S	N	S	S	Tolerance
Friends SW Centr		86	AZ		R	74	17	0	35	Y	Y	Y	Pu	N	C	N	N	Y	N	Y	Y	L	Cb	F	N	2-3		S	N	Qk	N	N	S	Y	Truth; Openness
Hohm Community		112	AZ		R	75	40-50	Incl		Y		Y			Cb	Y	N*					L	Cb	F	Y			Y	Mo	Ecm	Y	N			NQ Right Living
Order Ecumenical		180	AZ*	14 units	U	54	14	7		Y	Y	Y	Pu		C	N	N	Y	N	N	Y	C	C	F	N	20	820	N	N	Ecm		N	N	Y	Worldwide Diversity + Partic.
Reevis Mountain		206	AZ		R					Y	Y						S								S									Y	NQ Self-Reliance
Caravan Theatre Farm		32	BC	80 ac	R	78	5	5		Y	Y	Y			Cb	Y	S	S	Y	S	Y	L			S				N			P	P	Y	NQ Stewardship
CEEDS		35a	BC	400 ac	R	72	15	0	N	Y	N	Y		N*	C	Y	Y	S	Y	N	Y	N	N	R	N			Y	N	N	N	N	Y	S	Ecology; Agriculture
Community Alt'natives		46	BC*	9 units	B	77	34	11	~Same	Y	Y	Y	Cb	Y	C	N	S	S	S	S	S	C	C	C	R	5		Y	N	N	N	Y	Y	Y	NQ Cooperative Social Action
Edenvale		73	BC*	117 ac	R	73	34	8		M	M	Y	Cb	N	N	N	Y	Y	Y	Y	Y	C	C	C	C			Y	N	EDL	Y	N	N	N	Honor Life's
Fraser Common Farm		85	BC	10 ac	R	77	4	2+2		M	M	Y	Cb	N	C	Y	Y	Y	Y	Y	Y	C	C	C	C			Y	Y			Y	Y	Y	NQ Permaculture
Hundred Mile Lodge		118	BC*	10 ac	R*	48	120	Incl		M	M	Y	Cb	N	Cb	Y	Y	Y	Y	Y	Y	Cb	Cb	Cb	S			Y	N	EDL	Y	Y	Y	S	NQ Attunement
Kootenay Co-op Land		132	BC	200 ac	R	69	18	9	12 Fam	Y	Y	Y	Cb	25+	C	N	N	N	Y	N	Y	C	N	F	N	5		Q	N	N	N	S	S	Y	Balance Ecology/Economy
Linnaea		144	BC	315 ac	R	79	8	8	<20	N	N	Y	Cb	N	N	Y	N	Y	Y	N	Y	L	L	F	N		<50	S	N	N	N	N	Y	Y	Environment
Salt Spring Centre		219	BC	80 ac	R	81	7	2	12-20	Y	M	Y	Cm	N	Cb	Q	Y	Y	Y	Y	Y	L	L	Cb	N	100	150	M	CHM	E	Y	Y	Y	Y	Daily Spiritual Discipline
Syzygy Cooperative		259	BC	80 ac	R	73	16	6?	Same	N	N	Y		N	C		S	N	Y			C	I	F	N			Y	N		N	S	S	Y	NQ Cooperation; Trust
3HO California		265	CA*	1+	U					Y	Y						Y	N	Y	Y	Y	C	I	F	N			Y	Ma	E	Y	Y	Y	Y	NQ Righteous Life
Alcyone		4	CA	360 ac	R	81	4+16	0	150	Y	Y	Y		Y	C	N	Y	Y	Y	N*	Y	Cb	Cb	Cb	N	50-8		N	N	Y		Y	Y	Y	Meditation & Unity
Ananda Village		6	CA	900 ac	B	68	400	125		Y	Y	Y	Cb	1,500+	C	Q	Y	Y	Y	N*	Y	C	C	F	N	Vol	Vol	Y	CH	CE	Y	N	Y	S	Non-Denominational
Atmaniketan		13	CA		B	72	25	6		M	M	Y	Cb	N	C		Y	Y	Y	Q	N	C	C	D	Q			N	C	E		N	N	Y	Dedication; Sincerity
Auroville Int'l USA		14	CA*	Network	B	68	400	200	~50,000	Y	Y	Y	Cb		N		Y	S	Y	N*	Y	L	L	Cb	S	120	(P)	S		E	N	Y	Y	Y	[Network] All Life Is Yoga
Big Wheels		18	CA	40 ac	R	71	3+10	1+3		Y	Y	Y		N	M		Y	Y	Y	N*	Y	C	C	F	N	40+	150	Y				Y	Y	Y	Extended Family
Black Bear Ranch		21	CA	70 ac	R	68	5	6	20	Y	Y	Y	Cb	Varies	C	S	Y	Y	Y	Y	Y	L	Cb	Cb	N			Y	N	N	N	N	Y	Y	Sustainable Living
Black Cat		22	CA	15 Rm	U	86	9	2	9a, 3c	Y	N	N		0	C	S	S	N	Y	Y	Y	L	L	Cb	N			Y	N		N	N	Y	S	Direct Action Politics
Black Oak Ranch		23	CA*	490 ac	B	65	26+	Y	N	M	M	Y	Cb	N	C*	Y	N	Y	Y	Y	Y	Cb	Cb	R	N		250+	Y	N	M	N	Y	Y	Y	Humor; Friendship
Brigid		26	CA	8 Rm	U	85	6	1	Same	N	N	S	Pu	N	C	Y	N	Y	Y	Y	Y	C	C	R	N			Y	N	Ecl	N	Y	Y	S	Personal Growth
Center/Examined Life		38	CA		U	66	7	0		Y	N	Y	Cb		Cb	Y	N	Y	Y	Y	Y	C	C	R	Y			Y		Y	Y	Y	N	Y	Human Potential
Community Evolving		47	CA	50 ac	B	88	4	2	32-40	Y	Y	Y	Hm	N	C	N	N	Y	Y	Y	Y	U	U	U	R			Y	N	N	N	P	Y	Y	Intimacy; Deep Ecology
Comptche Farms	(F)	50	CA	100 ac	R	87	6	2	6 Fam	Y	Y	Y	Hm	Y	Y	Y	Y	Y	Y	N	Y	C	C	F	N	40	750	P	HMo	N	N	N	N	Y	Diversity; Stewardship
Consciousness Village		51	CA		R	74	6	3	15	Y	Y	Y	Pu	Y	C		S	Y	Y	N*	Y	I	Cb		Y	75	140	Y		N	Y	N	S	Y	Rebirthing

Key to the Headings: **Map#:** Corresponds to numbers on the maps. **More?** [A]Adults, [C]Children **Sch?** Kind of Schooling? **Gen?** Gender: Women or Men only?
Decis? [C/M]Consensus or Majority? [Wt?]Weighted Decisions? **Food/Diet?** [Gr]Grow Own? [Ea]Eat Together? [Or]Organic/Whole Grains? [Vg]Vegetarian? [Fl]Flexible?
Ownership: [Ld]Land? [B]Buildings? [Rm]Rooming/Accommodations Style? **Economic Sharing:** [S?]Income Sharing? [L/mo]Labor/Month? [$/mo]Cost/Month
[Op?]Income-Earning Opportunities? **Spirituality:** [B]Basis? [L?]Leader? **Values:** [P]Pacifist? [Fl]Feminist? [VS]Voluntary Simplicity?

North American Communities: Cross-Reference Chart

Sorted by State/Province

Chart Codes explained on Pages 144-145

Map #	Community Name	Forming?	State/Prov	Land/ Bldgs	Rur/ Urb	Year Est?	Adults	Chld	Max?	More? A	More? C	Visitors?	Gen?	Join Fee	Decis? C/M	Wt?	Gr	Ea	Or	Vg	Fl	Ld	B	Rm	Econ S?	L/mo $/mo	Op?	Sexual Restr?	Spirit Basis	L?	P	F	VS	Other Values / Remarks
74	Ellis Island		CA	11 BR	U	69	11		Same	M	M		M	N	C	Y	N	S	N	S	Y	C	C	R	N		Y	N	N	N	N	N	Y	No Dogmas
77	Essene Mother Earth		CA	140 ac	R	82	4	3		Y	Y	Pu	Y	5,000	N	Y	S	S	Y	N*	Y	C	C	F	N		Y	CMo	Ecm	N			S	Essene Lifestyle
87	Full Circle Farm		CA	5 ac	R	84	14	4	N	M	N	Cm	N	N	Cb	Y	S	Y	Y	N*	S	I	I	R	I	5-10	N	N	N	N	N	Y	P	S	Non-Violence
92	Glen Ivy		CA*		B	77	66	10	125			Pu	Y	N	N	Y	S	Y	Y	Y	N	C	C	Cb	N	180		N	EDL	Y	N	N	N	Selfless Service
93	Goodlife		CA	1 hs	U	68	6	2	Same	M	M	Cb	Y	100	C	N	Y	Y	Y	Y	Y	I	I	R	S	300+	Y	N	N	N	Y	N	Y	Urban Extended Family
101	Group W		CA	5 Rm	U	85	5	0	Same	P	N		S	N	C	N	N	S	Y	Y	Y	N	C	Cb	N	65	N	N	(P)	N	Y	N	N	Political Activism
103	Harbin Hot Springs		CA	1,100 ac	R	71	120	10	N	Y	Y	Cb	Y	1,001	N	Y	N	N	S	Y	N	N	N	R	N	s		N	Ecl				Y	Land; Human Potential
104	Harvest Forum	(F)	CA	11 Rm	R	87	4	0	12-16	Y	Y		Y	N	C	S	S	Y	Y	N*	N	N	N	R	N	12		N	Ecm	N	P	Y	P	Alternative Lifestyle
110	Hillegass House		CA	11 Rm	U	79	11		11	N	N		N	N	N	N	N	Y	Y	Y	N	C	C	R	C	10		N	N	N	N	N	N	Respect; Tolerance;
111	Hog Farm		CA*	490 ac	B	65	26+		N	M	M	Cb	Y	N	C*	Y	Y	Y	Y	Y	Y	Cb	C	R	N	250+	Y	N	M	N	Y	Y	Y	Humor; Friendship
117a	House, The		CA	8 Rm	U	72	6	2	N	Y	M		N	N	C	N	S	Y	N	N	N	C	C	R	N	10-15		N(P)	N	N	N	S	Y	Enjoy Shared Living
128	Kerista		CA	4 Hs	U	71	28	4	N	Y	Y	Hm	N	N	C	N	N	Y	N	N	Y	C	Cb	R	Y			N	Y	N	N	N	Y	Growth; Communication
129	Kidstown	(F)	CA		B	90	1	0	N	Y	M	Hm	N	N	Cb	M	N	Y	N	N	N	Cb	Cb	R	N	Vol	M	N(P)	Ecl	N	N	N	Y	Love One Another
134	Krotona		CA	118 ac	R	24	40										P	Y	Y	N*	Y	F			Y			N	Y					NQ Theosophy
149	Madre Grande		CA	1 Hs	R	75	10	3	N	Y	Y	Pu	Y	N	N	N	Y	Y	Y	Y	N	C	C	C	N			N	Ecl	N	N	N	N	New Age Monastic
150	Magic		CA		U	76	8	0	N	Y	Y		Y	N	C	S	S	Y	Y	M	N	L	L	D	S	--450		N	Ecl	N	S	S	Y	Science & Loving
151	Mariposa Group		CA		B	84	3	1	40	Y	Y	Pu	Y	350	Cb	N	N	N	N	N	N	C	C	C	Y		N	Q	Y	N	N	N	N	Honesty
156	Monan's Rill		CA	440 ac	R	73	17	6	40	Y	Q	Pu	Y	2,500	C	N	Y	Y	Y	Y	Y	C	C	F	N	16	Ngo	CHLG	Qk	N	Y	Y	Y	Brother/Sisterhood
157	Monarc-Christiania	(F)	CA		R	70	1+	0	Billions	Y	P	Hm	N	N	N	N	M	M	M	N	Y	Q	N	F	Vo	Vol		CP	CO	Y	Y		Y	Free Will
163	Mount Madonna		CA	355 ac	R	78	~65	~40	N	Y	P	Cm	Y	N	Cb	Y	Y	Y	Y	Y	Y	C	C	F	N	170	125	Q	E	Y	N	N	Y	Positive Thought & Action
165	Murphy Street		CA	2 Hs	U	85	5	0	N	M			Y	N	C	N	S	Y	Y	Y	N	I	I	F	N		Y	N	Ecm	N	Y	Q	Y	Emotional Healing
170	New Moon		CA	12 Rm	U	83	10	2	N	N	N	W	Y	N	C	Y	N	Y	Y	Y	N	N	N	F	N	250+		N	N	N	Y	Y	Q	Living Happily w/o Structure
176	Ojai Foundation		CA	40 ac	R	79	20	2	N	M	M	Pr	Y	M	Cb	Y	N	N	N	N	Y	C	C	C	N	140	N	N	Ecl	Y	Y	Y	Y	Education
182	Our Land (Int'l.)		CA	4 Rm	B	80	59	157	N	Y	Y	Cb	Y	N	C	N	N	N	N	N	Y	L	C	Cb	N		Var	N	N	N	Y	Y	Y	Universality:
184	Ozone		CA	4 Rm	U	85	4	0	Same	N	N		Y	N	C	N	S	N	N	N	Y	C	C	R	N	Var	Var	N	N	N	Y	Y	P	Eat Together; Family
189	Peace Gardens		CA	6 units	U	83	8	2	6	Y		Cb	Y	S	C	N	N	Y	Y	N	N	L	L	F	N			N	N	N	Y	Y	Y	Land Trust
190	Phoenix		CA	4 Rm	U	83	3	0	6	Y	N		Y	N			N	N	N	N	N	C	I	F	N			N	Ecm	N	N	N	N	Psychospiritual Growth
197	Prudence Crandall		CA	4 Rm	U	72	4	0	Same	N	N		W Y	N	C	N	N	Y	Y	Y	N	C	C	R	N		Y	N	N	N	Y	Y	Y	Global Conscience
198	Purple Rose		CA	10 Rm	U	78	9	0	9	P	N		P	50	C	N	N	N	Y	Y	Y	C	C	C	N		Y	N	N	s	s	Y	Y	Openness; Directness
201	Rainbow Junction	(F)	CA	40 ac	R	89	1-3		50+	Y	Y		Y	U	Cb	Y	Y	U	Y	N*	N	C	C	F	N	U	M	N	Ecl	Y	Y	Y	Y	No Drugs or Alcohol
208a	Revolutionary Tomato		CA	1 Hs	U	83	5	2	Same	Y	N	Cb	Y	N	N	S	N	Y	Y	N*	N	I	I	R	N	375+		N	N	N	Y	Y	Y	Communal Living
209	Riparia		CA*	12 ac	B	87	8	7	Same	S	S	Cb	Y	Sliding	C	N	N	Y	Y	N*	N	C	C	Cb	N		Y	N	N	N	Y	Y	Y	Peace Activism
220	San Fran Zen Center		CA		U	69	25-40	0	N	Y	Y		Y	Sliding	N	Y	N	Y	Y	Y	Y	Y	Y	Cb	N		Y	Y	Zen	Y	Y	Y	Y	Daily Zen Medtation
223	Santa Rosa Creek		CA	27 units	2 U		27	?	Same	Y	Y		Y	Y					Y			C	I	F	N		Y	N						NQ Limited Equity Co-op
226	Seeds of Peace		CA	Duplex	(B)										C				Y			I	N	Y	S	50%					Y			NQ Political Action
229	Shenoa		CA		R									C				Y																NQ Teach Community
234	Sierra Hot Springs		CA	600 ac	R	88	10	0	120	Y	M		Y	U	N	Y	N	Y	S	Y	N	N	N	Cb	N	Y-Y		N	Ecm	N	Y	Y	Y	Spirituality; Healing
241	Spaulding Unit		CA	5 Rm	U	78	6	0	6				Q	Q	Cb	Y	S	Y	Y	N*	N	C	C	R	N	8	300	N	N	N	N	N	N	Collectivity
248	Suburban Palace		CA	1 Hs	U	82	7	0	Same	N	N		M	N	N	C	N	N	N	N	N	N	N	R	N			N	O	N	N	Y	S	Post-Hippy Anarkids
254	Sunset House		CA*	7 Rms	U	77	7	2	Same	S	S		Y	N	S	Y	S	Y		S	S	I	I	R	N	5		N	N	N	Y	Y	Y	Urban Co-op
258	Syntropy Institute		CA	1 Hs	U	86	6	0	40+	Y	Y		Y	N	N	Y	Y	Y	Y	Y	N	Cb	Cb	R	N	600+	Y	N	N	N	N	N	N	Philanthropic Service
277	Urban Stonehenge		CA	8 rm	U	82	5	5	5-10	M	M		Y	Y	C	N	N	Y	Y	Y	Y	N	N	R	N		Y	N	N-(P)	N	s	Y	Y	AntiAuthority;Humor;Politics

Directory of Intentional Communities
Page 161

North American Communities: Cross-Reference Chart

Sorted by State/Province

Community Name / Forming?	Map #	State/Prov	Land/ Bldgs	Rur/ Urb	Year Est?	Adults	Child	Max?	More? A	C	Sch? Visitors?	Gen?	Join Fee	Decis? C/M	Wt?	Gr	Ea	Or	Vg	Fl	Ownshp Ld	B	Rm	Econ S?	L/mo	$/mo	Op?	Sexual Restr?	Spirit Basis	L?	P	F	VS	Other Values / Remarks
Vedantic Center	279a	CA																																NQ No Info Available
Villa Sarah	280	CA		U	73	13	2		S	S	Y		N	C	N	N	N	N	Y		C	C	R	N	20	170+	N	N		N	N	N	N	Group Process
Zen Center (Los Angls)	302	CA		B	68	40	3	N	Y	Y	Pt	Y	N	N	Y	N	Y	N*	Y		Y	Y	Y	N	4	40	N	CHLG	Zen	Y	Y	S	Y	The Buddha Way
Bijou Community	19	CO		U		3+15	2															L							Ecm	N			Y	NQ Peace & Justice Work
Denver Space Center	62	CO		U	79	5	0		Y	Q		S	N	Cb	Y	N	N	N	N		N	N	R	N	8	150	N	N	Q	N	S	P	S	Good Company &
Hooker House	116	CO	1 Hs	U	77	4	0	8	N	N		Y	N	C	N	N	Y	N	N		C	C	F	N	15		N	N	N	N	N	S	S	Middle Class Cooperative
Lamborn Valley (F)	139	CO	120 ac	R	89	11	14	40	P	P	Cb	P	U	U	C	Y	Y	N	N	Y	Cb	C	Cb	F	N	U	U	H	CE	S	S	S	Y	Interpersonal Relations
Truth Consciousness	273	CO*							Y	Y		Y		N	Y											Y			E	Y	E	Y	N	NQ Spiritual Growth
Deer Spring	61	CT*		R	74				M	M	Cm	Y		N	Y	Y	Y		Y									M	HB	Y	Y	N	Y	NQ Hutterian
New Haven Zen	166a	CT																																NQ No Info Available
Community: CCNV	48	DC		U	70	45	1		Y	Y	Pu	Q	N	C	Q	N	Y	N	N	Q	N	N	N	N	N	N	N	N	Ecl	N	N	Q	Y	Resist Injustice
Finders	82	DC	Various	B	70	15	2		M	M	Cb	Y	N	Y		N	Y	Y	Y	Y	C	C	R	Y	Y	Y	Y	N	Ecl	S	S	S	S	Life is a Game
Sojourners Community	238	DC	Non-res	U	75	30	10					Y			Y				Y				Cb					N	C	N	S	S	S	NQ Neighborhood Service
Arden Village	10a	DL	<200 ac	U*	00	400	100	Same	N	N	Cb		N	M	N	N	S	N	N	Y	L	I	F	N	N	Y	S	N	N		S	S	S	Artistic Enclave
Grassroots Co-op	95	HL	258 ac	R	82	44	31		M	M	Cb		N	Cb	N	N	N	N	Y	Y	Cb	N	F	N	N	N	N	N	N		N	S	S	Environment; Peace
Jubilee Partners	126	GA	258 ac	R	79	9	6	N	Y	Y	Pu		0	Cb	N	Y	Y	Y	Y	N	C	C	Cb	Y	Y	Y		CHM	C	N	N	Y	Y	Resetting Refugees
Koinonia Partners	131	GA	600 ac	R	42	22	10	55	Y	Y	Pu		N	Cb	N	Y	Y	Y	N	Y	C	C	Cb	Y			Y		C	N	N	Y	Y	Service to Others
Metanoia (F)	153a	GA	1 Hs	U	80s	2+2	0		Y								N	Y				C						CMa	C	N	N	S	Y	NQ Demilitarization
Open Door	179	GA		U	81	32	2	Same	Y	Y	Pu	Y	N	Cb	Y	N	Y	S	N	S	C	C	Cb	S	A Lot	N		HGMo	C	N	N	S	Y	Solidarity with Poor
Dolphin Society (F)	63	[HI]	CA now	Q	84?				Y	Y		Y																		Y			Y	NQ Undersea City
Mother Earth Opihihale	162	HI	9 ac	R	78	7	1	10-12	Y	Y	Cb	Y	Negot	Cb	Y	S	Y	Y	N	Y	C	N	F	S	10-2	125+	N		Ecm	N	Y	Y	Y	Unconditional Love
Organic Kauai Prod (F)	181	HI		R	89	6	5	20	Y	Y	Hm					Y	Y	Y	N*	Y	L	L	Cb	Y	Y			N	Earth	N	Y	N	Y	Simple Living
ReCreation Center	205	HI		R	86	12	6	20	Y	Y	Cb	Y	300	N	N	Y	Y	Y	Y	Y	C	C	R	Y	40-6	300	Y	M	CE		Y	Y	Y	Water Therapy/Birth
Communia	45	IA	300 ac	B	76	30	6		Y	Y		Y	N	C	N	N	N	N	N	N	C	C	F	N	N	25	N	N	CE	N	Y	Y	Y	Spiritual Growth
River City	211	IA	5 Hs	U	77	30	0	75-100	Y	Y	Cb		20	M	N	N	Y	S	S	Y	Cb	Cb	R	N	16	~250	M	N	Ecm	N	N	S	S	Low Cost Housing
Thoreau Center	263	IA	3 Hs	U	79	12+	1+	~Same	Y	Y	Cb	Y	N	C	Y	S	S	Y	N*	S	I	I	R	I	5-4000		Y		Ecm	N	P	Y	P	Art, Environment, Spirit
Casa Grande	33	IL		U	70	6	1		Y	Y	Hm		N	C	Y	Y	Y	Y	Y	Y	L	C	R	N	15	200	Y	Y	N	N	Q	Y	Y	Egalitarian; Environment
Plow Creek Fellowship	193	IL	189 ac	R	71	33	36		Y	Y	Cb		N	C	N	Y	Y	Y	Y	Y	C	C	Cb	Y				CHMa	C		Y	Q	Y	Mennonite
Reba Place	204	IL	40 Units	U	57	60	35	N	Y	Y	Cb	Y	N	C	N	N	Cb	S	S	Y	C	C	Cb	N	Vol		N	CM	CEcm	S	Y		Y	Christian Living
Stelle	245	IL	240 ac	R*	73	102	38	250,000	Y	M	Cb		N	C	N	S	S	Y	N	N	N	Co	N	Y	Y			N	CEO	N	S	S	N	Self Sufficiency
Vivekananda Soc	282	IL*		B	30	15	1		N	N		Y	25		Y	N	Y	N	N	N	C	R	Y	Y				C	E	Y			Y	Vedanta; Mission
Center/Peace & Life	37	IN		R	72?			N	Y	Y	Cb	Y	N	C	Y	N	N	N	Y	N	C	I	F	N	N	N	N		C	N	Y	Y	Y	Broader Community
Earthworks (F)	70	IN	1 ac	R	88	1+6	0+1	N	Y	Y	Cb	Y	N	C	N	N	N	Y	Y	N*	N	N	F	N	N	M			EDL	Y	N	N	Y	Ecology; Art; Prayer
Oakwood Farm	175	IN*	326 ac	B	73	25	5		M	M	Pu		N	N	Q	N	N	N	S	N	I	C	R	N	N	N	M	Ma			N	N	N	Y	Prctical Spirituality
Padanaram	185	IN	2,000 ac	R	66	100	100		Y	S	Pr	Y	N	C	N	Y	Y	N	N	Y	Cb	Cb	F	Y				CH	EDL	Y	N	N	N	Internat'l Communal Utopia
Patchwork Central	187	IN	Non-res	U	77	20	6	6	Y	N	Cb	Y	N	C	N	S	S	N	Y	Y	N	N	R	N	N	N		C	Ecm	Y	N	N	Y	Urban Mission Work
Midwest Community (F)	155	KS	1 Hs	U	83	2	0	6	Y			Y	N	C	N	N	N	Y	Y	Y	C	N	F	N	D	Y	N	Y	C	O	Y	N	S	Y	Accountability Now
Planetary Project (F)	191	KS	100 ac	R	89				Y					C		Y	Y	Y	Y	Y		C							Y		P		P	NQ Integrate Spirituality
Rainbow House	200	KS	9 Rms	U	81	10	1/2	Same	Y	M	Cb	Y	N	Cb	N	S	S	Y	Y	Y	I	I	R	N	2	200-		N	N	N	N	S	S	Gender/Ethnic Balance
Sunflower House	252	KS	30 Rm	U	69	25	0	30	Y	N		Y	160	C	N	N	N	Y	N	S	L	L	R	N	25	150+	N	N	N	N	N	S	P	Carry Your Weight
Futures Inc.	88	KY	73 ac	R	88	7	1	250	Y	Y	Cb	Y	Varies	Cb	N	P	Y	Y	Y	N	L	C	Cb	N	170			U	Ecm	M	S	N	Y	Soul Fraternity
Spiral Wimmin's	242	KY		R	88	5	0	10-20	W	Y		W	Y	W	Y	Y	Y	Y	N	N*	L	I	F	N	Y	50+					Y	Y	N	Permaculture

Key to the Headings: *Map#:* Corresponds to numbers on the maps. *More?* [A]Adults, [C]Children *Sch?* Kind of Schooling? *Gen?* Gender: Women or Men only?
Decis? [C/M]Consensus or Majority? [Wt?]Weighted Decisions? *Food/Diet?* [Gr]Grow Own? [Or]Organic/Whole Grains? [S?]Vegetarian? [Vg]Vegetarian? [Fl]Flexible?
Ownership: [Ld]Land? [B]Buildings? [Rm]Rooming/Accommodations Style? *Economic Sharing:* [S?]Income Sharing? [L/mo]Labor/Month? [$/mo]Cost/Month
[Op?]Income-Earning Opportunities? *Spirituality:* [B]Basis? [L?]Leader? *Values:* [P]Pacifist? [F]Feminist? [VS]Voluntary Simplicity?

North American Communities: Cross-Reference Chart

Sorted by State/Province

Community Name	Map #	State/Prov	Land/Bldgs	Rur/Urb	Year Est?	Adults	Child	Max?	More? A	More? C	Sch? Visitors?	Gen? Visitors?	Join Fee	Decis? C/M	Wt?	Food Gr	Food Ea	Food Or	Food Vg	Food Fl	Own Ld	Own B	Own Rm	Econ S?	Econ L/mo	Econ $/mo	Econ Op?	Sexual Restr?	Spirit Basis	Spirit L?	Val P	Val F	Val VS	Other Values / Remarks
Holy City	113	LA	Non-res	B	70	33	41		Y	Y	Cb	Y	N	C	Y	N	N				Cb	Cb	F	N	10%	10%	N	CMa	R/C	Y	N	N	N	Gospel Poverty
Suneidesis	250	LA	117 ac	R	77	11	6	30	Y	Y	Cb	Y	N	C	N	Y	Y	Y	Y	N	N	N	N	Y				N	Ecm	N	Y	Y	Y	Self-Motivation/Correction
3HO Massachusetts	264	MA*		R																								Ma	E	Y				NQ Individual Excellence
Ark/Amherst	11	MA		B	84	10	2	12	Y	Y	Pr	Y	N	C	Y	N	Y	N	N	Y	N	N	N	N	10		N	N	Ecl	N	Y	Y	Y	Children
Earthdance	69	MA	180 ac	R	86	10	3	20-28	Y	Y	Cb	Y	N	C	N	S	Y	Y	N*	Y	Cb			N	32+	425	U	N		Y	N	S	S	Dance, Joy, Hard Wrk
Gould Farm	94	MA	600 ac	B	13	120	18		Y	M	Pu	Y	N	C	N	Y	Y	Y	N	N	C	Cb		N			Y	(M)**	CJ	Y	N	S	S	Care for Mentally Ill
Kripalu	133	MA	300 ac	R	71	280	7		Y	N		Y	0-100	N		N	Y	N	N	N	C	Cb		Y	168+		N	CMa	E	Y	Y	Y	Y	Service
Montebello	159	MA		U	82	6	0		N	N				Cb	M	N	N	N	N	N	N	R		N	243		N	CHM	C	N	N	N	N	Evangelic Christians
Renaissance	208	MA	80 ac	R	68	12	12		S	S	Pu	Y	AA	M	Y	Y	N	Y	N	N	C	F		Y		Y	CHP	C	N	Y	Y	Y	Love
Rowe Camp	216	MA		R	74	7	0	8	M	M	Pu	Y	N	N	Y	N	Y	N	N	N*M	C	F		N	160+		N	N	UU+P	N	Y	Y	Y	Hard Work
Sirius	235	MA	86 ac	R	78	21	12		Y	Y	Cb	Y	N	C	Y	Y	Y	Y	N	Y	C	Cb		N	32	50	Y	N	Ecm		Y	Y	Y	Findhorn Influence
Top O' The Ten	270	MA		U		6										Q	Y	Y	Y	Y	L	L	Cb	N		500	Y	N		C	N	Y	Y	Y	NQ Urban Co-op
Wellspring House	287	MA		B	81	5			Y	Y		Y	N	C	Q	Y	Y				L			Y				N		C	N	Y	Y	Y	Homeless Shelter
Crystal Spring	55	Man	*	R				150?	M	M	Cm	Y	N	N	Y	Y	Y				L	N	F	N		60	M	M		HB	Y	N	N	N	NQ Hutterian
Duck Mtn Circle (F)	66	Man	160 ac	R	87	3	3	10 Fam	Y	Y	Hm	Y	3,000	C	N	Y	Y	Y	Y	Y	L	N		N			M	N		N	N	N	N	N	"People Garden"
Heathcote	108	MD	35 ac	R	65	4	0	N	Y	P		W	250	C	Y*	Y	Y	Y	Y	Y*	L	L	Cb	N	30-4	300+	N	N		N	Y	Y	Y	Ecology Action
Intergenerat'n Women (F)	122	MD		B	89			N	Y			W				Y																		Y		NQ Living/Retirement
Woodburn Hill	295	MD	128 ac	R	75	7	3	N	Y	Y	Cb?	Y	Varies	C	N	Y	N	S			C	C	Cb	N	12		Y	N		N	N	S	S	Play; Love; Learn
SEADS of Truth (F)	225	ME		R	80	5?			Y	Y		Y	N	C		Y	N				L	Cb	F	Y			Y			N		Y		Y	Co-op Self-Sufficiency
Krutsio	135	Mex		R	76				Y	Y	Hm					Y	Y				C	C	R	Y						N		Y	Y	Y	NQ Egalitarian; Esperanto
Los Horcones	146	Mex		R	73	20	10		Y	Y	Cm	Y	Varies	C		Y	Y	Y	N	Y	C	C	Cb	Y			Y	Q		N		N	Y	Y	Behavior Change
Earth Community	68	MI	40 ac						Y	Y						Y	Y	Y	Y	N	C	C	Cb	Y			Y			N		N	Y	Y	NQ No Info Available
Heartlight	107	MI	360 ac	R	80	12+5	0+4		Y	Y	Hm		N	C		N	Y	Y	Y	Y	N	N	D	N		200+	N	CM	Ecm	N	Y	N		Love, Joy, Peace, God
Kuntree Bumpkin	136	MI	80 ac	R	81						Pu		AA			Y	Y	Y	Y	N								CHMa	C	Y	Y	Y	N	NQ No Info Available
Rivendell Co-op	210	MI	1 Hs	U	74	7	1	7	M	M	Cb	Y	200	C	N	N	Y	N	N	Y	C	C	R	N	12	205	N	N		N	N	N	N	Work on Problems Openly
Sky Woods Cosynagle	237	MI		B	72	7	0		Y	Y	Cb	Y	N	C	N	N	Y	Y	Y	Y	C	Cb	D	Y			Y	N		N	P	Y	Y	Greater Quality
Sylviron (F)	257	MI	Looking	R	89				Y	Y	Cb	Y	N	C		Y	S	Y	Y		C	C	Cb	N			Y				Y	S		Co-op Trainings
Vivekananda Mon	281	MI*	108 ac	R	68	12	0		Y	N	Cb	Y	Varies	Cb	Y	N	Y	Y	N	Y	Cb	Y		Y	S	N	C	E	Y	S	S	Y	Work; Acceptance
Zen Buddhist Temple	301	MI		U					Y	M		Y				Y					C	C	R	Y			Y	Y	E	Y	S		Y	NQ Zen Monastery
Bethany-Fellowship	16a	MN																											Y					NQ No Info Available
Camphill Vill/Minn	30	MN	360 ac	R	80	31	13	~90	Y	Y	Hm	Y	N	C	N	N	Y	Y	N	Y	C	C	Cb	Y			Y	N**		Y	N	Y		Anthroposophy
New Prairie	171	MN	10 ac	R	81	4	3	25-30	Y	Y	Pu	Y	AA	C	N	N	Y	Y	Y	N	C	C	F	Y			M	CHMa	C	Y	Y	Y	Y	Sharing & Service
Starland	244	MN*		R					M	M	Cm	Y	N	N	Y	Y					C	N	F	N			Y	M	HB	Y	N	N	N	NQ Hutterian
Wiscoy Valley	292	MN	356 ac	R	76	18	10		Q	Q	Cb	Y	3,000	C	N	N	Y	N	N	Y	C	N	F	N	4	25	Y	N		N	N	S	S	Sustainable Agriculture
East Wind	71	MO	160 ac	R	74	40	8	300-750	Y	Y	Cb	Y	N	M	Y	S	Y	Y	N	Y	C	C	D	Y			Y	N		N	N	N	P	Egalitarian; Environ;
Greenwood Forest	99	MO	1,000 ac	RR	79	45	8	N	Y	Y	Cb	Y	12,500	M	M	S	N	N	N	N	Cb	I	F	N	Vol	8	N	N(Mo)	N	N	N	P	S	Land Stewardship
Hearthaven	106	MO	1 Hs	U	88	5	0	N	Y	N	Cb	Y	Y	C	Cb	N	N	N	N	N	C	C	R	N			Y	N	Ecm	N	Y	Y	Y	Peace; Joy; Hospitality
Meramec	153	MO	213 ac	B	88	40	10		M	M	Cb	Y	Y	Cb	Y	N	N	N	N	N	Cb	Cb	F	N	Vol	15	Y	N		N	N	N	N	Ecological Practice
Moniteau Farm	158	MO	465 ac	R	79	24	37		Y	Y	Cb	Y	Y	C	Y	N	N	N	N	Y	L	N	F	N	8		Q	CH		N	N	N	N	Macrobiotics
Sandhill	221	MO	135 ac	R	74	7	2	15-20	Y	Y	Hm	Y	N	C	Y	Y	N	N	N	Y	C	C	Cb	Y			Y	N		P	Y	Y	Y	Respect for Earth
Seven Springs Farm	227	MO	120 ac	R	72	10	0	10	Y	Y		Y	N	Cb	Y	Y	N	N	N	N	Cb	N	F	N	2	10	N	N		Y	N	N	Y	Stewardship; Community Life
Shepherdsfield	230	MO	95 ac	R	69	<100	Incl	100a	Y	Y	Hm	Y	AA	Cb	Y	S	Y	Y		Y	C	C	F	Y			Y	CHM	C	Y	N	N	Community of Goods

Chart Codes explained on Pages 144-145

North American Communities: Cross-Reference Chart

Sorted by State/Province

Community Name (Forming?)	Map#	State/Prov	Land/Bldgs	Rur/Urb	Year Est?	Adults	Chld	Max?	More? A	More? C	Sch?	Gen?	Visitors?	Join Fee	Decis? C/M	Wt?	Gr	Ea	Or	Vg	Fl	Own Ld	Own B	Own Rm	Econ S?	L/mo	$/mo	Op?	Sexual Restr?	Spirit Basis	L2?	P	F	VS	Other Values / Remarks
Sunnyside (F)	253	MO		(R)	89	7	2	N	N	N	Cb		N	U	C	N	P	Y	Y	N	Y	N	N	Cb	N			M	N	N		N	S	S	Equality; Self-Sufficiency
Sweetwater CLT	256	MO	480 ac	R	81	6	2	14 Hs	Y	Y			Y		C		N	Y	Y	N	Y	L	I	F	N			Y	N	N		N	N	Y	Environmental Protection
Third Avenue Co-op	262	MO	3 Hs	U	79	8	4	N	M	M			Y		Cb		N	Y	Y	Y	Y	C	C	R	N		130	Y	N	N		N	S	Y	Anti-Athoritarian
Woolcroft (F)	297	MO	73 ac	R	88	1	0	10?	Y	Y			Y	100	S		Y	Cb	Y	N*	Y	Cb	Cb		N		85	M	N	N				P	NQ Permaculture; Livestock
Laurel Hill (F)	140	MS	1400 ac	R	79	4	1	N	M	N	Pr		Y	Y	N		N	N	N	N	N	N	N	Cb	N		Y	N	HGMo	N	N			Y	Honest, Industrious, Clean
Celo	36	NC	1200 ac	R	39	43	25		S	S	Cb		Y	Q	C		N	N	S	N		L	I	F	N		Y	N		C	N	N	S	S	Community Service
Jubilee House	125	NC		U	79	13	4		S	S			Y	Y	C		N	S	N	Y	N	C	C	Q	N	Vol		S	(Mo)	C		S	S	Y	Homeless Shelters
Long Branch	145	NC	126 ac	R	74	6	3		Y	Y			Y	AA	C			S	N	Y	N	L	L	Cb	Y						N	N	Y	Y	NQ Environmental Education
Union Acres (F)	276	NC	110 ac	R	89	10	5	50	Y	Y	Pu		Y	Y			M	Y	Y	N	Y	C	N	F	N		8	Y		Ecl	Y	Y	Y	Y	Spiritual Ecology
Green Pastures	96	NH*	160 ac	R	63	68	11	80	Q	Q	Pu		Y	N			Y	Y	Y	Y	Y	C	C	Cb	N		20	Y		EDL	Y	N	Y	Y	Stewardship
Namasté Rainbow (F)	165a	NH	49 ac	R	84?				Y	Y			Y	100			Y	Y	Y			C	C	Cb			Y	N	N	Ecl		Y	Y	Y	NQ Greens Camp
Tobias Community	268	NH		R	88																										Y				NQ Anthroposophy
Homeland (F)	114	NJ	Looking	R	89	9	2	<100	Y	Y	Cb		Y		C	N	P	Y	Y			L	C	Cb	N		8	Y	N	Ecl	N	Y	Y	Y	Soc. Responsible Development
3HO New Mexico	266	NM	40 ac	B	69	100	0	20	Y	Y	Cb		Y	N	Cb	Y	N	Y	N	Y	N	N	N	N	Y				Ma	E	Y	N	N	N	Sikh Religion; Yoga
Ecological Village (F)	72	NM	Not yet	B	88	20-70	?	700	Y	Y	Cb		Y	25	C	N	N	Y	S	Y	N	L	I	Cb	N					Ecl	N	N	Y	Y	Planetary Regeneration
Jemez Bodhi Mandala	123	NM																																	NQ No Info Available
Lama Foundation	138	NM	80 ac	R	68	14-70	?	N	V	V	Cb	S	S		C	Y	S	Y	Y	N*	M	L	L	Cb	N	A lot	200+	Y		Ecc				Y	Awakening Consciousness
Ojito	177	NM	20 ac	R	88	1+4	0	8	Y	Y		Y	Y	Negot	Cb	Y	S	Y	Y	N*	M	I	I	Cb	Y	40+	S	M	CH	Ecl	S	N	N	N	Earth; Individual; Spirituality
Santa Fe Com. School	222	NM		B	68	11	13	80	Y	Y	Cb		Y	N	Cb	Y	S	Y	Y	N	Y	C	C	F	N	30-	300	Y		N		N	N	Y	Summerhill Philosophy
Baxters Harbour Co-op	15	Nov		R	74	15	10	N	N	N	Pu		Y	1,000	Cb	N	N	N	Y	Y	N	C	N	F	N		20	N	Q	Ecm	N	N	U	Y	Individual Lifestyles
Builders	28	NV		B	69	40	25	40	Y	Y	Cb		Y		Cb	Y	N	N	Y	Y	Y	C	N	Cb	N		3	Y	(CHM)	Ecl	Y	N	N	Y	Feedback & Free Choice
Abode of the Message	1	NY	430 ac	R	75	43	18	50a25c	Y	Y	Cb		Y	500	Cb		N	Y	Y	N	Y	C	C	Cb	N	16	<405	N	N	Ecl	Y	S	S	Y	Sufism
Adirondack Herb	2	NY	40 ac	R	82	6	0	20	Y	Y			Y	N	C	N	Y	Y	Y	Y	N	L	C	Cb	N					N		N	N	N	Conservation
Birdsfoot	20	NY	73 ac	R	72	11	0	N	M	M				N		Y	N	Y	Y	N*	N	C	C	N	N		64	Y	CHLP	C	Y	N	N	N	Individual Spirituality
Camphill Vill/U.S.A.	31	NY	600 ac	R	61	180	40	220	Y	M	Pr			N	C		C	F	Y	N	Q	C	C	Cb	N	18+	160	Y		C				Y	Social Therapy
Common Ground	42	NY	70 ac	R	89	3	0	N	Y	Y				N	C		N	N	Y	Y	Y	C	C	F	Q		50	Y		C		N	N	N	Trust
Common Place	44	NY		R	76	7+4	3	40	Y	Y	Cb	Y	Y	Y	C	N	S	S	Y	P	Y	L	N	F	N	3	60	M		N		N	N	Y	11 Core Ideals
Dayspring	59	NY		R	75	8	9	30+	Y	Y+	Cm				Y		N	N	Y	Y	N	L	L	Cb	Y					Y	Q	Q	Y	N	Org.Agricultr; Psych
Fellowship Community	81	NY	7 bldgs	U*	67	105	20	N	M	M	Pr			Y	C		N	Y	Y	N	Y	C	C	Cb	N			Y	CHM	C	Y	N	N	Y	Anthroposophy
Ganas	84	NY	40 ac	U	78	9+35	0	55	Y	Y	Cb		Y	450	Cb		N	N	N*	N	Y	C	C	R	S		150+	Y		N		N	S	S	Communication & Feedback
Griffin Gorge	100	NY		R	77	8	3	10-12	Y	Y	Cb				Cb		N	Y	N*	N	Y	L	N	F	N			Y		Y		N	N	Y	Self Esteem; Earth
Pleasant View	192	NY*		R					M	M	Cm				C		Y	N	Y	Y	N	L	N	F	Y				M	HB	Y	Y	N	N	NQ Hutterian
Sivananda Ashram	236	NY	80 ac	R	75	10	0	N	Y	Y			Y	200	N		S	Y	Y	Y	N	N	S	Cb	N		Var	N	CMa	E	Y	N	Y	Y	Vedanta Yoga
Triform	272	NY		R	77	27	6		Y	Y	Pu				C		N	Y	Y	Y	N	C	C	F	N			Y		C		N	N	Y	Camphill Community
Woodcrest Bruderhof	296	NY*	100 ac	R	54	300	Incl	N	M	M	Cm		Y	N	C		Y	N	N*	Y	N	Q	Q	R	Y				M	HB	Y	Y	N	N	NQ Hutterian
Yoga Soc. Rochester	299	NY		U	73	5	1	7	Y	Y				N	C	S	N	N	N*	Y	Y	Cb	Cb	R	N	8	65	Q	N	Ecl	N	Y	N	N	Mutual Support
Catholic Worker/ Cleve	35	OH	Houses	U	84	20	0	N	Y	N				N	C		N	N	S	Y	N*	C	C	Cb	N			Y	N	C/Ecl	N	Y	Y	Y	Live with Poor
Currents	56	OH	163 Ac	R	81	11	6	30	P	P		Y	Y	13,800	C		N	S	Y	N	Y	C	C	Cb	N	12	88+	N		N		N	Y	Y	Cooperation
Deep Woods	60	OH	310 ac	R	78	7	0	30-50	Y	Y	Cb		Y	9,000	C		Y	Y	Y	Y	N	C	N	F	N		10+	Y	CMo	Ecl	N	Y	Q	Q	Sharing; Neighbors
Far Valley Farm	78	OH	234 ac	R	80	12+2	8	N	P	P	Cb		Y	5,000	C		N	N	Y	Y	Y	C	I	Cb	N	10	25	Y		N		N	N	Y	Organic Structure
Middle Earth (F)	154	OH		R	76	2	0	5-7	Y	Y			Y	Negot	M		N	Y	Y	Y	Y	L	L	F	N			Y	HBLP	CP	N	N	N	Y	Community Commitment
Moonridge	160	OH										W																							NQ No Info Available

Key to the Headings: **Map#:** Corresponds to numbers on the maps. **More?** [A]Adults, [C]Children **Sch?** Kind of Schooling? **Gen?** Gender: Women or Men only?
Decis? [C/M]Consensus or Majority? [Wt?]Weighted Decisions? **Food/Diet?** [Gr]Grow Own? [Or]Organic/Whole Grains? [Vg]Vegetarian? [Fl]Flexible?
Ownership: [Ld]Land? [B]Buildings? [Rm]Rooming/Accommodations Style? **Economic Sharing:** [S?]Income Sharing? [L/mo]Labor/Month? [$/mo]Cost/Month
[Op?]Income-Earning Opportunities? **Spirituality:** [B]Basis? [L?]Leader? **Values:** [P]Pacifist? [F]Feminist? [VS]Voluntary Simplicity?

Directory of Intentional Communities
Page 164

Community Name	Map #	Forming?	State/Prov	Land/Bldgs	Rur/Urb Year Est	Adults	Chld	Max?	More? A	More? C	Sch? Visitors?	Gen?	Join Fee	Decis? C/M Wt?	Food Gr	Ea	Or	Vg	Fl	Own Ld	B	Rm	Econ S?	L/mo $/mo	Op?	Sexual Restr?	Spirit Basis	L?	Val P	F	VS	Other Values / Remarks
New Covenant	166		CH	—	R 77	3	1	N	Y	Y	Hm	Y	AA	C	Y	Y	Y	N	Y	C	C	F	Y			CM	C	N	Y	Y	Y	Anabaptist
New Jerusalem	167		CH	Non-res	U 71	170	150	N	Y	Y	Cb	Y	N	N	N	N	S	N	Y	N	N	F	N		N	CHM	R/C	Y	N	Y	Y	Work for Social Change
Raven Rocks	203a		CH	1047 ac	R 70	11	0	30	Y	Y		Y	N	Cb	S	S	Y	N	Y	Cb	Cb	Cb	S		N	N	QEcl	Y	N	Y	Y	Education; Ecology; Sharing
Sunflower Farm	251		CH	152 ac	R 75	13	10	30	Y	Y	Pr	Y	5,500	Cb	N	Y	Y	N	Y	Cb	N	F	N		N	N	N	N	N	Y	Y	Self-Reliance
Susan B.Anthony	255		CH	152 ac	R 79	4	0		Y	N		W Y		C	N	N	N	N	Y	C	C		N	150			N	N	N	Y	Y	Economic & Social Change
Vale	278		CH	40 ac	R 59	9	10		Q	S	Cb	Y	50	C	S	Y	Y	N	Y	L	N	F	N	50			Y	N	N	S	S	Family Oriented
Sparrow Hawk Village	240		OK	332 ac	R 81	72	8	300	Y	Y	Pu	Y	N	M	S	Y	Y	Y	N	L	C	Cb	N	8	5	N	Ecm	Y	N	S	S	Spirituality; Service
Walden Hill	283		OK		R 81	2	1		Y	Y	Hm	Y	N	Cb S	P	Y	Y	N	Y	L	C	Cb	Y		Y	HMa	C	N	N	S	Y	Rainbow Family
Crieff Hills	53		Ont		75	2-20	0	N	Y	Y	Pu			N	N	N	P	N	Y	L	L	F	N		Y		N	N	Y	S	Y	Christian Hospitality
Dandelion	58		Ont	50 ac	R 75	4	1	12-15	Y	Y		Y	LoanAA	C	Y	Y	Y	Y	Y	C	C	R	Y	30	Y		N	N	P	P	P	EcoFeminism; Self-Sufficiency
Dragonfly Farm	65		Ont	250ac	R 78	10	1	1	Y	Y	Cb	Y	3,000	C	Y	Y	Y	Y	Y	C	I	F	N				N	N	N	P	P	kAos
Hailos	102		Ont	320 ac	R 81?	6	5		Y	Y	Cb	Y	10,000	Cb Y	S	S	Y	Y	P	C	I	F	N				N	N	N	P	P	Cottage Industries
Headlands	105		Ont		R 71	4	2		N	N	Pu	Y		M	Y	N				N	N	Cb	N	300	Y		N	N	N	N	N	Ideological Void
King View	130		Ont*	87 ac	R	50	Incl	Incl	M	M	Cb	Y		Cb	Y	Y	Y	Y	Y	Cb	Cb	Cb	S		Y		EDL	Y			S	NQ Hospitality
Morninglory	161		Ont	100 ac	R 69	7	7	7 Fam	Y	Y	Cb	Y	5,000	Cb	Y	Y	Y	N	Y	Cb	Cb	F	N	N	Q	N	Ecm	N	N	S	Y	Respecting Earth
Rowanwood	215		Ont	92 ac	R 80	12	6	30	Y	Y	Cb	M	Y	C	Y	S	Y	N	Y	C	I	F	N	Var 85	Y	N	Ecl	N	N	S	S	Extended Family Caring
Stone Soup	247	(F)	Ont	Non-res	U 88	6-10	0	N	P	P	P	N	N	Q	N	Y	N	N		Cb	S	R	N				N	N	N	N	N	Human Wholeness
Toad Hollow	267		Ont	100 ac	R 86	4	3	~20	Y	Y	Pu	Y		C	Y	Y	Y	N	P	C	I	F	N	Var 50+	Y	LGMo	Y	Y	Y	Y	Y	Support; Deep Relationships
Zen Lotus Society	303		Ont		U				Y	M		Y	AA													Y	E	Y				NQ Zen Monastery
Alpha Farm	5		OR	280 ac	R 72	18	4		Y	Y	Pu	Y	N	C	Y	Y	Y	N*	Y	C	C	Cb	Y		Y	N	Ecl	N	Y	Y	Y	Group Process
Appletree Co-op	7		OR	23 ac	R 74	13	10	10-25	Y	Y		Y		Cb	S	S	Y	N*		C	C	R	N	S	S	N	N	N	Y	Y	Y	Ecology; Comunications
Breitenbush Hot Spgs	25		OR	86 ac	R 77	36	10	40a,10c	Y	Y	Pu	Y	500	M Y	N	Y	Y	S	Y	C	C	F	N	40/w	Y	N	Ecl	N	Y	N	S	Energy Self-Sufficiency
Cerro Gordo	40		OR	1200 ac	R 73	7F	3	2,500	Y	Y	Pu	Y	500	M Q	S	Y	N	Y	Y	L	N	F	N	N	Y		N	N	N	Y	S	Symbiotic Comunity
Earth's Rising Co-op	69a	(F)	OR	60 ac	R 70s	<10	>10	12-15		M		M		C	Y	N	Y	N		C	C	F			Y		N		Y			NQ Simple Living
End of the Road	76		OR	40 ac	R 81	4	2	12-15	Y	N		Y	N	C	Y	Y	Y	N*	N	L	L	Cb	Y	150	N	N	N	N	Y	Y	N	De-Consumerizing; 3rd World
Galilee	88a	(F)	OR	140 ac	R 90	2	0	N	Y	Y	U	Y	N	C Y	P	Y	Y	N	N	U	U	P	U		U		Ecm	N	Y	Y	Y	Environmental Consciousness
Lichen	142		OR	140 ac	R 71	3	0	12-15	Y	Y	Pu	Y	3,000	C	N	Y	Y	N	N	L	L	F	N	30	N	(CH)	N	N	Y	Y	Y	Ecology & Environment
Lost Valley Center	147		OR	90 ac	R 89	13	3	30-40	Y	Y	Cb	Y	100	Cb	S	Y	Y	N	Y	L	L	Cb	N	20/w	Y	N	Ecl	N	Y	N	S	Mutual Cooperation
Mountain Grove	164		OR	400+ ac	R 70	4+8	2		Y	Y	Cb	Y	N	Cb	N	Y	Y	Y	N	L	N	F	N		Y	N	N	N	N	S	S	Non-Doctrinaire
Owl Farm	183		OR	147 ac	R 76	5	2		Y	Y	Cb	W Y	Y	C	Y	Y	Y	Y	Y	L	L	F	N		Y	N	P	N	Y	Y	Y	Earth as Mother
Rootworks	214		OR	160 ac	R 70s	~60	~4	N	Y	Y	Cb	W Y	N	(C)	Y	S	Y	N	P	N	N	Cb	N	40 - 100	N	CLP	(P)	N	N	P	Y	Women's Network
Seven C's	226a	(F)	OR	160 ac +3R	89	6	0	15+kids	Y	Y	U	Y	U	M Y	Y	S	Y	N	N	I	I	Cb	N	100	N		N	N	N	S	N	Lasting Relationships
Still Meadow	246		OR	50 ac	R 76	21	Incl	Incl	M	M	Cb	Y		Cb Y	Y	Y	Y	N	Y	Cb	Cb	Cb	S		Y		EDL	Y			S	NQ RadiantTranquility
Wolf Creek Sanctuary	293		OR		R 85				Y			M Y		C						L	L											NQ Radical Faerie
Womanshare	294		OR	23 ac	R 74	4	0	8	Y	Y	Cb	Y	N	C M	Y	Y	Y	Y	Y	C	C	Cb	N	110+ 40	N	CLP	N	N	N	Y	S	Workshops/Concerts/Gatherin
Aquarian Research	8	(F)	PA	1 Hs	U 69	3	2	N	Y	Y	Cb	Y	N	N C S	Y	N	S	N	Y	N	Y	Cb	(P)		Y	N	CO	Y	N	N	N	Concern about World Situation
Bryn Gweled	27		PA	240 ac	U 40	136	65	Same	Y	Y	Cb	Y	Y	C	S	N	S	N		C	N	F	N		N	N	N	N	N	N	N	Diversity
Camphill Spec'l School	28a		PA	57 ac	R 63	60	80+		Y	Y	Cm	Y		C	N	Y	N	Y	N	L	L	F	N			N	N	O					NQ Anthroposophy
Camphill	29		PA	410 ac	R 72	100	30	160	Y	Y	Pr	Y	Vol	C	N	Y	N	Y	N	L	L	Cb	Y	Vol		N**	O	N				Anthroposophy
Gita Nagari	91		PA	600 ac	R 74	51	23		E	Y	Cb	Y		C	Y	Y	Y	Y	Y	L	L	Cb	Y		Y	CMa	E	N	N	N	Y	High Thinking
Greening Life	98		PA	135 ac	R 73	8+2	1+2	30-35	Y	Y	Cb	Y	5,000	C	S	N	Y	S	Y	C	N	F	N	8-10 95+	N		Ecm	N	S	N	Y	Growth in Spirit
Julian Woods	127		PA	140 ac	R 75	16	6	N	Y	Y	Pu	Y	3,700+	Cb N	S	N	Y	S	Y	L	I	F	N	21	Y		Ecl	N	S	S	S	Permaculture; Stewardship

North American Communities: Cross-Reference Chart

Sorted by State/Province

Community Name	(F)	Map#	St/Prov	Land/Bldgs	Rur/Urb	Year	Adults	Chld	Max	More A	More C	Gen/Vis	Sch	Join Fee	C/M	Wt	Gr	Ea	Or	Vg	Fl	Ld	B	Rm	S?	L/mo	$/mo	Op	Sexual	Spirit B	L?	P	F	VS	Other Values / Remarks
Kehillat Mishpakhot		127a	PA	Non-res	U	82	6	fam	N	Y	Y	Cm	N		(C)		N	S				F			F		N			J					NQ Tribe of Families
Life Center Asso.		143	PA	4 Hs	U	71	31	1		Y		Cm			C	Q	Q	N				L	L	Cb	N	30					N	N	Y	Y	Economic Democracy
New Meadow Run		169	PA*		R					M	M	Cm	Pu		N	Y	N	Y				N	N	Cb	Y		~250	S	M	HB	Y	Y	N	N	NQ Hutterite
Northeon Forest		173	PA&	AZ	R	73				Y	Y	Y	Pu	N	C		Q	N				N	N	Cb	N	30				O	Y	Y	Y	Y	Gurdjieff Philosophy
Tanguy Homesteads		259a	PA	100 ac	U*	45	102	53	Same	M	M	Y	Cb	30	C		N	S				Cb	I	F	N	Var	30		N	(C)	N	Y	Y	Y	Racial Equality; Change
La Cité Ecologique		137	Que	800 ac	R	84	102	53	N	Y	Y	Hm		100,000	Cb		Y	Y	Y	Y	Y	L	L	F	Y				N	N	Y	N	Y	Children's Education
Providence Zen Center		196	RI	50 ac	R*	72	10	2	15	Y	N	Pu	S	350	Cb		N	N	N	N	N	C	C	D	20		370			E	Y	N	N	N	Zen Meditation
Agape Community	(F)	3	TN	300 ac	R	72	2	4	N	Y	Y	Hm	Y	N	Cb		S	S	S	S		Y	F	F	Y	Y	Y		CMa	C	Y	C	Y	N	Shared Spiritual Life
Dunmire Hollow		67	TN	160 ac	R	74	10	4		Y	Y	Cb	N	N	Cb		N	S	Y	S	N	Y	Y	F	S	N	25	S		N	C		N	N	N	Stewards; Comunity
Farm, The		79	TN	1,750 ac	R	71	125	175	800	Y	Y	Cm		3,000	Cb	S	Y	S	N	Y	N*Y	Y	C	C	F	S		110+	M	N	Ecm	N	Y	Y	Y	Universal Oneness
Flatrock		83	TN	27 ac	B	79	8	6		Y	Y	Pu			N		N	Y	N	Y	N*Y	L	N	F	N	Y	35+		N	N		Q	Y	Y	Y	Je Ne Sais Quoi; Funk
Short Mountain		232	TN	200 ac	R	80	8	0		Y	N	Hm		N	C		N	N	Y	Y	Y	L	L	Cb	N	Y	75	N		N	PO	N	Y	Y	Y	Radical Faeridom
Sundance		249	TN	7 ac	R	78	2	2	N	P	P	Hm		N	C	N	N	N	Y	N	N	Cb	C	F	N	Y				N	N	N	Y	S	Y	Harmony with Earth
Panhandle Permacultr		186	TX	20 acres	R	88	7	4	N	Y	Y	Cb	Y	N	(C)	Y	S	Y	Y	N	N	(L)	N	F	N	7	20	Y		N	N	N	Y	Y	Y	Permaculture
Peace Farm		188	TX		R	86	3	0	6-8	Y	Y	Cb		N	C	N	P	Y	Y	N*Y	Y	C	C	R	Y		200	N		N	N	N	Y	Y	Y	Nonviolence; Peace
Rainbow Valley		202	TX	220 ac	R	80	15	4	50	Y	Y	Pu		5,000+	Cb	N	M	N	Y	N	N	L	I	F	Y	4	20+	N		Earth	S	Y	Y	Y	Energy Self-Sufficiency
Saint Benedict's Farm		217	TX		R	56	5			Y	N			N	C		Y	N	N	Y	N	C	C	D	Y				C	R/C	Y	N	N	Y	Catholic
Whitehall Co-op		289	TX	13 Rm	U	49	13	0	13	S	Q	Pu		27	C	N	N	N	Y	N	N	C	C	R	N	16	360		N**	N	N	N	S	N	Support; Family Bonding
Zendik Farm		304	TX	300 ac	R	69	40	8		Y	Y	Hm		AA	N		Y	Cb	Y	N	Y	C	U	C	Y			Y	N	Ecl		P	Y	Y	EcoLibrium
Common Ground		43	VA	77 ac	R	80	10	5	18 Fam	Y	Y	Hm		Y	C		S	S		N*		L	I	F	Y			Y		Ecl		Y	Y	Y	Ecology; Non-Exploitation
Community, The		49	VA	6 Hs	U	66	5	4		N	N	Hm		N			N	N	N	N	N	C	C	Cb						Ecm	N	Y	Y	N	Communication
Gathering, The		89	VA	10 ac	B	69	14	0		Y				N	Y		Y	Y	Y	Y	Y	C	C	D	Y				Y	Y	Y	Y	Y	N	Spirituality; Communal Life
Innisfree		120	VA	400 ac	B	71	70	1	90	S	Y	Pu		N	C		N	Y	N	N	N	C	C	R	N				N**	N	N	N	S	S	Disabled
Inst Sustain Living		121	VA	5 ac	U	89	10	1	~200	Y	Y	Cm		U	N		N	Cb	N	Y	N	C	U	C	Y			Y	N	Ecl		N	P	Y	Sustainability
New Land		168	VA	750 ac	R	79	37	8	200	Y	S	Cb		N	M	Y	N	S	N	S	N	N	N	F	N	Vol				N	N	M	Y	S	Consciousness
Oak Grove	(F)	174	VA	52 ac	U	89	1	0	12-15	Y	N		S	U	C		P	P	P			L	U	Cb	U			U	U			Y	Y	Y	Simple Living Center
Reina del Cielo		207	VA	52 ac	R	72	16	8	N	Y	Y	Pu		N	Cb		N	N	N	N	Y	C	N	F	N	Var	175	N	Mo	CE	Y	Y	N	Y	Ancient Mysteries
Shannon Farm		228	VA	490 ac	R	74	60	21	N	Y	Y	Cb		Y	Cb		N	S	N	N	N	C	C	Cb	Y	12	7%	S		N	Y	Y	N	Y	Tolerance; Freedom
Sojourners' Orchard		239	VA	211 ac	R	83	6	1	N	N	N	Cb		Y	Cb	M	N	Y	N	Y	N	I	I	I	N	Y	1200	Q	N(Mo)	N	N	S	S	N	Tolerance; Environment
Springtree		243	VA	120 ac	R	71	5	2	10	Y	S	Cb		AA	Cb		Y	Y	Y	Y	Y	C	C	D	Y					N	Y	Y	N	Y	Living Lightly; Joy
Twin Oaks		275	VA	400 ac	R	67	75	15	200	Y	Y	Cb		Y	Cb		Y	Y	S	Y	S	C	C	R	Y			Y		N	Y	Y	Y	Q	Non-Violence; Anti-Racist
Winged Hrt. Homstd.	(F)	291	VA	283 ac	R		1	0	20	Y	M	Pu		V			N	Y	S	Y	N	N	C	Cb	N	Y	30+	Y		ECO	N	Y	N	N	Sufism
Yogaville		300	VA	750 ac	R*	66	200	50	N	Y	Y	Cm		N	Cb		Y	Y	Y	Y	Y	C	Cb	Cb	Y			Y	CM	Ecm	Y	Y	Y	Y	Interreligious Peace
Greenhope Farm		97	VT	17 ac		83						(w)										C	F							Ecm					NQ No Info Available
Asponola		12	WA*	40 ac	R	60	45	Incl		M	M	Cm	P		N	Y	Y					C	F						Y	HB	Y	Y	N		NQ Agriculture
Bear Tribe		16	WA	40 ac	R	70				Y		Y					Y	Y	Y	N		C	C	Rm				P		NAm	Y			Y	NQ Permaculture
Goodenough		92a	WA	Non-res	U	81	100	12	300	Y	Y	Cb		25/Yr	C	Y	N	N	Y	N	Y	L	L	Cb	N				N	Ecm	Y	Y	Y	Y	Covenant
Homestead Co-op	(F)	115	WA	290 ac	U	89	35+	?	10,000	Y	Y	Cb		V			N	Y	Y	Y	N	L	L	Cb	N	Y	Y	M		N	N	S	S	S	Freedm & Mutul Aid
Love Israel Family		148	WA		R	68	39	46	144,000	Y	Y	Cb		AA	N		N	Y	N	N	Y	C	C	F	Y	Y	N=		Y	C	Y	Y	Y	N	Love is the Answer
Old McCauley Farm		178	WA		R	75	15	8+4	N	Q	Q	Cb		Y	Cb		Q	Q	N	N	Y	C	N	F	N	N	25		Y	N	N	N	S	S	Owners Agreement
Ponderosa		194	WA	1,000 ac	R	79	36	15		Y	Y	Pu		N	C		N	Y	Y	N	Y	N	N	F	N			N	M	S	N	N	S	S	Self-Reliance
Prag House		195	WA		U	72	10	5	10a,5c	N	N	Pu		N	M	N	Y	Y	Y	N	Y	L	L	F	N	8	5%	N	Mo		N	N	S	S	Liberal Politics

Key to the Headings: *Map#:* Corresponds to numbers on the maps. *More?* [A]Adults, [C]Children *Gen?* Gender: Women or Men only? *Sch?* Kind of Schooling? *Food/Diet?* [Gr]Grow Own? [Ea]Eat Together? [Or]Organic/Whole Grains? [Vg]Vegetarian? [Fl]Flexible? *Decis?* [C/M]Consensus or Majority? [Wt?]Weighted Decisions? *Economic Sharing:* [S?]Income Sharing? [L/mo]Labor/Month? [$/mo]Cost/Month *Ownership:* [Ld]Land? [B]Buildings? [Rm]Rooming/Accommodations Style? *Spirituality:* [B]Basis? [L?]Leader? *Values:* [P]Pacifist? [F]Feminist? [VS]Voluntary Simplicity? [Op?]Income-Earning Opportunities?

Directory of Intentional Communities

North American Communities: Cross-Reference Chart

Sorted by State/Province

Community Name	Map #	Forming?	State/Prov	Land/Bldgs	Rur/Urb	Year Est?	Adults	Chld	Max?	More? A	More? C	Visitors?	Gen?	Join Fee	Decis? C/M Wt?	Gr	Ea	Or	Vg	Fl	Ld	B	Rm	Econ S?	L/mo $/mo	Op?	Sexual Restr?	Spirit Basis	L?	P	F	VS	Other Values / Remarks
Raj-Yoga Math	203		WA		R	74	6	0	10-12	Y	N		Y	N	N	Y	Y	Y	Y	Y	N	N	N		Var	N	Y	C	E	Y	N	N	N	Directness
River Farm	212		WA		R	71	9	5	12a, 6c	P	P	Cb	Y	Varies	C Q	Y	S	Y	N	Y	L	Cb	Cb	N		Y	N		N	N	N	Y	N	Practical Homesteading
Saint Clares Hermitage	218		WA		R	80	4	0	12	Y	N	M	Y	N	N	Y	Y	Y	Y	Y	N	N	Cb	N	80	N	Y	CMa	CEO	Y	N	N	N	Renunciation; Solitude
Teramanto	260		WA	3 Hs	R	75	7	3	40	Y	Y	Cb	Y	5-	C N	Y	Y	Y	Y	Y	C	C	Cb	N	Y -or- 75	Q	N	Y	Y	P	P	Y	Y	Activism
Tolstoy Farm	269		WA	440 ac	R	63	27	22	100	Y	Y	Cb	Y	N	C N	Y	Y	N	Y	Y	L	N	F	N	N	N	N	N	N	N	S	S	Organic Farming
Twin Brooks	274		WA	250 ac	R	89	4	1	U	Y	Y	Pt	Y	Y	Cb Y	Y	Y	Y	N	Y	N	N	Cb	N	P <100 S	CH	Ecm	N	P	P	S	Casualness
Walker Creek	284		WA		R		8	5													L									L				NQ Evergreen CLT
Waukon Inst	285	(F)	WA		R	87	7	0	20-30	Y	Y		Y		C	Y	Y	Y			C	C	Cb		Y	Y		P			Y		Healing & Nutrition
Wesleyan Christn	288		WA	68 ac	B	77	28	20	Same	Y	Y	Cb	Y	N	C N	Y	Y	Y	N*	Y	C	C	F	N	56 293 +	CM	C	Y	N	N	N	Honesty & Integrity
Bounty	24	(F)	WI	12 ac	R	89	3	3	N	Y	Y	Cb	Y	7,000	C N	P	N	Y	N		Cb	I	F	P	N	Y	N	N	N	S	S	Y	Good Neighbors
Casa Maria	34		WI		U	68	15	3		Y	Y	Cb	Y	N	C	N	Y	Y	N	Y	L	Cb	Cb	N	Y	N	N	R/C		N	Y	Y	Non-Violence
Dancing Waters	57		WI		R	82	8-10	3	N	Y	Y	Cb	Y	N	C N	Y	Y	N	Y	N	C	C	F	N	Y 140	N	N		N	N	Y	Y	Communication; Land
DOE Farm	62a		WI	80 ac	R	77			35	Y	Y	W	Y		C Y	S	S	Y			C			N	Y .3%	N			Y	Y	Y	NQ Womyn's Land
Dorea Peace Commty	64		WI	89 ac	R	80	8	8	10a+?c	Y	Y	Pu	Y	N	C N	N	Y	N	N		Cb	N	F	N	F 175	N	Ma	C	N	N	Y		Justice Issues
Farm Home Center	80	(F)	WI		R	87	3	0	N	Y	Y		Y	U	M U	N	N	N	N		N	N	F	U	U N	U	Ecl	N	U	U	Y	Alternative Agriculture Center
High Wind	109		WI	46 ac	R	81	15	6	60	S	S	Pu	Y	N	C N	Y	S	Y	N*	Y	Cb	Cb	F	N	80+ 50+ S	N	S	N	N	S	S	Y	Living/Learning Center
House of Lavendar	117		WI	1 hs	U	74	7	2	9	S	Q	Pu	Y	50 Dep	M	N	Y	N	N		C	C	D	M	175	N		N	N	N	S	Y	Progressive Social Change
Martha's Housing	152		WI	1 Hs	U	70s	30	+	Same	Y	Y	Cb	Y	35	Cb N	N	N	N	Y	P	C	C	R	N	20-2 200	N	Q	N	N	Y	N	Cooperation; Consensus
Rock Ridge	213		WI		R	71	3+3	3		Y	Y		Y	N	C	N	Y	N	N	Y	C	C	F	N	8 235	N	Q	N	N	P	P	Y	Stewardship; Peace
Sichlassenfallen	233		WI		U		5	0	6-7	Y	Y			N	C	N	Y	N	N	Y	N	N	N	N.	8-10 200	N	Ecl	N	N	S	Y	P	Democracy; Environment
Wellspring	286		WI	100 ac	R	88	3	0	10-20	Y	Y		Y	N	C Y	Y	Y	Y	N	Y	L	Cb	R	N	5-10 350	N	Ecl	N	N	Y	Y	Y	Deeply Value Earth
Yahara Linden	298		WI	8 Rm	U	74	4	2	8	Y	M	Pu		N	C	N	Y	N	N	Y	L	L	R	N	10 190	N	N	N	N	N	N	Cooperative Diversity
Gesundheit	90		VA	310 ac	B	71	9	5	150	M	M	Cb	Y	N	Cb Y	S	Y	Y	N	Y	L	L	R	S	Y	N	N	N	P	P	Y	Serve People & the Planet
New Vrindaban	172		WV	5,000 ac	R	68	300	120		Y	Y	Cb	Y	N	C Y	Y	Y	N	Y	M	C	C	Cb	Y	240	Y	CHM		Y	N	P	P	Y	Surrender to God
Sassafras Ridge	224		WV	240 ac	R	72	10	7	15-20	N	N	Cb	Y	N	C S	Y	N	N	F		Cb	N	F	N	Y M	N	PJ	N	Y	Y	Y	Shared Responsibility

Chart Codes explained on Pages 144-145

Directory of Intentional Communities

The Abode of the Message

Route 1, Box 1030-D
Shaker Road
New Lebanon, NY 12125
(518) 794-8090

The Abode of the Message is a thriving spiritual community of 50 adults and 25 children living on 430 acres in the Berkshire Mountains. It was founded in 1975 by Pir Vilayat Khan, head of the Sufi Order in the West. The Abode has many purposes. It is an expression of spiritual freedom in which people of diverse interests are striving to fulfill their spiritual ideals in everyday life. It is an esoteric school for the Sufi Order in the West, and a spiritual center for the message of the unity of all religions and all people. It is a retreat center for those who seek the opportunity to withdraw from the world for a period so they may commune with their innermost being.

The Abode was started to provide an environment conducive to the fulfillment of human potentialities, and a supportive and creative framework within which self-discovery would be fostered. It was formed as an experiment, with the hope that individuals of varying beliefs, interests, and desires could live together harmoniously and successfully, learning how to share cooperatively the bounty which life offers. It is this vision, this ideal, which is the continuing purpose and goal of the Abode of the Message.

Most individuals at the Abode earn a living in the surrounding community or are self-employed. Each member of the Abode is responsible for his or her financial contribution to the community, paying a fixed monthly fee for housing and food. Community members share kitchen and cleaning responsibilities, with each adult contributing 3 to 4 hours of their time weekly. One half day each month is set aside as "community workday," sharing chores such as gardening, wood gathering, cleaning of common areas, etc. Common meals are served three times daily, and all community members have private rooms or houses on community property.

Decision-making is both democratic and hierarchical, with community members participating in policy formation through monthly "Family Meetings." Most decisions are implemented by an appointed executive committee. Though total consensus is not required, a sincere effort is made to consider the wishes and interests of all community members when making decisions. Family meetings are open forums, and are an important vehicle for communication within the community. Write or call for further information. 1/22/90

Adirondack Herbs

Box 593
Broadalbin, NY 12025
(518) 882-9990

A small, non-sectarian community welcoming folks that follow different spiritual paths or none at all. A basic requirement is a commitment to conservation in the field of the environment, energy, and resources. Our income derives from the sale of herbs to health food stores. Depending upon abilities, visitors might have the choice of working with herbs, bees, greenhouses, building construction and repair, hydroponics, electronics, vehicles, alternative energy projects. Choose from different levels of involvement, from guest status (six hours of work per week) to full-time partnership. If you work more than 16 hours per week you share in the profits of the farm. Diet: vegetarian or not, plenty of fruits, nuts, cheese, tofu, tahini, squid, and weird stuff like that. No heavy drinking, drugs, or hunting. Location: 40 acres in the Adirondacks, minutes from Great Sacandaga Lake (great sailing), close to wilderness, skiing, Saratoga Springs, railroad. Cold winters, private rooms or cabins, good library (science, technology, literature, history — over 50 journals and magazines). 12/20/88

Agape Community (Forming)

Route 1, Box 205
Liberty, TN 37095
(615) 536-5239

Agape Community is a residential settlement of the Russian Orthodox Church Outside of Russia. It is located in a remote rural area of mountain hollows some 60 miles SE of Nashville. Permanent residence is open to those who share fully with the Community in the Faith, either as landholders purchasing neighboring property, or as leaseholders on property owned by the community. Temporary residence on community property is possible for those who seriously seek instruction in the Faith. Visitors who seek information concerning the Orthodox Christian Faith and an experience of a life centered therein are welcome for short periods of time by prior arrangement ... but should be prepared for primitive living conditions and a diet and daily life conditioned by the discipline of the Church.

The community operates a small religious press and publishes a bimonthly magazine, *Living Orthodoxy,* at $8/year (USA). Inquirers for further written information are asked to provide adequate funds to cover the cost of response ... our resources are severely limited (SASE appreciated too). [cc] 2/7/90

Alcyone Light Centre

1965 Hilt Road
Hornbrook, CA 96044
(916) 475-3310

Alcyone is a creative spiritual adventure balancing the energies of heart and mind to enhance life as a co-creative enterprise in harmony with nature and all life, recognizing and affirming our unity in diversity. We wish to demonstrate and encourage a holistic, self-reliant lifestyle; serve as a strategic link in raising the vibrational quality of the planet in cooperation with other centers, groups, and individuals; and provide an educational environment in which regenerative ecology, sacred architecture, integrated healing/wholeness, love and inner peace are all studied and lived within a spiritual context.

Alcyone's 360 acres of rolling meadows and tree-covered hills are located on the California/Oregon border west of I-5, fifteen miles south of Ashland, Oregon. Majestic Mt. Shasta can be seen to the south, and Mt. Ashland hovers over us to the northwest. Our land is diverse in terrain and potential usage, with south-facing slopes, flat agricultural valleys, generous wells, and seasonal creeks.

Alcyone's first building, a "bioshelter" called Ariesun, will be self-sufficient in its use of solar energy, rammed earth walls, photo-voltaics, and other thoughtful new age innovations. Nearing completion now, it will house six permanent residents and up to fifteen guests/students.

There are a number of ways to become involved with Alcyone, including Charter Membership, Residential Charter Membership, or various levels of financial support to help us reach our goals. We encourage visits by prior arrangement. For more information, please write. 3/24/91

Alpha Farm
Deadwood, OR 97430

(503) 964-5102 Farm
268-4311 Alpha-Bit

Alpha Farm is a close-knit, extended-family-style community on 280 acres in the Coast Range of Oregon. Consensus, our decision-making process, is also a metaphor for the ideal world we seek to create here — and so help create in the larger world. We seek to honor and respect the spirit in all people and in nature; to nurture harmony within ourselves, among people, and with the earth; and to integrate all of life into a balanced whole. We value service, and work as love made visible. Group process is a strong point; we meet regularly for business and sharing.

Founded in 1972, we average 15-20 adults, and now have three young children. New people spend a year as residents (trial members) before committing to membership. Members and residents work on the farm, in community-owned businesses (a cafe/bookstore, contract mail delivery, and construction), and in freelance professional work. We also offer workshops on consensus and facilitation several times a year. All income and resources are held in common. Individuals have private rooms; other living space is common, and evening meals are communal.

We are open to new residents; visitors are welcome for a three-day initial visit. Please call or write well ahead. 6/1/90

Ananda World Brotherhood Village
14618 Tyler Foote Crossing Rd.
Nevada City, CA 95959

(916) 292-3065 / 292-3464

Ananda World Brotherhood Village is a spiritual community based on the communitarian principles taught by Paramahansa Yogananda. Founded in 1968 by the master's disciple, Sri Kriyananda (J. Donald Walters), Ananda now has several branch communities, including one in Europe, and numbers some 500 members.

Dedicated to a life of high ideals and simple living, members of Ananda share their teachings and way of life through The Expanding Light Retreat, through books and tapes, through tours and pilgrimages, and through urban teaching centers and meditation groups. Ananda embraces nearly 900 acres of woods and meadows in the Sierra Nevada foothills, in Northern California. Members support themselves through a variety of community and private businesses. The Ananda "how-to-live" school is open to children from both within and without the community.

Voluntary cooperation is the norm in community activities. Democratic sharing at every level comes effortlessly, without rancor. The prevailing mood at Ananda is one of friendship and harmony, together with a cheerful spirit of service to God; respect for individuals and their privacy; and freedom to learn and grow at one's own pace. A balance is sought between spiritual guidance and self-motivation. 6/19/89

Appletree Co-op
Box 5
Cottage Grove, OR 97424

(503) 942-4372

Appletree Co-op, first established in 1974, has approximately 10 adult members and 6 children living on 23 acres located four miles from Cottage Grove. We have four separate households on the land, one being fairly communal with two single mothers, one couple, and four kids. We were an income-sharing community for nine years, but recently returned to a co-op structure (our original form).

We have feminist, non-violent, non-racist and ecological values. Co-op decisions are made by consensus, and daily decisions are made by managers or individual households.

People earn their own livings. We have a large organic garden and orchard, and plan to raise some food and livestock for our use. We have meetings as we need them. Children are raised by household, and there is some informal sharing between houses. Inquire about visiting... we need some time to regroup. New members have a 1-year residency before becoming full members. Please write or call in advance. 3/21/91

Aprovecho
See: End of the Road House

Aquarian Research Foundation (Forming)
5620 Morton Street
Philadelphia, PA 19144

(215) 849-1259 / 849-3237

Aquarian Research (tax-exempt since 1970) helps to develop a positive future for the planet. Its founder, Art, started living communally in Paraguay in 1948. The shoestring operation has an 8-room house in Philadelphia for people working on exciting projects with Art and his wife and partner, Judy. We worked on ending the arms race, and in 1988 Gorbachev's advisor, Georgi Arbatov, sent a Soviet scientist to accompany Art (in our 1958 Cessna) on a tour of U.S. communities. *Where's Utopia?* (58 min. VHS) was produced as a part of that tour, to document the wide variety of successful cooperative systems. We're now marketing the video, and working on the Turner Tomorrow Award — to produce a realistic film showing a loving, cooperative future for Earth in 10-15 years. Art is also working to abolish military systems worldwide, and seeking cooperative solutions to homelessness that combine human potential and communal movements.

With years of experience with communal movements and with many different human potential movements, Aquarian is seeking to unite these two movements to create a real solution to the the problem of Homelessness in America; please contact us if you can assist in any way. Another project, The Caring Alternative, helps people meet and develop better love relationships. Call or send SASE for more information.

We also have a free national computer network for communities and others working for a positive future, publish *Aquarian Alternatives News-*

Aquarian Research *(Cont'd.)*
letter, and do assorted organizing and referrals (see Resources listing). We're funded by donations and video sales.

We seek co-workers to share a drug- and smoke-free environment, and (as a couple with 2 children aged 5 & 10) seek a larger community in which our work could continue and grow ... to build a cooperative world based on free and loving relationships. 1/21/90

Aquarius Ranch (Forming)

#1 Aquarius Plaza, Box 669
Vail, AZ 85641

(602) 449-3588

Aquarius offers 30 acres of rugged mountain terrain — secluded, but easily accessible to Tucson (we're 40 miles from downtown).The scenery is "out of this world." The property is owned by three people forming a community, relating intimately, and building an exclusive clothing optional resort. We have opportunities for employment in the construction and servicing of communication towers and equipment, and concessions are available for breeding saleable exotics (mushrooms, flowers, and herbs). A five-acre parcel is available for sale.

We make decisions by consensus, though we may use a majority rule if deadlocked. A major value we share is preserving as much as possible our unspoiled natural surroundings, and to share space with other living things. Are you daring, adventurous, mature, open, independent, honest, trustworthy? Please write for details. 7/6/89

Arcosanti

HC74, Box 4136
Mayer, AZ 86333

(602) 632-7135

Arcosanti is an urban experiment under construction since 1970 at Cordes Junction in central Arizona. The inspiration of Paolo Soleri, it is an attempt to solve the problems of overpopulation, pollution, energy and natural resource depletion, food scarcity, and quality of life. By reorganizing sprawling landscapes into dense three-dimensional cities, people will be more closely integrated with nature, culture, and each other. When finished, Arcosanti will be a 25-story structure, heated by a 4-acre food-supplying greenhouse. Of the total 860 acres, 846 will remain in

their natural state or be used for the farming or recreational needs of the projected 5,000-person community. We also own over 3,000 additional acres which are leased and not developed.

Presently, Arcosanti has 60-75 resident members who guide the students and professionals who pay about $550 to participate in 5-week construction workshops. Participants learn skills and the joys of shared accomplishment. 1/20/90

Arden Village

The Highway
Wilmington, DE 19810

(302) 475-3912

Arden Village was founded in 1900 by disciples of philosopher-economist Henry George — based on his theory of the Single Tax (abolishing all taxes except a single tax, levied on the value of the land, irrespective of the value of improvements on it). They believed that this system would distribute income and wealth more justly, on the basis of the output of a person's labor rather than their ability to monopolize land and other natural resources. They created a living community, one that would change over time at the direction of its residents. Unlike other experimental communities, Arden founders did *not* believe in selecting the people who would live there ... it was open to people of all beliefs, creeds, and cultures.

The development of an experimental rural colony was an inviting challenge to a multitude of people who shared a fascination with ideas and a concern for making a better world. The village attracted artists, musicians, craftsmen and women, builders, and dreamers — of diverse interests and beliefs: some of them were vociferous *opponents* of the founders and their Georgist ideas!

Almost half of Arden's acreage was set aside for the use of all residents: in greens, forests, roads. The perimeter of the settlement was maintained in woodlands, a fortunate design that has served to insulate the village from the intrusion of adjoining suburbia.

The core ideals have remained in effect over the years. The residential land is still owned by a board of trustees, and the rest of the land is communally owned through the incorporated village. Rent is still collected on residential land, and used for the benefit of the residents. Though Arden has always based its

government on a board of trustees and a town meeting, in 1967 the Town Assembly became the legally constituted legislature of the Village, and its committees are the executive branch of the government. Meetings are held quarterly, with the voting membership comprised of every resident who is at least 18 years old and who has lived in the village for six consecutive months immediately preceding the meeting.

Today there aren't many Single Tax disciples living in the village, although every fall Arden does offer a course in the theory. It is still an artistic enclave, with over 40 professional artists currently living and working in the village. Write for more information; SASE appreciated. 3/15/90

The Ark

Box 605
Amherst, MA 01004

The Ark is in the early stages of creating extended family together. We are located in a friendly, cooperative neighborhood called Hearthstone Village (pop. 70+); we are also part of a larger friendship network. The house is 7500 sq. ft. of mostly finished, flexible spaces — designed to support needs for both community and personal sanctuary. We are looking for a family and children-loving folk who: •connect energetically with us, •are interested in exploring long-term community, •want to be learning relationship skills in the context of living together, •enjoy creating gatherings and events, and •are interested in exploring co-ownership

The "village" is in the Pioneer Valley of western Massachusetts, where major cultural, political, artistic, and alternative events abound. We aspire to a state of dynamic stability in which we may expect miracles in our daily life while also knowing that our lives and our lifestyles are an integral part of the manifestation of miracles on a planetary scale. Please write (include SASE) — sharing your vision of living together, and we'll send more information about us. 3/1/89

Asponola Colony

Hutterian Brethren, Inc.
Route 1, Box 6-E
Reardon, WA 99029
(509) 299-5400

A Hutterite colony, engaged chiefly in agriculture. They raise wheat, hay, barley, peas, and potatoes. They also

N. America

market several thousand geese and ducks yearly, have 6,000 laying hens, and seventy milk cows. A garden, hogs, sheep, and a small orchard are maintained , but not on a commercial basis. The community is relatively self-sufficient, but markets excess to accumulate the cash necessary to acquire more land to serve their growing population. See main listing for "Hutterian Brethren." 3/14/89

Atmaniketan Ashram

1291 Weber Street
Pomona, CA 91768

(714) 629-8255

2621 W. Highway 12
Lodi, CA 95240

(209) 339-1342

Atmaniketan Ashram is a living laboratory for the practice of Sri Aurobindo's Collective Yoga of Integral Perfection. All seekers sincerely aspiring to become a selfless instrument in the progressive manifestation of a "Divine Life" upon earth are welcome to collaborate. This is not a meditation retreat—but a place for those who, with their whole heart, mind, life and body, wish to serve the Divine with dynamism and concentration.

Intimate spiritual guidance is provided by Ashram Founder Swami Sadhu Loncontirth, an Indian Yogi who has confirmed Sri Aurobindo's Teachings in his life experiences. Swamiji comes twice a year to America from the main Ashram in West Germany and India. The Ashram is glad to announce the opening of a new center in Lodi, California, which will soon be open to collective activities. Please call either location for further information. 12/24/89

Auroville International USA

Box 162489
Sacramento, CA 95816

(916) 452-4013

Auroville is a "universal township" of over 500 people living and working on 2000 acres near Pondicherry, India. Auroville was created in 1968 to realize the ideal of Sri Aurobindo who taught the Karma Yoga.... Auroville is for those who want to do the yoga of work. It is designed to bring about harmony among different cultures, and for understanding environmental needs of man's spiritual growth.

Services, made up of the persons actually involved or interested in a particular work, do the necessary administration and coordinating in specific areas. There is no institutionalized authority as such, and major policy decisions are referred to the general meeting in which all members of Auroville are free to participate.

Auroville is in a rural setting, and conditions are simple in most of the 40 different settlements. The electrical supply, telephone service, and water supply are subject to breakdown. Health services of various kinds (including dental) are available. Food in the common kitchens is basic, and mostly vegetarian. For purposes of external communication, they publish the *Auroville Review* and various newsletters.

Auroville International, an international body, has its main offices in Holland and its secretariat in Paris. It has members in most parts of the world and centers in Holland, France, USA, Canada, Sweden, Italy, Germany, Switzerland, and the United Kingdom. These centers are bases of support for and information about Auroville. 3/15/88

Baxters Harbour Co-op

Route 5, Canning
Nova Scotia, CANADA B0P-1H0

At this time we are in a "quiet" state. Not much is going on collectively though this may not be a permanent state. About half the membership lives elsewhere — in nearby Wolfville, or as much as 350 miles away. Recently three-quarters of the community lands were sold to individual family groups. The community still holds 32 acres, including a common garden area and several small buildings. County by-laws are restrictive in terms of new dwellings or further subdivision — this is a problem for new membership.

Members pursue individual careers and lifestyles, including sociology, political science, nursing, various environmental concerns, international relations, carpentry.... fund-raising remains a problem. Our

"central plant" remains minimal, though our list of possible projects is extensive: from pond-building and field-reclaiming to various study group possibilities. 1/24/89

Bear Tribe Medicine Society

P.O. Box 9167
Spokane, WA 99209

(509) 326-6561 M-F(9-5)

The Bear Tribe is an intentional community of people working together for the common goal of understanding and healing ourselves, others, and the Earth. The community was founded in 1970 based on the visions of Sun Bear, a teacher of sacred knowledge. His message is that we must be responsible in all our actions to all beings in Creation, not just for this generation, but for all generations to come.

The Bear Tribe relates to the world at large by teaching and communicating what its members have learned through study and through their own experiences about self-knowledge, healing, ceremonies, the Medicine Wheel, bioregional awareness, the ways of indigenous peoples, networking, the earth changes, relationships, living in intentional community, and becoming more self-sufficient. We teach through our speaking, workshops on Vision Mountain, Medicine Wheel Gatherings, and the books some of our members have written. We publish a magazine called *Wildfire*. Our work also consists of permaculture site development and teaching, self-reliance programs, book sales, and vision quests.

Because we maintain and live on a land base, we are able to remain aware, and grow in our awareness of the Earth and all beings on her. Sun Bear's vision of the earth healing through the healing of living things is a vision for the world — not just for one specific ethnic group. It is for anyone who feels a desire and a commitment to re-establish a loving and responsible relationship with Creation. 6/17/88

Bethany Fellowship

6820 Auto Club Road
Bloomington, MN 55438
(612) 944-2121

The Directory received a postcard from this group stating their desire to be included — later confirmed by a phone call. We have no further information. 1/13/90

Bhaktiras (Forming)

6713 E. Kiami Street
Tucson, AZ 85715

We are in the early stages of creating a family-sized community consisting of eight yogi-yogini pairs, with their children, whose main desire in life is the achievement of non-dual consciousness culminating in ecstatic love of God. By working together, supporting each other, and serving the outside world, our spiritual goal is more readily attainable. Bhakti Yoga — loving God and seeing God in each other — would be the primary practice.

We are envisioning a home with land and pond in a sun-filled climate, accessible to a nearby city. Co-housing arrangements would be a combination of private and shared space. We would share ownership, income, and expenses as a cooperative corporation. Our financial goal would be reasonable independence based upon right living. Responsibilities for earning, cooking, coordinating, creating, and so forth would be distributed based upon need, talent, and desire. Life-filled food, carefully prepared, would be a highlight of each day. Meditation, chanting and dancing, worship, scripture reading, physical training such as Hatha Yoga, and sharing would be integral to our way of life.

We plan to utilize the best of modern technology, but combine it with simplicity of lifestyle. We are excited about the decade ahead, and see global activities connecting us to communities around the planet.

If you share our dream ... we'd love to learn more about you, your goals, and what you could potentially commit to this effort. Please write either to the address above, or to Brother Hannes; R.D. 1, Box 319; Moundsville, WV 26041 (SASE requested). We promise to get back to you as soon as possible. 1/24/90

Big Bend Hot Springs

Big Bend, CA. See:
Essene Mother Earth Church

Big Wheels Ranch

Route 2, Box 32
Montgomery, CA 96065
(916) 337-6206

Big Wheels Ranch is a 40-acre homestead located midway between Mt. Shasta and Mt. Lassen, in the northernmost part of California. We bought the land in 1971, and there has been a fairly stable core group of members living on and off the land ever since.

Title to the land is held by an owners association comprised of present and past members: 3 resident adults and one child, and 10 non-resident adults with 9 children among them. We make decisions by majority rule, though there is a strong effort to try to accommodate everyone's needs to the greatest extent possible. Daily decisions are made by the group in residence as we go along, and long-term decisions are made by the owners association at quarterly meetings (often planned to coincide with a celebration and a work weekend). All members, resident and non, share the costs of taxes, general maintenance, and community improvements. Members living on the land pay a monthly fee, and are expected to work on community projects.

Big Wheels has the feel of a large extended family, and most of the non-residents plan to eventually return here to live. Over the years there have been some tough decisions that have stretched and strained us a bit, but we have come to know each other well and care about each other a lot — so we have a fairly solid basis for working things out in the long run. We're not actively seeking new members. SASE appreciated. [cc] 1/12/90

Bijou Community

411 West Bijou
Colorado Springs, CO 80905
(719) 635-5078

We are an ecumenical group that practices simple living and works for justice. Our residences are held in a land trust, housing 2 children and 3 adults. We have a Hospitality House for people in need, and a soup kitchen that serves 350 people a day. 5/18/91

Birdsfoot Farm

Star Route, Box 138
Canton, NY 13617
(315) 386-4852

We are a 16-year-old agricultural community of 11 adults, in a very rural area near the Adirondack Mountains. We work the land, growing a large percentage of our food, and marketing vegetable crops, herbs, fruits, and crafts for part of our cash income. During the growing season we host farm apprentices. We also have many skills and activities other than farming. Several members have part-time or full-time jobs off the farm.

Our 73-acre farm has fertile loam, woods and streams, barns, and five houses. We are in transition to cooperative ownership; the vegetable business is a separate partnership. We envision a cautious expansion in membership, including children. New members have a 6-month trial period. Initial financial investment is not required. We each pay a monthly "rent" for living expenses, and purchase equity in the property in monthly installments.

We are concerned with problems like sexism, racism, violence, poverty, and environmental destruction. We care a lot about each other, and find time for many kinds of communication and sharing—such as communal meals, group work, meetings, rituals, parties, etc. Each individual follows his/her own path. Some of us are exploring and borrowing from a variety of spiritual traditions. We create our own rituals. We welcome open-minded people from diverse backgrounds. For more information please send an SASE. 2/10/89

Black Bear Ranch

Box 645
Forks of Salmon, CA 96031

Black Bear Ranch is a former gold-mining town that was reinhabited in 1968. We are located in steep mountain terrain, with four creeks that supply water for the gardens and the pond. In 1987 the seventy acres was put into a land trust with six trustees. The beneficiaries are the people who have lived at or are now living at the ranch.

Currently there are a dozen adults and children, with fluctuation due to friends and visitors. Much activity centers around the communal kitchen and meeting space, both located in the 120-year-old main house. Also there are six individual cabins, some dormitory-style sleeping spaces, a barn, and a woodshop. The ranch's emphasis is on communal and sustainable living. There are four acres of certified organic gardens where we raise vegetables, herbs, grapes, berries, and apples. We weave our gar-lic into flowered braids and wreaths which we sell at fairs. We are slowly expanding the herbal gardens into a cottage business.

In reinhabiting this place we accept our responsibility to live here harmoniously — so that we and the forest ecosystem live healthily into

N. America

the next century. Please include SASE with correspondence [cc]. 6/29/89

Black Cat House

San Francisco, CA

Black Cat Collective is a housing collective with two bases of unity — feminist witchcraft or compatible spiritual focus (we have an engaged Buddhist, etc.) and direct action politics. We have a large house owned by several of the members, located in the Mission district of San Francisco. We were formed as a group of friends who decided to live together. Some of the friends have since moved on; and we have some new members — friends from the larger community who have recently joined us.

We are nine adults and 2 children (none yet of school age). All major decisions are by consensus, and we eat together regularly. We garden and have a rock & roll band. 8/25/89

Black Oak Ranch

Box 1288
Laytonville, CA 95454

We are an extended family, not a collective or commune. We have many family units and individuals within the Hog Farm. 26 Hog Farmers are partners in our rural land, others are not. Not all of our land partners live on our property. Those of us living together on our land cook together for the most part. We have individual sleep spaces.

Some of us are hippies, some of us are yuppies, some defy description. We are farmers, doctors, musicians, store-keepers, artists, carpenters, clowns, nurses, chefs, etc. We have children of all ages, and some of our friends also spend time living with us.

We have built a beautiful camping facility on our land which we rent to our own performing arts and circus camp — Wavy Gravy's Camp Winnarainbow for kids and adults. We are also open to renting to other groups. Mail inquiries only — and sometimes we're slow to respond. See also: The Hog Farm. 9/16/89

Bounty (Forming)

Route 3, Box 191-AA
New Auburn, WI 54757

(715) 967-2730

We are a community in formation located in the rolling country of northwest Wisconsin. We have purchased 12 acres of land on a beautiful little lake. Each member owns a small lakefront lot (1 acre) to build on — the rest of the land is held in trust. We are starting as good neighbors, and hope to learn to cooperate and share in other ways: income producing activities, food growing (we are finishing our solar greenhouse), etc.

New members would need to help finance new lands, so some investment (about $7,000) would be necessary. We feel a combination of private land (for privacy) and community land (for sharing) is a good combination. We encourage energy self-sufficiency, ecology, freedom. We are non-sexist, and non-religious. We welcome inquiries (please enclose SASE). 1/15/90

Brandywine Forest

Deming, WA
See: River Farm

Breitenbush Hot Springs

Retreat & Conference Center
P.O. Box 578
Detroit, OR 97342

(503) 854-3314 Message

Breitenbush has reorganized dramatically in recent years. Officially we are now a worker-owned and operated corporation, though in many ways we are still a community. We are philosophically similar to before — we honor all spiritual traditions, and are intentionally creating an energy self-reliant model for ourselves and the world (geothermal heat and hydro-electricity).

We are involved in raising public consciousness about ecology issues, and are deeply involved in trying to save the remaining temperate rain forest of our area. We still strive to serve the highest social good, and to achieve our own highest individual good.

Currently there are 16 workerowners, and 20 other workers who are at various stages in the 18-month membership process. One automatically becomes a worker-owner after 18 months, and pays a $500 nontransferable membership share. Dividends vary according to the performance of our hot springs business.

The worker-owners hold an annual meeting at which they elect a board of directors. The board in turn chooses a general manager who oversees the day-to-day operation of the business, and who appoints team leaders to coordinate the five areas of operations: kitchen, housekeeping, office, maintenance, and marketing/publicity. Everyone else who works is a team member; non-working spouses of workers are considered community members.

The community lives across the river from the retreat/conference center, in a village of approximately 24 cabins. Every other week we hold a community sharing in the sanctuary. Three times each year we schedule a four-day community renewal — when guest facilities are closed and the community joins together for sharing. 9/19/89

Brigid House

2012 Tenth Street
Berkeley, CA 94710

Brigid is a collectively-owned home in Berkeley, begun in February of 1985. Currently there are 6 adult residents (aged 33 to 48, five of whom are owners) and one 9-year-old boy. All of us are white; four are women; two are gay/lesbian, two straight, two bisexual, and one undecided. Our class backgrounds vary. We work at a variety of jobs: computer programming, job development for adults with developmental disabilities, carpentry psychotherapy, therapeutic bodywork, etymology, and book publicity.

Our house (originally a duplex) has separate bedrooms, an assortment of common space, and a large yard. It includes office spaces for computers and bodywork/psychotherapy. The house is our home — it's NOT an investment.

Our agreements include a meeting and two dinners weekly, sharing food, quarterly retreats, regular upkeep and renovation of our home, and most important — clear communication and consensus process. We value emotional sharing, and are supportive of each other's growth. We are a combination of spiritual ritualists, mediators, environmentalists, and feminists — and are involved in healing ourselves. We value our friends outside the house, our families, work, and leisure. We strive to give our 9-year-old artist his space, some continuity, and our listening side. SASE appreciated [cc]. 8/30/89

Bruderhof

International
See: Hutterian Brethren

Bryn Gweled Homesteads

1150 Woods Road
Southampton, PA 18966
(215) 357-3977

The School of Living is proud that it helped to stimulate the organization of BGH in 1940. The diverse founders of BGH sought a friendly neighborhood cherishing individual responsibility, honesty, family autonomy, and extreme diversity of culture, wealth, religion, politics, lifestyles, etc. Persons going through the membership procedure visit with each of the 75 families and qualify as Approved Applicants if they get 80% positive vote in a secret written ballot. Many more reject BGH after being fascinated by it, than BGH has rejected by the voting process. Conformists are repelled by the wide spectrum of non-conformists at BGH.

Homes sell at prices typical for Philadelphia suburbia, notwithstanding the fact that the land is owned by BGH. Being a lessee of a 2-acre tract and being a member are synonymous. Membership should be investigated only by those having adequate capital to buy a suburban home and those free to allocate evenings during several months for the membership visits. In joining BGH an Approved Applicant buys the home of a withdrawing member. Most members withdraw only after homeowning for more than 30 years. Land use rent to BGH (as advocated by economist Henry George) pays for maintenance of the roads, swimming pool, 80 acres of common ground about a mile north of the northernmost tip of Philadelphia, etc. Each member owns a non-interest-bearing debenture (redeemable when leaving) corresponding to the capital involved in the land, roads, swimming pools, tennis courts, community center, etc. Most of the founders are dead, but the few remaining are pleased that the current membership is fulfilling the dreams of the founders better than seemed plausible in 1940. To our knowledge, no member has left BGH because of dissatisfaction with the community. In fact, alumni typically take part in celebrations, and we are hoping to have as many as possible gather for our 50th anniversary in 1990. 12/12/88

The Builders

Box 2121
Oasis, NV 89835
(702) 478-5112

The Builders, founded in 1969 by Norman Paulsen, direct disciple of Paramahansa Yogananda, offers instruction in the Sun Technique of Meditation. A lifestyle incorporating Twelve Virtues and Eight Paths of right action assists us in accessing the higher brain and the cosmic sense of illumination. Individual commitment to, and relationship with Mother/Father/Creator, *"I am that I am"* is vital. We also value our association with like-minded souls.

We are self-motivated, self-responsible individuals. There is no formal membership or membership committee. Builders reside in four western states, where Builder-owned businesses exist and Builder-owned property and/or housing is maintained. Current businesses include: natural food stores and cafes, demolition and excavation, motel, gas station, mobile home park and sales/installation, apartment complex, typesetting, affordable gemstones, commercial art, and sailing ship restoration. We have 20 years experience in community living. We notice society's evolution towards cooperative community and responsible world citizenry. We invite hardworking sincere seekers of Truth to explore the possibility of working with us. Visitors by appointment only; please include SASE. 8/3/89

Camphill Special Schools

Beaver Run
Route 1, Box 240
Glenmoore, PA 19343
(215) 469-9236

Camphill Special Schools, Inc., is a community of 60 adults and their children who live with, work with, and educate a population of about 60 children in need of special soul care. These are children with varying degrees of mental retardation or other handicaps.

The school offers a three-year seminar in Curative Education for those who come to live with and learn to educate the special child. The foundation of the work and education is based on Anthroposophy — a holistic approach to life developed by Rudolf Steiner, an Austrian philosopher, educationalist, and artist. Camphill is an international movement, with more than 70 centers throughout the world.

Life is intense and demanding here, but very enriching. Please call for further information. 2/26/90

Camphill Village Kimberton Hills. Inc.

Box 155
Kimberton, PA 19442
(215) 935-0300

Camphill Village Kimberton Hills is one of seven North American communities in the Camphill movement — each one unique, yet all with similar purposes. We seek to create a renewed village life, and to establish social forms of human interdependence between disabled and non-disabled people. Our approach is a non-denominational, Christian way of life based on the inspirations of Rudolf Steiner's Anthroposophy, which allows each person to evolve to their potential as a respected individual.

Started in 1972, our 410-acre biodynamic farm is run by a community of 130 members including some with mental disabilities. Scattered around the farm are fifteen houses which shelter "extended families" who work the farm, gardens, orchard, bakery, cheese house ... and sell surpluses in the small coffee shop and farm store. We have a strong cultural life which involves many visitors and neighbors. Visitors are welcome to share in the life and work here — for shorter or longer periods as space permits. We also have a small apprentice program in biodynamic agriculture which brings 4-6 students per year for "on the job training." All visits are by appointment *only* — and letters are preferred to phone calls (SASE appreciated). 1/22/90

Camphill Village Minnesota, Inc.

Route 3, Box 249
Sauk Centre, MN 56378
(612) 732-6365

Camphill Minnesota is one of 70 Camphill communities around the

N. America

world. 38 of us — children, adults, and adults with mental handicaps — live in extended families in six houses on two adjoining farms which total 360 acres.

We live together for a variety of reasons which all come together in the quest to bring the needs of the land, people, and animals into harmony with the needs of the Spirit. All of our work is based on Anthroposophy (literally, "the wisdom of man"), which came about through Rudolf Steiner (1861-1925), an Austrian-born philosopher, artist, and scientist.

We farm/garden biodynamically, an approach that combines organics, the rhythms of the planets, and other factors. Through a creative approach which uses art to introduce subjects to the children, the goal of our home school is to bring the child's thinking, feelings, and will into harmony. In all that is done (including our houses, weavery, woodshop, and bakery) the dignity of humanity is enkindled collectively and individually. We are open to new members as space is available. Please inquire by letter or phone. 3/2/90

Camphill Village U.S.A.,Inc.

Copake, NY 12516

(518) 329-7924 / 329-4851

Camphill Village is an international community of 220 people, about half of whom are adults having mental disabilities. We are situated on 600 acres of wooded hills and farmland 110 miles north of New York City. The Village includes a farm, a large garden, workshops, a community center, giftshop, co-op store, and 17 family-size houses (each shared by 6-8 adults having disabilities, and 2 to 4 co-workers and their children).

We are part of the wider Camphill movement, and based on the innovative therapeutic work of Karl Koenig, M.D. Village life includes work on the land, in crafts, and on household chores; worship; and cultural activities. Co-workers live in Camphill Village as full-time volunteers, receiving no salary but working in answer to the needs of others; in return, their own needs are provided for. Through this viable alternative to the wage system, it becomes possible to develop a sense of mutual responsibility and brotherhood.

Skills: the only requirement is a dedication to maintain active interest, care, and concern for one's fellow man. Camphill Village offers a 3-year training in Social Therapy. 12/20/88

Caravan Theatre Farm

R.R. #4, Comp. 1
Armstrong, B.C.
CANADA V0E-1B0

(604) 546-8533

Originally part of the Caravan Stage Company (Est. 1978 — see Resources section), the groups separated in 1987. Year-round membership is usually 4 to 5 adults and a similar number of children. Each spring the community-in-residence swells to around 40 members who collaborate in the production of 2 or 3 major innovative and colorful productions (which draw sell-out crowds for the duration of the 3-week runs). They also offer a two-week Children's Theatre Workshop which covers voice, music, movement, clowning, characterization, rehearsal, and the performance of a play.

Their 80-acre farm is owned and operated by the Bill Miner Society, a non-profit group. They also have entered into a stewardship agreement with the Turtle Island Earth Stewards (a Canadian land trust organization) to assure that the land is used in an environmentally sound way. The Farm offers clinics in the use of alternative energy and its rural application, and conducts workshops in theatrical skills such as voice, movement, and scenic art for the novice and advanced. 6/1/88

La Casa Grande Colectiva

906 South Maple
Urbana, IL 61801

La Casa Grande Colectiva is a housing cooperative situated on 2.5 acres of land in Urbana, Illinois. The town just grew up around this secluded little haven of an old farmstead. The house has been a cooperative for about 18 years. Recently — when our landlord threatened to develop the area — we began the process of incorporation, and initiated steps among ourselves towards building an intentional community.

Our dream is to purchase the land, a parcel at a time, and place it in a land trust. We hope to move old Victorian houses (ones that are

threatened with demolition) to the periphery for renovation into additional low-cost housing. We plan to keep the center area as a parkway and for communal gardens. The barn will become workshops and/or a community center.

We are actively involved with other cooperatives here in Champaign/ Urbana — such as the food co-op, and a network of student housing cooperatives. Several of our members have been living here for nearly a decade, and we hope to attract others with long-term commitments to intentional community.

What follows is our statement of purpose as formally recorded in our articles of incorporation:

•To provide low-cost, not-for-profit cooperative housing that is operated and governed in a participatory and democratic manner.

•To serve as a resource center that provides technical assistance and educational service about cooperative living.

•To develop relationships with other cooperatives in order to exchange information and services.

•To work towards a society based on cooperation, sharing, and equality.

As part of this process we hope to promote a living situation that strives to be ecologically sound and egalitarian. Please include SASE with correspondence. 2/5/89

Casa Maria

Catholic Worker Community
1131 North 21st, Box 05206
Milwaukee, WI 53205

(414) 344-5745 / 344-0300

The Casa Maria Catholic Worker House has been fundamental in housing and feeding the homeless for 50 years. It is based on the philosophy of non-violence, voluntary poverty, and helping those in need. The community is large enough to house 4 families and 3 single women until they find another place to live. The community also gives out food, clothes, and used furniture to those in need. There are about 25 people who work at the house now. No one is paid because it is done in the Christian conviction that we should take care of our sisters and brothers in need without seeking any reward for this. We are interested in rooting out the violence in our society and the causes of hunger and homelessness. As a result we do not cooperate with

Casa Maria *(Cont'd.)*

the governments of this society and its system. We receive no funding from the Church, government, or large corporations, nor do we accept tax exemptions.

We are always looking for new members since the more people we have the more we can do to care for the needy and try to non-violently destroy the causes of poverty and build a new society of generosity and caring. 12/13/88

Catholic Worker Community of Cleveland

4241 Lorain Avenue
Cleveland, OH 44113

(216) 281-6854 / 631-3059

Deeply convinced of the radical truth of the Gospel, we strive to follow a Catholic Worker philosophy. We emphasize the corporal works of mercy — identifying with and ministering to the homeless, poor, sick, imprisoned — and radical action against the causes of poverty and oppression. We seek to be non-violent and opposed to all war, and to answer Jesus' call to be peacemakers. We recognize the continual need to clarify our thought through prayer, reflection, dialogue, and action.

We are forming a loving and caring resistance community with a strong spiritual base which will enable us to share our lives with those who are broken — not just for their sake but ours as well, knowing that we are all sisters and brothers. Come to Cleveland! We need new community members to live in our intentional community and to help in our work with the homeless on Cleveland's west side. Our ministry includes a cooperative community, a drop-in center, several small houses of hospitality, a newspaper, and efforts in resistance to violence and militarism. We invite those interested in this possibility to write us at 3601 Whitman Avenue, Cleveland OH 44113, or call (216)631-3059 and ask for Joe, Jane, or Paul. 12/12/88

CEEDS

Box 8 Miocene
Via Williams Lake, B.C.
CANADA V2G-2P3

(604) 296-3216

Members of the Community Enhancement and Economic Development Society (CEEDS) look upon ourselves as the seeds of a movement to change the disastrous present-day methods of agriculture. The majority of our members are in their early 30s, and have spent their entire adult lives working toward that aim. During our early years we squatted on a natural meadow, and were what might be called radical environmentalists. We now consider ourselves to be ecologists deeply concerned and actively working in the defense of Mother Nature.

CEEDS rents and operates four small farms in the South Cariboo, and a large organic garden on an Indian Reserve near Kamloops. We raise and breed cattle, pigs, work horses, sheep, goats, a variety of poultry, and honey bees. Our surplus organic meat and vegetables are sold at farmers' markets and at the farm gates. Special activities include our sheep project (we believe, and have demonstrated, that sheep are a viable alternative to herbicide spraying for weed control), horse logging (to provide an alternative to the devastating logging practices now in common use), preservation of rare breeds of plants and animals, foster parenting, providing a home and meaningful lifestyle for street people, operating a school for our labor-intensive organic farming methods, and working for and bartering with our neighbors and friends.

We have 15 full-time members, both Indian and White, who live on and manage our farms. There is no private property. There are also 6 Indian street people who live and work with us, fluctuating between town and the farms. We have several sustaining members who have supported us financially with small loans which we repay with organic meat and vegetables from our farms. More such support would help strengthen our programs, and help us establish more CEEDS farms in communities throughout the province. Our deeds do match our words. 3/8/90

Celo Community

Route 5, Box 79
Burnsville, NC 28714

(704) 675-5525

Founded in 1937, Celo Community is the oldest land trust community in America, and one of the most successful. It comprises some 30 family units living on 1200 acres owned by the community. Members purchase "holdings" which are confined to the realistic needs and uses of each family. Group ownership and control is designed to exercise wise stewardship of the land. A portion of the community land, by agreement of the members, has been set aside as a wildlife preserve.

Celo community members are diverse in background, in occupation, in religion — and make their livings independently (membership includes craftsmen, farmers, teachers, and doctors). The simple lifestyle pursued by Celo members helps free them to take a vigorous part of the cultural and civic life in the area.

Community members have initiated a variety of projects, all of which serve the wider community as well — and which, in some cases, enjoy a national clientele. The Celo Health Center emphasizes health care, and provides high quality health service at moderate cost; The Arthur Morgan School, a boarding and day school which accommodates 24 junior high students, is a living/ learning/working community in which study, work, play, and decision-making are shared by students and staff; Camp Celo is a "Farm Home" camp serving children ages 7-12 and emphasizing a non-competitive philosophy; Ten Thousand Things is a food co-op which provides wholesome food to its members, in bulk, at low cost; The River Craftsmen is a cooperative retail outlet for a great variety of craft wares produced in the area; Celo Friends Meeting (Quakers) was organized by community members in about 1950; Cabin Fever University facilitates the sharing of knowledge and skills among area adults — with no money changing hands; Celo Press operates a nationwide publishing business on a modest scale. It is significant that although all of these projects were organized by Celo Community members, the overwhelming majority of participants (including much of the ongoing leadership) is drawn from outside the community. We have a 2-year waiting list. 2/12/90

Center for the Examined Life

1525 Hornblend Street
San Diego, CA 92109
(619) 273-4673

Founded in 1966. Former church buildings in beach community. Seven members (17-22 years involvement).

Also seven residential work-exchange spaces (minimum 3-month commitment; philosophical participation not required). Visitors welcome by appointment. No short-term accommodations. Send SASE for brochure, or $2 for literature.

We consider ourselves primarily a "mental" rather than a physical community, a research project that started with encounter groups and the vision of our director, Constance Lerner Russell. We are developing new social and personal processes for living and wish to be a rallying place for people interested in truth as the radical basis for change. We are tackling the deepest issues of the human predicament — as embodied in ourselves — including power, sex, neuroses and defenses, good and evil in everyday life. Our members are dedicated to facing and correcting their deep emotional errors, no matter how severe. Our work includes the rehabilitation of an autistic woman.

We believe: That vulnerability should be the basis for living; That life is meant to be a glorious adventure; That if individuals are truthful about their inner processes, they can learn to operate "normally"; That if a committed group does this together, they can work down to their roots and start a new non-defended (non-neurotic) life based on love and joy.

Our core group must necessarily be closed, but we welcome sincere participants and volunteers in our open activities. Future plans include classes, groups and inspirational services. Send SASE for brochure; $2 for literature package. Formerly known as The Center for Psychological Revolution. 12/19/88

Center for Peace & Life Studies

**2010 W. County Road 1270 N
Muncie, IN 47303**

(317) 396-3508

CPLS is really a community within a community. The families that live on the grounds form the nucleus of a larger community which meets regularly to promote peace and foster our own spiritual growth. In the summer the CPLS offers family campers recreational and community-building experiences. Six cabins and a dining hall are available spring through late summer. A chapel/meeting hall and winterized cabin are available year round for group gatherings.

Community members are dedicated to building a peaceful world, to living simply, to sharing resources with those in need. To this end, the center has a mission in Haiti where a founding member is currently working.

We welcome inquiries about participating in family camp or using facilities for a group sharing. 2/15/90

The Center for Psychological Revolution

*San Diego, CA. See:
Center for the Examined Life*

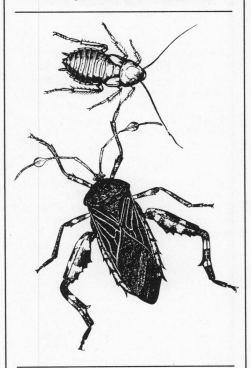

Cerro Gordo Community

**Dorena Lake, Box 569
Cottage Grove, OR 97424**

(503) 942-7720

Cerro Gordo is a community of residents, future residents, and supporters who are planning, financing and building an environmentally sound, human-scaled new town for 2,500 people on 1,200 acres near Eugene, OR. Homes, businesses and community facilities will be clustered in and near a pedestrian village — preserving 1,000 acres of forest and meadows in its natural state. Private automobiles will be replaced within the townsite by community transit, bicycling, walking, horseback, and a community delivery service. The community will recycle materials and rely upon sun, wind, water, and biofuels for power as much as possible. The community plans to be self-supporting, with jobs provided by light production companies, education and publishing, community shops, and intensive agriculture. The town school will involve community people in providing learning opportunities for the children. While homes and homesites will be privately owned (there are presently seven households on site), all residents will be members of the Cerro Gordo Cooperative, Inc., which will own and maintain community open space and utilities, and will facilitate community decisions and activities. The community *building* process emphasizes participation in a diverse yet mutually supportive community. Cerro Gordoans are seeking to build a neighborly community living in harmony with the natural environment. We invite you to take part in our project and our extended community. Send $2 for "Cerro Gordo: Plans, Progress and Processes," which provides a basic introduction and overview, together with our "Visitor's Guide." 5/15/87

[Ed note: A feature article about Cerro Goro published in issue #71/72 of Communities prompted a barrage of criticisms and rebuttals in issue #74.]

Child's Garden (Forming)

**c/o Gary & Carole Sugarman
7887 East Uhl Street #905
Tucson, AZ 85710**

(602) 886-5514

We call it Child's Garden because, for us, it is the nurturing and honoring of our children (folks without kids are also very welcome) and it is the healing of the children inside ourselves and each other which we feel to be our most sacred task. And it is the process of awakening and opening and yielding and surrendering — which this task so continually requires of us — which we see as our most sacred, daily, ongoing spiritual practice. It is not always an easy path. And that is especially why we are so much in need of each other's support, inspiration, camaraderie, and deep and close friendship.

We begin with ourselves: to heal our own families, to create a loving model together. Hopefully, later, we will have a healing retreat center for others as well. *(Cont'd.)*

Child's Garden (Cont'd.)

Child's Garden is still in the formative stages. We don't yet have our permanent location (as of March '89). For more information please write in care of the above address, or leave a phone message (the phone number is an answering service). 3/16/89

Christmas Star

2300 Dripping Springs Road
Winkleman, AZ 85292

(602) 280-9992

Without seeking to make a better world, which requires an individual to equal and best the meaningful achievements of the present cultural state, there can be no Karmic Freedom. To nurture the dreams of the Sacred Agenda (goals that represent exalted progressive states), or without reductivism of this agenda by a coherent body of people, is a great task for any subsociety — to understand the magic it is involved in, without creating circles of vanity.

Experience from building microenvironments (alien outposts) develops a common frame of reference, so the caravans of these eclectic oases have an understandable language and become necessary parts of the geopolitical entity. Neither Nature nor scripture can provide all the contextual or conceptual models needed for the path to freedom. Nor is it the state of an individual that is important, but the state of existence. Spiritually-committed people will never have any time left over; it takes full use of their energy to produce evidence of real progress.

Christmas Star was born from concepts like these mentioned, with people who hold the Earth closely, feel the Spirit of the Christ, and perceive the Mission as endeavors of music, art, and high culture. It is located at 3,000' in a lush, hilly valley in central Arizona, surrounded entirely by mountains. The rich loam soil provides a nourishing home for the thousands of fruit trees, indigenous plants, and small dome structures set about the slopes. There is abundant pure water, and the Gila River is nearby. We have occasional gatherings involving the sweat lodge, music, and dancing.

Members and leaders seem to be chosen by themselves from one's abilities, skill, and time involved pertinent to the projects occurring. There are greenhouse and farming plans being implemented, a creative

tile business in production, and the Wind Spirit Landscape Company that works outside the community.

Visit or write anytime — bring your best self. In order to grow spiritually, we must trade information. 3/17/90

Common Ground (Forming)

P.O. Box 710
Saugerties, NY 12477

(914) 246-7219

Common Ground of New York is an intentional community currently living on rural property that we intend to purchase — with plans to develop a conference/education center which demonstrates conservation of energy resources and sustainable agriculture. Originally a 70-acre family farm that grew into a summer resort for 120 guests, this vintage Catskill mountain lodge (with fields, woodlands, and stream) will be used to sustain 12 to 15 live-in staff members. We wish to live in a community of trust while developing an organic farm, remodeling the buildings for energy-efficient year-round use, cooking, and otherwise managing the conference facilities. We cater to groups and guests from all walks of life and all disciplines — hence the name "Common Ground" — in a homey, rural atmosphere 100 miles from New York City.

There is no spiritual focus other than a shared reverence for divinity in all beings, and personal responsibility for one's own life. We are generally a mature, middle-aged group with successful business/professional backgrounds, who have found a beautiful view of the mountains and a peaceful lifestyle — all within the context of a pleasant business environment. Like-minded persons who are ready to explore themselves in a setting of openness and trust are invited to inquire about Common Ground — either as a prospective member (live-in, occasional visitor, or supporter), investor in a socially-responsible business, or advisor. SASE appreciated. 4/25/89

Common Ground

Route 3, Box 231
Lexington, VA 24450

(703) 463-9422 / 463-9451

Our intentional cooperative community holds a perpetual lease on 47 acres of land owned by the

School of Living — a regional community land trust. Our members hold lifetime subleases, and own the "improvements". A major goal is to maintain a natural balance between the personal and social needs of people, emphasizing self-improvement in all areas of life, and enthusiastic sharing of our lives with others.

In members we look for caring persons of good will who know how to listen and how to work cooperatively with others on mutual concerns. We also share a deep ecological interest in the land, and a non-exploitive attitude toward people. Members follow their own spiritual leadings. Most prefer a vegetarian diet. Our children (ages 2-12) are homeschooled by choice, and meet with other homeschooled children twice a week in our learning center. We have monthly business meetings which use consensus decision-making; meetings are open. Managers are selected to coordinate and supervise community work; it is common to have Work Days where the whole community turns out to work in the community garden, on building the shop shed, etc.

Each household has two-plus acres to develop privately. Something over half of our acreage is being developed cooperatively by the community. A yearly budget is adopted, and each household is assessed a monthly rental fee to cover expenses. We have two carpenters, a car mechanic, a store manager, a homemaker, a lawyer, an entrepreneur, a teacher, and three retired persons. One makes his living on the land. We look for excuses to celebrate such things as birthdays — through potlucks, songfests, etc. (a number of us play the guitar). Every now and then we share a VCR movie. We also play baseball, volleyball, etc., and are building a pond for swimming and skating. Visitors are welcome upon pre-arrangement; tenting and camping space is available. 8/5/89

Common Place Land Cooperative

4211 Cuyler Road
Truxton, NY 13158

607) 842-6849 / 842-6858

CPLC is a rural cooperative land trust located in the rolling hills of central New York State. Currently we are 14 adults and eight children living on the land. We are actively seeking new members to join us. In the future we look forward to evolving a small-scale community of perhaps 35 households, working towards greater self-sufficiency in food and energy. Over the last ten years six new solar homes have been built on the land. The original farmhouse serves as rental space for prospective members or those in the process of building their homesteads.

Some of the interests and skills of current community members are: organic gardening, market gardening, ecological land use planning, solar and wind-powered electricity, passive solar and superinsulated home construction, political activism, home birth and midwifery, natural continuum style parenting, home schooling, puppet theater, music, and worker-owned cooperative businesses.

Over the last ten years we have defined a set of *Core Ideals* which form the common ground for our community. These core ideals are: 1) stewardship, 2) consensus decision making, 3) holistic perspective, 4) holding land in trust, 5) voluntary simplicity, 6) sense of moral responsibility, 7) sharing long-term goals, 8) welcoming diversity, 9) rural revival & reinhabitation, 10) economic self-reliance, and 11) community participation.

In addition to our desire to grow as a community, we invite participation at a variety of levels. Visitors are always welcome on the land. Camping is available for a nominal $2/night fee. We hold two large festivals on the land each year — the Strawberry Festival in late June, and the Summer Gathering in mid-August. They are a fun way to meet the larger Common Place community. 1/2/90

Communia

P.O. Box 1188
Iowa City, IA 52240

Communia is a lay contemplative community devoted to meditation; spiritual growth; contemplative living; service to the physical and spiritual needs of those "in need"; the concrete creation of a retreat facility for peace restoration, meditation, and contemplation toward the deepening of spiritual life; and the mindful stewardship of our land.

Communia is an open concept, respecting all forms of dedication to the spiritual path — and as such includes people in both Judeo-Christian and Buddhist practices. Our experience of community integrates the personal and group consciousness, and accelerates growth on many levels. It is the work of a peaceful world in miniature.

Communia Farm/Deep Mountain Retreat Center is located on 300 acres of rolling hills and deep valleys in the "driftless area" of northeast Iowa. The retreat center is the primary project of our community. It provides an all-faith/traditions, year-round facility for renewal, rest, and restoration of the spirit; it is available for individual, group, or family retreats. There is a small contribution for short or extended retreats.

Our community has evolved over a period of 14 years, a process and experience of dynamic change in growth, insight, and form. At present we all reside in Iowa City, 100 miles south of the farm. We meet on a weekly basis, and spend one weekend a month of work and meditation at the retreat center. Please include SASE with inquiries. 1/18/90

The Community

414 North Edgewood Street
Arlington, VA 22201

(703) 528-3204

The Community is an intentional family, a neighborhood, a network of friends, and a way of living. A dozen or so folks live here, ranging in age from 8 months to 71 years. Many of us have lived together for a decade or more. Our goal is to be a loving family and good neighbors in whatever way we can.

We have several houses on a city/suburban block, though many people in our network live elsewhere as well. We see community as an attitude and a lifestyle rather than a particular set of buildings — loving communication is the glue that holds us together. There are no membership lists; people establish the connections that they feel are best for themselves.

We tend to be individualists, living with few formal structures. Over the last ten years there have often been more businesses than members! Our current businesses include a chain of computer stores, a drug education program, property management, and commercial art. Our network includes artists, carpenters, musicians, teachers, healers, inventors, entertainers, writers, and "guerrilla capitalists." Our three pre-school children are the focus of much of our daily recreation and joy. We especially welcome other parents who want mutual support in the child-raising process — sharing child care, chores, and play. We are also considering homeschooling in the future.

We share a strong sense of spirituality, without endorsing any particular guru, dogma, or religion. Our celebrations are created by borrowing from many traditions. Our lifestyle centers on everyday living, with a little extra consciousness and concern about the world around us. Other special joys are acoustic music and group singing, bicycling, hiking, conversing, eating healthful foods, and laughing. (We try to avoid drugs, quarrels, and artificial flavoring.)

We intend to be lifelong friends and family, living together as best we can. We seek new members in a rather relaxed way; we are open to expanding our family circle, but don't feel compelled to do so. Visitors are welcome, and are expected to share in our work as well as our play. If you would like to visit, please contact us at least a week in advance. You may arrive by car or public transportation — we live a short Metro ride and walk from downtown Washington, DC, in an area with lots of greenspace and towering oak trees. Please do not bring alcohol, tobacco, or other drugs. Give us a call if you'd like more information. Please include SASE with correspondence [cc]. 6/13/89

Community Alternatives Co-op

1937 West 2nd Avenue
Vancouver, B.C.
CANADA V6J-1J2

We are 53 members (ages 2 to 75) living in a cooperative community located in the city of Vancouver. We are interested in, and working on/towards: alternate family groupings, community-scale economics, meaningful employment, appropriate technology, consensus decision-making, and collective social action. Projects initiated by some of our members include a cooperative restaurant, a gourmet garnish and salad company, a retail/wholesale muffin business which trains mentally disabled young people and adults, and another communal housing cooperative in our neighborhood (which shares a similar vision of community). We are part of the Community Alternatives Society which has 10 non-resident members, and which also owns a 10-acre organic farm one hour from town (see listing for Fraser Common Farm). Prospective visitors should please write first. 9/15/89

Community for Creative Non-Violence

425 Second Street NW
Washington, DC 20001

(202) 393-1909

The Community for Creative Non-Violence is an 18-year-old community of resistance and service that is rooted in spirituality. We attempt to share our lives and our resources with the poor whom we encounter daily through our soup kitchen, shelter, and drop-in centers. At the same time we seek to educate, confront, and change those institutions and structures that make each of us a victim. We see community as a means of living which is healthy, and one which frees us up to do our work.

Brochures will be sent upon request. Visitors with a serious interest in sharing our life must contact us in advance so that housing can be arranged. 2/1/89

Community Evolving

Box 208
North San Juan, CA 95960
(916) 288-3600

Community Evolving is a close-knit intentional family of 6 adults and 2 children committed to living, working, learning, and growing together in a healthy emotional and physical environment in the Sierra foothills 30 miles N.W. of Nevada City, California. We place much value on raising our children and ourselves in a healthy emotional environment. We are looking for more people to join our household, and for more households to form — creating a broader, land-based community on our 50 beautiful acres.

At present, we gather several times a week without the children for business and emotion-sharing meetings; and weekly for a family meeting where children participate fully. All our decisions are made by consensus. In our daily lives we like to experiment with various structures gleaned from many sources.

We envision the creation of a tribal village consisting of several extended families clustered on the land. Each group household would form around affinities on issues of lifestyle, personal chemistry, and areas of interest. Households will come together forming a tribal council where broader, community-wide issues will be discussed and decided.

Underlying all this is the desire to be deeply involved in each others' lives, to be sources of inspiration and learning for each other, and to grow older and wiser together. 4/7/91

Community of Families

Upper Darby, PA
See: Kehillat Mishpakhot

Comptche Community Farms (Forming)

P.O. Box 167
Comptche, CA 95427

Comptche Community Farms currently consists of three families with two young children. We are in the process of purchasing and moving onto 100 acres of beautiful land 12 miles east of the coastal town of Mendocino, Northern California. We are in the early stages of forming, but have already established the basis for a rural farming community — with a balance between individual homes and shared facilities. Members will share in the work of developing our organic farm, on a part or full-time basis, and also have their own cottage industry or professional work. Two acres plus a small fruit orchard are now under cultivation, with plans to expand. Gentle parenting, home education, and the creation of a loving environment for our children in the midst of a rural farm setting guide our overall vision of intentional community.

We are seeking up to three more financially responsible and compatible families (with young children and an interest in home schooling) to share in the group purchase and development of our community-owned land and to help us evolve a more fulfilling and community-oriented way of life. For further information send a legal sized SASE (52¢) and information about yourselves. 1/25/90

Consciousness Village

P.O. Box 38
Campbell Hot Springs Rd
Sierraville, CA 96126
(916) 994-8984 / 994-3737

Consciousness Village/Campbell Hot Springs is an international rebirthing center for the purpose of spiritual purification using earth, air, fire, and water. Our founder is Leonard Orr, the originator of the rebirthing movement. We have a weekly training session which includes three seminars, three rebirths, and one day of fasting and fire purification. We also have special guests come from outside once a month to give trainings and seminars, usually on weekends. It takes six weeks to become a permanent resident, including three weeks of training and three weeks of working guest status. Most members are between the ages of 20 and 40, and are into high levels of spiritual purification. We are open to more people who share these interests and would like to join our community. For information about training and/or membership, please write or call. 5/1/91

Cooper Street Household

Triangle F Ranch Cooperative
Box 238
Vail, AZ 85641

Cooper Street Household is a cooperative intentional household living in a suburban home in Tucson and on a 22-acre primitive "ranch" in an isolated foothills canyon. These two settings permit flexibility in responding to differing needs for togetherness.

We are six adults living within an organizational structure which is loose. There are few rules, but tolerance for the lifestyles of others is expected. Consensus is used for major decisions such as the acceptance of a new family member.

We feel that we can lead a better life together, living in community, than separately. Despite the diversity of our occupations and cultural backgrounds we have a common value system related to right treatment of ourselves, right treatment of others, and right treatment of the environment. Visitors are welcome, but should be prepared to camp if facilities are crowded. 12/13/88

Crieff Hills Community

Retreat & Conference Center
RR 2, Puslinch
Ontario, CANADA N0B-2J0

(519) 824-7898

Crieff Hills Community is a retreat and conference center dedicated to preparing Christian lay people for the work of ministry in the world, and to the building up of community within congregations and the whole Church (the body of Christ). We provide short-term accommodations, facilities, and training which enables people to experience Christian community, to grow spiritually, and to develop their gifts for serving others. We also emphasize the building of Christian leadership skills.

Through our work we serve many

groups and individuals who come with varying needs, and who seek a quiet setting apart from the pressures of daily life. We seek to be a Christian community that facilitates community in others. Please keep inquiries brief and simple, and enclose an SASE. 1/24/90

Crosses Creek Youth Ranch & Christian Community

Route 2, Box 185-A
Elkins, AR 72727

(501) 643-2338

Crosses Creek is a small community established to give spiritual healing to youth and adults, where individuals and families are living on the premises and working together. We are located on a river in the midst of the scenic Ozarks.

We maintain a number of cottage industries, to provide both income for the community and valuable work experience for our youth. We desire new members with skills in building, maintenance, housekeeping, kitchen service, education, sewing, crafts, and greenhouse work. Must be willing to work. All members share income. 3/12/89

Crystal Spring

Hutterian Brethren
Ste. Agathe, Manitoba
CANADA R0G-1Y0

(204) 433-7634

See main listing under "Hutterian Brethren." 3/1/89

Currents

13177 Concord Church Road
Glouster, OH 45732

(614) 448-4141/6545/7251

Currents Community formed in the late '70s as an outgrowth of our regional food co-op network. We became a legal entity in 1981 and bought a 163-acre farm which is home to the 9 members, 2 residents exploring membership, and 6 children. One common bond is a commitment to non-violent social change activism. Located in the Appalachian hills of southeast Ohio, we are 16 miles from the university town of Athens, a very supportive macro-community environment. We are attempting to create a replicable model of joint land ownership and stewardship based on

cooperative principles and requiring only modest capital investment. Home-based economic enterprises and development of sustainable land use practices are in their beginning stages. We are currently building new housing and expect to have room for a few new residents in the near future. 12/14/88

Dancing Waters

Permaculture Co-op
Route 2, Box 69
Gays Mills, WI 54631

(608) 872-2333
872-2533

Dancing Waters, established in 1982, is a cooperative community with a major focus on permaculture. Other values essential to our group include tolerance; flexibility; honesty; willingness to communicate; and sharing song, food, love of our land, sweat, and spirit. We have 8-10 adult members, and 3 children. The community owns the land and the houses, and housing is organized into individual family units. We also grow a substantial amount of our food. We are open to visitors, but *only* if arrangements are made in advance, please! 1/31/89

Dandelion

RR1
Enterprise, Ontario
CANADA K0K-1Z0

(613) 358-2304

Dandelion is a small co-operative, established in '75 on 50-acres of mixed bush, farmland, and marsh, located in the rolling lowlands of southeastern Ontario, near Kingston. Dandelion has been a member of the Federation of Egalitarian Communities for the past 15 years, and the basic ideals of equality, nonviolence, and cooperation are still intrinsic to our operation.

At this time we are undergoing a transition from being a strictly income-sharing community, to a broader-based co-operative in which various levels of community can exist. We expect to derive our income in a variety of ways, including outside work and crafts, and possibly by reviving our rope-products cottage industry. We also plan to develop the farm and other businesses over time.

The situation at the moment is formative; anyone interested in visiting or more information should contact us for an update. 5/10/91

Dayspring

Four Chimneys Farm
Route 1, Box 176
Himrod, NY 14842

(607) 243-8868 / 243-7502

We are a community of about 20 people on one of the Finger Lakes in New York State. We share all things in common, drawing our income from organic agriculture - vegetables and fruits - along with processing and retail sales. We have a school for children, grades K-12. The base of our community life is spirituality and a psychological work aimed at helping each other develop and mature. Our scope is international. We sponsor a chamber music series. We are involved in the hospitality industry and are expanding our gourmet restaurant endeavors. We are especially interested in networking with other communities, both in the U.S. and abroad. 12/12/88

Deep Woods Farm, Inc.

24851 State Route 56
South Bloomingville, OH 43152

(614) 332-6976

310 acres, mostly forested, with hills, rocks, creek, orchard, garden, and some pasture-land. Three couples, several individuals, two homes completed, three rental cabins. Deer, wild turkey, ruffed grouse, woodcock, other wildlife, and a rich variety of plants share their space with us.

•The aims of Deep Woods Farm are to provide a place where people of like minds can practice a sense of caring stewardship of the environment ...

•To learn to live more simply and self-sufficiently, and to explore new methods of independent living ...

•To promote cooperation with each

Deep Woods Farm *(Cont'd.)*
other, neighbors, and the larger communities ...

•To promote mental and physical health, and to encourage creativity and spiritual development.

We welcome inquiries — we are seeking new members who share our vision and want to live in the hills of Ohio. 1/7/89

Deer Spring Bruderhof

Hutterian Society of Brothers
207 West Side Road
Norfolk, CT 06058

(203) 542-5545

See main listing for "Hutterian Brethren." 2/2/89

Denver Space Center

Northeast Denver, CO
(303) 296-8061

We are an urban cooperative household established in 1979 — more intentional than a boarding house, less intense than a commune; more civilized than a fraternity, less crowded than a dormitory. We have relatively few rules, though relatively much experience in this lifestyle. We share the rent, the common spaces, the housework, a piano, a big yard with gardens, and make decisions by consensus when possible. We encourage friendships, good company, interesting conversations, aesthetic ruminations, and connections to a developing circle of friends. We have a non-biological resemblance that eludes prosaic description. [cc] 8/8/89

DOE Farm

Wisconsin Womyn's Land Co-op
Route 2, Box 42
Norwalk, WI 54648

(608) 269-5301 (Summer only)

D.O.E. (Daughters of the Earth) Farm is an indescribably beautiful 80-acre farm/campground/home located in west central Wisconsin. The land was acquired in the spring of 1977 by the Wisconsin Womyn's Land Co-op, our organizational structure. No one presently lives at the farm full time, though our organization is strong and spread out over the entire Midwest. Membership in WWLC is required of all womyn who use the land, and is based on a sliding scale of $3 per

$1,000 of net annual income, adjustable for womyn with dependents.

Our founding vision included some very general, yet significant, concepts: self-sufficiency, an environment conducive to personal and collective growth, a non-hierarchical political and social structure with consensus among those living there (WWLC decisions are made at monthly business meetings), being open to visits from non-resident womyn, organic gardening (but *not* large-scale farming), and an atmosphere of learning and skill sharing. We agreed that all womyn living on the land needn't necessarily live together, but must meet a determined minimum energy exchange with regard to the land, maintenance, and other womyn in the living collective.

The structure is designed to give power to members who take responsibility, who commit themselves to do the work. Directions have changed; policies have come and gone; some policies have been kept for a very long time. Some of us feel it is particularly hard to incorporate womyn into the community who don't have a strong grounding in the reality of how difficult it is — because it's hard work, and we are so few in number. More womyn would make it seem less like an endurance test and more like living in the land of bliss. Womyn wishing more information should write, and please enclose SASE (two stamps). 1/6/89

The Dolphin Society (Forming)

1425 West 221st Street
Torrance, CA 90501

We are organizing an interspecies community of dolphins and people on the Big Island of Hawaii. The purpose is to communicate and have cultural contact with dolphins and whales.

The Dolphin Society is planning to buy a ship and build an undersea village, to be called Atlantis. Atlantis will be a place to live in harmony with nature, surrounded by the awesome beauty of the Sea. Because Atlantis will be a sharing, caring society free of status and competition, it has the potential to grow into an ecologically healthy nation with the resources to heal the Earth. Come, join the Dolphin Society, and live in freedom in the Sea. Together we can bring a new age of peace, love, freedom and play to Earth. 1/3/89

Dorea Peace Community

1645 - 60th Street CTHD
Turtle Lake, WI 54889

We are a community of married couples who own their own homes, and each of our 4 families supports itself. We work in the surrounding towns, and are not a self-sufficient community. We have 89 acres, five of which are held in common, and one acre which each family owns. We do not allow home schooling or drugs. We gather four times a week to share meals together, and hold a meeting once a week for business and spiritual reading. Justice issues are a focal point for us, and we are all involved in many activities which contribute to that purpose. 9/28/89

Dragonfly Farm

Mink Lake Road
Lake Saint Peter, Ontario
CANADA K0L-2K0

(613) 338-2709

Dragonfly Farm was established in 1978 by a political collective from the city. We have 250 acres of bush and farm land in the backwoods of eastern Ontario. Six adults and a child belong to the commune on the land, and other original landowners still hold an interest in the property. We are working towards becoming self-sufficient in food with gardens, fields and livestock. While there is no agreed upon set of principles, most of us share an interest in paganism and anarchism. Decisions are made by consensus after a process of discussion during daily interactions and occasional meetings. As well as expanding the farming operation and performing the regular chores, we are involved in the local community and help publish a small journal. This year, we are hosting a radical pagan festival, a new age gathering, and a kids' camp.

Membership is open. Interested parties can write to us or drop by anytime — we like surprises. 12/20/88

Duck Mountain Circle (Forming)

c/o Ron Tremback
Boggy Creek, Manitoba
CANADA R0L-0G0
(204) 935-2238

Duck Mountain Circle is a developing intentional community located in the hills of western Manitoba. Our common ties will be a love of the earth, a reverence for its life forms, and a commitment to individual and collective psychological and spiritual growth. Our goal will be to create a "people garden" where life will positively evolve and flourish indefinitely into the future, and will provide individual residents with the opportunity to be directly responsible for meeting their needs in a gentle way.

We will also create a Duck Mountain Wellness Centre to assist participants in the process of becoming "vibrantly alive", facilitated by holistic therapists and experts in alternative living techniques. One of our main focuses will be "Progressions" (long-term residency programs) which will allow participants to completely immerse themselves in various disciplines away from the distractions of our present civilization. We also plan to offer shorter "gentle living programs" including: dwelling construction, home schooling, alternate energy generation, natural childbirth, organic gardening, yoga, cooking with natural foods, meditation, etc.

The land is 160 acres blessed with inspirational forests, fields, hills, lakes, streams, springs, and marshes. A great variety of wildlife either lives on or visits the land. The legal structure will be a land trust so that the land can remain a haven for all form of life for perpetuity. Individual residents and families will pay an entrance fee and a yearly fee, and they will receive a parcel of land on which to construct a dwelling. We are looking for "pioneer-type" people who want to become involved with the initial development of the Circle and the Wellness Centre. We also encourage potential future residents to become involved. We have available several papers describing our philosophy and plans, and also have an application kit available. Please write for more information. 2/1/89

Dunmire Hollow

Route 3, Box 449
Waynesboro, TN 38485

(615) 722-3078/9201/5096

Dunmire Hollow (est. '73) is a community of about a dozen people sharing their lives and 160 acres in a magic hollow in Tennessee. We have fields, orchards, gardens, woods, springs, creeks, a community center, woodshop, sauna, county-wide food co-op, etc. Each family is economic-

ally independent; we make our livings in a variety of ways: construction, auto repair, teaching, woodworking, sewing, nursing, truck driving, small engines sales and repair, crafts, and from providing for ourselves more directly through domestic economy and barter.

We wish to communicate with people who are interested in rural community living. We enjoy visitors; please write for more information or to arrange a visit (please include an SASE). 5/10/90

Earth Child

Davenport, WA
See: Tolstoy Farm

Earth Community

19731 Forrer Street
Detroit, MI 48235

(313) 273-1407

The Directory received a postcard from this group stating their desire to be included — later confirmed by a phone call. We have no further information. 1/18/90

Earth Cyclers

Edwall, WA
See: Waukon Institute

Earthdance Cooperative

HC - Box 77B
Prospect Street
Plainfield, MA 01070

(413) 634-5678

Earthdance Cooperative is a non-profit arts-oriented community based on 180 acres in rural western Massachusetts. We are creating an egalitarian economy with home-run businesses and schooling. Dance is a primary tie. Currently 8 adults and 3 children, in the process of growing to 15 adults and 6-7 children. Expanding from a "family" structure to the next level of intimacy, friendships, and commitments. We have an intention of land trust ownership. Please include SASE with correspondence [cc]. 7/5/89

Earth's Rising Co-op Farm

25358 Cherry Creek Road
Monroe, OR 97456

(503) 847-5434

Earth's Rising is a cooperative corporation owning 60 acres in the foothills of the Coast Range at the edge of the Willamette Valley, about three miles west of Monroe, Oregon. The land is inhabited by a loosely knit group who share some common ideals: simplicity of lifestyle, land stewardship, cooperative decision making. The group is small — less than 10 adults, less than 10 children. We are presently vegetarian, and our household conveniences and machinery are minimal by American standards. We are a Tilth Certified Organic Farm, and there are provisions in our bylaws limiting exploitation of natural resources. Decisions involving the normal operation of the farm are made by consensus of all resident members at periodic meetings.

We see ourselves as a community rather than an extended single household. Separate families and individuals maintain separate incomes and private living spaces. Personal belongings exist along with community property. Earth's Rising is not a financially self-supporting entity; each resident contributes a small monthly payment for general maintenance.

We do not consider ourselves to be a public networking organization, but we do answer most of our mail, and people do occasionally visit us. 3/9/90

Earthworks (Forming)

9805 Union Road
Plymouth, IN 46563

(219) 935-4164

Established by 7 persons in August 1988, Earthworks is located in north central Indiana. The convent of the Poor Handmaids of Jesus Christ sits directly across a 38-acre lake from the Earthworks farmhouse. Our community has as its focus: 1) living as ecologically as possible — ministering to the Earth; 2) ministering to the creativity of people through the arts — especially art and prayer; 3) helping others while finding our own place in the community of all beings.

At present one person lives on the one-acre site (there is possibility of

N. America

Earthworks *(Cont'd.)*

expansion) and works in the organic garden. We are new, and welcome visitors. Please call in advance to arrange a visit [cc]. 7/11/89

East Wind Community

Box CD-90
Tecumseh, MO 65760
(417) 679-4682

East Wind is a community owned and operated by its members, who share all income and expenses and rear their children communally. Established in 1974, East Wind is located on 160 acres in the Missouri Ozarks. We lease 190 acres of government land adjacent to our own, which is bordered by Lick Creek and includes 85 acres of good agricultural land.

Supported entirely by our community enterprises, we produce rope hammocks and sandals and a line of natural nut butters. We maintain an organic garden, beef cattle, and chickens. Communal facilities and services provide for child-rearing, food, clothing, health care, and other needs and amenities.

East Wind is a member of the Federation of Egalitarian Communities — a network of groups devoted to building a society rooted in the values of equality, cooperation, and non-violence. We work on shedding ourselves of oppressive and competitive habits. We try to distribute authority and responsibility so as to empower us all, primarily through democratic decision-making.

We presently number about 40 adults and 8 children. We are eager to become a group of several hundred. We welcome visitors and new members. Write or call (please *don't* drop in) for more information or to arrange a visit. 11/21/89

Ecological Village Community (Forming)

1807 Second Street, Studio #2
Santa Fe, NM 87501
(505) 986-1401

In 1987 we began a community-building process in New Mexico, the goal being to create a new village community which will foster both personal well-being and planetary regeneration, and to serve as a model for ecological land development which is economically viable and socially desirable.

We are presently in the "formative" stages — we do not yet have the land,

but are building the relationships and the organizational foundations of community. Presently, we have a core group of about 20, and 50 more in an extended group in the Santa Fe area. Our vision is to establish an advanced Ecological Village Community of 700 people in northern New Mexico. This development will include several neighborhoods of privately-owned homes, a variety of non-polluting commercial enterprises, research and educational facilities, and ecologically sound systems for energy, building, land regeneration, organic food production, transportation, and waste management. The land itself will be held in a community land trust.

Key elements will include: global exchange programs, creative learning opportunities, economic self-reliance, multi-generational balance, holistic healing, individual freedom, and decision-making by consensus. We are manifesting a community of caring people whose livelihoods enrich their Spirit and nurture the Earth. With this vision and our organizational frameworks in place, we are now focusing on the finer points of strategic planning, site criteria, and finance. We welcome others who would like to support or actively participate in this pioneering project. (See also: "CEED Institute" in the Resources listings.) 4/30/91

Edenvale

Box 1269
Aldergrove, B.C.
CANADA V0X-1A0
(604) 856-3388

Edenvale, home of 34 adults and 8 children, is located in the heart of the Fraser Valley in southwestern British Columbia. Its rich and fertile setting has led naturally to the establishment of its Stewardship Farm, which yields a variety of organic produce. Residents also work at a number of community businesses, and offer a variety of classes and workshops. See main listing under Emissaries of Divine Light. 1/12/89

Ellis Island

1204 W. 27th Street
Los Angeles, CA 90007

"Hang loose but don't fall apart." We are fond of certain slogans, including "Keep it clean, pay the rent, contribute...." Founded in 1969, we were

a somewhat classic hippie commune. Over the years there have been plenty of changes, the house always reflecting its current membership. We're now more eclectic, maybe even with a touch of bourgeoisie in a few isolated corners.

We are currently remodeling our 11-bedroom house, with some house members being hired by the group. Four members are the legal owners, but function as stewards rather than as landlords. It's definitely a mid-city urban environment. We're mostly anarchistic and non-hierarchic. We have no particular dogmas or religious focus, although we lean to the left politically and are generally anti-war. Several members have a background in Transactional Analysis; although it's not "practiced" here per se, it does provide a basis for "straight talk". Among our members there is also an incredible diversity of attitudes and interests — including some into cooperatives, creative arts, and/or loud music (Rock & Roll).

We are not soliciting new members — they come regularly through our network of friends and acquaintances (we have at least a 6-month waiting list for new residents). Prospective visitors need to make arrangements in advance, and should direct inquiries to Rush Riddle. 1/16/90

Emissaries of the Divine Light

The "Emissaries" are an association of individuals in many countries who share the premise that the same spirit that creates and sustains life is also a source of wisdom and direction for those who find attunement with it. Self-discovery is only possible in the context of a greater whole, and is known through giving whatever is practical, helpful, and balanced in any situation.

Over a dozen Stewardship Communities, situated around the globe, comprise the backbone of the network (see resources entry). While there is no official organization to join, an ongoing context is provided for shared creative work. All of these centers have literature available; most offer seminars, regular weekly meetings, and spiritual leadership classes.

Emissary communities listed in this directory: Edenvale, Glen Ivy, Green Pastures, Hillier Park, Hohenort, Hundred Mile Lodge, King View, La Vigne, Mickleton, Oakwood, Still Meadow. 3/15/91

N. America

End of the Road House

Aprovecho Institute
80574 Hazelton Road
Cottage Grove, OR 97424

(503) 942-9434

End of the Road Community members support projects sponsored by the Aprovecho Research Center (Aprovecho is a non-profit, tax-exempt organization which collaborates with indigenous organizations to present major permaculture courses in Mexico, Guatemala, and other Third World countries). Extensive publications and courses in permaculture are used to educate North Americans about worldwide agricultural innovations and resource utilization techniques. The Research Center is a daily demonstration of a deconsumerized lifestyle — aiming to make the best use of available resources, and continually redefining the terms "prosperity" and "quality of life".

Land resources are developed for sustainable orchards, forestry, wildlife habitat, plastics sacrifice, water sources, experimental building sites, and extensive gardens. Community members have experienced interaction with the younger generations through children's camps and, more recently, a multi-ethnic children's magazine *Skipping Stones* (see Resources listing). Please include SASE with correspondence. 4/29/90

Essene Mother Earth Church

196 Hot Springs Row
Big Bend, CA 96011

(916) 337-6680

Our community's initial inspiration was drawn from the lives of the early Essenes who lived outside the cities of their day — finding them, even back then, to be centers of dissolution, corruption, and decay. They lived in small groups, grew their own food, and were self-supporting. They were the natural teachers and healers of their day, and we are attempting to follow a similar path.

Cooperation is one of our strong motivations. Although individual activity is at times necessary, the spirit of people working together for mutual benefit must prevail at all times. We also believe that organization and strong central leadership are of utmost importance for a continually growing and expanding cooperative community.

Our initial living areas are rustic cabins and spacious camping areas, while the changing seasons of this tree-covered mountain area add a dimension to our living and organic gardening activities. Each family or group owns its own parcel of land on which we are developing clusters of carefully planned self-sufficient homes.

Our healing and refreshing hot mineral springs (open to the public) go well in this retreat environment, and we offer seminars on survival, nutrition, cooperative living, alternative energy sources, and abundant living. We operate Big Bend Hot Springs to preserve the American heritage of free independent people working together to rebuild the natural way of life that will build a strong, healthy, independent nation. 1/13/90

Family-Community Movement

Upper Darby, PA
See: Kehillat Mishpakhot

Far Valley Farm

12788 New England Road
Amesville, OH 45711

(614) 448-4894

We are 14 adults and 8 children living in sub-Appalachia on 234 acres of open and wooded land in S.E. Ohio (near Athens, the home of Ohio University). We incorporated with the state of Ohio in 1980, and recently gave ourselves a new name — Far Valley Farm. We are multi-skilled and are moving toward a goal of relative self-sufficiency. We regard ourselves as stewards of this land, sharing sort of an overall respect for life and the life force which includes self respect, growth, and love. We have grown fairly organically, are pretty tolerant, and tend to be honest and up front with each other. Please, written inquiries only (SASE appreciated). 2/16/90

The Farm

34, The Farm
Summertown, TN 38483

(615) 964-3574 (Main Gate)

The Farm is a cooperative community of families and friends living on 1750 acres in southern middle Tennessee. We started the Farm in 1971 with the hope of establishing a strongly cohesive, outwardly-directed community — a base from which we could, by action and example, have a positive effect on the world as a whole. The Farm is a community where ideals can find expression in daily life, and it has pioneered in the fields of midwifery, soy technology, Third World relief, solar energy, and cooperative living.

The Farm School is a unique alternative education center offering basic skills plus foreign languages, fine arts, and apprenticeship training. Since 1984 the school has been a member of the National Coalition of Alternative Community Schools [see NCACS listing in "Resources" Section]. The Farm is still home to the Midwife School, and babies are delivered regularly. Although PLENTY's business offices have been moved to California, the One World Trading Company continues to market Guatemalan goods; the Natural Rights Center thrives under Albert Bates' directorship; and Kids to the Country maintains a nature enrichment program for urban children

Approximately 250 residents and about 40 businesses (including the Soy Dairy, Solar Electronics, the Book Publishing Co., and the Dye Works) contribute funds to maintain the community. Please write or call for further information. 11/5/89

The Farm

Lopez Island, WA
See: Old McCauley Farm

Farm Home Center (Forming)

P.O. Box 1208
Milwaukee, WI 53201

The Farm Home Center is a shareholder-owned company whose primary purpose is to establish an alternative agricultural center — one which demonstrates natural methods of gardening and small-scale farming (production, processing, and distribution) on an individual, family, and

Farm Home Center *(Cont'd.)*
commercial basis. Our vision incorporates social and environmental values which promote the development and management of the "Farm" as a living ecosystem. (This does not mean, however, that all chemicals must or will be eliminated.) The Company will develop a Residential Home and Retreat Center for its shareholders who will establish gardens and livestock — enabling them to become self-sufficient. Future plans include the development of a Study and Conference Center which is non-sectarian (open to all races, religions, and beliefs), focusing on alternative agriculture, holistic healing and health maintenance, and a holistic approach to our food system. The basic philosophy is that as shareholders and associate members we are stewards of the soil, and are responsible for our own bodies — that the health and well-being of the ecosystem and of ourselves is of utmost importance. 11/5/89

Fellowship Community

Rudolf Steiner Fellowship
241 Hungry Hollow Rd.
Spring Valley, NY 10977

(914) 356-8494 / 356-8499

We are an intergenerational care community centered around the care of the elderly but taking up the care of handicapped young adults, children in need of special help and one another. Our care extends to the land, animals and objects we are responsible for. We are very hard working, seeking to incorporate ideas from the spiritual world into our daily life rather than merely talking about them. Our impulses come from the work of Dr. Rudolf Steiner.

We live a rural type existence in an urban setting and have a varied life. We support ourselves through social, therapeutic and educational efforts such as our medical practice, biodynamic farming, metal shop, wood shop, candle shop, gift shop, print shop, weavery, pottery as well as our care activities. We do most of our own small building and maintenance work. We have a children's garden for our preschoolers, and our children attend the local Waldorf School. We have a rich study and cultural life. Music and art are emphasized.

Our spiritual ideas permeate our community organization, economics, work activities, education and cultural life. We are open to new co-workers who have at least an interest in learning more about Rudolf Steiner, want a full and varied life and who are unafraid of hard work - inner and outer - in the service of others. We welcome inquiries and pre-arranged work-along visits. 2/15/90

Fellowship of Reconciliation

Renton, WA
See: Teramanto

The Finders

Washington, DC

The Finders have been around for over 20 years, living and working together in a rather spontaneous non-organization. The group of 15 adults and 2 children has no official name, but "Finders" is the label most often used by outsiders to describe the community.

Their overall approach to life is to make it into a "Game" — a challenging and educational process where the rules change from week to week, day to day, sometimes even by the hour. Members often "volunteer" to each other, informally rotating leadership roles depending on the project at hand, the experience of the people involved, and the prevailing mood of the moment. The head game caller is usually Marion Pettie, the originator of the adventure.

Their cooperative lifestyle is usually incredibly efficient, and a fertile arena for personal growth. They own an apartment complex; a huge warehouse which has been converted to a library, resource center, gathering space, and crash pad; a several hundred acre farm less than four hours from town; and several other properties. They often share communal meals, pool most resources, and operate several consulting and research businesses — for business organizations, computer users, and people in need of virtually any type of information. They thrive on challenges to their creativity.

The Finders welcome visitors who share their zest for learning and adventure. They'd enjoy hearing from you — if you're friendly, open minded, and resourceful enough to find them.... 10/1/89

Flatrock Community

2720 Hutchinson Road
Murfreesboro, TN 37130

(615) 895-2841

Flatrock Community is 8 adults and 6 children working to develop creative responses to competitive economics, sexism, racism, wasteful resource use, disintegration of supportive community, and other problems facing our society. The ten-year-old community owns 27 acres of land, predominantly cedar glade, three miles from a city of 50,000 with a medium-sized university, and thirty-two miles from Nashville. Interests include intensive organic gardening, appropriate technologies, a project on new protein sources with third world application, crafts & cottage industries, and a biannual conference on voluntary simplicity. We live in simple houses and share a community house. Although separate finances are maintained, our monthly community dues are used to purchase tools and improvements on the land. We make group decisions through consensus. We welcome new members and visitors — prior arrangements preferred. Please include SASE with correspondence. 6/13/89

Foundation for Feedback Learning

Staten Island, NY
See: Ganas

Four Chimneys Farm

Himrod, NY
See: Dayspring

Fraser Common Farm

1356 - 256th Street
Aldergrove, B.C.
CANADA V0X-1A0

Fraser Common Farm, established as a registered co-operative in 1977, is a 10-acre organic farm located an hour's drive from Vancouver. We are part of the Community Alternatives Society, and are home to a salad and garnish business that is collectively-owned. Our goals are: 1) to provide recreational and educational opportunities for the urban and resident members; 2) to do research and experimentation in small-scale farming and appropriate technology; 3) to produce quality in-season food; and 4) to work towards economic viability. We are farming by the "permaculture" model, and now have 100 laying hens, two hives of bees, nut trees, fruit trees, raspberries, and a 3-acre market garden. We presently are 4 adults and 4 children (2 part-time). Prospective visitors should please write first. 5/30/89

Friends Southwest Center

Route 1, Box 170
McNeal, AZ 85617
(602) 642-3729

Friends Southwest Center is a small land trust in the high desert, with independent living and commitment to Quaker principles of truth, non-violence, and simple living. We have excellent water, clean air, year-round cool nights — and this is possibly the most economical place to live in the United States. The corporation is not-for-profit, and is solvent. Few jobs are available. Our land is in the Gadsden Purchase, twenty miles from the Mexican border, and we shop in Mexico once a week. A sojourning period is required for your protection and ours. Hook-ups are available. Write (send SASE) or call for more information. 4/1/89

Full Circle Farm

c/o Suzanne Riordan
P.O. Box 23635
Santa Barbara, CA 93121

We are a fairly easy-going group of struggling artists and other well-meaning, ecology-minded individuals who live on a farm located in the hills about an hour away from Santa Barbara. We're mostly in our mid-30s to 40s in age, and our main focus is in the kitchen/dining room of the main building where we share communal dinners 7 nights a week. Kids and adults get together several nights a week with popcorn and comforters around the TV/VCR in the adjacent family room. We also share chores.

Most members have jobs or businesses which take them into the adjacent towns during the day,

though several work on the property as craftsperson or teacher, or maintenance person. The main house also functions as a school for children ages 6 to 11. Two of these live in the community, and the remaining twelve come from an adjacent intentional community or from town.

The property is owned by one member who collects monthly rent and utilities. Inherent in this situation are certain inevitable tensions and a sense of insecurity regarding the future — yet the sense of family and fellowship is quite genuine, and the group at this time is remarkably cooperative and tolerant. 2/11/90

Futures, Inc.

111 Bobolink
Berea, KY 40403

(606) 986-8000

Futures is a new 100 percent co-op community for all ages, open membership, self-financed, self-governed, ecological, and deeply spiritual but not fanatical. Retired people furnish most of the money and younger people furnish most of the skill/labor. Seniors function as a subsidiary, and crew members function in four ways: food and noon meals, builders of beautiful warm/dry living units with spacious community hall over 10 years, a services crew for transportation and education and home clinic with a skilled nurse.

The cement that holds members together is a two-hour noon gathering five days a week. Here the people commune with food, then with worship, then with business (each crew reports weekly), and fellowship of fun. Members can forget the jalopy and ride the shuttlebus. They can abandon the supermarket and get well on home grown organic foods. Believe it or not, costs run about three quarters of condos. Each occupant lends for cost of constructing his unit; then his loan is refunded when a new occupant takes over.

We own 75 good acres, five miles from Berea College and I-75. Our forefathers pioneered the great West. Futures pioneers the great New Age with 38 innovations in farming, housing, services and spirit domain. $3 brings a packet (contains a 30-page description, bylaws, a form for prospects, etc.). We also offer a 1-hr. video, *Sacred Soil and Soul*, which documents some of our work and the wonders of cooperation. Futures pioneers have renounced oligarchy,

monopoly, bureaucracy, legalized poaching and paternalism. Simple living and austere at first, but glorious if you can qualify. "Ain't gonna study war no more." 12/14/88

Ganas

135 Corson Avenue
Staten Island, NY 10301
(718) 720-5378 / 981-7365

You are invited to explore a non-religious, NYC community of about 40 adults of all ages, types, and cultural and socioeconomic backgrounds. We live together in a cluster of 7 large, attractive houses (5 with adjoining yards) that we remodeled to suit our needs and our pleasure. We enjoy comfortable private rooms and excellent space and equipment for work, study, play and just relaxing. Our Staten Island location is near the ferry, and 1/2 hour from downtown Manhattan — and yet our gardens, fireplaces, porches and views feel quite rural.

We share a healthy respect for personal privacy, dreams, preferences, ideological differences and truth. We aim for individual autonomy in cooperative community; for better learning skills; for ability to share thoughts and feelings more easily and accurately; and for a good quality of life in a safer, happier world. We work very hard at trying to accomplish these things, and succeed only a little. We welcome new ideas for how to do better. We care deeply for people in general, and for each other in particular.

Our projects involve innovative use of video and other feedback devices for learning many things, but mostly for learning how to learn. Our businesses (recycling furniture, clothing, and household goods) are co-operative, interesting, useful, and do well. If you're interested and we decide to try living together for a while, you can work in the city and pay $500 a month to cover all of your expenses here — or you can pay your way by working with us. Write or call for more information. [Note: Formerly known as the Foundation for Feedback Learning, a non-profit organization still operated by members of the Ganas community.] 10/21/89

The Gathering

Box 179, Riverside Drive
Schuyler, VA 22969

(804) 831-2354

We are a spiritual group whose aim is a closer relationship with God as individuals and as a group. We came together in New York City in 1968, and began moving onto 10 acres in Virginia in 1975; at present we have 14 members. We have our own system of economics, combining elements of income-sharing as well as individual finances. We work for the refinement and uplifting of the quality of life expressed in our spiritual practices, our creative endeavors (nursing, art, carpentry, design, carving, building, medicine, etc.), the enhancement of our environment, our relationships with each other, our economic systems, and the development of our menus and cooking practices. We pray and meditate together on a daily basis, and our spiritual format incorporates elements of the Old and New Testament, as well as a wide range of Eastern and contemporary teachings.

We believe that the communal style of living is the future and the key to survival. It is the best format for development of the individual and the evolution of civilization. 6/13/89

Gesundheit Institute

HC64, Box 167
Hillsboro, WV 24946

(304) 653-4338

2630 Robert Walker Place
Arlington, VA 22207

(703) 525-8169

Gesundheit Institute is a holistically-oriented health care community. Our principle project is the creation of a 40-bed, free, community-based hospital on 310 acres of land in rural West Virginia. Our dream is to create a truly ecumenical healing center with all types of healers (from Western allopaths to spiritual healers) treating all types of illness (mental, physical, and spiritual). Humor, clowning, art, nature, and good old-fashioned love and friendship are important ingredients in our healing work.

We have one building already built (a 4,000 sq. ft. workshop) and are in the planning stages of the main (40,000 sq. ft.) facility. A comprehensive land use plan has been drawn up so that we can develop our property as ecologically as possible. We also have a suburban home in Arlington,

Virginia, where we do fund raising and administration.

There are 6 adults and 3 kids living at the Arlington center; and 3 adults, 2 kids, numerous volunteers and short-term residents at the West Virginia site. Volunteers are being sought to help with the building project (West Virginia) and to do clerical work (Arlington). Visitors of all kinds (whether visiting in sickness or in health) are expected to work and participate in the community as fully as possible. The "spirit of community" itself is used as medicine. If you would like to work hard while building a dream with a group of enthusiastic do-gooders, please get in touch. 9/28/89

Gita Nagari Village

ISKCON Farm
Route 1, Box 839
Port Royal, PA 17082

(717) 527-4101

"Plain Living and high thinking" is the motto of Gita Nagari, the Hare Krishna movement's 600-acre farm community in central Pennsylvania's Juniata Valley. Begun in 1975 by the movement's founder, Srila Prabhupada, the community raises crops, protects cows, works oxen, schools children, publishes a farm journal, and lives life in the loving spirit of Lord Krishna's *Bhagavad-Gita*, Gandhi's favorite book of truth. Krishna's devotees love to share, and Gita Nagari has a lot to offer: farm-fresh vegetarian foods, spiritual ecology, bhakti-yoga culture, and deep friendship on the path to self realization. Weary of the modern wasteland? Visit Gita Nagari and drink deep at the reservoir of pleasure — Krishna consciousness. For more information write to ISKCON Farm. 12/28/88

Glen Ivy

25000 Glen Ivy Road
Corona, CA 91719

(714) 735-8701

Glen Ivy (est. 1977) is the community name of the Southwest Regional Center of the Emissaries of Divine Light (see main listing). It is a spiritual education community where people may come for an experience of the Art of Living. Communal living is not an end in itself for the Emissaries but is used to create a still environment that makes it easy for an individual to have a greater experience of his or

her true identity. The permanent residents are charged with the task of putting this expansive spirit into practice in everyday duties and relationships. Such harmonization with the currents of life is seen as essential for personal, as well as global, fulfillment.

Glen Ivy is internationally renowned for its hot springs resort, its spa, and its vivacious hospitality. Approximately 85 people of all ages make Glen Ivy their home. We invite you to come visit on Sunday and share in our morning radiation service which begins at 10:30 a.m. If you find yourself resonating with the values outlined above, we encourage you to attend a 1- or 5-day Art of Living seminar. All correspondence may be addressed to Robert Kauffman. 9/11/88

God's Valley

Williams, IN
See: Padanaram Settlement

The Goodenough Community

2007 - 33rd Avenue South
Seattle, WA 98144

(206) 323-4653 / 323-6782

Founded in 1981, the Goodenough Community (the American Association for the Furtherance of Community, a non-profit educational corporation) is an organized response to its members' need to participate in a social process that builds character, strengthens will, and teaches relational skills. Though it is not a residential community, it is a transformation community — a way of life that shares responsibility for a relational environment in which to accomplish personal and social change. It provides culture, safety, order, and prioritization as expressed in its covenant:

"The purpose of the Goodenough Community is to create a way of life through the relationship we share.

"By entering into this covenant, we define the Goodenough Community and shape the relationship between and among us. We agree to be accountable to each other for upholding the covenant.

"As part of the Goodenough Community, I commit: •To make and keep agreements with great care; •To remain constant through conflict; •To trust the good intentions of each of us; •To relate with acceptance and respect; •To enter fully into life's experiences; •To acknowledge the inner connectedness of all creation; •To awaken my awareness to my unique role in the Universe. •So be it!" 7/17/89

Goodlife Community

2006 Vine Street
Berkeley, CA 94709

(415) 525-0251

Goodlife is a cooperative household with (at present) seven members. Our location is a large house near the center of Berkeley. Our group is similar to the many other communal/collective/cooperative living groups that exist in the San Francisco Bay area. We eat together; have weekly house meetings; share cost of food, utilities, etc.; share household work; and raise a garden. We are committed to peace, ecology, and freedom for everyone. Because of our small size and urban location we are not set up for drop-in or overnight visitors. Our household was established at the beginning of 1969 as Harrad West. Please include SASE with correspondence. 7/20/89

Gould Farm

Monterey, MA 01245
(413) 528-1804

Founded in 1913 on an abandoned farm in the Berkshire Hills of western Massachusetts, Gould Farm provides a secluded retreat that offers emotionally exhausted and disturbed human beings the healing fellowship of a "family" community. We are not a classical intentional community, but a psychiatric treatment and rehabilitation community where staff and staff families form the more or less permanent community. Most basic to our program is providing a warm and caring atmosphere in which the healing process can take place. The necessary work of a community and a farm are at the center of our program.

Each guest is expected to take care of his/her own room, participate in common chores such as helping with meals and dishes, and for several hours each day assist staff in varied farm and domestic activities. We balance work with recreation and community events: square dances, discussions, coffee houses, parties, swimming and a sauna, games, picnics, trips....

We are a non-sectarian and interracial recuperation center offering a healing milieu: care, work, rest, counseling, and accommodations for 40 guests (mostly between the ages of 19-40). Our full-time staff numbers over 35. Our 600 acres includes a 100-acre working farm, high hills, a brook with summer swimming, miles of hiking trails through beautiful woods, New England stone walls.... Here individuals suffering from mental illness, anxiety, depression, situational difficulties, and fatigue have found help in community living, in work, in the friendship of another human being, and in quiet places of natural beauty. Each guest has a private room.

No one is ever turned away from Gould Farm for a lack of money — if the applicant and family are willing to pay a fee appropriate to their income and resources. We do not offer a permanent home to any guest, nor are we able to accept those who are retarded, have brain damage, are assaultive or suicidal, or are addicted to alcohol or illicit drugs. Mail inquiries only. 3/1/89

Grassroots Community

5075 Sweet Basil Lane
Tallahassee, FL 32301
(904)   877-0765

Grassroots is a land co-op community of 44 adults and 31 children. There are several values essential to our group's purpose: support for the environment; peace and disarmament; hunger and habitat issues; and a focus on the quality of life. Individuals own their own parcels and their own homes; as a community we hold 4% of the land in common, and the community assesses itself for road repair, etc. We make all major decisions by consensus, but fall back on majority rule if consensus fails three times. Currently all 27 parcels of land are sold. We are open to new members only if we find more land or if existing members leave. 2/5/89

Green Pastures Estate

Route 3, Box 80
Ladds Lane
Epping, NH 03042

(603) 679-8149

Green Pastures is the New England headquarters (since 1963) for the Emissaries, a worldwide association of wholesome men and women devoted to allowing full release of the natural qualities of life's spirit in practical, everyday living. We love revealing true being by truly being. Green Pastures is one of the educational sites for Emissary Art of Living seminars, Spiritual Leadership classes, and a variety of conferences.

Eighty-five men, women and children ranging in age from eight to eighty live here in a spirit of agreement. The 160-acre estate is comprised of woodland (source of our heating fuel), pasture fields, and a garden of several acres (worked with drafthorses). Visitors are welcome any time. Overnight guests should make arrangements prior to arrival and we suggest a contribution of $25/night's stay. Green Pastures is located one quarter-mile east of the intersection of Routes 125 and 27 in Epping, NH (about an hour's drive north of Boston). Dave and Dianne Pasikov, Coordinators. See the main network listing under Emissaries of Divine Light. 12/14/88

Greenhope Farm

Route 1, Box 226
East Hardwick, VT 05836

(802) 533-7772

Confirmed by a phone call: "This is a women's community, and we wish to be included." No additional information was received. 1/15/90

Greening Life Community

Route 1, Box 265
Shermans Dale, PA 17090

(717) 582-4363

In 1972, Greening Life, Inc. purchased a 135-acre farm in South Central Pennsylvania for the purpose of establishing a planned community. Working together, we put in roads and a community water system, and built our homes.

We follow organic farming practices on our fifty acres of tillable land and in our two-acre garden. The garden produces the majority of our vegetables and our orchard is beginning to provide us with fruit.

The effort to create a balance of cooperative living, with time for individual and family has been a rewarding struggle. Growth in spirit, both individual and community is an important part of our life together. We respect all persons and value their opinions as a voice to guide us. We are interested in sharing our resources and spirit with other individuals and groups. Come and join us for a visit or a lifetime! 12/14/88

The Greenwood Forest Association

Star Route, Box 70-H
Mountain View, MO 65548

(417) 934-2893

Greenwood is a land trust of 1,000 acres in Shannon County, Missouri, located near Mountain View. It is bordered by the Jacks Fork River, about 100 miles east of Springfield. It has been in existence for ten years. There are 45 landowners who each own a 5- or 10-acre parcel. Approximately 540 acres are owned in common by the membership, which elects a board of directors. Decisions are made by majority rule. We meet for potlucks, swimming, annual meetings, etc. Each owner lives on their own parcel, and is required to abide by a set of restrictions designed to protect the environment. The common ground acts as a buffer between parcels, ensuring privacy. Greenwood members are diverse in our backgrounds, belief systems, and personal lifestyles — though the major conviction which binds us together is stewardship of the land. Many of our members are environmental activists and are working toward world peace. We have a few 5 and 10-acre parcels for resale, and would welcome inquiries. For more information write (or call) Don Wilson, Bear Ridge Homestead, at the address listed above. Please enclose an SASE with correspondence. 1/24/90

Griffin Gorge Commons

Route 30, Box 341
Wells, NY 12190

(518) 924-2112 / 924-2335

This community consists of 7 adults and 3 children (ages 5, 8, 13). We are currently working together doing carpentry, woodworking and other crafts. We are building a health food store and restaurant and greenhouse in spring 1989, with long-range plans of developing into a resource center for group encounters and seminars to do with all forms of healing, rejuvenating and replenishing ourselves then the planet. We are located in the Adirondack Mountains on 40 acres of land with a pond, a chapel, 3 homes, a woodworking shop and barns. All inquiries are welcome — call, write, or simply drop by. 1/8/89

Group W House

3788 Army Street
San Francisco, CA 94110
(415) 821-3392

Group W was established by a group of friends who knew each other through an anarchist network in San Francisco. Some were politically active working on group projects, and others were working individually and supported by the rest of the group. Now, in 1990, although only one of the original group still lives here, it is still a group of politically active folks. Several of us are also active in cultural arts on several levels ... for instance we have a performance artist/singer, a political singer/songwriter, and a filmmaker.

In terms of the workings of our household as a unit ... first of all, we are currently 1 man and 4 women ... not an intentional imbalance, but we liked a female subletter so much that we asked her to move in anyhow. We are all very busy with our work (whether working for money, or all of the rest of our "work"), and some are in school. So sometimes the house is empty, but more often than not, someone's home. We buy our food together ($15 into the money jar each week) but do not have a set weekly meal together because our schedules don't allow for it. We don't have house meetings often, and that seems to be a problem for us now in terms of house chores and group decisions. Ideally we make decisions by consensus, but we typically end up using a looser style of "check it out with the housies and if no one objects in any major way go for it." Right now some household issues don't get dealt with — since there's no "forum" for them. We've just decided to do house meetings once a month; things feel more together since we made that decision. 1/29/90

Guru Ram Das Ashrams
See: 3HO Centers (pp. 224 & 267)

Hailos Community
P.O.Box 8, Lumby
British Columbia
CANADA V0E-2G0

A New Age community of "free-spirited" brothers and sisters from different backgrounds — all seeking truth and happiness along their path. We are developing a lifestyle in harmony with nature, based on mutual respect and love — a community where we look for the One-ness beyond our differences. We're primarily vegetarian, and grow some of our food on 320 acres in a secluded valley in northern BC, and are working to establish cottage industries to support ourselves. Each member is responsible for his or her own home, personal needs, and income. We maintain a new age learning centre, and are in the process of establishing a Wholistic Health Centre to provide educational programs on Natural Healing arts and Macrobiotic dietary practices. We offer weekend and week-long retreats — details available upon request. We're seeking a lifestyle where there is time and room to explore the spiritual and social aspects of life. We prefer to stay away from drugs, alcohol, and other stimuli. After a 1-year probationary period, new members make an initial payment of $1500 before beginning construction of a permanent home, and pay a total of $10,000 over a period of up to 40 months. Hailos is a home for those who share high ideals and who know that tomorrow is built today. For more information or a proposal, please write to us. 6/1/88

Harbin Hot Springs

Heart Consciousness Church
Box 782
Middletown, CA 95461

(707) 987-2477
(800) 622-2477 (CA only)

Harbin Hot Springs is a clothing-optional, 1100-acre New Age community/teaching center nestled in a quiet valley with clean air and pure spring water. We have been in existence since 1972, and have well over 100 adult members who operate, maintain, and improve a hot springs retreat and conference facility.

There are many challenging opportunities here for those skilled in construction, housekeeping, computing, healing, administration, mechanics, carpentry, etc. If you are interested in applying for residency, or wish to consider establishing a program of your own here, your inquiry is invited. Financial assistance for projects is sometimes available.

There are many important details concerning visiting, meals, workshops, pets, children, and residency that are not covered in this listing — so we recommend calling or writing

(Attention: Community Relations) before visiting us. Please enclose $1 for postage.

How to get here: Take Highway 29 north from the Napa Valley to Middletown, turn left (west) at the Union 76 gas station; then right at the stop sign and continue four miles, keeping left at the fork in the road. Use of drugs or alcohol is not permitted. Open 24 hours a day, 365 days a year. 1/3/90

Harvest Forum (Forming)

1406 Cole Street
San Francisco, CA 94117

(415) 566-0513

Members of the Harvest Forum Community are looking for creative and responsible people to share in shaping and realizing a cooperative vision of communal living. We are creating an alternative lifestyle focusing on personal growth, quality relationships, and a sense of balance with the earth. Plans so far include the purchase of about 160 acres of partially gardened, partially wooded land for approximately a dozen community members of diverse backgrounds, including various ethnic, age, gender, and sexual orientations. Acceptance of diversity, subversive tendencies toward art and play, and respect for personal and community space are necessary for participation.

Accomplishments so far include community meetings, the publication of several issues of a newsletter, preliminary investigation of land sites within three hours' drive of San Francisco, and application for non-profit status. We are establishing a trial living situation in the San Francisco Bay Area before moving to a rural site. Write us to find out more, to meet with us, or to obtain a free subscription to our newsletter (see Resources listing). 11/23/89

Headlands

Route 1
Stella, Ontario
CANADA K0H-2S0

(613) 389-3444

Headlands is a non-profit consumer cooperative. As of September '89, we are 3 men, 2 women, and 2 children (eight and five years old). Our hope is that Headlands will evolve toward a larger community of individuals living and working together in small inter-related and overlapping consumer and producer cooperatives. Members are involved in a commercial sheep farm (600 ewes) and various revenue-generating activities. Our own livestock provide much of our food.

We live on Amherst Island in Lake Ontario near Kingston, Ontario. Individually, we are active in the social and political life of this 380-person un-intentional community. Collectively we produce a monthly newsletter, the *Amherst Island Beacon*, keeping everyone up to date in all the news and views that are fit to print in this somewhat conservative rural area. Please include an SASE with any correspondence. 5/24/89

Heart Consciousness Church

Middletown, CA
See: Harbin Hot Springs

Hearthaven

3728 Tracy
Kansas City, MO 64109

(816) 531-8164 / 561-0531

Hearthaven is a community of 5 permanent members who seek to model a way of living "from the heart." We care about people, the earth, and the universe; we seek to express with joy, creativity, imagination, and love the basic fact that our creator has given us everything we need to live life abundantly, without fear, and in harmony with all of creation.

We are willing to provide temporary housing and life support for one or two individuals at a time who may be going through emotional or spiritual difficulties and wish to experience the healing ways of our household. Terms are negotiable, based on the needs and desires of all concerned. We impose no specific religious creed or doctrine, although all permanent residents are members of the same ecumenical faith community — "ecumenikos".

ecumenikos is an alternative house-church style faith community formally affiliated with the United Methodist, United Presbyterian, Mennonite, United Church of Christ, and Christian (Disciples) denominations ... but open to people of any faith, as well as those who are "spiritual seekers." We have no formal membership requirements, and make all decisions by consensus. We place a high value on living one's life in a way that is consistent with what one believes — whatever the belief. We do advocate seeing Jesus as a model for that kind of living, and for the value of living life based on love, rather than fear. Our involvement in various collective ministries reflects those areas where individual members have felt called, and also reflects a strong commitment to ecumenical efforts, particularly in peace and justice areas. 1/12/90

Hearthstone Village

Amherst, MA
See: The Ark

Heartlight Center

67138 Shimmel Road
Sturgis, MI 49091

(616) 651-2234

Heartlight Center is a Spiritual Light Center for Peace and Wholistic Education. Its total focus is upon knowing our connection with Our Heavenly Father, and then manifesting His Will for us in service to the world. It is a place where people are truly striving to live the Kingdom of God here on earth.

It is also a place where all people can come together in work and in play and learn how to live the Will of Our Heavenly Father in their everyday lives. Heartlight is a Center of Light where people can come to experience a new, yet infinitely old way of life — a life of love, joy and peace. 12/21/89

Heathcote Center

21300 Heathcote Road
Freeland, MD 21053

(301) 343-0280

Nestled in a narrow valley 35 miles north of Baltimore, Maryland, Heathcote has been home to many people over the past 25 years. Though the players have changed as people moved along their paths, the spirit of the place has remained one of earth care and earth repair. Since 1982 the residential group has been women (both lesbian and heterosexual) who run our Conference/Retreat Centre, focus on our own personal healing, and care for the land (35 acres, mostly wooded, with organic gardens, small orchard, etc.).

We are involved with an ecological design system/philosophy called Permaculture, and we function as an education/information center within the North American and International

Heathcote *(Cont'd.)*

Permaculture Networks. Seeing a direct connection between healing the earth and healing ourselves, we support and encourage members to create their own personal programs (12-Step or other) to recover from our addictive society and various dysfunctional family-of-origin experiences. Our spiritual practices include earth-centered celebrations, Vipassana meditation and various Buddhist practices, Christmas... we're an eclectic group, but no gurus and no dogma here.

We are looking for several new members and interns who want to take part in the development of a permaculture education program, and in practicing applications on the land. Major requirements: must like to laugh, be silly, and enjoy life while working your butt off. If it's not fun, *why* are you doing it?! Please enclose an SASE with correspondence. 2/4/90

High Wind Association

Route 2
Plymouth, WI 53073

(414) 528-7212

"To walk gently on the earth, to know the spirit within, to hear our fellow beings, to invoke the light of wisdom —and to build the future now."

This vision has attracted thousands worldwide to High Wind's experimental exploration of ways for people to live more harmoniously with nature and each another. High Wind Community is located 55 miles north of Milwaukee on a 128-acre farm with high rolling meadows, woods, and springs.

High Wind's founders first organized innovative seminars — which examined new values from a global perspective. In 1980 a task group formed to build a passive solar "bio-shelter" — a residence with attached greenhouse. The community evolved from this group, combining education around alternative thinking with interests in ecology, shelter-building, and renewable energy — all within the context of an overarching sacred intent. Many of our current educational programs are held in conjunction with the University of Wisconsin.

Seventeen people (14 adults) live in the community, engaged in guest/ learning programs, networking, on-site enterprises (subscription farming, woodcraft, desktop publishing, a national think tank), some outside jobs, and site maintenance. All acreage is currently being placed into a land trust, with sites leased for businesses and homes. High Wind offers diverse options for lifestyles, with varying degrees of collectivity and autonomy.

We also operate a major alternative bookstore in Milwaukee (see Resources listing). *Windwatch,* our semi-annual journal, details the philosophy and challenge of life and personal growth in the community, evolution toward a sustainable village, and the relationship between alternative models and mainstream culture. 5/18/89

Highland Center

Dalton, PA
See: Rabbity Hill Farm

Hillegass House

3056 Hillegass Avenue
Berkeley, CA 94705

Hillegass House is an eleven-member, decade-old collective in Berkeley. We began as a (mostly) single-parent house made up of six adults who wanted to share the burdens (and joys) of parenting. The age spread of the current membership runs from the early-twenties through late-fifties, with the median age being 40-plus. Our group is relatively stable — we've had no openings for new members for nearly two years now, and two of our original members still live in the house.

We are an exceptionally diverse group in most regards (i.e., interests, spirituality, diet, sexuality, employment, etc.) and we think that's important. We blend together so well because we balance a strong commitment to group living and a real enjoyment of group dynamics on the one hand with a healthy respect for one another's privacy because we realize having time to one's self is absolutely vital.

Other factors of our success? Well, it helps that we live in a lovely house that can accommodate our number pretty graciously. Even more signifi-cantly, dinners are shared and we all perform at least honorably in the kitchen (and we have several really outstanding cooks in the crowd). Written inquiries only, with SASE (we're sometimes slow in answering correspondence). 5/15/90

The Hog Farm

1301 Henry Street
Berkeley, CA 94709

The Hog Farm is a commune that began 24 years ago in southern California. We treasure our freedom and try to have rules only when they become necessary. Everyone is expected to contribute financially and through work in the communal scene. We spend lots of time and energy on fund raising for various non-profit entities. There is no way to "join" except through a long experimental time of living with us. We have land in Northern California and a house in the San Francisco Bay area. We focus on hard work, helping others, maintaining our individual freedom, and creating an economic and social base that makes sense. We have meetings when necessary, and those of us who own the land each get a casual vote. Written inquiries only; please include a SASE [cc]. You may also write for a copy of our catalog and our newsletter *Hog Callings.* [See also: Black Oak Ranch.] 9/16/89

The Hohm Community

P.O. Box 4272
Prescott Valley, AZ 86302

(602) 778-5947 / 778-9189

The Hohm Community was founded in 1975 by Lee Lozowick, a Western Spiritual Master, and his students. Our approach provides an alternative to the conventional way of viewing life, the unconscious context from which life is habitually lived. We draw from all traditions, and our daily lives include the practices of exercise; meditation; study; right relationship to diet (lacto-vegetarian) and sexuality (monogamous relationships); and daily support of the community through work and financial contributions. We also strive to be sensitive to others, and to the environment.

Our community is comprised of approximately 250 students and friends — intentionally kept small in numbers to allow direct interaction with the Master and a sense of bonding among community members.

We attempt to carry a mood of celebration throughout our lives, and hold formal gatherings three times yearly. We move to produce revelation through radical, direct, hands-on experiential work in travel, theater, and other art forms; and we also offer a "householder" lifestyle for those more drawn to that form.

We have a main center in Arizona, and "outreach groups" throughout the US and Europe. We welcome questions, interest, and correspondence. A prerequisite to visiting Hohm Community is reading the extensive introduction to our principles, *Black and White* ($10 postpaid). 10/1/89

Holy City Community

Route 7, Box 390
Lake Charles, LA 70611

(318) 855-2871 / 855-1235

We are sixteen families, more than 70 people, at the end of 1988. We are making a directed, self-conscious effort to create a new society based on Gospel values. We support one another prayerfully and materially. We tithe, birth lots of babies, and celebrate the Sacraments joyfully together. Our efforts are directed toward re-forming our personal and family lives, creating a new set of peer relationships, and growing in our lifetime commitments to one another. In all of this we purposely try to become detached from many old ways of being and acting.

Presently, community members are selling their homes and moving together in urban and rural "clusters". In a cluster neighborhood, we buy, rent, or build homes next to one another with the desire and intent to live together in a back-door relationship. We want our children to grow up with many "aunts and uncles", and are anticipating the day when we have our own school.

The words of our covenant describe us and guide us on our journey to the New Pentecost: "We are a covenant community in the Roman Catholic tradition, subject to the authority of our Bishop and our designated leadership. Our life is centered in God the Father, the Son, and the Holy Spirit, our model of perfect community. We understand ourselves to be in God's image most fully as a community rather than as individual persons; and together we aspire to a life of gospel poverty." Shalom. 12/14/88

Home Front

Seattle, WA See: Homestead Cooperative Land Trust

Homeland Community (Forming)

c/o Susan Wynne Topf
2 Ann Terrace, East Brunswick
P.O. Milltown, NJ 08850

(201) 821-8515 (eves)

The purpose of Homeland, Inc. is to acquire and retain property for socially responsible development. This shall occur by leasing only to parties committed to the development and maintenance of structures that: • protect open space and natural resources; • are ecologically sound and energy efficient; • are governed cooperatively; • support sharing of resources; • foster community involvement; • promote limited equity and attitudes of land stewardship.

Our current group of 9 adults and 2 children have come together in an urban setting, and are presently looking for a farm... our target date is 1992. On our seal we say that Homeland is community at its best — with consensus decision-making, loving neighbors, lifelong friendships, and heartfelt living. 8/17/89

Homestead Cooperative Land Trust (Forming)

c/o Freedom Fund
4534-1/2 University Way NE
Seattle, WA 98105

(206) 547-7644 (Msg)

We are a community in formation, with a primary commitment to work with homeless and very low-income people in housing crises (evictions, building closures, etc.) who live here in Seattle. Participatory consensus-oriented democracy is our goal; right now a core group is actively forming by-laws/process proposals. Shared values include mutual aid, community autonomy, individual freedom, and direct action.

Our housing ranges from squatting, to limited-equity co-op living within a land trust arrangement. Our umbrella organization, HCLT, is becoming a tax-exempt non-profit corporation; its purpose is to acquire abandoned but restorable properties, and coordinates homesteading projects through which homeless and low-income people can repair and maintain the properties — and who then may reside permanently in land trust housing. We are not looking for out-of-towners to live with us.

We are in need of information, volunteers, organizational assistance, funds, etc. We are presently sponsored by the Freedom Fund (listed in the Resources section). Please include SASE with inquiries [cc]. 2/23/89

Hooker House

3151 West 24th Avenue
Denver, CO 80211

(303) 477-5176

Hooker House was begun in 1977 as a middle-class, urban cooperative. Our residence is a wonderful old house built in 1890. We have found cooperative living to be extremely practical, comfortable, and economical — allowing us more time and resources for life's other pleasures.

Decisions are by consensus. All members have employment outside the house. Grocery and house costs are shared, as is cooking, cleaning, and other work necessary to maintain the house. We have almost no solid injunctions, allowing consideration for others and negotiation to govern our behavior.

We currently have four residents, and discourage new membership at this time. Visitors must contact us and receive confirmation before arriving. 5/14/89

The House

Oakland, CA

The House is presently 6 adults and 2 toddlers sharing an old eight-bedroom home near the northern border of Oakland, California. There is also a network of ex-residents who share an interest in perpetuating our focus on group living. In effect the house is owned by an association comprised of all present and past members. Selling the house would require agreement of this rather diverse collection of "owners", thus we feel that the deed to our home is quite secure.

Members eat together regularly, and share equally in most of the household chores. We regularly schedule work weekends to tackle major projects, and friends often materialize to pitch in with the work and the fun. We have a pragmatic orientation, and not much ideology. Politically, there is a tendency for members to lean toward the liberal left. What we emphasize most is the enjoyment of shared living. 1/16/90

House of Lavendar

2455 W. Juneau Avenue
Milwaukee, WI 53233

(414) 933-3033

A "Community House" near the center of downtown Milwaukee. We have 5-7 members with a variety of backgrounds and experiences, but sharing a commitment to good energy conservation practices, nutritious food, progressive social changes, and alternative developments in our city. Since '68 we have had 50 members — educators, counselors, artists, public health workers, students, community activists. A few former members still live in the neighborhood and continue to enrich our lives. 1/1/89

"The Hundred" 100 Mile Lodge

Box 9
100 Mile House, B.C.
CANADA V0K-2E0

(604) 395-3397

Established in 1948, the 100 Mile House Emissary Community is located in the Cariboo country of British Columbia's central interior. Many of its 120 residents play integral parts in area businesses — including a deluxe lakeside resort, a bustling hotel, a 12,000-acre cattle ranch, a weekly newspaper, and the area's largest land development company. The Canadian headquarters for The Emissaries (see main listing), "The Hundred" welcomes a steady stream of visitors from around the world, and has a reputation for longstanding stability. Among its inhabitants are artists, musicians, and authors whose work is being recognized in ever-broadening circles. The Hundred is the home of Michael and Nancy Exeter, directors of the international Emissary program. 11/15/89

Hutterian Brethren

In Reformation times, a group of Anabaptists decided to pool their goods and unite in Christian brotherhood. Jakob Hutter became their leader five years later in 1533. They believe in the Apostles' Creed, baptism of adult believers, the Lord's Supper as a Meal of Remembrance, community of goods, leadership in the Church, Church discipline, and lifelong faithfulness in marriage. They refuse to do military service or use violence, hold public office, or swear oaths.

Today there are over 300 Hutterian colonies and Bruderhofs in Canada and the USA, as well as communities in South America and Europe. There are four large Bruderhof communities in the eastern USA and one in England — each with 150 to 400 residents.

Family life is important, with father at the head of the family, and mother at his right hand. Single members are included in family households. Divorce and remarriage are not allowed. Unmarried visiting couples may not share overnight accommodations. They educate their children in their own schools and day nurseries. Each colony has common work and a common purse. Hutterite groups manufacture Community Playthings (educational play equipment) and Rifton Equipment for the handicapped. Hutterian Anabaptists, mostly in the West, farm on a large scale. For more information send for their Plough Publishing House catalog, and a free issue of their periodical, *The Plough*, which discusses current issues, and is a platform for keeping us in touch with fellow Christians and interacting with other movements.

Individual Community listings in this directory: Asponola (WA), Crystal Spring (Manitoba), Darvell (England), Deer Spring (CT), Michaelshof (West Germany), New Meadow Run [also known as Spring Valley] (PA), Pleasant View (NY), Starland (MN), and Woodcrest (NY). 2/2/89

[ED NOTE: A Hutterite Directory is available c/o Dr. Lawrence C. Anderson, Dept. of Geography, Mankato State University, Mankato, MN. It includes addresses for over 200 other colonies, with size & date of origin.]

Innisfree Village

Route 2, Box 506
Crozet, VA 22932
(804) 823-5400

Innisfree Village was founded in 1971 as a creative alternative to institutional or homebound care for adults who are mentally handicapped. Innisfree is located on a 400-acre farm, about 20 miles from Charlottesville, Virginia, and also operates two group homes and several supervised apartments in Charlottesville. In both the village households and in-town residences, co-workers (as people with mental handicaps are called at Innisfree) and volunteers (staff who live full time in the village) live and work in an interdependent environment and share a mutual respect.

The 20-25 volunteer staff make a minimum one-year commitment. Longer commitments are encouraged to increase the community's stability. Policies and decisions about daily matters are made during weekly meetings, preceded by a Steering Committee which sets the agenda. The Board of Directors, composed mostly of parents of the co-workers, deals with finances, building, co-worker admissions and areas of overall welfare.

Innisfree volunteers and co-workers live together in family-style homes and work in a weavery, woodshop, bakery, pottery, and in the garden. For the volunteer, Innisfree provides the opportunity to both live in a community and contribute to the lives of persons often excluded from alternative communities.

We invite you to visit Innisfree, but please call or write in advance. Overnight visits can be arranged. 7/14/89

Integral Yoga Institute

Buckingham, VA
See: Yogaville

Institute for Sustainable Living

Route 1, Box 35
Check, VA 24072

(703) 651-3412

The Institute for Sustainable Living has been created to support research into ecological community design, and we currently publish a quarterly newsletter. We currently have a small farm, but expect to move to a larger property in 2 to 5 years. We are committed to creating a largely self-sufficient community which blends all of the parts of our lives — physical, spiritual, emotional, and intellectual — into an integrated nourishing whole. Many of us are educators or work in human services; an alternative school is part of our vision.

People within our group are on varied spiritual paths, and we look forward to sharing our traditions with each other and to creating celebrations, life-cycle ceremonies, and meaningful ritual. Our concept of sustainable community includes:

•Personal responsibility for ourselves, each other, and the natural world; a commitment to direct energy to healing the ills of society; and outreach to organizations with similar goals and values, so that we might share experiences and knowledge.

•Loving, respectful attitudes toward each other and our children, embodying our shared values of egalitarianism and non-violence.

•A focus on ecology and land stewardship, spirituality, education, and childrearing — including the creation of a school for our own children and for those from the surrounding community.

•We support both alternative and traditional means of maintaining and healing our bodies, minds, and spirits — emphasizing personal growth and creative expression.

•Economic, architectural, and consensus decision-making systems which support all of the above — including the sharing of work responsibilities on the community, and sharing the income we bring in. 2/26/91

Institute of Cultural Affairs

International
See: Late Entries

Intergenerational Women's Community (Forming)

c/o Kate McEvoy
51 Walnut Avenue
Takoma Park, MD 20912

We are the research committee of an intergenerational women's group seeking to encourage the development of a women's living and retirement community (or communities). We live near Washington, DC, and would like to build a network of intentional communities that will help us find a community in which to live — or to form our own.

One of our goals is diversity in our membership, however, at this time we are primarily feminist, lesbian, and white. We are not yet differently abled, skilled, or classed, nor do we have yet a woman of color involved in our group.

We are not yet a "we" that has a defined final vision of a singular community. Rather, we hope that several communities and connections may grow from an umbrella organization that provides information and communication. We are just beginning, and hope to eventually collect information from communities from across the U.S. and make it available

to interested women.

As a first step we have prepared a survey that we have sent to various communities, gathering information about the groups that already exist. We presently have a newsletter in the planning stage. 1/12/89

Jemez Bodhi Mandala

Box 8
Jemez Springs, NM 87025

The Directory received a postcard from this group stating their desire to be included. We received no further information. 2/2/89

Jesuit Volunteer Corps

Northwest Center
Box 3928
Portland, OR 97208

(503) 228-2457

The purpose of the JVC is to promote justice and peace through direct service with the poor and through structural change. Volunteers commit themselves for one year at a time to do full-time ministry. They strive to build community by a simple lifestyle and mutual encouragement of their service. 21 or over, male or female, without dependents. One year commitment, August to August. Receive room & board, health insurance, stipend. Interdenominational, but strongly affiliated with the Catholic Church. Needed: flexibility; enthusiasm; sense of humor; commitment to values of community, simple living, spirituality and social justice.

JVC East:
  18th & Thompson Streets
  Philadelphia, PA 19121
JVC Midwest:
  P.O.Box 32692
  Detroit, MI 48232
JVC South:
  P.O. Box 3126
  Houston, TX 77253
JVC Southwest:
  P.O. Box 23404
  Oakland, CA 94623   1/15/90

Jubilee House Community

902 Boulevard
Statesville, NC 28677

(704) 872-4045

The Jubilee House Community, established in 1979, is an intentional Christian Community with 13 members. We have numerous ministries which are governed by a Board of Directors, and which receive wide community support from churches, individuals, and various civic and charitable organizations. We operate an Emergency Shelter which provides room and board for seven days to the temporarily homeless — the jobless, highway accident victims, hitchhikers, etc. JHC also provides a shelter for victims of domestic violence and/or sexual assault; known as "Sanctuary", this shelter provides room and board for women and their children, for a maximum stay of three months. A third ministry is our Winter Shelter for the permanently homeless — the "street people" of Statesville and our surrounding county; approximately 150 different guests are housed each winter (from November 1 through March 31), being provided with supper, overnight lodging, and breakfast. We also staff a 24-hour Crisis Line which offers crisis intervention and advocacy for victims of sexual assault and domestic violence. Members of our community live together, share their income, and make household decisions by consensus. 2/2/89

Jubilee Partners

Box 459
Comer, GA 30629
(404) 783-5131

Jubilee Partners is a Christian community that was started in 1979 on 258 acres of land in north Georgia. The community is comprised of approximately 30 adults and 10 children. Around half of these folks are resident partners, and half are volunteers who stay for periods of 3-5 months. Jubilee's ministries include resettling refugees who have fled persecution in Central America, raising money to assist amputees who are victims of the war in Nicaragua, and ministering to the needs of some of the people on Death Row in Georgia. We are open to new members, though everyone interested in living here must come as a volunteer for the first year. 8/28/89

Julian Woods Community

Route 1, Box 420
Julian, PA 16844
(814) 355-5755 / 355-8026

Julian Woods Community is a non-profit corporation on 140 acres of hillsides and woodland in central Pennsylvania, 16 miles from Penn State University. We presently have 11 adult members, 4 children, and 8 non-member residents. We live in families or small family-like groups in separate homes which are clustered within a short walk of each other.

We recently received a grant to construct an evapotranspiration greenhouse for sewage treatment. Potential liaison with Penn State provides cultural and educational opportunities. The Science, Technology and Society Department is a source for alternative ecological material.

A guiding principle here is land stewardship. Otherwise, we enjoy our diversity and the challenge to live cooperatively on shared land.

Organic, biodynamic gardening, foraging and herbal healing are practiced. Simplicity; sustainable living and farming habits; bioregional, decentralist self-sufficiency are primary goals. Learning to live gently is our urgent task: to treat our bodies and our earth in holistic ways.

Ideas for future growth include cohousing, home schooling, acquiring more land for farm and forest. We seek people with resources to help realize these projected ecologically-based ideals. Adjacent land is available for sale to like minded groups. Please include an SASE with correspondence. 5/17/91

Kehillat Mishpakhot

c/o Ernest & Elaine Cohen
525 Midvale Avenue
Upper Darby, PA 19082
(215) 352-2689

Kehillat Mishpakhot ("Community of Families"), established in 1982, is comprised of about a half-dozen families — adults and children. Our goal is to develop a life pattern which markedly improves upon two aspects of modern American society: 1) Relations of people with each other (Community), and 2) Relation between humans and Planet Earth

(Ecology). Members will live within expanded family units to the greatest extent possible. These are of mixed ages, of the size of large natural families, and often are natural families. Several nearby family units form a cluster, functionally equivalent to a tribe or village. Several clusters work together as a "Community".

Kehillat Mishpakhot was started in Upper Darby (suburban Philadelphia) because our philosophy is "build where you are." The religious component of this subculture is derived from Judaism — basically rational, but with the dedication to protect and perfect Planet Earth as "stewards of the Creator." Kehillat Mishpakhot is egalitarian and co-operative, but focused on life in (expanded) families.

In some ways, Kehillat Mishpakhot is like a Havurah. We celebrate life-cycle events and holidays together. There is an affiliated preschool which is being expanded into a "Family School." We are also planning to build an appropriate business for our members.

While we enjoy occasionally talking with people about what we are doing and what we stand for, we cannot provide bed and board for people traveling across the country, nor a sheltered environment or housing for the physically or emotionally disabled. Also — we do not wish to be on any additional bulk mailing lists. However, those who wish to know more about our program and philosophy, please write. Effective participation requires time and commitment. 2/25/90

Kerista

547 Frederick Street
San Francisco, CA 94117
(415) 681-6598

Founded in 1971 in the Haight-Ashbury (where it still exists today), Kerista blends hippie idealism, rock-'n'-roll, and real world practicality. We are non-separatist feminists and Utopian futurists, with a highly evolved strategy for building an international commune movement to solve global problems.

We practice orthodox polyfidelity (coined the word, in fact). There are 27 adult members in the commune, living totally without jealousy or possessiveness. The largest family cluster at present (early 1989) numbers 15 people (8 women, 7 men). We're raising two kids, but have become

non-breeders (will not have any more babies ourselves). All Keristan males get vasectomies within one year of joining (the best birth control option available right now).

Our business, Abacus, Inc., is successful in the Macintosh computer field. We do Mac sales, service, training, networking, graphics and animation. We also publish The Node (a computer paper) and RockHEAD (a rock music journal) in the San Francisco Bay area.

Our structure is democratic, with an emphasis on shared, team leadership and worker self-management. We live by a clearly defined social contract, studied and agreed to by members before they join. A key element in our ongoing existence and a secret of our success is the Gestalt-O-Rama process. This is a rational, verbally direct, open style of interpersonal relating and self-development that goes on all the time among members. It's not for lightweights ... people who don't want to think or change. Being a Keristan is a total-involvement trip. We are evolving a new religion of humor, equality and liberation, and are actively engaged in "culture sculpture" as we move along in life.

Free literature is available for those interested in learning more about us. We do want to find more kindred spirits. People are also welcome to come to our Gestalt-O-Rama Growth Co-op (rap groups) at 8pm any night except Saturdays and Mondays. It takes place at 543 Frederick Street (near Stanyan) in San Francisco. Write for free information/correspondence. 7/20/89

Kidstown (Forming)

c/o Bob Brown
P.O. Box 826
Middletown, CA 95461
(707) 987-0669

"Kidstown", started January '90, is an intentional community designed primarily to provide a wholesome family environment for kids 12 to 17 years old. Our kids have been separated from their families, and either don't want to return to an unwholesome living atmosphere, or have no family home to return to. Staff and children will reside on the premises, with the children taking an equal part in our democratic process when they reach and maintain a defined level of responsibility.

The Kidstown "Questing Game" (a collective search for the truth) will be the primary growth process, and each individual will be responsible for determining their own pace. The staff will be expected to play the game with the kids, and the underlying standard is that everything can be questioned.

Initially all staff will be volunteers, and we will encourage seniors from nearby housing developments to share their experiences and skills with the kids. When we are financially able, we will pay the earliest volunteers (for up to 20 of their weekly hours) at a rate slightly above the minimum wage. Some badly needed skills may be paid at a higher rate.

Our project is set in the clean air and pure water of Lake County, just two hours north of San Francisco. We are seeking socially responsible investors to support our program, requiring capital for both land acquisition and building construction (we'll share 50/50 any capital gains realized). The land and housing wil be managed by our non-profit organization, Solutions For Today, Inc. (SFT). Our books are open to inspection by any authorities or officials.

The first new building to be constructed will be an energy-efficient passive solar house. A second priority is to develop an organic greenhouse and garden—to grow food for present occupants, and to allow the kids to enhance self esteem and earn spending money by developing produce sales.

A major goal of Kidstown is to promote greater self-esteem, primarily by living on our own efforts, without government aid. We are guided by a spiritual/rational/pragmatic force which, if trusted completely, causes everything to work out for the betterment of everyone. We welcome donations from folks who feel kinship with what we are doing. If you like children and want to help them find a better life for themselves (and perhaps for yourself), write or call for a copy of our brochure. We are open to visitors. 2/6/90

Kibbutz Movement (Israel)
See Yad Tabenkin (p. 290)

King View
P.O. Box 217
Aurora, Ontario
CANADA L4G-3H3
(416) 773-2241

Stewarding an 87-acre farm in a wealthy equestrian countryside, King View is known as a place of integrity and hospitality. Its 50 residents provide an elegant home just 30 miles north of Toronto, where they host diverse public events and cultivate a living understanding of spiritual purpose. Through business interests, artistic endeavors, and a welcoming hearth, this maturing community extends its quiet influence into Canada's most populated region. Contact: Ron Polack. (See main listing for Emissaries of the Divine Light.) 1/6/89

Koinonia Partners
Route 2
Americus, GA 31709
(912) 924-0391

Koinonia Partners is a Christian community dedicated to being a demonstration plot of Christian principles. Ministries include, but are not limited to, building homes for low-income families, child development center, youth program, peace witness. Simple lifestyle supported with income from pecan, fruit cake, and candy mail-order business and farming. We welcome volunteers and visitors when arrangements are made in advance. 5/1/89

Kootenay Cooperative
Land Settlement Society
General Delivery
Argenta, British Columbia
CANADA V0G-1B0
(604) 366-4472 (msg)

We are 18 adults and 9 children living on 200 acres of forested hillside at the north end of Kootenay Lake in southeastern British Columbia. Our community, established in 1969, is striving for a balance of ecology and human economy on our land and within our group. We have a system of 12 individual homesites surrounded by common lands. Our decisions are by consensus, and members are expected to contribute at least 5 hours of labor per month. We appreciate visitors and letters, but prospective visitors *must* write in advance. We are not looking for new members. 2/4/89

Kripalu Center
for Yoga & Health
Box 793
Lenox, MA 01240
(413) 637-3280

Originally located in Summit Station, Pennsylvania, our center is now nestled in the Berkshire Mountains of Western Massachusetts. Kripalu Center is an oasis where you can rediscover the beauty of your own life, a unique environment to support your search for greater health and happiness — your potential for abundant energy, long-lasting contentment, and limitless ability to love. We offer year-round programs in Yoga, Personal Growth, Bodywork Training, Health and Fitness, Spiritual Attunement, Yoga Teacher Training, and the Spiritual Lifestyle Training Program—a unique opportunity to experience the yogic lifestyle practiced by our 280-member resident staff. We also welcome guests on a daily-rate basis for yoga and dance class, sauna, whirlpool, experiential workshops, and delicious vegetarian cuisine. Call for a complete program guide.

We have also had a center in Sumneytown, Pennsylvania — the site of Gurudev's first ashram. This property is being transformed as the present staff moves to the new center in Massachusetts. Our vision is to establish a residential community here for those wanting to be involved in a Kripalu lifestyle, but who could not live in the program center due to family or career considerations. We want the community to be independent from the existing Kripalu structure — a completely autonomous entity. Members of the new community will have both the responsibility and privilege of translating this new concept into reality. If you have interest in becoming involved in Sumneytown's next phase, please contact Baladev at the Lenox center. 3/1/89

Krotona Institute
46 Krotona Hill Road
Ojai, CA 93023
(805) 646-2653

The Krotona Institute was established in 1924 as a center for students of Theosophy—a philosophical system which brings together science and religion, East and West. We have 40 residents living on 118 acres, and offer classes and retreats on spiritual and esoteric subjects. We also operate a press and a bookstore, and maintain an extensive library. 1/16/90

N. America

Krutsio, Comunidad

Apartado Postal 174
Guerrero Negro
Baja California Sur
MEXICO

Founded in '76, Comunidad Krutsio is an intentional community that goes beyond basic survival — our main goals are individual development, community development, and the promotion of the communities movement. We are attempting to become a cellular community, that is, a social cell of the future planetary organism which incorporates the best of rural and urban traditions. The cellular community is a new social unit based on psychological, economic, and ecological guidelines. Emerging cellular communities must interconnect, and this process is facilitated by the use of a common language — for this reason we practice Esperanto as a second language.

Krutsio is located in a small desert valley between the mountains of Baja California and the Pacific Ocean. Our weather is mild thanks to the fresh onshore winds, with winter lows around 50° and summer highs at about 78°. The scarce rainfall (4" annually) occurs mainly in the winter. In spite of the aridity, the indigenous flora of the area is particularly varied and abundant.

Our community is built and maintained by our own hands. Work for us is a pleasant activity and an excellent means of self-fulfillment ... not a sacrifice. We work about six hours a day, six days a week. We try to let everyone work in what he/she likes most and does best. The more routine jobs are equally shared or are rotated. Work includes agriculture (on a small scale), building, carpentry, cooking, design, education and care of children, food preserving, harvesting and processing of sea resources, mechanics, solar distillation of sea water, etc. In our spare time, we regularly cultivate all the principal areas of human development: spiritual, intellectual, physical, interpersonal, creative, and recreative. We are open to visitors as long as they respect our intent and are willing to exchange knowledge. Volunteers and visitors normally don't give or receive money for staying at Krutsio, but are expected to participate on the same basis as members — although the demands in general are less. 5/8/90

Kuntree Bumpkin

Hickory Farms
9765 Scully Lane
Whitmoor Lake, MI 48189

(313) 449-0001

Confirmed by phone that they'd like to be included in the Directory. If you plan to visit, please give a call first. No further information available. 1/15/90

La Cité Ecologique

(The Ecological City)
Ham-Nord, Quebec
CANADA G0P-1A0

La Cité Ecologique, founded in 1984, is a model society that emphasizes an ecological lifestyle. Over 150 residents enjoy the unspoiled environment of our 800-acre center located in the Bois-Francs region of Quebec. We place a priority on 1) the education of children, 2) the practice of pedagogical principles, 3) the acceptance of self-transformation, 4) keeping har-   mony in family & community, and 5) the finance of all activities. Our approach is a marriage of spiritualism and capitalism, and work is our meditation. Mutual respect and harmony are our basis for individual liberty.

We have 7 legally recognized companies, each with an executive staff and an administrator board. The board of La Cité is, in turn, formed of representatives from each company. These companies include: 1) the Solar Arising Center, a guest facility for visitors and those coming for training; 2) Bio-Solar Farm, which owns the land & buildings, and produces much of the food; 3) the Jivot Research Center, for research in organic agriculture, alternative energy, holistic medicine, etc.; 4) the Communication Jivot, which edited 3 books and 60 one-half-hour programs about La Cité, and which does advertising for each of the other businesses here; 5) Bio-Solar Greenhouse (25 acres), which produces tomatoes, cucumbers, and other organic foods; 6) Bio-Solar Gardens, which manufactures

pies, bread, other foods, and operates a restaurant and market; and 7) Bio-Solar Economical Center, which manages funds for investors. 2/19/89

Lama Foundation

Box 240
San Cristobal, NM 87564

(505) 586-1269 M-F(9-11am)

Lama, founded in 1968, is an ecumenical community located at an elevation of 8600 feet in the wilderness of the northern New Mexico mountains. Lama exists for the purpose of *Awakening Consciousness*. We try to match people with the spiritual practice and/or religion which will deepen the experience of *Reality*. The flavor of our group changes as the group changes — and we allow a maximum continuous residency of seven years.

An Indian saint named Neem Karoli Baba once said *"Love everyone, serve everyone, remember God."* Taking these words to heart, the Lama Foundation is dedicated to service. We serve as 1) a community model — an ongoing experiment in group relationships, right livelihood, and simple living; 2) a school and retreat center — where people come to learn about the deeper aspects of themselves and their relationships with others, with the earth, and with God; and 3) an oasis where people can rest and breathe deeply and reconnect with what is essential.

Lama's cottage industry centers around silk-screened prayer flags from many religious traditions. Hermit huts are available to the public for solo retreats up to two weeks long. New staff are always welcome to help serve our summer programs. The smaller winter community of 14 to 25 members is dedicated to spiritual practice. 5/2/91

Lamborn Valley Community (Forming)

1559 - 4110 Drive
Paonia, CO 81428

Lamborn Valley Community is still in the formulation stage of development. The eight founding members' main focus is spiritual. A major part of community life is work and play with children. We want our children to grow up among us sharing our learning and working. The community's resources include a 120-acre organic farm, 9 dwelling units, a com- munity center, a river, and plenty of irrigation water. Work is scarce and wages are low in the small town of Paonia (one mile away). We are looking for one or two permanent families who share our vision and are willing to work hard to attain it! Please include SASE with inquiries [cc]. 1/2/89

Laurel Hill Plantation (Forming)

1054 Lower Woodville Road
Natchez, MS 39120

Laurel Hill is a "Land Grant" Plantation belonging to Pierce Butler, a descendant of the original recipients of a Spanish Land Grant in Adams County, Mississippi. The 1775 plantation house burned in 1968, but the outbuildings remain and are used. The property includes modern barns, a woodworking shop, a hunting camp, and an 1839 Episcopal Chapel. Most of the 1400 acres is under lease to a hunting club. The main housing area is a mile down a dirt and gravel road.

We are members of the Mississippi Organic Growers Association, but our orchards and vineyards are only family-size, not commercial ventures. There are three large fenced gardens for anyone who wants to try their hand at growing organic vegetables. We enjoy wild pawpaws in August, wild lemons in September, and pecans in October and November.

We would welcome one or two visitors at a time who have the energy and enthusiasm to check out what life in rural Mississippi is all about — but we cannot afford to pay. Visitors should be forewarned that it is *hot* here in the summer, and *cold* in the winter — and that we have neither adequate heating or cooling! Please include SASE with correspondence. 3/12/91

Lavendar House

Milwaukee, WI
See: House of Lavendar

Lichen

P.O. Box 25
Wolf Creek, OR 97497

(503) 866-2665 (7-8am best)

Lichen was established in 1971, and is a community land conservancy/ trust. Our facilities include a community building, four satellite retreats, a lab, sawmill, shop, and garden area. Most of our 140 acres is

devoted to a wildlife refuge and environmental sanctuary. We derive our income from contract services and/or individual home industries — including laboratory work in electronics (non-defense); field recording, editing, and duplicating cassette tapes of nature sounds (especially birdsong); and various craft activities. Agreed-upon expenses for space, utilities, food, taxes, and capital development are shared. The remainder of personal earnings are used at the discretion of the individual. We like a varied diet, mostly vegetarian. We come together for evening meals, work projects, and weekly meetings. Child care, though generally by family/ parent(s), is often shared by others. Visitors are welcome, though it's essential to make advance arrangements. If you'd like to know more about us, please write (we're not likely to respond unless you include some information about yourself) and enclose *at least* an SASE (a dollar or two to cover our expenses would also be appreciated). 5/7/89

Life Center Association

Land Trust
4722 Baltimore Avenue
Philadelphia, PA 19143

Originally started as a support community for MNS (Movement for a New Society), we are now a land trust that owns four cooperative houses with 6 or 7 people each, plus two apartments that each hold one or two people (or possibly a 3-person family in close quarters). We also have a hostel and conference center with three or four long-term residents. Most members are somewhat politically involved. Each house chooses its own members and is fairly autonomous. All major group decisions are made by consensus. 3/27/91

Linnaea Farm

Box 98, Manson's Landing
Cortes Island, B.C.
CANADA V0P-1K0

(604) 935-6370; Fax 935-6424

Linnaea Farm is a land trust under Turtle Island Earth Stewards. The Farm, in part an ecological reserve, encompasses 315 acres of forests, fields, orchards, gardens, and lakefront.

The members of the Linnaea community share a commitment to ecological stewardship of the land and its people. We are responsible for

day-to-day operations, financial matters, and various agricultural and educational projects. Farm decisions are made by the group at weekly meetings.

The community operates much like a village, with separate dwellings for families and single people. Each member is responsible for utilities, upkeep, and a small monthly rent. We earn our own livelihoods, and for the most part this means at least some employment off the Farm. Housing is limited, and we are at current capacity with five dwellings housing 8 adults and 8 children in total.

In accordance with our charter the Farm offers educational outreach programs. These include: • the Ecological Garden Program, an eight-month residential course for up to six adults; • the Linnaea School, an alternative school for island children aged 5 to 11; and • a variety of Summer Workshops, including an annual hands-on Permaculture Workshop.

While not currently seeking new members, we welcome inquiries and visitors (prearranged, please). 4/15/91

Fellowship for Intentional Community

•

Alliance Building Support Services & Referrals for:

• **Intentional Communities**
• **Community Networks**
• **Individuals**
• **Support Organizations**

•

The Fellowship nurtures a sense of connectedness and cooperation among communitarians and their friends ... by providing a forum for sharing among a wide range of intentional communities, networks and support organizations, and people who are seeking a home in community.

See article p. 123; listing p. 267.

N. America

Long Branch Environmental Education Center

Big Sandy Mush Creek Rd.
Route 2, Box 132
Leicester, NC 28748

(704) 683-3662

We are a small group of people who are deeply concerned about the interwoven and accelerating problems of population growth, natural resource depletion, and environmental degradation. We are a community of individuals who have chosen to live cooperatively and steward this land... caring for it in a way that it will be healthy and beautiful for our children's children. We align ourselves with all the groups and centers across the country that are dedicated to helping heal the earth. As our particular focus we have chosen to demonstrate specific, practical strategies by which individuals can simplify their lifestyles and become more self reliant — with organic gardening, ecological agriculture, solar energy, and appropriate technology.

Our land is an ecological sanctuary and land trust, and we have developed a small, hands-on environmental education center. We have staff, interns, and a volunteer program. We are open to the public every Saturday, and frequently offer weekend workshops on a variety of topics including organic gardening, greenhouse design, country crafts, natural cooking, composting toilet systems, natural history, massage, and nutrition. 10/15/89

Los Horcones

Apartado Postal # 372
Hermosillo, Sonora
MEXICO 83000

Los Horcones began in 1973, located on 250 acres in Sonora, Mexico. Our basic objectives are to design a society where members cooperate for a common good, have shared or communal property instead of private property, and promote equality and pacifist solutions to problems (non-violence). Our community is ecologically oriented and tries to become self-sufficient in all areas. We also value community child rearing and education, satisfactory interpersonal relations, and good health.

Life here is experimental, and non-dogmatic. We apply the data obtained from various scientific fields. Our main tool for achieving our objectives is the application of scientific principles derived from the experimental analysis of behavior — used to teach the members communitarian behaviors and to reduce noncommunitarian behaviors.

The community provides all the goods and services needed by our members: kitchen dining room, community living room, private bedrooms, laundry, children's house, school, library, workshops, garden, orchards, and livestock. The way we organize our work changes, always directing itself toward a system that is more satisfying (reinforcing) for all members. Members are sometimes required to do certain jobs, and at other times may choose their own work. We work 6-9 hours daily, giving women and men equal opportunities to choose tasks. We have work managers for each area (agriculture, construction, animals, etc.) within an overall egalitarian government (managers have no special privileges).

We invite others to get to know our community by living with us for a while, but please write ahead to make arrangements. We publish a bimonthly newsletter which is available for $10/year. 12/14/88

Lost Valley Center

81868 Lost Valley Lane
Dexter, OR 97431

(503) 937-3351

Basic ecological principles provide the focus and inspiration for our community... we live in a way that is self-sustaining, yet as abundant as possible in today's world. We all believe very deeply that the Earth needs our conscious effort and healing in order to survive; therefore, one of our primary focuses is to restore the land. Our facilities are presently very moderate, and need to be modified into simpler and more appropriate housing and conference spaces. We are demonstrating and educating others how to make this transition. Also, we are experimenting with energy systems that best conserve our resources.

With over five acres of land devoted to permaculture experiments, we are creating an organic garden that is quite spectacular — beautiful as well as functional. We will cultivate fruit and nut orchards, and grow some grains and hay as well. We feel deeply rooted to this land and want to help restore it to a fertile condition. In acquiring our land we also inherited 50 acres of clear-cut land which we are reforesting with a variety of trees and polycultures... creating a sacred grove.

In addition to being a community, Lost Valley Center is developing many businesses. Our present focus is on organizing a conference and retreat center, food service, and an organic farm. We have facilities here for 150 visitors and 30 residents, plus classroom spaces for seminars. Other projects include Earth Books, One World Family Travel Network, Fresh Wave Productions, a resource library and networking center, audio & visual production, a General Store, and an American Youth Hostel.

At Lost Valley Center we are creating a family that most of us have never before experienced — functional, honest, integral, and concerned with healing. Presently we are nine adults and three children, and are actively seeking new members to make the vision grow. We would like 20 people for the winter season, and 30 for next summer. If you would like to come for a visit, we can arrange for 2-3 days on a work exchange basis. Then, if we all agree, we can offer a 1-3 month trial period. Long-term residency is determined during the trial period. Mail inquiries only, please, and an SASE is requested. 9/15/89

The Love Israel Family

14724 Mattison Road
Arlington, WA 98223

(206) 435-9679

"When the seers come together, then the watchers will see."

Now that we've seen that we are the Family of God, what are we going to make of our relationships?

Now that we've seen that we are eternal beings, what kind of a culture can we create that will last forever?

Now that we know that we are One Person, how do we fit together to fulfill our wholeness?

Now that we can agree that *Love is the Answer*, how can we translate that love into ongoing daily life together, forgiving and remaining loyal to one another?

After 21 years, we continue to address these challenges together: learning, growing closer, overcoming our weaknesses, and carving out a new reality for ourselves and our children.

Inspired by the revelation of Jesus Christ, the Family began gathering around Love Israel in 1968. Currently 85 people are integrating their lives on a 300-acre ranch, 50 miles north of Seattle, Washington. 8/14/89

Madre Grande

Mountain Sanctuary
18372 Highway 94
Dulzura, CA 92017

(619) 468-3810

As a new age monastery, we have monks who are men or women, of any spiritual persuasion, and we only require our members to be working on a positive path to perfection. Individual dedication to our unification varies from annual to life terms and voting rights progress accordingly. Our officials who make the decisions are annually elected and are answerable to the body of monks. Retreat guests take part in community functions according to their abilities and length of residence. Membership in the monastery is not a requirement. We wish to develop a spiritual and meditation retreat facility and a body of monks dedicated to operating and preserving it with representation from as many spiritual paths as we can. Ability to work cooperatively and selflessly are valued above all, but special skills in gardening, building, child care are needed. We raise our own honey, publish our own literature and have monks who are highly skilled in their professional occupations. 11/22/88

Magic, Inc.

P.O. Box 5894
Stanford, CA 94309

(415) 323-7333 / 325-2786

Magic is a non-profit corporation operated entirely by volunteers, heavily supported by gifts and in part by fees for services. The Magic Household is one of several experiments in community sponsored by the corporation, and is home to 8 people active in our work. We live here in intentional community to experiment with lifestyle changes which we perceive to be   steps along the path to peace among humans and harmony with nature. We make little distinction between home and office, work and play.

Since 1979, we have opened the household to more than 400 different overnight guests, and to more than 1,500 different people who came to participate in Magic-sponsored activities. We describe our various activities in terms of four overlapping programs: 1) Ecological Philosophy — using lectures, seminars, and publications to re-examine the concepts of value and purpose; 2) Personal Awareness — offering classes, workshops, and individual counseling in which we examine and alter patterns of everyday life ... like language, eating, movement, planning, and relaxation; 3) Cooperation — sponsoring experiments in intentional community, founding and providing continuing support to a neighborhood association, and offering lectures and workshops about cooperative resolution of conflict; and 4) Environmental Protection — providing a variety of ecosystem protection and restoration services with the dual purpose of caring for the earth and engaging others in doing so. Specific environmental activities include ecological analysis of land use alternatives, urban and rural tree-planting and care, comprehensive urban forest planning, urban forest modeling software, and redesign of street networks to improve safety and comfort in residential neighborhoods.

We enjoy sharing our small home, eating nourishing, tasty food, laughing a lot — and we welcome opportunities to meet new people and to explore how we may interact to mutual benefit. Please enclose an SASE with inquiries; $1 is requested to cover costs. 3/15/91

The Mariposa Group

21450 Chagall Road
Topanga, CA 90290

(818) 340-1146

The Mariposa Group, a Conscious Community: We are creating an environment which promotes more joyful and fulfilling conditions for work, play, and interpersonal relationships. Our emphasis is on fully using the interpersonal support, personal skills, education, financial resources and group energy available to us in a community — such that each of us may achieve our fullest human potential and happiness. We are actively seeking new members who are willing to commit to making themselves, and this community, all that they can be. Send SASE for more information. 1/5/89

Martha's Housing Cooperative

225 Lake Lawn Place
Madison, WI 53703

(608) 256-8476

Martha's Housing Cooperative is one of 8 houses in the Madison Community Co-op. All decisions are made by consensus at the house level, and by majority rule at the board level. Our particular house is a diverse group of 30 workers and students who strive for a high degree of intimacy and involvement with each other.

We are committed to cooperation, consensus, feminism, anti-racism, peace, caring for the environment, and many other issues. Individuals have their own rooms, and share the rest of the house. We share a vegetarian meal every evening, and all interested folks are invited to share our food. We ask a one-year commitment of all new members. Children are welcome. [cc] 1/16/90

Meramec Valley Community Land Trust

Eastern Missouri
(314) 775-2329

We are a new land trust which in June of '88 bought 213 acres along a crystal clear, canoeable tributary of the Meramec River in rural Missouri. We comprise 22 families and individuals who mostly live and work in St. Louis. A few of us have immediate plans to establish homesteads. Many plan to use the land for recreation. We are a diverse group with ecological interests as our common factor. We practice a blend of consensus and majority rule in our decision-making. Membership is currently fully subscribed. We would, however, like to network with other interested investors to try to purchase adjacent land. We hold approximately 50% of our total land for common use and management. The most noteworthy qualities of our community land trust are the harmonious interaction of persons from diverse lifestyles, and the pristine environment, which includes springs, caves, bluffs, creeks, fields and forests. 2/12/89

North American Communities

Metanoia Community

1702 Highway 40 East
St. Marys, GA 31558

(912) 882-4820

Metanoia is a community of resistance on the southern coast of Georgia, near the Trident submarine base there. We've bought land near the base, built a house to establish a permanent peace presence, and keep very busy working to free the world of nuclear weapons in general, and the Trident program in particular.

We demonstrate non-violence as a way of life, through a compassionate and ecologically sensitive lifestyle which affirms life and resists the dehumanizing systems of militarism, racism, sexism, and materialism. We make local presentations, invite neighbors in for open houses, offer workshops, and have made friends with the local Catholic priest and parishioners. We minister to the poor and those who suffer, physically or spiritually, in a spirit of hospitality and support — as space and circumstances allow. 3/5/90

Middle Earth (Forming)

1250 Sullivan Road
West Union, OH 45693

(513) 549-2241

Hi! We are 39 (female) and 50 (male); tall, slender, liberated, even-minded, independent individuals committed to expanded family living, cooperative sharing, peer relationships, and an intentional community-based economy.

After working through the grief we experienced subsequent to the death of one of our original family members, we are looking for a serious persons or persons, who in doing their homework find themselves ready to make a commitment to an expanded family kind of lifestyle. We are looking for A) a couple with or without children, or B) a woman with or without children. Such person(s) would enjoy: 1) a holistic approach to living; 2) a very rural setting; 3) organic farming, gardening, and orchards; 4) self-sufficiency and independence; 5) emotional and sexual intimacy and commitment among adults; 6) hard work, outdoors, animals, plants, and trees; 7) shared parenting (perhaps leading to development of an alternative form of education for children); and 8) the joy of family life, the fun of living, the enrichment of self and of others.

Our house, Middle Earth, is 132 acres of hilly farm land evolving into a self-sufficient homestead. Music, crafts, books, fun, sharing and joy are very much a part of our daily lives. We are located 90 minutes from a major city that offers many cultural/educational opportunities. Our climate is very Midwestern, with all four seasons to enjoy.

Both of us operate from a land trust point of view. Consequently, financial arrangements relative to sharing Middle Earth and our lives as an extended family are negotiable and will evolve as we get to know one another. Interested? Please call or write Dena Morris/Parker Moore at the above address. 1/6/89

Midwest Community (Forming)

c/o Aurora Mendia
& Ray Anderson
P.O. Box 20341
Wichita, KS 67208

(316) 686-7100

Two of us are trying to find other people in Kansas or surrounding states who would like to get together for a couple of days to check each other out as to our compatibility for living and working together in a small (5-7 member), leaderless, urban group. The central purpose of the group is to do everything we can to bring about an alternative social order, one giving top priority to the process that generates ever new levels and dimensions of mutual understanding and appreciation. The group will feature direct communication, giving and receiving feedback, no-lose conflict resolution, and openness to new possibilities of constructive action. Please phone or write if you'd like to join us in a mutual check-out, or would like information about the World Federation of Small Urban Groups. 1/21/90

Monan's Rill

Northern California
(707) 539-9351

Monan's Rill, established in 1973, is an intentional community of 22 people ranging in age from kindergarten to the 70s. We live on 440 acres of beautiful wooded hills about one hour north of San Francisco. Our name comes from a small creek running through the property.

We are committed to helping and encouraging each other as members of our chosen family, and to care for the land together. Some of us are

Quakers, and our business meetings are conducted in the manner of Friends. Decisions are by consensus.

We are a general partnership, and no one holds individual title to houses, land, or improvements. We share the responsibilities of taking care of our large garden and orchard (certified organic), the gravel roads, the water and septic systems, the fencing, the woodcutting, the care of equipment, and the care of animals. We have a variety of occupations including carpentry, nursing, psychotherapy, and teaching. As a group we have no creed, but we all share a concern about the social chaos around us; we each reach out to do what we can.

We do not claim to have a solution to the world's problems — or even our own. We believe we are making steps in the right directions, and we know that good things are happening here. If you reach an answering machine when calling, please leave your address. 5/12/89

The Monarchy of Christania (Forming)

2262 San Marcos Pass
Santa Barbara, CA 93105

(805) 964-3136

Christania is a forming Spiritual Love Community patterned after The Spiritual Love Community at Capernaum Jesus presented to The Jews as their Messiah to show higher human potentials. Members are able to consider themselves God's People by practicing The Golden Rule, giving Good For Evil, going Second Miles to show contempt for persecution, and gain Good Karma necessary for Touch Love that climaxes in healing flows of aura energies, rather than intercourse that wastes them.

Christania's 40 acres is an island surrounded by forest overlooking the Pacific at 12,000 feet, yet only five miles from shopping on a state highway. Water and stone sales provide income, with proven potentials for farming. There are twelve homesites along its mile of roads. Prospective members must be unmarried, and free of obligations to (or so-called "benefits" from) Family, State, or Church. Forcing oneself to give Good for the worst Evils that can be recalled should make intense feelings of love seem less intimidating for non-virgins. Questions will gladly be answered in an SASE, but actual practice of Christian customs and separation from Church People with hopes of salvation after death must precede visits to, or thought of living on, The Land.

Possibility of immortality in this life should soon come clear when one is surrounded by Lovers and feels new strength in his aura he knows delights them. Health and social problems just dissolve, and struggles to pay bills will be a thing of the past. Raising oneself and others to higher levels replaces desires to raise children, and Christania's way of life is a true hope for world peace in the coming Millennium. 12/13/88

Moniteau Farm
The Spiral Inn
Route 1, Box 9
Jamestown, MO 65046
(816) 849-2189 / 849-2587

Moniteau Farm is a macrobiotic homesteading community. 25 private land tracts, one 60-acre community parcel, total 400 acres. Seeking harmony through closer relationship to the land, changing diet and lifestyle with the seasons, growing our own food. Diet centers around grain, vegetables, and beans. No illicit drugs. Extremely unbalanced foods, such as red meat, dairy foods, sugar, chemicalized foods, etc. are avoided.

Most members build their own homes, have home industries, and do cooperative homeschooling. Established in 1980. Landowners Association approves land use. Some tracts still available. Interested visitors are welcome to camp, up to five days. Write for more information. 12/12/88

Montebello Community
74 Montebello
Jamaica Plain, MA 02130

We are a community committed to Evangelical Christianity, with some interest in urban ministry. Members share the household chores, and we each pay $243 per month for rent and food. Decisions are made by a combination of majority rule and consensus, depending on the issue. We are not presently open to new members, but welcome visitors who make arrangements in advance. 2/17/89

Moonridge
Route 1, Box 240
Guysville, OH 45735

The Directory received a postcard from this group stating that "We are an intentional women's community, and wish to be listed." No further information was received. 3/1/89

Morninglory
Route 4
Killaloe, Ontario
CANADA K0J-2A0

Seven children and seven adults live on the land now (six of the kids are home birthed, a practice we highly value). An essential value of our group is respecting the Earth. As an intentional community we seek to preserve and foster the simple way of life, and to protect the land and the wildlife for the enjoyment of future generations.

Organic gardens & orchard. No electricity. Five private all-weather dwellings scattered on 100 stony, hilly, and wooded acres in the foothills overlooking the Bonnechère Valley. Music is highly valued, as is dance. Anyone wanting to visit please write ahead. Yes, we may wish new members. No, we're not quick correspondents —we're child-oriented, and their needs and survival come first. Please include SASE with correspondence. [cc] 2/20/90

Mother Earth Church of Opihihale
Box 172
Honaunau, HI 96726
(808) 328-9267

We are a cooperative community of 7 adults and 4 children living on 9 acres of rainforest on the Kona coast of the island of Hawaii. Rain, mosquitoes, few nearby beaches or jobs, 20 miles from town.

We're planting orchards and gardens, building a community kitchen. Eventually, we'll be making the land available for New Age workshops and spiritual healing retreats to help pay expenses, but for now it all comes out of our pockets.

If you're honest, keep your word, and are willing to do your share; if you enjoy living with a group of people who resolve conflicts as they arise; if the idea of community service appeals to you; drop us a line.

Short-term internships available in landscaping and gardening. Short-term visitor camping space and work trade arrangements available. 12/14/88

Mount Madonna Center
445 Summit Road
Watsonville, CA 95076
(408) 847-0406
722-7175/5983

Mount Madonna Center is a 355-acre intentional community, retreat, and seminar facility developed on a former ranch in the foothills east of Santa Cruz. A public non-profit educational organization, the center teaches adults in programs on personal growth, spiritual pathways, and alternative health sciences —plus the administration of a private school for 109 children from preschool through high school. Groups of up to 300 can be accommodated with programs lasting for a weekend or longer.

The inner life of the center is inspired by its spiritual leader, Baba Hari Dass. It is a home to people on a quest for spiritual and personal enlightenment — individuals of all religions, and of different philosophies. There are daily rigors of rising at early hours, and practicing yoga exercises and meditation.

With major contributions of time and money by members, the center's approximately 30 buildings were paid for pretty much as they were built. Some staff residences are clustered in groups, and others dispersed individually about the acreage. Some people still live in one-room huts. Near the lake are a woodshop and a mechanics' shop. A garden provides vegetables for the center's vegetarian diet, and flowers to beautify the buildings. Five campgrounds provide tent housing in mild weather.

Key staff members pay the same $125 monthly for room and board as other residents who work outside the community. Only the Mount Madonna School teachers are paid salaries — about half of what they could earn in public schools — and they, too, pay if they live at the center.

The 225-member Hanuman Fellowship has the final say, each member having one vote. It elects annually a 10-person board of directors whose members tend to be those really taking responsibility. The board in turn appoints a seven-person administration, on the scene to handle the daily business. That group meets weekly, or more often as circumstances require. Its areas of responsibility are finance, personnel, office, programs, and kitchen. Middle managers are responsible for areas such as landscaping, garden, maintenance, and so on. 3/16/89

N. America

Mountain Grove

Center for New Education
Box 818, 785 Barton Road
Glendale, OR 97442

(503) 832-2871

Our community is small — 4 adults and 2 children — but we've plenty of room to expand with over 400 acres for all of us to share and explore. We are open to anyone who has a willingness to become a part of our lives, with a commitment to strive for better personal relationships, both with themselves and with others. Spiritual growth, honesty, hard work, sharing love and laughter, and an open mind are needed to make our community grow and prosper. People seeking a community are asked to correspond first, so that we may mutually determine compatibility. The next few years will be crucial in involving new energy and focus for our dreams of what can be a reality here. The possibilities here are only as limited as your dreams and commitment. 4/1/90

Murphy Street House

116 Murphy
Grass Valley, CA 95945

(916) 272-4111

We are a core group of four with a large house, a small house, and a vegetable garden on a city lot in a small town. We've had as many as ten on the property. Our purpose is to live cooperatively and ecologically as an intentional family, to celebrate life and love God/Goddess, to support Peace and Social Justice causes, and to support each other in our own unfolding and healing. We have supported an excellent local candidate for congress, organized the local Greenpeace boycott of Burger King, and helped start the Neighborhood Garden Project. Most importantly, we support each other in our emotional healing with unconditional acceptance, and with techniques for mirroring, getting clearer on our contexts, and taking responsibility. Telephone inquiries only. 5/26/89

Namasté Rainbow Living Greens

Route 2, Box 578
Center Barnstead, NH 03225

(603) 776-7776

Namasté Community is not a community yet. A community is where people are attuned to one another, to themselves, and to nature... and where communication from the "heart" flows from a sense of trust and love. Community is hard to actualize in this world of fear, hunger, torment, weapons, greed, and environmental degradation. Green Bio-Community is where groups of best friends bond their lives together to synergize and perfect communication while co-creating green policy, economics, and culture.

Namasté Rainbow 1990 is a living Green bootcamp. From April 1 to November 22 there will be crude camping, permaculture practice, biodome construction, natural living group projects, and harmonious relationships focused on local and global sustainability via lifestyle. Fee is $100/adult; voting members are those who co-participate for at least two weeks and who are active in a personal or group project. 2/23/90

New Covenant Fellowship

13206 Dutch Creek Road
Athens, OH 45701

(614) 592-4605

We are located near Athens, Ohio, the home of Ohio University and a center for alternative lifestyles. We have been active in local movements for peace and social justice.

At the present time our community consists of one family and one single person — and we hope to grow. Our basis is a commitment to following Jesus, seeking to be guided by God's Spirit in everything we do, both in our personal lives and in social action. Our theology is Anabaptist. The major support for the community comes from growing organic vegetables, which we sell at the local farmers market. 1/23/90

New Haven Zen Center

193 Mansfield Street
New Haven, CT 06511

(203) 787-0912

The Directory received a postcard from this group stating their desire to be included. We received no further information. 7/5/89

New Hope

Berea, KY
See: Futures, Inc.

New Jerusalem Community

745 Derby Avenue
Cincinnati, OH 45232

(513) 541-4748

New Jerusalem, established in 1971, is a lay community of 170 adults and 150 children who have chosen to live as neighbors in a working class enclave in Cincinnati. Each Sunday and Wednesday we worship together, and during the rest of the week we seek to live out the Gospel message as extended family to one another and to our other brothers and sisters down the street and around the globe.

We have become aware that dignity is denied to many of those around us, and so we pray and work for justice in many areas. Some of our current involvements include care of Central Americans, for whom we provide a temporary home en route to Canada; housing rehabilitation for the poor; work with youth and the elderly; and work to protect the environment. Over 25% of our annual income is given away to those in need outside the community, and to those laboring for social change.

For our first 15 years we were guided by our charismatic teacher-founder, Richard Rohrer, who discerned a call to move on to another ministry in 1985. The three years after his departure were a time of struggle, soul-searching, and finally renewal — as each of us was asked to re-choose the community and to accept full responsibility for our own lives. We have selected three lay members as a leadership team to help us move ahead. We also rely on the vital assistance of ordained priest-friends (who aren't members of the community), and maintain ties with the Catholic Church.

Our life is rich, full, and challenging... as we try to integrate our personal journeys, families, careers, and community. We are pleased to welcome you, or to serve you however God leads, trusting that God will continue to bless us all with more abundant life. 2/21/90

New Land

Route 1, Box 174-A
Faber, VA 22938

(804) 361-1252

The New Land is an intentional community of individual homesites in a beautiful rural setting, with mountain views, access roads, and a lake, on land shared with the Monroe Institute — a research and educational organization dedicated to the study and development of human consciousness through the use of audio stimulated brain hemispheric synchronization and other scientific techniques. Residents and land-holders who chose to join the New Land come mostly through experience with the Institute. Homes are privately owned, and most members are self-employed (in a wide range of professional fields) or retired. Personal freedom and evolving consciousness are shared values. Occupations, types of homes, and land use are a matter of individual choice (i.e., gardens, greenhouses, horses, llamas, etc). Members get together as desired to share in special projects, social affairs, and spiritual growth. Some homesites are available. 7/25/89

New Meadow Run

Hutterian Society of Brethren
Farmington, PA 15437

(412) 329-8573

Also known as Spring Valley. See main community listing for "Hutterian Brethren." 2/2/89

New Moon

1516 Guerrero
San Francisco, CA 94110

We are a house of communication and child-raising, established in '83, living together happily without a formal structure or community goal. We are presently 10 adults and 2 children, with a woodshop, a library, a free store, and an organic backyard garden. We live in an old Victorian house on a noisy city street, and come together for dinner every night where we share tales of our city adventures. Expenses and chores are shared, and we make group decisions

through a consensus process. We are TV-free, mostly vegetarian and non-smoking. We are very interested in knowing and communicating with other communities. Please write first if you would like to visit. 8/24/89

New Prairie Fellowship

Route 1
Farwell, MN 56327

(612) 283-5849

New Prairie Fellowship is a community of 2 families; a third family is living in community as guests at the present.

The community began in 1981 arising out of a commitment to living an alternative lifestyle based on Christ's teachings concerning love, peace, justice, and non-violence. Our lifestyle emphasizes cooperation and active, mutual support (economic, spiritual, and emotional) among the members and for those around us.

We are located on 10 acres of land in West Central Minnesota and are concerned about the care and nurturing of the earth as well as of human relationships. We grow as much of our food as possible, all organically. We have built three homes for the community and guests - each building incorporating as much recycled material as possible; all dwellings are heated by wood heat.

Income is generated both inside and outside of the community and all is shared. During the week (Monday-Friday) we share communal evening meals; weekend meals are family-centered.

Our goals as a community are to continue to discover ways in which we can care for and nurture our relationships with god, one another, and all people. Our hope is to enrich and enhance life through sharing and service. Visitors and those just traveling in the area are welcome to come and stay with us. 12/12/88

New Vrindaban

(League of Devotees)
Route 1, Box 320
Moundsville, WV 26041

(304) 843-1600 / 845-2290

New Vrindaban is the headquarters of the League of Devotees, an international interfaith organization whose goal is to establish a God-centered human society. Founded in 1968 in the Appalachian foothills, New Vrindaban now covers 5,000

acres, and has 500 residents, a school system, a cow-protection program, and one of the largest dairy herds in West Virginia. The community features West Virginia's second-largest tourist attraction, Prabhupada's Palace of Gold, now hailed as "America's Taj Mahal."

All activities within the community are directed for the pleasure of the Supreme Lord, Sri Krishna, under the auspices of His Divine Grace Srila Bhaktipada. Visitors are welcome — indeed, all are invited to "experience the heavenly life — even on earth." Special festivals, which include outdoor drama, fireworks, huge feasts, and special speakers, are on Memorial Day weekends, Fourth of July weekends, and Labor Day weekends. Guest rooms are available year-round with advance reservations.

For those who want to make this lifestyle theirs, all necessities are provided with the understanding that one must adhere to four basic principles of morality: no intoxication, no illicit sex, no gambling, and no meat-eating or hunting.

New Vrindaban residents are currently constructing a 300-acre City of God that will give spiritual shelter to people of all faiths. It will be able to accommodate 12,000 persons. Proposed completion date is the year 2000. 12/14/88 [Ed Note: New Vrindaban has been at the center of a nationally publicized court case. Swami Bhaktipada was recently convicted of racketeering and mail fraud, and is now serving a 90-year prison term. Community members maintain that Bhaktipada is the victim of religious persecution — that he is being held accountable for the actions of a few disloyal followers — and are now working to raise the funds necessary for an appeal. — 5/1/91]

Northeon Forest

Route 4, Box 517
Easton, PA 18042

(215) 258-9559

10200 N. Camino Valdeflores
Tucson AZ 85737

(602) 742-7445

Founded on a tree farm in Pennsylvania by an architect named Beidler, The Search at Northeon Forest now has adherents worldwide. The underlying philosophy reflects the ideas of Gurdjieff integrated with the ideas of anagogic adepts in Middle and Eastern Asia. A core of hardy seekers presently live in the colonial buildings at the edge of the forest. Assisted by a growing number of adherents, they maintain the dynamics found

Northeon Forest *(Cont'd.)*

stimulating for individual research beyond conventional expectations. Adherents are scattered in small bands and include farmers, janitors, Buddhists, Christians, doctors, Jews, waiters, architects, teachers, nurses, entrepreneurs, engineers, musicians, journalists, artists, writers, officials, taxi drivers, dish washers, salesmen, horse trainers, ministers, etc. Seeking an awareness of their own significance in a cosmic order, they embark on an exploratory inner journey and begin to contend with what they find.

Gradually they reach a deeper participation in a transformation from what is found to be largely an involuntary life-denying reality, to a life-affirming attitude of involvement. The recommended practices tend to upset complacency, and make adherents more aware of their actual condition. Seekers need the support of their co-seekers ... the Search attracts those who find that they must look for truth within themselves, without overt distortion from the normal context of their daily lives. 4/24/89

Oak Grove (Forming)
Route 1, Box 455
Round Hill, VA 22141

Oak Grove is an old 18th century mountain farm on the edge of the Blue Ridge Mountains, 60 miles from Washington, DC. The community, just beginning, will soon need experienced person(s) with some professional experience in the fields of either orcharding (fruits and nuts) or house building — to help develop a small community of three or four projected households.

Part of the community's emphasis will be on the development of a center for more simple living, in harmony with nature, with a spiritual orientation. Small conferences and workshops have already been taking place in the summer. At this very beginning stage, Oak Grove consists of one writer (a Quaker) and one medium-sized passive solar house. Please include an SASE with inquiries, and include a description of yourself, goals, and experience with orchards and building. 3/31/89

Oakwood Farm
Route 1, Box 659
Selma, IN 47383
(317) 282-2024 / 282-0484

Oakwood Farm is a place of stillness set in verdant, central Indiana. The farm setting has a serene and wholesome atmosphere where 30 individuals, aging in range from 3 to 74, practice the daily "art of living" through spiritual expression. "Let our hearts rest, all is well, trusting Life to govern all things" is the approach experienced in the kitchen, in the garden, on the farm, and in our friendships.

Oakwood Farm is a member of The Stewardship Community and is a practicing organic grower. There are a number of homes and a community building located on the 326 acres of farm land and woods. Oakwood Farm is located one hour northeast of Indianapolis.

Oakwood Farm is an Emissaries of Divine Light community and serves as the Emissary Midwest Headquarters. Individuals living at Oakwood are actively dedicated to the purpose of the spiritual regeneration of mankind. Those who resonate with this central purpose may want to visit.

Visits may be arranged by contacting Daryl Petersen. See main listing under Emissaries of Divine Light. 11/5/89

Ojai Foundation
Box 1620
Ojai, CA 93023
(805) 646-8343 office
646-0902 kitchen

The Ojai Foundation is a non-sectarian educational and retreat center located 95 miles northwest of Los Angeles on 40 acres of ancient Chumash Indian grounds. We bring together leading teachers from all over the world — from many different spiritual traditions, scholarly disciplines, and artistic pathways — to participate in interdisciplinary and intercultural dialogue, explore social and environmental issues, lead vision quests, and engage in individual and group practice. In 1987 we established the Foundation School, which works with the basic view that to educate ourselves means to understand deeply our own lives and the world around us, and to recognize our undeniable relationship to all living things.

The community itself has been comprised of some 15-18 core staff

members who live in yurts or tipis, with a very simple lifestyle. Due to recent interactions with county officials, we are in transition to a smaller staff (perhaps six people) living together in a caretakers' home we will build on the land; we are now engaged in related planning and fund raising activities. We are also planning to construct 10 to 15 canvas domes which will be used as hermitages for solitary retreats (easier to bring up to code than tipis or yurts). Our main continuing programs will be the solitary retreats and our youth programs (coordinated with several private high schools in the L.A. area). We are also contemplating becoming a university without walls — holding accredited workshops in rented facilities. Please call for more information and our catalog of programs. 4/15/91

Ojito
Box 152
Velarde, NM 87582

Ojito (pronounced "Ohito") at this stage is essentially a "place" with potential. Primitive and remote, it is capable of nurturing a small, earth-rhythm, cooperatively oriented tribe. Self esteem and individual spirituality with the space to evolve are possible group values.

We have offered seven-month internships for several years — a seasonal experiment in cooperative living. At this point we hope to chose a core group of summer/winter residents (potential co-owners/co-leasers) based on compatability evaluations of fellow participants involved in the spring work camp (May 1st-15th).

Our 20 acres are beautiful, and include rich earth, dwellings, vegetable gardens, orchards, a vineyard, and a field for small grain experiments. Often our 5-mile dirt access road requires four-wheel drive during the rainy season.

When corresponding please express your needs and expectations, and describe how you feel you could contribute. If you would like photos of the farm, please enclose $5. 3/22/91

Old McCauley Farm
Route 1, Box 1400
Lopez Island, WA 98261
(206) 468-2696

Old McCauley Farm, established in 1975, is presently full with 15 adults and 8 children (under 18) living on the farm. A membership share is 1/15th of the cost of the land, half the cost of all community improvements to date, plus the cost of the member's home. We use the original farmhouse and buildings communally, and each family unit has been built by members. There is a community fee of $25 per month, and each member is expected to regularly contribute labor to the group. We are not all the same in any way, nor do we want to be — we all expect to change. Our Owners' Agreement (legal) is what holds our cooperative together through its changes and through our changes as individuals. 12/13/88

Open Door Community
910 Ponce de Leon Avenue NE
Atlanta, GA 30306
(404) 874-9652 / 876-6977

The Open Door Community is a residential Christian community which shares life with the homeless and hungry and those in prison, especially those under the sentence of death. We live together to enable our work for justice and righteousness rooted in the non-violent love of the Cross. We struggle to resist the idols of money, power, violence, sexism, racism, death, war, and the self. We share worship, work, parenting, visiting, playing, meals, friendship, and study.

Everyone participates in daily decisions; our leadership team (members with lifetime commitments) makes financial and policy decisions. Our ministries include permanent housing for 30, twice-daily soup kitchens, showers and clothing, visitations and letter writing to prisoners, anti-death-penalty advocacy, advocacy for the homeless, medical services, free eye exams, a "Hospitality" newsletter, daily worship, weekly Eucharist, and Bible study. Members are expected to *not* earn any income. Visitors are limited to a one-month stay. 1/20/90

Open House Community
Lake Charles, LA
See: Holy City Community

Order Ecumenical
Institute of Cultural Affairs
4220 N. 25th Street
Phoenix, AZ 85016
(602) 468-0605

Order Ecumenical, part of the international ICA network (see main entry in Late Entries), owns three adjacent apartment buildings in Phoenix. Two of the 18 apartment units are used as office space, with plans to expand to 40 units in 1992. Our residents include 14 adult members and 7 children. Group decisions are made by consensus, with power shared equally among the membership. After 30 years of income sharing, the Order is moving toward more cooperative financing by resident members, and adding a new non-resident category of membership to encourage growth. 3/30/91

Organic Kauai Produce (Forming)
George & Anna Hadley
Box 1613
Kapaa, HI 96742

A community of Light is forming on the beautiful garden island of Kauai. It will use biodynamic sustainable agricultural methods supporting a natural health and education research center that will foster a joyous expression in art, music, dance, and creative crafts.

Children will be home schooled, and all decisions will be made by consensus. We are a group of egalitarian, spiritually eclectic individuals aware of our co-creative abilities and responsibilities.

The emphasis of living at the community will be — "simply". The emphasis on diet will be — "lightness". The land will be held in trust, supported financially by on-site cottage industries, a vegetarian restaurant, organic farming, and various human services that promote self-awareness and self-healing. Other interests include communication, consciousness, ecology and environment, energy alternatives, consumer and worker and housing co-ops, networking and referrals, and Utopianism.

We will live and work in harmony with ourselves, each other, and God. There will be various entry levels for members, and no one will be turned away who is willing to work for the benefit of all. Write for more information, and please include an SASE. 10/1/89

Our Land Cooperating Community
P.O. Box 185
El Nido, CA 95317
(209) 383-2690

Our Land Cooperating Community is dedicated to humanitarian socioeconomic development. We are in need of socially responsible, liberated activists to increase our capacity to utilize many worthy opportunities. We currently have projects in the United States, Mexico, and Vietnam.

Our lifestyle is kibbutz type. The goal is to develop an efficient, positive way of life, motivated by love and vision, capable of competing successfully against wasteful socio-economic systems based on alienation and exploitation. Some participants have developed parallel partnerships as a result of a commitment to going beyond culturally-induced neurotic patterns. In addition to providing positive role models, we seek to apply technology appropriately for the benefit of nature — including humanity.

Our personal relationships should rationally be the result of our applied philosophies. Liberation is to be free from ignorance, fabricated restraints, and imposed limitations — not to be exploited, and not to exploit. With love as the basic building block, humanity thrives. Let us put our lives together in an effective cooperating community and expand our human potential.

We encourage you to contact us, regardless of your present status. We desire to create intentional communities that are happy, healthy, worthy environments — to assist us in fulfilling humanity's individual and collective potential. Creative, productive struggle will help to bring the dream of a better world into reality. 6/13/89

North American Communities

Owl Farm

P.O.Box 133
Days Creek, OR 97429

(503) 679-3266

Women need to have time, space, and resources to develop their own culture. We are feminists working against racism, ageism, classism, and we share our love for Mother Earth. Our land is owned by the Oregon Women's Land Trust (see Resource listing). Payments for this land come from contributions by women across the country, often in the form of monthly pledges. Policy on the farm is decided by the women who live here. Women and children can visit and/or live. Limited housing and ample camping space are available. Visits and inquiries are welcome. Send an SASE with all correspondence, please. 1/7/89

Ozone House

1209 Villa Street
Mountain View, CA 94041

(415) 964-1468

Ozone House started as a bunch of friends, mostly in their early to mid-twenties, who thought it would be economical — and fun — to live together. So in 1985 we rented a house together and began sharing meals, chores, and the ambiance of an extended family. As our incomes increased (most of us work in the computer industry) we decided to buy a house together — even though most of us could, at that point, easily afford to live alone somewhere.

We have developed a rather elaborate ownership structure where everyone has an equal vote, but with widely varying equity positions based on individual incomes and preferences. We have also developed what amounts to a sliding scale "rent" which covers the monthly operating and maintenance costs, and a buy-out scheme that protects the house from a financial catastrophe should someone leave holding a sizable investment.

But the essence of Ozone is not the financial structure, it's still the family environment and the sense of commitment. We get a lot of nurturing and mutual support from this arrangement, and also enjoy frequent outings, shared dinners most evenings, and a diverse network of friends. 1/17/90

Padanaram Settlement

Route 1, Box 478
Williams, IN 47470

(812) 388-5571

Padanaram Settlement, established in 1966, is a spiritually oriented community of individuals. It operates its own schools, kitchen, bakery, and craft shops. The economic base is sawmilling, log cabin construction, and compost and bark mulch companies. We are not affiliated with any one group, but seek friends among other communities. We envision the ICU, an International Communal Utopia made up of a network of smaller communities. We hold bi-annual conventions, and an open house yearly during mid-October. For more information write Attn: Rachel Summerton. 11/12/89

Panhandle Permaculture Group

P.O. Box 248
Bushland, TX 79012

(806) 426-3393

The people who formed the Panhandle Permaculture Group live and work in a rural village west of Amarillo, Texas. We began in March of '88 with 8 adults and 4 children as resident members of the community Sunat Center. Together we have increased our involvement in alternative technology and group process. Seven adults now manage and staff the non-profit Permaculture corporation. Our purposes are to develop, demonstrate, and teach principles of functional design and sustainable agriculture in the Panhandle region of Texas and in similar bioregions.

We have a variety of concerns which increases our need for group purpose and definition. Community members are working with the consolidation of the theories and strategies of permaculture, and a substantial number of permaculture projects are in progress on over 20 acres of prairie land bordering the Canadian River breaks. Folks who

would be interested in interning with us could, for example, be involved in building their own shelter from indigenous materials. We welcome any serious inquiries. Please prearrange visits, and enclose SASE with correspondence. 11/21/89

Patchwork Central

100 Washington
Evansville, IN 47713

(812) 424-2735

Patchwork Central is a Christian community located in the central city of Evansville, Indiana. It is a gathering of about 20 persons whose primary focus is urban ministry. We use a consensus style of making decisions, and a shared leadership administration. The common life of the community centers around worship on Sunday evenings, followed by a shared meal; other regular parts of the common life are a community meal on Thursday evenings, morning prayers, meetings, occasional study groups, task-related events, and celebrations. There are specific ministries which the community supports — an economic development center, a children's program, and a food pantry — as well as a strong participation in the life of the neighborhood and an open door for people with individual concerns. There is a lively sense of the importance of being in mission, of developing one's own life of faith, and of pursuing the path of peace with each other and for the world.

People at Patchwork Central must be self-supporting. Some of the members do specific work for the community and receive salary, but many members work outside the community. Several people live within the neighborhood, others live in various parts of Evansville. There are single and married, young and old, male and female. Though the life of faith in God is important, there is a wide tolerance for the paths of beliefs. [cc] 1/29/90

Peace Farm

HCR 2, Box 25
Panhandle, TX 79068

(806) 335-1715

The Peace Farm is a 20-acre farm located across from the rail exit of the nuclear train at Pantex — the United States' nuclear weapons assembly plant. The Peace Farm's mission is to create an environment for peace through peaceful means, to assert that peace can exist only where there is justice, and to develop an ecological model for non-violent social change. Subscriptions are $5/year for their bimonthly newsletter, *The Advocate*. 1/25/90

Peace Gardens

484 - 36th Street
Oakland, CA 94609

(415) 652-0598

Peace Gardens was made into a land trust through the cooperative willingness of the property owner and the residents living there at the time, and is now owned by the Northern California Land Trust. Lovely gardens had been and still remain an important part of the residence — providing herbs, flowers, and vegetables (to a small extent) in the summer. Located near downtown Oakland, a freeway, and a major avenue, this landscape gives a much-needed sense of serenity and view of greenery.

Half of our 8 adult members have lived at Peace Gardens for most of the past five years, and others have come and gone. We request a minimum of a year's stay. Our adult members are presently earning income from part-time outside jobs. Two of us women have one child each (a girl three years old; a boy of six) and both work in the field of child development. Residents share a commitment to sanctuary for Latin Americans, and some members do volunteer work for this cause. One of our units has been set aside for Spanish-speaking friends. Please enclose an SASE with correspondence [cc]. 1/26/90

Penny Royal Education Center

Floyd, VA
See: Winged Heart Homestead

Phoenix Community

257 Wetherly Drive
Beverly Hills, CA 90211

(213) 275-3730

Phoenix, our group marriage, is based on deep and intense love. We reach casual levels of mind and reality together, and discover and mediate awesome psychospiritual phenomena, processes, and energies —

including archetypes, Kundalini, and mind fusion. Our vision is to share these with many others for healing, growth and transformation ... and for planetary survival and wellbeing.

We are unabashedly serious, bright, upscale, urban and competent. Our work is primary ... but we also jog, ski, and backpack. We're non-smokers, moderately health-oriented, and intensely heterosexual — fidelitous to each other (polyfidelity). Now two women (37 & 50) and one man (49), we welcome visits from like-minded potential new members (temporary or permanent) and people desiring intense psycho-spiritual work. We expect ourselves and all visitors to open the heart level and to put aside all personal defenses. Mail inquiries only — and if you write, tell us about yourself. 8/20/89

The Planetary Project Foundation (Forming)

Route 5, Box 53-A
Newton, KS 67114

(316) 799-2837

The intent of the Planetary Project Foundation is to provide an environment which nurtures the essential spirituality within the individual, integrating it into daily activities and cooperative living. A site of 100 acres is being developed as a sanctuary in rural Harvey County, Kansas. Through group process we have designed a central gathering/living structure which is currently under construction. Our general goals include: 1) to serve as a sanctuary for the communion of all life; 2) to develop a small community dedicated to serving the goals of the project; 3) to establish an experimental/spiritual center for holistic living and the integration of body-mind-spirit; 4) to experience co-creative learning of the principles of ecology, bioregionalism, and permaculture; 5) to share information gained in the development of the project; and 6) to serve as a place of connection for individuals who are working as planetary healers.

The way of the Project is to experience the reverence with all of life, and to feel the common union with nature, each other, and the essence of life itself. All decisions are made through the process of "attunement" and consensus. 8/28/89

Pleasant View

Hutterian Brethren
300 Rosenthal Lane
Ulster Park, NY 12487

(914) 339-6680

See main listing under "Hutterian Brethren." 3/21/91

Plow Creek Fellowship

Route 2, Box 157
Tiskilwa, IL 61368

(815) 646-4264

Plow Creek Fellowship, an intentional community established in 1971, is a congregation of Christians who have joined their lives together in a common search for the Kingdom of God. The home base of this intentional community is a 189-acre farm located in the north-central part of Illinois. Members come from various denominational backgrounds and from various parts of the country. The Fellowship is affiliated with the Mennonite church. Members make a commitment to Jesus as Lord, pacifism, fidelity in marriage and chastity outside of marriage, consensus decision-making, and a communal economic life.

There are 30-plus adult members ranging in age from early 30s to early 60s, and over 35 children. Most children attend public school, though some are being home schooled. Fellowship life is supported by a number of Fellowship-owned businesses (vinyl repair, a medical clinic, a building crew, a law office, and others) and by some members who work at outside jobs. Other major activities in our lives include gardening, raising cattle and sheep, woodcutting, food preserving, and operating a U-pick berry operation.

We worship together on Sunday mornings, have common meals twice a week, meet in weekly sharing groups, have a weekly full members' meeting, and regularly schedule fun events together. We get together Saturday mornings for various work projects. We have been involved in several different ministries such as the Overground Railroad (hosting refugees), assisting dysfunctional families, care of individuals having trouble adjusting to their life situations, and support and care for workers in other countries (to name a few). We welcome anyone who would like to come visit with us for a short or longer period of time! 12/20/88

Information is current to date printed at end of each listing.

N. America

Ponderosa Village

203 Golden Pine
Goldendale, WA 98620

(509) 773-3902

We are deeply involved in a most interesting and demanding adventure — creating a satisfying place to live! We are located on a 1000-acre property in south-central Washington State. The concepts behind the village are self-reliance, freedom, voluntary cooperation, personal growth, a place of security in case of serious problems — economic, war, whatever. Land, houses, gardens are individually owned. Living and gardening with nature are encouraged. 51 people live here now, all ages, many backgrounds. We started eight years ago. Visitors are welcome any time – a call beforehand is appreciated. Camping area available. We offer self-reliance seminars in summer. 12/14/88

Prag House

Seattle, WA
(206) 329-0922

The Prag House is an urban collective residing within a turn-of-the-century Gothic Colonial mansion on Capitol Hill. It was purchased in 1972 by a community of graduate students and professors who saw it as a way to continue their pro-peace and environmental work in a mutually supportive social environment. Title to the property is held by the Evergreen Land Trust [see Resources listing].

Members are involved in promoting peace in Central America, supporting local democratic issues, and pursuing more personal interests. Individual house members host numerous fund-raisers and meetings of the broader alternatives community. 2/21/90

Providence Zen Center

528 Pound Road
Cumberland, RI 02864

(401) 658-1464

Providence Zen Center is a community of Zen meditation practitioners with a lay residential facility located on 50 wooded acres in southern New England. About one in ten members lives in residence, participating in an ongoing process of Zen meditation under Guiding Teacher Jacob Pearl, JDPSN. Residents organize and join in public programs including twice-daily meditation practice, monthly retreats, meditation instruction, talks and tours, introductory workshops, and an annual Summer Training Period. Most residents hold jobs in the outside community and pay training fees to live at the center. There are also staff scholarships available for limited periods, trading work for the training fees. No paid jobs are available. All residents participate in "together action" by contributing energy to the preparation of community meals, and to the cleaning and maintenance of the household. A complete package of information about our programs and residencies is sent upon request; visitors are welcome for scheduled public programs only. 1/26/90

Prudence Crandall House

Oakland, CA
(415) 652-7600

The Prudence Crandall House is a long-term (17 years for two of the original three, 12 years for a third one) intergenerational (ages 45 to 72) collective house of three independent women. We are all in different fields of work, and have a mutual interest in each others' activities. What we all share is deep concern for peace, ecology, feminism, and justice.

Sounds pretty serious? We also do fun things like sharing meals and outings, taking a winter vacation, celebrating our birthdays, and being owned by three cats.

We own our lovely 80-year-old house and garden, and share large expenses based on income. Each one has a bedroom and a work room or office, and the common space gets decorated on a revolving basis. No, we don't all have the same taste — but it works! A short summary of our communal living might be: a combination of any desired privacy, and near familial cooperation.

Who is Prudence Crandall? A teacher, white, who before the Civil War illegally admitted black students to her school. 8/10/89

Purple Rose

1531 Fulton Street
San Francisco, CA 94117

Purple Rose is an active collective household. We take our collectivity seriously — but also enjoy our playtime together, and the closeness that the whole experience brings about.

Collectively owning our old Victorian house means freedom from landlord-imposed restrictions, but also means more responsibility for maintenance. (Two previous housemates are on the title as a matter of form, but they don't "own" the house.)

Most evenings we share family-style dinners, which are primarily vegetarian. We also value being very open and direct — talking a lot with each other in a very personal way, about very personal things. Some of this happens at our weekly house meetings.

Presently we have 10 members who can only be classified politically as independents — though we lean towards working for a better life for all people, not just a favored few. We are avid recyclers, do our best to maintain the planet, and use organic products when feasible. We feel we are working for the future in the present time. Please include an SASE with inquiries. 4/15/90

Rainbow Farm

Selma, IN
See: Oakwood Farm

Rainbow House

1115 Tennessee
Lawrence, KS 66044

(913) 843-3704

The Rainbow House is a cooperative consisting of 10 women and men who are interested in using creative ideas to maintain a peaceful and enjoyable living situation. We share the responsibilities of the House's operation — from housework, to decision-making on house policy. There is no manager, and no leader. We are a group of equals working for ourselves and for each other.

We have a magnificent old house in Lawrence, Kansas, which has (among other things) a solar greenhouse and a huge organic garden. Everyone at the house has his/her own room; we share a living room, dining room, kitchen, bathrooms and workshop. Although we require group interaction to function, the house is large enough to afford each person the privacy he/she needs.

House members devote some time each week to the House's operation. This includes a weekly house meeting, some housework, and an occasional fix-up project. We feel that the time spent is well worth the benefits of living in such a fun and enjoyable place. 1/4/90

Rainbow Junction (Forming)

Box 291
Adin, CA 96006

Rainbow Junction is an alternative community now forming in Northern California's Modoc County. A 40-acre community of adventuresome and resourceful-minded individuals, we will begin our "official" status as a community when 2-3 community members begin to lay out and assess the potential of Rainbow Junction as a viable community site. The land is at an elevation of about 4225 feet, with water abundantly supplied by springs. It slopes to some degree, and at present the only vegetation is a form of sagebrush. Animal life includes deer, antelope, coyote, and an assortment of large birds. It had originally been intended that Rainbow Junction be a community of bus people, but incoming members have expressed an interest in more conventional housing. We hope to grow not only in numbers but in size, and our end goal is as a private township. *Positive* Rainbow energy needed! We are currently looking for a membership of at least 50 people. We would like to stress that we are looking only for people desiring a drug-, alcohol-, and violence-free environment. 1/29/89

Rainbow Valley

Agricultural Cooperative
Route 2, Box 28
Sanger, TX 76266

(817) 458-5122

We are an alternate lifestyle/appropriate technology type of community, structured as an agricultural cooperative occupying a 224-acre valley east of Sanger, Texas. All members hold in common about 120 acres of bottom land, creeks, plains, and deep woods. The remaining 90-95 acres are divided into homesites ranging in size from 1 acre to 4 acres. There are a dozen owner-built structures on our land — a few wooden homes, but mostly earth-sheltered ferro-cement

domes. We have our own well, and water is available from our own water cooperative. Telephone lines have been brought into the valley (underground) but *no power lines.* Our goal is to be a totally energy self-sufficient community. Our charter prohibits connections to the nuclear grid. Each member is responsible for his/her own power needs (photovoltaics, wind generators, or gasoline-powered generators).

We want to enable individual freedom, privacy, and self-determination to the greatest extent possible. At the same time we intend to create a community of cooperative work and play. We are looking for new members — not unannounced drop-in visitors — but serious, mature persons who want to join as equal members in our community. Mail inquiries only, and please include SASE. 9/26/89

Raj-Yoga Math and Retreat

Box 547
Deming, WA 98244

Founded in 1974 with one Guru, one caretaker, and six students. *Purpose:* to provide a self-sufficient consciousness-liberating Chakra in which individuals spiritually grow away from self-orientation, toward a deep and total purification (not just healing). To return to God's Dharma and give all the brothers and sisters needed Divine Guidance — Bodhisattvas and Divine Mothers. The methods are Kriya-Kundalini Yoga, taught and lived within a Vedantic framework and lifestyle of surrendering to the One in the All.

Hopes: To be more self-sufficient through earthworm farming, and relevant to those seeking a new start in this lifetime. Dreams: Total purification of this tired, dross-laden earth of what we call "our world," into a new spiritually-oriented civilization open to Divine Direction and Guidance. Environment: Located at the base of Mt. Baker's foothills among tall cedars, spruce, alders, pine, and vine maple trees. Cold streams flow quietly into the nearby Nooksack River.

Government: By Guru compassion and guidance. *Visiting Policy:* Write a long letter, no drop-ins please. *New Members:* Only after completing a three-month retreat intensive within the Guru's Fire. Then as a semi-hermit without social, interpersonal interaction, and reinforcing goodies. Five years of prior spiritual

training required. Mail inquiries only, and please enclose SASE. 1/12/89

Raven Rocks

Southeastern Ohio

Raven Rocks is a small rural project in the northern edge of Ohio Appalachia. Begun in 1970 with 19 members, it is probably best described as a community of purpose, brought together and held together by common values and goals which have found focus in the effort to pay for, restore, and set aside for permanent preservation what are now more than 1,000 acres of hill and ravine lands. The original environmental concern, to rescue the property from strip mining for coal, has grown to include a variety of member-financed projects. These include several structures, above and underground, that utilize a wide range of conservation techniques and solar strategies. The larger of two underground buildings was designed for public demonstration, and will incorporate seven solar strategies in one structure. Also part of this demonstration will be a bio-intensive garden. All agricultural projects — beginning with the Christmas tree operation, and including a small grassfed cattle project and gardens at all the homes — have been organic since the initial purchase. Most of the Raven Rocks acres have been set aside for natural restoration of the hardwood forest that is native to the area. The entire property, including the homes and other improvements, is designed as permanent preserve, and hence not available for sale or development.

Of the 11 current members, ten are from the original group. Members earn their own livings, then volunteer the time required (about 7,000 hours annually) to raise Christmas trees that pay for the land, and to do the work of the corporation, which was set up as legal owner.

Education — or re-education, for those of us who are adults — has been a fundamental interest of this group. Most of our efforts, therefore, have an educational intent — whether to educate ourselves or others. We are striving to get more of our multi-faceted public statement and demonstration into place, and fear that the effort could be jeopardized by too much premature publicity and traffic. Hence, for the immediate future we are withholding phone number and information about location. 4/27/91

N. America

Reba Place Fellowship

727 Reba Place
Evanston, IL 60202
(708) 328-6066 (8am-5pm)

Reba Place Fellowship was established in 1957 in Evanston, Illinois, just north of Chicago. Our basis for membership is that this is a Christian lay community: we support each other, and those in need, in all aspects of living a "whole" life. We are associated with both the Mennonite Church and the Church of the Brethren, although in practice we are ecumenical.

We have about 60 adult members and 35 children living in the Fellowship's 40 residences. This includes both families and singles, with some shared living households. Our diet varies from one subgroup to the next, and a majority of us are vegetarians. We practice total income-sharing at the community level. Some members have outside careers, but their income goes into the common fund.

Ministries include shelter for the homeless, work with refugees from Cambodia and Central America, low-income housing, many types of personal counseling, a peace witness program, and others.

Anyone who embraces this lifestyle and wants to participate is welcome. Please write if you'd like more information. Written inquiries preferred. 4/13/90

ReCreation Center

P.O. Box 1653
Pahoa, HI 96778
(808) 965-7880

The ReCreation Center is situated on a 5-acre solar farm with pond. We've been here in Hawaii for three years now, and have an exotic fruit tree orchard which provides our primary food: bananas, macadamia nuts, breadfruit, coconuts, limes, avocados, and pomelos. We also have taro and garden vegetables, and are developing a nursery and seedling business. We have a 5-bedroom home with three cabins which allow us to accommodate bed-and-breakfast guests on a nightly, weekly, or monthly basis; we accept tourists and those who are interested in the research we have completed on water therapy and water birthing.

Three of our four children were born in a water bath. Our 8-year-old's birth was documented in Karil Daniel's award-winning videotape *"Waterbaby: Experiences of Water-*

birth." We have available a library of books, tapes, and resources — as well as the 100-page *ReCreation* by Marilyn Rodgers (one of our founding members).

We use Montessori home-style teaching for our children, and encourage (but don't require) personal Bible studies for full-time residents. We have enough land to sublease half of our beautiful Hawaiian island paradise ... near natural warm ponds, steam vents, and the ocean. We also provide office space for the Allright Family Band, the *Entertainer News* and Network, and a recording studio which offers video and audio opportunities. 2/1/90

Reevis Mountain School of Self-Reliance

HC02, Box 1534
Roosevelt, AZ 85545

(602)467-2536

We are a New Age, vegetarian, self-reliant community and school. We are dedicated to teaching native herbology, outdoor self-reliance skills, natural healing and health, metaphysical philosophy, compassion for the Earth and the family of humankind. We are open to new members, including children, but prospective members must be like-minded and should first communicate by mail. Write for a free brochure of our weekend and week-long classes. [cc] 7/15/90

Reina del Cielo

Route 4, Box 123
Lexington, VA 24450
(703) 261-1219

Reina del Cielo (Queen of Heaven), was founded in 1972 in Louisiana. Our community now numbers 16 adults, including 5 ministers and 8 children. Reina del Cielo was established to provide a spiritual atmosphere for the study of ancient wisdom as revealed through the Una Kenya Mystery School ... a continuation of the ancient wisdom as brought to earth by the sons of God. It has continued through the ages in a direct link through its initiates who are keepers of the ark of the covenant. While the community has always been open to public view, the School itself operated under the hermetic seal of silence until recently. Now we feel that contact with other groups is an important part of our mission; so we offer lectures and classes to the public.

Our community is a living experiment where families live, work, and pray together. We govern ourselves by an elected board of officers, from among our Church organization, under the guidance of our Minister and Church Board. Our whole structure is based upon "Love is the fulfilling of the Law." We study the ancient scriptures, and teachings of all ages and cultures. We follow the teachings of the Christ, and work toward the day when that Love will manifest throughout the earth. 2/18/90

The Renaissance Community

Box 272
Turners Falls, MA 01376
(413) 863-9711

The Renaissance Community, founded in 1967, has over 100 members, roughly two-thirds adults and one-third children. Our intent is to foster personal growth, creative expression, and growth of consciousness through the incorporation of spiritual values into our daily lives, and affirming our lives as a creative adventure.

We started as a backwoods agricultural commune, yet have evolved into a diverse and dynamic community. Our major projects at present include 1) The 2001 Center — building an energy-efficient village on 80 acres in Gill, Massachusetts; 2) Rocket's: running a business that builds and leases custom coaches; 3) operating a recording studio, fully equipped with an 8-track music studio; and 4) doing varied contracting projects: painting, carpentry, excavation, etc. — including work outside the community as well as maintenance and development on the home front.

All inquiries and visitors are welcome. Please write first if you plan to stay overnight, and call in advance for day visits (for which weekends are more suitable). We are interested in pursuing any ways we can work together. 6/24/89

Riparia

P.O. Box 4812
Chico, CA 95928
(916) 895-8786

Riparia is a community of 12 adults and 9 children living on 12 acres near the edge of Chico, California. The land has 8 dwellings, a creek, gardens, pasture, and a pear orchard. We are active in peace and environmental issues, sell organic produce locally, and actively promote organic farming. We make decisions by consensus. Much of our community life centers around our children. We welcome visitors who make arrangements in advance. 1/21/90

Rivendell Cooperative

731 West Genesee
Lansing, MI 48915
(517) 485-6520

Rivendell is a seven-person vegetarian cooperative in an older neighborhood of Lansing. A mixture of students and non-students of different ages, we are concerned about such issues as the environment, peace & justice, local community, etc., and attempt to provide a non-sexist, non-racist, egalitarian, and low-cost household in line with these values. Our food is purchased in bulk, providing healthful meals at a low cost. House decisions are made by consensus. We share a willingness to work out problems in the open, and to give up some privacy. Members each have about 10 hours of jobs each month. We have a variety of links with local peace & justice and folk music communities. Openings occur randomly; current monthly charges are $285. 6/22/89

River City

Housing Collective
802 E. Washington Street
Iowa City, IA 52240

(319) 337-4733 Anomy House
354-6768 Kazan House

River City Housing Collective is a University-affiliated organization whose goal is to provide quality housing for students and community members at a cost below the Iowa City average. Quality housing includes good maintenance, caring landlords (ourselves!), a healthy social environment, and responsible cooperative people to live with. The co-op's five houses (we own two of them) are all located close to campus and bus lines. One of the houses, Anomy House, is mostly non-students.

Each member does at least 16 hours of work each month, half for the organization, and half for the house they live in. Each house buys food as a unit, and house members share cooking, cleaning, and maintenance duties. Each house member is expected to cook one meal per week, and to learn bookkeeping, maintenance, communication, and

compromise. We are people of diverse backgrounds, interests, and lifestyles drawn into a cooperative community that promotes friendships, greater human understanding, and an exchange of knowledge. People often join the co-op for economy, but stay for community. 10/9/89

River Farm

3231 Hillside Rd
Deming, WA 98244
(206) 592-5222

We live in the Pacific Cascadia bioregion in the northwest corner of the United States, and are one of the five communities in the Evergreen Land Trust. Eight adults and four children live here, and there is some yearly turnover.

Our community is maintaining protected wildlife areas; practicing organic, ecologically sensitive farming; and acting as an educational source for the community and each other. Our farm is a mixture of forest, gardens, and fields. We also have sensitive areas of marsh and streams, a good size river, and mountainside.

We value independence and practical homesteading. We help each other with living, and work to improve our communication skills and to widen our views. We are open to written correspondence, and endeavor to network with similar folks — especially those battling clearcuts near your land, as we are. Please, mail inquiries only [cc]. 8/6/89

Rock Ridge Community

Route 3, Box 228-A
Dodgeville, WI 53533

We live with Quaker simplicity — living simply that others may simply live. Three adult members live here on the land, and three others come out for weekends. We love and support each other in our various ministries. Our basic focus includes the stewardship of our healing land, peace and justice issues, inter-racial summer visitations with Mississippi, and learning Spanish for Central American concerns. 2/18/90

Rootworks

Wolf Creek, OR 97497

"Rootworks", where *Womanspirit* magazine was published until 1984, is one of a number of woman-owned lands in southwestern Oregon. All the land is privately owned with the

exception of the Oregon Women's Land Trust Farm (see separate listing) which is open to all women who can abide by certain agreements. The women who live on these large and small parcels near the I-5 corridor, along with women of nearby towns, constitute a self-defined organic open community.

Feminism, lesbianism, love of nature, recovery, and women's spirituality are major components of the affinity these women share. Creativity is encouraged and supported in long-standing writers' and visual artists' groups. We also celebrate seasonal holidays and birthdays. Work exchanges, dances, workshops, performances, and conferences bring the women together frequently throughout the year.

This community is remarkable for its friendliness and creativity. There is usually a small daily charge for visitors, and an expectation that "daily bread" labor will be contributed. Please send SASE with $1 for further information. 2/21/90

Rowanwood Conservers Society Co-op

RR 2, Oro Station
Ontario, CANADA L0L-2E0

Rowanwood is a residential cooperative community on 92 rolling acres in rural Ontario. We're here because we enjoy doing things together, and spending time in each other's company. We share a commitment to conservation, to steward our farm, to be an extended family, to care for each other, and to share our learnings in cooperative living.

Member families live in individually built houses on one-acre sites owned by the cooperative. Our membership meets twice monthly for business, making decisions by consensus, and once for a potluck supper. Other committees (e.g., conserver, finance) meet as necessary. Each member shares in the work of the community — contributing as individuals, in small teams, and at community work parties. Children are encouraged to participate in the work as well.

Relationships are characterized by respect for individual differences, trust, clearness, and openness. We value personal and family privacy, an openness to resolving conflict, and a sense of humor. We acknowledge and respect a variety of spiritual values and motivations, and recognize that

Rowanwood *(Cont'd.)*

the spiritual dimension of our community is fundamental to what we do and how we do it. If you write, an SASE would be appreciated [cc]. 2/14/90

Rowe Camp & Conference Center

Kings Highway Road
Rowe, MA 01367

(413) 339-4216

We are a small community, founded in 1974, committed to offering weekend retreats and a summer camp for teenagers (see Resource listing). Members of our "intentional community" are here to do *that* work first (160+ hours each month) ... living as a loose-knit community comes second. We are also affiliated with the Unitarian Universalist Association. Visitors are welcome, but they must pay and/or work. [cc] 2/3/89

Rudolf Steiner Fellowship

Spring Valley, NY
See: Fellowship Community

Saint Benedict's Farm

Box 366
Waelder, TX 78959

(512) 540-4814

St. Benedict's Farm was founded in 1956 as a lay Christian community, based on the Rule of St. Benedict — the first word of which is "Listen". We are fervent Catholics, though not "officially" sponsored by the church. Presently we are three men and two women.

Our family is *Monastic* — that is, concerned with our day-to-day living and growing together toward God. Our lifestyle includes poverty, celibacy, simplicity, obedience, prayer, study, work, and worship. We have a lot of concern for the substance of monasticism, but very little for its forms — thus it is difficult for some to see our life as really being monastic.

We earn our living by running a photography business, a beef cattle breeding operation, and a recording studio. We believe strongly in self-support, and in the idea of working together as a family at whatever we do to earn a living. No special skills are required, only willingness to contribute whatever one can. Our dress is simple and uniform — made of blue denim. In our daily life we operate largely on consensus and consultation, though we have an abbot as our teacher and primary decision-maker. We are open to new members who are willing to make a whole-hearted dedication, without reservation. 6/14/88

Saint Clare's Hermitage

5984 Rutsatz Road
Deming, WA 98244

(206) 855-1498

Purpose: We offer to qualified serious men the time and space to live in the style and search of Thomas Merton. Work, study and meditation compose the lifestyle within the Prominent Ideals of Renunciation and Solitude. Tools or vows are not fixed as solid realities but provide useful approaches to deep Spiritual Growth. Through Simplicity/Sanctity/Surrender a seeker can become Transformed and enter into the path to Sainthood.

Hopes: To provide Christian Saintly Teachers and Guides for many seekers who see the need to be in Conscious Union with Christ, not just be good moral Christians.

Members: One abbot, four hermits, one oblate.

Dreams: To cleanse this earthly world of desire-oriented games and roles moving toward a real 1000 years of True Peace and Spiritual Conscious Communing.

Environment: Many evergreens populate the area, which is surrounded on one side by an organically alive 12-foot wall and forest vine maples laden with green moss.

Government: By the founding priest and deep consideration of those present and their needs. Benevolent dictatorship!

Visiting Policy: Long letter first — no drop-ins.

New Members: One-month workshop intensive must be completed first. Suggest monastic training in a Catholic monastery but not always necessary. Must have good health and

sound emotional control and an open mind and heart. 1/12/89

Salt Spring Centre

Box 1133
Ganges, B.C.
CANADA V0S-1E0

(604) 537-2326 / 537-9596

Salt Spring Centre is a spiritual community based on the principles and practice of Ashtanga Yoga, the eight-limbed Yoga path. This includes practice of ethical principles, yoga postures, breathing exercises, and meditation. We are blessed to have the guidance of a living master, Baba Hari Das.

In addition to our spiritual practice we have an alternative school with about 24 children, and a large garden with fruit orchard, vegetables, flowers, and culinary and medicinal herbs. We also provide week and weekend retreats for individuals and groups. Along with these retreat programs we offer various types of healing treatments such as massage, reflexology, sauna, and an herbal steambox.

Presently our community is made up of 12 adults and 4 children, as well as an "extended family" of contributors throughout the island community. All the adults who live at the community make regular work and financial contributions to the centre, and we are currently looking at expanding our cottage industry potential. Members contribute approximately 100 hours per month and $150 per person. We are vegetarian, and try to maintain a balanced and wholesome lifestyle. We live a non-violent and simple life. We welcome visitors, guests, and potential community members ... though we advise people who might be interested in joining our community that it is based on Yoga and a selfless service — and consequently requires a substantial commitment. 10/21/88

San Francisco Zen Center

300 Page Street
San Francisco, CA 94102

(415) 863-3136

The San Francisco Zen Center is a Zen Buddhist Meditation Center which offers daily meditation and weekly lectures to the public. It also has residential facilities for up to 40 people. Other programs include guest students (short-term residents who pay $10/day), classes in Buddhist Sutras, and meditation intensives (sesshins) from 1-7 days. Meditation instruction is given on Saturday mornings at 8:30. [cc] 1/22/90

Sandhill Farm

Route 1, Box 155-D
Rutledge, MO 63563

(816) 883-5543

Sandhill Farm is a family of friends living in northeastern Missouri. We've been here for 15 years and currently number six adults and one child. We produce most of our own food, on our 135 rolling acres. Some of our land is planted, some wooded, some pasture, and some ponds. We keep cows, poultry, and bees. Every year we plant a large organic garden. We get satisfaction from doing things ourselves, whether it is making cheese, repairing machinery, playing music, or constructing our own buildings. Resource consciousness and harmonious relations with the land are highly valued at Sandhill.

Our main source of income is from organic agricultural products, including sorghum syrup, honey, tempeh, garlic, horseradish, and herbs. The sorghum is our best seller. It is a traditional sweetener in our area, and we devote most of September and October to its harvest and processing, in a fun and energetic group effort. We also run Community Bookshelf (see its listing in Resources) — a small mail-order bookselling business featuring titles on community and cooperative living.

We share our land, our work and play, and our appreciation and love for each other. We try to be supportive of individual interests and needs as well as those of the group. Communication, honesty, equality, and non-violence are strongly held values. There is structure in our lives, but we try to get along with as few rules as possible.

We are nearing completion of a passive solar, earth-sheltered residence which will allow us to consider new members. We are open to both non-parents and adults with children.

We welcome visitors, especially during sorghum season. Please write first, and tell us something about yourself, and when you'd like to visit. We are active participants in the Federation of Egalitarian Communities. 5/20/90

Santa Fe Community School

Box 2241
Santa Fe, NM 87504

(505) 471-6928 / 471-3912

Santa Fe Community School is a community which welcomes children. Currently 5 adults and 5 children. We live in trailers and share a community center on 5 acres at the edge of the city. We are expanding to Paonia, Colorado where we can grow food organically, raise animals, and develop our spiritual awareness. Some members move back and forth between these "sister" community locations. Solid organization based on consensus decision-making, personal growth through problem solving with group support, and low cost through cooperation and work exchanges make this community possible for anyone. The school was founded 1968 to offer a non-coercive approach to education. Now, with the same educational goals, it is evolving into a community where parents, children, and teachers live, learn, work, and play together. Visitors are welcome. Contact us for application procedure to arrange for fees and living space. 12/12/88

Santa Rosa Creek Commons

887 Sonoma Avenue #16
Santa Rosa, CA 95404

(707) 523-0626 / 527-7191

Santa Rosa Creek Commons is a limited-equity housing cooperative for all ages, located near central Santa Rosa, 50 miles north of San Francisco. We have 27 units (studio to three-bedroom), a community room, laundry facilities, and a wooded area on the creek at the rear of our two acres. Members serve on committees, and are responsible for managing and maintaining the property. Members purchase shares, based on the size of the unit occupied, at the time of occupancy. We reserve ten shares for low-income members, and these range from $680 to $2,080. Unassisted shares range from $5,800 to $10,800. We pro-rate the monthly carrying charges to meet expenses. Applications are being received for future occupancy. 1/15/90

Sassafras Ridge Farm

Buck Route, Box 350
Hinton, WV 25951

Sassafras Ridge Farm is a community of several households with adults in their 20s to 40s and seven girls aged 3 to 14. Each household owns a few acres, and some of us have jointly owned the bulk of common land since 1972.

The farm consists of 240 acres of mountain and valley, with about 20 acres in crops and hay, 40 in pasture, and the rest wooded. There are several creeks, two ponds, and just a mile away is a clean, canoeable river.

Activities include gardening, greenhousing, animal care (cows, goats, chickens, horses, and mule), fencing, firewood, construction, tractoring, cropping, and haying — along with household tasks and child care, based on equal access and responsibility. We celebrate earth holidays.

Within the community, our household invites people to come share in the experience. We offer to trade accommodations and meals for a few hours of your labor daily. We insist on prearrangements and request that the initial stay be 3-7 days. Some compensation could be arranged for additional work including childcare, although the farming in itself is not income-producing. Most income is earned outside. Written inquiries only, and please include an SASE. [cc] 8/12/89

Satchidananda Ashram

Buckingham, VA
See: Yogaville

SEADS of Truth, Inc. (Forming)

P.O. Box 94
Harrington, ME 04643

(207) 483-9763

We are a not-for-profit group establishing a "self-sufficient" alternative energy community and seminar center in rural Maine. We are using a community land trust model, and stress voluntary cooperation and mutual aid — working with others, using group consensus and sharing. Families will have their own living space (bedrooms, kitchen, bath) and share "common" space, greenhouse, and independent electricity. We're still in the formative stages. Please write or call. 5/23/89

Seeds of Peace

**2440 - 16th Street, Box 241
San Francisco, CA 94103**

(415) 420-1799

Seeds of Peace is a collective of consensed members and friends — we live and work together using the consensus form of decision-making. We are currently living in a duplex in Berkeley, and hope to add a farm in Oregon this summer. Each individual has made a commitment to contribute half of their earned income to the collective while living here; exceptions are made. Each member also agrees to work directly on Seeds of Peace projects. We all help around the house, and recognize that there will be times when an individual will need to pass up an action, stay home, and keep the basics together.

On the road we work in various service capacities: managing food, water, sanitation, transportation, peacekeeping, and a variety of other functions as required by the circumstances. Seeds does not design these actions — we are called in to work with sponsoring organizations.

Politically we are a diverse group, and our communal commitment is to non-violence, nuclear disarmament, and social justice. We work with a broad spectrum of groups — from the Oregon Country Fair, to the International Peace Walk, to the Rainbow Gathering. As a group, our foremost priority is to maintain life support services. 5/12/89

Seven C's (Forming)

**P.O. Box 801
Medford, OR 97501**

Cripple Creek Cross Circle Cedar City Co-Camp (7-C's) is a newly forming community based on a vision of togetherness, lasting relationships, and hard work for the common good. We are presently six adults living together on 100 acres in a very high private valley of cedar, scattered oak and conifer trees. We have two other dairy farms as well.

At this point members earn money at outside jobs while we develop several worker-owned and -operated businesses. Work initiatives include forestry, horse and beef breeding, a hydroponic greenhouse, commercial seed growing, truck/auto repair apprentice school, horse shoer & wrangler apprentice schooling, a Christmas tree farm, and a 22-room tourist dude ranch with bed and breakfast.

7-C's has no formal religion on the grounds. We do respect short silent grace at meals, and welcome mature people of any denomination. No headbands or strange religious garb or clothing is permitted on the grounds. Men are expected to maintain a hair style no longer than three inches, and any beards must be well trimmed. We have a non-drugs, non-drinkers, non-smokers policy.

We are seeking people who are receptive and friendly, and who notice eye contact. It's important to not bury feelings — to cure problems you must be able to open up! The 7-C's vision includes the elimination of racism, ageism, and sexism. We are open only to heterosexual relationships, monogamous or not, though those in open relationships must use a calendar (a proven practice that works).

We also take time for rest and play. Regular activities include music evenings, western swing dancing, outdoor sing-alongs, riddles and jingles, campfires, ocean trips, picnics, and barbecues. Visitors are welcome, and are asked to contribute 4 hours each day (whether as teacher, student, or laborer). We also appreciate any information and network contacts with others who are committed to this type of lifestyle. 3/26/90

Seven Springs Farm

**Route 1, Box 95-D
Mountain Grove, MO 65711**

(417) 948-2687 / 948-2662

Seven Springs is an intentional community with an 18-year history. We each hold the deed to a five-acre parcel, and hold the balance of our 120 acres in common. Our community is nestled in the Missouri Ozark Mountains approximately 80 miles from Springfield. Currently our population consists of a mixture of single and family households — with ages ranging from teenagers to 51. We support ourselves through outside employment. We are bound together by our philosophy of ecological land stewardship and our choice to live in community. We have no other underlying philosophy. We are actively seeking new members. 10/15/89

Shambala Community

*Originally in Louisiana
See: Reina Del Cielo,
Lexington, VA*

Shannon Farm

**Route 2, Box 343
Afton, VA 22920**

(804)361-1180 / 361-1417

Shannon Farm is an eclectic, rural, multi-generational intentional community spread over 490 acres of farm and woodlands. We are in a beautiful river valley in central Virginia, on the eastern crest of the Blue Ridge Mountains, and enjoy mild winters and cool summer nights. We value personal freedom of choice because 1) people can change lifestyles or belief systems and remain in the community, and 2) our diversity maintains a dynamic, continually evolving community.

We strive to cultivate an enduring spirit of cooperation in our community life together. At the same time we seek to strengthen our connections to the larger society around us through business activities, civic groups, sports and fitness programs, political activities, and alternative and public schools. Shannon is active in local networking with ten other intentional communities in our area, and national networking through the Fellowship for Intentional Community.

We make decisions by consensus in our committee meetings and monthly business meetings — so we are continually working to improve our skills in non-competitive conflict resolution. Although we reserve the option of deciding by 60% majority vote, we have not resorted to the vote in over ten years. Formal leadership roles are rotated among the membership on a voluntary basis. Day-to-day management is decentralized to the simplest function level possible.

Our 60 members (approximately half women, half men) and 21 children range in age from infancy to over 70 years. Almost half of us have been here for over twelve years, another quarter for over eight. We value consensus decision-making, feminism, equality, diversity, environmental concerns, and individual initiative and responsibility.

Our members have built 19 family homes, 3 group houses, several cabins, a wood shop, lumber kilns, and warehouses. While all the buildings are owned jointly, those members responsible for financing hold long-term leases on the structures. Leases may be sold to other members or, at a discount, to the community as a whole. Matching loans for construction or lease transfer financing are available to some extent. We paid off our community mortgage in 1987. To cover common expenses and projects, we each pay dues of 7% of after-tax income (a minimum of $42.50/month) and contribute 1-1/2 days of labor per month.

We have several gardens, an orchard, a vineyard, and a raspberry patch. Two or three members work part-time with farm animals, haying, and other farming activities. Some members have organized worker-owned businesses, including a 6-person woodshop (on the farm) and a computer systems outlet (in Charlottesville, 25 miles away). 60% of us commute to work, mostly in health services and education.

We are open to new members of diverse ages; ethnic backgrounds; political, spiritual, and sexual orientations — those who want to help build Shannon and the global intentional communities movement. 5/20/90

Shenoa Community
P.O. Box 43
Philo, CA 95466
(707) 895-3156 (10am-6pm)

The Shenoa Community, a Findhorn-inspired retreat center 2-1/2 hours north of San Francisco, regards "growing community" as a primary reason for its existence. Besides sponsoring events such as their "Growing Community in our Lives" workshop, Shenoa offers informal community gatherings at the retreat center throughout the year. We have a core staff and a large extended community. Our facilities are also available for conference and workshop reservations. Please write or call for information, reservations, or a calendar of events. 9/13/89

Shepherdsfield
Route 4, Box 399
Fulton, MO 65251
(314) 642-1439

Shepherdsfield is a Christian fellowship which tries to live as the Early Christians did and as recorded in the Acts of the Apostles, including the "sharing of all things in common". We have accepted Jesus Christ as the Way, the Truth and the Life. Through Him we have found answers to the

many questions that arise in trying to live together, and in reaching out to others.

We presently have about 100 souls associated with our community. We are located in a farming area within driving distance of Columbia and Jefferson City, MO. We earn our living through an organic bakery, a wallpapering and painting company, several cottage industries, and some printing and publishing. We have a large ministry that reaches over the world in studies of Scripture and principles of Life. We operate our own school for our children, and take seriously the task of raising children in an environment of "purity and childlikeness."

Our desire has been to show others that Christianity is not limited to the institutional forms that have so disenchanted many people and led them to reject the claims of our Master, Jesus of Nazareth. We would not want to mislead anyone by claiming our life is a Utopia that requires little or no effort for the individual. Quite the contrary, true peace and brotherhood can be accomplished only when the utmost of diligence is applied in living out and promoting the necessary qualities. That requires struggle in order for the goodness of God to be "fleshed out" in us. However, we find great joy in living for Him in the present, and seeing ourselves and others changed from day to day.

If you would like to visit us, please write or call in advance. We have varying lengths of visitation before a person may apply to become a novice, which can eventually lead to becoming a member. 12/13/88

Shiloh Community
P.O. Box 97
Sulphur Springs, AR 72768
(501) 298-3299 / 298-3297

Shiloh has actively followed a communal way of life since 1942, when E. Crosby Monroe retired from designing battleship interiors to pursue his spiritual beliefs. He purchased a 500-acre farm in southwestern New York, and opened his home to those who would join him there, including some young servicemen. Rev. Monroe died in 1961, but the community has continued to thrive. By 1968 the community needed an improved setting for its family and businesses. Drawn to the beautiful Arkansas Ozarks, the group acquired a grand hotel with a colorful history.

A self-supporting community since its inception, the Shiloh Community has followed a progression of occupations — from general farming, dairying, meat processing, flour milling, baking, retail, then wholesale distribution. At this point the community's main business interests are Sun Rise Acres Bakery, Shiloh Farms Inc., The School of Shiloh Inc., and the Shiloh Christian Retreat Center. The bakery now uses only stone-ground whole grain flours and natural sweeteners and oils in the manufacturing of Shiloh Farms bread.

The community's ventures and philosophy are based soundly on a verse from Isaiah 55:2 — "Wherefore do ye spend money for that which is not bread? Harken diligently unto me, and eat that which is good, and let your soul rejoice." 2/26/89

Short Mountain Sanctuary
Route 1, Box 84-A
Liberty, TN 37095
(615) 536-5176

Short Mountain Sanctuary (SMS) is a not-for-profit corporation chartered in Tennessee to hold land, and to keep it free from private exploitation. SMS also provides a place for its residents and members to undertake projects in sustainable agriculture, wholistic forestry, low-cost shelter, and alternative energy.

The residents of SMS are gay men and lesbian womyn, their families and friends. On the land they work on self-reliance and celebrate the earth's cycles. All major decisions are made by consensus.

SMS is a working farm with a herd of goats, organic garden, chickens, bee hives, fruit trees, and herb beds. The main structures are a pre-Civil War cabin with additions, a large barn, and other outbuildings. Organizational income derives from annual membership dues ($75), and registration fees for two 9-day gatherings in May and October. Residents pay a fixed amount each month for food and supplies. Visitors are welcome, but need to write in advance (please enclose SASE). Daily fees for food and land use are $5 for non-members, and $2.50 for members.

SMS is presently the home of *RFD: A Country Journal for Gay Men Everywhere.* RFD has been in production now for 15 years, and is a reader-written magazine (see resource listing). 3/1/90

Sichlassenfallen

1139 North 21st Street
Milwaukee, WI 53233

(414) 933-2063

Sichlassenfallen is a place called home by 5 unrelated adults, who have interest in finding one or two more compatible housemates (a parent with child is a possibility). Members each pay a monthly share of about $200, and are expected to contribute 8-10 hours per month. We emphasize democracy and ecology, and make all major decisions by consensus. 1/13/89

Sierra Hot Springs

P.O. Box 366
Sierraville, CA 96126

(916) 994-3777

Sierra Hot Springs has a colorful history. Native Americans held it sacred and revered it for healing and ritual. Later, it provided the early immigrants and miners of the Gold Rush with the luxury of a hot bath.

The attractiveness of the hot springs has been carefully preserved. Its few buildings are unobtrusively set where nature left a place for them in the shadows of elegant pine trees on the steep Sierra slopes, 5,000 feet above sea level. In the springtime the alpine meadow, clad in pastel blooms, becomes a feast for the spirit. Deer, raccoon, chipmunks, squirrels, porcupines, and many species of birds drink and forage there.

Today this 600-acre, beautifully-located hot springs has evolved into a spiritual community dedicated to the protection of these magical waters while keeping them open to the public. It is on land formerly a part of Campbell Hot Springs (see separate listing). Training is available in techniques of spiritual enlightenment and healing methods to integrate spirit, mind, and body.

Sierra Springs Community is currently seeking skilled members. The community is especially interested in people who have construction skills. A non-denominational spiritual lifestyle is supported, with an emphasis on holistic health. Please, no smoking or drugs. For more information, call Carol at (916)994-3777. 1/28/90

Sirius Community

Baker Road
Shutesbury, MA 01072

(413) 259-1251

Sirius Community, named after the star known esoterically as the source of love and wisdom for the planet, was begun in 1978 on 86 acres of land by former members of the Findhorn Community in Scotland. Today we are about 20 Full Members from many spiritual paths, and 10 children. We have many Associate Members across the country and the world.

Our vision — molding us even as we all mold it — is a vision to attain the highest good in all levels of God's creation: field and forest, plants and animals, humans and angels, earth and stars. We strive to embody a faith in God, love, truth, cooperation, honoring the oneness of all life, detachment from desire, meditation, and service to the world. We are a group of diverse people from different backgrounds who are working to respect and appreciate our differences, yet joyfully cooperate. What we are doing can be applied globally, for the tensions between nations pose a similar challenge.

In any polarity or conflict, we work to create balance and focus on the wholeness of the system, rather than the separateness of the parts. Our tools include a weekly meeting and open discussion by all adult members; governance by group meditation and consensus; attunement to God, to nature, and to each other. We strive to live close to the earth without being bound to it. For us, "appropriate technology" is computers as well as composting toilets and wood stoves.

We also strive toward right livelihood — earning our living through loving, non-exploitive ways. A few of us work at Sirius or in our own businesses, but most of us are employed outside the community. We work in such fields as social and health services, domestic service, solar construction, whole foods distribution, socially responsible investment, media, publishing, and educational services.

We grow some of our vegetables, and build our own houses. We share equally the expenses of the land, and work on community projects one day a week. Most of us participate in community evening meals and a food buying club.

We host visitors from many countries, and make ourselves available to those on a spiritual quest and those in transition seeking a better life. As a non-profit, tax-exempt educational center, we continue to offer a variety of educational programs — from solar construction to new age politics, from organic gardening to wholistic healing. Each Sunday we offer a spiritual service, and on the first and third Sundays of the month, an open house.

More importantly, we serve the world through our meditation. We work to create positive thought-forms of peace and healing for the world, as we know that energy follows thought. We are striving together to build Sirius into a center of Light, a place where cooperation is a dream that works. Our vision of service is to help build a Network of Light which radiates positive energy and hope for the future throughout the world. 5/15/90

Sivananda Ashram

Yoga Ranch Colony
P.O. Box 195
Woodbourne, NY 12788

(914) 434-9242

An international network of Sivananda Yoga Vedanta Centers are thriving in major cities on four continents — founded by Swamiji (Swami Vishnu Devananda) to spread the teachings of Swami Sivananda. The organization is staffed by volunteer "karma yogis", and student membership is well over 80,000. The Yoga Ranch, in the Catskills of southeastern New York, was established in 1975, and is presently the home to 10 resident adults and no children. Our focus is on five basic points for radiant health and inner peace: proper exercise, proper relaxation, proper breathing, proper diet, and positive thinking and meditation. Our daily practice includes meditation, yoga, chanting, and vegetarian meals. We also enjoy a sauna, pond, and cross-country skiing.

Come as a guest, a karma yoga volunteer (requiring a 6-month commitment), a resident, or a Teacher Trainee. We also have ashrams in Canada, California, India, and the Bahamas. For more information, write for our brochure. 5/26/89

Sky Woods Cosynegal

Box 4176
Muskegon Heights, MI 49444

We believe the heart of our humanity is an essentially social nature whose fullest realization is one with the destiny of community. We believe that global survival depends on compassionate commitment of all our resources to create a truly advanced social and ecological awareness. We affirm that we are one with all our sisters and brothers and with nature. We must replace competition and aggression with mature skills of cooperation and humanization.

We are not merely utopian dreamers. We have experienced the agony and ecstasy of shared lives for 15 years. We believe that the trials of our forebears may have granted the conceptual, technical and spiritual resources to achieve a consistently cooperative lifestyle. Community has given us the high privilege of real life participation in mutual self-creation.

We think we have made credible advances over sexism, ageism, racism, and possessiveness toward material resources or others. Those advances have been based on rational self-criticism; democratic consensus/majority decision-making; full disclosure relationships; ample group communication and expression; collective sharing and control of all socially significant material resources; and a firm rejection of one of the last strongholds of the competitive mentality — preferential monogamy or possessive relationships. Even as we seek to replace individual possession of resources with sharing, so too do we leave behind jealous possession of others for a diverse network of support and love. Our exhilaration and sustaining ideal is a fully egalitarian community.

Some among us have already committed ourselves to a lifetime together. We have a few acres of beautiful wooded hill country on the shore of the inland sea, a small organic farm, a home and several thriving cottage industries. We produce some arts and crafts, are deeply into alternative energy, holistic health, nutrition, organic gardening and orcharding.

We are ready for a limited increase in our numbers. We will gladly mail a statement of our beliefs and purposes, or answer other questions. Simply drop us a note with an address and/or phone number. We welcome visitors, but request that arrangements be made in advance. 12/14/88

Sojourners Community

1323 Girard Street NW
Washington, DC 20009

(202) 636-3637

Sojourners is an ecumenical community church, rooted in biblical authority and moving in the stream of historical Christian orthodoxy. The vision of our community has always been to bring together that which has often been divided in the history of the church: prayer and ministry, worship and politics, evangelism and social action. We are mutually accountable to one another for our commitments to simple lifestyle, shared decision-making, personal conversion, spiritual growth, economic sharing, peacemaking, and involvement with poor and struggling people.

The community currently has 30 adult members, both single and married, and 10 children. Most of us live in a variety of houses and apartments within a several-block area in an inner city neighborhood. Commitment to this neighborhood is a central part of our life together. Leadership is exercised in the community by a team of pastors, both women and men, whose authority has been recognized by the community. Other small committees oversee various aspects of our life. We meet every Wednesday night in large or small groups to celebrate, share and worship, and discuss business.

The community carries out a variety of ministries in our neighborhood. We distribute food on Saturday mornings to residents of the neighborhood, and during the week to pregnant women, mothers with young children, and the elderly. We coordinate a children's program, offer mothers' support groups and nutrition education, and provide support to a local tenants organization. Our outreach ministries include a magazine, *Sojourner*, a peace ministry that works on peace & justice issues, a resource center, a speaking and teaching ministry, a guest ministry, and an internship program.

Many community members work in other service-related jobs around the city, including a nurse, a social worker, a medical technologist, an occupational therapist, and a researcher. We also have a mechanic, two teachers, two staff workers at homeless shelters, a counselor, a secretary, and a director of a church-based housing organization. These varied jobs reflect the diversity of our community.

Our commitment to feminism and to children has led the families among us to seek ways to co-parent creatively. The work and joy of raising children in a faithful community context is a very central part of our life. Our worship service is held Sunday evenings at our neighborhood center, and is open to the public. 12/12/88

Sojourners' Orchard

HCR 02, Box 530
Madison, VA 22727

(703) 923-4671

Sojourners' Orchard and Farm is located on 211 acres of rolling and mountainous land at the foot of the Blue Ridge. 6 adults (three couples) and 1 infant comprise the current membership. The land, originally purchased by the 3 original members, is still fully owned by them. Common values for members are a concern for the environment and an acceptance and tolerance for others.

Although some members have outside jobs, there are currently three enterprises being pursued at Sojourners: 1) The conversion of approximately 30 acres of old commercial apple and peach orchards into an organic operation; by-products include apple cider and vinegar. 2) The sheep operation, with a flock of about 70 ewes, is primarily for meat production. This project is also moving toward organic. An addition to the sheep operation is raising and showing Border Collies (working dogs). 3) Avalon Conservation Club (our most unusual venture) is on 40 acres set aside for clothing-optional family recreation such as swimming, volleyball, hiking, and simply relaxing and getting close to nature in a natural way. Operated as a private club with about 100 members at present, Avalon conducts conservation and environmental education programs for members and guests.

Sojourners does not currently have housing for additional members, but does expect to increase available housing over the next few years. At present, room and board can be provided for participants in our organic farming apprenticeship program. Please write for more information. [cc] 1/23/90

Sparrow Hawk Village

Box 1274
Tahlequah, OK 74465

(918) 456-3421

Sparrow Hawk Village, established in 1981, is an intentional community of 80 seekers representing a blend of beliefs, backgrounds, ages, and talents. Villagers are dedicated to harmony, individual growth, responsibility, and developing as world servers. We have daily meditations, and an active program of open classes and workshops in the Wisdom Teachings, Christian Origins, and Spiritual Studies. An excellent bookstore, library, and Community Church are enjoyed by all. We are situated on 400 wooded acres on scenic river in the Ozark foothills. We have a community garden, orchard, horse pasture, and our own deep well and central water system. Guest rooms and campgrounds with full hook-ups are available *(Reservations, Please)*; we also have single-family homes and homesites. Please enclose an SASE when writing. Come to visit, to study, or to live. 5/31/89

The Spaulding Unit

2319 Spaulding
Berkeley, CA 94703

The Spaulding Unit, started in 1978, is an urban household of 6 adults. We make decisions through a process much like consensus. Each person has their own room, and we share the rest. Members typically spend a couple of hours a week doing work for the group. We are primarily vegetarians, sharing family-style meals. Individuals are fairly independent, with interests ranging from gardening to political activism and collectivity. Please include an SASE with inquiries. [cc] 1/4/90

The Spiral Inn

Jamestown, MO
See: Moniteau Farm

Spiral Wimmin's Community

P.O. Box 337
Monticello, KY 42633
(606) 348-6597 / 348-7913

Spiral Wimmin's Community (Spiraland) is 250 acres in the foothills of south-central Kentucky, in the Cumberland Valley. Covering a ridge and valley of forest and cleared land,

Spiral includes three springs, a good barn, a log cabin, and new dwellings wimmin are building.

We recognize that the land is a sacred heritage, belonging to herself — part of the complex web of life in which we learn to play our part harmoniously with the rest of her creatures and plants. Our community is based on permaculture principles. Our actions on the land are to en-   hance the diversity and abundance of life forms, to preserve and build the soil, to work with the cycles and forces of nature. We look at the land as a self-sustaining ecological system capable of fruitfulness for all time.

We are currently 4 wimmin living on the land. There are two houses, with a third house in the planning stage. We offer room and board to wimmin in exchange for help in building. Skilled workers would be welcomed, but any help is appreciated. Please write (include SASE) or call for more information. 1/26/89

Spring Valley

Farmington, PA
See: New Meadow Run,
Hutterian Society of Brethren

Springtree Community

Route 2, Box 89
Scottsville, VA 24590-9512
(804) 286-3466

We are a group of five adults and one child living together as an extended family. Our home (est. '71) is on 120 acres in central Virginia. We live together in two houses, eat our meals together and share all income. Today, as in the past, children have been raised collectively, but parents have retained primary responsibility for them.

Living frugally is important to us, and we try to live as ecologically as possible. We grow much of our own food, maintaining an organic garden and orchard, chickens, and bees. We support ourselves by pooling income from outside jobs, farming, and a home-based book indexing business. An experimental agroforestry project — combining a variety of tree species with pastures and animals — is one of our important activities.

We intend to remain a small group, considering 10 adults a maximum. We are interested in frugality, commitment, compatibility. We meet weekly to plan and to discuss issues.

We advise a two-week initial visit

for those interested in membership. We offer internships in organic gardening and country living skills to those interested in spending several months with us. To arrange a visit or for more information write and tell us about yourself, or call Tom. 5/6/91

Stardance

San Francisco, CA
See: Purple Rose

Starland

Hutterian Brethren
Route 2, Box 133
Gibbon, MN 55335
(507) 834-6601

See main listing under "Hutterian Brethren." 3/1/89

Stelle Community

127 Sun Street
Stelle, IL 60919
(815) 256-2212

Stelle was founded in 1973 in Illinois by The Stelle Group, a not-for-profit organization, in order to create a supportive environment where individual human development would be made a foremost priority. The founding values of personal responsibility, lifelong education, positive attitude, and cooperation still remain a vital part of the community. Today no single organization oversees all aspects of community life ... instead, different groups play various roles in the community. The Stelle group is now only one small organization among many, including the Stelle Community Association and the newly formed Stelle Area Chamber of Commerce. The Stelle Group continues its philosophical and educational pursuits — running an award-winning, accredited school and publishing a quarterly, *The Philosopher's Stone* — whereas governing of the community and promotion are left to other organizations.

Education continues to be a keynote in Stelle, with a variety of study groups and classes periodically available. Stelle owns and operates its own water and sewage treatment plants and telephone mutual. Almost all of the community's 44 homes are now owned privately. Residents support themselves in a variety of pursuits, several of them within the community, with a high number of privately owned businesses.

Efforts at creating beauty in a challenging prairie environment were rewarded when, in 1985, Stelle became the smallest community to receive the Tree City Award from the National Arbor Day Foundation. For more information write to the Stelle Area Chamber of Commerce at the address listed above. 4/18/90

Still Meadow

16561 SE Marna Road
Clackamas, OR 97015

(503) 658-2477 / 658-2544

The spirit of Still Meadow is best described by the words "radiant tranquility." Located in the foothills of the Cascade Mountains twenty miles from Portland, Still Meadow is lush and heavily forested — a dwelling for osprey, owl, heron, deer, coyote, and fox. Our Stewardship Farm encompasses hydroponic gardening, turkey- and cattle-raising, and hay and herb production. This is home to twenty-one members, many of whom work in a variety of businesses. Still Meadow is also a regional center for the Emissaries (see main listing). This is a quiet place, a naturally abundant and peaceful setting where people may come to know true purpose in living. 6/17/89

Stone Soup Collective (Forming)

16 Omaha Avenue
Algonquin Island
Toronto, Ontario
CANADA M5J-1Z7

(416) 360-5510

We are a group of 6 adults who began meeting in January of '88 to talk about community, utopia, and life in general. We formed a collective, the purpose of which is to form a community. Our vision is a social, economic, emotional, and political community where we can live more wholly as human beings — providing alternatives to wage labor, the nuclear family, consumer mentality, etc. We see our community as a practical option for living and growing (who can deal with a mortgage in reality?), and plan to locate in rural southern Ontario. We are not religiously based, nor are we adopting a pre-fab dogma. There is no "charismatic leader," rather we consist of charismatic individuals who participate equally. We emphasize our commitment to diversity in the population of the community.

We stopped meeting regularly in the fall of '89, though we are still informally committed to each other as we continue to develop and pursue our visions somewhat more independently. Some of us hope to reform as a group, to redefine our shared vision. We welcome inquiries from community-minded people, and seek new and different perspectives. [cc] 8/25/89

Storefront Classroom Community

San Francisco, CA
See: Kerista

Suburban Palace

San Francisco, CA
(415) 386-5386

The Suburban Palace is situated in the heart of sub-urban San Francisco, and is comprised of a polymorphous perverse mixture of sexual persuasions and age groups — from retro-bohemians to post-modern anarchists. We believe in our inalienable right to live with many of the modern conveniences (VCRs, computers, pushbutton phones with "Call Waiting," espresso machines, refrigerators) as they free our time for more productive activities such as saving the world from itself and from people like us.

Femina-anarchist/pagan eco-freakism is our favorite section of the video rental store. (We request that any FBI agents reading this not raid our house on Tuesday or Thursday nights as we will be watching "Thirty Something" or "L.A. Law.") We hate house meetings and would rather go bowling. Who are we, but our own contradictions?

Members work for many diverse causes from AIDS Prevention; to fostering cross-cultural relationships between Japan and the U.S.; to ensuring that tie-dye standards are kept high; and protecting the environment. If you call and don't reach a live one (we have a machine), leave a message if you don't mind accepting a collect call [cc]. 1/21/90

Sunat Center

Bushland, TX
See: Panhandle Permaculture

Sunburst

Originally in Stanta Cruz, CA
See: The Builders, Oasis, NV

Sundance

Route 2, Box 170
Whitleyville, TN 38588
(615) 621-3474

Sundance is looking for people of political purpose to support the soon-to-be land trust, and would appreciate input in the endeavor. Sundance is a handful of acres with a house (The White House, built first in 1860 and then rebuilt around WWI) wanting loving attention. The land was homesteaded in 1978 with the intention of providing an example of alternative living. Electricity is from solar sources, heat is from wood, water is spring-fed, and food is grown on the land, purchased from a co-op, or grown by friends. We have a home school group, and offer a place to connect with craftsworkers, organic farmers, home educators, musicians, and people seeking new ways (or renewing old ways) to live in harmony with the earth. Do write, and please include a SASE Thanks. [cc] 6/13/89

Suneidesis Consocation/ Touchpoint South

Box 628
Velaashby Island
Buras, LA 70041

The Suneidesis Consocation is based at Velaashby Island — 117 acres in the Mississippi River delta, 65 miles south of New Orleans and a 10-minute boat ride from the mainland. Our residential community is small; our extended family network spans from eastern Texas to central Florida.

We sponsor five annual gatherings and various workshop/retreats throughout the year. We also host such for other groups or individuals.

We are a spiritually-based people who draw from many paths. We are convinced that the all-effective way to heal the earth is through the alignment of our hearts and minds in consciousness and through the directing of this energy into creating a new human consciousness.

As we wish to remain a small community, we do not actively seek new residents. However, we do seek those few who might find great alignment and walk with us.

We seek always to network with others. In our different ways, we are working toward the same goal of common-unity that transcends our diverse ways. Our searches are to rediscover our unity in our oneness with the Source.

Visitors are most welcome. We ask only that each contribute in such ways as s/he is able. 12/14/88

N. America

Sunflower Farm

12900 Parmiter Road
Amesville, OH 45711

(614) 448-6688 / 593-7456

Sunflower Farm, established in 1975, is a community of seven families on 100 acres in southeast Ohio near Athens. Sunflower is an alternative of independence and interdependence and a response to dependence on costly, impersonal, large-scale institutions. There are five-acre private homesteads and 50 acres owned in common. Adults' ages range from 30s to late 40s, 11 children (oldest is 15). We have artisans, engineers, computer specialists, social service workers, teachers, and more.

Athens allows us outside and in-community jobs, and has a 15,000-student university and medical school, excellent cultural and recreational resources. Cooperative activities include gardens, orchard, laundry, dining, community meetings, childcare program, stained glass, woodworking, beekeeping workshops, and intermediate technology weekend workshops. We encourage new intentional community development and hope prospective members will be able to help with our programs and workshops in self-reliance skills. We are demonstrating that creative living and caring, cooperative environments are possible. 12/14/88

Sunflower House

1406 Tennessee
Lawrence, KS 66044

(913) 841-0484

Sunflower House is a 30-member student housing cooperative founded in 1969 (formerly the Campus Improvement Association — CIA House). We have three major purposes: 1) to provide high-quality, low-cost, student-managed housing for University of Kansas students; 2) to provide an educational environment where students can learn practical skills (cooking, carpentry, plumbing, bookkeeping, supervising or coordinating the work of other members, etc.); and 3) to serve as a research site for the design of procedures that promote cooperative relations among individuals (the Experimental Living Project).

Each of the 30 members of Sunflower House has his or her own bedroom, while we share a variety of other spaces (6 bathrooms, 2 kitchens, lounge, TV room, game room, shop). We work 5-10 hours per week within the community. The money we contribute through monthly fees covers our expenses, and any surplus is rebated to members at the end of the year. Major decisions are made at weekly meetings of the membership. A board of directors, consisting of KU students and faculty, meets infrequently to provide guidance on the overall direction of the cooperative. We employ a project director who oversees the research, development, and ongoing operation of our program. Mail inquiries only. 5/12/89

Sunnyside Collective (Forming)

167 E. Cedar Street
Columbia, MO 65202
(314) 443-8012

We are a group of good friends who met as members (mostly long-term) at East Wind Community in Tecumseh, Missouri. We are in the very first stages of creating our own community, so many of the details of exactly what we want are still to be worked out.

There are some things that are already clear. We make decisions by consensus. We are partial income sharing. We want people to be close, and to work problems out with each other. We strive to be non-sexist, non-violent, non-racist, and as open as possible to the different needs of individuals. We like to work hard, joke with each other, and play games.

At the moment we are living in Columbia and seeking employment to earn money. Eventually we want to start our own business, be economically self-sufficient, and live rurally. We envision a variety of living situations ranging from communal houses to private homes. Mail inquiries only, and please include an SASE [cc] 2/15/90

Sunrise Homestead
See: Sweetwater CLT,
Mansfield, MO

Sunset House

2708 Sunset Avenue
Oakland, CA 94601
(415) 534-9276

One member bought the house in April '77, and two friends moved in almost immediately. In the intervening 13 years we've had many long-term members (for 3 to 8 years), although there has been no cement to hold us together beyond sharing vegetarian food, cooking, and maintenance. There have been a number of romantic connections. We do share part of our lives, and have similar values since we admit new members by consensus. We also enjoy occasional reunions with former residents.

We grow quite a bit of our food during the summer months, and try to live in balance through energy conservation, recycling, etc. The house is now at capacity with 7 adults and one child — ranging in age from 83, 62, 60, 43, 43, 32, 20, to 2 years. We get along well with each other. 9/21/89

Susan B. Anthony Memorial Unrest Home

13423 Howard Road
Millfield, OH 45761

We are a community of 3 women, ages 40 thru 63, living on a 152-acre tree farm in beautiful, Appalachian Ohio. We are 10 miles from Ohio University in Athens, Ohio — a campus of 15,000 students. Our remodeled farmhouse has 3 bedrooms, an upper deck, 2 baths, large kitchen, living room with fireplace, and parlor with a grand piano. Our garden is large — with flowers and vegetables, fruit trees, and grape vines. We also have 2 dogs and 3 cats.

The Suh-BAM-Uh (S.B.A.M.U.H.) campground for women is quite successful. It includes wooded and mowed grass tent sites, a field kitchen with running water, logs for sitting around a fire circle, outhouse with picture windows, solar-heated shower, and a half-acre swimming pond. It is available for use by individuals and groups (by reservation only).

We would like other women to join us, come for a camping visit, talk with us about ideas for living in community. Women could possibly build their own dwelling, bring in a mobile home, convert an outbuilding into a living unit, or share the farm house. Please write us for further information and an opportunity to visit. 2/2/89

Sweetwater

Community Land Trust
Route 3, Box 177
Mansfield, MO 65704
(417) 741-7363

Sweetwater Community Land Trust holds 480 acres of rural land on the

N. America

Gasconade River. 60 acres are farmland, the rest is wooded. Our community structure is a hybrid of communal and private: 1) all land is owned and managed by the Trust, which gives 99-year leases for 10-acre homesites. The Trust is governed by a council composed of all leaseholders; decision-making is by consensus. 2) Buildings, tools, vehicles, businesses, etc. are privately owned. Individuals and families manage their own finances.

Sweetwater operates like a "neighborhood" where members develop and regulate their own levels of involvement, cooperation, support, and sharing within the community — from totally private at one end, to cooperative housing, gardens, businesses, etc. at the other.

The Land Trust is not a community government — it's sole legal purpose is holding and leasing land. We are "social anarchists" — we govern by developing cooperative arrangements rather than creating and relying on governmental controls. Our primary focus as a community is land stewardship and environmental protection, along with the optimization of human well-being and relationships. [cc] 7/22/89

Sylviron (Forming)
4771 Rolland Road
Blanchard, MI 49310
(517) 561-5037

Sylviron is a cooperative village in formation, presently existing only as a model in the novel "Sylviron". We are searching for land somewhere in southern Michigan. The first phase will be a conference facility, self-reliant but not isolated, intended to serve cooperatives and other community organizations. We will expand from that beginning into other activities.

The buildings will be earth-sheltered and super-insulated to conserve energy, and will be built for an economic life of centuries. Food production, recreation, and education for personal growth will be the foci of what we do. We use negotiation of consensus (not traditional rules of order) as described in *Welty's Book of Procedures for Meetings, Boards, Committees and Officers* (available through the Institute for the Development of Cooperation (see Resources). We seek voluntary, cooperative, and non-governmental solutions to society's needs. 3/21/91

Syntropy Institute
302 College
Palo Alto, CA 94306
(415) 325-7529

Syntropy Institute is a small California non-profit corporation dedicated to supporting the development of sustainable prosperity in ways open to all humanity. We emphasize the development of personal creativity, philanthropy, financial independence, and broadening of practical knowledge. Our activities are primarily local in nature, and include free seminars, vocational counseling, authoring of public domain computer software, and technical assistance to groups in the developing world.

Several supporters of Syntropy Institute currently live together in a six bedroom house in Palo Alto (near Stanford University). Some of us have serious interests in spirituality, polyfidelity, and use of computers to aid democratic decision making — but these are not the primary basis of our sense of community. Most of us work for our collective business, Aard•deus Inc., which provides computer and artistic services. Our finances are integrated at a level similar to business partnerships — individuals assume primary responsibility for their personal expenses. Some of us have been quite successful in business, and have helped others to establish rewarding careers.

We may be moving to a more rural area in 1990. We would like to expand our publishing and artistic activities, and are planning to build some ecologically sound innovative housing. 11/27/89

Syzygy Cooperative Community
R.R. #1
Hornby Island, B.C.
CANADA V0R-1Z0
(604) 335-0325

Syzygy is a place where we can live our individual and family lives in a spirit of trust and cooperation. Eighteen of us are agreed to be mutually responsible for 80 acres of land on Hornby Island in the Straight of Georgia. We have been here as a group since 1973, and govern our group by emergent consensus. We help each other when asked, but are careful not to impose our wills on each other. While each individual is paramount, our mutual trust, love, and respect allow us to place high value on the collectivity. We often join together spontaneously to accomplish whatever project is at the forefront. We have an annual group project — a pizza booth at the Vancouver Folk Festival — which provides financial support for the cooperative; the individual families financially support themselves. 7/15/88

Tanguy Homesteads
54 Twin Pine Way
Glen Mills, PA 19342

Tanguy Homesteads began in 1945 as an *intentional* community. One of the primary goals of the six founding families was to develop low-cost housing that would be cooperatively owned, with no limitations on membership with respect to color, race, or creed. They divided the original 100-acre tract into lots of about two acres each, with 10 acres of community land. Lots were leased to member-owners whenever possible; deeds were given when needed as a base for obtaining mortgages.

These objectives and the original character of the community have been maintained over the years (though most of Tanguy's houses are now on deeded rather than leased land, and few could still be characterized as low-cost). Our present membership is 38 families, and our backgrounds vary in race, political preference, religious point of view, and job skills.

Tanguy is guided by a set of by-laws and some standard operating procedures and policies. Nothing, however, is static here ... change has been our rule, and changes are our source of continued renewal. We often explore fresh ways to use Tanguy's land, buildings, flexible structure, and tradition of cooperation to meet common needs. Each resident adult in a member family is expected to regularly attend our monthly membership meetings, take part in work days, and serve on at least one committee — where most of our organization and program are carried out. At present we have committees for Community Life, Recreation,

Tanguy Homesteads *(cont'd.)*

Homestead, Junior Membership, Nominating, New Members, Community Buildings, Pond, Tractor, Community Land, Publication, and Finance. Members vote for officers and directors, and are welcome to attend Board meetings.

The monthly meetings are where we make decisions as a community. No votes are taken ordinarily; our decisions are reached instead through what we call "substantial agreement." Workdays are important in getting many projects completed, including maintenance on roads and buildings, pond work, cleaning and repairing the Community Center, and helping neighbors with projects bigger than they can handle alone. Celebrations, holidays, an annual camping trip, pottery classes, dances, and weekly potlucks all contribute to our spirit of community living.

We have a monthly assessment (currently $30) which is used to maintain community-owned land, buildings, and the pond; to pay the community's taxes and insurance; and to support various community activities. It is preferable for people considering living here to get to know the community before a house becomes available (which is often unexpectedly). Prospective members are encouraged to attend potlucks, membership meetings, other community events — and to discuss with various members the many aspects of our community. [cc] 3/2/90

Teramanto

**10217 - 148th Street SE
Renton, WA 98056**

(206) 255-9573 / 255-3563

Teramanto (est. 1974) was formed by A Pacific Group — developed in 1971 by Fellowship of Reconciliation members and friends. It is now several adults plus children in two adjacent houses 15 miles from Seattle. We are in the May Valley Coop [MVC] Homeowners Association. Tera has 1-1/2 acres and lots adjacent for more building. It also has use of the MVC organic garden and 21-acre forest.

Most Tera residents contribute to the small cash household expenses — and work in community maintenance and subsistence production. Those without enough outside income can work more inside for cash.

We endeavor, partly through simple living, to contribute more to a better world, and to do for others as one does for self. We participate in co-op, peace, and environmental activities. We are building alternative-energy housing and exploring community enterprises. Decisions are by consensus. Membership is open. Visitors should contact us well in advance. 12/13/88

Third Avenue Co-operative

**Columbia, MO
(314) 875-8668**

The Third Avenue Cooperative is an urban community which presently consists of 8 adult members and 4 children living in two adjacent households in Columbia, Missouri. (We own a cluster of 3 houses, but the third is rented to friends who aren't members.) The title is held by our cooperative corporation, which is managed by the group as a whole. We aspire to make all decisions by consensus, although our bylaws specify majority rule in certain instances; in practice, a vote hasn't happened in many years.

Our primary shared value is cooperative anti-authoritarianism — and most members are active in grassroots organizations working toward that goal. Some of our involvements include: local and global environmental issues; peace and justice work; equality for all ... regardless of gender, age, or race; printed and audio-visual media.

Our lives are quite independent, though we share ownership expenses, regular meetings, and occasional meals. We welcome visitors only with adequate advance notice, since guest space is limited. Please call for more information, and be prepared to leave a message if no one's around (we call collect when returning long-distance calls). 2/6/90

Thoreau Center

**3500 Kingman Boulevard
Des Moines, IA 50311**

(515) 279-7311

The Thoreau Center is an alternative community full of people committed to peace and social justice who are artists, environmentalists, and other creators. Overall focus: an integration of the arts, the environment, and spiritual growth. Most members are vegetarian, all group meals are. For income, subgroups do workshops, book sales, etc. Members operate a

Creative Arts Collective and the Solar Energy Collective; our Feminist Creationist Group does lots of Earth rituals and workshops; one of the houses is a lesbian/gay center. Please enclose an SASE with correspondence. [cc] 1/16/90

3HO Guru Ram Das Ashram

**438 Long Plain Road
Leverett, MA 01054**

(413) 548-9344

We are a center of the Healthy, Happy, Holy Organization (3HO) — a worldwide association of people dedicated to the excellence of the individual. See main listing in Resources section. 2/2/89

3HO International Headquarters

**Guru Ram Das Ashram
Box 35006
Los Angeles, CA 90035**

(213) 550-9043

The 3HO Foundation is an international educational and spiritual organization exemplifying the standards of righteous living and service to humanity that is the foundation of the Sikh Dharma (founded in India in the 15th century). See main listing in Resources section. Other headquarter locations:

•*Eastern US Region* — 1740 White Wood Lane; Herndon, VA 22070 (703) 435-4411

•*Canada* — 346 Palmerston, Toronto, Ontario, Canada M6G 2N6 (416) 964-0612

•*European Region* — Dan Texstraat 46, Amsterdam, Holland 10 17 (Telephone: 24-19-77) 12/20/88

3HO New Mexico

**Hacienda De Guru Ram Das
Route 3, Box 132-D
Espanola, NM 87532**

(505) 753-7832

3HO has centers throughout the world (see Resource listing). Our lifestyle is based on the yogic practices of vegetarianism, abstinence from drugs, Kundalini Yoga, and meditation. We practice the Sikh religion. Our center also hosts an annual camp for women — where women break from their routines to experience their individual identities as women and their lives as a seeker of truth. 3/31/89

Toad Hollow Community Farm

Route 2
Bracebridge, Ontario
CANADA P0B-1C0

(705) 645-3716 / 645-3831

We are at present a family-centered community of two households. We aspire to live as gently on the earth as possible, growing and storing food for our own consumption. Our food growing and shared meals follow vegetarian, organic principles ... although we do include milk and eggs in our diet.

Our intention is to create an open, affirming, caring space in which all members can grow as individuals while sharing the loving support of the other members. Members value openness to and desire for personal growth and intimate, supportive relationships.

There is a high level of social consciousness among the members which is expressed individualistically. We share an underlying goal to, as much as possible, maintain a lifestyle free of violence in all its various forms. We are particularly interested in confronting sexist, stereotypic roles, and in raising children who are centered in their own beings and are capable of consciously directing their own lives. 9/20/89

Tobias Community

Route 1, Birch Hill Drive
Wilton, NH 03086
(603) 878-3939

Tobias Community is an Anthroposophically oriented initiative that is just one year old. Our approach to work with handicapped people incorporates vocational, social, and expressive arts therapies, as well as psychotherapies. We further include the medical arts, whole nutrition, body therapies, and spiritual aspects as part of our striving to create a healing environment.

We presently have a live-in position available for a female coworker or a couple, to work with developmentally disabled adults who are dually diagnosed. The work is intense,

but rewarding. Applicants should be committed, creative, and centered. Send resumé and cover letter to Charles W. Frank, Route 1, Birch Hill Drive, Wilton, NH 03086. 10/2/89

Tolstoy Farm

Route 3, Box 72-R
Davenport, WA 99122
(509) 725-6497 (machine)

Tolstoy Farm (est. 1963) is an eclectic community stewarding 460 acres of canyon land in six different parcels. About the only thing all have in common is avoidance of chemically dependent farming methods. The largest piece, 160 acres (Mill Canyon Benevolent Society — MCBS), is corporately owned, with land designated for common use and several leased "homesteads".

At MCBS 40 percent are kids, and over half of those children of school age are home-schooled. Members earn money working in outside jobs, and some have home businesses. Most homes here are solar electric.

Other corporately owned land is 80 acres, Sunrise Hill Free School. Legal operation of the school ceased 10 years ago, but seven adults and nine children live here currently. Most homes here are "on the grid" for their electric supply.

Occasional openings for new member(s) occur when a departing family or individual sells their improvements to move. No profit or capital gain is allowed. Some households will take-in apprentices who wish to experience our lifestyles.

We try to respect Mother Earth, ourselves, each other, and the world. We believe that individual freedoms can co-exist with community consensus, and encourage peaceful communication to solve whatever problems may need to be worked out. We are tolerant, liberal, and ethical. Except for weekly potlucks, we find need for community meetings rare — one to six times a year. Those wishing "all your info" should tell us about themselves and enclose SASE. 6/23/89

Top O' The Ten

10 Royal Street #2
Allston, MA 02134
(617) 782-9559

Six adults in an urban cooperative household. They asked to be included, but no additional information has been received. 8/16/89

Trails End Ranch

Route 2, Box 924
Royal, AR 71914

(501) 767-2431

Trails End Ranch (near Hot Springs, in north-central Arkansas) was established in 1983. We are a group of like-minded people interested in our physical and emotional well-being, and we are moving toward self-sufficiency and environmental development. We are looking for sincere, dedicated individuals to help us build a life in this beautiful, semi-mountainous region with an abundance of lakes, streams, and timber.

Cottage industries will provide our small group free time to travel and camp; to enjoy and participate in liberal arts or other creative endeavors; to study nature and the environment; to garden organically; to visit and network with other communities; and to pursue other hobbies or avocations.

We have a modified lifestyle of family network — social equality and decision-making. We strive to help those around us and the animals of our local environment.

Purposes: improve social/economic standard of living, reduce overhead, joint efforts on community projects, social interaction and cooperation (being there for each other through bad and good times, such as happiness and sorrow), upgraded lifestyle, increased security and ecology.

The members think this is a unique community for selective individuals. Applicants with a sincere desire to work and play as a group may reply. 12/12/88

Triform

Route 4, Box 151
Hudson, NY 12534

(518) 851-9320/21

Triform is a Camphill Community located in New York State. Many people who join us have had difficulties finding their place in life. All are looking for an appropriate social setting where everyone is willing to live and learn together. Most of the young people are in their early 20s; however, we are open to answer inquiries from any person looking for community life.

Work provides a meaningful learning experience for the young person. On the farm and in the

N. America

Triform (Cont'd.)

garden, we care for the plants and animals which feed us. In our houses, we learn to deal with our physical environment as well as with people. Through craft work, cultural activities, and artistic and academic courses, we share with each other.

"The important issue here is that our teaching lives. We are not content for the growing person to acquire certain ideas, feelings, abilities ... but that he or she takes with him into life something that is in itself alive." (–Rudolf Steiner)

We are working towards an understanding of the whole person and his destiny. Our whole approach is to overcome labels and work towards the sharing of life in all aspects of the threefold social organism — leading to an awareness of the person as an agent of change and responsibility. 2/2/90

Truth Consciousness

Sacred Mountain Ashram
3305 County Road 96
Ward, CO 80481

(303) 447-1637

Truth Consciousness was founded in 1974 by Swami Amar Jyoti as a vehicle for spiritual awakening. The primary focus is the uplifting of human consciousness into a life in tune with the Divine. The organization presently maintains ashrams in Ward (CO), Tucson (AZ), and Rockford (MI); and Community Centers in Boulder (CO) and Tucson. These five centers provide a setting for devotees and disciples to grow spiritually under the direct guidance of the Master. Meditation, yoga instruction, frequent retreats, and weekly Satsangs (Spiritual Discourses) are open to all sincere seekers. Guests are welcome to visit or stay at the centers by special arrangement. While there is never a fee for any of these programs (other than retreats), donations are always welcome. 3/23/91

Twin Brooks Farm

644 Lucas Creek Road
Chehalis, WA 98532

(206) 262-3169

Our community of 4 adults and 1 child is just developing on land that has been owned by two of our members since 1953; we have talked of land trust or incorporating. We honor a diversity of paths, and greet a great many friends new and old throughout the year (in the last 10 years we have had about 1,000 visitors). We try to produce enough in our organic garden to provide most of our vegetables for the year, and there is potential for selling at the local farmers' market. We raise chickens, ducks, and geese to help fertilize, weed, lay eggs, and provide meat. We also have goats, sheep, a Great Pyrenees dog, orchards, a greenhouse, woodshop, and sawmill.

We all contribute financially, and most are active in the surrounding community (including in a cooperative preschool). We try to eat healthfully, and do hikes, hot tubs in old bathtubs, sweat lodges, singing, playing, and work parties. Individual members are involved in alternative building, woodworking, social and political activism, local church activities, graphic design, nursery work, and tree doctoring. Call or write for more information (SASE). 12/20/88

Twin Oaks

Route 4, Box 169-D
Louisa, VA 23093
(703) 894-5126

Twin Oaks is a community of 85 people living on 400 acres of farm and forestland in rural Virginia. Since the community's inception in 1967, our way of life has reflected our values of equality, ecology, and nonviolence.

We are economically self-sufficient. Our hammocks and casual furniture business generates most of our income, with our book indexing and software services providing much of the rest. Still, less than half of our work goes into these income-producing areas: the balance goes into a variety of tasks that benefit our quality of life — including milking cows, gardening, cooking, and communal child care. Most people prefer doing a variety of work, rather than the same job day in, day out.

A number of us choose to be politically active in issues of peace, ecology, anti-racism, and feminism. Each summer we host a women's gathering ("Women — Celebrating Our Diversity"), and each spring we host a men's gathering ("Softening the Stone").

To arrange a visit, write us a few weeks in advance. Potential members visit for three weeks and later participate in a six-month provisional period. There is no membership fee — we want to encourage people of diverse economic and racial backgrounds to live here. 5/10/90

Union Acres (Forming)

Route 1, Box 61-G
Union Hill Road
Whittier, NC 28789

(704) 497-4964

Union Acres is based upon principles of equality, consensus, simplicity, and wholesome living. Our purpose is "to live as neighbors in peace, harmony, and ecological balance; to respect and support one another and all forms of life; and to attune to and act in harmony with the Universal Life Force which is the essence of all existence." Guidelines for harmony and conflict resolution are provided, but the freedom and privacy of individuals is maintained. There is no requirement to ascribe to any religious or political ideology other than attunement to the "good of the whole."

Eighty beautiful acres in the Great Smoky Mountains have been surveyed into 24 lots for sale (between one and four acres), with seven acres set aside as common land. Community development moves ahead as lots are sold, and includes a budget for roads, nature trails, and community buildings. Decisions are shared by members of our non-profit Landowner Association; after 80 percent of the lots are sold, decisions will be made by consensus of the residents. Future projects planned include community organic gardens, a recycling center, a food co-op, an alternative children's school, a chapel, cooperative businesses, retreats and workshops. We seek like-minded families to join us — please call. 8/31/89

Urban Stonehenge

1998 - 25th Street
San Francisco, CA 94107

We are a collective household of five adults committed to political activism and cultural work in pursuit of social change. We are feminist, anti-authoritarian, and work as part of a larger community of 15 other anarchist, collective, or pagan households in the S.F. Bay Area. Our activities run the gamut from traditional direct action organizing to large performance/spectacle events. We provide meeting, rehearsal, and events space for our community — reserving one floor for those purposes (our building is an ex-church). Though we don't own our space, we share all expenses and chores, and operate by consensus ... having meetings as mood or necessity strikes us. We tend to be ideologically impure, sweetly cynical, convinced that revolution is a blast. We also like to dance. If you write, an SASE would be nice. 10/23/89

The Vale
Box 207
Yellow Springs, OH 45387
(513) 767-1461

Established in '61, we are five members and five non-member families living on 40 acres of woodland, two miles from the center of Yellow Springs. Each family lives in its own home and earns its own living. The land and utilities are managed together.

We govern by consensus. Many of us are Quakers; some are vegetarians. Most garden extensively.

We are family-oriented, and desire families who share concern for nature, the wider society, and for the well-being of the family unit. Interested people must live here for a year before a mutual decision about membership is made. 4/28/90

Valley of Light
HC 289
Hagarville, AR 72839
(501) 443-2127 (ans. svc.)

Valley of Light is a spiritually oriented community whose emphasis is on self-realization and self-sufficiency. It is located on 60 acres in a secluded valley inside 15,000 acres of a National Wilderness. The land is divided into three areas: community activity, residential, and cropland/pasture.

Goals: Create a time/space where the self-realization of each member is fully supported and nurtured. Live in harmony with each other — with love, trust, openness, honesty, and shar-

ing. Share spiritual life together. Live in harmony with nature, having respect for all living forms. Flow with Universal Energy so all actions are appropriate. Become self-sufficient to the extent that conditions "outside" have a minimum effect on the community.

Notes: The community is Egalitarian (one vote per adult). The structure consists of Goals, Membership Requirements, Membership Rights, and Community Agreements. There is a three- to six-month trial membership period before permanent membership is granted. The community is vegetarian. The children will be schooled by the community at the Valley. Separate sleeping quarters are planned for each "family"; all other facilities are communal. The community population is currently limited to 14 adults plus children. The Valley is a "multi-path" community. 3/1/89

Vedantic Center
c/o Harold Jones
3528 Triunfo Canyon Road
Agoura, CA 91301
(818) 706-9478

The Directory received a postcard from this group stating their desire to be included. No further information was received. 3/12/89

Villa Sarah
1134 E. Palm Street
Altadena, CA 91001

What makes us special? Our surroundings and our individual differences. We're suburban, 15 miles north of Los Angeles, yet we live in a reconverted 1912 mansion of sorts, a few blocks from the San Gabriel Mountains. We do the groundskeeping — including tending a vegetable garden and composting organics — ourselves. (These are valued — and worked at — more by some than by others.)

We're white, all (adults) are employed, lesbian/gay and straight, most of us are parents, many of us are coupled. We're committed to: cooking for each other, sharing household tasks, meeting weekly. At the meetings we do the routine (schedule tasks, meals, guests ...) and the special (take turns facilitating and leading an activity which enriches our time together).

And continuously our politics and philosophies meet real life — some of us care about (not) financing

socially (ir)responsible corporations — some of us begrudgingly participate in boycotts. Some of us have pets — others have personal/political feelings against pets, their care and expense. Some of us are vegetarians, and we try to accommodate each dietary need and preference. Most of us are familiar with (white middle-class type) group process, but we are more or less comfortable with group facilitation and sharing intimacy. As a group we are committed to being a working community amidst these differences. Please include SASE with correspondence. 1/3/89

Vine & Fig Tree
11076 County Road 267
Lanett, AL 36863
(205) 499-2380

Vine & Fig Tree, established in 1986, is presently 4 adults sharing a house on 240 acres near the eastern edge of Alabama. We are very serious gardeners, share meals, share costs on a variable basis, try to make all decisions by consensus, and plan to put title to our land into a land trust.

We want spiritual growth for all members, with affirmation of diversity. "Vine and Fig Tree where all shall live in peace and unafraid" is a vision and challenge for us to grow in loving non-violence among ourselves (including regular sharing of deep feelings) and with all of creation. Thus we participate in voter registration, the annual Sing Out for Peace, marching in Selma, walking "From Trident to Life," refusing to pay for death subs and death squads – and we actively work for the abolition of the death penalty, war, imperialism, racism, environmental degradation, anti-Semitism, homophobia. ...

An occasional gathering place for small groups, we dream of large gatherings/workshops, e.g., orientations in non-violence, cultural sharing, permaculture classes. We want a land-based economy, and envision the possibility of alternative schooling that can also benefit the local schools, of services that can benefit the county: recycling? weatherization? health care?

We need fiscal and physical resources to help us care for at least two elderly parents, to help us plan and repair, and to help us build Vine & Fig Tree. We are open to new members. Please call if you'd like more information. 6/5/90

Vivekananda Monastery & Retreat

6723 Fenn Valley Road
Fennville, MI 49408
(616) 543-4545 / 543-4114

Situated on 108 acres of land, the Vivekananda Monastery and Retreat offers a quiet rural setting with facilities for individual and group retreats. This is a branch of the Vivekananda Vedanta Society of Chicago. Our residential community is presently 12 celibate adults who share a willingness to work, and acceptance of the path of others. We offer regular classes, and a schedule of conferences, concerts, and meditation workshops. Write for more information. 7/12/89

Vivekananda Vedanta Society

5423 South Hyde Park
Chicago, IL 60615
(312) 363-0027

The Vivekananda Vedanta Society of Chicago is a branch of the Ramakrishna Math and Mission which has its headquarters at Belur Math, India. The Chicago Center was founded in 1930, although Swami Vivekananda participated in the Parliament of Religions held in Chicago in 1893 — becoming the first Hindu monk to bring the message of Vedanta to the West.

The society maintains a temple, monastery, and guest house in Chicago, and a monastery with retreat facilities in Michigan. Both centers maintain bookshops which are open every day, and libraries of books on Eastern and Western religion and culture. There are 15 resident members who live at the Chicago center. 7/12/89

Walden Hill

Route 5, Box 152
Stillwater, OK 74074
(405) 372-3287

Walden hill is a community organized for the improvement of the spiritual and material welfare of the Rainbow Family... an all-inclusive family which disregards all distinctions of color, race, or creed. It includes everyone on planet Earth who has a belly button.

We are creating a peaceful, sober, cooperative society where individual differences of belief, opinion, taste, and behavior are mutually respected and tolerated. Equality of creed, sex, age, and race are promoted. This is a child-life sanctuary, a wildlife sanctuary, and an alcohol-free (not allowed) zone.

We seek an ecologically-sound way of life, making use of appropriate technology with maximum dependence on renewable resources and solar energy. We emphasize voluntary simplicity, and aim to be self-reliant and self-supporting. Any trade or commerce we engage in will promote and contribute to the maintenance of a non-exploitive world economy. Most of our group decisions require the unanimous consent of the circle (a decision-making council of all residents).

Our income is shared through what we call the Magic Hat, and our books are open to any resident at any time. On any job over $300 that we do as a group, 20% is divided by those who did the work, 10% by the other residents of the Hill, and 70% goes into the Magic Hat. On jobs yielding less than $300, the residents will decide what is fair—based on current priorities and outstanding bills. On all personal jobs landed, 50% goes to the worker, and 50% to the Magic Hat (all expenses come off the top).

To head off interpersonal tension, we encourage direct communication and emphasize the importance of listening carefully to the other person's feelings and perceptions. Hearsay is usually inaccurate, if not grossly distorted — it is probably best disregarded, and not even repeated, unless you go directly to the object of the hearsay and tell him/her what is being said.

A *Guest* is someone dropping by, in from the road, needing a calm, peaceful place to crash. We welcome visitors, and figure a week is long enough; but of course there are exceptions — which will be dealt with accordingly in the circle. If a guest would like to stay on, the next step is to become a *Working Visitor.* The circle will decide if they will be an asset and compatible with our community, and we figure that a month is a reasonable time for that process. Before becoming a *Resident*, they will submit a Statement of Intent. Visitors should call first to make arrangements. If you write, an SASE would be great (but isn't required). 5/19/89

Walker Creek Farm

1802-C Peter Burns Road
Mt. Vernon, WA 98273
(801) 422-5709

Members of Evergreen Land Trust. 8 adults and 5 children. Although they did ask to be included, no other information has been received. 9/11/89

Waukon Institute for Co-Creative Art

Route 1, Box 9-C
Edwall, WA 99008
(509) 236-2265

The members of Earth Cyclers and Zaishta Church have come together to form this new community. WICCA will manage and operate a holistic self-healing camp conjunctively with a natural food farm providing staff, space, and facilities on 600 acres for camping and a wide variety of groups, activities, and workshops on practical, spiritual, ecological, and self-actualizing subjects (see Resource listing).

A healthful diet of whole, natural foods will be grown on Earth Cyclers Farm and other local organic farms.

We seven are looking for more partners who are into healing and nutritional arts. We also intend our community to be a focus of Gylanic Art Expression — that is, music, poetry, dance, painting, sculpture which comes in an egalitarian tribal society. 8/1/89

Wellspring

4382 Hickory Road
West Bend, WI 53095
(414) 675-6755

Wellspring is a year-round retreat and conference center located just 25 miles north of Milwaukee. Wellspring, Inc. was founded as a non-profit educational organization in '82; we moved to the land and became a community in '88. We are presently 3 adult members, with leadership provided by our Board of Directors, and a Center staff made up of volunteers. We have 2 houses on 32 acres now, and are buying another 68 acres in 1990. At that point there will be room for more homesites, and more community members.

We respect each person's truth and spiritual path, and deeply value the Earth and our place in the planetary community. Our educational programs include wellness education, the arts, ecology & gardening, and personal growth. The organic gardens provide hands-on experience in bio-dynamic gardening methods, and quality food for Wellspring guests and Garden Club members (for $25/year members can harvest their own produce, paying 25% less than super-market prices). We also offer associate memberships for those who would want to use the Center as though it were their vacation home — with the facilities available on a first-come basis. Write or call Mary Ann Ihm at the office for more information on pro-grams, reservations, and rates. 1/9/90

Wellspring House, Inc.
302 Essex Avenue
Gloucester, MA 01930
(617) 281-3221

Our community operates a shelter for homeless families, and our life-style reflects our commitment to social change. Our successful mem-bers, both past and present, came because they cared about the work and wanted to do it in a cooperative style — not because they wanted "community." All major decisions are made by consensus. Small salaries are paid to our staff who are not strictly in "community" with our many volunteers and Board of Directors. This varied circle of friends and fel-low workers means that we are not a closed circle but rather a small "center" around which many gather, sharing their gifts in all kinds of ways and degrees. 12/14/88

Wesleyan Christian Community
Box 668
Vashon Island, WA 98070
(206) 463-9123

The Wesleyan Christian Community was formed in 1977, growing out of a Church congregation which desired the richer and more fulfilling Christian experience and life experi-ence that community can provide. We have also organized a Retreat Center to provide a haven where people — no matter what their religion, race, or nationality — may come for help to deal with their spiritual, emotional, and relationship problems. This inner-healing ministry, developed over a period of 22 years, is accom-plished through counseling, work-shops, and in-residence programs. The only charge while here is for the food.

We also provide for the staff and their families (28 adults, 20 children)

a warm, loving, and supportive ex-tended family environment in which to live and work. Each family lives in their own quarters, and handles their own money. Each member presently makes a monthly contribution to finance a major construction project, and tithes 15% to finance our inner-healing ministry.

The community is governed by the members through a weekly meeting, where a unanimous vote is required on all issues. 7/12/89

Whitehall Co-op
2500 Nueces
Austin, TX 78705
(512) 472-3329

Founded August 6, 1949, Whitehall Co-op is Texas' oldest housing co-operative. The 13-member house-hold includes a variety of ages and occupations, and everyone contri-butes equally to monetary costs and household labor. Whitehall is a non-sexist, non-racist, non-competitive living environment. All decisions are made by consensus.

Our goals include obtaining intimate, meaningful tribal/familial bonds, emotional support, and spontaneous and planned creation and play. We are learning proper use of resources, non-competitiveness, and communication skills. We want to be a part of a significant, non-exploitive socio-economic movement.

The household is vegetarian, though fish meals are occasionally prepared. No smoking of any sort is allowed in Whitehall. All members have individual rooms with semi-private bathrooms. Whitehall was the first Texas recipient of funds from the National Co-op Bank (Washington DC) in '79 for use in construction of a professional-grade kitchen. 5/19/89

Windspirit
Los Angeles, CA
See: Christmas Star (AZ)

Winged Heart Homestead (Forming)
& The Penny Royal
Education Center
P.O. Box 552
Floyd, VA 24091
(703) 763-3728

The Winged Heart Homestead em-phasizes healthy living, spiritual

growth, respect for ecology, and research on holistic healing and methods of organic farming/gardening. Members are accepted on their compatibilities to our ideals of Universality, and active interest in spiritual growth. We prefer families with children.

We have added the Penny Royal Educational Center (now incorpora-ted) to the homestead, and will give a number of seminars this summer. The seminars are moderately priced, and barter arrangements will be given in certain cases. The following topics are planned: psychic attunement and readings, telepathy, house construc-tion using native materials, sweat lodge ceremony, and Sufi spiritual healings. We work closely with other organizations in Floyd County who have related ideas. Our brochure is available upon request.

We are planning to build a Univer-sal — a Sufi temple building which will be used for Universal worship honoring all world religions. It will also serve as a place for healing, music, and theater performances.

Our homestead is 283 acres, and includes camping facilities. Those wishing to camp here are requested to make reservations in advance. Mail inquiries only, please; include SASE if available. 5/5/89

Wiscoy Valley
Community Land
Cooperative Association
Route 3, Box 163
Winona, MN 55987
(507) 452-4990

We are a group of 20 adults and as many children living on 356 acres of land in beautiful southeastern Min-nesota. Our land is valley and ridge, field, forest, prairie and open — with a small creek running through the valley and a few small ponds. We are individually minded folks with no common dogmatic ideology. We try to treat the land with respect and man-age it in common, keep membership reasonable, and cooperate with each other. We've been established for 13 years in co-op form, building our own houses and generally trying to be self-reliant. Our adult ages range from 28 to 48, and children's ages range from 1 to 17. We are open to a few more responsible people to join and grow with us. Please write before visiting. 12/13/88

Wolf Creek Sanctuary

c/o Nomenus
P.O. Box 312
Wolf Creek, OR 97497

Wolf Creek Sanctuary is situated on a land trust owned by Nomenus, a non-profit corporation founded to locate and purchase land for faeries (see Resources). We have hosted three large West Coast gatherings of the Radical Faeries, and are involved in other organizing and networking for the Men's Movement. 12/14/88

WomanShare

P.O. Box 681
Grants Pass, OR 97526

(503) 862-2807

WomanShare Feminist Women's Land (established in 1974) is a home and family of Lesbians on 23 acres of hilly forest land in southern Oregon. We welcome women visitors and their girl children, and are periodically open for new collective members. We have a main house with kitchen, living room, and shower room. We also have six women-built cabins, one reserved especially for our visitors. The other cabins are the living places of collective members.

We have a large garden, trails to hike, and work projects to share with women who would like to contribute their energy to women's land. We ask visitors to contribute $5 to $20 per person, sliding scale, for each day of your visit. This includes lodging or camping, land use, and food. We also hold workshops, concerts, and community gatherings here on the land. Please call or write before coming so that we can be prepared, and so you know that there is space available. When writing, please include an SASE (and please, no inquiries from men). 3/15/91

Woodburn Hill Farm

1150 Woodburn Hill Road
Mechanicsville, MD 20659

(301) 884-5615

Woodburn Hill started off approximately 15 years ago with total income sharing, much shared child rearing responsibility, and many communal activities such as meal prep and eating. Over the years we've gradually gotten away from that, and now we're pretty independent. There could be a return to more shared communal activities and responsibilities with the right energy and people.

The land and houses are owned by a corporation with about 23 shareholders who have somehow been connected to the farm over the years. Shareholder decisions are by consensus. Residents can be shareholders or not, but both types of residents pay rent to the corporation. All the residents are expected to share in the upkeep of common grounds — it's 128 acres of woods and fields, barns, lawns, a pond, and Amish neighbors. There's one main house and two smaller houses organized by families, one trailer, and another house which we hope to use more as a retreat center for appropriate groups.

We hope to nurture the land and derive quiet and sustenance from it. Hopefully everyone is open to progressive and alternative lifestyles and beliefs. Some are into vegetarianism. Telephone inquiries only. 2/14/90

Woodcrest Bruderhof

Hutterian Brethren
P.O. Box 903
Rifton, NY 12471-0903

(914) 658-3141

Christian, rural, communal. Visitors arrange in advance. Write for information. See main listing for the "Hutterian Brethren." 3/25/91

Woolcroft Farm (Forming)

Route 1, Box 69-13
Couch, MO 65690

(417) 938-4549

I have 73 acres, approximately 55 in woodland, with several nice homesites. The couple who were buying the land with me changed their mind (due to a lot of personal, family, and financial problems), so I am attempting to farm alone at present. I would still like to find some others with common interests to join me.

I have a small flock of beautiful sheep (long-wool "spinners" for yarn), Angora rabbits, and a few chickens. The house is large but old. It needs work but is livable. I have two extra bedrooms and a large attic that could be finished into a large room or rooms. I am trying to use some "Permaculture" methods and erosion control. We do have an organic gardening association going here, and so can get marketing for organically grown vegetables and fruits. 1/25/89

Yahara Linden Co-op

2117 Linden Avenue
Madison, WI 53704

(608) 249-4474 / 249-4131

The Yahara Linden Gathering is comprised of 7 adults and 1 child who share a comfortable, three-story Victorian home, garden, greenhouse and common meals. Individuals have professions and personal income within this vital Midwestern city. The co-op is political and into civil liberties and human rights. Religion, politics, and sexuality are one's personal choice. Decision-making is by consensus. A non-equity co-op, Yahara Linden has existed since '74; as a household we are involved in environmental and peace issues. This co-op is an alternative to landlord-owned rental housing in Madison. Visitors are welcome as guests of individual members. 12/15/88

Yoga Society of Rochester

93 Spruce Avenue
Rochester, NY 14611

(716) 235-1810

While we are not exactly an intentional community, we are community-oriented and have a strong emphasis on education, personal growth, and cooperative alternatives.

Actually, the Yoga Society has two identities: firstly, we are an educational membership organization, offering a wide range of classes and workshops in yoga and other personal growth modalities. Overall governance is in the hands of a board of 9 trustees. Secondly, we are a core group of, presently, 6 adults who live together in the Yoga Society Center.

We have a minimum of formal rules, and operate by consensus of the core group.

Our facilities consist of a large house in an urban setting close to the University. This structure provides both instructional and residential space. We have an extra lot adjacent which we use for recreation and growing vegetables.

We are always open to expanding our membership and educational program, and we sometimes have openings in our core group. We can accommodate small numbers for brief periods of time, and can arrange special programs for small groups. Our quarterly newsletter will be sent upon request. 12/13/88

Yogaville

Satchidananda Ashram
Route 1, Box 172
Buckingham, VA 23921

(804) 969-3121

Satchidananda Ashram/Yogaville is the international headquarters for the Integral Yoga Institutes (we have many associated urban centers). Yogaville is situated on 750 secluded acres of wooded hills and fields in rural Virginia, with a panoramic view of the James River and the Blue Ridge Mountains. Here, under the guidance of the Reverend Sri Swami Satchidananda (Gurudev), people of all faiths and backgrounds have come together to study and practice the principles of Integral Yoga to attain mental and physical health, ease, and peace. Yogaville is designed to serve as a model of how we can all live and work together in harmony while still enjoying our individual differences. Residents include both singles and families, and individuals who have chosen to make a formal commitment as monastics or as ministers. Our children's education programs include a preschool, primary school, and high school.

At the center of Yogaville is the Light Of Truth Universal Shrine (LOTUS), dedicated to the Light of all faiths, and to world peace. It houses altars for all the major world religions, and representative altars for other known and still unknown faiths. The LOTUS is a center for silent contemplation and meditation, and embodies the message "Truth is One, Paths are Many." We also publish and/or distribute many spiritual materials including books, magazines, videotapes, and cassettes. 1/19/90

Zaishta Church

Edwall, WA
See: Waukon Institute

Zen Buddhist Temple

1214 Packard Road
Ann Arbor, MI 48104

See listing for "Zen Lotus Society — Toronto." 12/20/88

Zen Center of Los Angeles

923 S. Normandie Avenue
Los Angeles, CA 90006
(213) 387-235

Located in the heart of the Wilshire District in Los Angeles is an urban Zen training center and residential community. ZCLA offers a year-round training schedule including daily zazen, weekly instruction, talks, interviews with a teacher, and intensive retreats ranging from two to seven days monthly. The schedule intensifies during a 90-day Winter Training Period. During the summer months, a second 90-day intensive retreat is held at our affiliate Zen Mountain Center which is nestled in the San Jacinto Mountains, 120 miles east of Los Angeles.

The 40-member residential community is composed of students, professionals, families, monks, and lay practitioners — all engaged in the Buddha Way under the guidance of Abbot Taizan Maezumi, Roshi. Residents are expected to participate in the daily schedule on a regular basis, to take part in the upkeep of ZCLA's facilities, and to provide help with ZCLA programs. Part of the Japanese Soto Zen tradition, the community also serves practicing members throughout California and affiliate groups throughout the United States. Short-term residential training opportunities are also available at both city and mountain centers. 1/24/90

The Zen Lotus Society

86 Vaughn Road
Toronto, Ontario
CANADA M6K-2M1
(416) 658-0137

We are a spiritual community focused on Zen training and manual work — under the guidance of Zen Master Samu Sunim of the Korean Chogye Order. We live a communal lifestyle based on the monastic model as it is adapting itself to North America. Some members hold jobs, others work within the temple(s) on projects including the publication of *Spring Wind — Buddhist Cultural Forum,* our international quarterly journal. We have an affiliate community in Michigan.

Our training is open to men, women, and couples (families, under special circumstances) and can lead to religious ordination (monk or nun) or lay orientation (Dharma teacher) for qualified individuals. Short visits can be arranged. A three-month trial residence period and a sincere mind for Zen training are prerequisites for full-time community membership. Inquiries welcome. 12/20/88

Zendik Farm

Arts Foundation
Star Route 16C-3
Bastrop, TX 78602
(512) 321-0712

We are a cooperative tribe based on a reverence for the Earth as a mother, and taking responsibility for everything that happens — to ourselves, to other humans, to plants, to all life forms — everything. We've recently relocated from Southern California to a 300-acre farm near Austin. Our aim is self-sufficiency: organic gardening, animal husbandry, home schooling, carpentry, mechanics, graphix, muzik. We bring in a majority of the money needed to support our group by publishing an underground quarterly environmental/arts magazine. We also have a rock band which plays clubs and concerts, and we have opened a storefront botique/art gallery/coffee house in Austin. Any and all money earned goes toward group support. We have started a political party called ZAP (the Zendik Action Party) in order to get mostly young people working together to throw out the old society and build an ecologically sound one to replace it. Call or write for further information; copies of our magazine are available on request. 4/29/91

The Renamed, Regrouped, Dead, Disbanded, Lost, & No Replies...

It seems that there are quite a few "community lists" floating around out there in the world that are actually compilations of other lists. In doing research for this Directory we integrated every one of those other lists that we could put our hands on — quite a chellenging (and often frustrating) undertaking!

The biggest problem was that mistakes on one list would be perpetuated in each succeeding generation. You could clean a list up one time, then the mistakes would reappear the next time you tried to integrate new groups.

Another major problem was duplications. A group might go by two different names, may have changed names, may have relocated at another address (or even to another state), or may have both a street address and a P.O. Box.

We've tried to clean all of those mistakes and duplications out of our data base, and have included this section so that others can clean up their lists too. Hopefully they'll give us feedback when they have information more current than ours.

A second benefit: when "seekers" come up with a lead for a group not included in our regular listings, this brief summary will indicate whether or not we have any information about the current status of that group. Again — please let us know if you come across any new information or any unlisted groups.

We do have old address and phone information for most of these groups in this section, but we've not been able to get a response from them. If we sent a letter and never heard any-thing in response, then that group's line will include the word "NoResp". If our letter was returned by the Postal Service, our code is "BadPO" and will be followed by the explanation given to us by the Post Office. Many of the groups in both of these categories are still likely to be around and viable — our letter may have been lost, the group may have forgotten to reply or might have been too busy at the time, they may have preferred to remain anonymous and figured that remaining silent was the best way to maintain a low profile. Or maybe the Post Office just made a mistake....

We did hear from over a hundred groups who told us that "We are still a community, but don't wish to be listed at this time." Those groups are not mentioned anywhere in this Directory.

Groups listed as "NoCon" are those we were unable to contact due either to insufficient address and telephone information, or to the fact that their referral came to our attention too late — this Directory would still be in the "idea" stage if we kept trying to chase down all of the leads that we dug up. In any event, we did not send a letter to any groups with this classification.

"Insuff" means that we had some contact indicating that the group still exists in some form, but we weren't sure what to say about them, and got no confirmation that they wanted to be included.

"Dupe" is a duplicate; the group either has another name or a new address. Some of these groups do have actual listings; many are merely cross-referenced to other names in this RRDDLNoR section.

"NLC" means the group responded that they are no longer a community (but may still be a loose cooperative or some other alternative form). "Never" means they said they have never considered themselves to be a community (though they may still look like one to us). "M/R" means the group has been moved to the Resources Section, usually at their own suggestion. If the group is also listed as "NoResp" or "NoCon", then we were considering them for the Resources Section but had no confirmed information.

"Limbo" groups are presently dormant or in transition ... still around in some form or other, but not feeling that they could represent themselves as viable communities at this point.

And last: "Defun". Some of these communities have folded entirely, others have re-emerged through new incarna-tions, still others have been absorbed by similar groups. We have tried to use reliable sources to verify these "defunct" list-ings, but often one person's first hand experience reads quite differently from the next person's. The rumor mill is tough to head off: please let us know if you have any new information.

Sorry about the fine print, but we ran out of space and still wanted to squeeze this in. Hope you find it useful. ❖

Groups are listed alphabetically within each state or province. Canadian RRDDLNoR listings are on page 236.*

First Church in Community	Fairbanks	AK	BadPO	"Insufficient Address"
Kenny Lake	Copper Center	AK	BadPO	"Return to Sender"
L'Arch Mobile	Mobile	AL	NoResp	
Land of Peace	Prattville	AL	NoCon	
Malbis Plantation	Daphne	AL	NoResp	
Morningside	Birmingham	AL	BadPO	"Return to Sender"
New South Lifestyles	Wetumpka	AL	BadPO	"Forwarding Order Expired"
So. Inst. for Appropropriate Tech.	Lineville	AL	Insuff	Contradictory responses
Foundation of Ubiquity	Jasper	AR	NoCon	
Ganashyam	Pelsor	AR	NoResp	
Heartsong Farm	Nail	AR	NoResp	
Leslie Folks	Leslie	AR	Dupe	"Addressee Unknown"
Little Portion Franciscans	Eureka Springs	AR	NoResp	
Living Lightly Village	Fayetteville	AR	BadPO	"Return to Sender"
Lothlorien Fellowship	Harrison	AR	BadPO	"Return to Sender"

Maud's Land	In the Ozarks	AR	Dupe	Fictitious name for a real group
Ozark Wimmin's Land Trust	Fayetteville	AR	NoResp	
Whypperwillow Land, Inc.	Eureka Springs	AR	BadPO	"No such Number"
Adobeland	Tucson	AZ	NoResp	
Buchanan Community	Phoenix	AZ	NoResp	
Capricorn Ranch	Yucca	AZ	BadPO	"Forwarding Order Expired"
Cascabel Clayworks	Benson	AZ	NoResp	
Children of Light	Dateland	AZ	NoResp	
Concord	Snowflake	AZ	NoResp	
Friends United Church	Bisbee	AZ	BadPO	"No Forwarding Address"
Leela Spiritual Life Community	West Sedona	AZ	NoResp	
Making Contact	Tucson	AZ	NoResp	
Miracle Valley	Miracle Valley	AZ	NoCon	
New Earth	Bisbee	AZ	BadPO	"Addressee Unknown"
People of Joy	Scottsdale	AZ	BadPO	"Forwarding Order Expired"

Community	City	State	Status	Note
Saint Francis in the Foothills	Tucson	AZ	NoResp	
Whetstone Community	Benson	AZ	NoCon	
Your Heritage Church	Kingman	AZ	NoResp	
AIM House	Oakland	CA	NoResp	
Annapolis Springs Ranch	Annapolis	CA	NoResp	
Aquarian Minyan	Berkeley	CA	NoResp	
Aquarian Research Group	Agoura	CA	Never	Never was a community
Avadhut Church	Santa Cruz	CA	Never	Never was a community
Babaji Yoga Sangam	Norwalk	CA	BadPO	"Return to Sender"
Bartimaeus Community Church	Berkeley	CA	Defun	Disbanded in '84
Bayland Family	San Jose	CA	BadPO	"Return to Sender"
Bee Song Honey Farms	Montague	CA	NoResp	
Beginnings	Garberville	CA	BadPO	"Forwarding Order Expired"
Bekins Hall	Redlands	CA	Insuff	Student Cooperative
Berkeley Poets Commune	Berkeley	CA	NoResp	
Boddhi Pacific	Los Gatos	CA	NoResp	
Bodega Livestock Pastures	Bodega	CA	NoResp	
Br. of the Holy Translators	Los Angeles	CA	BadPO	"Forwarding Order Expired"
Catholic Worker Farm	Sheepranch	CA	NoResp	
Cave, The	San Francisco	CA	Defun	Folded in '90
Cedar	Camptonville	CA	BadPO	"Addressee Unknown"
Center of the Pumpkin	Occidental	CA	NLC	No longer a community
City of Friendship	New Cuyama	CA	Limbo	Not developing; see Geltaftan [R]
Co-op Communities Project	San Francisco	CA	Defun	Folded in '83; See Kidstown
Colony, The	Burnt Ranch	CA	NoResp	
Community Christi	San Anselmo	CA	NoResp	
Cmty. for Emotional Self-Develpm't.	Santa Cruz	CA	Defun	Dissolved '80
Cooperative Village	Ukiah	CA	Defun	Disbanded '80
Cornucopia West	Soquel	CA	NoResp	
Daga-Ray	San Francisco	CA	NoResp	
Dawn Horse Communion	Middletown	CA	NoResp	
Dhyanyoga Centers Inc.	Soquel	CA	NoResp	
Djarma Community	Ojai	CA	BadPO	"No Forwarding Address"
Earth First! Household	San Francisco	CA	BadPO	"No Forwarding Address"
Empty Gate Zen Center	Berkeley	CA	NoResp	
Farallones Rural Center	Occidental	CA	Never	Never was a community
Firestone Community	Los Angeles	CA	NoCon	
Forever Forests	Redwood Valley	CA	NoResp	
Forever Young	San Mateo	CA	Defun	Folded
Freeman House	Petrolia	CA	NoResp	
Garden Community Land Trust	Covelo	CA	NoResp	
Good Times Commune	San Francisco	CA	Defun	Disbanded '81
Greenfield Ranch	Ukiah	CA	NoResp	Reported still to be at it
Greenhouse	Goleta	CA	NLC	No longer a community
Hanuman Fellowship	Santa Cruz	CA	NoResp	
Harmony Farm	Fallbrook	CA	NoResp	
Harrad	San Francisco	CA	BadPO	"Addressee Unknown"
Harrad West	Berkeley	CA	Dupe	See: Goodlife Community
Harrarian Minyan	Berkeley	CA	Dupe	See: Aquarian Minyan (above)
Harwood House	Oakland	CA	NLC	No longer a community
Heartland	Berkeley	CA	NoResp	
Heliopolis	Oakland	CA	Defun	Regrouped '84; see Brigid
Holy Order of Mans	San Francisco	CA	NLC	No longer a community
House of Love and Prayer	San Francisco	CA	BadPO	"No Forwarding Address"
Human Potential Foundation	Los Olivos	CA	NoResp	
ICSA Ananda	San Francisco	CA	NoResp	
Ilarne	Crockett	CA	BadPO	"Addressee Unknown"
Institute of Mentalphy sics	Yucca Valley	CA	NoResp	
Int'l Buddhist Meditation Center	Los Angeles	CA	NoCon	
Jungian-Senoi Institute	Berkeley	CA	NoResp	
Kailas Shugendo	San Francisco	CA	NoResp	
Kerensa Co-op Community	Menlo Park	CA	Never	Never was a community
Kids-ll-eat Ivy Farm	Cool	CA	BadPO	"Forwarding Order Expired"
Kilowana	Calistoga	CA	Defun	Folded c. '86
Land House	Monte Rio	CA	NoCon	
Landlab	Los Angeles area	CA	NoCon	
Lavender Hill Womyn's Retreat	Elk	CA	Defun	Folded
Limesaddle	Oroville	CA	Defun	Folded in the '70s
Lyons Valley Co-op	Talmage	CA	BadPO	"Addressee Unknown"
Mariposa School	Ukiah	CA	NLC	No longer a community (5/90)
Martin De Porres Catholic Worker	San Francisco	CA	NoResp	
Meadowlark Healing Center	Hemet	CA	NLC	No longer a community
Medicine Ways	Valley Ford	CA	NoResp	
Meditation Mount	Ojai	CA	Never	Never was a community
Mount Baldy Zen Center	Mount Baldy	CA	NoResp	
Mt. Kailasa Farm	Hopland	CA	NoResp	
Multibear Family	San Jose	CA	NoResp	
Murrieta Hot Springs	Murrieta	CA	NoResp	
Naturalism	Los Angeles	CA	BadPO	"Addressee Unknown"
Nityananda	Sebastopol	CA	NoResp	
No Name Given	Berkeley	CA	BadPO	"No Forwarding Address"
Omega Fellowship	Los Gatos	CA	NoResp	
Omega Salvage	Berkeley	CA	NoResp	
One Life Family	Santa Monica	CA	NoResp	
One World Family	Stockton	CA	Defun	Folded
Order of St. Benedict	Central Valley	CA	NoResp	
OSA Rainforest Reserve Coalition	Eureka	CA	NoResp	
Pacha Mama	Susanville	CA	BadPO	"Return to Sender"
Peace House	Pittsburg	CA	NoResp	
Peralta	Sacramento	CA	NoCon	
Pier House	Santa Monica	CA	NoResp	
Plenty International	Jamul	CA	NoResp	
Plow Creek	Carpella	CA	Never	Never was a community
Psico	Pasadena	CA	NoResp	
Purple Submarine	San Francisco	CA	Dupe	Subfamily of Kerista
Radiance Media Ministry	Eureka	CA	NoResp	
Rainbow Star Community	Hornbrook	CA	NoResp	
Ranch, The	San Francisco	CA	NoResp	
Redwood Monastery	Whitethorn	CA	NoResp	
Religious School Natural Hygiene	Santa Cruz	CA	Limbo	Presently dormant
Rio Bonito Cooperative	Sutter Creek	CA	NoResp	
River Spirit Community	Mad River	CA	NoResp	
Roandoak of God Chr. Com.	Morro Bay	CA	NoResp	
Round Mountain Co-op	Ukiah	CA	Defun	Folded c. '87
Russells Mill	Murphys	CA	Defun	Folded '87
St. Herman of Alaska Mon.	Platina	CA	NoResp	
Sanatana Dharma Foundation	St. Helena	CA	NoResp	
Self-Sufficient Community	Beverly Hills	CA	NoResp	
Sivananda Yoga Center	West Hollywood	CA	NoCon	
So. Calif. Alliance for Survival	Los Angeles	CA	BadPO	"Return to Sender"
Spiritual Community/NAM	Berkeley	CA	NLC	No longer a community
Star Mountain	Bodega Bay	CA	BadPO	"No Forwarding Address"
Starcross Monastery	Annapolis	CA	NoResp	
Stardance	San Francisco	CA	Dupe	See: Purple Rose
Stonesthrow	Ukiah	CA	NoCon	
Storefront Classroom	San Francisco	CA	Dupe	See: Kerista
Summerfield School	Santa Rosa	CA	Never	Still a Waldorf School
Summerland Inn	Summerland	CA	Insuff	No Response
Sunburst	St. Barbara	CA	Moved	Builders, Nevada (p. 174)
Sunrise House	Berkeley	CA	Insuff	Forming summer '89
Sweetwater Community	Guerneville	CA	BadPO	"Insufficient Address"
Synergy House	Stanford	CA	NoResp	
Table Mountain Ranch	Albion	CA	NoResp	
Tahl Mah Sah Zen Center	Los Angeles	CA	NoResp	
Taorima	Ojai	CA	NoResp	
Transpersonal Institute	Stanford	CA	NoResp	
Treehouse	Oakland	CA	NLC	No longer a community
U-Lab 2	San Francisco	CA	Dupe	See: Purple Rose
Ukiah Research Institute	Ukiah	CA	Defun	Dissolved mid '80s
University of Trees	Boulder Creek	CA	NLC	Not currently a community
Urban Ecology House	Berkeley	CA	NoResp	
Village Oz	Point Arena	CA	Defun	Faded mid-80s; sold land in '90
Wholistic Counseling	Berkeley	CA	NoResp	
Willow	Napa Valley	CA	M/R	Possible Resource listing
Y.C.C. Communities	Three Rivers	CA	NoResp	
Yana Trails Community	Cohasset Stage	CA	BadPO	"No Forwarding Address"
Yorkville Women's Land Collective	San Francisco	CA	BadPO	"Forwarding Order Expired"
Zen Mountain Center	Carmel Valley	CA	Never	A Buddhist monastary
Adventure Trails Survival School	Black Hawk	CO	NoResp	
Auroville (CO)	Boulder	CO	NoResp	
Blossom Family	Denver	CO	BadPO	"No Forwarding Address"
Catholic Worker	Denver	CO	NoResp	
Center for United Endeavors	Aspen	CO	NoResp	
Circle of Friends	Boulder	CO	BadPO	"Addressee Unknown"
Cochetopa Dome Ranch	Conifer	CO	NoResp	
Community of Celebration	Colorado Springs	CO	NoCon	Merged with CoC in Pennsyl.
Crestone Mountain Zen Center	Crestone	CO	NoResp	
Divine Light Mission	Denver	CO	BadPO	"No such Number"
Episcopal Community	Denver	CO	NoResp	
Family, The	Littleton	CO	NoResp	
Jubilee Brotherhood	Colorado Springs	CO	BadPO	"No Forwarding Address"
Nairopa Institute	Boulder	CO	Never	Never was a community
Ontological Society	Loveland	CO	NoResp	
Paradise Valley Commuity	Saguache	CO	NoResp	
Rocky Mountain Dharma Center	Livermore	CO	NoResp	
Stillpoint	Wetmore	CO	NoResp	
Sunset Goodearth Farm	Fort Collins	CO	Never	Never was a community
Universal Ashram & Sanctuary	Denver	CO	BadPO	"Forwarding Order Expired"
Bonsilene	New Haven	CT	NoResp	
Community of Saint Luke	Stamford	CT	NLC	No longer a community
East River Community	Guilford	CT	NLC	No longer a community
Emmaus Community	Stamford	CT	NoResp	
San Daimiano Community	New Britain	CT	BadPO	"Addressee Unknown"
Black Hebrew Israelites	Washington	DC	NoCon	
Community of Hope	Washington	DC	NoResp	
Community, The	Washington	DC	BadPO	"Addressee Unknown"
Devadeep Rajneesh Sannyas Ashram	Washington	DC	NoResp	
Dunamis Vocations Church	Washington	DC	NoResp	
Eighth Day Community	Washington	DC	BadPO	"No Forwarding Address"
One World Family Commune	Washington	DC	NoResp	
Society for Human Development	Washington	DC	NoResp	
Believers Fellowship	Naples	FL	NoCon	
Belleview Gardens	Archer	FL	NoResp	
Dayglo	Gainesville	FL	BadPO	"Addressee Unknown"
Florida Group Retreat	Leesburg	FL	NoResp	
Gentle World, Inc.	Umatilla	FL	NoCon	
Heart Lodge	De Leon Springs	FL	NoResp	
Highland Gospel Fellowship	Sebring	FL	NoResp	
Iskon Farm	Alachua	FL	NoResp	
Kashi Ranch	Roseland	FL	NoCon	
Long Leaf	Melrose	FL	NoResp	
Peckerwood Community	Tallahassee	FL	NoCon	
Rainbow Ranch	Jupiter	FL	NoCon	
River Sink Community	Tallahassee	FL	NoCon	
Spes Nova Community	Tampa	FL	NoResp	
Sycamore Land Co-op	Greensboro	FL	NoCon	

Other Communities: RRDDLNoR*

Name	City	State	Status	Note
Villa Serena	Sarasota	FL	BadPO	"No such Number"
Walking Wood	Miami	FL	NLC	No longer a community
Wetumpka Farms	Quincy	FL	NoResp	
Woodville Grapevine	Tallahassee	FL	NoCon	
Albemarle Organic Cmty. Garden	Atlanta	GA	NoResp	
Alleluia	Augusta	GA	NoResp	
Atlanta Community	Atlanta	GA	NLC	No longer a community
Community of Hospitality	Decatur	GA	NoResp	
Featherfield Farm	Albany	GA	NoResp	
Home In America	Jefferson	GA	BadPO	"Forwarding Order Expired"
King of Kings	(?)	GA	NoCon	
Logos	Atlanta	GA	BadPO	"Insufficient Address"
Sevananda	Atlanta	GA	NoCon	
c/o Ben Hopkins	Haleiwa	HI	NoResp	
Dharma Buddhist Temple	Honolulu	HI	NoResp	
Good Karma Farm	Captain	HI	NoResp	
Hawaii Center for Ecological Living	Keaau	HI	NoResp	
Hui Io	Kailua	HI	NoResp	
Maui Zendo	Haiku	HI	BadPO	"Forwarding Order Expired"
Ohana Aloha	Waumanlo	HI	NoResp	
Ohana Mauka	Pahala	HI	NLC	No longer a community
Amana Society	Amana	IA	NLC	No longer a community
Arch, The	Clinton	IA	NoResp	
Catholic Worker Community	Davenport	IA	NoResp	
Kindred Community	Des Moines	IA	Defun	Disbanded 12/89
c/o Alan Krivor	Sandpoint	ID	NoResp	
Friendship House	Boise	ID	NoResp	
Lucark Community	Hope	ID	BadPO	"No Forwarding Address"
Two Rainbows	Boise	ID	BadPO	"Addressee Unknown"
Aquarius	Phillips Township	IL	NoCon	
Austin Fellowship	Chicago	IL	NLC	No longer a community
Bonhoffer House	Chicago	IL	NoCon	University of Chicago
Chicago Meditation Center	Chicago	IL	NoResp	
Children of God	Chicago	IL	BadPO	"Addressee Unknown"
Covenant Community	Evanston	IL	NLC	No longer a community
Dharmadhatu Meditation Center	Chicago	IL	BadPO	"Forwarding Order Expired"
Hudgeons Creek Farm	Carbondale	IL	BadPO	"Addressee Unknown"
Jesus People USA	Chicago	IL	NoResp	
Kishwaukee Tribe	De Kalb	IL	BadPO	"Forwarding Order Expired"
Medicine Wheel	Alto Pass	IL	BadPO	"Return to Sender"
Midwest Collective	Chicago	IL	NLC	No longer a community
Monroe Street Living Collective	Bloomington	IL	BadPO	"No Forwarding Address"
New Earth	Oblong	IL	Never	Never was a community
Salem Communal Brotherhood	Rock City	IL	NoResp	
Synergy	Carbondale	IL	NoResp	
The Community	DeKalb	IL	NoResp	
Brothers of the Holy Cross	Notre Dame	IN	NoResp	
Chrysalis	Helmsburg	IN	NLC	No longer a community
Cygnus, Inc	Richmond	IN	NoResp	
Fellowship of Hope	Elkhart	IN	NoResp	
Kneadmore Life Community Church	Nashville	IN	Defun	Court action dissolved fall '89
Light of the World Mission	Evansville	IN	NoCon	
Plum Creek Community	Nashville	IN	Dupe	See: Kneadmore Life (Defun)
Saint Meinrad Seminary	Saint Meinrad	IN	NoResp	
Blue Moon Ranch	Lawrence	KS	NoResp	
Children Kansas	Wichita	KS	NoResp	
Kansas Zen Center	Lawrence	KS	Never	Never was a community
Marion Mennonite Brethen Church	Hillsboro	KS	BadPO	"Return to Sender"
New Creation Fellowship	Newton	KS	Never	Never was a community
Sungreen Co-op	Wichita	KS	NoResp	
Y.C.C. Communities	Wichita	KS	NoResp	
Cedar Hollow Community	Milltown	KY	BadPO	"Addressee Unknown"
Cornucopia	St. Mary	KY	Dupe	See: Ken Keyes College [R]
Covenant Community	Lexington	KY	NoResp	
Earthward Bound	New Haven	KY	BadPO	"Return to Sender"
Gathering	Louisville	KY	NoResp	
Godsland	Kettle	KY	NoResp	
Lexington Zen Center	Lexington	KY	NLC	No longer a community
Longcliff Collective/Community	Sunnybrook	KY	NoResp	
Middle of the Rainbow	Tompkinsville	KY	NLC	No longer a community
New Age CLT	Milltown	KY	Dupe	See: Cedar Hollow (BadPO)
New Covenant Fellowship	Beverly	KY	Never	Never was a community
Passionist Religious Order	Erlanger	KY	NoResp	
Polestar	Elkton	KY	BadPO	"Return to Sender"
Quaker Action	Hindman	KY	BadPO	"Forwarding Order Expired"
Rainbow Ridge	Richmond	KY	NLC	No longer a community
Tupelo Ridge	Huff	KY	BadPO	"Return to Sender"
Windspirit Farm	Kettle	KY	NLC	No longer a community
Alive	New Orleans	LA	NLC	No longer a community
Jesus the King Community	New Orleans	LA	NoResp	
Open House Community	Lake Charles	LA	Dupe	See: Holy City
AAO Boston	Somerville	MA	NoResp	
Agape Fellowship House	Jamaica Plain	MA	BadPO	"Forwarding Order Expired"
Antrockies	Amherst	MA	BadPO	"Forwarding Order Expired"
Battlebrook Farm	Cambridge	MA	NoResp	
Beacon Hill Friends Meeting	Boston	MA	NoResp	
Bebop Co-op	Allston	MA	NoResp	
Broadway House	Cambridge	MA	NoResp	
Brookside Community	Jamaica Plain	MA	NoResp	
Cambridge Zen Center	Cambridge	MA	NoResp	
Center of the Light	Great Barrington	MA	NLC	No longer a community
Centerpeace	West Medford	MA	NoResp	
Community of Jesus	Orleans	MA	NoResp	
Cummington Community of the Arts	Cummington	MA	Never	Never was a community
Ecologos	Milton	MA	NoResp	
Family Tree	Acton	MA	NoCon	
Fare-Thee-Well Center	Huntington	MA	NoResp	
Fort Hill	Roxbury	MA	NLC	No longer a community
Friends Crossing Community	North Easton	MA	NLC	Did not develop as envisioned
Haley House	Boston	MA	NoResp	
Healing Grace Sanctuary	Shelburne Falls	MA	NoResp	
Institute for Cooperative Community	Cambridge	MA	BadPO	"Addressee Unknown"
Interface	Newton	MA	BadPO	"Forwarding Order Expired"
Island	Belchertown	MA	NoResp	
Kindred Spirits	Allston	MA	BadPO	"Addressee Unknown"
L'Abri Fellowship	Southborough	MA	NoResp	
Maji	Jamaica Plain	MA	BadPO	"Addressee Unknown"
Millenium Fellowship	Reading	MA	Never	Never was a community
Random People House	Somerville	MA	NoResp	
Shim Gum Do Zen Sword Center	Brighton	MA	NoResp	
Spanish House	Brookline	MA	BadPO	"Addressee Unknown"
Spring Hill	Ashby	MA	Dupe	See Resources listing
Temenos Retreat Center	Shutesbury	MA	Never	Never was a community
Unadilla Farm	Gill	MA	NLC	No longer a community
Waldo Collective	Somerville	MA	NLC	No longer a community
Woolman Hill	Deerfield	MA	NLC	No longer a community
Arrowhead Farm	Crofton	MD	BadPO	"Return to Sender"
Casa Caritis/ Emmanuel House	Baltimore	MD	NoResp	
Covenant Life Christian Community	Wheaton	MD	NoResp	
Dayspring Church	Germantown	MD	NoResp	
Deva Community	Burkittsville	MD	NLC	No longer a community
Downhill Farm	Hancock	MD	Defun	"Forwarding Order Expired"
Friends of the Retarded, Inc.	Towson	MD	Never	Never was a community
Giza Farms	Waldorf	MD	NoResp	
Koinonia	Stevenson	MD	Defun	Folded
Lamb of God	Tinmonium	MD	NoResp	
Lamb of God Communities	Baltimore	MD	NoResp	
Metanoia House	Baltimore	MD	NoResp	
Network of Light	Chevy Chase	MD	NoResp	
Pilgrim Community	Annapolis	MD	NoResp	
Savitria	Baltimore	MD	NLC	No longer a community
Society for Human Development	Cheverly	MD	NoResp	
Waterfarm	Chestertown	MD	NLC	No longer a community
Atkins Bay Farm	Phippsburg	ME	NLC	No longer a community
Battlebrook Farm Trust	Danforth	ME	NLC	No longer a community
Birdsong Farm	North Berwick	ME	BadPO	"Forwarding Order Expired"
Downeast Community	Freedom	ME	Defun	Defunct
Energy Systems Parameters	Unity	ME	NLC	No longer a community
Fayerweather	Freeport	ME	BadPO	"Forwarding Order Expired"
Hardscrabble Hill Center	Orland	ME	NoResp	
Leavitt Hill Farm Community	New Vineyard	ME	NLC	No longer a community
Nancy's Farm	Thorndike	ME	NLC	No longer a community
Osprey Community	Penobscott	ME	NLC	No longer a community
Saint Francis Community	East Orland	ME	NoResp	
Whiten Hill Farm Community	Thorndike	ME	NoResp	
Womonground	Troy	ME	NoResp	
Ann Arbor Shim Gum Do Zen Cntr.	Ann Arbor	MI	NoResp	
Aradia Inc	Grand Rapids	MI	NoResp	"Forwarding Order Expired"
Balanced Life Center	Davisburg	MI	NoResp	
Belanger Creek Community	Suttons Bay	MI	Never	Never was a community
Christ's Community	Grand Rapids	MI	NoResp	
Church of the Messiah	Detroit	MI	NoResp	
Detroit Peace Community	Detroit	MI	NoResp	
Farm, The	Allegan	MI	NLC	No longer a community
Great Lakes Rainbow	Ann Arbor	MI	BadPO	"No Forwarding Address"
Heiwa House	Ann Arbor	MI	NLC	No longer a community
Hickory Farms	Whitmore Lake	MI	BadPO	"Return to Sender"
House of David	Benton Harbor	MI	BadPO	"Return to Sender"
Lake Village	Kalamazoo	MI	NoResp	
Liberty Community	Vassar	MI	BadPO	"Return to Sender"
Menominee River Fellowship	Wallace	MI	BadPO	"No Forwarding Address"
Saint Agnes Community	Detroit	MI	NoResp	
Saint Gregory's Abbey	Three Rivers	MI	Never	Never was a community
Sherwood New Age Community	Williamstown	MI	BadPO	"Return to Sender"
Wellness House	Okemos	MI	NoResp	
Word of God	Ann Arbor	MI	NoResp	
Agora Community	St. Paul	MN	NoResp	
Disciples of the Lord Jesus Christ	Winona	MN	BadPO	"Insufficient Address"
Linden Tree Community	Underwood	MN	NLC	No longer a community
Plowshare Collective	Minneapolis	MN	BadPO	"Forwarding Order Expired"
Sacred Heart Community	Duluth	MN	BadPO	"Return to Sender"
Ananda Marga	Willow Springs	MO	NLC	No longer a community
Broadway Covenant Community	Kansas City	MO	NLC	Still exist as a church
Brookside Fellowship	Kansas City	MO	NoResp	
CSA/Zarephath-Horeb Cmty. Church	Pontiac	MO	Dupe	Same as U&I (folded)
Cass Catholic Worker	St. Louis	MO	NoResp	
Covenant Community	Kansas City	MO	NLC	No longer a community
Gathering	Kansas City	MO	BadPO	"No such Number"
Hawk Hill Land Trust	Brixley	MO	NoCon	
Ironwood	Birch Tree	MO	BadPO	"Forwarding Order Expired"
Jesus People USA Farm	Doniphan	MO	NoResp	
Karen Catholic Worker House	Saint Louis	MO	NoResp	
Little Farm	Stanberry	MO	NLC	Never really got off the ground
Meramec Watershed CLT	Jamestown	MO	NoResp	
Morning Glory Community	Arnold	MO	NLC	No longer a community
New Life Farm	Brixley	MO	NoResp	

Name	City	State	Status	Notes
Shining Waters Ashram	Frederickstown	MO	NoResp	
U & I Cmty.("United & Individual")	Eldridge	MO	Defun	Folded fall '86
West Walden Farm	Anderson	MO	NoResp	
Zions Order	Mansfield	MO	NoResp	
Int'l. Soc. of Krishna Consciousness	New Talavan	MS	NoCon	
Old South Vedic Society	Washington	MS	NoResp	
Bitterroot SP Healing Community	Hamilton	MT	NoResp	
Community Covenant Church	Missoula	MT	NLC	No longer a community
Friends Unlimited, Inc.	St. Ignatius	MT	BadPO	"Forwarding Order Expired"
Frontier Life	Alberton	MT	Never	Never was a community
Species Life House	Missoula	MT	NLC	No longer a community
Turah	Bonner	MT	Never	Never was a community
Universal Healing Arts & Research	Lavina	MT	Never	Never was a community
Aionic Talents	Chapel Hill	NC	BadPO	"Return to Sender"
Aloe Community	Cedar Grove	NC	Defun	Folded in '80.
Bonnie Haven Inn	Hendersonville	NC	BadPO	"Return to Sender"
Center of Light	Chapel Hill	NC	NoResp	Possible Resource group
Commune De Green Bean	Chapel Hill	NC	NoResp	
John C. Campbell Folk School	Brasstown	NC	NoResp	
Light of the Mountains Community	Leicester	NC	NLC	No longer a community
Lindenself Foundation	Chapel Hill	NC	Dupe	See: Center of Light (above) [R]
Running Water	Bakersville	NC	NoResp	
Schola Contemplationis	Pfafftown	NC	Defun	Disbanded in '86
Shalom Community	Brown Summit	NC	NoResp	
Singing Water Assoc.	Purlear	NC	NLC	No longer a community
Solar Chariot Schools, Inc.	Greenville	NC	BadPO	"No Forwarding Address"
Star Farm	Star	NC	NLC	No longer a community
Stillwind Community	Sugar Grove	NC	NLC	No longer a community
Suburban Partners	Durham	NC	BadPO	"Addressee Unknown"
Toehold	Burnsville	NC	NoCon	
Twin Streams Educational Center	Chapel Hill	NC	NoResp	
c/o Sandy Parsons	Mekinock	ND	NoCon	
Daystar-Gardner	Fargo	ND	NoResp	
Another Place	Greenville	NH	NLC	See Resources listing
Brookwood	Greenville	NH	Dupe	See Another Place (Resources)
Meeting School	Rindge	NH	NoCon	
Merriam Hill Community	Greenville	NH	Never	Never was a community
Mettanokit Community	Greenville	NH	NLC	See Another Place (Resources)
Sant Bani Ashram	Franklin	NH	NoCon	
Shaker Farm	Enfield	NH	BadPO	"Forwarding Order Expired"
Circles of Light New Age Resr. Cntr.	Bridgeton	NJ	NoResp	
Community of God's Love	Rutherford	NJ	NoResp	
Family of Friends	North Bergen	NJ	BadPO	"Forwarding Order Expired"
Hermitage, The	Bridgewater	NJ	BadPO	"Addressee Unknown"
Holistic Community	Mt. Freedom	NJ	BadPO	"Addressee Unknown"
Intentional Family	Stillwater	NJ	BadPO	"Addressee Unknown"
Labsum Shedrub Ling	Washington	NJ	NoResp	
Mill Hill Community Land	Trenton	NJ	NoCon	
People of Hope	Covenant Station	NJ	NoResp	
Agape Lay Apostolate	Deming	NM	NoResp	
Alamosa Farm	Monticello	NM	NoCon	
ARF	Santa Fe	NM	NoResp	
City of the Sun	Columbus	NM	NoCon	
Eden Community	AZ/NM Border	NM	NoCon	
Fiesta Family	Dixon	NM	NLC	No longer a community
Jerusalem Community	Belen	NM	NoResp	
New Age Co-op	Silver City	NM	BadPO	"Forwarding Order Expired"
New Buffalo	Taos	NM	BadPO	"Insufficient Address"
Osha Commune	Albuquerque	NM	NoCon	
Water Creek Cooperative Village	Santa Fe	NM	BadPO	"Addressee Unknown"
Water Creek Partnership	Tesuque	NM	Defun	Disbanded; land sold in '90
Willow Southwest: The Galisteo Inn	Galisteo	NM	NoResp	
Eckankar	Las Vegas	NV	BadPO	"Insufficient Address"
Meta Tantay	Carlin	NV	NoResp	
Acharya Sushil Jain Ashram	Staten Island	NY	NoResp	
Akwenasa	Ghent	NY	BadPO	"Forwarding Order Expired"
Albany Christian Community	Glenmont	NY	BadPO	"No Forwarding Address"
Ananda Ashram	Monroe	NY	NoResp	
Arunachala Ashram	New York	NY	BadPO	"No Forwarding Address"
Barry Hollow Land Co-op	Brooktondale	NY	NoResp	
Beachtree, The	Monticello	NY	BadPO	"Forwarding Order Expired"
Bear Tribe	Harriman	NY	NoResp	
Beech Hill Pond	West Danby	NY	NoResp	
Catholic Liturgy Community	Staten Island	NY	NoResp	
Chogye International Zen Center	New York	NY	BadPO	"Forwarding Order Expired"
Community of God	South Glen Falls	NY	NoResp	
Covenant House Community	New York	NY	NoResp	
Covenant Love Community	Freeville	NY	NoResp	
Dandelion Hill	Newfield	NY	NLC	No longer a community
Dawes Hill Commune	West Danby	NY	NoResp	
Energy System Parameters	Albany	NY	NoResp	
Everything for Everybody	New York City	NY	NoCon	
Farm Club Collective	Geneva	NY	NoResp	
Fish Cove Inn	Hampton Bays	NY	NoResp	
Friends of the Mountain	New Paltz	NY	Dupe	See: Unison (below)
Havagoats	Binghamton	NY	NoResp	
Hilarian	Slatterville Springs	NY	BadPO	"Addressee Unknown"
Household of Faith	Bronx	NY	NoResp	
Institute for Evolutionary Research	New York	NY	NoResp	
Integral Yoga Institute	New York	NY	NoResp	
Jews for Jesus	New York	NY	BadPO	"No Forwarding Address"
Kairos	New York	NY	NoResp	
Kriya Babaji Yoga Sangam	New York	NY	BadPO	"Addressee Unknown"
L'Arch Syracuse	Syracuse	NY	NoResp	
Lily Dale	Lily Dale	NY	NoResp	
Love Inn Ministries	Freeville	NY	NoResp	
Ma Yoga Shakti	South Ozone Park	NY	NoResp	
Matagiri Sri Aurobindo Center	High Falls	NY	NLC	No longer a community
New Covenant Community	Oswego	NY	BadPO	"Forwarding Order Expired"
New York Catholic Worker	New York	NY	NoResp	
Northwoods	Alpine	NY	NoResp	
Omega Institute	Rhinebeck	NY	M/R	See Resources listing
Omviron	New York	NY	NoResp	
Oneonta	Oneonta	NY	NoResp	
Pax Christi	Bronx	NY	BadPO	"Addressee Unknown"
Peter Maurin Farm	Marlboro	NY	NoResp	
Phoenicia Pathwork Center	Phoenicia	NY	M/R	Possible Resource listing
Pumpkin Hollow Farm	Craryville	NY	NoResp	
Quarter Moon Farm	Ithaca	NY	BadPO	"No Forwarding Address"
Religious Society of Families	Frewsburg	NY	BadPO	"Insufficient Address"
Saint Sebastian's Parish Association	New York	NY	NoResp	
SEADS of Truth, Inc.	Massapequa	NY	Dupe	See affiliate in Harrington, ME
Sivananda Yoga Vedanta Center	New York	NY	NoResp	
Sufi Order	Lebanon Springs	NY	NoResp	
Syda Foundation	South Fallsburg	NY	NoResp	
Turtle Creek Farm	Spencer	NY	Never	Never was a community
Unison	New Paltz	NY	M/R	Possible Resource listing
Watson Homestead	Corning	NY	BadPO	"Return to Sender"
Weed Mine Farm	Copake	NY	BadPO	"Addressee Unknown"
Zen Studies Society	New York	NY	NoResp	
A.S.	Mount Vernon	OH	NoResp	
c/o M. Winegarner	Monroeville	OH	NoCon	
Golgonooza	Millfield	OH	NoResp	
Goss Fork Community	Whipple	OH	NLC	No longer a community
Grailville	Loveland	OH	NoResp	
Laughing Buddha Farm	Amesville	OH	Defun	Folded c. '84
Lookout , The	Cincinnati	OH	NoResp	
Our Kibbutz	Ewington	OH	NoResp	
Our Retreat	Ewington	OH	Dupe	See: Our Kibbutz (NoResp)
Raven Rocks	Beallsville	OH	NoResp	
Servant Community	Cincinnati	OH	Defun	Disbanded 12/87
Sisters of St. Joseph	Cincinnati	OH	BadPO	"Addressee Unknown"
Southern Rainbow	Cincinnati	OH	BadPO	"No Forwarding Address"
Sun Circle Family	Akron	OH	NoResp	
Tucker's Cabin	Athens	OH	NLC	No longer a community
Way, Inc. (The)	New Knoxville	OH	NoResp	
Community of the Servant	Oklahoma City	OK	NoResp	
Hummingbird Medicine Society	Stillwell	OK	BadPO	"Forwarding Order Expired"
Aprovecho	Cottage Grove	OR	Dupe	See: End of the Road House
Bee Farm	Ashland	OR	BadPO	"Return to Sender"
Blue River	Finn Rock	OR	Never	Never was a community
Celebrations	Yamhill	OR	NoResp	
Center for Well-Being	Creswell	OR	NLC	3/91: "No longer a community"
Cherry Grove Center	Gaston	OR	Defun	"Forwarding Order Expired"
China Gardens	Cave Junction	OR	NoResp	
Crabapple	Eugene	OR	Defun	Defunct; see Polyfidelity Ed. [R]
Crack of Dawn	Ashland	OR	NLC	No longer a community
Folly Farm	Grand Ronde	OR	Defun	"Forwarding Order Expired"
Food Farm	Days Creek	OR	BadPO	"Forwarding Order Expired"
Goldenwimmin	Wolf Creek	OR	Defun	Disbanded
Hearthwind	Umpqua	OR	Defun	Disbanded '83
Highway Missionary Society	Wilderville	OR	Defun	Disbanded 12/87
Human Dancing	Ashland	OR	NoResp	
Illuminati Family	Cloverdale	OR	NoCon	
Ithifien	Sheridan	OR	NoResp	
Jeshua Ben Josef	Eugene	OR	Never	Never was a community
Land House	Forest Grove	OR	NoResp	
Land Lovers	Portland	OR	BadPO	"Return to Sender"
Living Love Center	Coos Bay	OR	Dupe	See Ken Keyes College [R]
Living Tree	Deadwood	OR	NoResp	
Lorien Family Land	Eagle Point	OR	Defun	Folded
May One Cooperative	Eugene	OR	NoResp	
McKenzie River Co-op	Finnrock	OR	Never	An alternative school
Mizpah Community	Woodburn	OR	BadPO	"Return to Sender"
Om Tribe	Veneta	OR	NoResp	
Planet Earth Clay Works	Myrtle Point	OR	Never	Never was a community
Portable Village	Philomath	OR	Limbo	See: Message Post (Resources)
Rainbow Farm	Drain	OR	NoResp	
Rainbow Tribe	Eugene	OR	NLC	No longer a community
Rainbow Valley	Eugene	OR	NoResp	
Rajneeshpuram	Antelope	OR	Defun	"Forwarding Order Expired"
Rivendell Farm	Cave Junction	OR	BadPO	"No Forwarding Address"
Rock Creek	Deadwood	OR	NoResp	
Seven Springs Community	Dillard	OR	Never	Never was a community
Shiloh Retreat	Dexter	OR	Defun	IRS battle '88; Now: Lost Valley
Sugar Loaf Mountain Family	Myrtle Point	OR	NoResp	
Syntony	Eugene	OR	Dupe	See: Polyfidelity Ed. (Resources)
Terracommun 2000	Portland	OR	BadPO	"Forwarding Order Expired"
Thunderhawk	Portland	OR	BadPO	"No such Number"
Universing Center	Cottage Grove	OR	BadPO	"No Forwarding Address"
Who Farm, Inc	Estacada	OR	BadPO	"Return to Sender"
Agape Campgrounds	Mt. Union	PA	NoCon	
Barkmill Hollow Commune	Airville	PA	Never	Never was a community
Blue Sky	Allison Park	PA	NoResp	
Body of Christ Community	Glen Mills	PA	NoResp	
c/o Alexandra Bricklin	Philadelphia	PA	NoCon	

Name	Location	State	Status	Notes
c/o David Kennedy (Forming)	Ontanna	PA	BadPO	"No Forwarding Address"
Circle of Good Hope	Landenberg	PA	NoCon	
Community of Celebration	Pittsburgh	PA	NoCon	Earlier name: Fisherfolk
Deep Run Farm	York	PA	Defun	Sold; became SoL Loan Fund
Fisherfolk	Pittsburgh	PA	NoCon	Community of Celebration
Hearth	Erie	PA	NoResp	
House of Umoja (Sister Fillacafata)	Philadelphia	PA	NoCon	
Int'l. Church of Ageless Wisdom	Wyalusing	PA	NoResp	
Jubilee Fellowship	Philadelphia	PA	NoResp	
Living Word	Philadelphia	PA	NoResp	
Mount St. Benedict Priory	Erie	PA	NoResp	
New Village	Fayette County	PA	BadPO	"Insufficient Address"
Pax Center	Erie	PA	NoResp	
Pendle Hill	Wallingford	PA	M/R	Possible Resource listing
Philadelphia Fellowship	Philadelphia	PA	Never	Never was a community
Pittsburgh Friends Meeting	Pittsburgh	PA	NoCon	
Rabbity Hill Farm	Dalton	PA	Defun	Folded; sold land 7/90
Sonnewald Homestead	Spring Grove	PA	Never	Was model organic farm
Copifawna	Foster	RI	NoResp	
Genesis	Providence	RI	NoResp	
Walden Three	Providence	RI	Defun	Folded in '76
Guardians of the Earth	Ruby	SC	NLC	No longer a community
Plainview Colony	Ipswich	SD	BadPO	"Forwarding Order Expired"
Abundance Land Community	Whitleyville	TN	Dupe	New name: See Sundance
Church of the Living God	McMinnville	TN	NoCon	
Far Away Farm	Sparta	TN	Defun	Disbanded '84
Nobodies Mountain	Livingston	TN	NLC	No longer a community
Okra Ridge Farm	Luttrell	TN	NoResp	
Pepperland Farm Camp	Farner	TN	NoResp	
Sycamore Hollow Farm	Celina	TN	NoResp	
Church of the Redeemer	Houston	TX	Never	Never was a community
College Houses Co-ops	Austin	TX	NoResp	
Community of God's Delight	Dallas	TX	NoResp	
Earth Current Farm	Red Rock	TX	NoResp	
East Side Group	Austin	TX	BadPO	"Return to Sender"
Ecumenical Monks of St. Benedict	Blanco	TX	BadPO	"Forwarding Order Expired"
Four Seasons	Call	TX	BadPO	"Forwarding Order Expired"
Greenbriar Community	Elgin	TX	NoResp	
Love Heals Family	Del Valle	TX	NoResp	
Metaphysical Institute for Research	Dallas	TX	NoResp	
Mill Fall Cooperative	Austin	TX	NoResp	
Quicksand Farm	Manor	TX	NoResp	
Rainbow Ridge Ranch	Kyle	TX	NoResp	
Sheltrano	Pearsall	TX	Defun	Folded
Shepherd's Bush Centre	Dallas	TX	NoResp	
Sunat Community	Amarillo	TX	NoCon	
Sunflower Cooperative	Austin	TX	NoCon	
Whitehawk Community	Sanger	TX	NoResp	
Alchemical Bakery	Monroe	UT	NoResp	
Eskdale Center	Murray	UT	NoResp	
Genesis I	Salt Lake City	UT	BadPO	"Return to Sender"
Associations of the Light Mornings	Copper Hill	VA	Update	Joined FIC spring '91
Blackwater Homesteads	Boston	VA	NoResp	
Broad Street Mennonite	Harrisonburg	VA	NoResp	
c/o Christa Phillips	Virginia Beach	VA	Insuff	Forming spring '89
Carmel-in-the-Valley	New Market	VA	NoResp	
Chrysalis	Mt. Sidney	VA	NoCon	
Community of the Servant	Richmond	VA	BadPO	"Return to Sender"
Fellowship of the Inner Light	Virginia Beach	VA	NoResp	
High Meadows	Clifton Forge	VA	NoResp	
Jordan Hollow Farm Inn	Stanley	VA	M/R	Possible Resource group
Jordan River Farm	Huntley	VA	NoResp	
Keshavashram Int'l. Meditation	Warrentown	VA	Never	Never was a community
Mulberry Group, Inc.	Richmond	VA	Defun	Folded
North Mountain Community	Lexington	VA	Future	4/91: Reported to be rebuilding
Partners	Virginia Beach	VA	NoResp	
Seekers Faith Communty	Mclean	VA	NoResp	
Society of St. Andrew	Big Island	VA	NoResp	
Stoneyfoot Farm	Rockbridge Baths	VA	NoResp	
Turtle Land for Wimmin	Arlington	VA	NoResp	
Zephyr	Floyd	VA	NoResp	
c/o Linda Sigel	Burlington	VT	NoResp	
Catalyst Group, The	Brattleboro	VT	NoResp	
Dimetradon	Warren	VT	NoResp	
Earth Bridge	Putney	VT	NoResp	
Earthwings	Orange	VT	NoResp	
Entropy Acres	Barton	VT	NLC	No longer a community
Frog Run Farm	East Charleston	VT	NLC	No longer a community
Heifer Hill	West Brattleboro	VT	NoResp	
Howl	Winooski	VT	NoResp	
Island Pond Community	Island Pond	VT	NoResp	
New Hamburger	Plainfield	VT	NoResp	
Quarry, The	(?)	VT	NoCon	
School House	Shelbourne	VT	BadPO	"Forwarding Order Expired"
Sunray Community	Bristol	VT	NLC	No longer a community
Abrupt Edge	Ione	WA	Dupe	Never a community; see Sarrodaya
Aliya	Bellingham	WA	BadPO	"Addressee Unknown"
Alom Community	Sumner	WA	NoCon	
Antahkarana Circle	Oroville	WA	NoResp	
Aushet	Tonasket	WA	NLC	No longer a community
Brandywine Forest	Olympia	WA	NLC	No longer a community
Can-Do Farm	White Salmon	WA	BadPO	"Forwarding Order Expired"
Center Family	La Center	WA	BadPO	"Return to Sender"
Crystal Seed	Seattle	WA	NoResp	
Earth Child	Davenport	WA	BadPO	"Addressee Unknown"
Goodearth Family	Olympia	WA	BadPO	"No such Number"
Ground Zero	Bangor	WA	NoCon	
Harmony Farm	Olympia	WA	NoResp	
Holden Village	Chelan	WA	NoResp	
Home Front	Seattle	WA	Dupe	See: Homestead CLT
Lanka	Republic	WA	Never	Never was a community
Light	Port Angeles	WA	NoResp	
Mill Creek Goat Farm Family	Colville	WA	NoResp	
Misty Mountain Farm	Curlew	WA	NoResp	
Nolla Journal	Bainbridge Island	WA	NLC	See In Context (Resources)
Pala	Coupeville	WA	NoCon	
Rainbow Nation	Tacoma	WA	NoResp	Probable Resource listing
Sarrodaya Community	Ione	WA	Never	Never was a community
Sarvodaya Communitarian Society	Oroville	WA	NoResp	
Seattle Dharma Center	Seattle	WA	BadPO	"No Forwarding Address"
Second Mile Community	Eatonville	WA	Defun	Disbanded c. '85
Seeseelichel	Bellingham	WA	NoResp	
SkySong	Issaquah	WA	M/R	See Resource listing
Sun at Midday	Olalla	WA	NLC	No longer a community
Sun Meadow	Tonasket	WA	NoResp	
Sunbow	Auburn	WA	Defun	Disbanded '88
Sunset House	Seattle	WA	NoResp	
Sunshine Family	Tonasket	WA	NoResp	
Wilderness Family	Tonasket	WA	NoResp	
Active Acres	Dodgeville	WI	NoResp	
Coldfoot Creek	Pembine	WI	NLC	Change '88; see Teaching Drum [R]
Harmony Valley Farms	Viroqua	WI	NoResp	
Shiloh Community	Lone Rock	WI	BadPO	"Addressee Unknown"
Taliesen	Spring Green	WI	Never	Never was a community
Wilderness Way	Wascott	WI	NoResp	
Agahpay Fellowship	Moorefield	WV	NoResp	
Catholic Worker Farm	West Hamlin	WV	NoResp	
Community of Saint Martin	Moyers	WV	BadPO	"No Forwarding Address"
Misty Bottoms Farm	Jumping Branch	WV	BadPO	"Forwarding Order Expired"
Mountain Land	Weston	WV	NoResp	
We Don't Have a Name Yet	Unger	WV	NoResp	

Canadian RRDDLNoR* Commnities

Name	Location	Prov	Status	Notes
Barnabas Christian Fellowship	Calgary	Alb	NoResp	
Common Ground Group	Olds	Alb	NoResp	Reported still active
Onoway Center	Onoway	Alb	NoResp	
Bread of Life	Abbotsford	BC	Defun	Folded
Doukhobors (Russian relig. sect)	Grand Forks	BC	NLC	Formerly on communal farms
Genesis Community	Lumby	BC	NoResp	
Gestalt Community	Kuper's Island	BC	NoCon	
Hollyhock Farm	Manson's Landing	BC	Update:	See Late Entries
Iskcon	Burnaby	BC	NoResp	
Lasqueti (Name Unknown)	Lasqueti Island	BC	NoCon	
Stock's Meadow	Kelowna	BC	NoResp	
Thera Community	Galiano Island	BC	NoCon	Reported active; healing focus
White Spruce Farm	Fernie	BC	NoResp	
Yasodhara Ashram	Kootenay Bay	BC	NoResp	Reported still active
c/o Pat Mooney	Brandon	Man	NoCon	
Common Ground	Winnipeg	Man	NoResp	
Land Co-op (several families)	Beresford, Alxndr.	Man	NoResp	
Matthew House Fellowship	Winnipeg	Man	NoResp	
Northern Sun Farm	Pansy	Man	NoCon	
Alternative Growth Institute	Ottawa	Ont	NoResp	
Alternative to Alienation	Toronto	Ont	BadPO	"Addressee Unknown"
Bakavi	Merrickville	Ont	NoResp	
Bright Community Farm	Bright	Ont	NoResp	
Chalbo	Holyrood	Ont	NoResp	
Cobwebs	Thunder Bay	Ont	NoResp	
Earth Bound	Maynooth	Ont	NoResp	
Family Pastimes	Perth	Ont	NoResp	(Dupe of Lanark Hills?)
Farm, The (Canada)	Lanark PO	Ont	NLC	No longer a community
Heartwood	Willowdale	Ont	BadPO	"Return to Sender"
I Am	Madoc	Ont	BadPO	"No Forwarding Address"
Ingersoll Fellowship AA	Ingersoll	Ont	NoResp	
L'Arche	Richmond Hill	Ont	NoResp	
Lanark Hills	Perth	Ont	NLC	No longer a community
Maple High Farm	Roslin	Ont	BadPO	"Addressee Unknown"
Marble Rock	Kingston	Ont	NoResp	
Nazareth	Hamilton	Ont	NoResp	
Ontario Zen Center	Toronto	Ont	Defun	Folded
Philoxians	Marlbank	Ont	NoResp	
S.O.I.L.	Toronto	Ont	NoResp	
Twin Valley School	Wardsville	Ont	BadPO	"No Forwarding Address"
Wilderness Seekers	Chapleau	Ont	BadPO	"No Forwarding Address"
Colonie Chetienne	Montreal	Que	BadPO	"Addressee Unknown"
L'Arche	Stanstead	Que	NoResp	
Les Plateaux Commun-ô-Terre	Anse St. Jean	Que	NoResp	
Terre De Vie	St-Aubert	Que	NoCon	

1991

Calendar of Major Community Events

April 6-7 CESCI Annual Meeting, Hosted by The Vale, Yellow Springs, OH Write: Herb Goldstein Rt . 3, Box 231, Lexington, VA 24450

April 9-11 FIC Spring Meeting, Hosted by The Vale, Yellow Springs, OH Write: FIC, 8600 University Blvd. Evansville, IN 47712

April 18-21 Communities Conference at Lost Valley Educational Center 81868 Lost Valley Lane Dexter, OR 97424

April 21 Earth Day — celebrations in over 100 countries, and at many communities

May 17-21 Spring Assembly: Federation of Egalitarian Communities Hosted by Twin Oaks, Louisa, VA Write: FEC Desk, Tecumseh, MO 65760

May 18-19 Community Workshop: "Thriving Through Change"; Sirius Community Baker Rd., Shutesbury, MA 01072

May 24-27 Open Convention on the Evolution of Human Society The theme: "Kindomism" Padanaram, Rt 1, Box 478 Williams, IN 47470

May 24-27 Men's Gathering at Twin Oaks Rt 4, Box 169, Louisa, VA 23093

June 4-13 "Alternative Communities Today & Tomorrow" — a 3-Credit Course through U.Mass &Sirius Community Write: Corinne McLaughlin Baker Rd., Shutesbury, MA 01072

June 15-16 Community Workshop: "Living Lightly on the Earth", at Sirius Community Baker Rd., Shutesbury, MA 01072

June 28-July 27 Living/Learning Adventure at High Wind Community (in Wisconsin) and at Findhorn (in Scotland) Write: Rt 2, Plymouth, WI 53073 (June 29 is their Annual Gathering)

July 1-7 Rainbow Gathering of the Tribes (Vermont site To Be Announced) Write: Box 116, Wilton, NH 03086

July 11-15 10th Assembly: 4th World Congress (Hosted near London, England) Write: Fourth World Initiative, Millbrook Ampthill, Bedfordshire MK45 2JB, UK

July 14-21 School of Living Quarterly Meeting Hosted at Julian Woods Community Route 1, Box 420, Julian, PA 16844

July 25-29 ICSA: Triennial Conference, hosted at Elizabethtown College. Write: Donald Kraybill, Elizabethtown College, Elizabethtown, PA 17022 (717)367-1151

This Calendar is continued on the next page ...

This is a calendar of:
1) events organized or hosted by community groups,
2) events specifically focusing on community living, and
3) major events with significant participation by members of "the movement".

Most of these events occur with some regularly, so this calendar is a reasonably accurate template for what to expect next year. Write specific groups for information about future events. Events listed as "hosted" are generally scheduled with a new site for each meeting.

Please send us suggestions of what to include in future calendars — thanks! Also note that the Fellowship publishes a newsletter several times a year (free to members) which includes announcements of and reports about similar events. Information about joining the FIC can be found on page 125.

Aug 9-15	Holistic Facilitation Training Alpha Farm, Deadwood, OR 97430
Aug 17-18	Community Workshop: "The Healing Power of Nature"; Sirius Community Baker Rd., Shutesbury, MA 01072
Aug 24-26	Women's Gathering at Twin Oaks Rt 4, Box 169, Louisa, VA 23093
Aug 30-Sept1	PEPCON 5 (Held in Berkeley, CA) Annual Conference on Polyfidelity Write: PEP, P.O. Box 6306 Captain Cook, HI 96704 (808)929-9691
Aug 15-21	4th Greens National Gathering, hosted at Davis & Elkins College, Elkins, WV Write: John Rensenbrink, 60 Hammond Street, Cambridge MA 02138
Sept 14-15	Community Workshop: "Creating Community Where You Are" Sirius Community, Baker Road Shutesbury, MA 01072
Late Sept	"Living More With Less" Dates are tentative, write to confirm. Annual CSI Fall Conference Box 243, Yellow Springs, OH 45387
Oct 1-3	"Preserving Affordable Housing: An Introduction to CLTs" (Hosted in Washington, D.C.) Write: ICE, 57 School Street, Springfield, MA 01105 (413)746-8660
Oct 10-12	CSA's 18th Annual Conference Host: Old Aurora Colony, Attn: Patrick Harris P.O. Box 202, Aurora, OR 97002
Oct 17-20	Padanaram's Open Convention on the Evolution of Human Society Rt l, Box 478, Williams, IN 47470
Oct 25-27	School of Living Quarterly Meeting Hosted at Common Ground Community, Route 3, Box 231, Lexington, VA 24450
Oct 27-29	FIC Fall Meeting Hosted at Lama, San Cristobal, NM Write: FIC, 8600 University Blvd. Evansville, IN 47712
Nov 7-9	Society for Utopian Scholars Annual Meeting (Hosted in Las Vegas) Write: Felicia Campbell, Dept. of English, UNLV, Las Vegas, NV 89154-5011 (702) 739-3457

Nov 9-13	Facilitation Training (Advanced) Alpha Farm, Deadwood, OR 97430
Nov 17-21	Fall Assembly: Federation of Egalitarian Communities Hosted by Sandhill Farm Rutledge, MO 65760

************** *Into the Future* *************

July or Aug 1992	Turtle Island Bioregional Congress-V Hosted near Dallas, Texas. [Their biennial conference. See Resources.] Write: TIBC, P.O.Box 140826, Dallas, TX 75214 Attn: Gene Marshall
June 24-29 1993	**Celebrating Community: An International Conference on Cooperative Living.** 5 days in late June, at Evergreen State College, near Olympia, WA. Sponsored by FIC, 8600 University Boulevard, Evansville, IN 47112

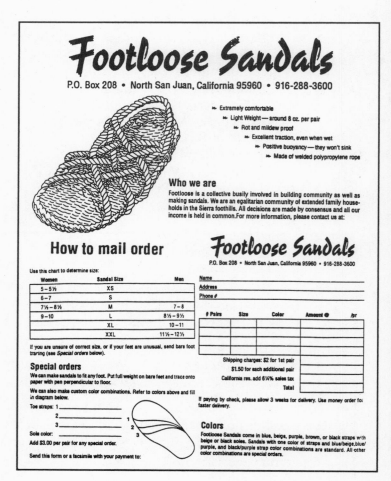

Footloose Sandals

P.O. Box 208 • North San Juan, California 95960 • 916-288-3600

➤ Extremely comfortable
➤ Light Weight — around 8 oz. per pair
➤ Rot and mildew proof
➤ Excellent traction, even when wet
➤ Positive buoyancy — they won't sink
➤ Made of welded polypropylene rope

Who we are

Footloose is a collective busily involved in building community as well as making sandals. We are an egalitarian community of extended family households in the Sierra foothills. All decisions are made by consensus and all our income is held in common. For more information, please contact us at:

How to mail order

Footloose Sandals
P.O. Box 208 • North San Juan, California 95960 • 916-288-3600

Use this chart to determine size:

Women	Sandal Size	Men
5–5½	XS	
6–7	S	
7½–8½	M	7–8
9–10	L	8½–9½
	XL	10–11
	XXL	11½–12½

If you are unsure of correct size, or if your feet are unusual, send bare foot tracing (see Special orders below).

Special orders

We can make sandals to fit any foot. Put full weight on bare feet and trace onto paper with pen perpendicular to floor.

We can also make custom color combinations. Refer to colors above and fill in diagram below.

Toe straps: 1 _____
2 _____
3 _____
Sole color: _____
Add $3.00 per pair for any special order.

Send this form or a facsimile with your payment to:

Name _____
Address _____
Phone # _____

# Pairs	Size	Color	Amount @	/pr

Shipping charges: $2 for 1st pair
$1.50 for each additional pair
California res. add 6¼% sales tax
Total

If paying by check, please allow 3 weeks for delivery. Use money order for faster delivery.

Colors

Footloose Sandals come in blue, beige, purple, brown, or black straps with beige or black soles. Sandals with one color of straps and blue/beige,blue/purple, and black/purple strap color combinations are standard. All other color combinations are special orders.

About the International Listings...

This section features communities in countries other than Canada, the U.S., and Mexico. Our research efforts were focused primarily on North America, so this sampling represents only a small fraction of what exists. For more extensive referrals on other continents, see "Communities Directories" and "Community Networks" in the index. There are also three articles in the Networking section that deal with this subject: "The Emissary International Communities," "Rural Communes in Great Britain," and "Global Networking."

This section is in three parts: 1) a cross-reference chart, arranged alphabetically; 2) an index of the communities, sorted alphabetically by country; and 3) a list of well over 50 international communities, including addresses and phone numbers where available.

Note: We didn't originally send questionnaires to any of these international groups, though we started doing so later in the going. For this reason we have included detailed chart information for less than half of the international entries.

The codes used in the Chart are identical to those used in the North American listings. See the brief description below for some of the more common abbreviations.

There's a lot of information in the listings that doesn't appear in the charts, so use both for the best overview of each community. You'll usually get a far better sense of a group by reading their descriptive listing — that's where we've given them license to tell their own story ... to share their visions, their histories, their daily life. Many of these descriptions go beyond the facts and figures, and give you a feeling for the community.

Some frequently-used abbreviations:

SASE   means enclose a self-addressed stamped envelope.

[cc]   means that the group cannot commit to responding promptly to written inquiries.

The date in small print at the end of a listing is the date the entry was submitted or, in some cases, the date that the group confirmed that the information is still accurate.

The information in the charts is based on community **responses to questionnaires** that we sent out, in at least three slightly different versions, over the 18 months of our research. **An "N/Q" in the "Other Values" column** indicates a group that did not submit a questionnaire; in these cases, we have tried to fill in some of the blanks based on other information (such as the group's descriptive listing, or our own personal knowledge).

The key for the chart codes: Since the meaning of some code letters varies from one column to the next, our key (pages 144-145) explains all the possibilities within each column. It is important to refer to this key when interpreting the chart ... a "C" in the "Decision-Making" column (indicating that the group uses consensus) means something very different from a "C" (community ownership) in the "Ownership Column" or a "C" (Christian) in the "Spiritual Focus" column or a "C" (celibacy) in the "Sexual Restrictions" column.

A few general disclaimers: As in most questionnaire-based research, different communities may have interpreted the same questions in different ways. It was sometimes impossible for us to tell if groups (including our own research team) had applied the same standards and definitions to each question that appears on this chart. Furthermore, it is impossible to do justice to the vast variety of communities and community experiences by attempting to quantify them in a yes/no or multiple-choice format.

We can't guarantee that the information in the charts and listings is accurate — each community decided what to say about itself, and changes may have happened over the past 6-18 months. We edited only for length and clarity. We caution each reader to verify all information before deciding to get involved with any of the groups listed.

At this point we're unclear about how extensively we will cover the international groups in future directories, but regardless, we do plan to continue expanding our international database. If you have any leads or new information about community groups living beyond the shores of North America, please drop us a line at FIC headquarters (see feedback section on the next-to-last page).

Clearly, the communities movement is a broad-based and dynamic reality — with valuable experiences and insights to share among ourselves and with those "other" realities. We hope this Directory will help us discover our common concerns, and provide opportunities for sharing that wisdom. ❖

International Communities: Cross Reference Chart

Sorted Alphabetically

Community Name	Country	Land/Bldgs	Rur/Urb	Year Est?	Adults	Chld	Max?	More? A	More? C	Sch?	Gen? Visitors?	Join Fee	Decis? C/M	W!?	Food Gr	Ea	Or	Vg	Fl	Own Ld	Own B	Own Rm	Econ S?	L/mo	$/mo	Op?	Sexual Restr?	Spirit Basis	L?	Val P	Val F	Val VS	Other Values / Remarks
Atlantis/Colombia	Col		R	87	5+2	3	N	Y	Y	Hm	Y	N			Y	Y	Y	Y		C	C		Y				N	N	N			Y	NQ Self Exploration
Atlantis/Eire	Eire		R	74	3+2	4	N	Y	Y	Hm	Y	N			Y	Y	Y	Y		C	C		Y				N	N	N			Y	NQ Self-Sufficiency
Auroville	Intl	2,000 ac	B	68	400	200	~50,000	Y	Y	Cb	Y	N	Cb		Y	S	Y	N*	Y	L	L	Cb	S	120	(P)	S	N	E	N		Y		All life is Yoga
Beeston	Eng	1 hs	U	75	6	0												Y		C	C		S					C	N			Y	NQ Worship; Family
Billen Cliffs	Aus	800 ac	R		75	45		Y	Y	Pu	Y				Y					C	C		R					C			Y		Y	NQ No Ideology
Birchwood Hall	Eng		R	70	14	7	~25	Y	Y	Pu	Y	N	Cb	N	N	Y	S	S	S	C	C	R	Y		~250	N	CHBG	N	N	N	S	S	Socialism
Black Horse Creek	Aus	967 ac	R		19	11		Y	Y		Y	N			Y					C			Y										NQ Community Minded
Bundagen	Aus	600 ac	R		80	60		Y	Y		Y				Y					C			Y										NQ Participation
Centrepoint	NZ		R	78	80	95		Y	Y	Pu	Y	AA	C	N	Y	Y	N	N	Y	L	L	D	Y				N	Ecm	Y	S	S	Y	Reality; Authenticity
Christiania	Den		U	60s	?	?		Y	Y	Cb	Y		Cb		S	S	S	S		C	Cb		Y					N	N	S	S		NQ Began as Squat
Christians	Aus		U		19	0		Y	Y		Y				Y					N	N		Y					Y		Y	Y	Y	NQ Share All Goods
Commonground (Australia)	Aus	95 ac	R*	81	7	4	30-40	Y	N	H	Y	Negot.	C	N	N	Y	N	N	Y	C	C	R	Y				CHBG	P	N	P	Y	Y	Activ Social Change
Community of the Ark	Fra	3villages	R*	48	22	18		Y	Y	Cb	Y	N	C	N	Y	Y	Y	Y	M	L	L	Cb	Y				CHM	Ecm	N	Y	S	Y	Non-Violence
Comunidad del Sur	Urug		B	56	14	4	400	Y	Y	Pu	Y	AA			Y	Y	Y	Y	Y	N	N	N	Y					N	N			Y	NQ EcoVillage
Comunidad - Nordan	Swe		U	77	7	5	20	Y	N	Pu	Y	AA	N	N	N	Y	N	Y	N	N	N	Cb	Y				N	N	N			Y	Change Society
Crabapple	Eng		R*	75	20	3	~Same	N	N	Pu	Y	N	Cb	N	N	Y	N	N	P	C	C	R	Y				N	N	N	S	P	S	Sustainability
Crescent Road	Eng		U	78				N	N	Pu	Y	N	Cb	N	N	Y	N	Y	N	C	C		N			Y	N	N	N	S	P	Y	Diverse Family
Darvell Bruderhof	Eng		R	20	134	132		Y	Y	Cm	Y				Y	Y	Y	Y		C	C		Y				Y	HB	Y	Y	Y	Y	NQ Hutterian
Finca Choconuevo	Ecu	80 ac	R	86				Y	Y	Hm	Y	N			S	Y				C	C		Y						Y			Y	NQ Environment; Harmony
Finca Jardin de Luz	Guat	100 ac	R	79				Y	Y		Y				Y								Y					C					NQ Cooperation
Findhorn	Sco		R	62	200	Incl	Incl	Y	Y		Y		C	Y	Y	Y	Y	Y	N	C	C	Cb	N					Ecl				Y	NQ New Age Spiritual
Fusion Arts Colony	Aus	2 ac	B		15	5	No	Y	Y		Y	Y	C	Y	Y													C				Y	NQ Visual Arts
Greuth Hof	Ger			77	10	2																						Ecl	N			Y	NQ Attunement
Hillier Park	Aus		B	79	25	10	No	Y	Y	Pu	Y	Y			N	N	Y	Y	N	C	C	Cb	N			N	N	EDL	Y	N	N	N	Inherent Life Design
Hohenort	SAfr		R					Y	Y		Y	Y			N	Y	Y	N										EDL					NQ Oneness
La Vigne	Fra		R	86	12	2	N	Y	Y	Pu	Y	N	N	Y	S	Y	Y	Y	N	C	Cb	Cb	N		310		N	EDL	Y	N	N	Y	Passion for life
Laurieston Hall	Eng	130 ac	R	72	20	10	N	P	P	Pu	Y	£1	C	S	Y	N	Y	N	Y	C	C	Cb	N	100	£60	Y		N	N	Y	N	Y	Cooperation;Growth;Fulfillment
Lebensgarten	Ger		R		80			Y	Y		Y				Y					C	C	C						N	N			Y	NQ Permaculture
Lifespan	Eng		R*	74	10	4	20-30	Y	Y	Cb	Y	N	C	N	S	Y	Y	Y	N	C	C	R	Y				N	N	N	Y	Y	Y	Work & Skill Sharing
Lower Shaw	Eng	3 ac	U*	78	6	7	3 Fam	P	P	Pu	Y	N	C	N	Y	Y	Y	Y	S	N	N	R	Y				N	N	N	N	N	Y	Conference Center
Mandala	Aus	278 ac	R		25	8		Y	Y	Pu	Y	N			Y	Y	Y	Y	Y	C			N				N	N	N			Y	NQ Conservation
Meitheal	Eng	5 ac	B	86	9	4	15-20	P	P	Pu	Y	N	C	N	Y	Y	Y	Y	Y	C	C	Cb	N	20/w	£120	P	N	Ecm	N	N	N	Y	Personal Growth
Michaelshof	Ger																											HB					NQ Hutterian
Mickleton	Eng	70 ac	U*	80	54	9	N	Y	Y	Pu	Y	N	C	N	N	Y	N	N	Y	Cb	Cb	Cb	N					EDL	Y	N	N	Y	Integrity; No "system" per se
Mitraniketan	Ind		R	56	100	300	300	Y	Y	Cm	Y	Y	Y		Y					C			Y									Y	NQ Grassroots Involvement
Monkton Wyld	Eng		R	83	9	6	18	Y	Y	Cb	Y	Y	Cb	Y	Y	Y	N*	Y		C	C	Cb	N					O	N		P	Y	Deep Ecology
Moora Moora Co-op	Aus	2760 ac	R	73	40	32	60+kids	Y	Y	C	Y	13,000	N	N	Y	N*	N	N	N	C	C	F	N	8		N	N	N	N		P	Y	Education; Conservation
Mt. Oak Community	Aus		R		25	3		Y	Y		Y				Y					C			Y							S	S	S	NQ Self-Reliance
New Goverdhan	Aus	1000 ac	R		70	30		Y	Y		Y				Y					C			Y					Y					NQ Glorify God
Nomadelfia	Ital	~1000 ac		31	300	Incl	Incl	Y	Y		Y				Y					C	C		Y					RC		S	S		NQ Brotherhood
Old Hall	Eng	74 ac	R	74	40	20	Same	Y	Y	Pu	Y	Y	C		Y	N	Y	N	Y	C	C	Cb	Y	40+		Q	N		N	S	S		Voluntary Cooperation

Key to Chart Codes is on Pages 144-145   1990/91 Directory of Intentional Communities

International Communities: Cross Reference Chart

Sorted Alphabetically

Community Name	Coun-try	Land/ Bldgs	Rur/ Urb	Year Est?	Adults	Child	Max?	More? A	More? C	Sch? Gen? Visitors?	Decis? C/M Wt?	Join Fee	Food/Diet Gr Ea Or Vg Fl	Ownshp Ld B Rm	Economic Sharing S? L/mo $/mo Op?	Sexual Restr?	Spirit Basis	L?	Values P F VS	Other Values / Remarks
Permacult'r Pyrénées	Fra	100 ac	R		<10		10	Y	Y				S						Y	NQ Autonomy; Creativity
Post Green	Eng				20	Incl		Y	Y	Y							C			NQ Christian Roots
Redfield	Eng		R	78	20	15	40	Y	Y	Pu	C	£1	Y Y Y Y N	C Cb	N Y Var Y	N	N	N		Housing Co-op
Shambala	Aus	640 ac	R		20	10				Y			Y	C		N	N	N		NQ Rural
Sharing in Developmnt	Scot		U	76	5	0	6	Y	N		C	N	S Y Y N Y	N	R N N	N	N	N	S S Y	Urban Household
Shrubb Family	Eng		R	70	7	0	N	Y	Y		C	N	Y Y Y Y Y	C C R	Y £68	N	N	N	M N	Family Closeness
Some Friends	Eng	Lg.Bldg.	U	73	15	0		Y	N		N	N	N Y Y Y Y	N C R	N £180 N	N	QO	N	Y Y Y	Inner City Co-op
Some People	Eng		U	78			N	Y	Y	CB	Y	N	N S s N Y	N N Cb	s N S	N	N	N	N Y Y	Cooperation
Svanholm	Den	1033 ac	R	78	75	60		Y	Y	Y	C		Y Y Y	C C R	R Y	N	N	N	N Y Y	NQ "Whole" Lives
Taena	Eng	135 ac	R	40s	6	?					S		S	F	N		RC	Y		NQ Weekly Mass
Tauhara Centre	NZ		R										Y							NQ Goodwill
Teachest	Wal	40 ac	R	74	12	9		N	N	Pu	C	N	S Y Y N* Y	N N F	N £100 Y	N	N	N	N N Y	Alternative Technology Centre
Terre Nouvelle	Fra	30+ ac	R	75	10	2		Y			C		Y Y		Y	Y	Ecl			NQ Joy; Tolerance
Wild Lavender	Eng		U	80	13	0	N	Y	N	M S	C	N	N Y S Y Y	N N R	Var N	CG	N	N	N	Gay Community; Love
Yamagishi Assoc	Jap	20 Grps	R		?	ea		Y					Y Y			N	N	N		NQ Communal Life

---

International Communities: Sorted alphabetically by Country

AUSTRALIA
Billen Cliffs (NSW)
Black Horse Creek (NSW)
Bundagen (NSW)
Christians (NSW)
Sydney South (NSW)
Commonground (Seymour)
Fusion Arts Colony (Victoria)
Hillier Park (Gawler)
Mandala (Queensland)
Moora Moora (Victoria)
Mt. Oak Community (NSW)
New Goverdhan (JD)
Shambala (NSW)
COLOMBIA
Atlantis/Colombia
La Atlantida
DENMARK
Christiania
Svanholm

ECUADOR
FincaChoconuevo
ENGLAND
Beeston (Nottingham)
Birchwood Hall (Worcestershire)
Crabapple (Shropshire)
Crescent Road (Surrey)
Darvell Bruderhof (East Sussex)
Lifespan (S. Yorkshire)
Lower Shaw Farm (Wilts)
Mickleton (Gloucestershire)
Monkton Wyld Court (Dorset)
Old Hall Community (Suffolk)
Post Green Trust (Dorset)
Redfield (Buckinghamshire)
Shrubb Family (Norfolk)
Some Friends Community (London)
Some People Community (Leicester)
Taena (Gloucester)
Wild Lavender (London)

FRANCE
Community of the Ark
La Vigne
Permaculture Pyrénées
Terre Nouvelle
GERMANY
Greuth Hof
Lebensgarten
Michaelshof
GUATEMALA
Finca Jardin de Luz
INDIA
Mitraniketan Community
IRELAND
Atlantis/Eire
Meitheal
ITALY
Nomadelfia
JAPAN
Yamagishi Association

NEW ZEALAND
Centrepoint
Tauhara Centre
SOUTH AFRICA
Hohenort
SCOTLAND
Findhorn
Laurieston Hall
Sharing in Development
SWEDEN
Comunidad - Nordan
URUGUAY
Comunidad del Sur
WALES
Teachest

Key to Chart Codes is on Pages 144-145

Directory of Intentional Communities

Atlantis/Colombia

c/o Ned Addis
Icononzo, Tolima
COLOMBIA, South America

Atlantis is a long-established commune consisting at the moment of 7 adults and 7 children living on a mountain farm in Colombia. We began as a therapy commune 20 years ago in London, and moved gradually away from "civilization". Our last stop before moving to Colombia was a tiny wild island off NW Ireland (see next listing). From there a pioneer group set off two years ago in search of an even wilder place away from the ever-lengthening tentacles of state control, social workers and pollution. They fell in love with Colombia and bought this beautiful forested farm, complete with streams and swimming holes. The climate is temperate with a lot of sunshine and rain every day. We grow a variety of crops, from Brussels sprouts to bananas. We're vegetarian, almost vegan, and we're aiming at self-sufficiency.

We don't practice formal therapy much anymore, although to keep clear and energetic we use a lot of techniques we've learned and made up over the years. We're a noisy, lively, humorous crowd. We're devoted to raising our kids to be as free and uninhibited as possible, though they get strong discipline when they (regularly) try to take over. In the evenings we talk and sew, do craft work, or play music and sing. We have no religion except Nature, and no time for anything modern (if you're hung up on medicines or technology, you won't like it here). We welcome long or short-term visitors, especially the open-minded, down-to-earth non-smoking variety (absolutely no drugs of any kind). We require no financial contribution, just that you join in with the work. Please write to us for directions on how to get here.

There are 7 books about us available from Pete Razzell, 17 South Hill Park, Gardens, London NW3, England. 11/9/89

Atlantis/Eire

Inishfree Island
Burtonport
County Donegal, EIRE

010353-75-21311

Atlantis is a commune that has been together in a constantly evolving form for the past 20 years. With our roots in C.N.D. [Campaign for Nuclear Disarmament] and the London encounter group movement, we have developed into a group aiming towards self-sufficiency living on a wild off-shore island of Eire. Here we grow our own vegetarian food organically; cut turf; keep goats, chickens, ducks, and donkeys; and give birth to our babies by the fireside without medical help. The island has no electricity, roads, or modern plumbing. Having found our feet on the soil of Donegal and become increasingly self-sufficient each year, we decided to adventure much farther from the illusory "safety" of modern life and emigrate to South America by sailing ship. This adventure came to pass in 1987, when most of our members left to start a sister community in Colombia (see previous entry). The Inishfree Island base will continue, remaining open to visitors and new members. Please contact us by mail or phone... or just arrive. 11/9/89

Auroville

Tamil Nadu, INDIA

Auroville is a "universal township" of over 500 people living and working on 2000 acres. For more information, see "Auroville International USA" in the North American listings. 4/1/89

Beeston Community House

4 Grange Avenue, Beeston
Nottingham NG9-1GJ
ENGLAND

0602 223886

Beeston Community House is a Christian house situated near the center of Beeston, Nottingham. There are six people living in the house, and a number of others who share the aims and commitment but are non-residential. We come from different church backgrounds including Anglican, Baptist, Methodist, and URC. Each member of the house is a member of their own local church as well — we are not a house church.

Living here is a moving, changing experience. Most people stay here for around three years, although there is no rule. We are male and female, young and not so young. There are tears and laughter, good times and bad — but for this short part of our lives we are here together, sharing our faith.

Four "senior" members of a local church bought our house in 1975, based on four aims: 1) to live together as an extended family, 2) to lead a life centered on prayer and worship, 3) to work for Unity in Christ among the local churches, and 4) to have outreach in the wider local community.

Over the years each fresh face of the community has tried to work out for themselves what that means in practice. One member of the house is supported financially by the others to do full-time community work. This has led to involvement in schemes such as refurbishing houses for the homeless, and initiating creative drama with handicapped children. We share meals, and entertain a lot of guests. We serve in the Oxfam shop twice a month, visit local churches, and publish a local ecumenical newsletter. Each member also enjoys their own particular interests... a list that is endless and growing. In between times we enjoy socializing with friends, perhaps a trip to the theater, or the cinema, or a pub. It's never boring. 1/6/89

Billen Cliffs Proprietary Ltd.

P.O. Box 685
Lismore, NSW
2480 AUSTRALIA

We are a large loose-knit community with 75 adults and 45 children living on 800 acres. Varying members of our community are engaged in food production, alternative economics and technology, permaculture, conservation, wildlife sanctuary, land reclamation, craftwork, spirituality, philosophy, healing, therapy, and personal growth. We have no ideological restrictions, and a lot of space for personal growth and enterprise. 7/21/89

Birchwood Hall

Storridge Malvern WR13 5EZ
Worcestershire, ENGLAND

08864-203

Birchwood Hall, established in 1970, has 14 adult members and 7 children. We are situated in a rural location, but are not agriculturally based. We share a political orientation, with a particular focus on Socialism. Most major decisions are made by majority rule, but include a bit of consensus process. 7/1/89

Black Horse Creek

c/o Sheri Coward
via Kyogle, NSW
2474 AUSTRALIA

We are 19 adults and 11 children living on 967 acres — a Proprietary Limited Company with 25 shares and several for sale. Some primary aims of the community include alternative technology, wildlife sanctuary, food production and economic viability. Visitors should be willing, community-minded people. 7/21/89

Bundagen

P.O. Repton
New South Wales
2454 AUSTRALIA

We are a community of 80 adults and 60 children living on 600 acres. Some of our concerns and aims include food production, alternative economics and technology, permaculture, conservation, wildlife sanctuary, spirituality, philosophy, healing, therapy, and personal growth. Please write for additional information. 7/21/89

Centrepoint Community

P.O. Box 35, Mills Lane
Albany, Auckland
NEW ZEALAND

Centrepoint is a self-reliant community with some 16 agricultural and craft-based businesses. For 10 years now its main center has been located in a lush green secluded valley, 14 miles north of Auckland, where a growing community of about 200 people (half of them children) live and work in an intensely cooperative and communal lifestyle. The community was originally founded and directed by its spiritual leader, Bert Potter, who (in March 1988) left the community to be run entirely by its members. Bert moved to a house just up the road on community property, and remains available for social visits and consultations.

Adults who become full members commit themselves to live and work together intimately, openly, and cooperatively — contributing all their worldly earnings and possessions to the community. They take only $2/week pocket money, and the community provides for all their basic needs. Community decisions are made by consensus at weekly business meetings.

Our fundamental "raison d'etre" is to encourage and provide the environment for the development of authentic, loving, and "responseable" individuals: men and women who want to discover more of their essential traits and capacities, and thus learn to take responsibility for themselves, their community, and their world. Our basic process is to promote open and honest communication and interaction among people — to develop affection, compassion, and trust for one another, and to reach a deeper level of understanding of our connection with all living things.

The community also provides members and visitors with opportunities for personal growth and transformation in the supportive environment of a wide range of workshops and personal counseling. Visitors are welcome, particularly at Saturday afternoon meetings when someone usually gives a talk, followed by an exercise or guided meditation, and a guided tour of the property for interested newcomers.

Workshop brochure and a pamphlet on the community are free of charge (we request postage for overseas: US $2 airmail). *Centrepoint* magazine (4 issues/year) costs US $13.50 airmail; $8.50 surface; $3 sample copy. 3/1/89

Christiania

DK-1047
Copenhagen K, DENMARK

Probably the biggest squat in Europe with a permanent population of some thousand people, rising to over twice that number in the summer. It is a melting pot out of which many initiatives elsewhere in Denmark develop. At a collective level they provide all their own services from street cleaning and rubbish collection, to keeping out violence and the abuse of hard drugs. The city of Copenhagen is sometimes actively disruptive and occasionally supportive — but never quite sure whether or not to accept Christiania as a part of the city. 1/15/89

Christians

P.O. Box A-678
Sydney South, NSW
2000 AUSTRALIA

We are 19 adults active in social and community work, and in non-violent protests against materialism in society. We also work with the poor in the Third World. All possessions are shared in common. Visitors participate in all group activities. 7/21/89

Commonground

P.O. Box 474
Seymour 3660, AUSTRALIA

057 922883

Commonground is a small rural community on 95 acres, 100 km south of Melbourne. At present we are 7 adults and 4 children. This community was first established in the city by a group of people committed to social change — searching for the most appropriate contribution we could make to building a better world. We express our social goals in two major ways: 1) by living in community, sharing our income and resources and the raising of our children, living lightly on the land, living as simply as we can, and challenging established social relationship patterns. We also act as a model to support others who wish to live this way. 2) Commonground is set up to be a resource for other social change groups. Groups (or individuals from those groups) can use Commonground as a place to get away from the city, to rest and recuperate from their struggles, or to plot and plan for the next one. We provide a place for gatherings, festivals, and other networking activities.

Commonground also runs workshops for groups — designed around each group's particular needs. Focus areas include group communication, personal process and empowerment,

International

Commonground *(Cont'd.)*

conflict management, decision-making and power sharing, direct action preparation, goal setting, and evaluation. Groups pay according to their ability to do so. These workshops provide some of the community's income, in addition to some highly paid workshops and two part-time jobs. All income is shared. Full members negotiate their financial contribution according to their assets. All land, buildings, and other resources (apart from personal items) are held in common.

Commonground has a commitment to shared child raising and all major decisions about children are made by consensus. The children are home schooled, with children's resource people scheduled from 7am until bedtime. Efforts are being made to incorporate children into the decision-making, especially the making of behavioral agreements. We do not require that members work a specified number of hours per week — we all work very hard at present (we are still in a building construction phase which requires a lot of energy).

We are a bit like an extended family, with all its costs and benefits. We work hard to support and challenge each other's personal growth and empowerment, and to disentangle some of the baggage we bring from our nuclear family socialization. We have a commitment to deal with conflict and personal issues that affect our relationships. We are open to new members, but reluctant to take people with children at present — until our adult/child ratio increases. 8/20/89

Community of the Ark

La Borie Noble
34650 Roqueredonde
FRANCE

La Borie Noble is the oldest of the communities of the Communauté de L'Arche (an order of nine communities in Europe and one in Canada), founded by Lanza Del Vasto after his encounter with Gandhi. Each community is composed of Companions, both men and women, married or single, who commit themselves to the service of others, following the way of Gandhian non-violence. This involves manual work, a search for inner knowledge, simple living and non-violent commitment for the cause of peace and justice.

Three communities live at the La Borie site situated on a vast and wild plateau of the Haut Languedoc. The ground is stony and not very fertile, but it provides a living for the 150 or so inhabitants of the three villages, and for their cows and their working horses. They produce the greater part of their own food, and have a daily schedule of work, exercise, vegetarian meals, and prayer. All resources are held in common; each person contributes what they can, and receives according to their needs. They consciously limit their needs to avoid falling into the traps of consumerism, and thus avoid contributing to the pillage of less developed countries. All important decisions are made by consensus, and they emphasize that conciliation and reconciliation among all is a necessary condition for a nonviolent community. Please include an SASE with correspondence. 4/1/89

Comunidad del Sur

Casilla de Correos 15229
Casa Encuentro, Millan 4115
Montevideo, URUGUAY

Comunidad del Sur, sister community to the group in Sweden (see following listing), runs a "meeting house" in Montevideo, and has initiated an ecological community village (Eco-Comunidad) outside Montevideo which eventually will be a training center for organic agriculture and appropriate technologies. Plans for the future include the establishment of ceramic, textile, and carpentry workshops; a library; a book cafe; and sales space for the products of the different groups.

The foremost objective of the projects is the creation of a new culture: to provide possibilities for people to study self-management and appropriate technologies, while exploring non-hierarchical forms of human association based on co-operation and direct democracy. This cooperative approach emphasizes interdependent and complementary attitudes, rather than competition and rivalry. 5/8/89

Comunidad - Nordan

Box 15 128
104 65, Stockholm
SWEDEN *(Tel: 08/41 01 47)*

Comunidad is an intentional community based on liberation and ecological principles. It was started 33 years ago in Uruguay under the name

"Comunidad del Sur." In 1977 the group moved to Sweden to escape political persecution. In 1985, after the military dictatorship ended, Comunidad del Sur was re-established in Uruguay and is now a "sister group" to the center in Sweden.

The purpose of living in community is to create a social structure where everybody can participate on all levels, and where all aspects of life (such as work, economy, education, and protective activity) are assumed in common. Comunidad has relations with many Latin American groups, and some of them have received support from an inter-communitarian fund. The intention is to grow as a movement for another development. In Sweden, Comunidad is a city-based group which runs a printing house and a publishing house. The group in Uruguay, "Comunidad del Sur", has both rural and urban centers (see previous listing). We do not respond to inquiries for alternative tourism or sleeping spaces. [cc] 5/8/89

Comunidad Rural "La Atlantida"

c/o Luis Adriano Calero
Apartado 7566
Cali, COLOMBIA (S.A.)

The Directory received a postcard from this group stating their desire to be included. We have no further information. 5/15/89

Crabapple

Berrington Hall
Berrington, Nr Shrewsbury
Shropshire, ENGLAND

0743 75 418

Our 200-year-old house, large and cluttered, was originally a rectory, and we are gradually making it more comfortable (though it can be very cold in winter). We have a 20-acre organic farm, but most of our income comes from our whole food shop in town — where we also sell books, and distribute information about food, green politics, and alternative lifestyles. All income is pooled, all bills are paid communally, and the members take pocket money to cover personal expenses. We share the jobs of bookkeeping, bill-paying, and accounting.

Normally 2-3 of us run the farm, with help from some of the others. We have cows, sheep, chickens, ducks, and bees. We raise hay & fodder for the animals, and grow vegetables for our own consumption and to sell in the shop. We make our own butter, cheese & yogurt, and we sell a lot of our eggs. We eat some of our own meat, but many of us are vegetarian. Our fuel wood comes from our own woods, and we've been doing considerable tree planting.

We are quite varied in our approaches to life, and there isn't any easily identifiable common aim. Though we each have our own interests, we do generally share a belief in non-racism, non-sexism, common ownership and co-ops, the fundamental madness of nuclear weapons and power and war-mongering in general. We are all concerned for our environment, and are into finding better ways of doing things (like organic farming). We meet once a week to sort out who's doing what when, to make any necessary decisions, etc. We also try to find ways of going deeper into issues and feelings, though we're often not very successful at it.

Visitors are welcome for up to four days (unless you are coming a very long distance). Please make advance reservations in writing, and enclose an SASE if possible. There are always things to do here, though we might not be able to give you as much time individually as we would like. We don't expect visitors to work all the time they're here, but expect them to join in with some of whatever is going on. We normally ask for a donation to cover our costs. Prospective members normally come for additional visits of two weeks and four weeks before we decide; they may take longer to decide for themselves. No capital is required, and we're not looking for any particular skills or types of people — what's important is whether we can live together or not. 2/1/89

Crescent Road Community

4608 Crescent Road
Kingston Hill
Surrey, ENGLAND

Formed in 1978, the Crescent Road Community presently has 20 adult members and 3 children. We live as an extended family group, with diverse interests and skills among our members. Our urban land and houses are owned more or less by our housing association. The more "major" a decision, the more we seek consensus. There is presently an internal discussion about how to share money to create common-wealth... whether to operate by contributing a percentage of our incomes, or to determine set levels based on the cost of living. Hospitality is also a consistent strand in our life. Please include an SASE with correspondence [cc]. 2/1/8

Darvell

Robertsbridge
East Sussex TN32 5DR
ENGLAND

0580 880 626

Membership requires a lifetime commitment. Our first call is to Christ and this cannot be separated from the brothers and sisters to whom we are pledged. We do not feel that any one pattern for daily life is the answer, but we do believe in a life of Christian brotherhood that comes from an inner change of heart, following Jesus completely in every aspect of life.

Our children are educated up to high school age by members in our own schools. Our principal livelihood is derived from the manufacture of nursery play equipment and equipment for the handicapped.

Inquiries are welcomed. Visits can be arranged, but please write in advance so as to ensure accommodation. Guests are asked to share in the work and life in an open and seeking way. (See main listing under "Hutterian Brethren".) 7/21/89

Finca Choconuevo

Galapagos 565 #27
Quito, ECUADOR
South America

Finca Choconuevo is an 80-acre farm in the rainforested foothills of the Andes mountains in NW Ecuador. Our conscious aim is to live in harmony with this special environment, and to promote and nurture the well-being of all within it. To this end, we are active in the local community — sharing freely of what knowledge, experience, and resources we possess or can attract.

Our practice is our service. We grow some of our food, and earn money from farming and crafts. We are an extended family (an informal group of fluctuating numbers) connected with other such groups in Ecuador and elsewhere, and united by our respectful love of the life and beauty all around us. Visitors are encouraged; they should be stalwart hikers (it's a *long* walk to town!) and willing to meet their own expenses. 2/13/90

Finca Jardin de Luz (Garden of Light)

Apartado Postal No. 10
Salamá B.V. 15901
GUATEMALA, Centro America

We hope to establish a non-denominational Christian community on our 100-acre tropical farm, which is half cleared of dense thorn bushes and ready for cultivation. We have been coming together for over ten years, but we're very isolated here, and the locals are not in any way interested in community life. We have obtained fair sized crops of corn and black beans (the local staple diet) and our most valuable asset is a perennial fresh water river; we are considering tomatoes as a future cash crop. One of our cherished dreams is to establish a bilingual Spanish-English school. For prospective members we would prefer young couples, with or without children, who are willing to work and who value cooperation. 1/27/89

International

The Findhorn Foundation

Cluny Hill College, Forres
IV36 ORD, SCOTLAND

0309 73655

The Findhorn Community, founded in 1962, soon became famous for growing very large vegetables on sand dunes by talking to the "nature spirits" and entertaining the notion that all life is one. Findhorn has subsequently grown into a center committed to deepening the understanding of all life's inter-connectedness, and exploring the emergence of a new culture in the world — believing that everything is alive and inter-dependent, and that we are all essential crew on Spaceship Earth.

The Findhorn Foundation is now a charitable educational trust whose conferences and workshops draw 5,000 visitors a year from all over the world. It is part of an international network of communities and community ventures, with links in politics, education, the arts, the spiritual growth movement, and environmental organizations such as Friends of the Earth and the World Wilderness Congress. Findhorn has inspired the formation of dozens of new age communities based on spirituality, interconnectedness, attunement, holistic health, and global peace.

At Findhorn's heart is a core of about 200 residents of all ages who strive to live and work in conscious awareness of the presence of God within all life. The community is the focal point for a growing network of independent businesses — a computer software company, the Moray Steiner School, a building company specializing in energy-efficient design, a graphic design company, a nursing home, a holistic health center, a bookshop, a health food shop, and a variety of individual projects which have grown from the Foundation or have been created by friends in the area. Findhorn distributes a wide range of tapes and literature — please write for details. Prospective visitors are requested to write well in advance to the Accommodations Secretary. 3/21/89

Fusion Arts Colony

Chris Neid, P.O. Box 293
Mornington, Victoria
3931 AUSTRALIA

A community of Christians concerned with developing skills and understanding in the visual arts. We have 15 adults and 5 children living on 2 rural acres. Other concerns and aims of the community include craftwork, philosophy, healing, therapy, and personal growth. Visitors should plan to share the cost of board. 7/21/89

Greuth Hof

e.v. Begegnungßtätte
D8966 Kimratshofen
WEST GERMANY

Established in 1977, we have grown into a living and working community of 10 adults and 2 children. We come from different countries and social conditions which lends much richness to our daily life and the workings of our group. We all have strong personalities but we place the emphasis on tolerance and attunement (harmony) — looking for and using that which unites rather than separates us. Everyone follows his/her own spiritual path (east/west) and our backgrounds in this area are varied: Catholic, Protestant, Jewish, Atheist.... 1/12/89

Hillier Park

Emissary Society - Australia
Hillier Road, Gawler 5118
SOUTH AUSTRALIA

08-22-5179

Hillier Park, situated on the banks of the Gawler River, is a regional center for the Emissary network, and home to 25 adults and 10 children. The community's primary livelihood has evolved from a simple mobile home park into a significant tourist park business. The community focus is directed towards a more effective and creative life experience, and spiritual awareness without dogma or belief. (See main listing under Emissaries of Divine Light.) 6/13/89

The Hohenort

P.O. Box 245
Constantia 7848
SOUTH AFRICA

021 743601

Surrounded by mountains, forest, and sea, The Hohenort ("high place") is a rich heartland setting for the restoration to wholeness of South Africa's diverse peoples. An Emissary community (see main listing under Emissaries of Divine Light.) and an operational hotel, it hosts events that welcome the participation of any who wish to harmonize with the way life works. The Hohenort is also well known as a hotel, pub, and restaurant — a hospitable setting for business seminars, conferences, receptions, and dinner parties. Because of the strong cooperation and teamwork among all involved here — and the shared perspective larger than the parochial and divisive issues of the day — the Hohenort is a strong symbol of oneness. 12/14/88

La Vigne

Velanne la Sauge
38620 St. Seoire-en-Valdaine
FRANCE

076 076040 / 071776

La Vigne has 15 full-time residents and a constant flow of visitors for various lengths of time. Situated in a tiny village in the foothills of the Alps, it has a rural quality to it. It provides a focus for Emissary activities throughout Europe. As the currents of unification move over the European Continent, La Vigne provides an example of harmony amongst its multinational residents. Our community offers a quality of atmosphere within which individual spiritual growth is fostered. "Art of Living" one-week seminars are offered three times a year while many other gatherings take place every week on themes ranging from therapeutic massage to English language courses to Bible classes. (See main listing under Emissaries of Divine Light.) 12/4/88

Laurieston Hall

Castle Douglas
Kirkcudbrightshire, S.W.
DG7 2NB SCOTLAND

064 45-263/275

We are a group of 20 adults and 10 children living in and around a spacious old mansion in the heart of the Galloway countryside. Founded in 1972, we own about 130 acres of land, live quite independent lives, and manage our collective affairs by consensus government at a weekly meeting. We place a high value on cooperation towards personal growth and fulfillment. Each adult is expected to contribute towards maintenance and support by working roughly half of the week on work for the community. We produce a large amount of our food and dairy products; wood for our woodstoves, gathered weekly from local forests; and electricity for lighting and hot water, generated by our hydro plant.

Between March and October we host conferences and events, with about 1500 paying visitors each year. We have our own lake, sauna, and large conservation area. Because of priority given to the activities of our conference center, we reserve two weeks each year for visitors who want to get to know us and experience living here. Other visitors are encouraged to come for weekend events, or to help during our tri-annual maintenance fortnights. All visitors must write to make advance arrangements. 1/10/89

Lebensgarten
(Permaculture Institute)

Akazienhain 4 (Ginsterweg 5)
3074 Steyerberg
WEST GERMANY

05764-2370/2158

80 members. The Permaculture Institute is just a part of the larger community. The buildings and land are held in common. Separate incomes: healing professions and seminars. Open to more members. 11/12/89

Lifespan Community

Townhead, Dunford Bridge
Sheffield S30 6TG
South Yorkshire, ENGLAND

0226 762359

Lifespan is a rural income-sharing community, committed to living and working together cooperatively, and to developing new sorts of relationships and ways of being that will offer an alternative to the nuclear family, consumerist society, and patriarchal values.

Our income comes mainly from our printing and publishing business, where we each work 2 or 3 days a week. We share childcare within a flexible system. We eat together, and all participate in domestic work. We have a big program of building and maintenance work to improve the property and to make more of it habitable. We have a large greenhouse, and a thriving organic garden. We aim to skill-share as a part of our commitment to power-sharing and breaking down traditional sex-roles. We spend time over our decision-making, trying to ensure that we are communicating honestly with each other, and that everyone has a chance to participate fully.

Our ambition is to see the community grow and develop — so that more of the houses are lived in or used as workshops, and so we have a wider variety of people living here. We are always open to new members. Write, enclosing an International Reply Coupon, and we will send you more information. 4/1/90

Lower Shaw Farm

Old Shaw Lane
Shaw, Near Swindon
Wilts SN5 9PJ, ENGLAND

In 1974 Lower Shaw Farmhouse was standing empty and unused, and the outbuildings were barely fit for even bovine residents. Since then the dairy and sheds have been converted to dormitories, meeting rooms, and workshops — and, thanks to the enthusiasm and effort of a succession of residents in the farmhouse, a sense of communal continuity has been established. There are now six adults and seven children living in the farmhouse, while the 'farm' itself is run as a flourishing meeting place for weekend and week-long courses, conferences, and learning holidays. We have a steady stream of visitors throughout the year. Though once

rural, we now enjoy a 3-acre 'oasis' in an area of 1980's development; the farm has nonetheless retained much of its character and atmosphere.

Our 'farm' has substantial organic fruit and herb gardens, and we keep an assortment of animals which provide not only farm products — but also a tremendous amount of enjoyment to residents and visitors alike (especially the childlike ones). We have no collectively stated religious or party political base, though we try to forge our diversity and attitudes into a core of common aims and values which include: to provide a meeting place where people can share ideas, information, experiences, and skills; to encourage ecological resourcefulness and due consideration for both our immediate and global environment; to increase individual sense of social responsibility; and to learn to live and work together well.

The nature of events here varies considerably. Some are instructive courses comprising both instruction and practical activity, while also being a social get-together for participants. Course subjects are wide ranging — from literature and the politics of food, to children's education, herbs, and health. Some courses are seen as informal learning holidays, and we have also hosted weekends for cycling, music, yoga, games, etc. In addition to running our own events, we also hire out our facilities to local and national groups such as work/study camps, community action and therapy groups, schools, and the Open University. If you would like to know more about our activities, or are interested in booking terms, please write enclosing a SASE. 3/1/89

Mandala

Mary Vale, MS 394
Warwick, Queensland
4370 AUSTRALIA

We are a community of 25 adults and 8 children living on 278 acres in rural Australia. The primary concern and aim of the community is conservation, and we try to provide sanctuary for wildlife. 7/21/89

International

Meitheal

Inch Fort, Inch Island
County Donegal, IRELAND

07760323

We are a spiritual community of 9 adults and 4 children who are living and working together to create both a home environment for ourselves and an educational center for exploring and demonstrating the holistic lifestyle — a way of living which seeks to develop our full potential for creativity and growth on every level: physical, emotional, mental, and spiritual. Each of us comes from a different religious background and is following his or her own spiritual path —but we all share a similar understanding of God, and recognize an essential "oneness" and unity in the rich diversity of all life. Three daily meditations are central to our routine, and we also have frequent silent attunements to bring us back to the spiritual focus of our work. We have weekly "family" meetings at which we discuss current administrative and organizational matters. We make all important decisions by consensus — and open communication is vital to keep things running smoothly. Regular "sharings" provide the opportunity to discuss the way we're feeling and know that we're being listened to, enabling us to resolve interpersonal conflicts as they arise.

We moved to our 5-acre site in 1986, and immediately began work on renovating our two cottages, and cultivating the organic garden. Although we had very little money, we trusted that the support would come — and it did. We are each self-supporting and contribute a weekly rent to cover food and expenses. The rest of our income is earned from organizing educational workshops and residential guest programs, and from donations. We will eventually be able to sell our free-range eggs and surplus organic produce from the garden, and we aim to become more self-reliant by starting a number of small businesses (including craft workshops). We run summer camps for children and parents, youth empowerment camps for teenagers, and have regular open house concerts.

We have an urban center as well, an office in Derry where we make connections with other groups working for positive social change — we are developing a resource center for support and information. We do welcome visitors, but ask that you confirm in advance. 2/27/89

Michaelshof

Hutterian Brethren
Auf der Höhe, 5231
Birnbach, WEST GERMANY

49 2681 6250

See main listing under "Hutterian Brethren." 3/1/89

Mickleton Emissary Community

Mickleton House, Mickleton
Gloucestershire GL55 6RY
ENGLAND

0386 438251 / 438308

Although we are a large intentional community and have quite a bit of through-traffic in short term residents, we are approaching our tenth birthday with no signs of coming apart. On the contrary, we are finding a degree of increasing harmony which most visitors find immediately remarkable. Yet nobody joins us because they're looking for a good community. (On that basis, they would probably be disappointed.) People find themselves living here because they have been attracted to something intangible about the central attitude to life of those who live here. They also come because they have a strong urge to change and to add their own personal contribution.

The community works without rules or belief system because we are able to trust one another. We can do that because of a basic agreement about our job on earth. We are part of a worldwide network of people, both in and out of communities, loosely known as Emissaries, who aim to "magnify the finest qualities of character in every field of human endeavor."

We live in communal and family homes in and around the village, and work at a variety of jobs both in and out of the village. In the central building, Mickleton House, we have community meetings three times a week, mostly open to the public — each accompanied by a meal for all of us and our visitors. (See main listing for Emissaries of Divine Light.) 12/20/88

Mitraniketan Community

Mitraniketan P.O.
Vellanad 695-543
Trivandrum, Kerala, INDIA

Mitraniketan ("the house of friends") is a rural educational community founded in 1956 with the aim to encourage people to "think globally and act locally," to develop the whole individual, and to offer a replicable model for Third World countries. It is a non-political, non-sectarian, non-commercial registered charity, and promotes grassroots development, training, and education.

Situated on 70 acres of green hilly land covered with tropical trees and vegetation, it is home for about 100 adults and 300 children and adolescents. Residents operate a farm, a spinning and weaving cooperative, a handicrafts cooperative, various shop facilities, a publishing unit, several schools, an arts and sports unit, a library, three hostels, a home for the aged, and a botanical garden for the production and sale of flowers and decorative plants. They host a number of regional, national, and international conferences and seminars on development, education, nature preservation, and other allied themes.

With the help of local conveners, Mitraniketan helps operate 100 adult education centers in local villages, 10 nurseries with 30-60 children each (with medical checkups and mothers' meetings for health and nutrition classes), and 20 youth clubs for environment protection. They also organize local farming efforts, construct local sanitation facilities, provide family counseling, and have built 20 low-cost houses.

Mitraniketan invites world servers from all over to come and offer their skills, time, talents, and funds. Mitraniketan provides food, accommodations, training, and a hearty welcome. For more details, please write about yourself and ask for our illustrated brochure. A voluntary contribution is appreciated from those who can afford it. 5/12/89

Monkton Wyld Court

Near Charmouth, Dorset
DT6 6DQ ENGLAND

0297 60342

Established in 1983, Monkton Wyld Court is a rural community with 9 adults and 6 children. Our shared spirituality focuses on deep ecology and a close relationship with nature. We also emphasize cooperation, non-hierarchical organization, and self responsibility. Most members' working time goes into the community. We have a kindergarten and a dayschool which several of our children attend. One of our children is homeschooled, one attends state school. We are open to a few more members, but children need to be seven or older. 1/6/89

Moora Moora Cooperative

P.O. Box 214, Healesville
3777 Victoria, AUSTRALIA

059 623749 / 624104

A rural cooperative community of 40 adults and 32 children, living mostly in individual family units. Members pay a joining fee of approximately $13,000 per adult, are expected to work eight hours per month, and to contribute financially each month to cover dues and their share of the mortgage. We emphasize the value of land and resource conservation, and of education. 1/12/89

Mt. Oak Community

P.O. Box 6, Cooma, NSW
2630 AUSTRALIA

064 544167

We are a community of 25 adults and 3 children living on 2,760 acres. Primary concerns and aims of the community include food production, alternative economics and technology, permaculture, conservation, wildlife sanctuary, land reclamation, craftwork, philosophy, healing, and personal growth. Visitors are expected to participate in community projects, and to have a responsible, self-reliant attitude. This is an arid environment, so be prepared. 7/21/89

New Goverdhan

Jaganananda Das
AUSTRALIA

066 724566 9am-1pm

Our community is based on simple living, high thinking, and making God the center of life and all activity meant for his glorification and satisfaction. Life is meant for engaging everything in God's service since he is the owner of everything. We are 70 adults and 30 children living on 2760 acres. Concerns and aims of the community also include food production and philosophy. Visitors should make arrangements in advance, and are expected to help out. 7/21/89

Nomadelfia

C.P. 178
58100 Grosseto, ITALY

0564-38243

"Nomadelfia" signifies "the law of brotherhood." It is the name of Catholic volunteers who live together to construct a new civilization based on the Gospel. It is not an institute nor a "boys' town", even if in its stride it has taken in those who have been abandoned — in particular minors. Today it is a group of 300 people (50 families) who live in an area covering four sq. km. in the Maremma, near Grosseto, in Tuscany.

Nomadelfia was founded by don Zeno Saltini (1900-1981) who at the age of twenty decided to change the world, starting with himself. In 1931, after becoming a priest, he adopted a young man who had been released from prison. Since then the families of Nomadelfia have accepted as their own children more than 5,000 young people.

Money does not circulate at Nomadelfia; there is no private property, no form of exploitation is admitted, and everything is held in common. It is in accordance with what Jesus said at the Last Supper: "Father, everything that is mine is yours, everything that is yours is mine, so be it...."

We are open to all, every year welcoming thousands of visitors. Members participate in meetings in parishes, schools, and associations. Come see us. If you wish to know more about us and receive our periodicals, please send us your address. 4/1/89

Old Hall Community

East Bergholt, Colchester
Suffolk, CO7 6TG ENGLAND

Old Hall Community is situated in an area of outstanding natural beauty. It is in the countryside seventy miles northeast of London, on the outskirts of the village of East Bergholt. Established in 1974, approximately 40 adults and 20 children live in a very large former manor house. Old Hall is a lay community where any religion or spiritual orientation is respected as long as it is not foisted on other members. Politically the community is Green or Socialist. All major decis-

ions are made at Friday meetings by consensus. Occasionally rows occur, but on the whole the community is convivial.

Money is earned by most members outside the community. A monthly maintenance charge goes towards the upkeep of the buildings and land, to pay the fuel bills, and to buy food that cannot be grown.

All community work is undertaken voluntarily by members and visitors. The 74 acres of land owned by the community is farmed and gardened organically. There are Jersey and Red Polled cows, Lincoln Longwool sheep, Toggenburg and Anglo-Nubian goats, chickens, and geese. Many of the fields retain their ancient names and are used for grazing, hay, cereal crops, and potatoes. There are two orchards and several areas of berries. A wide variety of vegetables are grown in the gardens for the kitchen. The meals served are delicious, with a choice of either a meat or vegetarian dish. Surplus produce is sold at the front gate to passers-by.

Old Hall is looking for new members. If you wish to be considered, or simply wish to visit, please write to the secretary. 8/8/89

Permaculture Pyrenées

Bourlège
11300 Limoux, FRANCE

68 31 51 11

We are a non-profit association whose purpose is the revival and maintenance of the Autonomous Native European Creativity — promoting arts, crafts, ecological agricultures, and science. Located in the foothills of the Pyrenées bioregion, with a house in a neighboring village where artistic activities and related workshops are offered to the local rural population. 100 acres, secluded, with difficult access. We are building our own living facilities, a communal house, with a barn also under way. Plans include a windmill, soft-tech pumps, and an irrigation system. Funding is needed. Visitors are expected to join in the work. Open to new members. Write before visiting. Not strictly vegetarians. Hope to grow to a stable group of about 10 adults. 3/1/89

International

Post Green Community Trust

56 Dorchester Road
Lytchett Minster, Poole
Dorset BH16 6JE, ENGLAND

0202 622317

We are currently about 20 people aged 7 years to 61 years, and are open to visitors and new members. Over the years our community has undergone significant changes, though we retain our roots in Christianity. Please write for more information. 4/6/89

Redfield Community

Buckingham Rd., Winslow
Buckinghamshire
MK183LZ ENGLAND

Redfield's 17 acres of land contain two small woods, a 7-acre field, a 3/4-acre vegetable garden and orchard, plus other gardens for herbs and flowers, a 50-room Victorian house, and a couple of cottages. A large stable block has been partially developed as a workshop space — so far with metal and woodwork shops, a black-smith's forge, a cowshed, and stores.

Redfield is a fully mutual housing co-op, established in 1978. Every adult who lives here must be a tenant and therefore a member. Being such a large group we are inevitably diverse. Some of us make a full or part-time living here; others work outside, or on state benefits. It has to be said that those doing nine to five jobs outside often find it difficult to meet the demands of the community as well.

We are united by our commitment to a lifestyle radically different from the norm... in a community rather than in isolated nuclear families or by ourselves. We do maintain our individual interests which include the Green movement, anti-nuclear struggles and environmental protection, yoga, knitting, carpentry, printing, playing musical instruments, art computing, Feminism, Third World studies, blues music, skiing, alternative medicine, and playing tennis (yes, we have a tennis court).

The community is run collectively and non-hierarchically in an atmosphere where sexism, racism, and ageism are not welcome. We have weekly meetings, and all decisions are made by consensus. The legal roles of Secretary and Treasurer, as well as our 'internal' jobs, are rotated mostly on an annual basis.

Most of the rooms on the first floor are for communal use, and the upstairs living units are to some extent private. All meals are cooked in the communal kitchen, and we are all responsible for cleaning the house. We also share the work of maintaining the house and tending the garden. We do not income share; rather, community expenditures are met by the members paying a monthly 'rent'. We are frequently looking for new members, and one of our most important criteria is that they would enjoy living and working here — and are prepared to contribute towards realizing the potential of the place. Please write for information about membership and visiting, and enclose an SASE. 2/12/89

Shambala

P.O. Box 10
Bellingen, NSW
2454 AUSTRALIA

Twenty adults and 10 children living on 640 acres. Primary aims of the community include food production, alternative technology, conservation, wildlife sanctuary, and craftwork. Short term visitors only. 7/21/89

Sharing in Development Group

26 Glen Street
Edinburgh EH3 9JE
SCOTLAND

We are an urban community of 5 adults, founded in Edinburgh in 1976. We grow some of our own food, and eat together daily. We make decisions by consensus, and expect members to regularly contribute labor to the group. Visits by prior arrangement only. Please include an SASE with correspondence. 1/22/89

Shrubb Family

Shrubb Farm Cottages,
Larling, Norwich,
Norfolk NR16 2QT CT
ENGLAND

0953 717844

Our family aims for the closeness of a family (though independent of any blood ties), and tries to live in harmony while being creative as a group and as individuals. We don't really have any rules here, though things are decided by tradition to a certain extent. We don't have any leaders either — it's good if every person here thinks of him or herself as the non-leader of the commune.

We all live under one roof, and much of the character of our commune is due to the fact that we do live in such close physical proximity to each other. A prospective member has got to want to live in a commune... not just be needing somewhere to live, or wanting to live with friends. We could do with some new female members to balance things up a bit.

The people are generous and selfish, loving, angry, busy, idle; they work, play, talk, laugh, quarrel, sulk, have some good times and — in short — do what people do. The dog and the cat behave more consistently. There is no hierarchy, no pecking order, no allocation of jobs — but work gets done. Meals appear on the table, the dishes get done, the house is cleaned sporadically. There are more jobs to do around the place than there is enthusiasm to do them.

Our farm house dates back to the early or mid 17th century, and is now owned by our own Limited Company. We have a workshop that needs building, and a wonderful garden that needs discovering. The greenhouse has been repaired and is in use; and we have recently acquired a full-size beehive, so now produce our own honey. Please include an SASE with inquiries [cc]. 6/1/89

Some Friends Community

128 Bethnal Green Road
London E2 6DG, ENGLAND

01 739-2301

Some Friends Community is an intentional community, with a current age range from seventy to twenty-two, plus a baby. We are non-hierarchical, making decisions by consensus at regular meetings. We all pay the same rent per month, but there is a sliding-scale charge for food. We do not share incomes. We have regular "relationships meetings" at which we share about how we are getting along—and we are committed to trying to resolve interpersonal conflict. Members work at a variety of outside jobs in London. Some are not employed at present. We currently live on three floors of a large building over a shop in Bethnal Green, an inner city area (parts of which are at present undergoing rapid commercial development — drawing a sharp distinction between rich and poor in the area). Each member has a separate room, and there are shared facilities. We are part of Some Friends Housing Co-op. We are open to inquiries, preferably by post. We emphasize non-violence, equality of the sexes, and vegetarianism. Also, about half our members are Quakers, and the rest are of varying spiritual persuasions. Written inquiries preferred. [cc] 1/6/89

Some People Community

12 Bartholomew Street
Leicester, LE2 1FA, ENGLAND
0533 545436/541403

Some People Community has no "members" as such, but we are an urban cooperative with rural links. Some of us are trying to pioneer a form of cooperative association which is *not* based on libertarian/egalitarian ideas, and yet which still aspires to be radical. Our overall organizing principle is cooperation, and we have a small income-pooling core group within the community which places a high value on commitment, loyalty, responsibility, and accountability. We also have a limited scope of income-earning possibilities via worker co-ops. Our land and buildings are stewarded by something resembling an informal trust. SASE appreciated with correspondence, if possible [cc]. 1/16/89

Svanholm

Svanholm Gods
4050 Skibby, DENMARK
02 32 16 70

The Svanholm Collective consists of about 75 adults and 60 children ranging in age from zero to 74 years. Most of us are around forty. We also have a number of agricultural trainees, and usually quite a few visitors on fairly long-term stays. We own an estate with 625 acres of farm land and 408 acres of park and woodlands. When we bought the property in 1978 we wanted to live in a production collective based on shared work, shared economy, and shared decision making. We wanted *whole* lives, with influence on our work and daily living, and a place where our children would thrive with animals and fresh air. We have learned how difficult it is to have all our dreams fulfilled, but we're still at it. Many new ideas and plans have emerged along the way, and never do we have sufficient money for all the experiments we'd like to put into action.

Most of us work at home, although around 30 people have outside jobs. Our main production is ecological farming (700 tons of organic produce last year). We operate a mill and a shop where we sell grain, flour, and fodder. We pool all income into a common fund, and we each receive a monthly allowance for clothes, amusements, and pocket money. Our decision-making authority is the communal meeting, which is held once a week. We do not vote, but discuss our way to agreement.

We live in "house-groups" in various buildings in and around the estate, and these are the centers of the daily social life. Households vary in size from 5-25 adults and children, and include families, couples, and singles. Everyone has a room of their own, with shared kitchens and living rooms. We all eat supper together in the large communal kitchen. A kitchen group takes care of daily cooking; cleanup and weekend cooking is rotated among everyone else. Small children spend the day in our kindergarten, and we have an after school "youth club" for the older ones.

We get a lot of inquiries, and like to meet these requests as far as possible — both by receiving visitors, and by going out to give lectures and slide shows. We also have a film under production, and sell a 20-page booklet which describes our experiment. Please call or write for more information. 6/21/88

Taena

Whitley Court
Upton St. Leonards
Gloucester GL4 8EB
ENGLAND
0452 68346

Six family houses on a 135-acre dairy farm are living as an intentional village. We began during WWII as a pacifist commune in Cornwall. After a few years we came under the influence of C.G. Jung, and this led to an interest in Yoga, meditation, and Eastern religions generally. We were then drawn to the Roman Catholic Church and, one by one, during the late 40s, were received into the Church. In 1952 we moved to our present home which adjoins Prinknash Benedictine Abbey.

In 1961 we changed to a village basis, and since then each family has been functionally separate and has developed varying interests and occupations. Though there are many living here who are not members of any church, our central act as a community is the weekly celebration of Mass in our chapel, offered by one of the monks from the Abbey. Occupations include: farming, painting, silversmithing, stone and wood carving, calligraphy, pottery, counseling, and teaching Tai Chi Ch'uan. Visitors are welcome, but please contact us first by letter. 2/1/89

Tauhara Centre

P.O. Box 125
Taupo, NEW ZEALAND
074 87-507

The Tauhara Centre is situated in park-like surroundings in Acacia Bay, overlooking Lake Taupo. It serves as a venue for people and groups of many differing viewpoints and methods of working who are united in their search for truth. Most of the staff are residential and live and work in close cooperation with each other — living in separate dwellings on the site, sharing meals and social gatherings.

The Centre can accommodate 40 people in its 10 four-berth rooms, though the dining room and main hall can cater for groups of up to 200 people. The main kitchen provides quality catering, but there is also a separate kitchen for those who wish to use it. The lounge is comfortable and suitable for more intimate gatherings. Trailer accommodations and campsites are available. The Centre was established to foster goodwill and understanding in the world, and to strive to serve this end in all its activities. 3/16/89

Teachest Centre for Alternative Technology

Machynlleth, Powys
WALES
SY20 9AZ
0654-2400

Set in a 40-acre disused state quarry, the center has working displays of small-scale solar, wind, and water power; low-energy buildings; organic growing; and nature conservation. The displays are designed to give practical ideas on how people can reduce the environmental impact of their everyday lives. The Centre is open to the public every day, and receives about 55,000 visitors each year — making it one of the largest attractions in mid-Wales. About a dozen staff members live at the Centre, making it very much a working example of alternative technology. Meals are served in our wholefood vegetarian restaurant.

The Centre was founded in 1974 as an educational charity. We are in a unique position to offer courses, as our staff have many years of 'hands on' experience, often backed by academic expertise in their subjects. We have been running courses for the public since 1979, and for academic establishments since 1981. Practical training courses were established in 1982 for people going into Third World countries as volunteers.

Our weekend courses cover water, wind, and solar power; organic growing; herbs; self-build; environmental education; and much more. The courses are suitable for beginners as well as those with a more advanced or professional interest in the subject. We also offer 'tailor-made' courses of any length for school children, teachers and trainee-teachers, university and college students — or indeed any interested group of people. For information about any of these programs, please write to us for a brochure, and include a SASE. [cc] 2/1/89

Terre Nouvelle

BP 52
05300 Laragne
FRANCE
92-65-24-25

Established in 1975, we are a living and working community of 10 adults and 2 children. We come from different countries and social conditions which lends much richness to our daily life and the workings of our group. We all have strong personalities, but we place the emphasis on tolerance and attunement (harmony) — looking for and using that which unites rather than separates us. Everyone follows his/her own spiritual path (east/west) and our backgrounds in this area are varied: Catholic, Protestant, Jewish, Atheist.... We come together and are united in daily periods of meditation and in the celebration of holidays and festivals throughout the year.

Everyone takes the responsibility of one or more work departments, but often has the opportunity to participate in all the work — in order to keep an overall vision of the community. We have weekly meetings for work and personal sharing, and we make decisions by consensus. For a long period of time our income was derived solely from our agricultural activities: goats, bees, and biodynamically grown produce. We are presently developing an "education department" which will add both a nursery school for the village, and conferences and workshops for a wider public.

Similar in spirit to the Findhorn Community, we have always been open to the 'outside', taking part in our civilization and our century. We know that very powerful healing and transforming energies are at work on the planet, and are convinced that the catastrophic 'end of the millennium' scenarios become obsolete as we wake to our new maturity. We participate in a variety of associations on the local, county, national, and international levels. We also enjoy an unending flow of visitors and, at their suggestion, have recently developed a week-long visitors program workshop. As we are a small community, all visits need advance confirmation by letter.

Joy, Richness, Intensity, Tolerance are words that speak best for our daily life; *Transformation, Exactingness, Clarity, Service* define our sense of commitment here; *Peace, Love, Light, Unity* describe our vision for this place and the planet. 9/27/88

Wild Lavender

34 Queensdown Rd, Hackney
London, ES 8NN, ENGLAND

We are an urban community of 13 men, established in London in 1980. Essential values of our group include Gay communality, and love. We are sometimes open to visitors, if arrangements are made in advance. Please include an SASE with inquiries. 6/1/89

Yamagishi Association

International Dept.
Toyosato Jikkenchi
5010 Takanoo-cho, Tsu-shi
Mie-ken 514-22, JAPAN

A network of more than 20 rural communities in Japan, each having around 200 members and a communal lifestyle. 1/12/89

Updates...

As people around the world attempt to create living environments that reflect their values and dreams, the number of intentional communities continues to grow. And as the members of existing communities continue to learn from new experiences, those groups grow and change to reflect new perspectives and priorities. It's all a very dynamic process.

Our aim is to publish a new Directory every 2-3 years, with information as current and comprehensive as possible— so we need your help. Please use the *Reader Response Forms* on the next-to-last page to share with us whatever information you have. We invite your participation. ❖

About the Resources

In this section we list organizations whose work could be helpful to those seeking, or already involved in, "cooperative alternatives." We also include publications which cover subjects relevant to shared living and shared work (such as personal growth), or topics that frequently come up as the focus for various communities (such as environmental advocacy). We cover areas as diverse as community organizing and networking, health care, economics, work, law, food, housing, communication and facilitation, family life and relationships, energy and environment, politics, education, decision making, self and spirit, and culture.

Our listings were solicited from people both in and out of community, and comprise a representative (but by no means exhaustive) overview of groups making significant contributions in the development of a more peaceful, just, cooperative, and ecologically harmonious world. Each of these groups was judged by at least one person we know to be worthy of inclusion; time and space limitations have undoubtedly meant that some other groups, equally worthy, have not been included.

We generally avoided listing groups that are specifically local in scope, preferring to chase down networks and umbrella organizations. Our rationale is that regional or national groups will likely be good sources of information and/or referrals — regardless of the locale of the person making the inquiry. For example, we've not included many of the food co-ops, alternative schools, or health clinics referred to us by the communities which responded. We made two notable exceptions to this policy: we've included local groups that 1) are projects or businesses organized/operated by one of the communities listed in the Directory, or 2) have such a unique focus or style of operation that a listing might serve as a model for replication.

We hope that the resources described in this section will provide you with access to the wide range of groups working for a better future. If you don't find specifically what you are looking for, we hope that — by starting with the groups that *are* listed — you will find a referral to the group or resource you seek. If you're lucky, it will be no more than an SASE or two away.

The feedback we've requested regarding the community listings applies to resource groups as well — if you know of any groups that you think should be seriously considered for the Resources section of future Directories, please let us hear about them. On the next-to-lastyou page we've included a description of the information that will be of use you to us, where to send it, and a sample form to make your part easier. you
Thanks for your participation! ❖

Resources

THE CRITERIA WE USED to decide which Resource groups to include is explained in the introduction to these listings. Use the index to locate specific topics of interest.

IF YOU KNOW OF AN UNLISTED GROUP that you think should be included in future editions, please send us a description and contact information.

Abundant Life Seed Foundation

P.O. Box 772
Port Townsend, WA 98368

(206) 385-5660

Abundant Life Seed Foundation is a non-profit organization whose purpose is: 1) to acquire, propagate, and preserve the plants and seeds of the native and naturalized flora of the North Pacific Rim, with particular emphasis on those species not commercially available — including rare and endangered species; 2) to provide information on plant and seed propagation; and 3) to aid in the preservation of native and naturalized plants through cultivation. The Foundation sponsors the World Seed Fund, which provides seeds to those who most need and can least afford them. For each $100 donated, we send 400 packets of fresh, open-pollinated seed, appropriately selected, postpaid for distribution through any agency in any country that is working to end hunger (donors may opt to specify a country). Members of Abundant Life Seed Foundation pay $5-$20/year (sliding scale) and receive the annual seed and book catalog as well as periodic newsletters. 11/12/89

Acres, U.S.A.

10008 East 60th Terrace
Kansas City, MO 64133

(816) 737-0064
737-3346 Fax

Acres, U.S.A. believes that in order to be economical, agriculture must be ecological. We publish a monthly newspaper featuring a wide range of articles on eco-farming and human health; operate a bookstore; and host an annual conference on sustainable agriculture. We offer information on soil dynamics, cultivation methods, organic soil amendments, and radical analyses of the American farm position vis-a-vis agribusiness, "Big Government", multinationals, etc. Subscription rates: U.S. $15 per year; Canadian and foreign $18, U.S. funds only; single copies $2.25. 11/12/89

Action Linkage

Ann Weiser, Editor
5825 Telegraph Avenue #45
Oakland, CA 94609

We are deeply concerned about the present challenges facing life on the earth — the problems and possibilities of rapid technological, socioeconomic, and cultural change on a global scale — and the potential for local, win-win solutions to these global challenges. However, unlike most organizations we have no specific *external* mission. Rather, our mission is *inner-directed* — helping you personally be more effective in bringing about the changes you desire. We operate as a laboratory for the open exchange and development of useful means and goals in every area of social and personal change.

We are a network of independent individuals who communicate with each other in an interactive dialogue style. Discussion groups through the mail are in progress on several topics, including career options, designing new civilization, Mondragon-type communities, etc. We also encourage other methods including face-to-face meetings which put members in touch with each other for mutual support and action. Our newsletter is $30/year. Please write for information about how you may become a member of the network. 5/11/89

Advocates for Self-Government

Main Office:
940 East Bremer Avenue
Fresno, CA 93728

(209) 441-1776
441-1866 (Fax)

Publications Office:
1115 Sundial Circle
Birmingham, AL 35215

(205) 853-9307

Advocates for Self-Government is a non-profit educational organization. Our purpose is to present the freedom philosophy honestly and persuasively — to opinion leaders — so that they can encounter, evaluate, and (when ready) embrace the ideals of self-government.

Self-government is the combination of responsibility and tolerance. Abundance springs from responsible economic behavior; harmony springs from tolerance of others. We hold workshops to help our members better communicate their beliefs to others, and also sponsor *Seminar One,* a nationwide program of study groups which introduce the principles of self-government. We also produce and sell tapes and books. Our newsletter is the *Liberator.* 12/17/89

Akwesasne Notes

Mohawk Nation
P.O. Box 196
Rooseveltown, NY 13683

(518) 358-9531 U.S.
(613) 575-2063 Canada

Akwesasne Notes, the official publication of the Mohawk Nation of Akwesasne, has reported on indigenous people's news and issues for the past 21 years. It is probably the most widely-known and respected Native American periodical in print. Self-described as a "Journal for Native and Natural People," it is produced six times a year by a non-hierarchical editorial staff through whom (in the words of one former editor) it's "connected to just about everything that's going on in Indian Country, and much of what's happening elsewhere." Subscriptions are $15/1yr, $27/2yrs, $39/3yrs. 12/21/89

All Ways Free

515 E. Grant Road #113
Tucson, AZ 85705
Vermont Gathering '91
Box 116, Wilton NH 03086
(603) 878-2022

All Ways Free, published Winter and Summer of every year, is absolutely free and non-commercial, all volunteer, and all donation-supported. It features news and networking for the Rainbow Gatherings, heartsongs, and stories of the Rainbow Family.

We council at the World Peace Gathering of the Tribes (commonly known as the "Rainbow Gathering") which is held the first week of July each year — and the paper goes home with a different circle of focalizers. Anyone who writes us gets added to the mailing list. Each year's focalizers will start a fresh list, so you need to write us every year to stay on the list (or sign up at the Gathering).

Heartsongs and artwork are welcome. Your donation, of course, is the only way to make sure that anybody gets an actual paper! (Rainbows everywhere — throw us a benefit and give away a bundle of *Free!*) We love you ... see you in Vermont in July '91! Namaste. 3/21/91

The Alliance

2807 SE Stark
Portland, OR 97214

(503) 239-4991

The *Alliance* is a grassroots, multi-issue community newspaper covering news about ecological, feminist, anti-racist, gay and lesbian, international solidarity and labor movements in Oregon and the Pacific Northwest. We also do social journalism, investigative muckraking, interviews, and commentary. There are local editions in Portland and Eugene. Subscriptions are $15/year. 3/22/90

Alliance for Survival

Box 33686
San Diego, CA 92103

(619) 277-0991

AFS is involved in environmental, anti-nuclear, and anti-intervention work in the community. We do primary organizing for Nevada Test Site actions, and we also do economic conversion work, i.e. planning to convert military facilities and factories to peacetime uses. We are the sponsoring group for the local Big Mountain Support Group, and for an affiliate organization called Ballast Point Organizing Project (BPOP) which is a coalition of affinity groups involved in CD in this area. 5/10/88

Alternative Press Index

P.O. Box 33109
Baltimore, MD 21218

(301) 243-2471

The *Alternative Press Index* has been published since 1969. It is the most complete index available for periodicals that chronicle social change in the United States and around the world. Published quarterly, the API is a comprehensive guide to over 200 alternative, progressive, and radical newspapers, journals, and magazines. Articles are indexed by their subjects in a format similar to the *Reader's Guide to Periodical Literature*. Over 10,000 citations appear in each issue, including over 400 book and film reviews. Institutional subscriptions are $125/year; individuals or movement groups $30. We also publish a *Directory of Alternative & Radical Publications* which is available for $3. 3/13/90

Alternatives

5263 Bouldercrest Road
P.O. Box 429
Ellenwood, GA 30049

(404) 961-0102

Alternatives is a nonprofit organization providing resources for responsible living and celebrating. Started in 1973 as a protest against the commercialization of Chrismas, our focus is to encourage celebrations that reflect conscious ways of living. To us, living responsibly means avoiding consumption for consumption's sake; being aware of the individual's role in protecting the environment; recognizing the reality of our relatedness to one another; and being intentional about working toward social, economic, and political justice.

We distribute various publications which challenge the commercialization of our holy days and provide study materials, workshop aids, ideas, and resources for more joyful and appropriate celebrations. *Alternatives: A Quarterly Review* is our 24-page magazine which makes critical links between how we live and celebrate, and global justice issues that challenge people of conscience. We also operate a mail-order book store. Annual memberships are: $25 for Individuals; $15 Student/Limited Income; $75 Institutional. Subscriptions alone: $8 Regular; $6 Student/Limited Income; $10 Foreign. 9/21/89

The American Natural Hygiene Society, Inc.

P.O. Box 30630
Tampa, FL 33630

(813) 855-6607

The American Natural Hygiene Society is a non-profit, tax-exempt education organization which teaches people how to live happier, healthier lives than is usually thought possible. We carry on a vegetarian, holistic system of health self-care that began in the United States in the 1830s. Members learn about the dramatic healing and recovery powers of their own bodies, and that health and healing come from within. Like all living things, we are self-constructing, self-regulating, and self-repairing. So we teach that, except in emergency situations, the only way to build health is by building it ourselves through our own good choices and actions. 5/16/89

Animal Town

P.O. Box 2002
Santa Barbara, CA 93120

(805) 962-8368 9-5 Mon-Sa

Cooperative games have been played in many cultures for centuries, but very few games today are designed so that all players strive toward one common goal. Most competitive games cause players to feel isolated or left out. Cooperative and non-competitive games encourage children and adults to feel good about each other during the game process... they like making joint decisions, sharing and helping one another. A good game has excitement, fair play, harmony, and a good challenge. We are a mail-order company that invents and manufactures cooperative board games for children and adults. Please write for one of our free catalogs. 3/20/90

Annals of Earth

10 Shanks Pond Road
Falmouth, MA 02540

Annals of Earth is a publication of Ocean Arks International and the Lindisfarne Association, both non-profit organizations. Ocean Arks disseminates the ideas and practice of ecological sustainability throughout the world; Lindisfarne is dedicated to fostering the emergence of a new global culture. *Annals* is available for an annual contribution of $10 or more (tax deductible). If your contribution is greater than ten dollars, you will be helping distribute the publication abroad — particularly in the third world. 6/21/89

Another Place Conference Center

Route 123
Greenville, NH 03048

(603) 878-3117
878-9883

Another Place, Inc. is a non-profit center for wholistic education and living managed by a cooperative community. We've been hosting lectures, gatherings, and conferences in New England since 1976. Regular topics include alternative healing, natural foods, art, parenting, homeschooling, and counseling work. Every fall we host a Healing Arts Fair. Write if you'd like to be on our mailing list. 3/5/90

Resources

Appropriate Technology Sourcebook

c/o Volunteers in Asia
P.O. Box 5006
Stanford, CA 94305

For more than a decade the *Appropriate Technology Sourcebook* has been the standard reference for people working in village technology and community development. The 1986 edition reviews 1150 of the most useful appropriate technology books from around the world, with complete pricing and ordering information provided for each book reviewed. Written by Ken Darrow and Mike Saxenian. 800 pages with 6500 illustrations, available through Volunteers in Asia. $17.95 paperback, $26.95 hardbound, plus $2 shipping. 5/21/88

Aquarian Research Foundation

5620 Morton Street
Philadelphia, PA 19144

(215) 849-1259 / 849-3237

The Aquarian Research Foundation is a resource center that educates about a wide variety of successful cooperative systems, and directs people to various communal and cooperative lifestyles. We are a source of information on many different groups. Our video *Where's Utopia?* (see Classified Ad) may be used to explain communal societies to inexperienced friends and relations, or school groups. We sometimes fly people on visits to communities in our four-place Cessna. 1/21/90

Australian Christian Communities Directory

Matthew C. Clarke
5 Muttama Road, Artarmon
2064 AUSTRALIA

(02) 412 2204

The aim of this Directory is to facilitate the exchange of ideas and resources between Christian Communities in Australia. The editors made no attempt to judge which groups to include — except that they must be in Australia, profess Christianity, and have some living together community-ness. Listings of two dozen communities, plus addresses for a dozen more. 80pp; $8 (Australian) includes postage. 8/12/88

Better World Society

1100 - 17th Street, NW #502
Washington, DC 20036

The Better World Society is a non-profit international membership organization dedicated to making people aware of the global problems that threaten life on our planet: the nuclear arms race, a burgeoning world population, and worldwide depletion of the environment. None of these threats can be resolved by one country or region — it is imperative that the world's citizens learn about the problems, communicate about possible solutions, and cooperate for mutual survival. The Better World Society produces, acquires, and distributes television programs on global issues — to point viewers toward constructive involvement in the issues. Members can purchase their own copies of BWS programs at cost and show them to local clubs, civic groups, issue forums, and in the schools. Write for more information. 11/12/89

Bikes Not Bombs

Inst. for Transportation &
Development Policy
P.O. Box 56538
Washington, DC 20011

(202) 589-1810

Bikes Not Bombs organizes cyclists, environmentalists, churches, and others to send bikes and spare parts to Nicaraguan teachers and health care workers. Since its formation in 1984, more than 1500 bicycles have been sent to Nicaragua by chapters formed all across the U.S. The organization has also established a bicycle and repair shop in Managua, and has plans for more. The project has caught the attention of government officials — the Minister of Transportation has announced Nicaragua's intention to import 50,000 bikes over the next five years to reduce dependency on foreign oil. 9/21/89

Bio-Dynamic Farming & Gardening Association

P.O. Box 550
Kimberton, PA 19442

(215) 935-7797

The Bio-Dynamic Farming and Gardening Association (founded in 1938) provides technical assistance, education, research, training, conferences, human support, bio-dynamic compost preparations, books, and magazines. It serves the USA, Canada, Central America ... and is connected with other bio-dynamic groups world wide. Membership dues are $20/year, and include the quarterly magazine *Biodynamics* and a bi-monthly newsletter. Write for non-US membership prices, bio-dynamic preparations list, and literature list. 12/14/88

Bioregional Project

c/o David Haenke
Route 1, Box 20
Newberg, MO 65550

(314) 762-3423

The Bioregional Project was created in 1982 to aid in the development of the Bioregional movement in North America. In the long term we work for the reformation and redesign of human societies according to ecological laws and principles, towards the time when human population can live in mutually beneficial cooperation with — and within — the planet's naturally occurring ecosystems.

Our work takes the following forms: 1) We can answer your general questions and put you in touch with people active in your area. 2) We write and publish booklets, pamphlets, and general information on bioregionalism. 3) We can come to your area to give lectures and other educational presentations. 4) We can help you organize bioregional events, conferences, or congresses.

The focus of bioregionalists includes sustainable economics and business, appropriate technology, organic agriculture/permaculture, renewable resource development, forest husbandry, water quality, land stewardship, peace, conservation and environment protection, "all-species" rights, holistic health and education, media and communications. 3/15/91

Bound Together Books

1369 Haight Street
San Francisco, CA 94117

(415) 431-8355

We are an all-volunteer, collectively operated anarchist bookshop ... now 13 years old. We carry a range of alternative political and cultural titles, both historical & contemporary, with a special emphasis on anti-authoritarian materials (although many gay, women's, and magic titles grace our shelves as well). We also carry magazines and a large array of pamphlets.

Our intent is to provide a cultural/political perspective to the public — something beyond the "fast food" mentality that prevails in book publishing — and to help sustain the small presses that put out alternative political/cultural materials. We also do a Prisoners Literature Project, and put out a mail-order catalog, regularly updated (just send two 29¢ stamps, for return postage). 6/30/89

Briarpatch Network

San Francisco, CA

The Briarpatch network started in 1974 in San Francisco, California, and has spawned local branches in several other cities in the US and abroad. Our primary purpose is to promote Right Livelihood (figuring out what creative socially responsible things you want to accomplish in life, then finding a way to support yourself by doing it), mutual support, and socializing through a very loose "personal" network. Network membership includes over 400 alternative business organizations ranging from benevolent dictatorships to worker-owned businesses ... which range in size from a single entrepreneur to a 600-person residential/meditation community that owns several different businesses run by its residents. The success rate for member businesses is 80% (a phenomenal accomplishment when contrasted to the 20% success rate of small businesses in the US). The network regularly sponsors workshops and networking socials, and has a team of roving consultants who visit member businesses every Wednesday (scheduled in advance, and by request only). Membership is open, and dues are voluntary — but to get involved you need to be introduced by a friend or acquaintance who is already a member (we have a "no publicity" policy). 12/12/89

Caravan Stage Company

P.O. Box 228, Wolfe Island,
Ontario, CANADA K0H 2Y0

(613) 385-2935

The Caravan Stage Company is a professional theater company that tours in the summer months with horse-drawn wagons, performing outside in a large tensile tent. The Caravan is dedicated to doing original plays of social/political concerns. Originally part of the Caravan Farm (see listing in Communities section), the Caravan has traveled and performed extensively in the western regions of Canada and the U.S., and is now concentrating on eastern North America.

The Caravan is not a fixed community, but a theater company that hires actors, musicians, and theater technicians on a seasonal basis. The company has operated on a level of cooperative responsibility, everyone sharing the moments of delight and depression, economically and spiritually. In the winter a small administration staff works at a rented winter headquarter base which can change from year to year. 6/23/89

CCEC Credit Union

2250 Commercial Drive
Vancouver, B.C.
CANADA V5N 5P9

(604) 254-4100

CCEC is the Community Congress for Economic Change Society, and the purpose of the CCEC Credit Union is to pool the savings and other financial activities of concerned groups and individuals in British Columbia to promote "group solutions to individual problems." We support co-operatives, and self-help and social action groups which deal with issues such as shelter, food, employment, sexual and racial equality, conservation, and social justice. Our current membership includes over 200 of these groups. 4/15/91

CEED Institute

1807 Second Street, Studio #2
Santa Fe, NM 87501

(505) 986-1401

The CEED Institute is developing ecological community models and new economic options for a sustainable culture — demonstrating that ecological and socially responsible enterprises and community capitalism really can be economically viable. Our Seed Ecological Living Center, opened on Earth Day 1990, provides a variety of practical environmental products and right livelihood support services. We are also beginning a Youth Ecology Corp, empowering teenageers to design and carry out ecological community service projects, and create jobs.

We actively network with national and local groups involved in creating sustainable communities. Long-range projects include developing a Santa Fe "Green City Village" and the formation of a rural village (see p. 184). Send $5 for our information packet including a sample *New Wealth Journal*, our latest *Seedling* newsletter, brochures, and other resource information. 4/30/91

*T*IES CONSULTING

101-5810 Battison Street
Vancouver, B.C. V5R 5X8
(604)432-9473

Planning T I E S that sustain
• Neighbourhoods • Communities • Bioregions

• Consensus Facilitation
• Multi-party Dispute Resolution
• Sustainable Development Planning
• Community Economic Development
• Stewardship Land, Forest & Agricultural Trusts

Resources

Center for Communal Studies

University of Southern Indiana
8600 University Boulevard
Evansville, IN 47712

(812) 464-1727; Fax: 464-1960

CCS — headquarters for the Fellowship for Intentional Community and the Communal Studies Association (see separate listings)— serves as an international clearinghouse for community information through its affiliation with these organizations and the International Communal Studies Association based in Israel. CCS is a research facility with a communal data base and an archival collection of manuscripts, photographs, recordings, publications, and artifacts from 100 historic and nearly 400 contemporary intentional communities. CCS sponsors conferences, classes, seminars, speakers, publications, small research grants, and related educational projects. We welcome inquiries, program suggestions, and materials for the Center archives. 5/12/91

Center for Conflict Resolution

731 State Street
Madison, WI 53703

The Center for Conflict Resolution is a non-profit educational organization. Through workshops, consultations, intervention, and a resource center we provide information on conflict, group process, and problem-solving. We have also sponsored several conferences on peace-related issues and social concerns, and have provided training for nonviolent action. Since our inception in 1970 we have been in a constant state of evolution as we attempt — both as a group and as individuals — to find ways of combining education and action in areas of peace and social justice. In 1971 CCR became a collective, replacing official leaders with facilitators and implementing a consensus decision-making process.

We have assembled two books: *Building United Judgment: A Handbook for Consensus Decision Making*, and *A Manual for Group Facilitators*. Workshop topics include: facilitation, communication skills, conflict resolution, decision making, meeting skills, program planning, and community organizing. Fees are on a sliding scale, and workshops are individually tailored to meet the needs of specific groups. 12/12/88

The Center for Cooperatives

University of California
Davis, CA 95616

(916) 752-2408 Fax: 752-5451

The Center for Cooperatives is intended to serve statewide, drawing its teaching and research resources from interested professionals from all UC campuses, the state university system, other colleges and universities, and the broader cooperative business community. The center 1) offers formal and informal education programs to those involved in cooperative management, and develops teaching materials for all levels of interest; 2) conducts research on economic, social, and technical developments — and refers researchers to cooperatives with need for such information; and 3) seeks to inform the public on cooperatives and their significance to the economy. 12/15/90

Center for Economic Conversion

222-C View Street
Mountain View, CA 94041

(415) 968-8798

The Center for Economic Conversion is a non-profit research and education corporation which promotes positive alternatives to military spending. CEC provides educational materials, speakers, workshops, and technical assistance. Subscriptions to their quarterly newsletter *Plowshare* are $25 yearly ($15 for limited incomes). A 30-minute video, *Building a Sustainable Economy*, is available ($20 per copy) which introduces the basic concepts of economic conversion, considers the economic consequences of the arms race, and describes creative strategies for redirecting resources for meeting critical needs. 7/12/89

Center for Educational Guidance

Sambhava & Josette Luvmour
P.O. Box 445
North San Juan, CA 95960

Towards Peace: Cooperative Games & Activities — selected for conflict resolution, communication enhancement, building self-esteem. Book includes 160 games. Send $7.95 plus $1 for postage and handling. 9/21/89

Center for Sacred Sciences

5405 Donald Street
Eugene, OR 97405

(503) 687-0148

The split between "subject" and "object" is illusory — for in reality, the observer and observed are united in a Transcendent Consciousness of which we all partake. We at the Center for Sacred Sciences believe that such a unity of knowledge can and will be achieved. As a non-profit organization of scientists and spiritual practitioners, our goal is to encourage and cultivate a dialogue between these two disciplines. Toward this end we offer varied educational programs including seminars, study groups, and meditation. Write or call for more information. 5/11/89

CESCI

Community Educational
Service Council, Inc.
c/o Shannon Farm
Route 2, Box 343
Afton, VA 22920

(804) 361-1417

CESCI was founded to help people learn how to live together — sharing their physical, intellectual, and spiritual resources to create a society based on cooperation and mutual respect — and then make the resources available to help people realize their dreams.

For over 35 years CESCI has offered short-term, low-interest loans to businesses owned by intentional communities from coast to coast. We would like to increase our endowment to make possible more and larger loans, and at the same time provide more educational services both to communities and to the public at large. Please write for more information about investment opportunities or loan applications. 11/9/89

Changing Men

306 North Brooks
Madison, WI 53715

Changing Men is a nationwide quarterly men's magazine with an anti-sexist focus. For ten years, *Changing Men* has brought to thousands of readers a candid look at contemporary masculinity from a profoundly male, pro-feminist perspective. Each 52-page issue is filled with analytical and personal essays, poetry, art, and more. Special focus issues have examined men confronting pornography, media myths, the reality of men's work, and black and Jewish prisms of masculinity. Annual subscriptions: $16 for Individuals, $30 Supporting & Institutional; $18 Mexico & Canada; $27 outside North America. 3/12/89

Children of the Green Earth

**P.B. Box 31087
Seattle, WA 98103**

(206) 781-0852

Children of the Green Earth is a non-profit educational organization committed to creating a global network of children who, by planting and caring for trees, experience themselves as stewards of the Earth and as part of one human family. Members receive periodic newsletters containing articles on tree planting projects being done worldwide, folk tales of tree planters, contacts for international partnerships, and a list of resources for teachers. Please write or phone for more information. 3/23/91

Chinook Learning Center

**Box 57
Clinton, WA 98236**

**(206) 321-1884
467-0384 Seattle**

Located on Whidbey Island, Chinook was founded in 1972 as a contemplative learning center and dispersed covenant community. The central dynamic of Chinook is education — the training and empowerment of people who are endeavoring to bring positive change to the world. Our work is based on the link between the inner transformation of the individual and responsible action in society. Chinook affirms the power of individuals and groups, acting from a new and hopeful vision of life, to impact creatively the social and political structures of our world. Chinook is a meeting ground for people who commit themselves to building an interdependent global future. Every first Sunday of the month is Open Day, including a tour, potluck lunch, and other activities. The Saturday before Open Day is a work day. There are also a limited number of places available for resident work/scholars (a 1-3 month position). 9/24/88

Christian Homesteading Movement

RD #2-G, Oxford, NY 13830

Started in 1963, our "school" is in reality a workshop homestead of 70 acres surrounded by woods and meadows on a hilltop in rural New York. We have chickens, ducks, cats, goats, cows, bees, a dog, and a work horse. Buildings are small and made of logs. Visitors are sometimes surprised by the primitiveness of our life.

Our family is living from the land as much as we are teaching other people how to do so. Our primary purpose is to better the world by helping both Christians and non-Christians to return to the land — through the teaching of basic homesteading skills, employing hand tools and horse power in harmony with a Christian philosophy of stewardship of the earth, the dignity of man, and a basic reliance on God. Guests and students camp in tents that they bring, and cook their food outdoors over open campfires. If you would like to visit, write ahead — we will be glad to pick a good time for you to come. We also publish a bi-monthly paper

called *The Homesteader*, which features articles on work horses, herbs, hand tools, etc. — as well as thoughts about our philosophy. Please enclose an SASE. 1/6/89

Christic Institute

**1324 North Capitol Street, NW
Washington, DC 20002**

(202) 797-8106

The Christic Institute is a non-profit, interfaith center for law and national policy in the public interest. We are supported by churches, Jewish philanthropies, foundations, and private citizens. Among other projects, we have been instrumental in the pursuit of lawsuits in the wake of the Iran-Contra scandal, and maintain a national citizens' action campaign, Democracy Watch ... designed to build a national consensus against the covert policies that resulted in illegal bombings, the Iran-Contra scandal, and the U.S. Government's complicity in drug smuggling. $20 entitles members to Christic Institute publications for one year, including our quarterly newsletter, *Convergence*. 6/21/89

The Truth Seeker

A quarterly journal of freethought and inquiry.

Pursuing reason and science on behalf of humanity

If You Believe:

- If Anything Is Sacred, The Human Body Is Sacred — Walt Whitman

- My Own Mind Is My Own Church — Thomas Paine

- In Every Country And In Every Age, The Priest Has Been Hostile To Liberty — Thomas Jefferson

- Men, Their Rights And Nothing More; Women, Their Rights And Nothing Less — Susan B. Anthony

- Love Is Our Response To Our Highest Values — And Can Be Nothing Less — Ayn Rand

Then, You Will *Want* To *Subscribe* To — *The Truth Seeker*

The Universe Of Human Love

Free color poster: *The Universe of Human Love* with paid subscription to *The Truth Seeker*. See us and the **Extended Family Network** at Booth #233. Subscription is $20 annually.

Name _____

Address _____

City/State/Zip _____

Please send check or money order in U.S. dollars to:
THE TRUTH SEEKER, P.O. Box 2832, San Diego, CA 92112

Resources

Resources

Circle Network News

P.O. Box 219
Mt. Horeb, WI 53572

(608) 924-2216   M-F 1-4pm

Founded in 1974, Circle helps people from many spiritual paths around the world connect with each other as well as deepen their relationships with the spiritual dimension of Nature. Circle is headquartered near Madison, Wisconsin, on a 200-acre sacred Nature preserve. It is a non-profit international Nature Religions resource center and a legally recognized Wiccan church. Our endeavors include mail-order books, tapes, and amulets; Nature preservation; and a wide range of educational, counseling, and networking services. The quarterly newsletter is $9 via bulk mail to USA subscribers, and $13 via first class to USA and Canada. A free brochure describing Circle's work is available upon request. 3/21/89

Circle Pines Center

8650 Mullen Road
Delton, MI 49046

(616) 623-5555

Circle Pines Center is a non-profit, educational and recreational cooperative located on 360 acres of meadows, forests, and a lake in southwestern Michigan. We operate a summer camp for families and children — featuring non-competitive games, cooperative work projects, peace education, group-building activities, canoeing and swimming, nature studies, and creative arts. Our work with peace education is based on the premise that the caring relationships we develop and model with each other will further efforts down the line in supporting each other in group actions.

We are open year-round, hosting a Winter Weekends cross-country skiing and natural healing program, and providing conference and seminar space in the spring and the fall. We are also an AYH hostel. 6/15/89

Citizens Clearinghouse for Hazardous Wastes

P.O. Box 926
Arlington, VA 22216

(703) 276-7070

CCHW is a national environmental organization which was started and led by grassroots leaders. Its principles and ways of working are based on the lessons learned at Love Canal — that the best policy comes from the bottom up, from grassroots efforts, when the people who are most directly affected speak for themselves. While other groups lobby for changes in national and state policy, CCHW sticks to the principle that people can and must speak for themselves ... thus CCHW devotes all of its energies and resources toward helping the people do that most effectively. We provide organizing skills, information, resources, and scientific and technical assistance. 3/21/89

The Cohousing Company

48 Shattuck Square #15
Berkeley, CA 94704

(415) 549-9980

The Cohousing Company is a design and development company formed specifically to build Cohousing communities. The principal members of our staff, Kathryn McCamant and Charles Durrett, authored the book *Cohousing: A Contemporary Approach to Housing Ourselves* which introduced this concept in the United States. Working with other real estate professionals, we guide resident groups through the entire development process. Our service areas include group formation and facilitation, site search and acquisition, real estate brokerage, land development, architectural design, project management, and finance. While our emphasis is in Northern California, we provide consulting services nationwide. Our book is available for $19.95 plus $1.50 shipping ($3 outside the U.S.). In California also add 6.5% tax ($1.30). 2/28/90

Cohousing communities combine the autonomy of private dwellings with the advantages of community living. Residents participate in the planning and design of the community so that it directly responds to their needs. Each household has a private residence, but also shares extensive common facilities with the larger group (such as a dining hall, children's playrooms, workshops, guest rooms, and laundry facilities). Although the individual dwellings are designed to be self-sufficient and each has its own kitchen, the shared facilities (and in particular the common dinners) are an important aspect of community life for both social and practical reasons.

Columbiana Magazine

Chesaw Route, Box 83-F
Oroville, WA 98844

(509) 485-3844

Columbiana is a bioregional journal of, and for, the Intermountain Northwest. It is published by a non-profit group, the Columbia River Bioregion Education Project, which offers space for the writers and artists of the region. All materials published are relevant to that particular bioregion, and include articles on environmentally sensitive political choices and visions; self-help health care and nutrition; home-based businesses; family concerns; alternative technology; sustainable agriculture/permaculture; urban and rural feminism; natural and regional history; international concerns; reviews of relevant books, magazines, and music; as well as regional fiction and poetry. 6/2/89

Common Ground

2225 El Camino Real
Palo Alto, CA 94306

Urban education center; Biointensive mini-farming. See also: Ecology Action (Willits, CA). 2/1/89

Common Ground USA

2000 Century Plaza #238
Columbia, MD 21044

Common Ground/USA is an educational non-profit organization devoted to the economic and social principles of Henry George, who wrote: "The progress of civilization requires that more and more intelligence be devoted to social affairs, and this not the intelligence of the few, but that of the many. We cannot safely leave politics to politicians, or political economy to college professors. The people themselves must think, because the people alone can act." An underlying "Georgist" principle is that all taxes should be abolished, save that on land — in effect, economic "rent" paid to Society.

There are Henry George Schools and other Georgist organizations in many areas; write Common Ground/USA for referrals to local chapters. CG/USA also publishes a bimonthly newsletter, *Groundswell*. 4/12/89

Communal Studies Association (CSA)

See: NHCSA (old name)
on page 279

Communes Network

c/o Lifespan Community,
Townhead
Dunford Bridge, Sheffield
S30 6TG ENGLAND

44 226 762359

Communes Network is a loose collection of people who are involved or interested in living collectively (some of us work together too). Our newsletter, also called *Communes Network*, is our open channel for communicating with each other — to exchange information, news, opinions, and our experiences of collective living. Production of the newsletter moves from group to group within the network, and there is a regular column devoted to *People Needing People Needing Places*. Subscriptions for 8 issues of this newsletter, which comes out every two or three months, are £7.50 in the UK; £9.50 for world surface mail ($15 USA); and £13.50 ($21) for USA Airmail. [Please add $4 to checks or money orders drawn in U.S. dollars.]

We have recently published a communities directory which concentrates on Great Britain (see the Resource listing for "Diggers & Dreamers"), and have an international directory in preparation. 2/15/90

Communities Access

Box 341, Spring Hill
Queensland
4004 AUSTRALIA

Communities Access publishes a directory of communities in Australia and New Zealand. If you would like to receive a copy, write for details (attn: Robin Goodfellow). 11/28/89

Communities: Journal of Cooperation

105 Sun Street
Stelle, IL 60919

Since 1973, *Communities* magazine has reported on the development of intentional communities — from people building together in urban neighborhoods, to rural farm communities — with articles examining community politics and group dynamics, family life and relationships, health and well-being, work and food cooperatives, and other areas of innovation and expertise developed or applicable to community living. "Reach" and "Resources" columns provide information on individuals, groups, publications, and other community-related resources and organizations. *Communities* is also a co-publisher of this directory. Subscriptions are $18 for 4 issues. 3/1/90

Community Bookshelf

Route 1, Box 155
Rutledge, MO 63563

(816) 883-5543

Community Bookshelf is a mail-order bookselling business which is co-operatively run by Sandhill Farm, a small rural intentional community in northeastern Missouri (see main listing). We at Community Bookshelf enjoy the quality of staying small — and try to answer each order quickly and personally. Write for our free catalog of books on community, co-ops, and other aspects of joyous alternative lifestyles and politics. 1/21/90

Community Catalyst Project

Geoph Kozeny
c/o 1531 Fulton Street
San Francisco, CA 94117

CCP provides research, networking, and support for intentional communities and cooperatives. Our ambitious staff (presently one full-time volunteer) has to date visited over 200 shared living groups. These field visits include research about each group's history, philosophy, and approaches to work, family, and daily life. This information is then shared with each subsequent group visited (and with the public) through slide shows and informal discussions.

CCP also provides referrals for people wanting to join a community (Geoph coordinated the listings section of this directory) and for communities in need of particular information or resources. CCP's special skills include planning, architectural design, and construc-

tion; publications and flyers (desktop publishing); photos and slide shows; facilitation and focalizing. The CCP newsletter (published on no particular schedule) is free; donations are encouraged. 2/1/90

Community Jobs

1601 Connecticut Ave N.W.
Washington, DC 20009

(202) 667-0661

Community Jobs is the only monthly listing of socially responsible jobs and internships nationwide. It lists jobs in peace and justice work, civil rights, women's issues, alternative media, social service, the environment, legal advocacy, labor, health, housing, and more. Each ad describes the hiring organization, lists the job's duties and requirements, and tells you how to apply. $12 for six issues (6 mo); $15 for one year. Job listers should call the editor at (202) 667-0331. 8/12/89

Community Service, Inc.

Box 243
Yellow Springs, OH 45387

(513) 767-2161
767-1461

Community Service is a non-profit educational organization started in 1940 by engineer and educator Arthur E. Morgan. His vision was to help small communities become better places to live — so that the most promising young people would not all move to large cities (where their families tend to die out). The small community, seen as the seed bed of future generations, needs to be nurtured and strengthened. Community Service concerns itself with the educational, economic, recreational, and spiritual aspects of community — addressing such issues as intentional community life, workplace democracy, community economics, community schools, bioregionalism, land trusts, and peace issues.

Community Service has a bi-monthly newsletter which carries articles and book reviews of interest to those concerned with improving their communities. It also operates a mail-order book service, and hosts an annual conference which explores various aspects of community (the '89 conference focused on "Creating The Regenerative Community"). Write or call for more information, a sample newsletter, and a booklist. 12/14/88

A coeducation boarding / day school for 24 students in 7th - 9th grades.
Students are involved in working, studying, hiking, caring, coping; learning and living in a small community in the Black Mountains of North Carolina.

Arthur Morgan School
1901 Hannah Branch Road
Burnsville, NC 28714 • (704) 675-4262

Resources

Resources

Connexions

**427 Bloor Street W
Toronto, Ontario
CANADA M5S 1X7**

(416) 960-3903

Connexions is a non-profit group which compiles, organizes, and distributes information about social, economic, and environmental alternatives. We work to build links between people who are striving to create positive solutions to critical social, environmental, economic, and international problems. We believe that real change can happen only through the active involvement of many people working to transform society from the grassroots up. We seek to nurture that involvement by making it easier for activists to share ideas, experiences, strategies, and information with each other — and with everyone who is concerned about our common future. We also promote the ideas, goals, organizations, and publications of the movement for social alternatives... to make them better known and more accessible to the general public. Connexions publishes the quarterly *Connexions Digest: A Social Change Sourcebook* and *The Connexions Annual* (a $25 subscription for both together). We also provide services for grassroots groups — such as mailing lists, consulting about computers, and teaching time-management skills. 5/9/89

Co-op America

**2100 M Street NW, Suite 605
Washington, DC 20063**

(800) 424-2667

Co-op America is a non-profit, member-controlled, worker-managed association dedicated to building a more cooperative, peaceful, and just economy... and a healthy, safe environment. By teaching people how to vote with their dollars we are changing the way America does business. Co-op America puts members in touch with an alternative marketplace of many businesses, co-ops, "green" producers, alternative trading organizations, and other groups that put their values into the way they do business. Member benefits include a quarterly magazine; a mail-order catalog of socially-responsible products; a *Socially Responsible Financial Planning Guide*; boycott updates; an annual Directory; and access to our travel service, investment service, and

health insurance program. Membership is $20 for individuals, and $50 for organizations. (Organizations receive different benefits, including reduced advertising, access to our mailing lists, a Discount Coupon Book, and more.) 12/14/88

Co-op Camp Sierra

**1442-A Walnut Street #415
Berkeley, CA 94709**

(415) 538-0454

Camp Sierra is a Co-op camp that will be celebrating its 51st season this summer. Camp is for families, single-parent families, and singles. Cooperators from all over California (and elsewhere) come to relax in the beautiful Sierra Mountains, to enjoy outings and recreation, to socialize, and to discuss issues related to worker and consumer cooperatives. Attendees are members of all types of cooperatives, and many get involved in planning and implementing camp activities.

A morning discussion series — facilitated by key resource people from the international cooperative movement — is at the core of the education program. To make it easier for adults to attend, there is a supervised children's program at this time. Afternoons are open for relaxing or for outings and adventures, and evenings are packed with optional slide shows, sing-alongs, carnivals, volleyball, and the like. There is also quite a teen scene.

The camp has a full array of facilities, and rates vary according to choice of accommodations — ranging from private cabins to tent camping. Traditionally camp has been held the first two weeks in July. Beginning in 1990, the Twin Pines Cooperative Housing Institute will be featured during the second week. There is also

---

CO-OP EDUCATION

New Mondragon Co-op	
VHS Video	$55.-
Plan & Facilitate Effective	
Meetings - 2 Videos	$95.-
(Ask about video rentals)	
European Co-op Systems	$4.-
Co-op Democracy - 320p.mss	$15.-
Limited Equity Housing Co-ops	$4.-
Democratic Bus. News (Subscr)	$7.-

**THE ALTERNATIVES CENTER
2375 Shattuck Berkeley CA 94704
(415)644-8336**

---

an annual winter trip during ski season. Written information available upon request. 1/14/90

Co-op Resource Center

**1442-A Walnut Street #415
Berkeley, CA 94709**

**(415) 538-0454 (w)
483-3467 (h)**

The Co-op Resource Center, established in 1980, has 17 cooperative member organizations. We publish a free catalog of resource materials available by mail. The 1990 catalog holds some 400 items ranging from books, to reprints, to T-shirts, and audio/visuals for cooperatives of all kinds. We also act as a clearinghouse for the sharing of information and related technical resources among cooperatives and like-minded organizations. 1/26/90

Council on Economic Priorities

**30 Irving Place
New York, NY 10003**

(212) 420-1133

CEP is a membership-supported public interest research organization. For over twenty years CEP has researched and produced hundreds of publications that 1) inform communities about corporate activity, and 2) convince companies that consumers care about corporate social responsibility. Our research is quoted in company boardrooms and in the media, and presented as testimony at state and federal hearings. It provides vital, timely information for investors, activists, and the general public.

CEP publishes monthly research reports, books such as *Rating America's Corporate Conscience*, and the pocket-sized *Shopping for a Better World*. We welcome any additional information on these and other companies that you may have. Regular membership is $25, or $15 for seniors and students. 1/12/89

Creation

**P.O. Box 19216
Oakland, CA 94619**

Creation is a forum for spirituality that seeks to heal the ancient wound of assumed antagonism between spirit and nature, soul and body, man and woman, God and the world. The source of this healing is an understanding of the cosmos itself as our richest source of revelation. Our forum brings together a rootedness in the Bible with the creation mystics of the West (from Hildegard to John Muir) and the wisdom of earth-centered native spiritualities, Green thinking, humanistic psychology, and the new physics. *Creation* provides practical ways to honor the artist in each of us and rituals which celebrate the sacredness of the earth and all its creatures. $20 for one year (6 issues), $35 for institutions, foreign add $8 for postage and handling. Send subscription requests to Creation Circulation Dept., 160 E. Virginia Street #290, San Jose, CA 95112. 8/12/89

CRSP

Cooperative Resources &
Services Project
Box 27731
Los Angeles, CA 90027
(213) 738-1254

CRSP is a 9-year-old non-profit tax-exempt organization which is an education, training, and development center for all kinds of cooperatives. We are located in the center of Los Angeles, we have a strong emphasis on urban intentional communities. We sponsor many projects: weekly drop-ins on intentional, shared, and cohousing communities; the Local Exchange Trading System (LETS); the Ecological Revolving Loan Fund (ELF); the Shared Housing Network (which meets monthly for potlucks and special events); the Jerry Voorhis Library on Co-ops; the Co-op Cafe (a monthly vegetarian restaurant); regular screenings of the videos "The Mondragon Experiment" and "Builders of the Dawn"; the ecological urban village; and our newsletter, *L.A. Co-ops and the Shared Housing Networker.* Membership is $25/yr. for individuals, $50/yr. for organizations — and includes a subscription to our newsletter, discounts on events and several other organizational memberships, and free library loan privileges. A subscription without membership is $10/yr. 8/12/89

Cult Awareness Network

2421 West Pratt Blvd., # 1173
Chicago, IL 60645
(312) 267-7777

The Cult Awareness Network is a national non-profit organization founded to educate the public about the harmful effects of mind control as used by destructive cults. CAN confines its concerns to unethical or illegal practices including coercive persuasion or mind control, and does not judge doctrine or beliefs. Funding comes exclusively from voluntary contributions and membership fees. We are the families and friends of past and present followers, as well as former followers. Some of us are interested mental health professionals, lawyers, physicians, legislators, clergy, law enforcement officers, and concerned citizens. We also provide information and support for families as well as assistance to former followers in their re-entry to society. Newsletter subscriptions are $25 in the US, $30 to Canada and abroad, $10 for former cult members. Our newsletter depends on our membership and friends for newsclips, original articles, and other factual data. 3/12/88

Dance New England

c/o Carolyn Fuller
12 Douglas Street
Cambridge, MA 02139
(617) 661-7138

Dance New England is made up of many city dances — from New England to New York — which run cooperative "alcohol-free, smoke-free, barefoot" dances on a regular basis (usually weekly). DNE was formed in 1980 as a way to bring all these dancers together to enjoy a week of dance and community-building at Another Place Farm in New Hampshire (see listing for Mettanokit Community). The idea flourished — and today we hold 3 or 4 weekend events for 100-200 people, hosted in varying cities, and a week-long event for 200-300 people held each August in Maine.

Dance and movement forms that we teach and practice include: contact improvisation, African dance, various martial arts, voice & movement, drumming, theater, mime, yoga, jazz dance, sleaze dance, etc. Dancing, working, and living together as a cooperative community raises challenges beyond learning choreography. Community meetings at every DNE event address such disparate issues as equity & volunteerism, dance & sexuality, sexism & racism, parenting within the community, and visioning for the future of the community. DNE wants to make dance and community available and accessible to any and everyone. Our membership directory, including a list of all our dances, is available for $3. 10/12/89

Democratic Business Association of Northern California

2375 Shattuck Avenue
Berkeley, CA 94704
(415) 644-8336

DBA is a regional association of worker-owned businesses, limited equity housing cooperatives, consumer cooperatives, other democratically owned and operated businesses, and supporting individuals. Its goals are to help improve the economic performance of member businesses; encourage mutual support among them; generate opportunities for dignified, decently compensated work; help create new democratic businesses; and promote the expansion of democratic businesses in the region. We facilitate mutual and professional technical assistance, provide education in technical skills and cooperative principles, publicly promote cooperatives as feasible and desirable enterprises, and publish a quarterly newsletter (non-member subscriptions are $7). 9/13/89

Diggers & Dreamers

1990/91 Guide to
Communal Living
c/o Lifespan Community,
Townhead, Dunford Bridge
Sheffield S30 6TG, ENGLAND
44 226 762359

Diggers & Dreamers is an up-to-date Communes Network Directory which lists nearly 60 communities in Britain and 20 community contacts abroad. The aim of the book is to increase public awareness of communal living, help people join or set up new communities, help existing communities find new members, and provide material for educational use and research. It includes an entertaining history of the movement, practical advice on setting up a communal household, topical stories, a comprehensive reading list, and more. 128 pages, perfect bound on 100% recycled paper; £6.75 ($11 USA) includes surface mail worldwide. 2/12/90

Diggers & Dreamers is also available in the United States for $9.50, plus $1.50 postage and handling, through Community Bookshelf, Route 1, Box 155, Rutledge, MO 63563.

Dormant Brain Research

Laughing Coyote Mountain
Box 10
Black Hawk, CO 80422

Cooperative living most often is destroyed by ego. The human brain is 90% dormant; this dormancy causes ego. It's equivalent to driving your 10-cylindered personality jeep, firing only one piston and trying to get over the Rockies of inter-personal trust.

Science has discovered a systematic, step-by-step method to self-circuit into more complete (up to 44%) use of the central nervous system — causing the ancient and venerable transcendence phenomenon known variously as "nirvana", "samadhi", "enlightenment", "rebirthing", "epiphany", "heaven", etc. The resulting increase in intelligence and innovation can be measured with standard tests. This is the neurological basis of perfect love community; the biological basis of a warless Earth.

Intentional communities are invited to become brain teaching centers. For more information, research reports, and/or social action guidelines — send a SASE (business sized) and a donation. 1/6/89

E.F. Schumacher Society

Route 3, Box 76
Great Barrington, MA 01230

(413) 528-1737

The E.F. Schumacher Society promotes a holistic approach to economics, emphasizing self-reliance... using local resources and serving local needs. They've done a lot of pioneering work on community financing: decentralized financial institutions and mechanisms for small-scale farming, cottage industries, and cooperatively structured small businesses. They have a Share program which works with alternative economics, and an alternative currency project called "berkshares". They also offer workshops and information about land trusts and low-cost housing. 12/13/88

Earth Care Paper Co.

P.O. Box 3335
Madison, WI 53703

(608) 256-5522

Earth Care strives to be an environmentally and socially responsible business. Our emphasis is to offer customers environmentally sound recycled paper products and educational information about recycling and other environmental issues.

Our catalog offers an attractive range of quality recycled paper products ranging from notecards to computer paper. Several artists are featured in the catalog, and are commissioned on items sold. Earth Care helps organizations raise funds with recycled paper promotions, and also donates 10% of its profits to organizations who are working to solve environmental and social problems. Please write us for a free catalog of recycled paper products. 5/11/89

Earth First!

P.O. Box 5871
Tucson, AZ 85703

(602) 622-1371

Earth First! is a movement, not an organization. Our structure is non-hierarchical. We have no highly-paid "professional" staff or formal leadership, no board of directors. There are various anonymous but cooperating elements within the Earth First! tribe — including dozens of local EF! groups, the Earth First! Foundation,the EF! Direct Action Fund, various task forces, the Earth First! Journal, and the Round River Rendezvous.

Earth First! believes in wilderness for its own sake, that it's not enough to merely preserve some of our remaining wilderness — we need to preserve it all, and it's time to recreate vast areas of wilderness in all of America's ecosystems. While many environmental groups are members of the American political establishment and essentially adopt the anthropocentric (human-centered) worldview of Industrial Civilization, we say that those values are anti-Earth, anti-woman, and anti-liberty. We are developing a new "biocentric" worldview based on the intrinsic value of all natural things: Deep Ecology, Lobbying, lawsuits, letter-writing, and research papers are important and necessary, but they are not enough. Earth First!ers also use confrontation, guerrilla theater, direct action, and civil disobedience to fight for wild places and life processes.

The EF! Journal is a 40-page tabloid published 8 times a year, and is a forum for discussion within the EF! movement. Subscriptions are $20 in the US; $30 in Canada, Mexico, and surface mail overseas. 3/12/89

Earth Island Institute

300 Broadway, Suite 28
San Francisco, CA 94133

(415) 788-3666
788-7324 Fax

Earth Island is a non-profit organization working for environmental preservation and hence, political reform. We publish a quarterly, the Earth Island Journal, which covers such topics as rainforest preservation, saving the dolphins, the Climate Protection Institute, dealing with nuclear and toxic waste, and information on bioregional and Greens groups. We sponsor twenty diverse projects working on these issues (including cooperative efforts with Central American and Soviet environmentalists), and have more than two dozen affiliated Earth Island Centers in the U.S. (and one in Italy). Annual membership is $25. 3/21/89

EarthSave

P.O. Box 949
Felton, CA 95018

EarthSave is a charitable organization that provides education and leadership for transition to more healthful and environmentally sound food choices, non-polluting energy sources, and a wiser use of natural resources. EarthSave promotes a vision of an ecologically sustainable future, in harmony and vital partnership with the web of life. EarthSave attempts to alert people to the terrible toll taken on the biosphere by modern systems of meat production, and educates the public about the health and environmental advantages of diets which are lower on the food chain and predominantly vegetarian or vegan. Activities include seminars and workshops; research and development of ecological alternatives; books, pamphlets and tapes; media campaigns; public policy work; and much more. Memberships are $20 for seniors and students, $35 for individuals, and $50 for families. 10/12/89

Eco-Home

4344 Russell
Los Angeles, CA 90027

(213) 662-5207

Eco-Home is a demonstration home and community resource center for ecological living in the city. It demonstrates physical systems needed to sustain concentrated human habitation non-toxically, such as solar technology, water-conserving organic gardens, recycling, and composting. Recognizing that 50% of the water used in Southern California residences gets poured on lawns and gardens, Eco-Home's front yard has been turned into a "Xeriscape" — a drought-tolerant landscape of plants that can survive on natural rainfall once they are established. Tours are conducted several days each week.

The Eco-Home Network is a membership organization and support group of people who are practicing or are interested in moving toward a more ecological life. Memberships are $15/year ($20 for households) and include a subscription to the quarterly *Ecolution;* discounts on events, books and other items; and access to the Eco-Home Library. 1/26/90

Ecology Action
Bountiful Gardens
5798 Ridgewood Road
Willits, CA 95490

We do research and training in Bio-intensive mini-farming methods and sustainable agriculture, and publish books and research reports on our work — including How to Grow More Vegetables by John Jeavons. Our retail store and urban educational center is located in Palo Alto, CA (see listing for Common Ground), and our rural research and training center is in Willits, CA. Please write to the Willits address for a free catalog of our mail-order seeds, books, and organic garden supplies. 2/1/89

EcoNet/PeaceNet
Institute for
Global Communications
3228 Sacramento Street
San Francisco, CA 94115

(415) 923-0900

EcoNet and PeaceNet are computer-based communication systems dedicated to helping the world environmental/peace movements communicate more effectively. Both are accessible, usually through a local phone call, in the U.S. and in 70 foreign countries. *The EcoNet News* is published quarterly in the *Earth Island Journal* (see listing). EcoNet offers more than 80 public "conferences" in which users can read valuable

information on a wide variety of topics — including news on Nicaragua, citizen diplomacy, offshore drilling, rainforest preservation efforts, toxic wastes, environmental legislation pending, the Greenpeace and Sierra Club newsletters, nuclear free zones, etc. PeaceNet has a similar index more oriented toward peace and justice issues. In most public conferences, users can also contribute information in response to others, or as new topics. Private conferences can also be set up to permit a selected group of users to conduct such activities as planning an event or writing a joint publication. There is a $10 joining fee, a $10 monthly subscriber fee, and a charge of $5/hour for off-peak computer time (or $10/hour during peak time). 8/18/88

Elfin Permaculture
7781 Lenox Avenue
Jacksonville, FL 32221

Elfin Permaculture provides lectures, workshops, and design courses on a free-lance basis. All Elfin PC events are initiated and organized by local hosts. We teach worldwide, and can arrange special terms for groups in poor countries. Upon request we can produce workshops and design courses geared to specific communities. Though we prefer to teach people to produce their own permaculture designs, we also provide consulting and design services.

We offer Advanced Permaculture Training (APT) programs in which each APT student designs (with guidance) his/her own program of permaculture research, outreach, design, and implementation. The APT course requires a minimum of one year, and a maximum of four. We are presently seeking a location to establish a teaching/learning center. For a list of Permaculture publications, send SASE to our sister enterprise, Yankee Permaculture, at this address. 3/26/91

Environmental Defense Fund
257 Park Avenue South
New York, NY 10010

The Environmental Defense Fund has been funding innovative and lasting solutions to environmental problems for more than twenty years. EDF's earliest work — following Rachel Carson's landmark publication of *Silent Spring* — led to the

nationwide banning of DDT in a triumph that has recently been called "one of the most important legal victories ever won for wildlife."

Since that time EDF's teams of scientists, economists, attorneys, and computer experts have won landmark achievements in the fields of acid rain, clean drinking water, endangered species, energy conservation, the Greenhouse Effect, hazardous waste, lead poisoning, marine animals, ocean pollution, ozone depletion, radon, solid waste management, tropical rainforests, wild and scenic rivers. We are also very involved in promoting the National Recycling Media Campaign to encourage mass education about the importance and efficiency of recycling programs, and to promote the development of recycling programs all across America. 1/12/89

Esalen Institute
Highway 1
Big Sur, CA 93920

(408) 667-3000

We are not an intentional community, rather we are an educational center offering various programs in personal growth and transformation — tools that can be of tremendous value when applied to community living. We have a full-time staff, plus a work-study program. Write for descriptions and dates of our various programs. 8/21/89

Evergreen Land Trust
747 Sixteenth Avenue East
Seattle, WA 98112

The Evergreen Land Trust owns five properties: two houses in Seattle, and three rural properties. Each property hosts a residential community which has complete responsibility for upkeep of the property, including all maintenance and payments. In return, the community controls the land as if it were owned by them. The only constraints are that the property cannot be sold, and its stewardship must meet the pro-environmental objectives of the land trust.

Each community is independent of the others. The ELT board, which acts as a clearinghouse for information and mutual assistance between the groups, consists of two representatives from each project. (See listings for Prag House and River Farm.) 2/21/90

Resources

Resources

Expedition Institute

National Audubon Society
Sharon, CT 06069

(203) 364-0522

High school, undergraduate, and graduate students participate in a consensus-run community-based expedition program which travels throughout the US and Canada... providing the opportunity to observe and study societal patterns of behavior and their impact on our fragile ecosystems. Students become active participants in a community and an educational process which emphasizes total involvement in the conservation and preservation of the planet Earth. 4/17/87

Experimental Cities

Box 731
Pacific Palisades, CA 90272

Experimental Cities is a non-profit education and research organization formed in 1972 to find innovative approaches to social and environmental problems. Its main contribution has been the conceptualization of the Earth Lab, a research center that would study and model solutions for today's common urban problems. Earth Labs would vary according to a given environment, culture, and set of problems (Experimental City I, designed for California, had a proposed population of 30-50 thousand). We are not and have never been a project designed to improve the living situation of a few dozen people (though that will surely result).

Our recent focus has been to study human relationships while continuing smaller studies (such as small hydro-electric power, new building materials which recycle waste, etc.) and working to increase cooperation among peace groups. Insofar as an Earth Lab would be free of the problems afflicting all cities, it would serve as an observable model and resource for other cities, both new and old. For more information, please send SASE. 1/2/89

Experimental Living Project

Dept. of Human Development
University of Kansas
Lawrence, KS 66045

(913) 864-4840

The Experimental Living Project is a research project in the Department of Human Development and Family Life at the University of Kansas. Established in 1969, its purpose is to investigate the application of the principles of behavioral psychology to the design of procedures that promote cooperative relations among individuals — especially those living collectively in a single household. The project is currently staffed by two faculty members and two students. Eight masters' theses and six doctoral dissertations have been completed on a variety of areas (e.g., egalitarian worksharing, participatory decision-making, new member education, officer accountability). Students spend at least 2 years living and working as members of the student housing cooperative that provides the research setting for the project (see listing for Sunflower House). Work with the project leads to a PhD in applied behavior analysis. 5/12/89

Factsheet Five

6 Arizona Avenue
Rensselaer, NY 12144

(518) 479-3707 (Ans)

A bi-monthly review of alternative/underground 'zines (small-circulation magazines of the fanatic, or devoted, depending on your view of the subject matter). Self-described as "the 'Zine of crosscurrents and cross-pollination," each issue includes hundreds of short, helpful, funny reviews covering 'zines of a confounding variety — anarchistic, evangelical, xerox- and mail-art, bioregional, libertarian, animal rights, music... and many more. Subscriptions are $2 per issue (or $2.75 first class); six issues for $11 ($15 first class). 8/28/89

The Farm School

50, The Farm
Summertown, TN 38483

(615) 964-3670
964-2325

The Farm School is an alternative education center located at The Farm, an intentional community in rural Tennessee. We have a small campus and two passive solar brick buildings — complete with science lab, art room, library, video, and satellite TV system. While most students come from the Farm community, there are children attending from the local area, and high school students from as far away as California.

We strive to maintain a friendly atmosphere among the students that is non-competitive — so that they may develop to their fullest potential. We foster the development of leadership qualities by having a democratic structure in which students have an equal voice, along with parents and teachers, in the decision-making process. Students learn to be responsible about many aspects of running the school: from cleaning, to fundraising, to dealing with disciplinary problems. Our curriculum emphasizes traditional academic subjects enriched with electives such as arts and crafts, drawing and painting, foreign languages, singing and musical instrument instruction, sports and gymnastics, and an apprenticeship program in the community. We are active in the National Coalition of Alternative Community Schools (see listing in this section). 6/12/89

Feathered Pipe Foundation

Box 1682
Helena, MT 59624

(406) 442-8196

Since 1975 we have enabled thousands of individuals to find new understanding, vision, and direction through our seminars, tours, publications, and other activities. We host programs such as yoga, health, astrology, shamanism, and personal transformation. As an emissary for planetary peace, the Foundation sponsors tours all over the world to study ancient traditions and experience the transformative energies that emanate from places of pilgrimage. We also co-sponsor a regional networking journal, Circle, and host community gatherings and ceremonies. Write for a free copy of our program schedule. 2/12/90

Federation of Egalitarian Communities

c/o East Wind Community
Box DC-9
Tecumseh, MO 65760

The Federation of Egalitarian Communities (est. '76) is a network of North American intentional communities. Each FEC community holds its land, labor, and other resources in common, and is committed to equality, cooperation, participatory government, ecology, and non-violence. There are six Federation communities ranging in size from small homesteads to small villages, and three "Communities in Dialogue." All of our groups have existed for at least 10 years, one since 1967.

We encourage social and labor ex-changes among member communi-ties, the pooling of some resources, and support of community-owned industries. We value cooperation a-bove competition, and the creation of a healthy, supportive environment above materialistic gains ... how we do things is as important as what we do. FEC assemblies meet twice a year. Write for a copy of our brochure ($2 donation requested).

Federation communities offer a clear alternative to traditional life-styles: men and women share nur-turing of children, making decisions, constructing buildings, preparing meals, and operating businesses. All our communities are seeking growth and generally welcome the oppor-tunity to share their lives with others. 2/1/89

Fellowship for Intentional Community

Center for Communal Studies
8600 University Boulevard
Evansville, IN 47712

(812) 464-1727

The Fellowship is a North American network that provides alliance build-ing, support services, and referrals for intentional communities, community networks, individuals seeking com-munity, and other interested organ-izations. Our major purposes are: 1) to facilitate the exchange of infor-mation, skills, and economic support among existing and developing communities; 2) to demonstrate and facilitate applications of intentional community and cooperative experi-ences to the larger society — through forums, talks, demonstration pro-jects, and workshops; 3) to build trust among communities and acceptance by others through a var-iety of celebrations and other joint activities; 4) to increase global aware-ness that intentional communities are modeling ecological alternatives, opportunities for personal and com-munity development, and methods for peaceful social transformation; and 5) to support resource centers and academic institutions in the

development of archives and pro-grams relating to the study of inten-tional communities.

The FIC has joined with *Com-munities* magazine to produce the directory you are now reading. We also maintain a Speakers Bureau, and are developing a Facilitation Referral Service. 2/1/89

First American Financial Co-op

410 North 21st Street
Suite 203
Colorado Springs, CO 80904

(719) 636-1045
(800) 422-7284

First American Financial Co-op is a member-owned cooperative associa-tion for people who want to make a difference through socially respon-sible investing. The Co-op provides members with up-to-date educational information on socially responsible investment alternatives and services. Member benefits include direct access to a network of socially conscious financial planners, brokers, and in-surance representatives. An initial membership fee of $25 is required, and a small annual renewal fee will maintain active membership. 12/2/88

Resources

Community Educational Service Council, Inc.

CESCI has been helping intentional communities grow since 1955, with educational services and over $200,000 in loans.

Intentional communities may apply to the CESCI Revolving Loan Fund for business development loans only. Loan requirements include:

* Personal acquaintanceship with at least some members of the CESCI board

* Personal guarantee of loans by three or more achievers, and

* Commitment for ongoing communication with CESCI

From $500 to $3000 may be borrowed for up to three years at about 10% interest; installments are due at the first of each calendar quarter. Larger loans may be available to communities that have established a payback record with the Loan Fund. For further information contact:

Community Educational Service Council, Inc.
Route 2, Box 343 • Afton, VA 22920 • (804)361-1417

Resources

Food First

145 Ninth Street
San Francisco, CA 94103

(415) 864-8555
864-3909 Fax

The Institute for Food and Development Policy, also known as Food First, is a non-profit research and education center that investigates the root causes of hunger in a world of plenty. Known for plain language and uncompromising analysis, Food First materials survey social conditions and development problems — tackling subjects ranging from population control to pesticides. The Institute has been credited with playing a key role in changing the global debate about the causes of and solutions to world hunger. Humanitarian responses to hunger, which formerly favored charity and development technology, now directly address the issues of poverty and powerlessness — the underlying causes of hunger.

Member support and revenues from book sales account for 85 percent of the Institute's income. By accepting no contributions from government sources, the Institute is able to carry out independent research, free from ideological formulas and prevailing government policies. Memberships are $25. Write for a copy of their book and resource catalog. 2/12/89

Foundation for Community Encouragement

7616 Gleason Road
Knoxville, TN 37919

(615) 690-4334

FCE was founded in 1984 to address the widespread desire for a social environment in which individuals could share their deepest fears and joys; needs or concerns; and be heard, accepted, and supported. Much of the philosophy is based on the writings of one of the founders, M. Scott Peck, author of *The Road Less Traveled* and *The Different Drum*. Their process is designed to help people achieve "community" — which they define as "a group of two or more people who, regardless of the diversity of their backgrounds (social, spiritual, educational, ethnic, economic, political, etc.) have been able to accept and transcend their differences, enabling them to communicate effectively and openly and

to work together toward goals identified as being for their common good."

FCE offers Community Building Workshops which seek to help participants learn to "empty" themselves of their natural defenses, prejudices, and personal barriers to effective communication and relationship building. FCE is also involved in community networking — aspiring to encourage and help strengthen all other communities and community building organizations. 10/15/89

The Fourth World Review

24 Abercorn Place
London NW8, ENGLAND

The Fourth World is a relatively new concept created by John Papworth, editor of this journal. The term denotes all minority and economically disadvantaged groups in all nations of the world — the poor and the oppressed who comprise a majority of the world. They would stand much to gain if the elite power structure and national governments withered away, if the world's financial and distribution systems fell apart. Hence The Fourth World is a drive to affirm the inalienable rights of rural villages and urban neighborhoods to make their own decisions about their own lives, for ethnic groupings to rule themselves, and to break down all big powers into ethnic or bioregional areas — not centralized world governments which send out directives, but rather free-will cooperation by various associations whose power comes from the bottom up. International Assemblies of the Fourth World have been held annually for the past 8 years; the three most recent were cosponsored by the School of Living (see separate listing). 12/13/88

Freedom Fund

4534-1/2 University Way NE
Seattle, WA 98105

(206) 547-7644 (Msg)

Freedom Fund is a worker collective (a union shop: Industrial Workers of the World) doing fund-raising and project/event organizing on human rights/liberation issues. Our work focuses on local and regional issues (such as housing, homelessness, and squatting; land trusts; racism; Native people's land use and culture; police violence and surveillance) and issues of broader solidarity (Latin

America, Eastern Europe, South Africa, and the Mid-East). We also publish a periodical, World Insight, which regularly considers these topics. 2/23/89

Freedom Song Network

131 Mangels
San Francisco, CA 94131

The Freedom Song Network affirms, through songs and music, the right of all peoples, at home and abroad, to establish more free, just, and equal societies... and to live in peace. We are multiracial, multicultural, intergenerational, and of all sexual orientations. We are part of a growing movement of people who see music as essential to our active involvement in our community. We will sing anywhere, from picket lines and demonstrations to songswaps and concert stages. We sponsor monthly songswaps in a half dozen cities from Santa Cruz to Sonoma County, and publish a bimonthly calendar of "progressive" benefits, concerts, and gigs in the area. 3/29/89

Friends of the Trees

P.O. Box 1064
Tonasket, WA 98855

(509) 486-4726

Friends of the Trees was founded to: 1) promote reforestation and Earth-healing activities throughout the world; 2) encourage self-employment and right livelihood using local, renewable resources and based on harmonious, non-oppressive relationships with nature and other people; 3) directly assist people in Earth-healing activities by distributing seeds, plants, and horticultural information; and 4) act as a network center for information on the worldwide "Green Front".

Friends of the Trees coordinates permaculture courses, sponsors seed and plant exchange days and tree sales, sells books, and publishes the Friend of the Trees Newsletter, the Actinidia Enthusiasts Newsletter, and the International Green Front Report. Our current major project is to set up a Travelers' Earth Repair Network (TERN) — a networking service for overseas travelers concerned about the issues mentioned above. TERN will seek out hosts in countries

TERN will seek out hosts in countries around the world... as well as organizations, notable periodicals, books or articles, travel guides, and other information of use to tree-sympathetic travelers. Memberships in Friends of the Trees cost $5 Low-income, $10 Regular, $25 Sustaining, and $100 Life. 5/21/88

FSC/LAF

100 Edgewood Avenue, NE
Room 1228
Atlanta, GA 30303

(205) 652-9676 (Alabama)

Since 1967 the Federation of Southern Cooperatives (FSC) has been the primary focal point for the rural cooperative movement among southern black and poor white farmers and rural residents. The Land Assistance Fund (LAF) was formed in 1971 to help black land owners across the South purchase "primary agriculture" land, and to retain property threatened by creditors, tax collectors, and unscrupulous land dealers. The FSC/LAF represents the merged program and shared history of both groups.

Building on the work of the Civil Rights Movement, the Federation has organized a community based cooperative economic development movement among 30,000 low-income families working in over 100 rural communities in eleven southern states. It provides services, resources, technical assistance, and advocacy to its membership of cooperatives and credit unions and their individual member families. Individual memberships are $100 per year, and can be paid in installments; family memberships are also available. 3/12/89

Garbage

The Practical Journal
for the Environment
P.O. Box 56519
Boulder, CO 80322

Ad Office :
508) 283-4721

Editorial Office:
Brooklyn, NY
(718) 788-1700

Garbage follows many environmental issues, keeping a close eye on critical areas. They are a good source of leads for paper companies that produce high quality, low-priced recycled products. $21/year. 9/23/89

Gardening By Mail III: A Sourcebook

Tusker Press
P.O. Box 1338
Sebastapol, CA 95473

(707)829-9189

By Barbara J. Barton This encyclopedia has over 2,000 listings of seed and plant sources, garden suppliers and services in the U.S. and Canada. Nurseries, seed companies, plant societies, libraries, magazines, books, and other related resources are indexed alphabetically, by location, by plant specialty, by brand name, and more. 280 pages. $16 plus $2.50 shipping. 10/12/87

Geltaftan Foundation

303 Georgetown Place
Claremont, CA 91711

(714) 624-5251

Geltaftan is a process of building with earth-and-fire, discovered by Iranian-born California Architect Nader Khalili, and developed along with his students and colleagues. This method uses the element of fire to bake and strengthen an already finished earthen structure from within, much like a conventional kiln. The interior of the building can be sculpted, then glazed during the firing process to integrate the arts of ceramics, sculpture, graphics, and architecture. We are currently working to establish the Earth Architecture Institute to provide education in this building technique. 2/2/89

Globe-Lib

1150 Woods Road
Southampton, PA 18966

(215)357-3977

If a global government is to effectively manage decentralization, conflict resolution, group process, peace, and justice — then we must use such approaches in striving toward such goals. Since 1979, the Corporation of Seekers for Global Liberty and Government (Globe-Lib) has been promoting the paradox that less total government could be achieved by strengthening the United Nations — with a primary emphasis on achieving the decentralization necessary to assure individual liberty. A strengthened UN would have goals similar to those it presently holds: abolish war; provide for individual freedom; reaffirm faith in human rights and the worth and dignity of all humanity; practice tolerance, peace, and justice among all global citizens; create an atmosphere in which a decentralist government may flourish; and provide for economic and social advancement for all people everywhere. Globe-Lib seeks to rely upon volunteerism, honesty, individual education, local autonomy, and gentleness. Any literate adult sharing such goals, without regard to their nationality or status, may sign our membership roll. 12/12/88

NATIONAL
DIRECTORY
of ALTERNATIVE SCHOOLS

Largest listing of alternative schools and educational resources published in this country

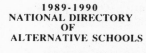

1989-1990
NATIONAL DIRECTORY
OF
ALTERNATIVE SCHOOLS

WITH SECTIONS ON FOREIGN SCHOOLS, RESOURCES FOR HOME SCHOOLERS, ALTERNATIVE COLLEGES, AND ALTERNATIVE BOARDING SCHOOLS

Produced by
THE NATIONAL COALITION OF
ALTERNATIVE COMMUNITY SCHOOLS

58 SCHOOLHOUSE ROAD
SUMMERTOWN, TN 38483
(615) 964-3670

Over 600 listings
Special sections on
Homeschool Resources
Foreign & Boarding Schools

published by NCACS
58 Schoolhouse Road, Dept CJ
Summertown, TN 38483
(615) 964 3670

$12.50 ppd

Resources

NOTE: Index Keywords also refer to groups in the Communities listings which offer specific resource services.

Green Committees of Correspondence

National Clearinghouse
P.O. Box 30208
Kansas City, MO 64112

(816) 931-9366
EcoNet: GCOC

Inspired by the ideals and growth of the worldwide Green movement, the GCOC was created in 1984 to provide a way for Americans to unite around common values. We believe that a moral, political, and spiritual renewal is due, and that a nationwide organization can make this vision a reality.

The Greens network has been built on a set of Ten Key Values — not a list of ten separate issues, but aspects of a unified world view. And it's not a final statement, but a basis for discussion among those desiring to work together for a more effective movement.

Currently Greens throughout the country are engaged in the participatory process of creating Green Program U.S.A. A preliminary draft, synthesized from hundreds of previous policy statements, will be reviewed at our national gathering to be held in Boulder Colorado in September 1990. We invite you to join our network. Supporting Members contribute $25 (or more) yearly, and receive our newsletters. Active Members participate in decision-making through local committees; if none exist in your area, we can help you organize one. 3/1/90

TEN KEY VALUES

Ecological Wisdom
Grassroots Democracy
Personal & Social Responsibility
Nonviolence
Decentralization
Community-Based Economics
Postpatriarchal Values
Respect for Diversity
Global Responsibility
Future Focus/Sustainability

Greenpeace

Box 3720
Washington, DC 20007

Greenpeace works to preserve the earth and all the life it supports, to stop the threat of nuclear war, to protect the environment from nuclear and toxic pollution, and to halt the killing of endangered animals. Their best known program is "Save the Whales." Greenpeace organizes non-violent direct actions to intercept whaling ships, tuna fleets, and other commercial fishing operations in order to stop their wanton destruction of thousands of magnificent marine animals. For a minimum contribution of $15, supporters receive the *Greenpeace* magazine. 11/12/89

Habitat For Humanity

Habitat & Church Street
Americus, GA 31709

(912) 924-6935

Habitat For Humanity is an ecumenical, grass-roots Christian ministry with the goal of eliminating poverty housing. There are over 330 affiliated projects in the U.S., Canada, and South Africa, and more than 58 projects in 24 developing countries. Funding comes from individuals, churches, corporations, foundations, and other organizations which are moved by concern and compassion to help those in need. Mortgage payments are put into a local "Fund for Humanity" and recycled to build new houses. No government funds are used. Habitat operates with a core group of paid clerical and support staff, but relies primarily on volunteer labor. Each affiliated project is run by a local board. 3/29/89

Harvest Forum

1406 Cole Street
San Francisco, CA 94117

(415) 566-0513

Members of the Harvest Forum Community (see main listing) publish a free newsletter which is an expression of shared thoughts, visions, and actions taken to create and nurture intentional communities. Readers are asked to submit stories about their daily lives, and ideas about how they'd like to live. Editorial decisions are made by consensus, and an edition is published when enough material is accumulated. Most material is not copyrighted. Donations to cover publishing and distribution costs are welcome. 5/15/91

Headwaters

P.O. Box 729
Ashland, OR 97580-0025

(503) 482-4459

Headwaters, founded in 1976, is a full-time environmental organization dedicated to tracking forestry issues. We consistently expose the negative impacts of logging on fish, wildlife, water quality, and aesthetics ... and promote alternatives to clearcutting, burning, and spraying. Pledges are welcome, and help fund: 1) research into the records and activities of the US National Forest Service and the Bureau of Land Management; 2) information sharing and support of citizens groups involved in forestry planning; 3) challenges of the administration's timber sales and questionable forestry management practices; 4) litigation (when necessary), and 5) a speakers' bureau. 4/18/91

Healthy Harvest III

c/o Potomac Valley Press
1424 - 16th St. NW, Suite 105
Washington, DC 20036

Healthy Harvest III is "A Directory of Sustainable Agriculture & Horticulture Organizations 1989-1990." Over 600 entries alphabetically arranged — full listings for over 400, complete with contact person and phone. The directory includes many international organizations, indexed by state, country, and the primary focus of each organization. The groups are described in their own words. $16.95 plus $2 shipping. 9/21/89

High Wind Books & Records

3041 North Oakland
Milwaukee, WI 53211

(414) 528-8488

High Wind Books & Records, owned and operated by the High Wind Association (see listing in the Communities section), is one of Wisconsin's leading alternative bookstores, and is a center for networking among alternative groups and businesses. 5/18/89

Holistic Education Review

P.O. Box 1476
Greenfield, MA 01302

The Holistic Education Review explores the frontiers of educational theory and practice. Each quarterly issue features provocative articles, book reviews, and comprehensive resource listings of organizations, publications, and conferences. Some topics covered in past issues: humanistic education, alternative schools, Montessori method, rites of passage, learning styles, whole language, home schooling, peace and global education, Waldorf schools, environmental education, and more. Individual subscriptions are $16/year; libraries $24/year. 9/21/89

Home Education Press

P.O. Box 1083
Tonasket, WA 98855

(509) 486-1351

Home Education Press is one of the largest publishers of home schooling books and special publications in the US. We believe that education should begin in the home, and that parents should be actively involved in their children's learning. We also publish the *Home Education Magazine*, a bimonthly known for its balanced, well-rounded approach to home schooling. 3/12/89

HortIdeas

Route 1, Box 302
Gravel Switch, KY 40328

A monthly which features abstracts and reports on the latest research, methods, tools, plants, books, etc. for vegetable, fruit, and flower gardeners — gathered from hundreds of popular and technical sources worldwide. Readers are encouraged to contribute ideas, clippings and reviews. Annual subscriptions are $15 for second class U.S.; $17.50 for first class U.S., Canada, and Mexico; Overseas $20 surface, $30 air mail. 9/28/89

Hospitality Exchange

4215 Army Street
San Francisco, CA 94131

(415) 826-8248

The Hospitality Exchange is a cooperative network/directory of friendly, travel-oriented people who have agreed to offer each other the gift of hospitality when traveling. Only people listed in the directory or who subsequently join may use the information. The entire household is involved in a membership because all

will be affected by a visitor's presence. So the fee of $15 for the calendar year covers any member of the household when traveling — whether it's a large communal group or an apartment. As of May '89 we have 175 member households in 22 countries and 32 states. 60% of our members are in the U.S. Europe is also well represented, and a few members live in Australia, New Zealand, Japan, and Thailand.

Members are sent the Spring directory, plus Summer and Fall updates. When planning trips, members call or write others they'd like to visit, asking for one or two night's lodging. If the timing is wrong, one may decline to host at all. When contacted about a visit, a member can look up the person's listing in the directory. 4/1/91

Hugs for the Heart

P.O. Box 85
Rainbow Lake, NY 12976

(518) 327-3020

Wholesome, alternative fun for kids. Hugs for the Heart is a new mail order company carrying only games, books, cassettes, and toys that address emotional and spiritual development, as well as that of the intellect — getting to the heart of education! Contact Linda for more information. 9/21/89

ICA/Earthcare

3038 Fall Creek Parkway
Indianapolis, IN 46205

(317) 925-9297

The "Indianapolis House" at 3038 Fall Creek Parkway is provided to the Institute of Cultural Affairs (ICA) by the Indianapolis Foundation. It is an office center by day, and a home for the four residential staff families by night. All staff earn their living in human service type jobs, and volunteer their time to maintain the ICA Program Center and coordinate its diversified program ventures. One of our programs, Earthcare, is a growing cross-cultural network of community leaders founded by the ICA in 1986. In promoting long-range, inclusive, ecological, and spirit-filled models for a healthy urban lifestyle of the future, Earthcare envisions a city that works in all of its parts for and by all of its people. (See also: Order Ecumenical in Communities section, and ICA in Late Entries.) 2/19/90

In Context

P.O. Box 11470
Bainbridge Island, WA 98110

(206) 842-0216

In Context is a quarterly which explores and clarifies just what is involved in a humane, sustainable culture, and articulates practical steps and useful insights to help us get there. Acclaimed as one of the six best alternative publications, it explores personal, cultural, and planetary change through in-depth articles and authoritative interviews. Sample topics: strategies for cultural change; living business; play and humor; USSR/USA human connections. $18/year; sample $5. 12/12/89

In These Times

Institute for Public Affairs
2040 N. Milwaukee Avenue
Chicago, IL 60647

(312) 772-0100

In These Times believes that to guarantee our life, liberty, and pursuit of happiness, Americans must take greater control over our nation's basic economic and foreign policy decisions. We believe in a socialism that fulfills rather than subverts the promise of American democracy, where social needs and rationality (not corporate profit and greed) are the operative principles. Our pages are open to a wide range of views, socialist and non-socialist, liberal and conservative. We welcome comments and opinion pieces. Published 41 times a year. Subscriptions are $34.95 ($59 for Institutions, $47.95 for outside the US and its possessions). 11/14/89

Industrial Cooperative Association

20 Park Plaza #1127
Boston, MA 02116-4303

(617) 629-2700

The ICA offers courses and training in the theory and practice of worker ownership. We offer two-day institutes at our offices, or under the auspices of businesses, regional development groups, unions, or church organizations in their own communities. The range of topics covered includes worker ownership fundamentals, starting a worker-owned company, converting an existing business to worker ownership, plant closing conversions,

Industrial Cooperative Assoc. *(Cont'd.)*
ESOPs, decision making and problem solving, feasibility studies, accounting, Third World worker ownership development, management and planning, and using computers in the worker-owned firm. Write or call for more information. 3/25/91

Institute for Community Economics

57 School Street
Springfield, MA 01105

(413) 746-8660

The Institute for Community Economics (ICE) is a national non-profit organization which provides technical and financial assistance to various community-based organizations working to produce and preserve affordable housing, land, jobs, and social services in communities where they are most needed. Our primary mission is to give communities the practical tools and skills for regaining control over their land in order to ensure its appropriate development and economically just allocation.

Our principal program for preserving affordable housing and farmland is the development of community land trusts, a model which we developed in 1967. We are the primary provider of technical assistance for developing CLTs in the U.S. — and currently coordinate a national network of over 90 CLTs operating in both urban and rural communities in 23 states. We also operate a Revolving Loan Fund which accepts loans from socially concerned individual and institutional lenders, and directs low-cost lending capital primarily to non-profit community groups which provide affordable housing. The Fund often provides the critical initial funding for start-up projects, money which enables them to develop a track record and approach conventional lenders. Write or call for free information about our programs. 8/21/90

Institute for the Development of Cooperation

4771 Rolland Road
Blanchard, MI 49310

(517) 496-3588

The Institute for the Development of Cooperation has been established as an active organizing instrument for new co-op villages, and is presently seeking land and development funds. The Institute has an Advisory Council of over a dozen experienced co-op and community people whose task is to find feasible sites, work out plans for developing the sites, recruit members, and establish business enterprises that will provide jobs for the members of the communities. IDC sees the development of businesses — right from the beginning of a community — as the key to success. In recent years they have conducted several dozen training seminars for co-ops and communities throughout the US and Canada, and are planning to set up a conference facility in the Midwest for continuing education in cooperative methods. (See "Sylviron" on pg. 223.)

COYOTE FOUND CANDLES

Quality Hand-dipped Candles at Low Wholesale Prices

Send $2.00 for catalog to:
Coyote Found Candles
P. O. Box 632, Port Townsend, WA 98368
(206) 385-5152

"No cheap earwax fillers"

Institute for Local Self-Reliance

2425 -18th Street, NW
Washington, DC 20009

(202) 232-4108

The Institute for Local Self-Reliance is a non-profit research organization which promotes healthy local economies, the concept of "waste as resource," and appropriate technology. We work with municipal governments and community groups to develop more efficient, self-contained waste management and energy systems, and can provide direct technical assistance for starting a recycling program in your neighborhood. Write for a list of our publications. 11/12/89

Institute for Social Ecology

P.O. Box 89
Plainfield, VT 05667

(802) 454-8493

Social ecology is an interdisciplinary path, integrating the study of human and natural ecosystems through understanding the interrelationships of culture and nature. The Institute for Social Ecology was established in 1974 at Goddard College, and was incorporated in 1981 as an independent institution of higher learning — to do research, education, and outreach in the field of social ecology. Studies have included appropriate technology and design, communities, community health, bioregional agriculture, eco-feminism, ecological anthropology, ecology and spirituality, wilderness studies, nature philosophy, and women in community development. College credit and an M.A. study option are available.

Community life is an important part of the summer semester ... the educational experience reflecting our belief in self-reliance and participation. Staff and students work together in the preparation of meals and the cleaning of common spaces; we share outdoor experiences and cooperative games; we create a supportive environment in part through informal men's and women's groups; our community meeting is a forum for discussing the issues we face together. As we come to know each other, our community deepens and develops.

Other projects of the institute include a study tour in Mexico, the *Social Ecology Newsletter*; a journal, the *Harbinger*; fall and spring workshops; and technical assistance to local community organizations. Write or call for more information. 3/20/89

Integrity International Publishing

Box 9, 100 Mile House
British Columbia
CANADA V0K 2E0

As the tides of change keep rising in our world, Integrity International (the Journal of Emissary Foundation International) plays an increasingly vital role — providing a balanced, penetrating perspective of what is happening, and highlighting creative endeavor wherever it occurs. Each issue covers a broad spectrum and introduces you to men and women all over the world whose concern is also for common sense and integrity in living.

We offer readers of this directory a special opportunity to subscribe to our journal at the introductory rate of $18 for one year (six issues, regularly $22 U.S.). 11/12/89

Intercommunities of Virginia (ICV)
See Late Entries

Interfaith Center on Corporate Responsibility

475 Riverside Drive
New York, NY 10115
(212) 870-2295

The Interfaith Center on Corporate Responsibility vigorously challenges corporations to make peace and social justice concerns part of the decision-making formula in business. The religious community, concerned about the quality and dignity of human life, has been one of the most active advocates of corporate social responsibility in American business.

Churches in America are stewards of billions of dollars of stocks and bonds in pensions and endowments. Members of the ICCR (churches, dioceses, and religious communities) accept the unique challenge of addressing issues of corporate responsibility with our resources, particularly our investments. Our covenant is to work ecumenically for justice in and through economic

structures, and for stewardship of the earth and its resources.

We publish The Corporate Examiner ten times yearly — reviewing publications and media, presenting opinions and ideas, and examining U.S. church and corporate policies and actions on South Africa, nuclear weapons, environment, foreign investment, minorities and women, health, hunger, energy, human rights, and alternative investments. Please write for membership and subscription information. 11/12/85

International Communal Studies Association

c/o Yaacov Oved
Yad Tabenkin Institute
Ramat Efal 52 960
ISRAEL

The ICSA was formed in 1985 during an international conference at the Yad Tabenkin in Israel. The purposes are to provide an international clearinghouse for research; to maintain and distribute lists of communal organizations and scholars; to conduct conferences; and to issue a journal, a bulletin, bibliographies, and conference proceedings. The next international conference will be conducted with the Center for Pietistic and Anabaptist Studies at Elizabethtown College, Elizabethtown, PA in the summer of 1991. Inquiries should be sent to Donald E. Pitzer, Center for Communal Studies, University of Southern Indiana, 8600 University Bouldvard, Evansville, IN 47712. Individual memberships are $15; Institutional $30. 6/22/89

International Communes Network

Communidad-ICN
Box 15128, S-10465
Stockholm, SWEDEN

The ICN was established in 1979 at the International Communes Festival held at Laurieston Hall, with stable contacts in 15 countries. We started with the conviction that living and working in a fellowship *is* a radical alternative to the present social structure. The main function of our network is to strengthen the ideological base — by supporting each other through the sharing of our ideas and expressions. Most often this happens through debates and dialogues, or as personal statements. We also have many opportunities for practical

cooperation through the exchange of members, services, goods, equipment, etc. And we can ask each other for help and advice in special situations, exchange news about conferences, campaigns and other activities.

The network is open to all communities who feel it has something for them. Communidad has produced a quarterly bulletin, and we publish a list describing who is active an the network. There is no fixed subscription, but a contribution is always appreciated. 9/12/88

Intinet
See Late Entries

Katúah Journal

Box 638
Leicester, NC 28748
(704) 683-1414

Katúah Journal is a bioregional journal of the southern Appalachian mountains, the oldest mountain range on our continent, Turtle Island. A small but growing group has begun to take on a sense of responsibility for the implications of that geographic and cultural heritage. Our editorial priorities are to collect and disseminate information and energy which pertains specifically to this region, and to foster the awareness that the land is a living being deserving of our love and respect. Subscriptions are $10/year Regular, $20 Sponsor, $50 Contributing. We welcome all correspondence, criticism, pertinent information, articles, poetry, artwork, etc. with hopes that Katúah will grow to serve the best interests of this region and all its living, breathing members. 9/21/89

Ken Keyes College

790 Commercial Avenue
Coos Bay, OR 97420
(503) 267-6412

In 1972 Ken Keyes wrote his most famous book, the *Handbook to Higher Consciousness*. Today the center in Coos Bay provides a nurturing environment where the staff assists people to heal their bodies, minds, and spirits. Workshops range from weekends to seven weeks, on topics including diet, exercise, and reprogramming of behaviors and core beliefs. Currently our Work/Learn Program is our only form of scholarship funding. 2/21/90

Resources

Kerr Enterprises, Inc

P.O. Box 27417
Tempe, AZ 85285

(602) 968-3068

The originator of the solar box cooker (see listings under Solar Box Cookers), Kerr Enterprises distributes plans, kits, and fully assembled cookers. Write for price list. 11/12/89

Kokoo

Huset, Rådhusstræde 13
DK-1466
Copenhagen, DENMARK

Kokoo is the Danish Communes Association — established in 1969 with offices in Copenhagen and Aarhus. The office has one staff person for a 7-month duty cycle; wages are paid by City Hall because we run a very efficient youth housing service. We run a matching service for communes looking for people and vice versa, and a free legal aid service staffed by experts on housing legislation. From time to time satellite Kokoo offices are set up around the country offering youth housing services and other networking activities. A small band of Kokoo activists produces a magazine, various folders on legal issues, communal cookbooks, etc. A larger more amorphous group of supporters are occasionally called upon to write articles, raise money, run campaigns, give talks at schools, etc. 4/3/89

Ladyslipper

P.O. Box 3130
Durham, NC 27715

(919) 683-1570 M-F(9-6)
(800) 634-6044 Orders

Ladyslipper is a non-profit tax-exempt organization which has been involved in many facets of women's music since 1976. Our basic purpose has consistently been to heighten public awareness of the achievements of women artists and musicians, and to expand the scope and availability of musical and literary recordings by women. We publish the world's most comprehensive Catalog & Resource Guide of Recordings by Women which has given hundreds of thousands of people information about and access to recorded works by an expansive variety of female musicians, writers, comics, and composers. Write for our catalog. 11/12/89

The Land Institute

2440 E. Water Well Road
Salina, KS 67401

(913) 823-5376

The mission of the Land Institute is to help transform agriculture to protect the long-term ability of the earth to support a variety of life and culture. We also operate The Grain Exchange, a parallel organization to the Seed Savers Exchange (see separate listing), founded to promote small-scale growing of diverse cereal crops. We are dedicated to good stewardship of the earth and the development of a sustainable agriculture — one that halts the damaging exploitation of the agricultural resource base and allows people to continue growing food.

The Land Institute is engaged in a range of interdependent activities including agricultural research, education, public policy work, and programs to conserve agricultural resources. 8/15/89

Left Bank Distribution

4142 Brooklyn NE
Seattle, WA 98101

(206) 632-5870

Left Bank Distributors, a project spawned by the Left Bank Books (a collectively owned bookstore in Seattle), sells books wholesale, retail, and as an international mail-order supplier. While we are "anti-state, anti-capitalist, and anti-authoritarian," we are by no means anti-people: in our diversity as a collective, our common belief is in people's ability to be autonomous and cooperative with one another as long as they are not constrained by governments, parties, religions, economic systems, or external authority. We carry a lot of books that reflect this attitude, plus a good selection of material in other "progressive" areas. We have published five of our own books, plus a half-dozen pamphlets. We carry 35 other radical presses, including over 400

TRANET

A TRANSNATIONAL NETWORK
OF, BY AND FOR PEOPLE WHO ARE
CHANGING THE WORLD BY CHANGING THEM-
SELVES.

POBOX 567
RANGELEY ME 04970
(207)864-2252

titles. The 10th anniversary issue of our International Blacklist is now available ... featuring over 5,000 listings from nearly every country in the world, filling 200 pages with information including anti-militarist, ecologist, indigenous, feminist, gay, sexuality, prisoner, punk, mail art, human rights, Latin American, middle east, eastern Europe, Asian dissidents, and other alternative points of view which don't follow some Party's line ($10 plus postage and handling). 1/2/90

Liberation Distributors

P.O. Box 5341
Chicago, IL 60680

(312) 987-0004

Liberation Distributors makes available progressive, radical and, especially, revolutionary books from a variety of publishers and covering a broad range of subjects. Central to our efforts is the distribution of the publications of the Revolutionary Communist Party USA and the international Maoist trend of which it is a part, as well as the writings of Marx, Engels, Lenin, Stalin, and Mao Tsetung. Publishers included in our catalog include RCP Publications, Banner Press, Monthly Review Press, Africa World Press, Progress Publishers in the USSR, Foreign Languages Press in China, International Publishers, Lawrence Hill & Co., Red Seas Press, Red Star Press in England, the Committee to Support the Revolution in Peru, Arab American University Graduates, and others. Many of our titles are also available in Spanish. Please write for our current catalog. 9/21/88

Meadowcreek Project

Route 1, Box D-14
Lineville, AL 36266

(501) 363-4500

The Meadowcreek Project is an educational center on 1500 acres in Fox, Arkansas. The project includes a 300-acre farm, demonstrations of alternative energy strategies and resource conservation, an education center hosting 1-7 day conferences and 3-week to 6-month internships (topics range from agriculture to architecture), and publications including Meadowcreek Notes.

We recognize that the natural world is both finite and fragile, and that all life forms are intimately connected. We take an integrative approach to education, building a curriculum which combines ecologically sound resource management, renewable energy systems, architectural design, and rural economic development. Curriculum for us is not abstract — it is what we must do to build, farm, live, and develop a sustainable economy. 3/16/91

Media Network

121 Fulton Street, 5th Floor
New York, NY 10038

(212) 619-3455

Media Network is the nation's premier broker of information on films and videos which foster social equality, cultural democracy, peace, and conservation of the environment. We operate an information center that compiles and disseminates information on available social-issue media, including: acclaimed media guides which evaluate new films and videos, a quarterly magazine, and fiscal sponsorship for independent producers. Our resources are used by schools, libraries, community groups, issue activists, media specialists, and concerned individuals seeking alternatives to Hollywood and mainstream television. 3/5/90

Message Post

Box 190-CD
Philomath, OR 97370

The Message Post is a portable dwelling info-letter. Information about living in tents, tipis, vans, trailers, boats, small cabins, etc. Letters, suggestions, candid product reports, contacts, events. SASE for information; sample $1. 2/12/89

Mobilization for Survival

45 John Street #811
New York, NY 10038

(212) 385-2222

MFS is a nationwide organization of grass-roots groups working for disarmament, non-intervention, safe energy, and human needs. Since its founding in 1977, MFS has worked to highlight the connections among the nuclear arms race, military intervention, nuclear power, and the lack of commitment to social and economic justice.

MFS's primary focus is to nurture the grass-roots movement for peace and justice by providing resources and assistance to carry out the work of community-based organizations. We promote a wide range of protest and educational activities — from non-violent civil disobedience to legislative lobbying. We also provide an opportunity for local organizations to join similar groups around the country in a common national multi-issue program. Local organizations interested in affiliating should contact us. Our quarterly newsletter is $15 ($7.50 for low-income). 3/21/89

Morningstar Adventures

Route 1, 13 Mile Road
Leroy, MI 49655

(616) 768-4368

Morningstar Adventures, Inc., is a non-profit organization formed to provide opportunities for women to develop their personal identity and to discover their uniqueness through the recognition of what God intends for them. We desire to share with other women the love, hope, joy, and peace we have found in the greatest adventure of our lives ... faith in Christ, the Morning Star.

Our lifestyle is committed to simplicity and service. Mornings are devoted to prayer, study, personal reflection, and solitude. Afternoons and evenings are given to creative work, hospitality, and play. Outdoor activities include walking, biking, snowshoeing, and cross-country skiing. There are also opportunities to participate in the labors of the land. Accommodations are rustic. Write for more information, or call after 12 noon. 2/20/90

Mother Jones

1663 Mission Street
San Francisco, CA 94103

(415) 558-8881

Mother Jones delivers a unique blend of tough investigative reporting, spirited writing on everything from politics to the arts, as well as humor and award-winning graphics. *Mother Jones* is published ten times a year by the Foundation for National Progress, a nonprofit tax-exempt organization which also operates The Mother Jones Investigative Fund — to research the controversial issues that lead to social change. In 1989 they pinpointed the highest industrial producers of ozone-destroying pollution — companies who were bragging about their high-tech, "clean" operations. Contrary to their big public relations efforts, behind the scenes these companies were actively lobbying to protect their ozone-depleting manufacturing methods. Subscriptions are $24 per year, foreign $29. 11/21/89

Movement for a New Society

The Movement for a New Society (MNS) disbanded in July, 1988, after 17 years as an activist organization dedicated to revolutionary non-violence, feminism, ecological sustainability, and social justice. MNS was committed to combining activism and fundamental social change with personal change and work against all forms of oppression. Many members lived in community, and the Life Center in Philadelphia continues as a living community for political activists (see the community listing).

Most former MNSers continue their social change activism, but came to feel that MNS as an organization was no longer a cutting-edge, vibrant, dynamic organization able to play a leadership role in such areas as building a multi-cultural movement in the '90s. New Society Publishers, an MNS spin-off, continues to publish excellent books (see listing); the Social Movement Empowerment Project (also listed) is another still thriving resource. 2/6/90

NACCCAN

National Centre for Christian Communities & Networks

Westhill College
Weoley Park Road
Selly Oak, Birmingham
ENGLAND B29-6LL

021 472 8079

Contact NACCCAN for information on Christian communities located in the United Kingdom. 1/6/89

NAEIR

National Association for the Exchange of Industrial Resources

P.O. Box 8076
Galesburg, IL 61402

(309) 343-0740

For a $495 annual membership fee, non-profit organizations have access to a huge warehouse of materials donated as tax write-offs by major

Resources

Resources

NAEIR *(Cont'd.)*
corporations. Member organizations receive quarterly catalogs (each 400-500 oversized pages) from which they order needed items. The goods themselves are free, although members are required to pay shipping on each order and a small handling fee.

Sample items available: computer books and supplies, heavy-duty pumps, motors, hundreds of small power and hand tools (saws, hammers, drills), maintenance supplies, triple-pane windows, and rubber tiles for outdoor decking. Drawbacks: many of the items are discontinued merchandise, odd-sized things, parts of things with the rest of the item no longer available. You can call and ask questions, though it makes sense to have people do the ordering who are familiar with the products being requested. 9/29/89

NALSAS

National Assoc. for Legal Support of Alternative Schools
Box 2823
Santa Fe, NM 87504

(505) 471-6928

NALSAS is a national information and legal service center designed to research, coordinate, and support legal actions involving non-public educational alternatives. We challenge compulsory attendance laws — as violating First Amendment rights and state provisions for non-compulsory learning arrangements (such as home schooling). NALSAS helps interested organizations and individuals locate, evaluate, and create viable alternatives to traditional approaches to schooling. We also accredit NALSAS members. Voluntary annual dues are $10-$20. 12/12/88

NASCO

North American Students of Cooperation
P.O. Box 7715
Ann Arbor, MI 48107

(313) 663-0889

NASCO works toward the vision of a socially responsible and financially successful North American cooperative economy. While much of our work is conducted on behalf of all people and organizations interested in applying the principles of cooperation, our efforts are especially concentrated on work with student cooperatives.

We provide them with operational assistance, encourage the development of new student co-ops, serve as an advocate for student co-ops to the U.S. and Canadian co-op movements, teach leadership development skills in student co-ops, and provide inspiration to co-op members.

We also maintain services for the co-op movement in general — including our publications clearinghouse and the annual Cooperative Education and Training Institute, which provides professional training for co-op members, staff, and board members. Write for more information. 9/21/87

National Co-op Bank

1630 Connecticut Avenue, NW
Washington, DC 20009

(202) 745-4790

The National Cooperative Bank is a private, cooperatively owned financial institution which provides commercial, investment, and development banking services to cooperative businesses nationwide. It provides a variety of financial services including short- and long-term loans at commercial rates of interest. Its affiliate NCB Development Corporation provides business planning and risk capital to start-up cooperatives.

NCB publishes a small booklet called "How to Organize a Cooperative," and offers some guidelines essential to the cooperative form of business: effective use of advisers and committees, keeping members informed and involved, maintaining proper board/manager relations, following sound business practices, conducting businesslike meetings, and forging links with other cooperatives. 10/15/87

National Federation of Community Broadcasters

666-11th Street NW #805
Washington, DC 20001

(202) 393-2355

The National Federation of Community Broadcasters is a membership organization formed to facilitate information, expertise, and program sharing between community-oriented public radio stations; to help groups start such stations; and to lobby for those stations with national fundors, public radio entities, and Congress. Each year NFCB hosts a 3-4 day conference with workshops covering topics important to community broadcasters.

Community stations usually encourage local people to learn how to host and engineer programs, to be news reporters, or to get involved in other ways. The programming on community stations is often quite diverse, often featuring alternate points of view and music not often played on other stations.

There are currently 65 participating member stations, and 150 associates in all parts of the United States. NFCB also has close ties with the worldwide radio association known as AMARC. To find out if there is a community station near you, or for help in starting a station, contact Lynn Chadwick (President) or David LePage (Member Services) at the Washington headquarters. 2/6/90

National Homeschool Association

P.O. Box 58746
Seattle, WA 98138

(206) 432-1544

The National Homeschool Association (NHA) is a nationwide, non-profit organization dedicated to supporting parents' rights to educate their children. Membership is open to all. We are working to increase the nation's awareness of home schooling as a viable educational option: keeping abreast of legislative developments that may affect home educators; developing nationwide information networks; encouraging a forum for those interested in home education; and more. We have a quarterly newsletter, a list of state support groups, a travel directory, an apprentice/mentor program, a single parents network, and an annual conference. Family memberships are $15/year. 2/19/90

National Organization for Changing Men

794 Penn Avenue
Pittsburgh, PA 15221

(412) 371-8007

NOCM is a comprehensive organization with chapters in many cities. We work towards personal growth for men, and broad social change from a feminist perspective. Our activities include support and education regarding fathering, ending men's violence, child custody legislation, lesbian and gay rights, and challenging homophobia. Have organized several national conferences, and Brotherpeace Demonstrations in over 50 cities worldwide. 12/22/88

National War Tax Resistance Coordinating Committee (NWTRCC)

P.O. Box 85810
Seattle, WA 98145
(206) 522-4377

Brochure explains legal rights and court precedents for non-payment of telephone excise taxes — a federal excise tax that has always been used to pay for war. "The phone company cannot legally disconnect your phone service for nonpayment of the excise tax and can be fined by the Federal Communications Commission if it does so." 3/12/89

Native Seeds/SEARCH

2509 N. Campbell Avenue #325
Tucson, AZ 85719
(602) 327-9123

Native Seeds/SEARCH is a non-profit seed conservation organization involved in collection, increase, distrib-

bution, research, and education. We focus our activities on the traditional native crops (and their wild relatives) of the U.S. Southwest and northwest Mexico. The food crops of this region are delicious, nutritious, and better adapted to the harsh environments of the low hot deserts and dry rocky uplands than are most modern vegetables. In addition, the native peoples and long-term residents of the Greater Southwest have a rich folk science associated with these fiber, dye, medicinal, ceremonial, and food plants.

We have a growers network, a quarterly newsletter, and 10 percent discounts for our members. All proceeds go toward our continuing efforts to preserve these plants in their native habitats and in seed banks, and to study their seemingly boundless benefits for humanity. Annual memberships are $10 Associate; $25 Contributing; and $100 Lifetime. 3/21/89

Natural Rights Center

P.O. Box 90
Summertown, TN 38483
(615) 964-2334/964-3992

The Natural Rights Center is a non-profit, public interest law project of Plenty USA (see separate listing), and

is associated with the United Nations' Department of Public Information. Philosophically we don't equate security with firepower, technology, or property. We hope to create real security by making the world a healthier, safer, and fairer place to live.

Our projects are directed towards averting future suffering. We fight industries that poison future peoples or squander their vital resources. We challenge agencies that discount future lives in order to gratify society's present desires. We work to improve the process of justice, and to enlighten the democratic discussion.

Current projects include: toxic waste dumping, atomic veterans and radiation victims, protection of natural areas and wildlife, human rights and voting rights, nuclear power and nuclear waste, nuclear weapons testing and deployment. The natural rights we're defending reach beyond the rights of the two-leggeds. They include the needs of the four-leggeds, and those with fins, and wings, and roots in the ground. 9/12/89

Nature Conservancy

1815 North Lynn Street
Arlington, VA 22209

A non-profit organization, formed in

NEW AGE FINANCIAL SERVICES
FOR INDIVIDUALS & COMMUNITIES

- Individual Money Management: Budgets, Cash Flow & Investments
- Consumer Debt & Credit Counseling
- Business Plans: Especially for Cooperatives
- Identification of Financial Resources: Especially New Age
- Loan Application & Packaging
- Affordable Related Legal Services, Including Do-It-Yourself Kits

••• Reasonable rates for all •••

We're dedicated to helping individuals & communities realize their financial abundance!

432 Livingston Avenue
Albany, New York 12206
(518) 436-1148

Communal Studies Association*

Center for Communal Studies
University of Southern Indiana
8600 University Boulevard
Evansville, IN 47712

Phone: (812)464-1727 Fax: (812)464-1960

The CSA invites you to discover its conferences, publications, and research facilities which unite the efforts of communitarians, scholars, and historic communal sites. The Center for Communal Studies is a clearinghouse for information, and an archival repository on past and present communities — for your use and for deposit of materials.

Membership: Individual $25
Institutional $50
Communal Societies subscription alone: $15

(*Formerly the National Historic Communal Societies Association)

Resources

Resources

Nature Conservancy *(Cont'd.)*
1951, which is dedicated to saving unique and important natural lands and the life they shelter. We seek out and identify natural areas that must be saved because of their ecological significance or the distinct wildlife they contain — and then acquire the land, either through outright purchase, gifts, or exchanges. The land is then managed by the Conservancy, or turned over to responsible public or private conservation groups or educational institutions. We own and manage more than 1,000 sanctuaries, encompassing nearly three and a half million acres in all 50 states. 9/23/89

NCACS

58 Schoolhouse Road
Summertown, TN 38483
(615) 964-3670

The National Coalition of Alternative Community Schools (NCACS) is an organization of individuals, families, groups, and private schools who are united in their desire to create a new structure for education. We are committed to a process that 1) empowers people to actively and collectively direct their lives, 2) requires active control of education by all involved, and 3) develops tools and skills for social change. We publish a quarterly newsletter and the largest directory of alternative schools and resources — with over 600 listings in 47 states and 18 countries. We also hold a national conference each spring. 6/12/89

The Neighborhood WORKS

Center for Neighborhood Technology
2125 W. North Avenue
Chicago, IL 60647
(312) 278-4800

In *The Neighborhood WORKS* you find out what's happening with community groups, neighborhood organizers, community development corporations, government, and funders. You learn about new ideas: land trusts to keep housing affordable; incubators to nourish small business start-ups; new financing vehicles like credit unions and community development loan funds; strategies to save local jobs and the environment too. You also discover the obstacles that community groups confront, the issues they debate, the projects they try — what works, what doesn't. A

$25 membership brings you our bimonthly newsletter and in-depth handbooks on various issues, showing how you and your organization can make a difference. 11/14/89

New Age Community Guidebook

Harbin Springs Publishing
P.O. Box 82
Middletown, CA 95461
(707) 987-2477

The New Age Community Guidebook, formerly of Eugene, Oregon, is now being published by Harbin Hot Springs (see listing). It includes articles and resources as well as community listings. The information in their '89 Directory is not as up to date as what we've printed here. Contact them if you'd like to be notified of future updates, or for a list of their other new age publications. 5/7/88

New Age Journal

P.O. Box 53275
Boulder, CO 80321
(Ads & Editorial Office:
342 Western Avenue
Brighton, MA 02135
(617) 787-2005

The New Age Journal is a bimonthly magazine that focuses on living a more natural and holistic lifestyle. We publish an annual directory of resources which features: Holistic Health & Natural Living, Personal Growth & Exploration, and Social Change. Our Winter 1990 Directory features over 800 groups offering everything from self-help options, to ecologically conscious household products, to socially responsible investing. Subscriptions in the U.S. are $24/year. 1/12/90

New Alchemy Institute

237 Hatchville Road
East Falmouth, MA 02536
(617) 564-6301

The New Alchemy Institute is dedicated to an ecological future. Founded in 1969, and located on 12 acres on Cape Cod, Massachusetts, New Alchemy serves students, teachers, households and small-scale farmers with research and education projects on food, energy, water and waste treatment systems. Current projects focus on resource-efficient housing, landscape design, organic market gardening, greenhouse horti-

culture, composting, and integrated pest management. Annual membership fee is $35, students and fixed income $20. We also sponsor children's programs, volunteer programs, tours and workshops, a speakers series, and a quarterly newsletter. Our mail-order catalog featuring publications, books, and organic gardening supplies is available upon request. 12/14/88

New Catalyst

P.O. Box 189
Gabriola Island, B.C.
CANADA V0R 1X0
(604) 247-9737

After five years of publishing a 36-page quarterly tabloid covering the environmental, bioregional, peace, feminist, and community movements in the west, *The New Catalyst* has now divided its publications in two: the tabloid still exists in a free 16-page version oriented mostly to local and regional issues, and the more enduring "feature" material of continent-wide relevance is now packaged twice yearly in book form as our Bioregional Series. An $18 subscription gives you the *The New Catalyst* magazine plus two books from the Bioregional Series. 3/8/91

The New Internationalist

P.O. Box 1143
Lewiston, NY 14092

At New Internationalist magazine we attempt to provide a precise, clear guide through the blizzard of information which bombards us all daily. We're not a newsmagazine, a daily newspaper, or an academic journal — every month we choose just one subject of vital importance to our battered old world. It's a valuable monthly reference work that builds into an encyclopedia of immediately accessible data and analysis on key global issues. We're fairly new to the U.S., but boast 100,000 readers in England, Canada, Australia, and more than 40 Third World countries. 3/12/89

New Options

P.O. Box 19324
Washington, DC 20036
(202) 822-0929

New Options is a monthly political newsletter which covers current events, social change groups, and political books from a decentralist/

globally-responsible point of view. It investigates new ideas and approaches that go beyond those of the traditional left and right. Each issue reinterprets national and international news, looks constructively and critically at social change groups and political books, and includes an extremely high-energy "Forum" section in which the new post-liberal/post-socialist ideas are debated by the readers. Subscriptions are $25/year (11 issues). 6/1/89

New Society Publishers

4527 Springfield Avenue
Philadelphia, PA 19143
(215) 382-6543

Publicity Office:
Box 582
Santa Cruz, CA 95061
(408) 458-1191
(800) 333-9093 Orders
M/C & Visa only M-F(10-5)

New Society Publishers is a not-for-profit, worker-controlled publishing house committed to fundamental social change through non-violent action. We are connected to a growing worldwide network of peace, feminist, environmental, and human rights activists, and we strive to meet their (your!) needs. We are proud to publish books by and for activists — books in which we try to see the world in new ways; to find new connections and repair old ones; to build a more just, peaceful, and joyful world. And we are proud of our efforts to practice what we preach in our organization and in the way we conduct business. For more information please call our publicity office. 10/4/89

Communal Studies Association (CSA)
[Formerly the NHCSA]

Center for Communal Studies
8600 University Boulevard
Evansville, IN 47712
(812) 464-1727 Fax: 464-1960

The CSA was founded in 1975 as the National Historic Communal Societies Association, which changed its name in 1990 to reflect its expanded emphasis upon current as well as historic intentional communities.

The CSA and its Pacific Coast Chapter each sponsor an annual conference at a historic or current community. CSA meetings are scheduled for Aurora, OR (Oct. '91); Nauvoo, IL (Oct. '92); New Harmony, IN (Oct. '93); and Oneida, NY (Oct. '94). Communitarians and anyone study-ing movements and groups organized in community are invited to submit proposals for sessions, presentations, formal papers, panels, and performances from their experience and research. For program consideration, please submit to CSA headquarters, at least six months before meetings, a brief presentation summary and personal qualifications.

We publish both a newsletter and a scholarly journal, *Communal Societies*. Newsletter items should go to Susan Matarese, Department of Political Science, University of Louisville, Louisville, KY 40292. Journal manuscripts are submitted in duplicate to Michael Barkun, Dept. of Political Science, Syracuse University, Syracuse NY 13244-1090.

Individual memberships are $25; Institutional $50; Journal subscriptions alone are $15. We welcome inquiries, conference presentations, and materials for the Center archives (which has already grown to include material on 100 historic and nearly 400 contemporary communities — see CCS listing). 4/26/91

Nolo Press

Box 544
Occidental, CA 95465

(707) 874-2818
(800) 433-6556 Orders (U.S.)
(800) 822-8382 Orders (CA)

Nolo Press is the nation's leading and most highly respected publisher of self-help law books. Nolo was founded in 1971 with the idea of making the law more accessible to ordinary people. Over the past 18 years our books have helped to demystify the legal system. Now with more than 60 titles, Nolo Press has saved consumers and business owners millions of dollars. We publish a quarterly, *Nolo News*, to keep readers up to date on law changes that affect Nolo books and to provide practical legal information to our readers. Subscriptions are $7 per year. Write for our catalog of self-help law books. 3/21/89

Nomenus

Box 11655
San Francisco, CA 94101
(415) 957-0514

Nomenus is a non-profit corporation which was originally founded (in 1985) to locate and purchase land trusts for faerie sanctuary space. Since that time Nomenus has broadened its base — we have hosted three large West Coast gatherings of the Radical Faeries, and produce the "Faerie Home Companion." Our promotion of radical awareness includes participation in bookstores, the California Men's Gathering, fundraisers, etc. We publish *Nomenews* to inform members of gatherings, projects, fund raisers, land reports, and land developments. We also maintain a computerized Faerie Data Base (fey dish). Correspondence about the Radical Faerie Gatherings should be directed to: Wolf Creek Sanctuary, P.O. Box 312, Wolf Creek, OR 97497. 12/14/88

Nuclear Free America

325 East 25th Street
Baltimore, MD 21218

(301) 235-3575
Fax: 462-1039
PeaceNet: "nfa"

Nuclear Free America is a non-profit educational resource center and clearinghouse for the Nuclear Free Zone movement. NFA works closely with existing Nuclear Free Zones and campaigns — providing them with a variety of legal, educational, and organizing resources. NFA also promotes socially responsible investing and purchasing (encouraging individuals, organizations, and communities to not do business with nuclear weapons contractors) and maintains a detailed database of nuclear weapons contractors. Contact NFA for information on how to declare your home, property, or community to be a Nuclear Free Zone. 12/14/88

Olympia Sustaining Fund
P.O. Box 10115
Olympia, WA 98502

The Olympia Sustaining Fund provides grants to progressive and community-oriented projects in Thurston County. Established in '85 (incorporated '87), OSF funds projects which promote community building, cultural diversity and awareness, and creative and conscientious local/regional development — groups working actively to educate and involve the community in challenging and correcting the social, political, and economic inequities around us. OSF is supported by local businesses which add a 1% voluntary surcharge to their prices (or make a regular contribution from their gross receipts or wages), and by individuals who voluntarily tithe 1% of their annual income. Although OSF is a non-profit, tax-exempt organization, contributions are not tax-deductible. We award grants quarterly. Please write for more information. 5/8/89

Resources

Omega Institute

Route 2
Lake Drive, Box 377
Rhinebeck, NY 12572

(914) 338-6030 Winter
266-4301 May 15 - Sept 1

Omega Institute for Holistic Studies, founded in 1977, is the largest non-profit vacation/learning center on the East Coast. Approximately 8,000 people participate in 200 week-end and week-long workshops during the 3-month summer season. We have an 80-acre lake-front campus located in the rolling hills two hours north of New York City. Workshops at Omega explore new ideas in the arts, psychology, health, fitness, business, global thinking, spirituality, and preventive medicine. Our faculty are the leaders and innovators in their fields. We also sponsor educational and wilderness trips throughout the world, 4-week winter programs on St. John's Island (in the US Virgin Islands), and winter courses at other sites in the Northeast. Write or call for more information and a free descriptive catalog. 11/12/88

Omega New Age Directory

6418 S. 39th Avenue
Phoenix, AZ 85041

(602) 237-3213
(800) 888-OMEGA

Since 1972, the *Omega New Age Directory* has been providing New Age news... important information and insightful articles about UFOs, holistic health, Earth changes, ESP, women's rights, astrology, and spiritual practices.

A real newspaper, the Directory covers local, national, and international news of interest to New Agers. We also have a comprehensive directory of all the New Age churches and study groups in Arizona; a directory service for psychic readers and counselors; and another directory for healing practitioners. 3/18/90

One Earth

The Findhorn Foundation Press
The Park, Forres, IV36 ORD
SCOTLAND

One Earth is a quarterly publication of the Findhorn Foundation (see listing in the "Communities" section) which covers a broad spectrum of topics relevant to their international network of communities and community ventures. Sex, politics, education, the arts, the spiritual growth movement, environmental issues, and more. 3/21/89

One World Family

Travel Network
81868 Lost Valley Lane
Dexter, OR 97431

(503) 937-3351

The One World Family Travel Network is a membership organization and support system for individuals who want to know about alternative and socially responsible travel options and organizations. The network emphasizes that travel which promotes cultural understanding and good will among people, and travel that helps appreciate and protect the natural environment we all share, can contribute to a more peaceful world. Options include educational & scientific, citizen diplomacy, environmental, retreats, volunteering, and more. Individual memberships are $15-35 (sliding scale) which includes a directory of 250 organizations that promote responsible travel. The directory alone is $7 postpaid. 12/12/89

Oregon Tilth

P.O. Box 218
Tualatin, OR 97062

(503) 692-4877

Oregon Tilth is a non-profit organization of people devoted to a clean and healthy food system — one that improves the quality of the soil in which food is grown, one that is locally based and nationally distributed, and one that provides nutritionally superior food with a diversity that arises form interest and enterprise by healthy, aware, and loving people. Tilth activities include bio-organic education through a bimonthly newsletter and other forums, conferences, nutritional database research, information distribution to government and private organizations, an organic certification program, and community development. Our members include farmers, small landholders, gardeners, health-conscious consumers, and people concerned about our legacy to future generations. 2/12/89

Oregon Women's Land Trust

Box 1692
Roseburg, OR 97429

(503) 679-3266

Oregon Women's Land Trust is a non-profit corporation founded to recognize that land is a sacred heritage and resource belonging to all people, to acquire land for women who otherwise would not have access, to develop harmonious and ecologically-sound land-based community, and to protect the land from speculation and overdevelopment. Women need to have time, space, and resources to develop their own culture. We are feminists working against racism, ageism, classism, and we share our love for Mother Earth. We have collectively acquired a 147-acre farm in Oregon (see Community listing for Owl Farm), thus eliminating owner/tenant power divisions.

Membership is open to any woman in agreement with our purposes who asks to be on our mailing list. We request a $3 contribution for the newsletter. Decisions are made by consensus at quarterly meetings which are announced in the newsletter. 1/7/89

Ozark Regional Land Trust

427 South Main Street
Carthage, MO 64836
(417) 358-4484

ORLT is a non-profit membership organization operating in the Ozark Mountain region of Missouri and Arkansas. Our purpose is to promote the appropriate environmental protection of land and resources. This is accomplished by permaculture design, community land trusts, and cooperative agreements and relationships. We have organized rural Community Land Trusts to bring permanent protection to the land and to foster cooperative relationships between its residential members. Several of these rural land trusts are seeking new members — Sweetwater CLT (480 acres), Hawk Hill CLT (240 acres), and Cave Creek CLT (55 acres). Write for information about these communities, or for assistance in organizing other CLTs in the area.

ORLT also protects sensitive ecological areas through land trusts and conservation easements on land. Our goal is to develop and implement models of permanent land protection whenever possible, using bioregional and permaculture concepts. 5/16/89

Pacific Publishers' Cooperative

P.O. Box 170052
San Francisco, CA 94117

The Pacific Publishers' Cooperative is an association of small independent publishers who share a common interest in publishing fine literature with a concern for social values. Most of the titles in our cooperative catalog are also available through other distributors. Member groups include Amazon Press, Barn Owl Books, Bootlegger Publishing, Frog in the Well, Pennypress, Regent Press, and Scribe & Son. Please write for a copy of our catalog. 7/12/89

Pattern Research

Box 9845
Denver, CO 80209
(303) 778-0880

Since 1975 we have been in the business of designing and maintaining what we like to call network generators. The Office for Open Network (flat fee: $50/yr) is our main project, with clients in most states and several foreign countries. We also do workshops on communication and information management, consult with individuals setting up network projects and other kinds of information projects. Although we are computer literate, we specialize in the human face of network building. We are fond of working with explorers — entrepreneurs, inventors, artists, writers, builders, and innovators. Call or write for free information. 5/17/89

Peacemakers

Box 627
Garberville, CA 95440

Peacemakers is a movement dedicated to the transformation of society through the transformation of the individuals therein. Our principles include 1) accepting non-violence as a guiding principle in our lives, 2) simplifying our lives, 3) forming closer knit communities, 4) believing we are part of earth's ecosystem, 5) using consensus, and 6) working for non-violent economic and social revolution. By committing ourselves to work toward living in line with our beliefs, we can each in a small but significant way begin to change the world. Although the movement is widely scattered, individuals within it try to keep in touch with one another for mutual support and occasional collective action. Our unity better enables us to search for truly non-violent ways of living for peace.

Peacemakers are those who accept and try to practice our philosophy and who consider themselves members. There is no statement to sign, no membership fee, no national office. 7/8/89

Penuel Ridge Retreat Center

Route 4, Box 304-2
Ashland City, TN 37105
(615) 792-3734 / 792-3534

Penuel Ridge is an ecumenical retreat center in the hills of middle Tennessee. It was founded in 1983 by a group of persons who identify with the Judeo-Christian tradition of pilgrimage, openness, and compassion. It offers a quiet, hospitable setting to all who seek time and space for reflection and renewal. In the silence and beauty of God's natural world, individuals and groups will have the opportunity to deepen relationships to God, to self, and to others.

Penuel Ridge is located on 100 acres which adjoins a 25,000-acre wildlife preserve. Trails wind through the wooded ridges and around a tranquil, spring-fed lake. This is an earth setting that offers its own healing, grounding touch. 6/10/89

People for a Change

(Gathering Resistance
Newsletter)
131 Mangels
San Francisco, CA 94131

People for a Change is a membership organization dedicated to building a grass-roots base for social/economic/political change. People for change believe in peaceful co-existance, favor an end to militarism and the arms race, put human needs ahead of profit, are concerned that millions of people are starving in the midst of plenty, want a world free of racism and ageism and sexism, participate in demonstrations, attend conferences, join organizations, make donations, write letters, sign petitions, work in political campaigns to elect progressives, sometimes run for political office, worry that the ecosystem is being destroyed faster than it is being restored. Membership includes a monthly newsletter, and every issue is filled with eye-opening statistics; historic and contemporary quotes; "movement" poetry, song lyrics, and update information. Memberships are $1/mo. or $10/yr. (U.S.), $1.25/mo. (Canada), and $2/mo elsewhere — and all memberships expire on May Day (international Workers' Day). Dues are half price for students, for the unemployed, and for the nearly broke of all nations. 2/21/90

PEP

P.O. Box 6306
Captain Cook, HI 96704
(808) 929-9691

PEP promotes "Polyfidelity", a sexually fidelitous marriage of more than two adults in which all partners are valued equally (all primaries). Although most people equate multiple relationships with a desire for promiscuity, often individuals who are polyfidelitous want as much commitment and sharing with their partners as anyone in a standard marriage situation.

PEP is a non-profit educational corporation. We publish learning materials and information about polyfidelity. Our materials describe direct experiences of polyfidelity, and the ideas and theories which have developed from it. Networking is one of our functions. Basic membership, including our quarterly newsletter, *Loving More* (formerly *Peptalk*), is $25 per year. Our *Polyfidelity Primer* (1989, 71 pages) describes the theory and essentials of the lifestyle, and is available for $12.00 postpaid. 4/10/90

The Permaculture Activist

P.O. Box 3630
Kailua-Kona, HI 96745

The *Permaculture Activist* is published quarterly to describe the activities of individuals and organizations throughout North America who are incorporating permaculture methods in their lives and work. The name of this newsletter/journal was chosen in order to promote an active approach to creating permaculture systems — rather than a passive, academic analysis. Permaculture activists are observing, planning, planting, building, growing, and maintaining sustainable food production systems, appropriate technologies, and econ-

Resources

Permaculture Activist *(Cont'd.)*
omic alternatives in all types of environments — temperate, tropical, urban, rural, humid, and arid lands ... in "under" and "over" developed nations. Most important, permaculture activists are creating changes in their own lives and lifestyles.

The *Permaculture Activist* relies on volunteer writers to contribute feature articles, press releases, news updates, drawings and photographs. Subscriptions are $16/year in Central and North America, $20 for overseas surface mail, $25 airmail. 11/12/89

Planet Drum Foundation

Box 31251
San Francisco, CA 94131

Planet Drum Foundation's primary focus is Bioregionalism, and they have recently completed an updated international directory that lists over 150 different bioregional organizations and contact people. The directory is included in issue #15 of *Raise the Stakes*, a regular Planet Drum publication. Annual membership (including RTS #15) is $15/year in North America, $20 outside North America. 11/12/89

Project Plenty

San Diego Center
14095 Proctor Valley Road
Jamul, CA 92035

In 1974 The Farm in Tennessee started an outreach program called Plenty. Over the course of its first ten years, Plenty established a clinic in Bangladesh, a tree nursery in Lesotho, and a wind-powered electric lighting system in a Carib Indian school in Dominica. It provided free ambulance service to the South Bronx. It went to sea with Greenpeace and gave the Rainbow Warrior its radiation monitoring equipment. Plenty put Native American FM stations on the air, and pioneered amateur-band television and radio to connect its remote outposts of volunteers. In 1978, Plenty formed a scientific research team and litigation project to work on environmental issues and human rights. In 1980, it founded the Natural Rights Center (see separate listing). 8/12/89

Pueblo to People

1616 Montrose Blvd. #3500
Houston, TX 77006

(800) 843-5257
(713) 523-1197 (in Texas)

Pueblo to People is a non-profit organization founded in 1979. We work at the grass-roots, supporting organizations of the poor themselves. Selling their products through PTP not only provides them with badly needed income, but gives them a chance to learn organizational skills and democratic methods many of us take for granted. With these skills other community problems are addressed; without these skills, many issues are never raised. Write for a free catalog of products from Central and South American Cooperatives. 9/1/89

R&E Miles Publishing

Box 1916
San Pedro, CA 90733

(213) 833-8856

We are a small publisher specializing in the environment (including a series of travel guides called EcoGuides) and American quilts. We will be pleased to send our book list to anyone requesting it. 6/12/89

Rainforest Action Network

300 Broadway, Suite A
San Francisco, CA 94133

The Rainforest Action Network is a non-profit activist organization which works internationally in cooperation with other environmental and human rights organizations on major campaigns to protect rainforests. Send for a free basic information packet or become a member ($25) and receive the *World Rainforest Report*, a quarterly newsletter. 11/12/89

Real Goods

3041 Guidville Road
Ukiah, CA 95482

(800) 762-7325
(707) 468-9214 (in CA)

Real Goods claims to offer the world's largest and most through selection of alternative energy products, and publishes an annual *Alternative Energy Sourcebook* which contains nearly 200 pages of products, charts, graphs, sizing, and design instructions ... everything you need to design and build a complete home power system from fantasy to electricity. $6.50 (ppd.) gets you the *Sourcebook* plus three issues of their quarterly update, the Real Good News! 9/21/89

Reclaiming

P.O. Box 14404
San Francisco, CA 94114

Reclaiming is a collective of San Francisco Bay Area women and men working to unify spirit and politics. Our vision is rooted in the religion and magic of the Goddess — the Immanent Life Force. We see our work as teaching and making magic — the art of empowering ourselves and each other. In our classes, workshops, and public rituals we train our voices, bodies, energy, intuition, and minds. We use the skills we learn to deepen our strength (both as individuals and as community), to voice our concerns about the world in which we live, and to bring to birth a vision of a new culture. We also publish a newsletter. 7/30/89

Regenerating America

Rodale Press
33 East Minor Street
Emmaus, PA 18049

News about what people and groups are doing to use the

NATIONAL
DIRECTORY
OF ALTERNATIVE SCHOOLS

Largest listing of alternative schools and resources published in this country.
Over 600 entries, with detailed descriptions of over 300.
Special sections on foreign schools, boarding schools, homeschool resources

Published by NCACS
(National Coalition of Alternative Community Schools)
58 Schoolhouse Road, Summertown, TN 38483

$12.50

talents and resources of their towns in building prosperity and a sense of community. Includes resource material and seminars. Bimonthly, $15/year. 11/12/88

Relocation Research

P.O. Box 1122
Sierra Madre, CA 91024

(818) 568-8484

Relocation Research is a national clearinghouse which assists individuals in planning a move from large urban centers to more livable environments (small towns and cities, islands, rural areas in general). We are interested not only in intentional communities... but in bioregions that embrace them, America's small-town Shangri-La's, survival retreats, last frontiers, regions of opportunity, etc.

We have knowledge about a myriad of organizations and resource persons assisting in seeking personal Edens. We publish "Greener Pastures Gazette" and Eden Seekers Guide. Please enclose SASE with specific requests. 7/12/89

Renew America

1400 - 16th Street NW, # 710
Washington, DC 20036

(202) 232-2252

Renew America is a non-profit, tax-exempt educational organization working towards a sustainable future by promoting a safe and healthy environment. Our main initiatives include: 1) the State of the States report, covering six different environmental topics each year. The report ranks each state on its program strengths and offers state and national environmental leaders important tools to create positive change. 2) Searching for Success, a nationwide overview of effective environmental programs and policies, identifying success stories to serve as models for policymakers, public interest groups, the news media, and government officials across the country. Memberships are $25/year, and include our quarterly newsletter and a copy of the State of the States report. Write for further information, and for a list of our available reports and focus papers. 6/21/89

ReVision

The Journal of
Consciousness and Change

Heldref Publications
4000 Albemarle Street NW
Washington, DC 20016

ReVision is a dense quarterly journal of consciousness and change. Each issue rigorously covers a theme with contributions from popular scientists, mystics, scholars, and others. Recent themes include "The Gaia Hypothesis", "New Paradigm Thinking", and "The Future of the World". ReVision has been described as "the academic journal of the New Age". Annual subscriptions are $35 for institutions, $18 for individuals, plus $8 for subscriptions outside the US. 8/12/89

RFD

Route 1, Box 84-A
Liberty, TN 37095

RFD is a reader-written journal for gay men which focuses on country living and encourages alternative lifestyles. Articles often explore the building of a sense of community, radical faerie consciousness, the caring for the environment, as well as sharing gay men's experiences. Editorship responsibility is shared between the Department Editors and the Managing Editors. The business and general production is centered at Short Mountain Sanctuary in rural middle Tennessee (see community listing). Features are often prepared in various places by different groups. Subscriptions are $15 per year (four issues). 9/21/89

Robert Owen Foundation

60 Lowther
Toronto, Ontario
CANADA M5R 1C7

The Robert Owen Foundation, founded in 1932, is a federally-chartered non-profit organization designed to encourage cooperative living and enterprise. It is run by a board elected by and responsible to the membership. We maintain a small endowment fund to assist in the establishment and operation of enterprises such as producers' cooperatives and cooperative communities. Specific services: we endorse projects, lend money, guarantee loans, reduce interest rates, provide organizational assistance, offer technical assistance and make small grants. We offer a set of questions, available on request, as a guide for writing applications. 9/3/89

Rocky Mountain Institute

1739 Snowmass Creek Road
Old Snowmass, CO 81654

(303) 927-3851

Rocky Mountain Institute is a research and education foundation whose goal is to foster efficient and sustainable use of resources as a path to global security. A membership is $10, and includes a subscription to our bimonthly newsletter. 12/14/88

Rodale Press

33 E. Minor Street
Emmaus, PA 18049

Rodale Press is the leading publisher of periodicals related to ecological alternatives and self-sufficiency. Some of their titles: Organic Gardening; New Shelter; New Farm; and Prevention magazines. They are part of the Regeneration Project, which advocates the principle of regeneration in areas of health, the economy, agriculture, etc. (see separate listing). Rodale's quarterly newsletter addresses regeneration at all levels from the personal to the community, and each issue features projects on urban economic revitalization. Newsletter subscriptions are $12 per year. 9/21/89

Rowe Camp & Conference Center

Kings Highway Road
Rowe, MA 01367

(413) 339-4216 Office
339-4468 Director

Rowe Camp & Conference Center, in the beautiful Berkshires 3 miles from Vermont, is an antidote to TV. Since 1924 we have run a small, intelligent and creative summer camp for teenagers. Since 1974 we have run weekends and week long retreats for adults and families on a wide variety of religious, political, psychological, and health issues. Are you a parent who wishes your children could get in touch with their innate idealism? Have you longed for a place to spend a weekend where people drop their masks but not their integrity, a place to meet a variety of different people, a place you could afford and still touch the beauty of the natural world? Write or call for a free copy of our beautiful flyer (see listing in Communities section). 2/3/89

Resources

Resources

School of Living

Route 1, Box 185-A
Cochranville, PA 19330

Founded in 1934, the School of Living explores options for decentralization, cooperative living, and land reform. SoL offers training conferences, financing for Community Land Trust (CLT) development, permaculture demonstrations, monetary and economic reform activities. It administers a regional CLT alliance for intentional communities, homesteaders, and other residential users wishing to place land in trust. 8/22/89

Seed Savers Exchange

Route 3, Box 239
Decorah, IA 52101

The Seed Savers Exchange is a network of mostly small-scale growers and gardeners dedicated to preserving our heritage of open-pollinated heirloom vegetables and other useful plant varieties. The network's underlying purpose is to protect the genetic diversity of our food crops. The SSE's winter yearbook lists varieties that have been saved ... then members exchange and grow each other's seeds. Two other valuable references works produced by the SSE are the *Garden Seed Inventory* (a complete listing of all commercially available non-hybrid vegetable and garden seeds), and the *Fruit, Nut, and Berry Inventory.* Write for information on membership. 1/21/89

Self-Directed Small Communities

Progressive Community Assoc.
P.O. Box 122-M
Athens, OH 45701

(614) 593-7456

SDSC is a group of individuals living and working in southeastern Ohio. SDSC offers a plan for alternatives in jobs, housing, and personal lifestyles — applying lessons learned from the movements of the '60s, '70s, and '80s. Emphasis is on developing small, land-based communities with access to towns and traditional opportunities. Within these communities people are encouraged to create their own basic institutions, offering options for independence and interdependence. Write or call for more information. 4/2/91

Seventh Generation Fund

Box 536
Hoopa, CA 95546

The Seventh Generation Fund is a national Native American public foundation which provides an integrated program of grants, technical and management support to Native people in their self-help efforts to rebuild their communities. The Fund is dedicated to maintaining and promoting our uniqueness as Native people and Nations. We believe that Native people must be empowered to define and create our own futures — to do our own community development. The Fund's role is to bring together the resources to support these self-help efforts toward positive change. We utilize an integrated and holistic approach, addressing all of the elements of community, to plan and develop processes for problem solving and community rebuilding. 3/25/91

Shaker Village, Inc.

Canterbury, NH 03224

Canterbury Shaker Village is a living museum — created and sanctioned by the Shaker Lead Ministry to rediscover, preserve, interpret, and celebrate the purposeful way of life led by the Shakers from the 1780s to the present. Serenely sited on a rolling hilltop, Canterbury Shaker Village guides the public through a world of beautiful images preserved through the ongoing stewardship of manuscripts, photographs, artifacts, and original buildings. Respectful interpretation of the Shaker traditions and demonstrations of their timeless crafts offer insights into the values lived by a utopian religious community. 7/12/89

Shared Living Resource Center

2375 Shattuck Avenue
Berkeley, CA 94704

(415) 548-6608

SLRC is committed to creating supportive shared living communities that integrate housing with cooperative living, affordability, and ecological design. SLRC's Community Core Group Process involves brainstorming of community design/lifestyle options, inspiring commitment, sharing fun and friendly exercises for learning more about your own motivations, looking at decision-making, considering how to select community mates, and resolving conflicts. Other services include workshops on designing shared living community, consultation sessions, slide-talk presentations, building and site surveys, architectural design, and construction drawings. 8/12/89

Sierra Club

730 Polk Street
San Francisco, CA 94109

(415) 776-2211

For almost 100 years the Sierra Club has been fighting to protect the earth's fragile systems. We have successfully lobbied for laws to limit air and water pollution, and to regulate poisonous toxic chemicals. We have won protection for swamps and meadows, rivers and mountains, deserts and prairies ... those natural places which permit the earth to heal and renew itself. We have constantly been an effective voice for a world healthful for all its inhabitants.

The unique power of the Sierra Club springs from our active grassroots membership ... volunteers who give freely of their time and expertise. Please write if you'd like to become a supporting member, or if you want to participate in our work. 11/12/89

Sirius Publishing

Baker Road
Shutesbury, MA 01072

(413) 259-1505

Members of the Sirius community have written a book, *Builders of the Dawn*, which surveys intentional communities around the U.S. and the world which have pioneered successful models of holistic health, worker-owned businesses, organic agriculture, solar energy, and conflict resolution techniques. They have also produced cassette tapes, slideshows, and videos on topics related to creating and living in community (available for sale or rent), and offer workshops, courses, and consulting services related to social change and building community. Write for a free brochure. 5/23/89

Skipping Stones

80574 Hazelton Road
Cottage Grove, OR 97424
(503) 942-9434

Skipping Stones is a multi-ethnic, international, non-profit children's magazine which encourages cooperation, creativity, and celebration of cultural and environmental richness — as a forum for communication among children from different lands and backgrounds. *Skipping Stones* is here to expand the horizons in a playful, creative way.

We accept original writings and artwork from all ages, in every language. Recent issues have included work by children from USA, India, Mexico, Nicaragua, Russia, Taiwan, Japan, Germany, Laos, Israel, Saudi Arabia.... *Skipping Stones* is a quarterly journal which will grow and change with the needs and input of our readers. We invite your submissions, subscriptions, suggestions, and support. Yearly subscriptions are $15 (overseas airmail: $20). Contact us about low-income and Third World reduced rates. 11/1/89

SkySong

3716 - 274th S.E.
Issaquah, WA 98027

SkySong is not an intentional community, although those who live here do live in community with each other. We use the studio for classes, workshops, and individual retreats. We are not seeking people (as our facilities are pushed to the limit), but we are always open to visitors and travelers. After two nights, guests pay $15 or offer a work/service equivalent for each day they are here. We've had some wonderful guests!

SkySong's philosophy is one of harmony with the environment, emphasizing permaculture and a sustainable ecology. We work mindfully, meditatively, and joyfully ... and enjoy sharing time with visitors, even briefly. We will likely relocate to Montana in the very near future. Please write before visiting. 4/15/91

Social Movement Empowerment Project

721 Shrader Street
San Francisco, CA 94117

(415) 387-3361

Our mission is to promote participatory democracy and progressive social change by helping citizens recognize their own power and be more effectively involved in grass-roots-based social movements. We develop practical strategic models and methods (called MAP: the Movement Action Plan) for analyzing, strategizing, and conducting social movements. Our tools include publications, consultations, talks, and training workshops. We work with groups the world round — activists working on critical social issues including peace, nuclear disarmament, justice, democracy, non-intervention, human rights, and the environment. A packet of our two basic publications is $4 postpaid. 2/8/90

Society for Utopian Studies

Attn: Lawrence Hough
Poli-Sci ECU
Greenville, NC 27858

Founded in 1975, the Society of Utopian Studies is an international, interdisciplinary association devoted to the study of both literary and experimental utopias. We have active members from a wide variety of disciplines — including Philosophy, Classics, Economics, Engineering, History, Literature, Political Science, Psychology, Sociology, Foreign Languages, and the Arts. Membership is open to all persons with utopian interests, and our ranks include architects, futurists, urban planners, and environmentalists. Membership includes announcements of meetings and our newsletter, *Utopis Discovered*, which contains information about upcoming conferences, workshops, and publications in the field. Dues are $10 per year ($5 for students and the unemployed). 6/6/89

Solar Box Cookers International

1724 Eleventh Street
Sacramento, CA 95814

(916) 444-6616
    447-8689 (Fax)

People have tried cooking with the sun for centuries, but early sun cookers were costly and impractical. In the 1970s two women in Arizona developed a simple box cooker that is convenient to use, inexpensive, and easy to build. Thousands of the new, simple solar box cookers have been used regularly for up to 14 years in the U.S. and elsewhere.

Solar Box Cookers International was formed as a non-profit organization in 1987 to promote solar cooking — for helping people and environments worldwide. Small pilot demonstrations in South and Central America, Mexico, and the Caribbean have been greeted with enthusiasm. SBCI works in partnership with other organizations to spread solar cooking, distributes teaching materials, provides training programs, and provides technical assistance for local production of solar box cookers. Write for literature/resource list and membership information. 12/5/89

Solar Box Cookers Northwest

7036 - 18th Avenue NE
Seattle, WA 98115

(206) 525-1418

An offshoot of SBCI (see previous listing), this group publishes a newsletter called *Solar Box Cooking*, available with a 1-year membership for $20. SBCN works to promote solar cooking both in this country and abroad, emphasizing local as well as international action, and invites participation in all forms. Becoming a voting member requires 12 hours of volunteer labor or $50. 12/5/89

Southern Dharma Retreat Center

Route 1, Box 34-H
Hot Springs, NC 28743

(704) 622-7112

Southern Dharma Retreat Center is a non-profit educational foundation, eclectic in nature, whose purpose is to offer meditation retreats and related workshops. Our goal is to provide a comfortable gathering place, removed from the hassles of everyday life, and to create an atmosphere of quiet calmness where one can nurture a sense of peace and uncover the truths within the heart. It is our intention to sponsor teachers from a variety of traditions, to maintain a supportive environment for meditation, and to keep costs to participants as low as possible. We are located in a remote, mountainous area. Facilities include a meditation hall, creekside campsites, and a dormitory which houses up to twenty-five. 1/12/89

Resources

Southwest Research & Information Center

Box 4524
Albuquerque, NM 87106

(505) 262-1862

SRIC provides timely, accurate information to the public on a broad range of issues related to the environment, human and natural resources, and consumer affairs. SRIC's programs and activities have twin objectives: 1) to promote citizen participation, and 2) to protect natural resources. We provide our services to community groups, policy makers, the media, national organizations, and individuals.

Locally, we provide site-specific technical assistance on such subjects as forest planning, the mitigation of water pollution, and the impact of mining. Nationally, we maintain a full-time staff person in Washington, D.C., to monitor nuclear waste developments at the federal level. We also provide a national clearinghouse for a network of citizen groups working on the issue of high-level nuclear waste disposal. We publish a quarterly magazine, *The Workbook*, which is national in scope. 5/15/89

Spring Hill

432 Columbia Street
Cambridge, MA 02141

(617) 864-9181 (10-4, M-F)

Spring Hill is the home of the Opening the Heart Workshops — a powerful experience that helps us heal old and current wounds, let go of heavy emotional baggage, contact our real selves, and find new momentum and direction. Since 1976 we have helped thousands of participants make significant changes in their lives. Besides the basic workshop, we offer specialty Heart workshops for Adult Children of Alcoholics, Survivors of Sexual Abuse, Lesbian and Gay Couples, Therapists, Men, Women, Teens, Recovering Alcoholics, and more.

Our business office is in Cambridge, but our workshops take place at our 80-acre retreat center near the New Hampshire border, an hour and a half northwest of Boston. It is an exceptionally safe and supportive environment for healing work.

The way of the Heart is to include rather than exclude, thus we have no rigid concepts or beliefs set up as a fence around our community. It is very easy to join us: just come to a workshop or community celebration... or one of our regular monthly get-togethers in Cambridge (MA), Hartford (CT), Burlington (VT), and Keene (NH). We welcome your participation in whatever form is right for you. 8/1/90

Sri Aurobindo Association

Box 372
High Falls, NY 12440

(914) 687-9222

The Sri Aurobindo Association is a non-profit organization dedicated to the vision of a transformed humanity as espoused by the Indian revolutionary and poet, Sri Aurobindo. His co-worker, known as the Mother, founded the international community of Auroville In 1968 — where people are trying to live together cooperatively based on spiritual values.

Our Association distributes books and information on the teachings of Sri Aurobindo and the Mother. We are not a residential community, but welcome inquiries concerning Auroville, Upon request we will send a free booklist and a sample of our newsletter, Collaboration. 5/11/89

The Stewardship Community

P.O. Box 9
100 Mile House, B.C.
CANADA V0K-2E0

The Stewardship Community is a non-profit educational organization of men and women around the world who are dedicated to the principles of earth stewardship. They are people of character and integrity who have chosen to realign their lives with higher purpose, respecting the natural laws of this living planet. We no longer view the global crisis as merely an environmental or technological problem, but as a call to basic change in consciousness and understanding of the real purpose of human life on earth. The central requirement is for personal responsibility and sensitivity to the interrelationship of all living forms.

Stewardship Farms and other associated communities apply these principles of stewardship by supporting sustainable agriculture, by developing wholesome food sources, and by using appropriate technology and management systems that enhance the ecological fabric of the earth. They offer an example of community spirit, where people of all walks of life transcend cultural, national, and philosophical identities — and allow a sense of family to emerge across the globe. These communities are the backbone of the Stewardship Community (see listing for Emissaries of the Divine Light in the "Communities" section). 6/21/89

Street News

1457 Broadway #305
New York, NY 10036

(212) 768-7290

Street News is "America's Motivational Non-Profit Newspaper — Helping America's Hungry," sold by homeless people. By April 1990, after just five months of publication, circulation in New York City exceeded 350,000 and involved over 1,500 sales people. Plans are being developed to establish offices in San Francisco, Washington D.C., and other cities across the nation.

Each issue features articles by "famous actors/actresses, singers/ musicians, artists, writers, fashion designers, models, performers, athletes" on such topics as "Parenting, Family & Career," "Jobs for the Homeless," "America's Entrepreneurial Spirit," the power of communication and the media, and personal and social responses to homelessness. Regular departments include listings of job training and work opportunities for homeless and/or undertrained men and women, sections on art, "the homeless poet," and a kids' page. Because 45¢ of the 75¢ cover price goes directly to the homeless sales representative, readers in those areas where Street News is available "on the street" are encouraged to buy it from homeless sales people instead of subscribing ($18/year, published twice monthly). 3/15/90

The Sun: A Magazine of Ideas

107 North Roberson Street
Chapel Hill, NC 27516

(919) 942-5282

The Sun is a self-described "magazine of ideas". Since 1974 they have explored the words of Ram Dass, Wavy Gravy, Patricia Sun, David Spangler and other luminaries through stories, essays, interviews, and poems. They also have a lively reader-submission policy. Every issue exudes a kind of warmth, integrity, and spirit of human discovery sorely missing from most publications (alternative or otherwise). Subscriptions are $28/year. 9/21/89

3HO Foundation

For Information & Referrals:
(505) 753-9438

The Healthy, Happy, Holy Organization (3HO) is a worldwide association of people dedicated to the excellence of the individual. 3HO brings to the public the science of Kundalini Yoga.

It offers complete lifestyle guidelines on nutrition and health, interpersonal relations, child rearing, and human behavior. You may choose from a wealth of knowledge to find exactly the techniques you have been seeking to upgrade your life. 3HO was founded by Yogi Bhajan, a yoga master who serves as a spiritual leader and guide for thousands of people worldwide.

There are many 3HO centers throughout the world that embrace the 3HO lifestyle based on the yogic practices of vegetarianism, abstinence from drugs, yoga, and medi-

tation. The Sikh religion is practiced in these centers — there are many paths to God, but only one God; all who worship, worship the same God; however a person worships, is what is good and right for them. However, you do not need to be a Sikh to practice or teach the 3HO lifestyle.

3HO hosts three worldwide yoga festivals each year, as well as a camp for women held in New Mexico — where women break from their routines to experience their individual identities as women and their lives as a seeker of truth. Call for more information on these gatherings, or to contact the center nearest you. [Note: several 3HO centers are listed separately in the Communities section.] 3/31/89

TIES - Turtle Island Earth Stewards

TIES Canada
101-5810 Battison Street
Vancouver, BC
CANADA V5R 5X8

(604) 432-9473

TIES USA
1420 NW Gilman #2346
Issaquah, WA 98027

(206) 391-3665

TIES is a non-profit charitable society incorporated in Canada in 1975 and in the USA in 1984. We are working with a new science of earth stewardship called TIES — Towards an Interdependent and Ecologically Sustainable Society. We help intentional communities place their land into public trusts which emphasize sustainable ecological stewardship of the land, and we promote the social and natural ecology of culture and place — to facilitate individual spiritual growth and develop a planetary consciousness. TIES works with groups to build consensus, resolve conflicts, and run more effective meetings. It also sponsors the Community Catalyst Project (see listing). 12/21/89

TraNet

P.O. Box 567
Rangeley, ME 04970

(207) 864-2252

TraNet is a transnational network of, by, and for people in all parts of the world who are changing the world by changing their own lifestyles — who are helping one another toward local

---

SECULAR COMMUNITY

✻ Towards a Sane and Strong
Collective Social Movement
and a Better Way of Life

✻ As a Primary Political Objective
Rather Than a Personal
Religious By-Product

A SUGGESTED CRITERIA OF SUCCESS

Will we benefit the cause
of human liberation and freedom?

Will we provide lifestyles
and benefits to our members
beyond those available
to society at large?

Will the ideas and
alternatives we generate
be accessible to and benefit
the rest of the world?

or will we become 20th Century Shakers,
leaving no legacy beyond finely crafted
furniture and unusual architecture?

for more information:

Low Consciousness Collective

c/o Shannon Farm
Route 2, Box 343
Afton, VA 22920

Resources

Resources

TraNet *(Cont'd.)*

self-reliance — who are adopting appropriate technologies (A.T.). TraNet holds that people themselves can and should be responsible for their own development and for the well-being of one another. Cooperative personal and community actions can replace reliance on the governments of nation-states which are inherently competitive and war mongering. Solidarity among people at the grass-roots can bring peace and equity.

TraNet has a primary goal of linking people with one another to raise the level of dialogue and practice of alternative and innovative ideas which will transform the whole Earth. Global problems of peace, pollution, and population must be solved by local actions. Members of TraNet are assisted in contacting other mem-bers and in establishing programs of mutual aid. Our Mini A.T. Library project puts each borrower into direct contact with the donor — the start of a cooperative linking which will bring intercultural understanding between the people of the world. 11/12/89

Transformation Times

P.O. Box 425
Beavercreek, OR 97004
(503) 632-7141

Transformation Times is a new age journal dedicated to expanding awareness of physical, mental, and spiritual resources. We believe that this awareness will enable a transformation of planetary consciousness to one of unity and love.

We accept articles on such issues as natural health, human potential, global responsibilities, occult sciences, and spiritual paths. We also provide information about services, products, and principles that we feel make a contribution to improving our world so that we all might live in harmony. Our goal is to provide a medium for expression of ideas and principles (both new and old) which help our lives work better. Subscriptions are $8/year for 10 issues. A sample issue is $1. 12/12/88

Turtle Island
Earth Stewards

(TIES) See previous page

Turtle Island Office

P.O. Box 955
Olympia, WA 98507

Turtle Island is a Native American

Indian word used to describe North America. The Turtle Island Office (TIO) is an information center for both the general public and the internal network of the bioregional movement. The office was created at the third North American Bioregional Congress held in August 1988 in Squamish, British Columbia, Canada. Current projects of the office are: a bioregional registry and archive, skills exchange, grant funding research, and the North American Bioregional Congress IV.

We do not have a national office. The function of the clearinghouse is to connect people and give background information. This structure was consciously chosen to embody decentralization. Every two years representatives from Turtle Island gather at the North American Bioregional Congress (see Calendar). We have two bioregional bookstores (see listings for *The New Catalyst* and for Planet Drum). 5/6/90

20/20 Vision

30 Cottage Street
Amherst, MA 01002
(413) 253-2939

You pay attention to what's going on in the world, and you've got some strong opinions about our government's military policy. But what are you doing with those well-thought-out opinions? How do you get them heard by the people who govern our democracy?

You're not ready to drop everything for a life of protest ... and you know that just voting, giving money, and talking to like-minded friends isn't enough.

If you've got 20 minutes a month, subscribe to our service. Every month we'll find you the best 20-minute action you can take at home to lobby policy makers to stop the arms race and improve global security. If you've got five hours a month, work with us to recruit local 20/20 Vision subscribers, and advise them about the best actions they can take. Either way, your time will be well spent. 3/21/91

Union of
Concerned Scientists

26 Church Street
Cambridge, MA 02238
(617) 547-5552

The Union of Concerned Scientists is a non-profit organization sponsored by donations from some 100,000 individuals, including many thou-

sands of scientists. UCS produces both printed and video educational materials on a variety of issues, including global warming, nuclear power, and renewable energy. It has been at the forefront of the movement to increase public awareness of the dangers of nuclear power and to promote safe, renewable energy alternatives. You may become a UCS sponsor and receive the quarterly publication, *Nucleus*, by making a tax-deductible contribution of any reasonable amount. 11/12/89

Urban Alternatives, Inc.

2375 Shattuck Avenue
Berkeley, CA 94704
(415) 644-8336

Urban Alternatives is a non-profit organization which provides support for the development and effective oper-ation of worker-owned and -managed businesses and non-speculative co-operative housing arrangements. We sponsor and develop organizations, help organize conferences, and op-erate the Alternatives Center, which offers a wide range of services including feasibility studies, financial planning, organizational development, and educational programs like workshops and consultations. We prefer to work with groups on an extended contract basis to assure long-term effectiveness. Training materials include video-workbook programs that teach how to plan and conduct more effective meetings, a new video on the Mondragon cooperatives, a guide to the development of limited equity housing cooperatives, a description of several European cooperative systems, and a monograph that tries to show that the social and economic concepts of cooperatives offer fundamental alternatives to the prevailing systems, and can be implemented in the U.S. through the formation of regional associations. 9/13/89

USCA

University Students
Cooperative Association
2424 Ridge Road
Berkeley, CA 94709

(415) 848-1936

The USCA is the largest student housing cooperative in North America, housing over 1400 people. Although a private non-profit corporation, the USCA works in cooperation with the University of California to provide housing for its students.

Over 1000 of the USCA's members live in room-and-board houses scattered around the Berkeley campus. There are also 15 large houses which each function as a separate cooperative household with elected managers for room assignment, work organization (housekeeping, food service, etc.), and maintenance. A central support staff of about 25 non-members provides technical information to members and oversees day-to-day administration (such as housekeeping applications and organizational financing). We also provide warehousing and support services to individual house food programs. 7/21/89

Utne Reader

P.O. Box 1974
Marion, OH 43306 [Subscriptions]

The Utne Reader offers "the best of the alternative press" six times a year, drawing articles from a wide range of alternative publications. Its aims are to "enlighten, incite, and encourage independent thinking." Through its "Off the Newsstand" section, it offers access to valuable and interesting periodicals that readers might not otherwise discover. Editorial Office address: 1624 Harmon Place, Minneapolis, MN 55403. New subscriptions cost $18 for one year; $30 for two years. 12/12/89

Veterans for Peace

P.O. Box 3881
Portland, ME 04104
(207) 797-2770

A world-wide organization of veterans working to abolish war in our lifetime, confident that we can change people's mindset about war and achieve multilateral disarmament. The founders' extensive military backgrounds give credibility to their stance as peace activists. Independent chapters take on diverse projects — ranging from working with the homeless, to starting clinics for young victims of war in various countries. You may join VFP if you are a veteran or the relative of a veteran. 8/12/89

The WELL

Whole Earth 'Lectronic Link
27 Gate Five Road
Sausalito, CA 94965
(415) 332-6106 (Computer)
332-4335 (Human Being)

If you have a computer and modem you can be part of a unique community of people that meet online. The Well is divided into conferences that discuss just about anything you can think of — mind, work, sexuality, Grateful Dead, and parenting are just a few. The Well is an on-line computer network affiliated with the Whole Earth Review (see separate listing). Rates are $8/month plus $3/hour for online time. 9/21/89

Whole Earth Institute

27 Gate Five Road
Sausalito, CA 94965
(415) 332-1716
332-2416 Fax

WEI is a newly-formed research and development arm of the philanthropic POINT Foundation — the parent organization of the Whole Earth Review. WEI is seeking contributions to finance special projects and to develop an endowment fund to support the magazine. Proposed projects: host new gatherings (such as their recent event for electronic hackers), promote habitat restoration tools, organize a populist video teleconference, experiment with buildings that learn, plant more WELLs around the country, or do a weekly national radio show. A history/possibilities packet is available upon request. See also: Whole Earth Review. 9/21/89

Whole Earth Review

27 Gate Five Road
Sausalito, CA 94965
(415) 332-1716

An "alternatives" general interest quarterly of "unorthodox cultural and technical news" which is wholly reader-supported (no advertising) and reader-driven (about half of the material in each issue is reader-suggested, or reader-written). The articles report on new products, promising books, art, cartoons, excerpts from hard-to-find books, and anything else that might qualify as conceptual news. They pride themselves in the incubation of half-baked ideas, a few of which survive. Subscriptions $20/yr (surface mail). See also: Whole Earth Institute; and The WELL. 9/21/89

Volunteer Co-Workers
Crozet, Virginia

Innisfree Village is an alternative lifesharing community with people with mental disabilities, situated on a 400-acre farm at the base of the Blue Ridge Mountains, 17 miles from Charlottesville, VA. Approximately 18 volunteers act as both house parents and co-workers in the bakery, weavery, woodshop, and garden in the Village. In addition, 4 volunteers live in Innisfree's two townhouses in Charlottesville, working on pottery. In a natural and humanistic environment, the emphasis is on the people-to-people relationships which develop in the course of daily family living and community sharing. Growth comes at a pace natural and therapeutic for the individual.

Duties: Share in cooking, cleaning, and other household management tasks; work in the work stations; attend community meetings and participate in community process.

Requirements: Patience; experience working with persons with mental disabilities helpful but not necessary; minimum 1-year commitment.

Salary: $150/month stipend. Room and board; health insurance; medical expenses (except for pre-existing conditions); dental expenses (up to $250); 15 days vacation at $28/day; severance pay accrued at $35/month.

To Apply: Contact the Office.

**Innisfree Village • Route 2, Box 506 • Crozet, VA 22932
(804)823-5400**

WICCA Camp

Route 1, Box 9-C
Edwall, WA 99008
(509) 236-2353

The Waukon Institute of Co-Creative Art [WICCA] intends to offer a summer self-healing camp with activities, workshops, and instruction in campcrafts, herb and food gathering, shelter making, footwear and leathercraft, herbal medicine, vision questing, crystals, yoga, meditation, addictions, relationships, gardening, food, horses and other animals, clothing, music, dance, and more. (See listing for Waukon Institute in the Communities section.) 12/12/88

Resources

Resources

Windstar Foundation

**2317 Snowmass Creek Road
Snowmass, CO 81654-9198**

**(303) 927-4777
927-3402**

Windstar is an education and alternative energy demonstration center located high in the Rocky Mountains near Aspen, CO. We offer educational programs in the fields of nutrition, education, and mind-body-spirit development. Topics range from world peace to energy conservation.

Our main building is heated by the sun, and powered in part by alternative energy sources. Our one-acre bio-intensive garden, greenhouse, and Bio-dome provide us with food, and we rejoice in our uniquely sublime climate, clean air, and good-natured staff.

Our programs are funded by John Denver, grants, and donations. Programs are priced moderately to allow them to be self-sustaining. Scholarships are awarded on the basis of applicant's needs, funds and space available for that program. Please write for more information and schedules. 3/28/91

Witness for Peace

**P.O. Box 567
Durham, NC 27702**

(919) 688-5049

Witness for Peace is a national organization of grass-roots activists working to mobilize public opinion and help change U.S. foreign policy to one which fosters justice, peace, and friendship with our Central American neighbors. WFP is developing an ever-broadening, prayerful, biblically-based community of U.S. citizens who are supporting continuous non-violent resistance to U.S. overt and covert intervention in the region. Many WFP delegations are visiting countries in Central America to document and report on the wars. Short-term delegates, long-term volunteers, media contacts, and legislative contacts are all needed. Our quarterly newsletter has a circulation of about 40,000; a suggested subscription donation is $25/yr. 12/18/89

Woman of Power

**P.O. Box 827
Cambridge, MA 02238**

(617) 625-7885

Woman of Power is a magazine of feminism, spirituality, and politics — a quarterly with exceptional literary and artistic works. "If we are to survive as a species, it is necessary for women to come into power and for feminist principles to rebuild the foundations of world cultures." Subscriptions: $28/year (4 issues), $46/two years; sample: $7. 12/12/89

World Future Society

**4916 St. Elmo Avenue
Bethesda, MD 20814**

(301) 656-8274

The World Future Society is an association of people interested in how social and technological developments are shaping the future. The Society was founded in 1966, and is chartered as a non-profit educational and scientific organization. We strive to serve as a neutral clearinghouse for ideas about the future — including forecasts, recommendations, and alternative scenarios. Membership is open to anyone who would like to know more about what the future will hold. We presently have 30,000 members in more than 80 countries, and over 100 local chapters worldwide. Annual dues, which include a subscription to our bimonthly magazine, are $30 in U.S. currency or its equivalent. 2/23/90

Worldwatch Institute

**1776 Massachusetts Ave, NW
Washington, DC 20036**

The Worldwatch Institute was founded in 1975 to inform policy-makers and the general public about the interdependence of the world economy and its environmental support systems. Our staff analyzes issues from a global perspective and within an integrated, interdisciplinary framework. We are an independent, non-profit research organization based in Washington, D.C.

Worldwatch's reports are designed to bridge the gap left by more traditional, specialized analyses. Our papers and magazines are distributed worldwide, responding to a strong demand for comprehensive public policy research. A $25 subscription includes all *Worldwatch Papers* released during the calendar year, plus a paperback edition of our annual *State of the World.* 3/21/89

Yad Tabenkin Institute

**P.O.B. Ramat Efal
52 960 ISRAEL**

**03-712221-4
03-344367**

Yad Tabenkin is the Research and Documentation Center for the United Kibbutz Movement. It offers a scholarship fund for research, and publishes a yearbook and selected works (including some by kibbutz members as well as papers from the labor movement and from the academic world). Yad Tabenkin also organizes Study Days and Symposia relating to both historical subjects and issues of vital immediate concern, and collaborates with different universities and institutes in the development of many projects. We have begun taping interviews with veterans of kibbutz and the labor movement — to preserve their stories of the early days. Current study circles are discussing specific problems including: questions of economics; political issues; Arab/Jewish relationships, security, and peace; kibbutz ideology; current kibbutz research; Israeli socialism and cooperation. 6/22/89

An Annual Gathering of womyn

late Aug. or early Sept.

Twin Oaks Community
Rt4 Box 169 Louisa, Va 23093
703-894-5126
for more info.

Yankee Permaculture

c/o Betsy Keenen
Box 264
Maloy, IA 50852

Yankee Permaculture publishes the world's largest collection of permaculture titles, including a species yearbook and a series of 15 Permaculture Design Pamphlets (placed in the public domain for free reproduction by all). We also publish a series of permaculture design slide/scripts, and distribute titles by important authors in the field. 5/22/89

Z (Zeta) Magazine

Institute for Cultural and
Social Change
116 Saint Botolph Street
Boston, MA 02115

We started Z two years ago because we thought the U.S. needed a periodical that would gather into one place in-depth news, opinion, and vision about the world and the Left. The result is a monthly 112-page, ad-free assemblage of news, analysis, vision, strategy, debate, reviews, interviews, cartoons, photo essays, and political art (deemed the best magazine of its class by *Utne Reader*). Our independent political magazine features critical thinking on the political, cultural, social, and economic life in the United States. We see that the racial, sexual, class, and political dimensions of personal life are fundamental to understanding and improving contemporary circumstances — and our aim is to assist activist efforts to attain a better future. Subscriptions cost $25 for one year (12 issues). 12/12/89

Reach Ads

Communities Forming:

Urban/Rural Peace Community: Philadelphia 50,000 sq. ft. building available 10 miles from downtown; residential area near playground. Cooperative and communal lifestyles devoted to peace and relationships, locally and worldwide. Will combine with rural community. Contact Aquarian Research (215) 849-3237 anytime or e-mail: AROSENBLUM on MCI or PeaceNet, TJCN72A on Prodigy.

Family with Land: Presently we live in Indiana, but we own a 75-acre farm in Kentucky which we would like to develop into a cooperative farm. We grow our food organically, and feel a spiritual connection with mother earth. We follow the Native American ways both in lifestyle and religion, and also belong to the Rainbow Family of Light. We have a business which is interior landscaping, done organically. Write: Carlos, Carol & Yolanda Alvarado, 4635 W. Franklin Road., Evansville IN 47712.

Couple seeks others who sincerely want to co-create an earth-healing intentional community. We are looking at land in the upper half of Indiana. We believe that creating the "social design" comes first, and are ready to jump into the challenging but rewarding process of collaborating in that design. Some pertinent features of the resulting community would probably be: regular community meetings; community decision making; in-house conflict resolution and arbitration process; cooperative projects; etc. Other features would include: ecological agriculture; alternative energy and technology; self-sufficiency; permaculture; earth-centered spirituality; bioregionalism; etc. Couples and families are encouraged in order to create a multigenerational community — and a community with heirs. Please contact Shepard & Tracy Hendrickson, 341 N. Hamilton, Indianapolis IN 46201. Phone (317)636-3977.

Namasté:
• Green/synergy center values
• 1600 hr/yr co-participation
• Consensus seeking
• Focus: "To enhance Life-Truth-Pursuit of Happiness"
• Holistic neighborhood, self-reliance as lifestyle
• Cohousing/personal sanctuary
• Conservancy/community land trust/permaculture
Namasté (603)776-7776, R2 Box 578, Barnstead NH 03225.

West Virginia: I would like to set up a small community here on my 142 acres in beautiful W.Va. Being a retired person this seems like a good way to perhaps not end up in a nursing home at great expense. For now I am in very good health and very active. I am interested in natural health, living within the ecological system, self-sufficiency, low-cost living, etc. Any who stay here need to be of the same inclination. Smoking, drinking, drugs, and junk food would not fit in. Interested in an herbalist, bee keeper, handy person with tools, farmer, or similar. Everyone would be independent, yet helpful when needed, cooperative in finding outside income. Interested in swapping when possible, using less electricity, growing food, canning, etc. ... whatever works. Write: High Horizons, HC-64 Box 169-A, Hillsboro WV 24946.

Help Wanted:

Wanted: people to fill two year-round positions: skilled maintenance person; cook. For 360-acre 52-year-old co-op camp and conference center SW Michigan Lake Country. Simple, rural, group lifestyle. Housing, board, benefits, modest salary. Write to:
Attn: Maintenance
Circle Pines Center
8650 Mullen Road
Delton, MI 49046

Products:

Great Alternative T-shirts. Peace & Environmental Messages. Top quality 100% cotton, multi-color printing. Free Brochure: Alternative T's, 411 W. Bijou, Colorado Springs CO 80905 (719)634-4622.

"Reach"...

is a regular feature intended to help match people looking for communities with communities looking for people. Please note that dated material requires a lead time of several months ahead of the anticipated publication date.

NOTE: Additional "Reach" and Classified Ads can be found on pages 310-311.

Late Entries

Ahimsa House

328 East William
Ann Arbor, MI 48104
(313) 662-2199

There are twelve of us "Ahimzoids" sharing a huge, 12-bedroom, beautiful old house in downtown Ann Arbor. We don't have much land to nurture, but are committed to supporting the earth by composting, recycling, reusing, etc. Our food is bought mostly in bulk; we have a working membership at the local food co-op, and a share in an organic farm nearby. Our house is vegetarian, with vegan options provided. We're famous for our superb dinners — each of us cooks once a week with a partner. There's also a list of house jobs that we choose from, and we come together once a month for house meetings. We each have varying schedules and lifestyles (with school, jobs, or freedom), but we try to accommodate different needs, and manage to have a fairly cohesive house ... usually. There are many popular Ahimsa activities — among them jam sessions, roof-top parties, yakking, and peace demonstrations. Being a hermit is acceptable, too. For those interested in joining, we usually have summer sublets, and September openings with one-year leases. Prospective Ahimzoids come to dinner to meet us, and may join if the house agrees by consensus. 5/30/91

Ananda Marga

97-38 42nd Avenue
Corona, NY 11368
(718) 898-1603

Ananda Marga (A/M) is a world-wide socio-spiritual group which was started in India in 1955 by Shrii Shrii Anandamurti, founded on the basic principle that all human beings should be given the opportunity to evolve themselves in all spheres of life — physical, intellectual, and spiritual. It now has Branches in more than 120 countries, and is devoted to bringing about a universal society based on love and Cosmic Brotherhood, "a new synthesis of spiritual and social values." Free instruction in meditation is available weekly at all Ananda Marga Centers.

A/M Schools synthesize the artistic expression of Rudolf Steiner with the all-round expansion of education. Their centers operate low-profit food stores and other industries — providing neighborhood residents with good products at a reasonable cost, and using the profits for local service projects. A/M has also estab-

lished an international relief organization that offers aid to those who suffer in the wake of natural disasters.

There are many Ananda Marga centers in North America, including: Denver, the Ozarks, D.C., and Memphis. The center in Corona, NY, serves as their North American headquarters. 5/21/91

Annwin

P.O. Box 48
Calpella, CA 95418

Annwin is a small neo-pagan/ecological community living on 55 wooded acres in Northern California. The residents here are caretakers of the land which is owned by the Church of All Worlds (see Late Entries/ Resources). We treat this land as sacred and hold our seasonal rites, festivals, handfastings, work parties, workshops, retreats, and staff meetings here. Annwin has a small pond, organic herb and vegetable garden, a small orchard, seasonal streams, hot tubs, a two-story Temple, two houses, and a canvas yurt. The land is semi-forested with Douglas fir, redwood, madrone, manzanita, bay laurel, introduced cedar, and various kinds of oak. We do *not* have electricity, hot running water, TV or telephones, and access is questionable at certain times of the year. We see ourselves as Stewards, not owners of this land, and we work hard to protect it. If you have a purpose for visiting our sanctuary, please write for our Visitors' Policy. 4/26/91

Atlantis Rising, Inc.

Silver Hill
Bradford, NH 03221
(603) 938-2723

Atlantis Rising, Inc. is a New Hampshire non-profit organization which has stewarded 128 acres since 1975. There is one family on the land and two others living in Massachusetts who split the taxes and the mortgage (now paid off); we are not looking for new members. Families sign 99-year leases to steward 5-acre parcels, upon which they can garden and build a home. Presently there is a small 3-acre garden and orchard; eventually we'll have 30 acres in agriculture.

Long-range plans include the construction of a 21st-century post-

industrial house, featuring solar design mixed with megalithic architecture inspired by Stonehenge and the Pyramids. We use mostly local wood, and minimal plywood. We have no utility electricity, and use sun energy. We are developing agriculture which respects the natural integrity of the existing ecosystem, and mimics the climax forest indigenous to the area. (Example: logging will be done very selectively, using horses to minimize the ecological disturbance.) We are also raising useful rare animals, including near extinct breeds of sheep and horses, to preserve genetic diversity. Visitors are welcome... please make arrangements in advance, and come prepared to camp. 4/25/91

Bear Creek Farms (Reforming)

c/o Bill Runner
Glenburn Star Route
Fall River Mills, CA 96028
(916) 336-5509

Bear Creek Farms was founded in 1985 by animation artist Sally J. Voorheis on a 26-acre backwoods mountain homestead dating back to 1856. We have access to a million-acre private timber preserve which surrounds our land. We are working to create a land trust, and there is also adjacent acreage for sale.

We are not plugged into "the grid", so produce whatever power we need through solar or hydro technology. In town (16 miles away) we own/operate a hostel, an animation studio, a gourmet restaurant, and commercial buildings. Consensus rule, spiritual tolerance, holistic lifestyle, and down-to-earth old-fashioned skills are blended here with high-tech solar equipment, blacksmithing, timber framing, and growing earthworms.

Membership is presently down to one couple plus an extended community of 15 others; we hope to grow to a maximum of 11 adults living on the land. We are looking for prospective members who are industrious, sober, organic, and creative. We can't accommodate single parents at this stage, and we 're not interested in welfare scams. Our politics are Libertarian; we are spiritually tolerant. No smoking or hard alcohol on the land. New members have a trail period. At this point we are only open to guests who are interested in joining — please enclose an SASE, a resume, and a description of what tools, finances, and expectations you would bring. 5/22/91

These late entries are included in the index that begins on page 314, and are summarized in the cross-reference chart on pages 302-303.

Catalyst (Forming)

RR #1, Box 3350
Plainfield, VT 05667
(802) 454-1032

A small group of friends is coming together to form a community in north central Vermont. We seek to be egalitarian, energy self-sufficient, and producing for our basic needs as much as possible. We are presently looking for additional members. 3/13/91

Cave Creek CLT

General Delivery
Bass, AR 72612
(501) 434-5265

Cave Creek Community Land trust is a non-profit open membership affiliate of the Ozark Regional Land Trust. Our 55 acres, acquired in 1987, has a land use plan that will meet the needs of the environment as well as future users. Approximately 40 elevated/forested acres are not suitable to agricultural production, but are ideal homesites which provide woodlots, road access, garden sites, water, and aesthetic surroundings. Five home sites of about 7 acres each are protected by conservation restrictions to prevent overcutting of the forest or contamination of the groundwater. The homesites are offered through low-cost lifetime leases, and the homes and other improvements on the sites will be owned by the lessees and may be sold when the lease is transferred or left to heirs.

The remaining 20 acres are in the heart of the watershed and serve as the principal demonstration site for our Keyline Project (an integrated system for managing the natural resources on a farm, and for accelerating the natural processes which restore soil fertility). A local agricultural cooperative is proceeding to develop and pay for the land project—members are joining together to cooperatively grow, process, and market food products of the farm. Equipment owned by the cooperative and its members is being used to develop the roads, housing, and water at minimal cost.

The CLT is the framework for demonstrating the important principle that application of Balanced Stewardship sustains the natural regenerative characteristics of the land and also sustains the people who must have affordable and productive land to live on. 3/21/90

Common Ground Farm

P.O. Box 2
Snow, OK 74567

These folks sent us a card stating "We do still exist as a community — how do we get listed?" We haven't heard any more. 4/10/89

Community Farm of Ann Arbor

8594 W. Huron River Drive
Dexter, MI 48130

(313) 426-3954

Community Farm of Ann Arbor, in existence since January 1988, grows organic produce for a community of people who live primarily in Washtenaw county. At this stage we are three growers and two apprentices, and none of us live at the present site. All of the agriculture is biodynamic (a system recognizing that food is not merely a chemical composition of matter, but also contains forces gathered from the sun, moon, and stars ... forces which nourish not just our bodies, but also our emotional and spiritual selves). In supporting Community Farm, our 170 members have chosen to assume a new kind of responsibility to the food system that nourishes them — members pledge both to support a social organization around the farm, and to provide its required financial support. Our goals:

• to utilize a sustainable method of agriculture, building and maintaining a healthy soil while producing high-quality food and providing the farmers with a just livelihood;

• to provide urban and suburban people access to a farm while putting "culture" (in the form of the rich relationships which result from community involvement) back into agriculture;

• to create a partnership in which the bounty and risks of production are shared by both consumers and producers; and

• to expand from our current vegetable production into a diversified dairy farm.

Our present 5-acre garden is on rented land; our goal for the coming year is to acquire a permanent site through the Potawatomi Community Land Trust. We also intend to add a team of draft horses, moving us toward diversity and away from fossil fuels. Our vision is that the growers and apprentices will live on the new land, and that the farm will become a self-contained organism (ecosystem). [There are more than 50 community-supported agriculture farms in North America — see Bio-Dynamic Farming & Gardening Association listing on page 256.] 5/21/91

Desiderata

c/o Gary Reynolds
404 Main Street
Smithville, TX 78957
(512)445-0233

Desiderata, established in 1975, is located on 120 acres north of Austin, TX. We have 11 two-acre homesites, and the rest of the land is held in common. Only one member family is presently living on the land; the other nine dwellings are either second homes, or retirement homes rented in the interim to non-members. One undeveloped lot is available; a couple of the homes are for sale. Most members needed to move back to town in order to finance the land and dwelling construction. 8/5/90

Duma

2244 Alder Street
Eugene, Oregon 97405
(503) 342-2656/343-5023

The Duma Co-op, established in '88, is a member-owned housing cooperative based on values of community, diversity & consensus (and we have a lot of fun). We have 15 members living in 2 households in Eugene, and are presently seeking new members. 5/26/91

Earth Family Farm

Box 241
Gardner, CO 81040
(303) 746-2332

Earth Family Farm provides an experience of living in community on a high mountain valley farm, as an extended family , while respecting each other's diversity, uniqueness, and solitude. We acknowledge the spiritual nature of all life forms and processes. Our common ground is a balance of ecocentric lifestyle and the search for our own inner ecology; this is a commitment to restoring the garden of Eden on earth through creating and teaching ways of nourishing ourselves which are sustainable and organic — including agriculture, foraging, diet, technology, architecture, relationships, healing arts, and living art.

Earth Family Farm is a vibrational dance of life upon the medicine wheel, gathering the four-directional teachings:

•North/simplicity: a purification and non-attachment to material things, possessions, ideas, and personalities; •South/nurturing: sharing, loving, growing with the spirit and family of all species; •East/celebration: a vision of gratefulness,

Late Entries

renewal, creativity, a rebirth of ancient memories while in the present; •West/emptiness: the inner journey of solitary dark and light while accepting the "creative void" within self and others, and the sacred completeness of all creation. 9/28/90

Ecanachaca Land Trust (Forming)

c/o Joan Thomas
P.O. Box 308
Sewanee, TN 37375
(615) 598-5942/598-5830

We are creating a land trust on 1100 acres situated on the Cumberland Plateau in Middle Tennessee. "Ecanachaca" is a Native American word meaning "holy ground." We plan to limit the number of households to 10 or 15. Our priorities are 1) to keep the land in one piece, with 2-5 acres entrusted to each member house-hold; 2) to create a sanctuary for all life; and 3) to encourage individual choice and responsibility within community. We are learning how to govern ourselves by consensus. At this time we have 5 adults and 1 child; we are open to meeting other interested people. 5/23/91

Eden Sanctuary (Forming)

2105 Scott Road
New Marshfield, OH 45766

"Go out from Babylon, declare this with a shout of joy, proclaim it, send it forth to the end of the earth."
—Isaiah 48:20

Babylon, capital city of the ancient empire castigated by the prophets of the Old Testament, epitomized a civilization gone wrong. Consumed with itself and the accumulation and protection of its material wealth, Babylon was encircled by armies and a huge wall. Within this wall, its people worshipped a god called Narduk that was symbolized by an 18-foot-high statue of gold.

We believe the modern industrialized nations of the world have become the new Babylon. Greed and materialism have again filled the vacuum to become the artificial and destructive deities for a people who have turned from the ways of God. There is again a massive "trusting in chariots" for its own "protection", and its collapse is equally inevitable.

The only functional difference today is the further development of technology which both increases Babylon's destructiveness and extends its ideology of greed worldwide through such insidious and seductive communication devices as TV.

Just as God called people out of ancient Babylon, so is God calling us today. Eden Sanctuary is being established as a refuge for those who hear this call. We consciously remove ourselves from the empire, refuse to participate in its obscene violence, and withdraw our consent from any claims regarding its legitimacy.

Although small in size (22 acres), we hope to catalyze the formation of other such sanctuaries. This beautiful hilltop land — being liberated from private ownership into a land trust — is blessed with fertile soil, abundant water, and an extensive growing season. Inspired by the Community of the Ark in France, which has successfully resisted assimilation for 35 years, we will ask people to take a vow of non-violence if they wish to become full-time residents. This vow helps bond us together to pursue a lifestyle in harmony with our beliefs regarding the sanctity of Creation. We seek total disengagement from the Babylon economy; we will use only ecological technologies (with an emphasis on hand tools); and we will act to alleviate hunger, reduce environmental degradation, and honor the sacredness of life through a vegetarian/ vegan diet. The community will be guided through collective discernment as we seek to follow the Voice within. For a more complete packet, please send an SASE. 4/9/91

Friends Lake Community

7700 Clark Lake Road
Chelsea, MI 48118
(313) 475-7976

In 1961 a group of Quaker families formed a cooperative community which emphasizes simplicity, ecology, and caring. We are a complex organization, open to persons of every faith and color, with diverse backgrounds and many overlapping areas of interest — our common ground is living with Quaker ideas as our guiding values. All community decisions are made using consensus.

Our 90 acres now has six families living or building on the land, with room for six more. We also enjoy an extended community of 150-200 members who use the land for retreat and recreation, and participate in meetings and celebrations. All members are expected to contribute three hours of labor per year, and are invited to participate in our work parties, educational programs, and monthly community/Board meetings (followed by potlucks or evening campfires and singing).

Sustaining members may acquire

life-time leases on cabin sites and home sites. All members have access to the many community facilities — the beaches, the boats, the lake and woods, the community buildings, and the campgrounds. We have also established a wildlife sanctuary, and a subgroup is developing a conference facility for activities consistent with our principles. 5/20/91

Gaia Community (Forming)

Route 1, Box 74
Mauk, GA 31058

Our "Gaia" Community is 30 miles east of Columbus, GA. We are an interracial group; Dee DeVille, our founder, is part Cherokee and part Afro-American. We are self-sustaining on the land, and a Land Trust. We are interested in staying connected with communities across the U.S. and the world, and could use referrals and information. 9/7/90

Galilee (Forming)

6215 S.E. 53rd Street
Portland, OR 97206
(503) 771-1491

Galilee is an egalitarian, non-denominational village of spiritual travelers who recognize the teachings of the world's religions as One Truth expressed as many truths. Each individual's truth is sacred and therefore honored as such. We encourage creative and artistic ways, and are an income-sharing cooperative corporation oriented toward networking with other groups for mutual economic, social, and spiritual benefits. We share a commitment to follow a spiritual path that is conducive to harmony within ourselves and with that which is all around us — separation from one another is a reality seen by the ego, but it is not the Truth. Our earth-oriented existence includes experiments with organic farming and indoor farming. At this point we have neither land prospects or financing. 6/5/90

Gorilla Choir House

Berkeley, CA
(415) 841-5367

The Gorilla Choir has been meeting every week for over five years, raising spirits in the flatlands of Berkeley. Our aim is to heal ourselves, heal the planet, demonstrate the Glory of the Presence in All, and have a good time.

Each week 10-40 people get together to sing songs from all of the world's spiritual traditions. Our material is all-inclusive, ranging from silly to sublime, and is never sung the same way twice. As we deepen our ability to hold, express, and empower the vision, we align ourselves with the Sacred Hoop of Life — just breathing, making sounds, and monkeying around.

Our small household exists to indulge the Gorilla Project — participants in the weekly sing came up with a downpayment to purchase the house. Choir members are all generic world servers; choir membership is determined by participation, and embraces a diverse range of individual philosophies (we have political radicals and pacifists, rich and poor, gay and straight ... you name it). Four choir members live here, living fairly independent lives while enjoying each others' company. 5/21/91

Greenbriar Community

Box 466
Elgin, TX 78621
(512) 285-2661

Established in 1969, we are a loose-knit community of 25 adults and 25 children living on 170 acres near Austin, Texas. What really holds us together is our school, which is based on "non-coercive alternative education." Our houses are arranged in a village cluster to allow lots of open land, including a 45-acre wildlife corridor. The community has no specific religion, but every aspect seems to be represented within our membership. Similarly, our dietary preferences range from Vegans to meat-eaters. We have limited facilities, so are not looking for more members and are not open to unannounced drop-in visitors. 5/22/91

Harvest Hills Association

14 Oak Hill Cluster
Independence, MO 64057
(816) 229-6836

Harvest Hills is still a viable entity after 20 years of learning about what it means to live in community. There are now 60 families with all ages represented — including 22 people over sixty-five years of age, and 46 children under the age of sixteen. The community owns outright about 40 acres of semi-wooded land, as well as a building consisting of six condominium units, a community center, and a community swimming pool.

Early members were involved in the Reformed Latter Day Saints church; it's still a major influence, but not a restriction. Our current membership in multi-racial, and there are at least a dozen different religious denominations represented in the resident families.

Our original philosophy remains intact, and many of the original signers of our covenant are still living in the community. Basically, we envisioned a community with all homes located around a common green in which children could play in view of all of the residents; automobiles are not allowed in this area. The arrangement of the community has been especially good for mothers and the rearing of children. Homes are owned by the individuals, and there are still vacant lots open for additional buildings. The community welcomes anyone who would like to be part of an intentional community based on Christ's values. For more information please write to the attention of: The President, Harvest Hills. 12/15/80

Hawkwind Earth Renewal Cooperative

P.O. Box 11
Valley Head, AL 35989
(205) 635-6304 eves best

Our 90-acre primitive retreat is nestled in the northern Alabama mountains, and is home to a developing healing arts center. We have/are creating co-ops for membership, organic gardening, livestock, food storage, arts & crafts — plus we have summer & winter campgrounds, a timesharing tipi, and a seminar center. We hold classes and public gatherings on a regular basis; facilities are available for private gatherings with 30 days advance reservation.

Our spiritual path is a combination of Native American, Earth traditions, and Paganism; we have many elders form many tribes. The community makes its decisions by majority rule, using a council process.

Our resident population varies with the seasons, ranging from 6 to 10 adults in the winter up to 15 in the summer, with 2-10 children. We have a support network of over one thousand members. Most members trade time to cover their monthly share of costs. 5/8/91

Hei Wa House

1402 Hill Street
Ann Arbor, MI 48104
(313) 994-4937

Hei Wa house was started in 1985 by a group of political activists with a vision of a communal house that would provide support for our political work. In the years that followed we have moved twice and many things have changed.

We are a vegetarian cooperative non-smoking household, with a membership that fluctuates between 8 and 12 people. We are a diverse group with a wide range of occupations and interests. We are working folks, artists, healers, radical faeries, and students. We pride ourselves in the diversity of our sexual orientations.

A countercultural and anti-establishment feeling pervades the house. While having no fixed ideology, many of us are influenced by anarchism, ecology, feminism, nonviolence, paganism, and socialism. Housemates have been involved in various political issues including gay rights, AIDS activism, hemp legalization, radical agriculture, urban issues, community organizing, women's rights, environmental issues, anti-militarism, and anti-war actions.

We try to live ecologically by recycling, conserving, and eating simple food grown locally and organically. We have a small urban garden, get most of our produce from a local biodynamic community-supported farm, and also support our local co-ops and cooperative warehouse. We are known to eat the wild plants that grow in our yard.

Our decision making is by consensus. If you are interested in visiting us you must contact us in advance. 5/22/91

Himalayan Institute

Route 1, Box 400
Honesdale, PA 18431
(717) 253-5551

The Himalayan International Institute of Yoga Science and Philosophy of the U.S.A. is a non-profit organization devoted to teaching holistic health, yoga, and meditation as means to foster the personal growth of the individual and the betterment of society. Founded in 1971 by Sri Swami Rama, the Institute combines Western and Eastern teachings and techniques to develop educational, therapeutic, and *(Continued...)*

Late Entries

Himalayan Institute *(Cont'd.)*
research programs.

The Institute provides a peaceful environment as well as training facilities at its beautiful headquarters in the Pocono Mountains of northeastern Pennsylvania. People of all ages, nationalities, faiths, and professions come to our seminars, classes, and workshops—which range widely from such subjects as meditation, Hatha yoga, and health awareness — to stress management, counselor/ therapist training, and biofeedback. Unique to the structure of our programs is a continuing synthesis of ancient teachings and disciplines with Western scientific and experimental traditions. Our research syste-matically explores such fields as medicine and psychotherapy — as well as diet, nutrition, and exercise in relation to their mutual influence upon an individual's growth in health and maturity.

Our courses emphasize the total integration of body, mind, and spirit. The faculty and staff have expertise in various professional fields and are also involved in their own self-training so that they bring reflective experience to their classes. In its practical philosophy the Institute looks upon the realization of human potentials as a lifelong experience leading to increased health, creativity, and happiness. 4/30/91

Hollyhock Farm

Box 127, Manson's Landing
Cortes Island, B.C.
CANADA V0P-1K0
(604) 935-6465

Established in '82, Hollyhock is a community and conference center on Cortes Island, surrounded by forest and beach. We provide retreat facilities, and sponsor summer workshops in the practical, creative, and healing arts. Highlights include morning yoga with a qualified instructor, and wonderful vegetarian and seafood cuisine — the garden supplies herbs, berries, vegetables, and flowers. 5/16/88

Human Potential Foundation

at Zaca Lake
P.O. Box 187
Los Olivos, CA 93441
(805) 688-4891/686-4678

In the heart of the San Rafael mountains there thrives a small community of 14 adults and 3 children drawn together as The Human Potential Foundation. Our goal is a gradual moving toward self-sufficiency, to be a model of balance in the interdependence between man and nature, to be a center of learning and a refuge for contemplation.

We have 320 acres fed year-round by natural springs. The land is a strange, beautiful blending of desert environment and rock mountains to the north, with pine forest to the south. There is a spectacular array of plants and wildlife living in and coming through the valley at all times of the year.

At the present time we are primarily a wilderness resort, however we are in a process of transition through which we are planning to integrate a work-study program with a broader program in holistic studies. We are a nonprofit organization which hosts such annual events as Special Olympics and Special Christmas. We also have seminar/workshop facilities, and operate a full-service restaurant in our main lodge which looks out over Zaca Lake.

We welcome any individuals who would like to become part of the community — come for a visit, and perhaps we can find a space for you. We offer room, board, a living allowance, and many fringe benefits in exchange for 40 hours a week of community service. 5/21/90

Institute for Cultural Affairs (ICA)

ICA Information Services
206 E. Fourth Street
New York, NY 10009

The Institute of Cultural Affairs, an international organization founded as the Ecumenical Institute in Chicago in 1954, is today active in some 35 countries. Our network has a spiritual focus which is inclusive of all faiths, and which places a high value on diversity, participation, and globality. Each center is staffed by a group of volunteers. The following are North American residential centers for the ICA, which may also be known as the Global Order, or Order Ecumenical:

Chicago/ICA
4750 N. Sheridan Road
Chicago, IL 60640
(312)769-6363

Indianapolis/ICA Earthcare
3038 Fall Creek Parkway
Indianapolis, IN 46205
(317)925-9297 (see p. 271)

Mexico City/ICA
Instituto de Asuntos Culturales
Oriente 158 No. 232
Colonia Moctezuma
15500 Mexico D.F., Mexico
(52-5)571-4135

Phoenix/Order Ecumenical
4220 North 25th Street #4
Phoenix, AZ 85016
(602)468-0605 (see p. 207)

Residential Learning Center
22421 - 39th Avenue SE
Bothel, WA 98021-7911
(206)486-5164

Seattle/ICA
1504 - 25th Avenue
Seattle, WA 98122
(206)323-2100/322-6266

Toronto/ICA
577 Kingston Road, Suite 1
Toronto, Ontario
M4E-1R3 Canada
(416)691-2316

Washington/ICA
1301 Longfellow Street, N.W.
Washington, DC 20011
(202)882-6284

There are also ICA residential centers in these cities on other continents; Write ICA Information Services (NY) for additional information: 3/30/91

Bombay, India
Brussels, Belgium
Guatemala City, Guatemala C.A.
Hong Kong
Kuala Lumpur, Malaysia
Nairobi, Kenya
Rio De Janero, Brazil
Sydney, Australia
Taipei, Republic of China
Tokyo, Japan

Institute of What Have You (Forming)

P.O. Box 82
Gays Mills, WI 54632
(608) 735-4878

The Institute of What Have You is — education, inspiration, and networking in sustainable community economics and interpersonal relationships. It is a space for those conscious of the effects of mindful action on the environment, psyche, soul, and heart. We inhabit a rambling old storefront/workshop which we are restoring into healthy home and work areas in a rural village in southwestern Wisconsin. We recognize the value of work, love, meditation, care, and cooperation. All of us here are members.

We have no hierarchy. We operate

by a consensus process facilitated by a council meeting every day consisting of at least three people. All consensus decisions are recorded and subject to a one-day evaluation.

Our projects include: Kickapoo Press, consisting of print and audio booklets, newsletters, factsheets, and children's books; audio/visual productions of ecological concern; a graphic activists network; handicrafts including jewelry, silk screening, tie-dye, pottery, and toys; Mississippi Watershed Alliance; free clothing and book exchange; Redirected Energies, which promotes alternative energy use; Bikes Not Bombs; Healthy Foods Network, which provides organic foods and sustainable agriculture within a 300-mile radius of Chicago; and the Organic Farm Labor Pool. Everyone is welcome to join in our activities and share their visions, love, and heartsongs. 9/1/90

Johnston Center for Individualized Learning (Bekins Hall)

**University of Redlands
1200 East Colton Avenue
Redlands, CA 92373**

**(714) 335-4071 Secretary
335-4059 Lobby**

An alternative education center based on the concept that each individual has the ability to create their own education through an individualized learning process. The atmosphere is "Living & Learning" (13 professors have offices within the student residence complex). Students live co-operatively, and are responsible for coming up with their own system of government. Meetings happen every week or two, and are by consensus; we handling everything from kitchen rules to how to allocate the budget (how much to spend on community activism, the garden, repairs, or to bring in a band for a party). We do our own policy about alcohol, etc., and attempt to take responsibility for how we live; sometimes we get to struggle with the administration over the issue of autonomy. 4/25/91

Light Morning

**Route 2, Box 150
Copper Hill, VA 24079**

Light Morning joined the Fellowship subsequent to the first printing of the Directory. No other information is presently available. 4/1/91

Maharishi International University

**Fairfield, IA 52556
(515) 472-5031; 472-6929 Fax**

Maharishi International University is a a fully-accredited university with teachings through the PhD level in many fields, with a curriculum based on a one-week block system. About one-third of the population of our small town is affiliated with the University. All in all, we have 1,800 faculty, staff, and students — plus 2,000 others associated with the international T.M. (Transcendental Meditation) movement.

There are now over three million T.M. meditators worldwide, and one of our goals is to get 7,000 meditators living in one place on each continent — to create a spiritual coherence which will provide the basis to help establish world peace. We already have centers in the U.S., Holland, Moscow, and India ... and we're now working on Japan.

Nearby we are building a totally integrated 5,000-room complex (houses, cabins, and dorms) on 1,500 acres (made of materials friendly to the environment). The financing is independent, but integrated, with a $150 million budget. In addition to creating jobs, the project will stimulate a retirement community.

Long-range plans include the development of an electric car system. This ties in well with our general tendency to pursue high-tech, environmentally friendly businesses. A high proportion of our members are new-age entrepreneurs — and the local economy is booming (in contrast to the rest of surrounding region). For example, one of our members has invented a computer shield which blocks out hazardous rays; another has developed an electric car business. 5/1/91

Maxworks Cooperative

**716 West Maxwell Street
Chicago, IL 60607**

(312) 226-3248

Pro-environment workers' cooperative, based in a historic downtown Chicago public market district, undertakes to retrieve, stockpile, re-process and remarket those rejected resources which are found in the waste product of Chicago's markets, industries and neighborhoods. Maxworks recycles cardboard, paper, glass, metals, plastics; designs and manufactures new product where possible rather than scrap the materials; convert pre-used lumber into appropriate carpentry: workbenches, shelving, lofts, ladders, recycling and compost bins, bike-tandem carts, alternative energy structures, bird houses, anti-overdose smoking systems, artparts, educative hardwood toys, building repair and restoration, landscaping and gardening. Art, graphics and publications; outings for pro-environment projects; Greens movement networking and provision of aid and lodging; exchange of visits, including extended residence, with workers and organizations of foreign countries; guests and members contribute $25/week Maxtax and 14 hours per week of productivity time.

Maxworks attempts to portray the idea that re-using a rejected 2x4 in downtown Chicago is tantamount to saving an equivalent poundage of living tree, together with its vegetative and animal dependencies anywhere in earthforest. Regional emphasis: save and revitalize the Maxwell Market (Jewtown), pre-eminent bastion of economic democracy in mid-America, with its tradition of one-on-one, co-operative trade between buyer and seller and resource sharing between barter-partners. 9/1/90

Methow Center of Enlightenment

**P.O. Box 976
Twisp, WA 98856**

(509) 997-3147

The Holy Wise Ones have designated the Methow Center of Enlightenment to be a major spiritual center in development upon this planet. It is the responsibility of each spiritual group upstairs to position their ground ambassadors, aligning them with their spiritual center of choice. It is unfortunate that so few can actually align with these centers, and ironic that the future of mankind lies in back country rural areas where natural uncontaminated resources are plentiful. Our inter-dimensional celestial project in north central Washington is designed to be a major Communications Command Post, Cultural Development Learning and Healing Center for all who have access to it. Space people (U.F.O. intelligences) from all dimensions will come and go freely from this Celestial City location.

We here at Methow are reaching out to gather in as many as Divine Guidance and time allow (earth and

Late Entries

Methow Center *(Cont'd.)*

economic changes). Naturally, they bring with them their inter-dimensional resources which adds to our strength here on all levels. Our goal of 2,000 to settle with us seems realistic. In addition to gathering our many cosmic friends, our top priority is the construction of pyramid green houses for high volume, high energy food production.

At Methow there are no rules or regulations of any kind, since the whole valley is our spiritual center, including everybody in it. This plan has been approved by the Holy Wise Ones. It is clean, simple, and allows for every one to do their thing naturally, finding their way in their own time. 7/15/90

Octagon Community

250 Bonita Glen Drive #E2
Chula Vista, CA 91910

(619) 426-2666

We are a small intentional community engaged in marketing and installing waterless toilets. Very little need be said about the tremendous waste of fresh water and loss of organic matter resulting from the current use of flush toilets. Our many successful installations lead us to believe that waterless toilets are most appropriate when used in households of more than 10 persons, so other intentional communities seem to be the best method of providing and publicizing this 200-year-old technology. We are happy to share our information. 2/23/91

Osho Ansu Meditation Center

P.O. Box 200-166
Lake Oswego, OR 97034

(503) 638-5240; 638-5101 Fax

A Garden of the Beloved...

"My function here is to make you aware of the false and the phony and the unreal and the superficial.

"Right now as you exist, you don't have any depth, you don't have any height. You exist as persona; you are not yet aware of the essence. And only the essence can have heights and depths. But to become alert that 'I am shallow' is good, tremendously important, significant. Don't forget it again: remember it. It will hurt, it will become a pain in the heart, it will become a wound. It will be like an arrow going deeper and deeper; and it will become more and more painful.

"That is the journey that every seeker has to go through. That is the pain which is needed for your rebirth ... great arrangements are needed before somebody can enter the collective unconscious, because so much is there, millions of experiences....

"The closed garden is needed — because it is not a question for the ordinary masses to know about; they will not be able to understand.... They cannot understand what; this is a scientific lab. People are being transformed; people are moving into new dimensions, taking quantum leaps, arriving into new spaces. You cannot watch these things from the outside."
—OSHO (Bagwan Sri Rajneesh) 4/24/91

Paideia (Forming)

Progressive Community
Associates
P.O. Box 122
Athens, OH 45701

Paideia is the word for the ancient Greek ideal that a humane culture and education would serve two basic tasks: 1) that of fostering all of one's native potentialities and giving them scope through a choice of contexts, and 2) cultivating a sense of social responsibility so that a person freely takes it upon oneself to improves one's community in every way.

A small, human-scale community, Paideia combines the best of professional and personal worlds, giving people with similar backgrounds and personal values the chance to join together to achieve new dreams and visions. The land consists of 70 acres divided into five-acre, wooded building sites, and 17 acres of common land. It is designed for people who want to pursue their private goals in the context of a larger, caring group of similarly-minded individuals. At Paideia the emphasis is on: the family, materially simpler living, creativity, communication, continued learning, ecological consciousness, shared planning, participatory democracy, and a full range of collaborative endeavors. Paideia is not a retreat from the "real world" but rather, an attempt to restore human-scale living and values in that world.

A wide variety of cooperative enterprises, from high-tech to low-tech, are anticipated. Among these may be electronic "cottage industries", mail-order companies, human services providers, greenhouses and small farming projects, communication/ publishing concerns, and small manufacturing companies.

At this point our main task is to form a community of people who share similar work and personal interests — so we have compiled a questionnaire to identify those similarities. Once a sufficient number of people with common interests have been identified, we will arrange exploratory weekend meetings to discuss cooperative work possibilities as well as the many other aspects of community life — a dynamic exchange of ideas, tours of the land and building sites, discussions about land acquisition and costs, and consultation on home construction. Residents will have the opportunity to make their own housing choices, spending as little or as much as they desire. If this may be what you're looking for, please write for more information and a copy of our questionnaire. 3/31/91

Port Centauri (Forming)

P.O. Box 11919
Pueblo, CO 81001

Port Centauri is stewarding 5,000 acres of beautiful high plains desert ranch in southern Colorado, land that has been untouched by mankind for hundreds of thousands of years — and most recently has been held sacred by the Native American Indians of this region, to be used when the collective consciousness was ready for the Great Spirit to reveal its Self in the heart of all beings. Port Centauri is about coming together as ONE, to exist totally in the Love vibration, to do the will of the Creator. We each have something to offer and some-thing to receive from the ONE as we create a new reality. Port Centauri is a Light Center for Mother Earth, located strategically in a network of centers to provide energy linkups for the planet as do the chakras for our bodies.

Today Port Centauri is being used to graze cattle and horses, and is a haven for those seeking peace and solitude on their paths to enlightenment. Over 300 guests blessed the land in 1989, many from the far corners of the world. We seek 400 individuals, each contributing $1,000, to pay off the debt of the ranch. Each contributor/participant will receive a share in the corporation that will own the property after the banks are out of the picture. This will give each individual a legal undivided interest in the entire 5,000 acres. In other words, if one is so moved to contribute $1,000 (or participate by just radiating Love), they will have unlimited use of the entire property. Come build a home, camp, vacation, play, and/or participate in endless creative opportunities.

Such creative expressions might include: raising organic food with or without greenhouses, reintroducing to the land buffalo and other native life, constructing a community lodge, developing springs, planting trees, building sweat lodges, constructing recreational facilities, utilizing the vortex/portals here to enhance spiritual development, creating healing centers, developing infrastructures to support space brother activities, expanding the network and its facilities and equipment, establishing a community newspaper, creating works of art, developing a global communications center, constructing an amphitheater for the performing arts, building learning centers to advance personal/planetary consciousness, establishing meditation facilities, organizing a library that supports expanding planetary consciousness, promoting research and development of science and arts, living your dreams without limitations. 12/15/90

Quaker House

Residential Program
5615 S. Woodlawn Avenue
Chicago, IL 60637

(312) 288-3066

The Residential Community at Quaker House (QHRP) is made up of men and women, students and working people — with various religious heritages and differing life goals. What we share in common is a desire to commit our lives to moral, purposeful action; to grow spiritually; and to seek ways of being of service to others. Most residents do volunteer work with public school kids.

Established by the 57th Street Meeting of Friends in Chicago, QHRP is an opportunity for 8 or 9 people to live together in community for one or two years, sharing the facilities of a large 19-room house which is also the Quaker Meeting House. Residents exchange ideas, work together, encourage one another, and enjoy each others' company. A residential director gives assistance in planning and realizing such community-building activities as outings, study groups, work projects, service projects, and many fun times together. Group decisions are made using the Quaker principles of clearness and unity,

though one needn't be a Quaker to live here.

Each resident has his/her own room, or may choose to share with another resident. Quaker House takes care of food purchasing and dinner preparations (five days a week) in order that residents can devote more time and energy to individual and group activities, spiritual growth, and service. Residents are responsible for minor household chores; a housekeeper maintains most areas of the house. 5/23/91

Quarry Hill

c/o Ladybelle Fiske
P.O. Box 301
Rochester, VT 05767

(802) 767-3902/767-9881

Quarry Hill, Vermont's oldest and largest alternative community, was founded in 1946 as an artists' retreat — Quarry Hill has been a haven for creative and open-minded people for 45 years. During the 1960s and '70s we experienced a surge in population and became a closely-knit community, though not a planned, "intentional" one. Among the few rules: *absolutely no violence towards children.* We run a small private school. Folks generally make their own expenses, though members help each other out as necessary. Families typically eat on their own, with occasional potlucks.

Visitors are welcome! We have a small dormitory. Bring tents for summer camping (the best season for visits). Possible longer residence — though we have 80 or more in our group, we are always happy to meet energetic, non-dogmatic, helpful people! We are looking for doctors, and teachers. Please write or call first, and ask for our brochure. Small financial contribution requested, or work exchange if broke. 5/2/91

Rejenneration House (Forming)

Box 42
Jenner, CA 95450

(707) 578-1951

Rejenneration is a family village cluster now forming on 5 knolltop acres in an ecologically diverse canyon on the Sonoma coast. Our current plans include building two or three buildings in which to live and work, and developing ample garden space. We are looking for 5-8 total partners with a

long-term vision of shared ownership. Values will be clarified as we evolve, and now include: simplicity; hard work; shared meals; earth stewardship; respect for biological, cultural, age, and spiritual diversity; and a healthful, balanced lifestyle. We have a long-term goal of becoming a sanctuary for our urban-dwelling friends — who can use our nearby variety of ecosystems to regenerate their personal spirit and connection with the planet. Please send SASE for more information; if you include your phone number, we may call you back if our schedule permits. 4/25/91

Revolutionary Tomato

Oakland, CA
(415) 547-8935

The Revolutionary Tomato is an urban household of 5 adults and 2 children who live together because we believe that communal living is healthy … it is our preferred lifestyle.

Our decision-making process might be best described as "benevolent anarchy" — housemates working on projects make decisions as things come up. If others question that decision, the matter is resolved, more or less by consensus. Basically things are decided by whoever is involved in any given project. Shopping and bathroom cleaning are the only rotating chores; all else relies on individual awareness and motivation. We eat together most nights, and really enjoy good food.

In raising our kids there is a lot of shared parenting, but the arrangements are mostly informal at this point. Several of our members are deeply involved in work for peace and social justice, though the house was not formed with that as a central focus. 8/20/90

Rosy Branch Farm

320 Stone Mountain Road
Black Mountain, NC 28711
(704) 669-6353

Rosy Branch Farm is a neo-indigenous forest community with an interest in ancient cultures and permaculture. Begun in '85, we originally came together through a meditation group with ecological and spiritual interests. We currently have 5 families living on the land (50 acres) with at least one more to come. We are not actively seeking new members, but we're into cooperation and *(Cont'd.)*

Late Entries

Rosy Branch Farm *(Cont'd.)*

the sharing of information — including labor exchange, trading visits, etc.

We're into what might be called high-tech simple living — fairly affluent, but downwardly mobile in a substantial sense. Economically each family is fairly independent, though we're developing right livelihood at the community level. We have created a non-profit project called Good Medicine which works to raise awareness of the large population of Mayan people in Guatemala and Mexico. We believe that indigenous values are valuable to the earth — there's a lot for our culture to learn about living within the limits of our resources. We arrange periodic trips to their region, help the weavers sell their goods, and publish a quarterly newsletter called *Maya Time*. Community and cooperation are very helpful in pursuing this work. 4/25/91

Sangamon River Community (Forming)

c/o Doug Hahn
106 N. Third St.
Champaign, IL 61820

(217) 355-1688

We are a group of five adults (two women, three men) and would eventually like to number around ten or so. We wish to live as a supportive family of friends. Our goal is to operate under the principles of egalitarianism, eco-consciousness, individual spiritual freedom, and consensus decision making.

Some of our collective and/or individual interests include: the partnership ideals in the book *The Chalice and the Blade*, alternative energy, eco-feminism, raising our own food, (eventually) unhooking from the grid, providing a space for creative expression and humor, group encounter, exploring positive gender roles, beginning a community-based business to become economically self-sufficient, pagan/earth-based spirituality, vegetarianism, and other neat stuff. Since we are just forming there are many possibilities.

As this listing goes to press we are going through the process of purchasing an 80-acre farm on the Sangamon river, 16 miles west of Champaign-Urbana, Illinois. It has a farm house, wooded areas, pasture, and a big old barn. We will need to build additional housing and community spaces before we can increase our numbers. 5/9/91

Shalom Community

6017 Bush Road
Brown Summit, NC 27214

(919) 621-5702

Shalom Community is a 46-acre housing cooperative, with present membership at 9 adults and 4 children. We hold 22 acres in common, and have with 18 individual lots. Joining costs are approximately $20,000 for a 3-acre lot. Decisions are made by consensus, and officers are rotated. We eat together weekly. [For more information see article on page 29.] SASE preferred [cc]. 4/15/91

Society of Love Alchemists (Forming)

c/o Paul Michael
P.O. Box 1119
Lake Stevens, WA 98258

We're just now beginning something we call the 'Delta 8 Game' and Friendship Arks. The vision is based upon the teachings of the audio cassette: *The Love Communalist Wo-Manifesto (A Planetary Partiers' Guide to Enlightening Up!)*. The teachings involve small communities made up of 4 men and 4 women holding things in common, co-parenting the children, worshipping Father/Mother God as the Personal Ground of Being, and engaging 'transterritorial' group tantra and rotational partnering. To create communal finances we sell a product called 'Excella' which is used for regenerating our bodies. Please write for more information. 9/12/90

Starseed Community (Forming)

Chapel Road
Savoy, MA 01256

(413) 743-0417

We are presently one family living on 130 acres in a remote area of Massachusets, up in the hills. Our six buildings include two houses and a cabin. We are interested in having others join us, but are presently trying to figure out our economic base — we are thinking about creating a retreat and recovery center here for people wanting to deal with stress and addictions. 4/15/91

The Third Place House

314 First Avenue North
Mt. Vernon, IA 52314

(319) 895-8517

The House is what we call a collective. We are four people living in a two-story, 4-bedroom house in lovely Mt. Vernon, Iowa. We share all incurred expenses, splitting bills equally. This allows us to exist comfortably within the limited budget of college graduates in the late 20th century. An individual's bills and debts are taken care of by that individual.

The most important feature of our shared reality is that we buy food as a household and fix homestyle dinners. Work and chores are distributed with relative equality in mind. We have a code of respect for individuals and privacy that seems to cover most circumstances. This is not a new idea. None of it is. But we have found that our "house" provides more than just an economic shelter, it allows us to communicate, interact, and share our learning and resources with one another — much to the benefit of everyone involve. It's difficult to imagine living any other way.

One member of the household (with lots of encouragement and support from the rest of us) publishes *The Box Elder Bug Oracle* — a quarterly art/fun/philosophy newsletter, funded entirely by donations, with the aim of creating a community in print. Submissions range from the pragmatic, to the esoteric, to the twisted. Please write or call if you'd like to know more about the Oracle, or just to say "Hi". 8/18/90

Veiled Cliffs Community (Forming)

15826 State Route 218
Scottown, OH 45678

(614) 256-1400

We're a new group living on a 145-acre farm in southwestern Ohio, with 7 members that share all income (three work at outside jobs full-time, one part-time). We have major financial debt which we hope to clear in two-year's time — to pay off the land debt, and to build a "home" place. We now live in the old farmhouse which has limited living space. Our plan is to begin a cottage industry which will permit most of us to work at home. We raise goats for meat, milk, and milk products; and also raise chickens for eggs and meat. We expect to raise all of our own vegetables and a portion of our fruit. We are not blindly committed to self-sufficiency, but acknowledge that the more we can do at home the better — so long as the cost does not increase unreasonably, and the things that we buy are "politically correct" and of acceptable quality.

Our purpose is to live with regard for other people, other living beings, and the earth. We share in the common belief that all life is growing and learning, and that we can benefit from honest association with all other life forms.

Though space here is at a premium, we would be grateful to have short visits from members of other communities. If you are passing through this area, stop by and share your piece of wisdom with us — we can certainly only benefit. 8/31/90

Whetstone Community (Forming)

P.O. Box 1798
Benson, AZ 85602

(602) 586-9356

Whetstone Community, established in '88, is comprised of 6 adults living on 275 acres located about fifty miles east of Tucson. We are open to children, though we have none presently. We have room for 69 households, and hope to be very self-sufficient. The land is in a privately-held land trust, and people can buy in; investment is mostly by building homes through a limited equity arrangement (the trust gets any appreciation).

The community was set up to provide affordable housing — members can build a pretty decent house for 20% of its assessed value. We work on each others homes, paying each other with credits — like a barn-raising, except with a bookkeeping system. The economic structure is independent, but we occasionally do custom work as a co-op. One member's livelihood is building rammed-earth, passive solar, energy-efficient designs — two on the property are complete, and another two shells are underway. Our long-range vision is to turn the building company into a cooperative, building up an alternative economy and doing for ourselves whatever we need.

We are trying to figure out how to do meetings, potlucks, etc. — ways to get together at least a couple of times a month. The details will be determined as we become a little more established. In the trust, decisions are majority vote based on equity. Community-level decisions are made through a Village Council. 4/26/91

The Wilfred

24 Dearborn Road
Medford, MA 02155

(617) 666-9849

The Wilfred is a seven-person cooperative house located in a working class neighborhood of Boston. The house is in its sixth year of operation, and the focus of our group is having shared dinners every night. We welcome visitors. 4/28/91

Windward Foundation

P.O. Box 51
Klickitat, WA 98628

(509) 369-2448

Single parents, retirees, gifted kids (human and caprine), and dreamers from 7 to 75 are pioneering a woodsy community, seeking saner social systems, practicing nearly-lost crafts, and enjoying the longest-running gathering of Mensans (since 9/88). Windward is a think tank, an operating farm, a school for self-reliance, and an extended family. It's a 60-acre research and development park with more than a hundred tons of tools of all kinds, including a foundry. It's a synergy machine that empowers people by combining their life experiences, training, and insights to minimize wasted effort. It's a place to hide away in peace and beauty to write a book or focus on a project you've always wanted to tackle.

Windward is a non-profit Washington corporation which owns the land and most of the tools and living spaces. Members retain ownership of other assets, and organize projects to suit their interests. It is cooperative in structure, and operates by the consensus process. We've been at this for 15 years and there are 16 members.

Our members have their own projects and interests, generally a combination of monetary and personal agendas. Various members raise goats, sheep, rabbits, geese, chickens, calves, and other animals; make cheese, sausage, soap, shoes, and circuit boards; design timber frames with ACAD; cut logs on a sawmill; shear sheep; spin yarns, knit, crochet, weave, and quilt; bake bread and pies from scratch, etc. What could you add to our concentric systems? 3/25/91

Zen Community of N.Y.

114 Woodworth Avenue
Yonkers, NY 10701

(914) 375-1510; 375-1514 Fax

The Zen Community of New York is an interfaith community which integrates meditation, livelihood, social action, and study. Our residents work and live in southwest Yonkers, an impoverished neighborhood just north of New York City. Since 1982 we have opened three businesses which have trained and hired hundreds of unemployed neighborhood residents in baking, office, and construction skills. In 1987 we began a not-for-profit so-cial service organization, Greystone Family Inn, which provides homeless families with permanent housing and services which they need to rebuild their lives and the lives of their children.

Ours is a remarkable network of organizations accommodating some 75 people of different national and religious backgrounds, committed to ending homelessness in our community within the next decade, while creating a model of community development that can be applied anywhere. We urgently need more staffing for our programs — child care workers, counselors, job trainers, secretaries — and volunteers from around the country who want to come here to help. We are also seeking financial help to start a development fund to be used to incubate new projects that address the needs of the greater community — such as an AIDS hospice, and the University of the Streets (a community-based education program designed to enable poor and homeless people to explore their potential as far as they wish to go). 1/25/91

Late Entries

Please send us:
information to update the listings in our 1993 edition:

- Address Changes
- New Phone Numbers
- Leads to New Groups
- Reports of groups that have folded
- Volunteers to serve as local or regional contacts for outreach
- Your Suggestions

Communities Directory
Sandhill Farm
Route 1, Box 155
Rutledge, MO 63563
(816)883-5543

Late Entries: Cross-Reference Chart

Sorted Alphabetically

Map #	Community Name	Forming?	State/Prov	Land/Bldgs	Rur/Urb	Year Est?	Adults	Chld	Max?	More? A	More? C	Sch? Visitors?	Gen?	Join Fee	Decis? C/M	Wt?	Gr	Ea	Or	Vg	Fl	Ld	B	Rm	Econ S?	L/mo	$/mo	Op?	Sexual Restr?	Spirit Basis	L?	P	F	VS	Other Values / Remarks
A	Ahimsa House		MI	12 Rm	U	80	12	0	12	S	M		S	235 Dep	C	N	N	Y	P	P	Y	N	N	N	N	25	340	N	N	N	N	N	P	P	S	Peace, Tolerance, Fun...
AA	Ananda Marga		NY	Network		54				Y	Y		Y		N	Y	N		V			C	C	Cb					N			N	Y	Y	Y	NQ Synthesize Spirit/Social
B	Annwin		CA	55 ac	R	80s				Y	Y	Qm	Y					Y		Y		C								P/Ecl		Y	Y	Y	NQ Sacred Land; Neo-Pagan
BB	Atlantis Rising	(F)	NH	128 ac	R	75	2+4			Y	Y		Y				S	Y				C	I	F	N	Y									Y	NQ Land Co-op; Stewardship
C	Bear Creek Farms	(F)	CA	26 ac	R	85	2+15	0+?	11a(+c)	Y	Y		N	N	C	N	S	Y	Y	N	Y	I	I	F	N	Y		N	Y	N	N	N	S	S	S	Holistic;Creativity;Libertarian
CC	Catalyst	(F)	VT	53 ac	R	90				Y	Y		Y				S		Y			F								F					Y	NQ Egalitarian;Self-Sufficient
D	Cave Creek CLT		AR	53 ac	R	87			5 Fam	Y	Y		Y					Y		Y		L	I	F												NQ Keyline Farming Project
DD	Common Ground Farm		OK		R																															NQ No Info Available
E	Com. Farm Ann Arbor		MI	7 ac	R	88	?	0		P	P		Y	Varies	Cb		Y	S	Y	N	Y	N	N		S	Y		N		N	N		N	S	Y	Community Sppt'd Agriculture
EE	Desiderata		TX	120 ac	R	75	17	?	11 Fam	Y	Y	Pu	Y	Varies	M	N	N	S	N	S	N	Cb	I	F	N	Var	80	N	N	N	N	N	N	N	S	Land Co-op; Rural Living
FF	Dirna		OR	2 Hs	U	88	15	?	?	Y					C	N		Y				C	C	R	N				N	N		N		N	N	NQ Diversity; Consensus
F	Earth Family Farm		CO		R																															NQ Ecology;Extended Family
FF	Ecanachaca		TN	1100 ac	R	91	5	1	15 Fam	Y	Y		Y		C	N	C	N	P		Y	L	I	F	N			Y	N	Y		N		Y		NQ Sanctuary for All Life
FG	Eden Sanctuary	(F)	OH	22 ac	R	91	1	0		Y	Y		Y		C	N	C	N	P		Y	I		F				Y		Y	Y			N		NQ Refuge f/ Consumerism
G	Friends Lake		MI	90 ac	R	61	?	?	12 Fam	Y	Y		Y	360	C	N	S	S	P	S	Y	C	I	F	N	3/yr	60	N	N	QkEc	N	P	P	P	Retreat,Recreatn,QuakerVals
GG	Gaia Community	(F)	GA		R					Y	Y		Y					Y				L													Y	NQ Int'l Netwrking;Interracial
H	Galilee	(F)	OR	4 Rm	U	90	2	0	N	Y	Y	U	Y	N	Cb	N	N	P	Y	Y	N	U	U	U	P	Y		N	U	N	Ecm	N	Y	N	Y	Environmental Consciousness
HH	Gorilla Choir House		CA	4 Rm	U	85	4	0	Same	N	N		N	N	Y	N	Y	Y	Y	N	S	Y	C	C	R	N		Y		N	Ed	N	S	S	S	Soul Singing Here Now
J	Greenbriar		TX	171 ac	R	69	25	25	Same	N	N	Qm	M		C	N															Ed					NQ Non-Coercive Education
JJ	Harvest Hills		MO	40 ac	R*	71	60	?	?	N	N		Y									Cb	I	F							C/Ecl					NQ Christ's Way; Multi-Racial
K	Hawkwind		AL	90 ac	R	87	10+5	2+8		Y	Y		Y	Varies	M	N	Y	Y	N	Y	N		I	F	N	2-7			N	NAm		S	N	Y	Healing Arts Center; Primitive
KK	Hei Wa House		MI	11 Rm	U	85	8-11	0	Same	P	M		Y	N	C	N	S	Y	Y	N*	Y	N	N	R	N	Y		Y	N	N		N	Y	Y	Y	Activists;Artists;Countrculture
L	Himalayan Inst		PA	Network		71	N.A		Hdqrtrs	Y	Y		Y																		E	Y		N	Y	NQ Yoga, Health, Meditation
LL	Hollyhock Farm		B.C.	20+ ac	R	82	16	?	Same	N	N	Cb	Y					Y	S	Y	N	C	I	F	N			Y	N	N		N		N		NQ Wkshop Cntr; Land Co-op
M	Human Potential Fdtn		CA	320 ac	R	85	14	3		Y	Y		Y					Y				C													Y	NQ Wilderness Retreat
MM	Instit f/ Cultural Affairs		NY	Network		54			Hdqrtrs	Y	Y		Y					Y				C	C	R	Y	Y		Y	N		Ecm		Y			NQ Diversity; Participation
N	Instit What Have You		WI	U*	90								Y		C	N		Y	Y	Y	Y	C	C	R				Y	N		N		Y	Y	Y	NQ Sustain Econ&Relatships
NN	Johnston Center		CA	Dorm	U	69				S			S	N	C	N		N	Y	Y	N*	N	N	R	N	Y		Y	N	N	N	N	P	P	S	NQ Alt. Education Center
P	Light Morning	(F)	VA		R		2	0		Y	Y		Y					Y																N		NQ Interested in Land Trust
PP	Maharishi University		IA	1500 ac	U*				5,000	Y	Y		Y												60	100				E	Y				NQ Transcendental Meditat'n
PQ	Maxworks Co-op		IL		U*	84				Y			Y					S																	Y	NQ Recycle Urban Waste
Q	Methow		WA		R		Small		2,000	Y	Y		Y																Y						NQ Learning/Healing; UFOs
QQ	Octagon		CA		U																								Y						NQ Waterless Toilets
R	Osho Ansu Medtn Cntr		OR																											E					NQ Rajneesh Teachings
RR	Paideia	(F)	OH	70 ac	R	91	1	0	10 Fam	Y	Y		Y	Y				S				Y	C	I	F				Y	Y	N	N	Y	Y	Y	NQ Human-Scale Community
S	Port Centauri	(F)	CO	5000 ac	R	87	1	0		Y	Y		Y	0-1,000				P				Y	C	I	F				Y	Y	N	N		Y		NQ Light Center; UFOs
SS	Quaker House		IL	9 Rm Hse	U	90	8	2	Same	P	P		Y	N	C	N	N	Y	S	N*	Y	C	C	R	N		525	N	N	N	N	N	Y	Y	P	Spiritual Growth; Service
T	Quarry Hill		VT	200+ ac	R	46	50	30		Y	Y	Qm	Y				S		Y										Y	N		Y	Y	Y	NQ Artist Retreat;Non-Dogma
TT	Rejenera'n House	(F)	CA	5ac	R	90	1	0	5-8adlts	Y	Y		Y		C	N		Y	Y	Y	Y	C						Y		Ecl	N				NQ Family Village Cluster
U	Revolutionary Tomato		CA	1 Hs	U	83	5	2	Same	Y	N	Cb	N	N	C	N		N	Y	Y	N*	I	I	R	N	P	375+	N	N		N	N		Y	Y	Communal Living
UU	Rosy Branch Farm		NC	50 ac	R	85	10+2	10+	Same	N	N		Y					S	S	Y	Y	C	I	F	Y			Y	N		N			N	Y	NQ Indigenous Values
V	Sangamon River	(F)	IL	80 ac	R	91	5	0	10adlts	Y	Y		Y		C	N		S	Y	Y	Y	C						M		P	N		Y	Y	Y	NQ Egalitarian; Ecology

Directory of Intentional Communities
Page 302

Key to the Headings: *Map#:* Corresponds to numbers on the maps. *More?* [A]Adults, [C]Children *Sch?* Kind of Schooling? *Gen?* Gender: Women or Men only?
Decis? [C/M]Consensus or Majority? [Wt?]Weighted Decisions? *Food/Diet?* [Gr]Grow Own? [Ea]Eat Together? [Or]Organic/Whole Grains? [Vg]Vegetarian? [Fl]Flexible?
Ownership: [Ld]Land? [B]Buildings? [Rm]Rooming/Accommodations Style? *Economic Sharing:* [S?]Income Sharing? [L/mo]Labor/Month? [$/mo]Cost/Month
[Op?]Income-Earning Opportunities? *Spirituality:* [B]Basis? [L?]Leader? *Values:* [P]Pacifist? [F]Feminist? [VS]Voluntary Simplicity?

Late Entries: Cross-Reference Chart

Sorted Alphabetically

Community Name / Map #	Forming?	State/Prov	Land/Bldgs	Rur/Urb	Year Est?	Adults	Chld	Max?	More? A	More? C	Sch? Visitors?	Gen?	Join Fee	Decis? C/M	Wt?	Food Gr	Food Ea	Food Or	Food Vg	Food Fl	Ownshp Ld	Ownshp B	Ownshp Rm	Econ S?	Econ L/mo	Econ $/mo	Econ Op?	Sexual Restr?	Spirit Basis L?	Values P	Values F	Values VS	Other Values / Remarks
YY Shalom		NC	40 ac	T	75	9	4	≈18a+8c	Y	Y	Ob	Y	≈20,000	C		S	Y	N	N	Y	C	C	F	F	N		Y	N	N	N	S	Y	S	Co-op; Informal Structure
W Soci. Love Alchem	(F)	WA		U	91			4w+4m	Y	Y														Y			Y	Y	Y				NQ Love Communalist Mnfsto
WW Starseed	(F)	MA	130 ac	R	89	2	?		Y	Y	Y					Y								Y			Y		Y				NQ Retreat/Recovery Center
X Third Place House		IA	4 Rm	U	86	4	0	Same	Y	N	Y		N	C		N	Y	N	N	N	N	N	R	N	10-2		N	N	N		P	P	Cappuccino Addictions
XX Veiled Cliffs	(F)	OH	145 ac	R	90	7	0		Y	Y	Y					Y	Y	Y	Y	N	C	C	R	Y		350	Y	N	N		N	N	NQ Regard Earth & All Beings
Y Whetstone		AZ	275 ac	R	88	6	0	60 Fam	Y	Y	Y	Varies	M	Y			Y	Y	N	Y	L	I	F	N			N						NQ Affordable Housing
YY The Wilfred		MA	7 Rm	U	85	7	0	Same	P											Y	N	N	R	N				N	N				NQ Shared Dinner Nightly
Z Windward Foundation		WA	60 ac	R	88	16	?		Y	Y	Y		C	N						C	N	N		N			Y	N	N				NQ Mensan Think Tank
ZZ Zen Community (NY)		NY		U	82	75	?		Y	Y	Y		C	Y						Y				N			Y	E	Y				NQ Meditation; Social Action

Late Entry Communities: Sorted alphabetically within State or Province

Alabama
Hawkwind, Valley Head, AL

Arizona
Whetstone, Benson

Arkansas
Cave Creek CLT, Bass

British Columbia
Hollyhock Farm, Cortes Island

California
Annwin, Calpella
Bear Creek Farms, Fall River Mills
Gorilla Choir House, Berkeley
Human Potential Fdtn., Los Olivos
Johnston Center: Bekins Hall, Redlands
Octagon Community, Chula Vista
Rejemeration House, Jenner
Revolutionary Tomato, Oakland

Colorado
Earth Family Farm, Gardner
Port Centauri, Pueblo

Georgia
Gaia Community, Mauk

Illinois
Maxworks Cooperative, Chicago
Quaker House, Chicago
Sangamon River Community, Champaign

Iowa
Maharishi Int'l. University, Fairfield
Third Place House, Mt. Vernon

Massachusetts
Starseed Community, Savoy
The Wilfred, Medford

Michigan
Ahimsa House, Ann Arbor
Community Farm of Ann Arbor, Dexter
Friends Lake Community, Chelsea
Hei Wa House, Ann Arbor

Missouri
Harvest Hills, Independence

New Hampshire
Atlantis Rising, Inc., Bradford

New York
Ananda Marga, Corona
Institute for Cultural Affairs, NYC
Zen Community of New York, Yonkers

North Carolina
Rosy Branch Farm, Black Mountain
Shalom Community, Brown Summi

Ohio
Eden Sanctuary, New Marshfield
Paideia, Athens
Veiled Cliffs Community, Scottown

Oklahoma
Common Ground Farm Snow, OK

Oregon
Duma, Eugene
Galilee, Portland
Osho Ansu Meditation Center, Lake Oswego

Pennsylvania
Himalayan Institute, Honesdale

Tennessee
Ecanachaca Land Trust, Sewanee

Texas
Desiderata, Smithville
Greenbriar Community, Elgin

Vermont
Catalyst, Plainfield
Quarry Hill, Rochester

Virginia
Light Morning, Copper Hill

Washington
Methow Center, Twisp
Society of Love Alchemists, Lake Stevens
Windward Foundation, Klickitat

Wisconsin
Institute of What Have You, Gays Mills

Key to the Chart Codes is on pages 144-145

Directory of Intentional Communities

California Action Network

P.O. Box 464
Davis, CA 95617

(916) 756-8518

CAN publishes an annual Organic Wholesalers Directory and Yearbook, a well-indexed listing of food growers, processors, manufacturers, organic farm supply sources, groups certifying organic products, and support groups located all across North America. The directory includes articles about the politics of the industry, i.e., how organic produce is documented and certified. Good for finding suppliers in your area, and locating farmers who sell via mail order. 9/21/89

Children & Community Network

14556 Little Greenhorn Road
Grass Valley, CA 95945

Children and Community Network (formerly known as "Making Contact") is for home schoolers, unschoolers, alternative schoolers — and those looking for child-oriented community, neighbors, and friends. For more information, please send an SASE. (Nationwide!) 8/1/90

Church of All Worlds & The Green Egg Magazine

P.O. Box 1542
Ukiah, CA 95482

(707) 485-7787

The Church of All Worlds, founded in 1962, is an organization of individuals who regard the Earth and life on it as sacred. Living in harmony and understanding with life's myriad forms is a religious act. In 1970 CAW was the first of the Neo-Pagan Earth Religions to obtain full Federal recognition.

While we prescribe no particular dogma or creed, our commonality lies in our reverence and connection with Nature and with Mother Earth, seeing her as a conscious, living entity. We are not only Her children, but evolving cells in Her vast, organic body. We embrace philosophical concepts of immanent divinity and emergent evolution. We are essentially "Neo-Pagan", implying an eclectic reconstruction of ancient Nature religions, and combining archetypes of many cultures with other mystic and spiritual disciplines.

But we are not just trying to recreate a Paradise Lost; we are actively involved in helping to save the present world as well as working to actualize a visionary future. We offer philosophical alternatives to present "life-negating" paradigms that produce war, profiteering, racism, sexism, exploitation and desecration of our natural resources. Instead we work to heal the splits. Some of our individual paths include Shamanism, Witchcraft, Voudoun, Buddhism, Hinduism, and Sufism — as well as science fiction, transpersonal psychology, bodywork, artistic expression, and paths of service.

Over the years, CAW has chartered a number of subsidiary branch organizations through which we practice and teach our religion. The Church owns "Annwin", a community in Northern California (see separate listing in Late Entries/Communities) which is our heart and sanctuary. We also publish a quarterly, *Green Egg* magazine, which features interviews, essays, fiction, comics, environmental action, columns, and an extensive reader forum. One-year subscriptions are $13 U.S., $18 Canada, $27 trans-Atlantic air, $30 trans-Pacific air; back issues are $5 U.S. postpaid. 4/26/91

Cooperative Grocer

P.O. Box 597
Athens, OH 45701

(614) 448-7333
(800) 878-7333

Cooperative Grocer is a bi-monthly trade publication reaching food cooperatives throughout the U.S. and Canada. Published since 1985, it offers professional advice and inspiring examples of successful co-op activities — written by people working in and with these co-op enterprises. It also features editorials, industry news, advertisements from suppliers to the co-op sector, and a regular column specially devoted to education and training for boards of directors. Cooperative Grocer can supply references to help find a co-op, and information about positions open in food co-ops. Subscriptions are $22 for 6 issues. The publication is also supported by and available through regional co-op distributors. [We expect to have new phone numbers as of 5/15/91.] 4/10/91

Deep Dish TV Network

339 Lafayette Street
New York, NY 0012

(212) 473-8933 Office
420-8223 Fax
PeaceNet: deepdish
Telex: 155258505 deepdish

Deep Dish TV is a national grassroots/public access satellite network which links community producers, programmers, activists, and people who support the idea and reality of a progressive television network. We assemble material from around the world and transmit it to community television stations and home dish owners nationwide.

Deep Dish is devoted to decentralizing media by providing a national forum — in addition to our own productions, we have a distribution cooperative for programs made independently and/or locally. Where commercial stations present a homogeneous and one-dimensional view of society, Deep Dish thrives on diversity and encourages creative programming that educates and activates the viewer. We seek out programs by and about people rarely seen on television: people of color, women, working people, people of different ages and from many regions.

Deep Dish TV is available on over 300 cable systems around the country, as well as selected public television stations. Call your local cable system for information; if they do not run Deep Dish programming, contact your local programmer and ask for it (they probably have a receiver which will work; if not, a local university, art center, or even a bar might be willing to help). Anyone with a home dish can receive Deep Dish — it's transmitted unscrambled on commercial "C" band satellite transponders. The exact times and channels vary from season to season, so check a satellite television guide or contact our New York office. 3/11/91

Family Tree

P.O. Box 315
Chestnut Hill, MA 02167
(508) 263-8629

Family Tree is an organization of people actively interested and/or participating in alternative relationship and family lifestyles. Our objectives are: 1) to provide a forum for the exchange of information and experiences, 2) to provide a meeting place and sponsor social and growth related events, and 3) to contribute to increased understanding and acceptance of alternative lifestyles. We are concerned with all forms of committed living styles which contribute to the fullest realization of the human potential for caring, intimacy, and growth. We do not press upon our members any specific behavior or values, but encourage and support individual freedom and interpersonal responsibility in the exploration and development of viable options for living. 4/3/91

Fourth World Services

P.O. Box 2154
Evansville, IN 47728

(812) 477-2730

The Fourth World in Hopi prophecy is our current era of materialism, in which the needs of the natural world are forsaken. The Fifth World is now dawning with our return to the practice of earth stewardship.

Fourth World Services provides access to information, products, and other resources necessary for a lifestyle which respects the integrity of the natural world, and which balances this concern with human needs. Human society is becoming more of a global culture, and so a corresponding need is for individuals to maintain control over the institutions which affect their lives. Consensual governing processes and economic democracy build a socially responsible culture, while affirming the inherent worth and dignity of every person. 4/27/91

Garden of Eden Project (Forming)

P.O. Box 303
Palermo, CA 95968

(916) 534-5150

The Garden of Eden Project will be establishing Essene health retreats for all to enjoy. All Essene Garden of Eden Health Retreats are to always be free — never a charge for anything, running on donations only. All retreats are going to be totally covered with all the good organic fruits, nuts, vegetables, grains, and flowers that each area will produce — 100% living foods for all! We will employ the best of technology and the great gifts of the Creation.

The so-called tide of civilization and its need of cars, trucks, etc. can be channelled into complete control

and harmony by the establishment of totally self-sufficient land parcels where cars are not allowed; where organic food, natural lifestyles, and safety for all living things are the highest priorities. 10/15/90

Green Letter

P.O. Box 14141
San Francisco, CA 94114

The Green Letter is a quarterly review of international events from a Green perspective. It is produced by a collective, and is an "official" vehicle for disseminating news from the Green Committees of Correspondence, a network of local groups spread across the U.S.(see separate listing on page 270). A one-year subscription is $20. 4/30/91

The Human Awareness Institute

1720 S. Amphlett Blvd. #128
San Mateo, CA 94402

(415) 571-5524

HAI offers workshops year round on "Sex, Love, and Intimacy" — held in Boston, Detroit, Australia, and at Harbin Springs (near Calistoga, CA). We have organized a support network in the San Francisco Bay Area which gathers once a month to reunite with old friends, introduce new friends, and to explore in depth the principles of unconditional loving; rap sessions and experiential exercises are often included. We also publish a bi-monthly journal which contains articles on living the principles, and disseminates information about parties, workshops, and informal gatherings of varying focus. Subscriptions are $18/year, payable to *Enlighten Journal*; all journal subscriptions and correspondence should be submitted to Chip August, 1905 Menalto Ave., Menlo Park CA 94025 (415)326-7712. 3/15/91

Innovative Housing

325 Doherty Drive
Larkspur, CA 94939
(415) 924-6400

Innovative Housing, a non-profit organization, has organized several hundred shared households on the West Coast — heavily concentrated in the San Francisco Bay Area, but also strong in the Pacific Northwest and in Southern California. They offer

workshops which introduce people to group living, then help them form compatible groups by clarifying needs and desires, and by teaching shared living skills. Usually, they hold "master leases" on rental properties, acting as go-between for conservative landlords and the more liberal householders. With a heavy ratio of low-income participants, almost half are single parents or elderly. Innovative Housing has worked closely with the Cohousing Company, and publishes a monthly newsletter. 7/15/90

Inter-Cooperative Council

Room 4002, Michigan Union
Ann Arbor, MI 48109-1349

(313) 662-4414

The Inter-Cooperative Council (ICC) was formed in 1937 by the housing co-ops on the University of Michigan campus — in order to gain greater efficiency and economy in certain functions, such as recruitment of new members, paying the taxes and mortgages, and overseeing large maintenance projects. In addition, ICC helps train new members and officers so that houses run more smoothly.

We are housing for students, owned and run by students, with 18 units ranging in size from 13 to 90 members, the average size being about 33. All are co-ed. The buildings range from wood-frame to brick, from historic to modern. We have non-smoking houses and houses that share vegetarian meals. Most houses serve lunch and dinner daily, while breakfast is do-it-yourself.

Houses are run democratically, each member having an equal voice. At house meetings students decide how much to spend on food, when quiet hours will be, what newspapers to subscribe to, what to do about a problem member, what work needs to be done, and so on. We rely on members to do all the work needed to run the houses — cooking, cleaning, planning, bookkeeping, recruiting, etc. — and each member puts in 4-6 hours of work per week. 5/9/91

InterCommunities of Virginia

[See page 135]

The InterCommunities of Virginia is an association of intentional communities. We are diverse in size,

Late Entries

InterCommunities *(Cont'd.)*

design, and intention... yet share many common values*: 1) an emphasis on cooperation and some form of resource/skills sharing, with norms of non-discrimination, non-sexism, and valuing individual equality and individual differences; 2) a commitment to personal and social change — the psychological and spiritual growth of our members, and service to society carried out in a community setting where individual needs are balanced with group needs; 3) a desire to "live lightly on the earth" — reducing consumption, recycling resources, embracing appropriate-scale technology and renewable energy sources; and 4) an awareness of the oneness of humanity and all life, and a conscious response to the global crisis through development of social and cultural designs for a more peaceful, ecological, and egalitarian world. We organize network gatherings twice each year, rotating host responsibilities among our member communities. 5/1/91

* Much of this list was adapted from *Builders of the Dawn* by Corinne McLaughlin & Gordon Davidson.

Intinet Resource Center

P.O. Box 2096-C
Mill Valley, CA 94942

(415) 507-1739

Intinet Resource Center was founded in 1984 by Dr. Deborah Anapol. Our mission is to serve as a clearinghouse for information on ethical multimate relationships, a network to link up people and organizations exploring new paradigms for sexualove, and a resource center to encourage designs for healthy and happy families. Members receive quarterly progress reports. For further information send an SASE.

IRC publishes *A Resource Guide for the Responsible Non-Monogamist*. Over 100 pages of hard-to-find information on ethical multipartner sexualove relationships. Includes annotated bibliographies, directory of organizations, articles, films, tapes, seminars, and other valuable tools for creating a multimate lovestyle. To order send $12.95 + $2 shipping and handling. 3/19/91

The Long Island Alternative

P.O. Box 452
Farmingville, NY 11738

(516) 737-1571

Provides a variety of viewpoints on the culture, politics, people, issues, and ideas that mainstream media ignores or just plain doesn't see. Features articles about such topics as the environment, homelessness, racism, reproductive rights, civil liberties, homophobia, capital punishment, and political activism. Although the fight for intellectual freedom is a serious matter and one not to be taken lightly, articles in the publication are apt to take a humorous slant as the editors strive to maintain that tenuous balance between scholarly discourse and side-splitting jest. Published bi-monthly. One year subscriptions are $6 for individuals, $10 for organizations; sample copies $1.50. 3/29/91

Parents Leadership Institute

P.O. Box 50492
Palo Alto, CA 94303

The Parents Leadership Institute offers classes and resource groups for parents who want to learn from one another as they build close relationships with their children, and good lives for themselves as parents. PLI publishes a series of useful pamphlets on parental listening skills — dealing with situations such as special time, building trust, "playlistening", tantrums, and indignation. Please write for more information. 3/21/90

Political Ecology Group (PEG)

519 Castro, Box 111
San Francisco, CA 94114

(415) 861-5045

PEG is s new, all volunteer, action-oriented research and public education group making the links between ecology, militarism, and social justice. Our first Action Paper, *War in the Gulf: An Environmental Perspective*, is a tool designed for activists, the press, and students — for educating themselves and others about the environmental impacts of the war. Please send $1.50 for a copy; $.50 each for orders of 100 or more (prices include postage). 2/7/91

Robert K. Greenleaf Center

1100 West 42nd Street, #321
Indianapolis, IN 46208

(317) 925-2677 (Phone & Fax)

Robert Greenleaf (d. 11/90) was Director of Management Research for AT&T for years, and was known as "The Conscience of AT&T". His focus was a humanistic approach to management. He retired in 1964 and founded the Center for Applied Ethics, and in 1970 wrote his famous "Leader as Servant" essay. In 1985 the center was moved to Indianapolis and renamed the Robert K. Greenleaf Center. The Center offers an insightful series of pamphlets and books about various aspects of leadership and service. 12/2/90

SEAC

Student Environmental
Action Coalition
P.O. Box 1168
Chapel Hill, NC 27514-1168

(919) 967-4600

SEAC is a grassroots democratic network of students and student groups on more than 1000 campuses across the country, all working together to build a strong student movement to save the planet. Students have been doing isolated organizing for too long — through sharing ideas, strategies, facts, and tactics we all grow more effective.

We are here to help students in whatever way we can. If you are doing an action and need lots of people — we can help hook you up with other active students near you. If you want to start a new campaign and don't know where to start, we can send you both factual and practical information written by students who started successful campaigns on their own campuses. If you've done incredible things on your campus and in your community, we can help you get the word out to motivate and inspire other students. If you need help finding speakers or getting in touch with media, we can provide names and numbers.

SEAC is what you make it... the more we hear from folks across the country, the better we are able to support student actions and initiatives. We publish a newsletter, monthly (ideally) through the school year, and once in the summer. Annual memberships are $15 for students,

$25 for student groups, and non-students/non-youth can become Friends of SEAC for $35. 4/12/91

Sing Out

P.O. Box 5253
Bethlehem, PA 18015-5253
(215)865-5366

Sing Out is a non-profit tax-exempt corporation dedicated to the preservation of the cultural diversity and heritage of traditional folk music; to support creators of new folk music from all countries and cultures; to expand the definition of folk music to include ethnic music; and to encourage the practice of folk music as a living phenomenon. A $15 annual membership includes a subscription to our folksong magazine, *Sing Out!*, which has come out quarterly since May of 1950. We also nationally syndicate a weekly one-hour folk music program available to all National Public Radio stations, and maintain a resource center — a multi-media library containing thousands of recordings, books, periodicals, photographs, video tapes, and ephemera. This is a free resource for members! We also publish *Rise Up singing*, a 288-page folksong sourcebook with words, guitar chords, and sources to 1200 songs of all sorts: traditional, political, folk, rock, Motown, children's, and more — $17.50 for one copy; $8 plus postage on full cartons(30 copies). 2/19/91

Sun Health Books

P.O. Box 1967-BH
New Haven, CT 06509-1967
(203) 498-2000

We are publishing the '91-'92 *Vegetarian Home & Travel Guide* (Eastern and Western editions) by Viktoras P. Kulvinskas, M.S.; Peter E. Firk; and Barry M. Harris, B.A. The guide features over 40 categories, including: New Age Communities & Homesteading, Organic Gardening, Natural Foods Restaurants, Vegetarian Health Resorts, Mail-Order New Age Prod-ucts, Health food Stores & Co-ops, Health Charts, Recipes, Ecology, Yoga, Macrobiotics, Films & Videos, Natural Childbirth, and much more. Color cover, 8-1/2" x 11" format, spiral bound, 1200+ listings. Projected press dates: Eastern U.S. (Fall '91), Western U.S. (Spring '92). Price: $9.50 per edition. Mention that you read about their guide in the "Directory of

Intentional Communities" and receive a $2.00 discount coupon/order form (no limit: please specify number). Wholesale and distributorship inquiries welcome. 4/15/91

Volunteers for Peace, Inc.

"International Workcamps"
Tiffany Road
Belmont, VT 05730
(802) 259-2759; 259-2922 Fax

Workcamps are an inexpensive and personal way that you can travel, live, and work in a foreign country. As an international short-term "peace corps", they are a fun-filled adventure in global education. The program allows people from diverse cultural backgrounds, with a wide variety of social and political viewpoints, to live and work together. — where the power of love and friendship can transform prejudice.

Workcamps are sponsored by an organization in a host country, and coordinated by people from the local community. Groups of 10-20 people live together, generally cooperatively like a family, in a school, church, private homes, or community center. Work-campers coordinate and share the day-to-day activities such as food preparation, work, and entertainment. The work atmosphere is casual, and typically involves construction, restoration, environmental, social, agricultural, or maintenance projects. The *1990 International Workcamp Directory* (112 pp.) contains over 800 listings of volunteer work camp opportunities in 33 countries. Individual memberships are $10, and include a copy of the directory. 3/15/90

Walden Two International Association

c/o Los Horcones
APDO 372, Hermosillo
Sonora, MEXICO 83000

This association was founded by Los Horcones for the purpose of sharing information about our developments and findings with those persons who would not live here but want to participate in some way in the development of a Walden Two community. We also disseminate information about the basic characteristics of a Walden Two and its social contributions — and to increase the degree in which we receive technical, economic, or any other kind of help. Members receive our newsletter,

articles published by and about Los Horcones, and invitations to seminars and other activities. Memberships are $17/year. 12/14/88

War Resisters League

339 Lafayette Street
New York, NY 10012
(212) 228-0450

Our work is to resist war in all its forms, by providing the public with information, materials, and workshops. To support our work we sell books that make a difference, plus T-shirts, posters, buttons, cards, pins, calendars, etc. Donations are always appreciated. Write if you'd like to know how to get more involved in your area. 9/21/90

Worker Owned Network

94 North Columbus Road
Athens, OH 45701
(614) 592-3854

Worker Owned Network (WON) is a cooperative economic development organization working in southeastern Ohio. WON has provided business development services to worker cooperatives since 1985. We have worked closely with about ten co-ops here in Athens county, and about five of those are currently active in our network (a Mexican restaurant, a commercial bakery, a recumbent bicycle manufacturer, a commercial cleaning business, and an "accessible housing" construction business.

Over the past two years, we have created a 12,000-sq.ft. cooperative business incubator to provide space and support services for new businesses. Recently we have begun extending our co-op organizing experience to the development of flexible manufacturing networks (FMNs) — creating temporary production networks wherein several firms can combine their resources and strengths, enabling them to manufacture and distribute products that none of the businesses could produce individually. 5/22/91

Directory of Intentional Communities

Sandhill Farm
Route 1, Box 155
Rutledge, MO 63563
(816)883-5543

GANAS COMMUNITY

A NYC group living experiment in open communication.
Committed to developing active motivation for
Truth, reason, love, & a better quality of life
established by the Foundation For Feedback Learning (F.F.F.L.),
a non-religious, non-profit, educational research organization.
135 Corson Avenue • Staten Island, NY 10301 • (718)720-5378/981-7365

A group of friends formed the FOUNDATION FOR FEEDBACK LEARNING in San Francisco in 1978. Six of us moved to New York together in the spring of 1979. We pooled our resources to buy and remodel a comfortable old 14-room house. By 1988 our numbers had grown a lot and we had acquired and renovated six more buildings. We expect to stop expanding at approximately 50 people. At that point, if we have developed a good model, we hope to be instrumental in helping other small communities to form, grow and prosper — as affiliated but autonomous self-governing cooperatives.

About 40 of us now live in five large, attractive, adjacent houses. Up to 25 of us work on the premises, or in the community's retail businesses housed in our two commercial buildings nearby. We are located in a lower middle income, integrated neighborhood in Staten Island, New York, one half-hour's ferry ride from downtown Manhattan. About 15 of the people who live in our community work in the city, or attend local universities.

Our ages have ranged from 18-80. The majority of us are between 30 and 45. No children live here at the moment, but they have in the past and probably will again. Many of us have lived and/or worked together on and off for from 5 to 25 years.

A number of us are in monogamous or open couples, some married, some not. The rest engage in the whole range of social practices usual for unattached people.

Representatives of almost every ethnic group, nationality, religious or other belief system, and socioeconomic, cultural background have lived here together in peace — and the differences are stimulating and enriching.

Between us we share a fine complement of skills, and we have access to resources in medicine; psychology and psychiatry; special education; community cable TV; video production; computer technology and graphics; management; product design and production; furniture repair and refinishing; retail marketing; theater, music, and art.

OUR LEARNING AND RECREATIONAL EQUIPMENT AND FACILITIES have expanded as rapidly as our housing and our numbers. They include: an excellent book, audio and videotape library; slide shows and projection equipment; a 3/4" and two 1/2" VCRs; several good stereo systems; cable TV in each house and in many of the rooms; a full range of biofeedback equipment; a good copy machine; several computers

and a range of software; an equipped computer graphics studio; sound, video filming and editing equipment; a carpentry shop, an exercise room, and a pool table. We expect to add an above-ground swimming pool and a ping-pong table.

Because we are situated on top of a hill, far back from the street, we have a nice view of the bay, and an unusual amount of privacy for New York City. The land between the houses is large enough for many trees, some of them fruit bearing; berries; flowers; vegetable gardens; fireplaces and outdoor eating space. We have six open porches and enough room to sit around and talk, play, party, or just retreat — outdoors as well as in. We also have 3 washers and dryers, and 15 modern bathrooms.

Our meals are well balanced and we try to cater to individual preferences whenever possible. Most of us eat dinner together most of the time. Well-stocked pantries, freezers, refrigerators, and two fully-equipped kitchens are available at all times for people who find our mealtimes inconvenient — or for those who prefer to do their own cooking, and for getting breakfast, lunch and snacks.

THREE POPULATIONS COMPRISE THE GANAS COMMUNITY

1. The Core group, which consists of 5 men and 5 women serves as the Board of Directors. We consider ourselves a self-selected family, love each other deeply, and plan to spend the rest of our lives together. Each of us is committed to doing whatever needs to be done. All our resources are pooled, including our money, talents, time, energy etc. Of course if one of the core group should choose to leave, they will take with them whatever money they put in. Those of us who work outside the community contribute our income, and help out at home when we can. We've agreed to try to support any career or non-income producing project, core group members choose to pursue.

The core group is open to, but not looking for new members.

2. The second group consists of about 15 people who live and work in the community, with varying degrees of closeness to the purposes, projects, and activities of the core group. Some form subgroups with philosophic objectives and activities of their own. Everyone who works here shares in the community's income to one extent or another, and expects to prosper as its cooperative businesses grow. Some will eventually join the core group. Others will leave when their course of study or interest in this lifestyle is over. The community is committed to providing them with whatever training they are interested in, and whatever help it can offer.

3. A third group of about 15 people just live here because they are interested in some form of training, in the community or because they like this lifestyle. They don't work with us.
Individuals in this third group contribute $400-500 a month to cover their in-house expenses. Some of them might also eventually join the core group. Like the second group, they have varying degrees of commitment and involvement, and are also offered whatever is needed and possible. Of course need and possibility are evaluated subjectively, and we do the best we can.

Because of our attempts at open communication, our work with behavior feedback, our proximity to Manhattan, and our incredibly varied population, we may be the only community of our kind. We talk to each other all the time about whatever is happening, and try to hold back as little as we can of either fact or emotion. It is important to us to try to get as close as possible to full, open disclosure and equally full response to everything disclosed. Getting as close as possible to each other has even higher priority.

Nobody who lives here is required or necessarily expected to accept or engage in any of the core group's commitments, conversations, or activities. Non-violence, non-exploitation, and agreement to abide by the laws of the state are the only requirements for residence.

Everyone who lives here is invited to core group meetings, and encouraged to make input to decisions. All opinions are welcome on every issue. However most decision-making authority requires membership in the core group and full sharing of resources.

Our government uses a participatory management system in which areas of responsibility determine the distribution of authority. We use either consensus or vote to arrive at major decisions only if those decisions affect the entire community.

THE MAJOR INTEREST OF THE FOUNDATION is the development of new methods for improving learning skills. The areas of learning we are involved with range from patient education, relaxation-mind quieting, language and music, to self-determined behavior change. Feedback educational methods use experiential or learn-by-doing approaches that offer on-the-spot performance information.

Projects in which the Foundation is, has been, or plans to be involved include participatory management systems that we design for use in our own residences and businesses, as well as for other enterprises and educational institutions. We have also done health education studies involving extensive training which prepares patients for active participation in their own treatment. We are producing videotaped instruction for this project, using dramatic as well as animated and other kinds of graphic presentations.

We also teach English as a second language; do neighborhood clean-up and beautification programs; provide biofeedback relaxation training; distribute tapes for becoming a non-smoker; work with housing renovation and maintenance, and the development of long-term plans for cooperative housing and businesses; and have several programs involving computer graphics and music. We have plans for a variety of public workshop programs; a news reporting project,;several public service TV shows; and C.A.S.E., Council for Alternatives to Stereotyping in Entertainment.

Our networking activities include collecting information about communities all over the world, and extend to a proposal to help establish a central communities office in NYC that would serve them all.

OUR FINANCING IS GENERATED BY OUR 2 RETAIL BUSINESSES AND OTHER INCOME-PRODUCING ACTIVITIES. Some specific undertakings are supported by private contributions. Our stores market artwork, crafts, clothing, jewelry, toys, stationery, greeting cards, books, records, china, glassware, appliances and other household things, as well as furniture, carpets, lamps, etc., etc., etc. Most of these are refinished and recycled. We produce some of them. A few are handcrafted. Many are new, purchased at auction and sold at very low prices. All of this happens in 2 large buildings, a few blocks from our residences. One houses our furniture store and a flea market; the other markets everything else. The stores are called, "Every Thing Goes."

Everyone that works here is compensated at the same rate, regardless of the job they do. If they work full-time, about 35 hours a week, they get $200 a month, plus all of their in-house costs. In addition, people receive commissions, payment for things they produced or refinished, and a share of our overall earnings. Everyone is encouraged to create their own products for distribution in our shops. Development of their own projects and businesses is also supported whenever possible, so that our cooperative might eventually expand to include many enterprises.

The goods and services of people in the larger community are also sold in our stores on a consignment basis. This includes over one hundred people not living in our community and not engaged in working with us directly.

Full partnership, in terms of equal shares of ownership of all the businesses and property involved is available to those who qualify and are willing to pool all of their resources. Only a small number of our total work force and residential population has elected to do that up to this point.

If you have questions, would like to visit, or are interested in setting up a similar living/working arrangement and need help, write or call Ganas. 135 Corson Ave, Staten Island NY 10301; (718)720-5378.

Announcements

A Celebration of Community: The Fellowship for Intentional Community is planning a *Celebration of Community: An International Conference on Cooperative Living,* tentatively scheduled for late June of 1993. If you are an intentional community, a seeker, a collective, a cooperative, an alternative village, or otherwise involved in a progressive endeavor—let us know your thoughts on such a large gathering of community-minded people. Your organizational involvement is welcome, and especially your suggestions and comments about activities, program, and funding sources. Contact: Community Celebration, Center for Communal Studies, 8600 University Boulevard, Evansville IN 47712, Attn: Joe V. Peterson. Let's celebrate community!

Call for Participation: The International Communal Studies Association (ICSA) will conduct its 3rd triennial conference July 25-28, 1991, at The Young Center for the Study of Anabaptist and Pietist Groups in Elizabethtown, Pennsylvania. The general theme, "Communal Societies: Values and Structures," will focus on the purposes of past and present communal societies, their structures to achieve these purposes, and their broader implications for contemporary worldwide developments. For additional information contact Dr. Donald Kraybill, The Young Center, Elizabethtown College, One Alpha Drive, Elizabethtown, PA 17022-2298. Phone: (717)367-1151 Ext. 440; Fax (717) 367-7567.

Call for Presentations: The CSA invites participation at its 18th annual conference — to be held Oct. 10-12, 1991, at Aurora, OR. If you wish to make a presentation or submit a formal paper, please send a brief statement about yourself and your topic to Patrick Harris, Old Aurora Colony Museum, P.O. Box 202, Aurora, OR 97002.

Your Archival Materials Wanted! Our future heritage of the study of communal history depends on our being alert to saving these materials *now:* communal publications (books, newsletters, flyers, leaflets), legal documents, written policies and agreements, correspondence, diaries, records, photographs, videos, and tapes. The Center for Communal Studies provides a temperature- and humidity-controlled environment to preserve such artifacts. Donors have complete access to their own materials and may specify limits on their use. In order to ensure your own community's materials a place in this collection, please contact the CCS director— Don Pitzer, 8600 University Blvd., Evansville IN 47712 (812)464-1727.

Books, Magazines, Videos

Diggers & Dreamers: an up-to-date *Communes Network Directory* which lists nearly 60 communities in Britain and 20 international communities. History of the movement, practical advice, comprehensive reading list, and more. £6.75 ($11 USA) surface mail. c/o Lifespan Community; Townhead, Dunford Bridge; Sheffield S30 6TG ENGLAND. Also available for $11 in the U.S. through Community Bookshelf, Route 1, Box 155, Rutledge, MO 63563.

Climate in Crisis: The Greenhouse Effect & What We Can Do compiles information from 3,000 reference works and offers a thorough and well-written look at this major environmental crisis. Written by Albert Bates (a long-term member of The Farm in Tennessee) and published by the Farm's publishing company. 240 pp, $13.50 (postpaid) available from the Natural Rights Center, P.O. Box 90, Summertown, TN 38483-0090.

Polyfidelity Primer: Polyfidelity is a sexually fidelitous marriage of more than two adults in which all partners are valued equally (all primaries). Often individuals who are polyfidelitous want as much commitment and sharing with their partners as anyone in a standard marriage situation. The *Polyfidelity Primer* (1989, 71 pages) describes the theory and essentials of the lifestyle, and is available for $12.00 postpaid from PEP, P.O Box 6306, Captain Cook, HI 96704-6306.

New Video: *Soviet Scientist Visits Communal America.* In 1988 Soviet social scientist Dr. Peter Gladkov, accompanied by a volunteer crew, took a whirlwind tour of successful cooperative communities in the U.S. *Where's Utopia?* (VHS, 58 min.) is the outcome of their trip. The video presents a rich diversity of cooperative systems, from housing to farming to food purchasing to insurance plans to neighborhoods and villages, pointing the way toward a future of people living in reverence for the earth and for each other. Educate classes, friends & relatives! Write: Aquarian Research; 5620 Morton St.; Philadelphia, PA 19144. Rent or purchase, $25 deposit. (Or call 215-849-3237 day/eve.) Low bulk prices available.

Read "Sylviron" — an exciting new novel about a cooperative village, set in the 21st century. $6.95 plus $1.25 postage. Joel Welty; 5902 South Carter Road; Freeland, MI 48623-9309.

Home Education Magazine has been offering more for home-schooling families since 1983. Write for our free catalog of home-schooling books — the most complete selection available! Box 1083; Tonasket, WA 98855.

Healing Arts Press: Free catalog of books and videos on psychic teachings, Tarot, channeling, self-help, spiritual counseling, and healing. Write Healing Arts Press; 13 Sartell Road; Grafton, MA 01519; (508) 839-0111.

Collective Yoga: extracts from the founders of Auroville on hierarchy, the individual, work, collective meditation. 75pp, $1.75. *A House for the Third Millennium:* essays of a priest who joined Auroville, the "city with a soul" to work on the Matrimandir, the place of concentration at its center. 100pp, photos, $6.95. Add $1.50 P & H. SAA / Box 372; High Falls, NY 12440; (914)687-9222.

Christ Consciousness, autobiography of Norman Paulsen, direct disciple of Paramahansa Yogananda. Personal account of one man's face-to-face contact with the Absolute. Includes story of creation and history of our universe. Encourages others to seek the ultimate experience for themselves. $12.45 from The Builders; Oasis, NV 89835.

Follow the Dirt Road: An Exploration of Intentional Communities in the 1990s is a new video documentary presenting a comprehensive introduction to the variety of today's communal lifestyles. Producer Monique Gauthier has been to over 25 communities with her partner Daniel Greenberg (See the "Children in Community" article on pg. 61). This unique video gives a voice to the peaceful communities striving to live in accordance with their ideals. For further information, write to Monique Gauthier / Follow the Dirt Road, 1325 West 27th Street #306, Minneapolis, MN 55408.

Support Organizations

Are You Forming a Community? Maybe we can help. Over the years members of the Federation of Egalitarian Communities have accumulated a wealth of experience about the nuts and bolts of community living. We've recently collected this information in a package of written materials, and it's now available at modest cost.

Our six communities represent a combined 80 years of making it work. Perhaps what we've learned about creating workable membership agreements, property codes, governance structures, bylaws, and visitor policies will help your community solve a problem. Or avoid reinventing the wheel.

For a free pamphlet explaining what's available and how to order, write: Systems & Structures; Federation Desk; Box C-7; Tecumseh, MO 65760

Community Service is an educational organization concerned with helping people improve their own communities. Bi-monthly newsletter; mail order book service; annual conferences on various aspects of community. Basic membership is $20. For a sample Newsletter and booklist write to Community Service; P.O. Box 243; Yellow Springs, OH 45387; phone (513)767-2161 or 767-1461.

Group dynamics a problem? Dealing with polarizing issues or interpersonal struggles? An outside facilitator or group process training may lead to a constructive solution. Referral service and training seminars. For a free brochure write: Alpha Institute, Deadwood, OR 97430; (503) 964-5102

Land Available

Pyramid on 40 Ocean View Acres For Sale. 2000+ square foot temple-home-retreat. Ideal for small group. Near San Francisco. $1000 reward to connect us with future purchaser. $344,000. Write "Pyramid"; General Delivery; Jenner, CA 95450.

Personals:

Life Partner Desired: Very intelligent, loving, and conscious man is looking for the same in a community-minded woman, age 25 to 38, who truly loves herself, enjoys life, and is open to having children. I'm strong and dynamic while also being playful, loving, and tender. Write and exchange photos: Eric; 21450 Chagall Road; Topanga, CA 90290.

Affordable Gemstones and custom jewelry. Let us supply your Hindu birthstone. Affordable Gemstones; Box 2121; Oasis, NV 89835 (702)478-5112.

Services

Aquarius Enterprises, Inc. offers to supply, install, service: Rammed Earth, Solar Buildings; Power Generation - photovoltaic, wind, water; Power Storage - Batteries; Power Distribution - 12v gadgets; Inverters - to operate 120v AC appliances; Solar Heating & Cooling - space, water; Propane Refrigerators, Freezers; Wireless Communication Equipment; Waterless Composting Toilets; Employment; Barter Accepted; Equipment Purchased. Box 669; Vail, AZ 85641-0669; (602)449-3588.

Reach Ads

Communities

Masters of our Own Destiny: Pot-luck Living for Mutual Minds; Self-Subsistence and Holistic. *Mission:* Multiply. Train leaders on our crews for new communities. Form network. *Purpose:* Communal Providence, ideals, values, methods, care, sharing. Non-regimented. *Method:* All generational. Seniors loan and share responsibility and are cared for. Workers, in crews; organic food production; build houses; wellness care (nurse), Montessori, public affairs; business and finance for persons as well as corporation.

Money: Occupants lend for their own living unit (refundable). Workers may lend at 20% of allowance. Non-workers pay $10/day. No rent. No interest. No profit. No war tax. Shuttlebus, no car needed. Own 72 good acres. *Work:* Produce fruit, nuts, fish, veggies, herbs, greenhouse. More perennials. Construct houses, apartments, community hall over a decade. Services from womb to tomb, wellness, education, care, guardian, companions, business, records, office, guardian for infirm or children. *Lifestyle:* Crews self-managed. Seniors self-directed. Noon fellowship on workdays. Consensus for most disciplines. "One Vote" when required. Soul fraternity. *Location:* 10 minutes to Berea (College) Kentucky on I-75. *Write or Call:* Futures (formerly New Hope); 111 Bobolink; Berea, KY 40403. (606)986-8000.

Ponderosa Village: Own land in our beautiful, established rural community! Live and raise your children among self-reliant friendly neighbors. Self-Reliance Life Seminars. Ponderosa Village, 203 Golden Pine, Goldendale, WA 98620 (509)773-3902.

New Age Community looking for new members to share in working, growing, living New Age ideals. Individual expressions of spirituality and lifestyle. Pay or work for rent. Seeking members skilled in mechanics, administration, bookkeeping, cooking, housekeeping. Write for information: Community, Dept CJ, Box 782, Middletown, CA 95461. Please enclose $1.00 for information.

New Age Spiritual Community now open to residents in the Sierra Mountains. Work in exchange for rent. Skilled and unskilled workers needed. For more information call (916)994-3773 or write: Sierra CJ, Box 366, Sierraville, CA 96126.

Communities Forming:

Community Forming based on sustainable agriculture. For more information contact George & Anna Hadley, Organic Kauai Produce, 6335 Waipouli Road, Kapaa, HI 96746. (See listing.)

Looking for co-workers and friends to help establish a community utilizing a profitable and growing forest products business as an economic base. I envision an egalitarian kibbutz-like organization, highly supportive of children, efficient enough economically to provide its members with a modest personal income and an opportunity for long-term members to accumulate equity in the community's assets. If you are secular, abstain from the use of drugs and alcohol, approach problems from a logical scientific perspective, and would like to build and live in a community of like-minded persons, then let's correspond. JEd. WIlbourn, PO Box 5025, Fredericksburg, VA 22403.

"Kidstown" will be accepting applications in late 1991 for resident kids who would like to make this "home" for a period of time (see our listing for complete description). Requests can come either from parents or the kids themselves. Kids have opportunity for cottage industry experience, a share of the income, community involvement. Call Bob at (707)987-0669.

Experienced Person(s) in fields of orchard and fruit/nut growing or in house building needed for a small community of potentially 3-5 houses, beginning in 1990. Oak Grove Farm, Rt. 1, Box 455, Round Hill, VA 22141.

People Looking

Hygienic, Spiritual Community: If yours is a hygienic, spiritual community in a warm, peaceful setting, with time for study, fasting, healing each other, and experiencing the Absolute, please write: Dean von Germeten, 314 Tenth #2, Racine, WI 53403.

Interracial Couple & Daughter: We are an interracial couple with a year-old daughter looking to join or start a community. We want to live self-sufficiently in harmony within our hearts by being in an environment which encourages spiritual growth without being dogmatic. Members might be pursuing meditation, healing arts, sacred dance, or other spiritual practices. Our passion is for the arts, and we'd love to create meaningful art with other members of the community. Parenting is very important to us, and we'd like to live with other dedicated parents interested in home schooling. Besides being a positive environment for growth and support, a community should ideally reach out to our ailing society through art, therapy, exporting agricultural knowledge, or other means. Any communities or people who are in harmony with our goals for community please contact us. Beth Aiken & Lycurgus Mitchell; P.O. Box 1110; Wellfleet, MA 02667.

Peaceful, Healthy, Cooperative brother and sister seeking/opening to group marriage/land cooperative. Working knowledge of cooperative living and decision making. Values deep friendships, shared parenting, enhanced economics, evolutionary personal growth. Assets include 24 secluded mountainous acres, lake frontage, self-sufficient skills, cottage industry potentials, resources towards shared construction of alternatively enlightened three master suites communal home. Children welcomed. Tumtum Heart Consociation; P.O. Box 57; Tumtum, WA 99034.

Political Activist, former East Wind member, looking for others interested in building an egalitarian-type community in the North Carolina mountains near Asheville, NC. Lots of opportunity here: high employment rate, low wages, medium cost of living. Non-sexist, non-racist, non-violent. Wish to avoid dogmatism. Please send SASE for details. Robert Carr, 32 Brookside Circle #6, Candler, NC 28715-9208. ❖

"Reach" is a regular feature intended to help match people looking for communities with communities looking for people. Please note that dated material requires lead time several months ahead of the anticipated publication date.

A Peek at the Team
That Assembled This Directory

Figuring that quite a few readers will be curious about the motley and dynamic crew that created this masterpiece, we've included brief biographic sketches of all the major actors (which also gives us one final opportunity to play with theatrical metaphors). Hopefully our dedication and sense of humor will share top billing. So — without further fanfare, here's the cast of characters (that phrase describes us perfectly, actually) in alphabetical order:

Anne Beck

is a member of East Wind community in southern Missouri, and is known for her informal networking among various community groups across the country. She was sporadically but enthusiastically involved in the Directory's research, information organization, and data cross-checking efforts — mostly during her visits to Sandhill, Shannon, and Twin Oaks. It may be an illusion, but it seems that she's had personal contact with at least a quarter of the groups listed in this Directory. When she's not busy visiting communities, or wading through lists, or networking ... you'll typically find her with glasses riding down the tip of her nose while she patches someone's britches or focuses on some needlepoint. She's camera shy, so it was impossible to get her to hold still long enough for a good photo.

Chris Collins

was active in a theater collective when she was first recruited to join the production staff for *Communities* magazine. That was over ten years ago, and she's been the magazine's production coordinator ever since. She's also a board member of Communities Publications Cooperative, the magazine's parent organization. From her home she runs a small publications business ... producing journals, newsletters, and promotional pieces. Write her at Farm River Publications (127 Highland Avenue, Branford, CT 06405) if you'd like to steer some business her way. When she's not staring at a computer screen and rattling its keys, you'll find her either working with land trusts to save local properties from the developers, or (more likely) cruising about in a sailboat. She has visions of sailing off for a week or a month — or maybe for the rest of her life.

Chris Roth

has been involved in the fields of ecology, organic horticulture/ agriculture, solar cooking, other forms of appropriate technology, and unintentional and intentional community for the past nine years. He has lived, among other places, on a traveling school bus, on the Hopi Reservation in Arizona, at End of the Road House/ Aprovecho Institute in Oregon, and at Sandhill Farm in Missouri ... and has left a trail of solar box cookers in his wake. He helped edit this Directory and created the reference maps while living at Sandhill — between bouts of directly experiencing life and nature, sleeping, eating, reading, writing, chasing cows, misidentifying birds, and getting pricked by honey locust thorns in Sandhill's maple grove. More recently, he has divided his time between Oregon, where he has edited *News from Aprovecho,* and New Hampshire.

Dan Questenberry

first published a manual for family planning clinicians while working in Atlanta in 1972. Then in 1976 he retired from public administration to answer the call of the Sixties at Shannon. In 1984 he co-edited three pages on Shannon Farm for *Builders of the Dawn* — and he's had a taste ever since for intercommunity networking. From his home base at Shannon he's become involved with InterCommunities of Virginia, the Fellowship for Intentional Community, and the School of Living Land Trust. Today he does member recruitment and integration, various development projects (roads, logging, home construction, lake, land purchase), and runs an insurance agency. A Capricorn with Sagittarius rising, he registered as a conscientious objector during the Vietnam war. The son of a preacher/deputy sheriff and a teacher, he's married to a farmer's daughter/Norfolk debutante. His communitarian objectives include maintaining a natural, fun-filled life of recreational, social and spiritual ananda, as well as experiencing mass land trust and co-op economic reform.

Elke Lerman

was born in New York City in 1955. As a "child of the left," she grew up seeing how inadequately the competitive, consumerist system took care of human needs. She sees her involvement in the cooperative and communal movements as political expression as well as individual lifestyle choice. She has been involved in consumer co-ops, worker co-ops, political action affinity groups, and communes in Virginia, California, Missouri, and New York since 1971. In 1986 she edited the Federation of Egalitarian Communities issue of Communities magazine. She now lives and works at the Ganas community in Staten Island, New York.

Geoph Kozeny
has lived in cooperatives and communities since 1973, and has also been quite active in various worker-owned businesses. He co-founded the Stardance Community in San Francisco in 1978, and lived there for ten years. In that time he was active in the Broom & Board construction collective, became a mainstay of the *Collective Networker Newsletter,* and helped publish six editions of the *West Coast Directory of Collectives.* On New Year's Day of 1988 he took a big leap, launching the Community Catalyst Project which takes him across the continent on visits to communities of all stripes. He gets involved in the daily routine of each group, asks about their visions and realities, takes photos and slides, and gives slide shows about the diversity and viability of the communities movement. He loves to entertain with his guitar and silly songs, and usually finds his best audiences in those under the age of 10. He is an incorrigible tease, and amuses himself with non-stop puns — simultaneously his most annoying and endearing qualities.

Jenny Upton
first produced commercial graphics for a brochure and portfolio for Heartwood Design, Shannon Farm's cabinetry and solar lumber-drying business. Today, nine years later, she's moved beyond marketing to designing furniture and producing custom cabinets. She's a strong believer in Heartwood's consensus decision-making and ethical capitalism. Acting with her collective partners, Jenny has reduced the use of toxic finishes and stopped selling rain forest products in their growing business. In the summer of 1989, Jenny was captivated by the experience of the Directory looming in her living room office. She took on the task of organizing photos for the Feature Articles. It complemented her interests in Shannon's communities movement committee and the InterCommunities of Virginia. Raised by a second generation farmer on the Virginia coast, Jenny moved inland to the mountains and Shannon Farm in 1976. Intentional community was not Jenny's dream, but it has become her place of bliss and harmony. She's mother to Conrad, her 14-year-old son.

Jim Estes
first experienced cooperative living as a member of the gigantic student housing co-op in Berkeley, where he attended the University of California after Navy service in World War II. In 1972 he became a charter member of Alpha Farm, in the Coast Range of Oregon, but he continued full-time newspaper work until 1987, when Social Security made him an offer he couldn't refuse. His newspaper venues included the *Stockton* (Calif.)*Record*, the *San Francisco Chronicle*, the *Salem* (Ore.)*Statesman-Journal*, and four hilarious months on *USA Today*. He keeps his hand in the business by freelance book editing at ridiculously low rates [call him for a quote] and putting out a monthly newspaper for the towns around Alpha. He is married to Caroline Estes, also a charter member of Alpha; they have two daughters and four grandchildren. Summing up his life so far, he says he's come a long way from Birmingham.

Julie Mazo
is both new and old in the communities movement. The early '50s found her intensely exploring intentional communities of that era, but it was almost 40 years before she became a community member at Shannon Farm in 1989. The time in between was spent on both coasts and in Canada as mother, administrator, writer, publisher, editor, business owner, management consultant, trainer, mediator, etc. Appreciation for the role played by the 1985 Communities Directory in her own search for community led Julie to jump eagerly on the bandwagon for preparing this edition — a jump whose wisdom she has sometimes questioned.

Laird Schaub
is a founding member of Sandhill Farm, and has lived there since 1974. He's been a delegate with the Federation of Egalitarian Communities since 1980, and involved with the Fellowship for Intentional Community since its revitalization in 1986. He does administrative/staff work for both groups. While he's written a few articles before, this is his first attempt at playing editor since he worked on his high school newspaper ... nearly 20 years ago.

Rebecca Krantz
of Sandhill farm is relatively new to community. She studied eco-feminist critiques of science in college (the University of Chicago), and graduated in 1988. She visited several communities, and spent two months at Springtree Community in Virginia. Since moving to Sandhill in June of 1989, Rebecca has been learning about farm and community life. In addition to work on the Directory, she attended the Fall assembly of the Federation of Egalitarian Communities, and has been practicing her spinning, exploring eco-feminist spirituality, and running Community Bookshelf, Sandhill's mail-order bookstore.

About the Index ...

The keyword index found at the back of this book, though by no means exhaustive, is a vital tool for rooting out some of the information hidden between the covers. To get the most out of the Directory, use the keyword index in conjunction with the map beginning on page 146 (a geographic index) and the chart following the map (an index of values and practices).

Our indexing is based primarily on information provided by the group itself, although in some cases we added information based on the personal knowledge of a member of our staff. **If a name is not indexed** under a particular keyword, that does **not necessarily** mean that the group is not involved with that particular value or practice. We can't list what we don't know, and it's likely that some groups gave incomplete information. Also, several very active groups listed so many keywords that we found it necessary to thin out their list — we tried to identify their most significant focus areas, and limited a group to no more than 8 or 10 index entries.

If an asterisk (*) precedes a keyword in the index, then that issue or value was addressed in our questionnaire, and there is a corresponding column in the reference chart which indicates how the group responded.

Because they aren't cross-referenced elsewhere in the Directory, we were more thorough in our indexing of the "Resource" listings. Still, we tried to index the communities on aspects not covered in the chart — based on resources they might offer our readers — or based on those recurring questions which arise in assisting people who are searching for their "ideal community."

Except for in the chart, we did not index the values or daily practices of a community. A group may practice meditation every day, but unless it regularly offers trainings in meditation, the group will not be indexed in that category. At least a quarter of the groups mention a goal of "self-sufficiency", but we have only indexed those which offer workshops or publications in that area.

We did, however, index several common community businesses — realizing that vocational considerations often play a major role in community searches. To the extent possible, we indexed such endeavors as restaurants, woodworking shops, food producers, etc. For the same reason, we've also indexed certain spiritual paths — such as Catholic Workers, Zen Buddhists, the Hutterian Brethren, Quakers, etc. In general it wasn't practical to index such broad categories as Christians, or Eastern Spirituality. Fortunately, those classifications are covered in the chart.

Two other areas of "overload" were conference/workshop centers, and publishers. Many groups offer services in these areas, but we decided to index only those which sponsor events or publish writings of individuals and groups outside their immediate community.

Some communities included in the listings do not appear in the keyword index even once. Their descriptive paragraph outlines their common bonds and their daily lives, but does not list any specific resources that they are actively making available to other communitarians. Similarly, if a group is just forming or merely "planning" to offer a training in a particular resource area, we've usually not indexed their intention unless it's a cornerstone of their vision.

Many of the index categories have **master listings and sublistings** (for example: Solar Energy is a subset of Alternative Energy; Workshop Centers are a subset of Conference Centers, usually with a smaller capacity). We've attempted to list a group only once in a particular area — so make use of the cross-references in the keyword index.

And now, a word about the **names used in the keyword index.** In the interest of enhancing readability and conserving space, we have used only short index names. In some cases this is the first word of a name, or the entire name if it's not more than about a dozen letters long. More often it's a shorthand blending of words and abbreviations — hopefully each is unique, yet easily identifiable.

The one-letter **abbreviations used in the index names** (such as "C-" for "Community") are explained in the footer at the bottom of each page of the index. If the name is preceded by an [F], it's included as a "forming" community in the North American Communities listings; an [I] prefix indicates an entry in the International section; an [R] is in the Resources section. If an index name has no prefix, then that community's description will be found in the North American listings.

Within the text following each keyword, the information is bunched into three groups — first the communities, then the resource groups, then the cross-reference information — with a "•" separating the three parts from each other.

A final note: we've included a section call "Late Entries", which begins on page 292, and has quick-reference index tabs; all of these groups have also been included in the index.

And remember — we need your feedback in order to make future directories even better! Send us your comments, ideas, and (especially) leads to groups you think should be included. May your search be fruitful. ... ❖

Section Codes: (No code) N. American   [F] N. American/Forming   [I] International   [L] Late Entry   [R] Resource
Abbreviations: (Cn) Center   (C-) Community   (LT) Land Trust   (N-) New   (Rb) Rainbow

Academic Programs
OjaiFndtn, [I]Teachest •
[R]CenComStudies, [R]ExpeditInst,
[R]ExpLiving, [R]InstSocEcolgy,
[R]IntComStudies, [R]NHCSA,
[R]SocUtopia, [R]YadTabenkin

Activism
(See: Peace & Justice;
Political Activism)

Agricultural Instruction
Birdsfoot, [I]Comunidad/S, Linnaea,
Sojourners(VA), [I]Mitraniketan •
[R]ElfinPC, [R]HealthyHarv,
[R]HortIdeas

Agriculture
(See: Bio-Dynamics; Bioregionalism;
Food-Producers; Organic Farming &
Gardening; Permaculture, Seeds;
Sustainable Agriculture)

Alternative Energy
EsseneMother, LaCitéEcol,
[F]SEADS/Truth • [R]Meadowcreek,
[R]N-Alchemy, [R]RealGoods,
[R]RockyMtnInst, [R]UConcernSci,
[R]Windstar • *(See Also:*
Appropriate Technology;
Conservation; Permaculture;
Solar Cooking; Solar Energy)

Alternative Lifestyles
[I]Crabapple, [F]DuckMtn,
HighWind • [R]C-Mag,
[R]FamilyTree, [R]Intinet, [R]RFD •
(See Also: Relationships)

Alternative Technology
(See: Appropriate Technology)

Anabaptist
N-Covenant • *(See Also:*
Bruderhof; Hutterian)

Anarchism
Dragonfly, Group-W,
SuburbPalace, Sweetwater,
U/Stonehenge • [R]BoundTogether •
(See Also: Self-Management)

Animal Rights
[R]BioregionProj, [R]NatRightsCen •
(See Also: Bioregionalism;
Endangered Species; Vegetarian)

Anthroposophy
Camphill, Tobias, Triform

Anti-Authoritarian
(See: Decentralization;
Self-Management)

Anti-Nuclear
(See: Nuclear Disarmament;
Nuclear Power Opposition)

Appropriate Technology
[I]Comunidad/S, LongBranch,
[L]Maharishi, [L]Octagon, Sirius,
Sunflower(OH), [I]Teachest,
[L]Whetstone(F) • [R]AppTech/SB,
[R]BikesNoBombs, [R]BioregionProj,
[R]Columbiana, [R]ExpCities,
[R]InstLocalSelf, [R]InstSocEcolgy,
[R]TraNet, [R]WhlEarthInst,
[R]WhlEarthRev • *(See Also:*
Alternative Energy; Permaculture;
Solar Cooking; Solar Energy;
Sustainable Agriculture)

Architecture
Alcyone, Arcosanti • [R]C-Catalyst,
[R]CoHousing, [R]Geltaftan, [R]Mea-
dowcreek, [R]Rodale, [R]Shared/LRC

Archives
(See: History; Museums)

Art
Arden, CaravanFarm, Earthdance,
[F]Earthworks, [I]FusionArts, Group-
W, Hohm, [I]PermPyrénées, [L]Quarry-
Hill, Rabbity-Hill, Rootworks, Thoreau,
Waukon, Wellspring(WI), Zendik •
[R]Another-Place, [R]CirclePines,
[R]N-Catalyst, [R]OmegaInst •
(See Also: Culture)

Art—Commercial
Builders, C-(Va), [L]InstWhatHav

Audio/Visual
[F]AquarResrch, [L]BearCreek,
[R][L]DeepDish, LostValley,
ReCreation, Renaissance, StBenedict's
• [R]BetterWorld, [R]MediaNet

Audubon Society
[R]ExpeditInst

Australia
[R]AustrCCDir; [R]C-Access • *(See:*
"Index by Country" that precedes the
International *listings)*

Bakeries
CamphillVill(PA), CamphillVill(MN),
Innisfree, LaCitéEcol, Shiloh(AR),
Shprdsfield

Barter
[R]CRSP

Bed & Breakfasts
(See: Hospitality)

Behavioral Psychology
LosHorcones • [R]ExpLiving,
[R][L]WaldenTwo

Bicycles
[L]InstWhatHav • [R]BikesNoBombs

Biodyynamics
CamphillVill(PA), Fellowship-C,
[F]OrgKauai, Wellspring(WI) •
[R]BioDynamFarm • *(See Also:*
Anthroposophy; Sustainable
Agriculture)

Bioregionalism
[R]BioregionProj, [R]Columbiana,
[R]EarthIsland, [R]InstSocEcolgy,
[R]Katúah, [R]N-Catalyst,
[R]PlanetDrum, [R] TurtleIsOff •
(See Also: Decentralization;
Environment; Permaculture)

Bodywork
Kripalu, SaltSpring

Books—Mail Order
BearTribe • [R]AppTech/SB,
[R]BoundTogether, [R]C-Bookshelf,
[R]C-ServiceInc, [R]CoResourCen,
[R]FdnPersC-Dev, [R]LeftBank,
[R]LiberatDistrb, [R]N-SocietyPub,
[R]NASCO, [R]Nolo, [R]PacPublCoop

Bookstores
Alpha, [I]Crabapple, Krotona,
Vivekananda(MI), Yogaville •
[R]HighWindBks

Boycott Info
[R]CoopAmer

Bruderhof
CrystalSpg, [I]Darvell, DeerSpring,
[I]Michaelshof, N-MeadowRun,
PleasantView, Starland, Woodcrest

Buddhist
Communia, Heathcote •*(See Also: Zen)*

Building Construction
Alpha, Builders, LittleFarm,
Padanaram, PlowCreek, Renaissance,
Shprdsfield, [L]Whetstone(F) •
[R]C-Catalyst

Index Keywords preceded by **an asterisk (*)** are also indexed in the Cross-Reference Charts.

Index

Section Codes: (No code) N. American   [F] N. American/Forming   [I] International   [L] Late Entry   [R] Resource
Abbreviations: (Cn) Center   (C-) Community   (LT) Land Trust   (N-) New   (Rb) Rainbow

316   COMMUNITIES: *Journal of Cooperation — No. 77/78*

Conferences
[R]AcresUSA, [R]AnotherPlace,
[R]BioregionProj, [R]CenComStudies,
[R]CirclePines, [R]C-ServiceInc,
[R]InstDevelCoop, [R]IntComStudies,
[R]Meadowcreek, [R]NHCSA,
[R]School/Living, [R]UrbanAlts

Conflict Management
[I]ComGro(Aus), Magic •
[R]CenConflictRes, [R]CenEd-
Guidance, [R]TurtleIsland

Consciousness
Lama, N-Land, RajYogaMath,
TruthConsc • [R]CenSacredSci,
[R]ReVision, [R]TransTimes,
[R]TheWELL

*Consensus
Alpha • [R]CenConflictRes,
[R]Peacemakers, [R]TIES

Conservation
[F]ComGro/NY, [I]Teachest •
[R]EcoHome, [R]ExpeditInst,
[R]NatConservcy, [R]Rocky-
MtnInst • *(See Also:
Environment; Recycling)*

Consumer Guides
[R]CoopAmer, [R]WhlEarthRev

Cooking
(See: Solar Cooking)

Cooperation
[R]AnimalTown, [R]CESCI,
[R]InstDevelCoop, [R]NASCO

Cooperative Living
CasaGrande, EsseneMother,
Magic, Ojito, Sunflower(KS) •
[R]AquarianRes, [R]CEED-Inst,
[R]Cohousing, [R]ComNetwork,
[R]Dig&Dream, [R]ExpLiving,
[R]FedEgalCom, [R]FellowIntCom,
[R]InstDevelCoop, [R]IntComNet,
[R]RobtOwenFnd, [R]School/Living,
[R]Shared/LRC, [R]SiriusPubl,
[R]TurtleIsland •
(See Also: Kibbutz)

Cooperatives
[R]C-Bookshelf, [R]C-Catalyst, [R]C-
Mag, [R]CCEC, [R]CenCoops(CA),
[R]CoCampSierra, [R]CoopAmer,
[R][L]CoopGrocer, [R]CoResour-
Cen, [R]CRSP, [R]DemBusiness,
[R]FedSoCoops, [R]IndusCoopAsso,

[R]InstDevelCoop, [R][L]IntCoopCncil,
[R]NatCoopBank, [R]Pueblo/People
[R]RobtOwenFnd, [R]UrbanAlts,
[R][L]WorkerOwnedNet

Cottage Industries
Appletree, CrossesCrk, Flatrock,
Hailos, [F]OrgKauai, [L]Paideia(F),
RabbityHill, [L]Sangamon(F),
Shprdsfield, SkyWoods, TrailsEnd,
[L]VeiledCliffs • [R]Columbiana,
[R]FedEgalCom • *(See Also:
Small Business; and specific
products and services)*

Crafts
Camphill-USA, Celo, Crafts,
[I]Centrepoint, Fellowship-C,
Flatrock, Innisfree, [L]InstWhatHav,
[I]Mitraniketan, [I]PermPyrénées,
SkyWoods • [R]R&EMiles

Credit Unions
[R]CCEC, [R]FedSoCoops,
[R]NeighbrWorks

Cult Awareness
[R]CultAwareNet

Culture
Goodenough • [R]AnnalsEarth,
[R]BoundTogether, [R]Columbiana,
[R]Dance/NE, [R]InContext,
[R]InstSocEcolgy, [R]Katúah,
[R][L]LongIsAlt, [R]N-Catalyst,
[R]OneWorldFam, [R][L]SingOut,
[R][L]VolPeace, [R]WhlEarthRev,
[R]Zeta

Dance
Earthdance, Waukon • [R]Dance/NE,
[R]WICCA/Camp

Decentralization
[R]AdvoSelfGovt, [R]FourthWorld,
[R]GlobeLib, [R]GreenComCor,
[R]N-Options, [R]School/Living •
*(See Also: Greens; Local Self-
Reliance; Self-Management)*

*Decision Making
*(See: Consensus; Facilitation;
Group Process)*

Denmark
*(See: "Index by Country" that
precedes the International listings)*

Desktop Publishing
HighWind • [R]C-Catalyst,
[R]N-AgeGuide

*Diet
(See: Food; Macrobiotic; Vegetarian)

Direct Action
[I]ComGro(Aus), SeedsPeace,
U/Stonehenge • [R]EarthFirst!,
[R]Greenpeace, [R]Mobilz-
Survival • *(See Also:
Grass-Roots Organizing)*

Directories
[R]AltPressIndex, [R]CoopAmer,
[R]HealthyHarv, [R]HospitalityEx,
[R]N-AgeJourn, [R]NatCoalAlts,
[R]NatlHmSchool, [R]Omega-
NewAge, [R]OneWorldFam,
[R]PlanetDrum, [R][L]VolForPeace •
*(See Also: Communities Directories;
Sourcebooks; and specific topics)*

Disabilities
C-Altrnatvs, [I]Beeston,
Camphill, Fellowship-C,
Innisfree, Jubilee(GA), Tobias

Draft Resistance
*(See: Military Resistance;
Peace & Justice)*

Drug Abuse
C-(Va), Heathcote • [R]ChristicInst,
[R]SpringHill, [R]WICCA/Camp

Earth Religions
[L]Annwin, Dragonfly, [L]Hawkwind,
SuburbPalace, Thoreau •
[R][L]ChurAllWlds, [R]CreationMag,
[R]Reclaiming

Eastern Spirituality
*(See: Hare Krishna; Sikh; Sufi;
Vedic; Yoga; Zen Buddhism)*

Ecofeminism
[R]InstSocEcolgy, [R]N-Catalyst

Ecology
Alcyone, Magic, RabbityHill,
Wellspring(WI) • [R]EcoHome,
[R]InstSocEcolgy, [R][L]PolEcoGroup •
(See Also: Environment; EcoVillages)

Economic Conversion
R]AllncSurvival, [R]CenEconConv,
[R]ComGro(USA), [R]IndusCoopAsso

Economic Development
OurLand, Patchwork • [R]CCEC,
[R]FedSoCoops, [R]Meadowcreek,
[R]NeighbrWorks, [R]OlympSustain,
[R]RegenAmer, [R]SeventhGen,
[R][L]WorkerOwnedNet

Index Keywords preceded by **an asterisk (*)** are also indexed in the Cross-Reference Charts.

Index

Economics
(See: Sustainable Economics)

Ecosystems
(See: Ecology; Environment)

EcoVillages
Arcosanti, CerroGordo, [I]Comuni-dad/S, [F]EcoVillage, LaCitéEcol, [L]Maharishi, Renaissance, [F]Sylviron • [R]AppTech/SB, [R]CRSP

Ecuador
(See: "Index by Country" that precedes the International listings)

Ecumenical
[I]Beeston, [I]FincaJardin, Hearthaven, [L]InstCulturAffairs, RebaPlace, Sojourners(DC) • [R]Habitat, [R]InterfaithCen, [R]PenuelRidge • *(See Also: Quakers)*

*Education
Camphill-SS, [L]Maharishi, [L]ZenCom/NY • [R][L]Child&Com, [R]HolisticEdRev, [R]NALSAS, [R]NatCoalAlts • *(See Also: Academic Programs; Home Schooling; Schools; or specific topics)*

Egalitarian
Appletree, [L]Catalyst), Dandelion, Earthdance, EastWind, [L]Galilee, [F]InstSustLiv, KehillatMishp, LosHorcones, [F]OrgKauai, Sandhill, [L]Sangamon(F), SkyWoods, Springtree, TwinOaks, ValleyLight, [L]VeiledCliffs • [R]FedEgalCom, [R]InterCom(VA)

El Salvador
(See: Non-Intervention)

Elderly
Fellowship-C, N-Jerusalem, Sojourners(DC) • [R]InnovHousing

Emissaries of Divine Light
Edenvale, GlenIvy, GreenPastures, [I]HillierPk, [I]Hohenort, HundredMile, KingView, [I]LaVigne, [I]Mickleton, Oakwood(IN), StillMeadow • [R]Integrity, [R]Stewdshp-C

Empowerment
[I]ComGro(Aus) • [R]Chinook, [R]SoMovEmpowr

Endangered Species
[R]AbundantLife, [R]EarthFirst!, [R]EarthIsland, [R]EnvirDefense, [R]Greenpeace • *(See Also: Animal Rights)*

Endowments
(See: Funds)

Energy
(See: Alternative Energy)

England
(See: "Index by Country" that precedes the International listings; See Also: Great Britain)

Environment
[I]Mitraniketan, OjaiFndtn, [I]Teachest, Zendik • [R]AllncSurvival, [R]AnnalsEarth, [R]BetterWorld, [R]CitHazWaste, [R]Connexions, [R]EarthFirst!, [R]EarthSave, [R]EcoNet, [R]EnvirDefense, [R]ExpCities, [R]ExpeditInst, [R]Garbage, [R]GreenComCor, [R]Greenpeace, [R]Headwaters, [R]InterfaithCen, [R]MediaNet, [R]MotherJones, [R]N-SocietyPub, [R]OneEarth, [R]OneWorldFam, [R]ProjPlenty, [R]R&EMiles, [R]Rainforest, [R]RenewAmer, [R]SierraClub, [R]SoMovEmpowr, [R]SW-Research, [R]VolForPeace, [R]Worldwatch • *(See Also: Alternative Energy; Bioregionalism; Conservation; Ecofeminism; Ecology; Forestry; Greens; Hazardous Waste; Nuclear Power Opposition; Overpopulation; Permaculture; Recycling; Sanctuaries-Wildlife; Socially Responsible Investing; Stewardship; Sustainable Agriculture)*

Equality
[R]Alliance, [R]LeftBank • *(See Also: Egalitarian; Human Rights; Peace & Justice)*

Esperanto
Krutsio

Essene
EsseneMother, [R][L]GardenEden

Facilitation
Alpha • [R]C-Catalyst, [R]CenConflictRes, [R]Fellow-IntCom, [R]TIES

Faerie
(See: Gay)

Family Therapy
PlowCreek • *(See Also: Therapy)*

*Feminism
Thoreau • [R]ChangingMen, [R]Columbiana, [R]N-SocietyPub, [R]NatOrgChgMen, [R]WomanPower • *(See Also: Ecofeminism; Equality; Lesbian; Women)*

Finance:
[R]CoHousing, [R]NatCoopBank

Findhorn Network
(See: Light Centers; Community Networks)

*Food
(See: Diet; Hunger; and next three categories)

Food—Information & Politics
Farm(TN), [F]FarmHome • [R][L]CalifAction, [R][L]Coop-Grocer [R]EarthSave, [R]FoodFirst, [R]N-Alchemy, [R]Windstar • *(See Also: Sustainable Agriculture)*

Food-Producers
Adirondack, Asponola, Birdsfoot, BlackBear, C-Altrnatvs, [L]C-FarmAnnArb, CEEDS/B.C., [I]Centrepoint, [I]Crabapple, Days-pring, [F]AquaRanch, Fellowship-C, FraserFarm, Headlands, HighWind, HundredMile, HutterBreth, Koinonia, LaCitéEcol, [I]Mitraniketan, N-Covenant, [I]OldHall, PlowCreek, Riparia, Sandhill, Shiloh(AR), Sojourners(VA), Springtree, StBenedict's, StillMeadow, [I]Svan-holm, [I]Taena, [I]TerNouvelle, Wellspring(WI)

Food Stores
[L]AnandaMarg, Builders, CamphillVill(PA), Camphill(USA), Celo, [I]Crabapple, GriffinGorge, [I]Svanholm

Forestry
[R]BioregionProj, [R]Headwaters, [R]Rainforest, [R]SW-Research • *(See Also: Trees)*

Section Codes: (No code) N. American [F] N. American/Forming [I] International [L] Late Entry [R] Resource
Abbreviations: (Cn) Center (C-) Community (LT) Land Trust (N-) New (Rb) Rainbow

Index Keywords preceded by an **asterisk (*)** are also indexed in the Cross-Reference Charts.

319

Index

Section Codes: (No code) N. American   [F] N. American/Forming   [I] International   [L] Late Entry   [R] Resource
Abbreviations: (Cn) Center   (C-) Community   (LT) Land Trust   (N-) New   (Rb) Rainbow

[R]AnimalTown, [R]CoopAmer, [R]EarthCare, [R]EcoAction, [R][L]ForthWorld, [R]HugsForHeart, [R]NAEIR, [R]Pueblo/People), [R][L]SunHealthBk • *(See Also: Books-MailOrder; Sourcebooks)*

Management
(See: Business, Leadership Training; Planning Skills; Property Management; Self-Management)

Massage
(See: Bodywork)

Media
[R]AltPressIndex, [R]BioregionProj, [R]C-Jobs, [R]CounEconPrior, [R][L]DeepDish, [R]EarthSave, [R]EnvirDefense, [R]Factsheet5, [R]MediaNet, [R]NatFedBrdcast

Meditation
Ananda/WB, Builders, , [L]HimalayInst, [L]Maharishi, MtMadonna, SaltSpring, Sirius, Sivananda/A, Truth-Consc, Vivekananda(MI), Yogaville • [R]CenSacredSci, [R]SoDharma, [R]3HO/Fdtn, [R]WICCA/Camp • *(See Also: Zen Buddhism)*

Men
WolfCreek • [R]ChangingMen, [R]NatOrgChgMen, [R]SpringHill • *(See Also: Gay)*

Mennonite
PlowCreek, RebaPlace

Mensa
[L]Windward

Metaphysics
ReevisMtn, [F]WingedHeart • [R]OmegaNewAge, [R]TransTimes • *(See Also: Consciousness; Spirituality; Transformation)*

Midwifery
Farm(TN) • *(See Also: Waterbirthing)*

Military Resistance
HutterBreth, Metanoia(GA) • [R]AllncSurvival, [R]CenEconConv, [R]Peacemakers, [R]20Vision, [R]VetsPeace, [R][L]WarResist • *(See Also: Non-Intervention; Nuclear Disarmament; Peace & Justice; War Tax Resistance)*

Minorities
(See: Human Rights; Multi-Cultural)

Monasteries
MadreGrande, StClare's, Vivekananda(MI), ZenLotus

Mondragon
[R]ActionLink, [R]CRSP, [R]UrbanAlts

Montessori
ReCreation

Multi-Cultural
Auroville, [L]Gaia(F), RockRidge, [L]RosyBranch • [R]FreedomSong, [R]ICA/Earth, [R]MediaNet, [R]OlympSustain, [R]SkipStones • [R]VolForPeace • *(See Also: Human Rights)*

Museums
[R]ShakerVill

Music
CaravanFarm, Dayspring, RabbityHill, ReCreation, [L]Gorilla-Choir, Waukon, Womanshare, Zendik • [R]Dance/NE, [R]FreedomSong, [R]Ladyslipper, [R]NatFedBrdcast, [R][L]SingOut, [R]WICCA/Camp

Native American
BearTribe, CEEDS/B.C. • [R]Akwesasne, [R]FreedomFund, [R]N-Catalyst, [R]NativeSeeds, [R]ProjPlenty, [R]SeventhGen • *(See Also: Earth Religions; Human Rights; Shamanism)*

Naturist
[F]AquarRanch, Harbin, Sojourners(VA)

Networking
HighWind, LostValley, [I]Meitheal, Shannon(VA) • [R]AllWaysFree, [R]Briarpatch, [R]C-Catalyst, [R]FdnComEncourg, [R][L]Forth-World, [R]HighWindBks, [R]PatternResrch • *(See Also: Clearinghouses; Community Building; Community Referrals; Community Networks)*

New Age
Dragonfly, [I]Findhorn, Harbin, MadreGrande, Sirius • [R]N-AgeGuide, [R]N-AgeJourn, [R]OmegaNewAge, [R]OneEarth, [R]ReVision, [R]TheSun,

[R]TransTimes • *(See Also: Health & Healing; Light Centers; Metaphysics; Spirituality)*

New Zealand
[R]C-Access • *(See Also: "Index by Country" that precedes the International listings)*

Newsletters
[L]InstWhatHav, [L]RosyBranch, [L]ThirdPlace • [R]AnnalsEarth, , [R]MsgPost, [R]N-Options, [R]NeighbrWorks, [R]PeopleForChng, [R][L]SEAC • *(See Also: Publications)*

Newspapers
[R]AcresUSA, [R]Alliance, [R]AllWaysFree, [R]InTheseTimes, [R]N-Catalyst, [R]OmegaNewAge, [R]StreetNews • *(See Also: Publications)*

Nicaragua
(See: Non-Intervention)

Non-Intervention
[R]BikesNoBombs, [R]ChristicInst, [R]MobilzSurvival, [R]PeopleForChng, [R]WitnessPeace • *(See Also: Peace & Justice; Military Resistance)*

Non-Violence
[I]C-Ark, Metanoia(GA), PeaceFarm, SeedsPeace • [R]CenConflictRes, [R]FedEgalCom, [R]N-SocietyPub, [R]Peacemakers • *(See Also: Peace & Justice)*

Nuclear Disarmament
PeaceFarm, SeedsPeace • [R]AllncSurvival, [R]BetterWorld, [R]Greenpeace, [R]MobilzSurvival, [R]NatRightsCen, [R]NucFreeAmer, [R]VetsPeace • *(See Also: Peace & Justice; Military Resistance)*

Nuclear Power Opposition
[R]NucFreeAmer, [R]UConcernSci • *(See Also: Alternative Energy; Environment)*

*Organic Farming & Gardening
CEEDS/B.C., [I]Comunidad/S, [L]InstWhatHav, LaCitéEcol, [F]LaurelHill, LongBranch, Riparia, Sojourners(VA), [I]Teachest, [F]WingedHeart • [R]AcresUSA, [R]BioDynFarm, [R][L]CalifAction, [R]EcoAction, [R]EcoHome,

---

Index Keywords preceded by an **asterisk (*)** are also indexed in the Cross-Reference Charts.

Index

[R]N-Alchemy, [R]OregonTilth, [R]Rodale • *(See Also: Gardening; Sustainable Agriculture)*

Overpopulation
[R]BetterWorld, [R]FoodFirst, [R]TraNet

Pacifism
(See: Peace & Justice; Military Resistance)

Pagan
(See: Earth Religions; Shamanism; Wicca)

Parenting
[R]AnotherPlac, [R][L]ParentLdrInste • *(See Also: Family Therapy; Home Schooling; Single Parenting)*

Peace & Justice
Dorea, Hearthaven, JesuitVol, Peace-Farm, SeedsPeace, Sojourners(DC) • [R]AllWaysFree, [R]Alternatives, [R]EcoNet, [R]FreedomSong, [R]GlobeLib, [R]InterfaithCen, [R]MediaNet, [R]MobilzSurvival, [R]N-SocietyPub, [R]NatWarTax, [R][L]PolEcoGroup, [R]TheWELL • *(See Also: Direct Action; Economic Conversion; Fourth World; Grass-Roots Organizing; Human Rights; Non-Intervention; Political Activism; Prisoners; Refugees; Social Change; Socialism; Third World; War Tax Resistance)*

Permaculture
BearTribe, EndOfRoad, Heathcote, [I]Lebensgarten, Linnaea, LongBranch, LostValley, [F]Namasté, Panhandle, [I]PermPyrénées, [F]Planetary, Spiral-Wimmin • [R]Columbiana, [R]ElfinPC, [R]FriendTrees, [R]Ozark-RLT, [R]PC-Activist, [R]School/Living, [R]YankeePC • *(See Also: Environment; Sustainable Agriculture)*

Personal Growth
Cn-WellBeing, [I]ComGro(Aus), FdnFeedback, Goodenough, HighWind, Kerista, Kripalu, Magic, MtMadonna, Phoenix(CA), Wellspring(WI), YogaRochestr • [R]ActionLink, [R]CreationMag, [R]Dance/NE, [R]DormantBrain, [R]Esalen, [R]FamilyTree, [R]FeatherPipe, [R]FdnPersC-Dev, [R]KenKeyColl,

[R]N-AgeJourn, [R]NatOrgChgMen, [R]SpringHill, [R]UtneReader • *(See Also: Communication-Interpersonal; Consciousness; Empowerment; Relationships; Therapy; Vision Quests)*

Photography
StBenedict's • [R]C-Catalyst

Planning Skills
[I]ComGro(Aus) • [R]CenConflictRes, [R]IndusCoopAsso, [R]PatternResrch, [R]RobtOwenFnd

Plant Closings
(See: Economic Conversion)

Play
[R]AnimalTown, [R]CenEdGuidance, [R]HugsForHeart, [R]InContext • *(See Also: Recreation)*

Political Activism
(See: Direct Action; Environment; Greens; Non-Intervention; Nuclear Disarmament; Peace & Justice)

Politics
Zendik • [R]BoundTogether, [R]ComGro(USA), [R]EarthIsland, [R]GreenComCor, [R]MotherJones, [R]N-Intnatlist, [R]N-Options, [R]PeopleForChng, [R]Woman-Power, [R]Zeta • *(See Also: Food-Information; Greens; Political Activism)*

Polyfidelity
Kerista, Phoenix(CA) • [R][L]Intinet, [R]Polyfidelity

Portable Dwellings
[R]MsgPost

Prisoners
Catholic(OH), Jubilee(GA), OpenDoor • [R]BoundTogether

Property Management
C-(Va), [F]Homeland

Psychology
See: Behaviorist Psychology

Publications
(See: Communities Directories; Journals; Magazines; Newsletters; Newspapers; Publications-Indexes; and specific subjects)

Publications—Indexes
[R]AltPressIndex, [R]Factsheet5, [R]UtneReader • *(See Also: Publications)*

Publishers
Celo, [I]Comunidad/N, Farm(TN), [I]Lifespan, [I]Mitraniketan • [R]N-SocietyPub, [R]Nolo, [R]PacPubl-Coop, [R]R&EMiles, [R]Rodale • *(See Also: Desktop Publishing)*

Quaker
Celo, FriendsSW, [L]FriendsLake, Monan'sRill, [F]OakGrove/Va, [L]QuakerHouse, RockRidge, [I]SomeFriends, Vale

Rainbow Family
[F]Namasté, [F]RB-Junction, Seeds-Peace, WaldenHill • [R]AllWaysFree

Rebirthing
ConsciousVill

Recreation
[L]FriendsLake • [R]CirclePines, [R]CoCampSierra, [R]Morning-Star(MI) • *(See Also: Play)*

Recycling - Raw Materials
[R]EarthCare, [R]EnvirDefense, [R]Garbage, [R]InstLocalSelf, [L]Maxworks, [R]Nat'lRecycling • *(See Also: Conservation; Environment)*

Recycling - Second Hand
FdnFeedback, Zendik

Referrals
(See: Clearinghouses; Community Referrals; Relocation)

Refugees
Jubilee(GA), N-Jerusalem, PeaceGardens, PlowCreek

Relationships
[F]AquarResrch, [L]SocLoveAlchem(F) • [R]ExpCities, [R][L]FamTree, [R][L]HumanAware, [R][L]Intinet, [R]WICCA/Camp • *(See Also: Alternative Lifestyles; Communication-Interpersonal; Family Therapy; Polyfidelity)*

Relocation
[R]RelocatResrch • *(See Also: Community Referrals)*

Resource Conservation
(See: Conservation)

Section Codes: (No code) N. American [F] N. American/Forming [I] International [L] Late Entry [R] Resource
Abbreviations: (Cn) Center (C-) Community (LT) Land Trust (N-) New (Rb) Rainbow

Restaurants
Alpha, [L]BearCreek, Builders, C-Altrnatvs, CamphillVill(PA), Dayspring, GriffinGorge, [L]Human-Poten, LaCitéEcol, [F]OrgKauai, [I]Teachest • [R]CRSP

Retreats
Abode, Ananda/WB, Breitenbush, Cn-Peace, [I]ComGro(Aus), Communia, CrieffHills, EsseneMother, GouldFarm, Hailos, Harbin, Heathcote, [L]HumanPoten, Krotona, Lama, LostValley, MadreGrande, MtMadonna, OjaiFndtn, RabbityHill, RoweCamp, SaltSpring, Shenoa(CA), Shiloh(AR), [L]Starseed(F), Suneidesis, TruthConsc, Vivekananda(MI), Wellspring(WI), Wesleyan(WA), ZenLosAngeles • [R][L]GardenEden, [R]Morning-Star(MI), [R]OneWorldFam, [R]Penuel-Ridge, [R]SkySong, [R]SoDharma

Right Livelihood
[R]Briarpatch, [R]CEED-Inst, [R]Frien-Trees • *(See Also: Career Options)*

Rituals
BearTribe, Rootworks, [F]WingedHeart • [R]Alternatives, [R]CreationMag, [R]FeatherPipe, [R]InContext, [R]Inti-net, [R]Reclaiming • *(See: Gatherings)*

Russian Orthodox
[F]Agape

Sanctuaries—Environmental
[L]FriendsLake, [I]Laurieston, Lichen, Linnaea, LongBranch, RiverFarm, WaldenHill • [R]CircleNet, [R]NatConservcy

Sanctuary Movement
(See: Human Rights; Refugees)

Schools—Adult Ed
Celo

Schools—Children
Ananda/WB, Celo, Dayspring, Farm(TN), Fellowship-C, [L]Greenbriar, [F]InstSustLiv, KehillatMishp, Koinonia, Linnaea, [I]Mitraniketan, [I]Monkton, MtMadonna, N-Vrindaban, Patchwork, Shiloh-(AR), StFeSchool, Stelle, [I]Svanholm, [I]TerNouvelle, Yogaville • [R]Farm-School • *(See Also: Home Schooling; Montessori)*

Science
LaCitéEcol, [I]PermPyrénées • [R]CenSacredSci, [R]CreationMag, [R]DormantBrain, [R]OneWorldFam, [R]ReVision, [R]UConcernSci, [R]WorldFutSoc

Scotland
(See: "Index by Country" that precedes the International listings; See Also: Great Britain)

Seeds/Seedlings
ReCreation • [R]AbundantLife, [R]EcoAction, [R]FriendTrees, [R]GardenByMail, [R]LandInst, [R]NativeSeeds, [R]SeedSavers • *(See Also: Agriculture; Gardening)*

Self-Government
(See: Decentralization; Self-Management)

Self-Management
[I]Comunidad/S, ThirdAve • [R]BoundTogether, [R]LeftBank • *(See Also: Anarchism; Collectives; Decentralization)*

Self-Sufficiency
BearTribe, [L]HumanPoten, ReevisMtn, Sunflower(OH) • [R]Rodale • *(See Also: Local Self-Reliance)*

Shakers
[R]ShakerVill

Shamanism
OjaiFdtn, [R]FeatherPipe • *(See Also: Native American; Earth Religions)*

Shelters—Women
Jubilee(NC) • *(See Also: Homelessness)*

Sikh
[R]3HO/Fdtn

Simple Living
(See: Sustainable Economics; Voluntary Simplicity)

Single Parenting
[R]InnovHousing, [R]NatlHmSchool • *(See Also: Parenting)*

Single Tax Theory
(See: Georgist)

Small Business
[R]Briarpatch, [R]CESCI, [R]DemBusiness, [R]EFSchumacher, [R]InstDevelCoop, [R]NeighbrWorks, [R]PatternResrch, [R]UrbanAlts

Small Community
[R]C-ServiceInc, [R]SDSC

Social Change
[R]ActionLink, [R]AltPressIndex, [R]C-Jobs, [R]CCEC, [R]Connexions, [R]FdnPersC-Dev, [R]InTheseTimes, [R]InContext, [R][L]LongIsAlt, [R]MotherJones, [R]N-Options, [R]N-SocietyPub, [R]NatOrgChgMen, [R]PacPublCoop, [R]Peacemakers, [R]PeopleForChng, [R]Reclaiming, [R]SoMovEmpowr, [R]StreetNews, [R]UtneReader • *(See Also: Peace & Justice)*

Social Justice
(See: Human Rights; Peace & Justice; Prisoners)

Socialism
[I]Birchwood • [R]InTheseTimes, [R]YadTabenkin

Socially Responsible Investing
LaCitéEcol • [R]CESCI, [R]CoopAmer, [R]CounEconPrior, [R]FirstAmFinan, [R]InterfaithCen, [R]N-AgeJourn, [R]NucFreeAmer • *(See Also: Funds)*

Solar Cooking
[R]KerrEnterpr, [R]SolarCookIntl, [R]SolarCookNW

Solar Energy
Farm(TN), LongBranch, Thoreau • [R]EcoHome • *(See Also: Alternative Energy; Solar Cooking)*

Sourcebooks
[R]AppTech/SB, [R]Connexions, [R]GardenByMail, [R][L]Intinet, [R]Ladyslipper, [R]RealGoods • *(See Also: Communities Directories; Directories; Mail-Order)*

South Africa
(See: "Index by Country" that precedes the International listings)

South American
(See: International; Non-Intervention)

Speakers Bureaus
[R]CenEconConv, [R]Fellow-IntCom, [R]Headwaters • *(See Also: specific subjects)*

Index Keywords preceded by an **asterisk (*)** are also indexed in the Cross-Reference Charts.

Index

Section Codes: (No code) N. American   [F] N. American/Forming   [I] International   [L] Late Entry   [R] Resource
Abbreviations: (Cn) Center   (C-) Community   (LT) Land Trust   (N-) New   (Rb) Rainbow

Wales
(See: "Index by Country" that precedes the International listings; See Also: Great Britain)

War Tax Resistance
[R]NatWarTax • *See Also: Military Resistance)*

Water Birthing
ReCreation • *(See Also: Midwifery)*

Watersheds
[R]Headwaters •
(See Also: Bioregionalism)

West Germany
(See: "Index by Country" that precedes the International listings)

Wicca
BlackCat, Waukon •
[R]CircleNet, [R]WICCA/Camp •
(See Also: Earth Religions)

Wildlife
(See: Endangered Species; Sanctuaries-Wildlife)

Women
Greenhope, Heathcote, [F]Intergen-Women, Moonridge, OwlFarm, SusBAnthony, 3HO(NM) •
[R]InstSocEcolgy, [R]Ladyslipper,
[R]MorningStar(MI),
[R]OrWomLand, [R]SpringHill,
[R]WomanPower • *(See Also: Feminism; Lesbian; Shelters-Women)*

Woodworking
Camphill(MN), Fellowship-C, GriffinGorge, Innisfree, Shannon(VA)

Worker Ownership
[R]Briarpatch, [R]DemBusiness, [R]IndusCoopAsso, [R]UrbanAlts, [R][L]WorkOwned • *(See Also: Collectives; Self-Management; Small Business)*

Workshop Centers
CrieffHills, [L]Hawkwind, [L]HimalayInst, LamaFdtn, [F]OakGrove/Va, [I]LowerShaw, Suneidesis, [I]Terra-Nouvelle, Thoreau, Womanshare •
[R]SkySong, [R]SoDharma •
(See Also: Conference Centers)

Yoga
Atmaniketan, Auroville, [F]Bhaktiras, [L]HimalayInst, [L]Hollyhock, Kripalu, MtMadonna, RajYogaMath, SaltSpring, Sivananda/A, TruthConsc, YogaRochestr, Yogaville • [R]Dance/NE, [R]FeatherPipe, [R]3HO/Fdtn, [R]WICCA/Camp

Youth
Camphill-SS, CrossesCrk, [F]Kidstown, Koinonia, [I]Meitheal, [I]Mitraniketan, N-Jerusalem, [I]Nomadelfia, RoweCamp, [I]Svanholm, Triform • [R]Kokoo, [R]RoweCamp, [R]SpringHill

Zen
N-HavenZen, ProvZen, SF-Zen, ZenBuddh(MI), [L]ZenCom/NY, ZenLosAngeles, ZenLotus

NOW, A COMMUNITY OF CONSCIOUSNESS WHERE YOU CAN...

...enjoy 400 wooded rural acres dedicated to spiritual discovery. An exciting place to visit, study, or live

...join with others for daily group meditations, full moon rituals, prayer vigils, sacred music, and choir.

...find qualified guidance in reaching your inner potential.

...examine the basis for religious thought, east and west.

...earn ordination as a New Age Minister through a residential or off-campus degree program.

...pursue a masters or doctorate in religious studies.

...Write or call the registrar:

SPARROW HAWK
VILLAGE
22 SUMMIT RIDGE DRIVE
TAHLEQUAH, OK 74464-9215
918 456-3421

Social Change Tool for the 90s

ALTERNATIVE PRESS INDEX

GCU 593M

This quarterly SUBJECT INDEX to over 200 publications will be an invaluable tool in your study of social change. So ask the folks at your library to subscribe to the *Alternative Press Index* — if they don't already.

Directory of Alternative & Radical Publications: $3

For more information write:
Alternative Press Center
P.O. Box 33109
Baltimore, Maryland 21218

Industrial Hair-Splitting

Even as we learn that "recycled" is a misleading label, it turns out that "post-consumer" is a bit slippery, too. People generally understand post-consumer waste to be that which has passed through its useful consumer life. By industry definition, though, paper becomes "post-consumer" when the product containing it is shipped from the printer's. It may have little to do with being "consumed". The paper might not be read, written on, or even thumbed through (much less used to wash windows or line a kitty box). Printing leftovers (overproduction, trimming waste, orders never picked up) are pre-consumer. Yet, if it's been delivered to the publisher, then it's post-consumer, even if the books containing the paper are scrapped out as overstock and have never left their shipping boxes. A fine distinction.

Index Keywords preceded by an **asterisk** (*) are also indexed in the Cross-Reference Charts.

Feedback

Directory Updates:
Your help is needed ...

Creating a directory of intentional communities is something like doing an ice sculpture for a summer solstice party — with a lot of work and skill you can craft something beautiful. Yet even as you present it, the accuracy of the details melts away from you. Soon the piece is lost in a flood of changes and the sculpture is more a snapshot of something that was instead of what is.

As near as we can tell, the changeableness of communities is not likely to change. Therefore we need your help to keep current. It's worth a lot to have one place where you can turn for the most up-to-date information on communities. The Fellowship wants to offer that service, but we can hardly begin to record all the changes without your help.

From the standpoint of the Directory, changes come in many forms, from the trivial to the essential. We ask you to use your judgment about what news we need to hear (bearing in mind that what is inconsequential to one person may be very important to another). We welcome input about all changes, but especially major ones like the birth of a new community.

Communities

The **most important news** is anything to do with existing **unlisted** communities (new or otherwise), and information about **listed** communities which have changed their phone number, their address, or their minds about existing as a community. See the **"RRDDLNoR"** **section on page 233** for a list of groups we tried to contact, but couldn't list because they didn't respond to our inquiries. Any information about these groups will be particularly appreciated. Please use the clip-out form at the bottom of the facing page, or send your updates and leads (including the name, address, phone number and contact person if possible) to the address listed below.

Resources

It is exciting and encouraging to realize how many "alternative" resources there are. Many more than we could possibly track down in the course of this project; and too many, of course, to list in this Directory. In creating the Resources section, we tried to include as wide a range of different types of organizations as we could while still being selective. Rather than include every organization that we came across, we tried to focus on groups that are regional, national, or global in scope. The few "local" resources we have included either are directly related to Communities which appear in the listings, or are fairly unique in what they do — and are probably worth replicating in other locales. Keeping these criteria in mind, please send us information about any resources which you feel we ought to know about. Use the clip-out form at the bottom of the facing page, or send the information (including the name, address, phone number, and contact person if possible) to the address below.

Do You Need More Information?

Can't find it in this Directory? Maybe we can help! Send your question and a self-addressed, stamped envelope to the address below. There may be a charge for this service, depending on the nature of the request, and on whether or not we can help.

The Directory Project

We put a lot of thought and effort into creating this Directory, and hope that the effort shows. Our overriding consideration has been to make the information accessible to potential users, and we invite your comments and criticisms. Please take a moment to let us know what you like about it, and how we can improve future editions. Thanks!

Communities Directory

Fellowship for Intentional Community • Center for Communal Studies
8600 University Blvd. • Evansville, IN 47712
(812) 464-1727; Fax (812) 464-1960

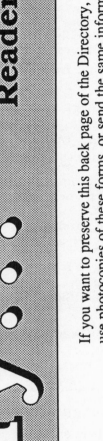

Reply...

A Request for Reader Responses

If you want to preserve this back page of the Directory, use photocopies of these forms, or send the same information on separate sheets of paper.

Subscribe to *Communities Magazine!*
NOTE: Prices in parentheses are for foreign orders and must be paid in U.S. currency.

- See inside front cover for a full description of *Communities: Journal of Cooperation.*
- Subscriptions: ☐ individual rate - $18 ($22) for 4 issues
  ☐ institutional rate - $22 ($26) for 4 issues
- Sample issue: ☐ $4 ($5)
- Check here for ☐ a list of available back issues $2 ($2.40)
  ☐ a set of all (≈35) available back issues $35 ($40)
- Check here for ☐ information about supporting the magazine by purchasing an extended subscription

Please print:

Name _____

Address _____

City _____ *State* _____ *Zip* _____

Total Amount Enclosed _____

For subscriptions or back-issues, send order to: **Communities Sandhill Farm • Rt. 1 Box 155 • Rutledge MO 63563**
If you're ordering additional copies of this directory as well, send your order to the address on the reverse of this form.

Do you have friends ...
who would want to see our *Bookshelf Catalog?*
Send us their names and addresses with your order, using the space below. (See address on reverse.)

Name _____
Address _____
City _____ *State* _____ *Zip* _____

Name _____
Address _____
City _____ *State* _____ *Zip* _____

Name _____
Address _____
City _____ *State* _____ *Zip* _____

———— *Thank You!* ————

Updates: The world of community is constantly changing. Please help us keep up to date! Send us the names and addresses of any new communities or resources, or old ones which you think should have been listed. Also, please let us know about any misinformation that you are aware of in this Directory. See facing page for more details. There's additional space on the reverse of this form.

Organization: _____

Address _____

City _____ *State* _____ *Zip* _____

Phone _____ *Contact Person* _____

Date _____

This is a ☐ correction
☐ new community
☐ new resource

Your Name _____

———— *Thank You!* ————

> Send to:
> **Communities Directory**
> c/o Fellowship for
> Intentional Community
> Center for Communal Studies
> 8600 University Blvd.
> Evansville, IN 47712

To order *Additional Copies* of this Directory:

For 1-9 copies .... $12.00 ea.

Postage & handling *requested: USA   Other

  First book $2.00 $3.00

  Each additional book $0.75 $1.00

Write for information on discounts for larger orders.

     Number of Copies Ordered _____

     Total Amount Enclosed _____

Please print your: *Name* _____

                  Address _____

           City _____ *State* _____ *Zip* _____

Make checks payable to Communities
Magazine and send to: **Communities Directory**
                   c/o Alpha Farm • Deadwood, OR 97430

*Optional for low income

**To order *Additional Copies*
of this Directory,** use order form
at left, or send your name, address,
and payment to:

   **Communities Directory
   c/o Alpha Farm
   Deadwood, OR 97430**

1-9 copies .... $16.00 ea.
10 or more copies, 40% off

Postage & handling: USA Other
  First book $2.00 $3.00
  Each additional $0.75 $1.00

**To Subscribe to *Communities*
Magazine** — or for information on
back issues, samples, and large
order discounts — please use
form on reverse of this page.

See inside front cover for more info.

DIRECTORY BOOKSHELF ORDER FORM

Book Title	Quantity	Price
Catalog		Free

Please print your:

Name _____

Address _____

City _____ *State* _____ *Zip* _____

Send to address at right.

Subtotal	
Postage (AT RIGHT)	
TOTAL	

(Thank You!)

To order the books on the
facing page, use the form at
the left, or send us a list of
the books you want.

When ordering, be sure to include:
✓ full name and address;
✓ postage and handling fees;
✓ U.S. funds (cash, check,
   or money order)

Postage & handling: USA Other
  First book $1.75 $2.00
  Each additional book.. $0.50 $0.75

Send to:
**Directory Bookshelf
Box 155
Rutledge, MO 63563**

Organization _____

Address _____

City _____ *State* _____ *Zip* _____

Phone _____ *Contact Person* _____

    This is a: ☐ community ☐ resource ☐ correction

Organization _____

Address _____

City _____ *State* _____ *Zip* _____

Phone _____ *Contact Person* _____

    This is a: ☐ community ☐ resource ☐ correction

Organization _____

Address _____

City _____ *State* _____ *Zip* _____

Phone _____ *Contact Person* _____

    This is a: ☐ community ☐ resource ☐ correction

Your Name _____ —*Thank You!* —

Updates:

The world of community is constantly changing. Please help us
keep up to date! Send us the
names and addresses of any new
communities or resources, or old
ones which you think should have
been listed. Also, please let us
know about any misinformation
that you are aware of in this
Directory. See facing page for more
details. There's additional space
on the reverse of this form.

Send corrections & leads to:
**Communities Directory
Fellowship for Intentional Community
Center for Communal Studies
8600 University Blvd.
Evansville, IN 47712**

(812)464-1727 • Fax (812)464-1960